Zoroastrianism in India and Iran

Zoroastrianism in India and Iran

*Persians, Parsis and the Flowering
of Political Identity*

Alexandra Buhler

I.B. TAURIS
LONDON • NEW YORK • OXFORD • NEW DELHI • SYDNEY

I.B. TAURIS
Bloomsbury Publishing Plc
50 Bedford Square, London, WC1B 3DP, UK
1385 Broadway, New York, NY 10018, USA
29 Earlsfort Terrace, Dublin 2, Ireland

BLOOMSBURY, I.B. TAURIS and the I.B. Tauris logo are trademarks of Bloomsbury Publishing Plc

First published in Great Britain 2024

Copyright © Alexandra Buhler, 2024

Alexandra Buhler has asserted her rights under the Copyright, Designs and Patents Act, 1988, to be identified as Author of this work.

For legal purposes the Acknowledgements on p. ix constitute an extension of this copyright page.

Series design by Adriana Brioso Cover image: Zoroastrian School, Iran, 1903.
(© Mary Evans / Grenville Collins Postcard Collection)

All rights reserved. No part of this publication may be reproduced or transmitted in any form or by any means, electronic or mechanical, including photocopying, recording, or any information storage or retrieval system, without prior permission in writing from the publishers.

Bloomsbury Publishing Plc does not have any control over, or responsibility for, any third-party websites referred to or in this book. All internet addresses given in this book were correct at the time of going to press. The author and publisher regret any inconvenience caused if addresses have changed or sites have ceased to exist, but can accept no responsibility for any such changes.

A catalogue record for this book is available from the British Library.

A catalog record for this book is available from the Library of Congress.

Library of Congress Cataloging-in-Publication Data

Names: Buhler, Alexandra, author.
Title: Zoroastrianism in India and Iran: Persians, Parsis and the flowering of political identity / Alexandra Buhler.
Description: London; New York: I.B. Tauris, 2024. | Includes bibliographical references and index. | Summary: "This book examines the strong relationship between the Zoroastrian community in Iran and the Zoroastrian community in India from the mid-nineteenth century to the 1920s. Using a variety of original sources from Britain, India and Iran, Alexandra Buhler looks at the political, legal, and social position of Zoroastrians in Iran and how different events impacted their attitudes as well as the attitudes of Zoroastrians in India towards their ancestral homeland"– Provided by publisher.
Identifiers: LCCN 2024009025 (print) | LCCN 2024009026 (ebook) | ISBN 9780755601608 (hardback) | ISBN 9780755655854 (paperback) | ISBN 9780755601639 (epub) | ISBN 9780755601622 (ebook)
Subjects: LCSH: Zoroastrians–Iran–History. | Zoroastrians–India–History. | Parsees–History.
Classification: LCC DS269.Z65 B84 2024 (print) | LCC DS269.Z65 (ebook) | DDC 305.6/950955–dc23/eng/20240513
LC record available at https://lccn.loc.gov/2024009025
LC ebook record available at https://lccn.loc.gov/2024009026

ISBN: HB: 978-0-7556-0160-8
ePDF: 978-0-7556-0162-2
eBook: 978-0-7556-0163-9

Typeset by Deanta Global Publishing Services, Chennai, India

To find out more about our authors and books visit www.bloomsbury.com and sign up for our newsletters.

For my mother, Monika, and in memory of my father, Michael.

Contents

Plates	viii
Acknowledgements	ix
Note on the text	xi
Map	xii
Introduction	1
1 Zoroastrian Philanthropy and Iran	15
2 Parsis and pre-Islamic Iran: A confluence of interests	33
3 Zoroastrians and the 'Great Game'	53
4 Arbab Jamshid and the Revolution: A new era	75
5 Struggles for justice: Zoroastrians and the law	99
6 Constitutional rule is restored: Nationalism in Iran and Parsi dreams of 'return'	123
7 The 'Awakening' of Pahlavi Iran	147
Conclusion	173
Notes	177
Bibliography	262
Index	285

Plates

1. A Picture from the Shah Nameh: Shah Kaekaoos Flying for a Kingdom in Heaven!   87
2. Afghan-Persian Parsis   89
3. The Fatherless Child!   91
4. Another Partition!   110
5. Under Protecting Wings   128
6. Mr Punch's Pateti Pictures – No. 1.: To Iran!   132
7. The Boa Constrictor   139

Acknowledgements

I am very grateful to everyone I have worked with at I.B. Tauris and at Bloomsbury for all they have done to help bring this project to fruition, and for their patience and understanding the countless times that I missed my deadlines. I would particularly like to thank Sophie Rudland, Faiza Zakaria, Yasmin Garcha and Nayiri Kendir, as well as Alex Wright, who I met with early in 2018 to first discuss my book proposal. I also wish to thank the two anonymous reviewers of my manuscript for all their comments and suggestions.

This book is based on the work I undertook as a PhD student at SOAS. I am deeply thankful to everybody who helped me during the years of my doctoral research, especially Sarah Stewart. I could not have had a more wonderful supervisor. Sarah inspired me to embark on my PhD, and her enthusiasm for my research has been a great motivation throughout the years that I was writing my thesis and later this book. I am also very grateful to the other members of my supervisory committee: Ben Fortna, Almut Hintze, and Derek Mancini-Lander, for their valuable advice, as well as to my examiners, Hugh Kennedy and Jenny Rose, for their insightful questions.

I was lucky to have been part of a lively and vibrant community at SOAS, and the friends I made at SOAS have continued to support me whilst I worked to develop my thesis into this publication. I would particularly like to thank Carys Barbour, Alex Magub, Neda Mohtashami and George Warner, for all their encouragement along the way.

During the time that I was conducting research for my thesis, I had the opportunity to travel to India. I am very grateful for the grants I received from SOAS and from INTACH (Indian National Trust for Art and Cultural Heritage) that enabled me to undertake this trip. At the end of my time in India, I was able to share some of my research findings in a talk that was organized by INTACH. I wish to thank Pheroza Godrej for her role in organizing this lecture and for her kindness throughout my time in Mumbai.

In terms of locating and accessing relevant sources in India, I benefitted hugely from the advice and the support that I received from the staff at the K. R. Cama Oriental Institute, the J. N. Petit Library, the Mumbai University Library, the Maharashtra State Archives, all in Mumbai, the staff at the National Archives in Delhi and from Bharti Gandhi at the First Dastur Meherjirana Library in Navsari. A heartfelt thank you to Aban Mukherji, who very kindly translated passages from Gujarati newspapers for me, as we sat together in the K. R. Cama and J. N. Petit libraries, and to Rusheed Wadia, who not only shared his deep knowledge with me and helped me with many practical matters, such as library passes, but whose friendship contributed greatly to the wonderful time that I had in Mumbai. I also have very fond memories of my breakfasts with Persis Sathe at her home in Colaba where I stayed, and I wish to thank Sonya and Sarojini Sapru, as well as Baby, Aditya and Shirin Malkani, for their hospitality and generosity. A big thank you also to Khojeste, Firoza, Kaiyan and Shireen Mistree, for warmly welcoming me to Mumbai and for making my time there very special.

Acknowledgements

Over the years that I was working on my thesis, and subsequently on this book, many people offered me advice, discussed ideas with me and helped me access useful material for my research. I would especially like to thank Malcolm Deboo for assisting me when I consulted the archives at the Zoroastrian Trust Funds of Europe and Dinyar Patel and Dan Sheffield for generously sharing resources. I also wish to thank Mansour Bonakdarian, Avan Engineer, Gerard Greene, John Gurney, Mehrbod Khanizadeh, Afshin Marashi, Vanessa Martin, Mandana Moavenat, Narges Nematollahi, Mitra Sharafi, Fatema Soudavar Farmanfarmaian, as well as the staff at various libraries and archives, particularly the British Library, the National Archives, Kew, and the Cadbury Research Library at the University of Birmingham.

There is another library that I have heavily relied on to complete this book and that is the library at King's College London, where I began working just a few days before my PhD viva. The ease with which I have been able to access relevant material has been incredibly helpful, and I hugely appreciate the work of my colleagues in the interlibrary loans team, who have ordered numerous books and articles for me over the past few years. As well as facilitating my research in practical terms, I have received wide-ranging support from my colleagues and friends at Libraries & Collections, particularly from everyone I have worked with closely, first in my role in the Customer Services team and now in the Learning Design & Delivery team. My deepest thanks to Holly Brown, Adam Garside, Rosemary Purr, Mary Walsh and Max Zanotti.

Around the same time that I began working on this book, I also joined the team at 'It's Not Your Birthday But . . .' (INYBB). I feel very fortunate to have met such inspiring people through this work, and I am grateful to Wendy Shepherd and everyone at INYBB for their support over the past few years. A big thank you to Fiona Whitelaw for all the encouragement and for our conversations about the ups and downs of writing and so much more.

I am very grateful, too, for the motivating conversations I have had with several friends who have been developing their theses into books at the same time as me, and for their support and their reflections on the process. In particular, I wish to thank Katherine Robinson, as well as Mark Stuart-Smith, who also kindly offered to read over sections of my work.

There are many individuals who have supported me in countless ways over these past few years to whom I would like to say a huge thank you. It has helped so much knowing that you are all there, and I am very lucky to have friends who have been so understanding when I was preoccupied with the book. Thank you too to Murat Cubukcu for all his encouragement in the final few months of the process. I have a feeling that the only one who will be disappointed that this book is finally finished is Dorothy the cat, as her 'lap time' will be much reduced. The companionship of Dorothy was a great help whilst I was writing, and I am very grateful to her for her calming presence.

Above all, I would like to thank my mother, Monika. I cannot thank her enough for all her love and support, for reading several versions of this book as I edited, re-edited and re-re-edited it, for encouraging me to persevere and not give up with the whole idea and for her endless patience with me.

Note on the text

In this book, the names I have used for geographical locations are those given in the contemporary sources that I have referenced – for example, Bombay rather than Mumbai. Likewise, India is used to refer to the territory known as India during the period covered by this book, rather than present-day India. In 1935, Reza Shah declared that Iran was the official name for the Iranian state, but in the sources used for this book, the country is sometimes referred to as Persia. Where there is no commonly used spelling for a Persian word, I have used a simplified version of the *Iranian Studies* transliteration scheme without diacritics for the long vowels. For consistency, all dates will be given in the Gregorian calendar. The Iran Chamber Society online 'Iranian Calendar Converter' has been used to convert dates when sources have used the Islamic Hijri calendar or the Iranian Jalali calendar.[1]

Map

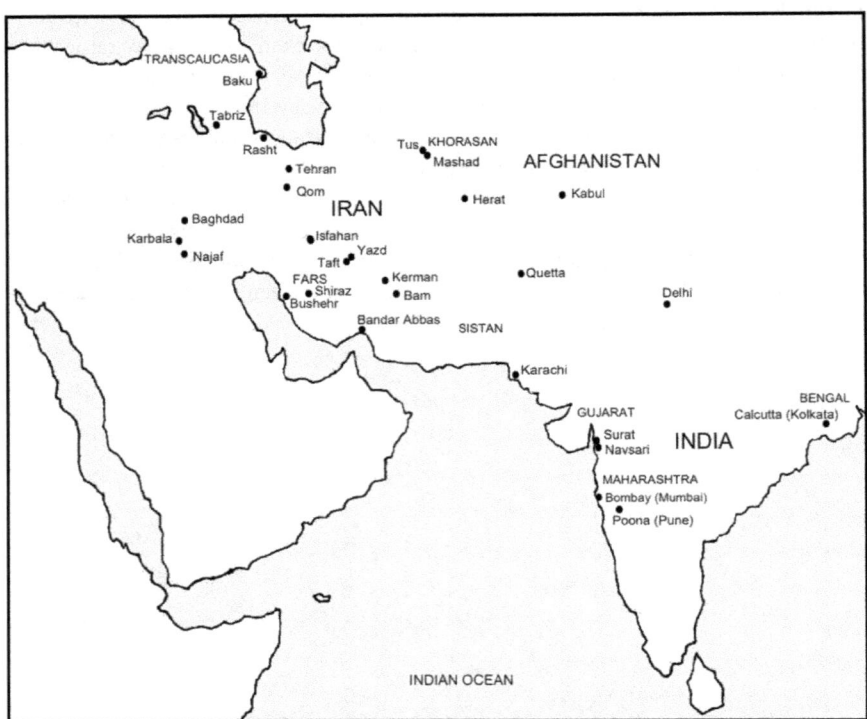

Introduction

Picture a busy Tehran coffeehouse in February 1907. A group of men have gathered; one has brought the latest issue of the *Neda-ye Vatan* newspaper to read and discuss with his acquaintances. The past few weeks had been momentous: the first Iranian constitution had been ratified by Mozaffar al-Din Shah, just days before he died. Printed in the pages of the newly established newspaper was a statement issued on behalf of Zoroastrians. This letter addressed recent events, principally the new laws and the death of the shah.[1] At the time, there were probably fewer than 500 Zoroastrians living in Tehran, a city with a population of around 200,000. Many of the Zoroastrians in Tehran were involved in trade, and perhaps the men at the coffeehouse had business relations with a several of these merchants. Maybe they had been surprised when Arbab Jamshid Jamshidian, the most prominent Zoroastrian merchant, had taken his place as the only non-Muslim deputy in the parliament. The creation of the Majles, the name used for the National Assembly, and the drawing up of a constitution were outcomes of the events now known as the Constitutional Revolution. Iranian affairs had attracted international interest, and the statement in the pages of *Neda-ye Vatan* was not in fact written by Zoroastrians who were living in Iran, but was a translation of an article first printed in Britain, in the *London Indian Chronicle*.

The editor of the *London Indian Chronicle*, Nasarvanji Maneckji Cooper, was a Parsi, a member of the long-established Zoroastrian community of India. At the turn of the century, Cooper left Bombay for London, where there was a small but expanding Zoroastrian community. He lived together with his sister Aimai, who is recorded in the 1911 census as the head of their household. Aimai moved to Ilford after studying medicine in Belfast, and she was the first female Indian doctor to have practiced in Britain.[2] Their father, Maneckji, had promoted Anglophone education in Bombay, and Nasarvanji began his career publishing educational books in the city.[3] Since settling in London, Nasarvanji established the *London Indian Chronicle*, as well as the Cooper Publishing Company. He also organized gatherings, where guest speakers delivered talks about Zoroastrianism and the Zoroastrian community. Reports about these events, which were well-attended by his co-religionists in London, contributed to debates taking place amongst Parsis in Bombay. The themes of several of Nasarvanji's printed works also reflect his interest in the history of his religion and the present-day situation of Zoroastrians in India and Iran.[4] Additionally, Nasarvanji dedicated two of his publications to prominent Iranian Zoroastrians who represented their community in the Majles: Arbab Jamshid Jamshidian and Kaykhosrow Shahrokh.

Reflecting a broader trend in the Parsi community, the attention Nasarvanji Cooper directed towards Iran, and to his co-religionists in the country was likely to have been encouraged by political developments in both India and Iran, as well as increased contact between Zoroastrians in the two countries in the preceding decades. This book will examine relations between Zoroastrian communities in India and Iran from the mid-nineteenth century to the 1930s, with a particular focus on how these links both impacted and were affected by political change. In the mid-nineteenth century, the outlook for Zoroastrians in Iran had been bleak, but by the time the First Majles convened in 1906, the situation for Zoroastrians had improved to the extent that the first non-Muslim in the National Assembly was a Zoroastrian. Conversely, with growing demands for self-governance being voiced in India, Zoroastrians, who had prospered under British colonial rule, questioned what the future would hold for their community. In contrast to India, Iran was not under direct colonial rule. However, there was widespread anger at the level of foreign interference in Iranian affairs. These feelings intensified after the First World War (1914–18), and when the Qajar dynasty (1796–1925) was superseded by the Pahlavi dynasty (1925–79), the state made efforts to secure the place of Iran as a strong and independent nation. Under the increasingly authoritarian rule of the first Pahlavi monarch, Reza Shah (r.1925–41), an emphasis was placed on the modernization and secularization of the country. The state promoted a form of nationalism that looked back to the strength of the Iranian empires during the pre-Islamic period, a time when Zoroastrianism was the dominant religion.

Named after the figure Zarathustra, or Zoroaster, alternative terms are also used for the Zoroastrian religion, including *Mazdayasna*, meaning 'worship of Ahura Mazda'.[5] According to tradition, Zarathustra received revelations from Ahura Mazda, 'Wise Lord', which he recorded in the *Gathas*, 'songs'. These poetic texts are composed in Old Avestan, an ancient Iranian language related to Sanskrit. Linguistic analysis has dated the *Gathas* to approximately 1500 BCE, but, similar to other Zoroastrian religious 'texts', the *Gathas* were transmitted orally for hundreds of years.[6] Geographical locations referenced in early Zoroastrian texts suggest that they were composed in Central Asia.[7]

Religious beliefs and practices do not remain static over time, and even at a particular moment in time, views will differ. Therefore, rather than thinking of one Zoroastrian community and of Zoroastrianism as a single entity, Jenny Rose has suggested that we might think instead of 'Zoroastrianisms': a plurality of beliefs, practices and communities.[8] Archaeological records reveal that forms of Zoroastrianism were practised in Iran during the periods of the three pre-Islamic empires: the Achaemenid Empire (*c.* 550–330 BCE), the Parthian Empire (*c.* 247 BCE–224 CE) and the Sasanian Empire (224–651 CE).[9] There were also Zoroastrian communities further afield, for example in China.[10] Under Sasanian rule, Zoroastrianism was closely tied to the state and was the dominant religion in *Iranshahr*, a Sasanian term meaning 'Land of the Iranians'.[11]

However, the situation changed after Arab forces succeeded in overthrowing the Sasanian Empire in 651 CE, establishing Muslim rule over Iran. Conversion to Islam was not initially widespread, and several centuries passed before the majority of Iranians were Muslims. By this time, Islam had been influenced by the existing cultural and religious environment.[12] In addition to instances of forced conversion, economic and political incentives were amongst the factors that drew people to Islam.[13] Partly for practical reasons, principally the number of Zoroastrians in Iran, Zoroastrians were sometimes regarded in legal terms as 'People of the Book' (*ahl al-ketab*). This meant that, similar to Jews and Christians, they were theoretically allowed to practice their religion but were not permitted to convert Muslims to their faith.[14] As *dhimmi*s, protected non-Muslims living under Muslim rule, Zoroastrians were subject to specific regulations, including payment of the *jezya*, a tax on non-Muslims which exempted them from military service.[15]

According to Zoroastrian tradition, a group of Zoroastrians fled Iran to safeguard their religion and found refuge in India. Various dates have been proposed as to when this migration occurred, usually between the eighth and tenth centuries. The story of the journey undertaken by these Zoroastrians and their arrival in Gujarat is related in the *Qesse-ye Sanjan*, an epic poem written in Persian *c.* 1599 by the Zoroastrian priest Bahman Kaikobad Sanjana, who based his work on earlier oral traditions.[16] Whilst the *Qesse-ye Sanjan* describes Zoroastrians leaving Iran to escape persecution, there were other factors which may have encouraged Zoroastrians to settle in India, including long-standing trade links between the western coast of India and Iran.[17] Members of the Zoroastrian community of India came to be known as Parsis, a term that denoted their Persian heritage, being derived from the name of the Iranian province of Pars, also known as Fars.

Although the historical accuracy of the *Qesse-ye Sanjan* has been questioned, the account it gives of the arrival of Zoroastrians in India is significant in relation to Parsi identity.[18] The epic offers an explanation as to how Zoroastrians were able to maintain their distinct religious identity and why a degree of cultural assimilation occurred.[19] According to the *Qesse-ye Sanjan*, before the Zoroastrians were given permission to stay in India, they had to explain their religion to Jadi Rana, the local Hindu ruler, and they had to make the following promises: that they would speak the local language, Gujarati; that Zoroastrian women would wear Indian dress; that they would lay down their arms, implying loyalty to their rulers; and that they would hold their marriage ceremonies after sunset. In return, they were allowed to practice their religion, and they were permitted to build a temple to house their sacred fire. Another Parsi text, the sixteen Sanskrit *Shlokas*, has traditionally been seen in the context of the overview of the religion requested by Jadi Rana in the *Qesse-ye Sanjan*.[20] In the *Shlokas*, there is an emphasis on the similarities between Zoroastrian and Hindu religious beliefs and practices, such as reverence of the cow and the purity rules observed by women.[21]

Parsi loyalty to local Hindu rulers is recounted in the *Qesse-ye Sanjan* in the description of a battle where Parsis fought alongside Hindus when Muslim forces attacked Sanjan.[22] This episode has been linked to instances of Hindu resistance to Muslim rule in Gujarat during the fifteenth century.[23] Following a period of unrest, between the years 1573 and 1660, Gujarat was ruled over by the Mughals. According to John Hinnells, life under this Muslim dynasty was a time of 'relative peace and security', resulting in improved conditions for the Parsi community.[24] In particular, the reign of Akbar (r.1556–1605) has been described as a period of religious tolerance. Akbar invited representatives from various religious communities to his court to discuss religion, including a leading Zoroastrian priest, *dastur*, Meherji Rana. The religion of the Parsis must have been of interest to Akbar, as the syncretistic monotheistic faith he developed, *Din-e Ilahi*, included elements that reflect Zoroastrian beliefs and practices.[25] Persian was the official language in Akbar's court, and he was keen to attract bureaucrats and intellectuals from Iran.[26] Two Zoroastrian priests were amongst the individuals who moved to India: Ardeshir Nushirvan, who was invited by Akbar to help compile a Persian dictionary,[27] and Azar Kayvan, who led a philosophical and mystical movement, the Zoroastrian *Eshraqi* (Illuminative) School.[28]

Between the fifteenth and the eighteenth centuries, there were also instances of Parsis travelling to Iran. As well as those who were engaged in commercial activities,[29] a few individuals were sent on missions to gather information from their co-religionists.[30] These Parsi laymen posed questions to Iranian Zoroastrian priests, who, as members of the 'original' Zoroastrian community, were considered to hold greater authority on matters relating to religious practice.[31] Collectively, the texts containing these questions and answers are known as the *Revayat*s. The first *Revayat*, dated to 1478, marked a revival of earlier exchanges between Zoroastrians in India and Iran, which had included the transmission of religious texts to India.[32] Additionally, in 1721 an Iranian Zoroastrian priest, Jamasp Velayati, travelled to India to offer instruction to Parsi priests; he spent a year in the port of Surat, a significant centre for the Parsi community.[33]

Through these interactions, differences between the ritual calendars used by Zoroastrians in India and Iran were brought to light. This realization led to discord within the Parsi community over the question of which calendar ought to be followed. Two factions emerged: the smaller *Qadimi* group, who argued that since the Iranian Zoroastrians belonged to the older tradition, their calendar was correct, and the *Shahanshahi*s, who held the view that the Parsi calendar was accurate.[34] In addition to the issue of the calendar, the *Revayat*s had also addressed the question of whether conversion was permissible, a topic that continues to be debated today.[35] By the late eighteenth century, communication between Zoroastrians in India and Iran via *Revayat*s came to an end. According to Jesse Palsetia, this may have been because Parsi lay leaders no longer accepted the authority of Iranian priests and their *Qadimi* followers in India.[36] Lay leaders had been heavily involved in the calendar dispute, and Daniel Sheffield has highlighted that during the mid-eighteenth century, the opposing groups were led by two wealthy businessmen who were also commercial competitors.[37]

The socio-economic status of these two men can be linked to broader changes that were taking place in the Parsi community. Following the arrival of European merchants on the western coast of India during the sixteenth and seventeenth centuries, greater numbers of Parsis began working in roles related to trade, rather than agriculture. Parsis took on positions as agents and brokers, facilitating trade between coastal towns and areas inland.[38]

Over time, Bombay replaced Surat as the most important trading port in the region. Amongst the first Parsis to settle in Bombay were individuals who worked with the Portuguese, who had conquered the islands in 1534. The territory came under British rule in 1661, having been included in the dowry of Catherine of Braganza, who married King Charles II of England. Charles II then leased the islands to the English East India Company (EIC) in 1668. Aiming to develop Bombay into an international centre for trade, the EIC encouraged immigration into the area by declaring that there would be religious freedom and legal equality, conditions that were not guaranteed in the surrounding area.[39] Land was offered to Parsis as a further incentive, including a site for a *dakhmeh*, a funerary tower.[40] Parsis were also pushed to move to Bombay due to unrest in Gujarat, linked to local power struggles, and periods of famine.[41] Dinyar Patel has highlighted that the impact of a famine that occurred in 1824, causing many Parsis to leave Gujarat for Bombay, was exacerbated by the actions of British officials.[42] As the Parsi population in Bombay grew, a council of elders, *panchayat*, was formed to deal with community matters. Likewise, other religious communities formed their own comparable councils. The initial members of the Bombay Parsi Panchayat were all laymen, and their authority over issues that would traditionally have been under priestly jurisdiction reflects shifts in power in the community.[43]

Members of the Parsi community played a critical role in the emergence of Bombay as a major trade centre. For instance, in 1736, Lovji Wadia moved from Surat to Bombay, as he had been commissioned by the British to construct what was to be the first dry dock in Asia. Members of the Wadia family were responsible for running the Bombay docks for 150 years and were also renowned for building ships. Parsis were prominent merchants and bankers, and members of the community both contributed to and benefitted from the rising commercial importance of Bombay. Indeed, the businesses of some Parsi merchants were so large that they had their own shipping fleets.[44] The relationship of economic 'interdependence' between Parsis and the British has been discussed by David Willmer, with reference to the Jejeebhoy family. Jamsetjee Jejeebhoy (1783–1859), who was the first Indian baronet, amassed his fortune by trading cotton, and later opium.[45] This trade was predominantly between Bombay and China, where some Parsi merchants settled, creating diaspora communities.[46]

Business relations between Parsis and the British were facilitated by the lack of religious constraints regarding the ability of Parsis to socialize with Europeans.[47] Furthermore, recognizing the potential socio-economic benefits of knowing English, Parsis took advantage of the education offered at Christian missionary schools. These were established when a ban on missionary activity in Bombay was lifted in 1813. However, when two boys attending a school run by John Wilson (1804–75), a Scottish missionary, converted to Christianity in 1839, most Parsis stopped going to missionary schools and Parsis began to direct funds towards setting up their own Western-style schools.[48] In addition, Parsis made up a significantly high proportion of the students at Elphinstone College, which was founded in 1835 to provide a 'modern' education for young men in Bombay. The college had received financial support from wealthy Indians, including Parsis, and it was run by the Bombay Native Education Society.[49] Dinyar Patel has highlighted that the Bombay Native Education Society had Indians and Britons amongst its directors, and the college also had some Indian members of staff. The professors at the college tended to be politically liberal, and accusations were made by missionaries that the college was anti-Christian.[50]

Following the conversion controversy of 1839, Wilson continued to campaign against Zoroastrianism. Citing texts he had read in translation, Wilson argued that Zoroastrianism was dualistic and polytheistic, and therefore inferior to Christianity.[51] Critical of the emphasis Parsi priests placed on ritual, Wilson also claimed that Parsis did not understand their own religious texts. Although it may have been true that priests did not know the ancient Iranian languages of Avestan and Pahlavi, Rose has pointed out that in terms of Parsi religious practice, the written text did not hold the position of authority that it did for Christians.[52] Nevertheless, aiming to equip priests with the tools that would enable them to counter such accusations, Parsis founded seminaries where students were trained in contemporary European scholarship as well as in priestly rituals.[53] The Parsi scholar Kharshedji Rustomji Cama (1831–1909), known as K. R. Cama, played a significant role in this respect. After studying in Europe in the 1850s, Cama returned to India, where he organized courses in Avestan and Pahlavi, promoted research into Zoroastrianism and helped to establish seminaries.[54]

The critical view of Zoroastrianism expressed by individuals such as Wilson was a factor that prompted a group of reformist Parsis to form the *Rahnumae Mazdayasnan Sabha*, Society of the Guides of the Mazdayasnan Path, in 1851. Many of the men involved in this society had studied at Elphinstone College, for example, Dadabhai Naoroji, who had also had a traditional education. In the same year, with the support of the wealthy reformist *shetia* (member of the commercial elite) Kharshedji Nasarvanji Cama, Naoroji also established *Rast Goftar*, a Gujarati newspaper that promoted social reform.[55] Eckehard Kulke has argued that the emergence of Parsi newspapers, such as *Rast Goftar*, strengthened a sense of community and facilitated the spread of reformist views.[56] Parsi reformers advocated a 'return' to the original Zoroastrian faith, emphasizing aspects of their religion that reflected contemporary British social values. The argument was made that the religion had been negatively impacted by the wider environment. Thus, if 'foreign' elements, such as child marriage, animal sacrifice and polygamy, were removed, its true essence would be revealed.[57] There were comparable reform movements in other religious communities, for example, the Hindu group Brahmo Samaj.[58]

Rather than viewing modernity as inherently European, Monica Ringer has argued that Parsis who called for social and religious reform held that modernity could be accessed through the revival of the true Zoroastrian religion.[59] Reformist Parsis were influenced by contemporary European views of religion, including the 'scientific' theories of evolutionism and historicism, which led to the idea that religions could be compared and situated on a scale, leading to the most advanced and 'civilized'. Echoing Protestant ideas as to what constituted a 'high' form of religion, Parsi reformers emphasized the status of the *Gatha*s as revelatory texts.[60] Additionally, they welcomed the opinion of the German scholar Martin Haug (1827–76), who, in contrast to Wilson, believed that the *Gatha*s provided evidence that Zoroastrianism was originally a monotheistic faith.[61]

Parsi reformers proposed various changes to religious practice, including the simplification of rituals, as well as the acceptance of *juddin*s, non-Zoroastrians, into the faith. These ideas were challenged by orthodox Parsis.[62] There was a higher proportion of reformist Parsis in Bombay than elsewhere in India, and, according to Mitra Sharafi, their 'flexible approach' to issues such as ritual purity 'accommodated the conditions of late colonial modernity'.[63] This gave Parsis an economic advantage as it eased relations with the British, including in the commercial sphere.[64] Although they were not treated as equals, Tanya Luhrmann has noted that Parsi reformers, who had 'distanced themselves from non-Parsi Indian communities', were praised by the British for their adoption of 'European manners and customs'.[65]

According to Ringer, a key aspect of this was the extent to which the societal position of Parsi women reflected European social norms.[66] Parsi reformers argued that in ancient Iran there had been a greater level of equality between women and men, indicative of the high level of civilization attained by Zoroastrians. Thus, rather than being viewed as the imitation of European manners, changes in the position of women in the Parsi community were presented as the restoration of authentic Zoroastrian customs.[67] This included the education of girls.[68] From the mid-nineteenth century schools were established for Parsi girls, and the 1901 census revealed that female literacy in the Parsi community was 63 per cent, with male literacy reaching almost 88 per cent.[69]

By 1901, there were 46,231 Parsis living in Bombay. This was approximately half of all Parsis in India, but only about 6 per cent of the population of Bombay,[70] which was, by the late nineteenth century, the second largest city in the British Empire after London.[71] Despite the comparatively small size of their community, Parsis were major landowners in Bombay, and the power and wealth of certain Parsis was visible in the public sphere, for instance in the form of statues and monuments.[72] The rise in the prosperity of the Parsi community under British rule encouraged expressions of Parsi loyalty towards the British.[73] As well as their success in the commercial sphere, due to their high level of education, Parsis were prominent in fields such as medicine and law.[74] According to Hinnells, after the 1857 'mutiny', or First War of Indian Independence, and the establishment of the British Raj, the British relied on educated Indians, including Parsis, to enable them to rule.[75] Parsis were numerically over-represented in local politics and some took on roles in the governments of the princely states.[76] In addition to the community in Bombay, there were Parsi communities elsewhere in India, particularly in Gujarat, and cities such as Poona (Pune), Karachi and Calcutta (Kolkata).[77] The economic and political power held by members of the highly urbanized Parsi community can be contrasted to situation of the majority of their co-religionists in Iran.

Over the centuries since the establishment of Muslim rule, the Zoroastrian population of Iran gradually decreased in numerical terms. In contrast to Jews and Christians, Zoroastrians were not involved in political matters during the medieval period. Zoroastrians were increasingly marginalized and the Mongol invasions of the thirteenth century also negatively impacted the community.[78] At the beginning of the sixteenth century, there was a significant development in terms of the religious history of Iran; the first shah of the Safavid dynasty, Ismail (r.1501–24), declared Twelver Shi'ism to be the state religion. Apocalyptic beliefs were widespread when Ismail became shah, and a related sense of urgency prompted campaigns to convert Sunni Muslims and non-Muslims to Shi'ism.[79] According to Aptin Khanbaghi, out of the non-Muslim communities, Zoroastrians were tolerated the least during the Safavid period (1501–1722).[80]

Despite this, there are instances when concerns were raised by the Safavid shahs regarding the position of Zoroastrians. For example, Shah Abbas (r.1588–1629) expressed an interest in the safety of the Zoroastrian community. According to Touraj Daryaee, this was linked to the fact that Zoroastrians played a prominent role in the Kerman wool trade.[81] The wealth accumulated by some Zoroastrians at this time is reflected in the ability of Rostam Bundar to personally fund the building, or rebuilding, of the Kerman fire temple in 1644.[82] Rather than being solely motivated by 'religious bigotry', Kioumars Ghereghlou has argued that the ill-treatment of Zoroastrians was often indicative of tension between central and provincial authorities. Zoroastrians were legally protected by the shah, and thus, local bureaucrats used the financial extortion of Zoroastrians as a way of displaying their power.[83]

However, there does appear to have been a rise in religious discrimination during the Safavid period, particularly in the latter years of their rule. By this stage, Zoroastrians were predominantly living in and around the cities of Yazd and Kerman.[84] Jamsheed Choksy has described how there was a 'rise in sectarian intolerance' during the Safavid period, with the derogatory term *gabr*, meaning 'infidel', widely used in reference to Zoroastrians, who were also misrepresented as 'fire-worshippers'.[85] There were instances of Zoroastrian fire temples being turned into mosques, and Zoroastrians resorted to hiding their fire altars in order to protect them from desecration.[86] The views of 'militant' clerics such as Mohammad Baqer Majlesi (d.1699) had a negative impact on members of non-Muslim communities. Majlesi wrote texts containing strict purity laws and within these works he promoted the idea that non-Muslims were physically impure, *najes*, and that contact with non-Muslims should therefore be avoided, including in relation to the preparation of food and drink.[87] Influenced by the views of clerics such as Majlesi, Shah Soltan Hosayn (r.1694–1722) issued a controversial decree calling for the whole population to convert to Shi'ism, if necessary by force,[88] but his lack of authority meant that the ruling was not fully imposed.[89]

In Kerman, Zoroastrians were made to live in a separate quarter outside the city walls; this was probably linked to the enforcement of Shi'i purity laws. Consequently, the community was in a vulnerable position when Afghan tribal forces advanced into western Iran during the final years of Safavid rule, reaching Kerman in 1719.[90] Although Zoroastrians suffered during this attack, according to Choksy, Zoroastrians did subsequently collaborate with the Afghan tribes, and were therefore targeted by local Shi'is after the Afghans were defeated.[91] The Afghan tribes were overpowered by Nader Shah (r.1736–47), who not only established control over the majority of the territory of the earlier Safavid Empire but also expanded his reach into India.[92] Contrasting accounts are given of the experiences of Zoroastrians under his rule.[93] For instance, the French traveller Ferdinand Méchin, who went to Iran during the nineteenth century, described positive relations between Zoroastrians and Nader Shah, whereas references to forced conversions are made in a book published in 1858 by the Parsi historian Dosabhai Framji Karaka.[94]

Following the assassination of Nader Shah in 1747, Karim Khan Zand, who had been one of his captains, gained power over most of present-day Iran (r.1751–79).[95] This appears to have been a period of relative tolerance, and in 1768, a Parsi *Qadimi* priest called Mulla Kaus travelled to Yazd with his son, Peshotan. Mulla Kaus had been commissioned to go on this journey to gather information regarding the contentious issue of the ritual calendar.[96] In addition to studying with Zoroastrians in Yazd and Kerman, Mulla Kaus spent several years in Isfahan, where he studied with Muslim scholars. Having gained a reputation for his expertise as an astrologer, Mulla Kaus served at the royal court in Shiraz.[97] Here, he succeeded in securing Karim Khan's support for the Iranian Zoroastrian community.[98] Meanwhile, Peshotan undertook priestly training in Yazd. After twelve years both men returned to India with copies of religious texts, and what was to be the last *Revayat*. Peshotan, who now used the name Mulla Firuz, later wrote an account of his travels, and he also published the *Dasatir*, based on a manuscript that his father had brought from Iran.[99] This text is likely to have been written by Azar Kayvan in the late sixteenth or early seventeenth century, but was for a time regarded as an authentic work from the pre-Islamic period.[100] According to Hinnells, both Mulla Firuz and his father were 'instrumental' in raising the awareness of Parsis about their links to Iran.[101]

By the end of the eighteenth century, the last Zand ruler, Lotf 'Ali Khan, was overthrown by Aqa Mohammad Khan, a member of the Qajar tribe.[102] There had been heavy fighting around Kerman in 1794, and a later account described how 'great numbers' of Zoroastrians were killed in the 'indiscriminate plunder and slaughter' of the Qajar attack.[103] Lotf 'Ali Khan was executed soon after, and Aqa Mohammad became the first Qajar shah.

At the start of the Qajar era, most Zoroastrians worked as agriculturalists and were geographically concentrated around Yazd and Kerman. Zoroastrians communicated with one another in their own dialect, Dari, which had regional variations and which was not understood by people outside the community.[104] In total, Zoroastrians comprised only about 0.1 per cent of the population of Iran, a country with ethnic, religious and linguistic diversity, and with a significant tribal population, some of whom were nomadic.[105] Whilst approximately 90 per cent of people living in Iran were Shi'i Muslims,[106] there was also a substantial Sunni Muslim community, as well as non-Muslim communities, including Jews, as well as Armenian and Assyrian Christians.[107] Although Zoroastrians were designated as 'People of the Book', they were sometimes subjected to greater restrictions than members of other recognized non-Muslim religions.[108] In addition to rules clearly linked to the idea of purity, other regulations served to humiliate and visibly distinguish Zoroastrians and members of non-Muslim communities. For instance, Zoroastrians were required to wear clothes of a yellow colour, and they were forbidden from building houses higher than those of Muslims and from riding on horseback in the presence of Muslims.[109]

According to Daniel Tsadik, rather than being regarded as 'non-affiliated, private individuals', non-Muslims living in nineteenth-century Iran 'were always classified according to their religion'.[110] Although the concept of 'minorities' as a political term became prominent in the early twentieth century, and can be seen as having developed alongside the establishment of nation states, the division of society according to religion had a long history in Iran.[111] Indeed, Michael Stausberg has highlighted that the Sasanian Empire was made up of a distinct dominant majority religion, Zoroastrianism, and subordinate minority religions.[112] The terms 'subordinate' and 'dominant' are used by Stausberg to stress the relative power of groups, which does not necessarily correlate to their numerical size.[113]

The position of Zoroastrians in Iran had changed drastically from the Sasanian period; Zoroastrians in Qajar Iran were not only a minority in numerical terms, but they were also a subordinate group. Whilst Zoroastrians in both India and Iran were numerical minorities, the socio-economic status of Parsis in India during the nineteenth century can be contrasted to that of the Iranian Zoroastrians. In this respect, the frequent use of the term 'elite', rather than 'minority', to describe the Parsi community can be seen in relation to the observation by Anh Nga Longva that semantically, 'minority' is often equated with 'inferiority, weakness, subordination'.[114] However, following the first census of India, which was carried out in 1871–2, Parsis were increasingly aware of, and concerned by, their status as a numerical minority.[115] In the census, Parsis were categorized as 'Asiatic foreigners', a terminology that emphasized the idea that Parsis were not Indian but Iranian.[116] Worries about the size of the Parsi community were exacerbated in the following years, as the British reaction to the Muslim-Parsi riots of 1874 suggested that the British were not willing to go against majoritarian religious feelings to protect freedom of speech when there was a danger of public disorder.[117]

Alongside members of the long-established Zoroastrian community in India, the 'Parsees' recorded in the census would have included much more recent Iranian Zoroastrian immigrants and their descendants. From the latter years of the Safavid period, a number of Iranian Zoroastrians had moved to India, where, to a certain extent, they formed a minority within a minority. Some stayed to work in India for a few years before returning to Iran, whilst others settled permanently. Initially, these immigrants and their descendants were called 'Parsees', or 'Persian Parsees', but by the early twentieth century, they usually referred to themselves as Iranis, thereby differentiating their community from the much larger Parsi community. According to Simin Patel, the motivation behind this change was for the members of the community to distance themselves from the associations that had been made between 'Persian Parsees' and poverty.[118]

Iranian Zoroastrians in India played a significant role in terms of strengthening ties between Zoroastrian communities in India and Iran during the nineteenth and early twentieth centuries. By focusing on these interactions and on the experiences of Zoroastrians over these years, an alternative view will be offered on the wider political developments during this period of Iranian and Indian history. Considering the marginalized position of Iranian Zoroastrians in the mid-nineteenth century and the geographical location of Parsis and Iranian Zoroastrians who were living in India, and in diaspora communities elsewhere, the perspective of Iranian history that is taken in this book might be described as 'history from the side'.

By adopting this approach, I hope to contribute to current discussions concerning the relations between Zoroastrian communities in Iran and India during the nineteenth and twentieth centuries. A number of the works referred to below were published during the time that I have been writing this book, and as far as possible I have addressed the points raised in this new research in my own work. Recently, transnational connections between Zoroastrians in India and Iran have been analysed from various angles. For instance, in *Exile and the Nation: The Parsi Community of India and the Making of Modern Iran*, Afshin Marashi has revealed the substantial impact that Zoroastrians had on the development of the form of Iranian nationalism promoted by the Pahlavi state, a nationalism that elevated the pre-Islamic era.[119] In his previous book, *Nationalizing Iran: Culture, Power, and the State, 1870–1940*, Marashi highlighted connections between Manekji Limji Hataria, a member of the Parsi community, and early Iranian nationalists who were writing during the late nineteenth century, and their shared interest in pre-Islamic Iran.[120] This subject has also been examined by Reza Zia-Ebrahimi and Michael Stausberg.[121]

Hataria spent many years in Iran, where he worked on behalf of the Society for the Amelioration of the Conditions of the Zoroastrians of Persia (Amelioration Society), which was founded in Bombay in the mid-nineteenth century. The strategies that Parsis used to support the Zoroastrian community in Iran have been addressed by Shervin Farridnejad, who has written about the campaign to end Zoroastrian payment of the *jezya* tax, and by Dinyar Patel, who has analysed the power relations between Parsis and the British and the implications for the success of Parsi campaigns regarding their co-religionists in Iran.[122] Patel has also researched the position of Parsis during the 1920s and 1930s in relation to nationalism in India and Iran, with particular reference to the Iran League, an organization established in 1922 in Bombay.[123] This period has also been the topic of recent research by Marashi, who has focused on Parsi proposals for economic investment in Iran, and by Murali Ranganathan, who has examined Parsi travelogues dating from the early 1920s.[124]

Covering a broader time frame, in *Pious Citizens: Reforming Zoroastrianism in India and Iran*, Monica Ringer has analysed the emergence of reformist views within the Parsi community in the early nineteenth century, and has examined the impact that these views subsequently had on Zoroastrianism in India and Iran, and on modernity and religiosity in Iran more broadly.[125] Talinn Grigor has also addressed the influence that Parsis had on modernity in India and Iran from the mid-nineteenth to mid-twentieth centuries, with a particular focus on revivalist architectural trends.[126] Whilst covering a similar period, in this book the emphasis will be on the political as well as the socio-economic significance of the ties between Parsis and Iran.

According to Janet Amighi, Zoroastrians were one of the most persecuted groups in mid-nineteenth-century Iran, but, by the Pahlavi period, they had become the symbol of Iranian nationalism.[127] The present book will examine the changes that occurred during this time, especially in the early years of the twentieth century, a transitional period for Zoroastrians in Iran, which have not received as much scholarly attention as earlier and later periods. During the Constitutional Revolution, the societal position of Zoroastrians and other recognized non-Muslim communities was brought into focus. The significance of links between Zoroastrians in India and Iran in the context of these political events has been outlined by Mansour Bonakdarian, in his article for *Encyclopædia Iranica* concerning relations between India and Iran at the beginning of the twentieth century.[128] In addition to the impact that political change in Iran had on the Iranian Zoroastrian community, and vice versa, events in Iran affected Parsi perceptions of their ancestral homeland. Attitudes towards Iran were also influenced by political developments in India, particularly the growing strength of the Indian nationalist movement.

Prior to the years of the Constitutional Revolution, significant links had already been established between Zoroastrians in India and Iran. The arrival of Iranian Zoroastrians in India was a key factor that led to an increase in Parsi interest in their co-religionists, and this prompted Zoroastrians in India to engage in philanthropy directed towards Zoroastrians in Iran. The Amelioration Society was founded in the mid-nineteenth century, and the organization had a profound and wide-ranging impact on the lives of Zoroastrians in Iran, not only in economic terms but also in relation to the legal position of Zoroastrians, as well as in terms of religious reform and access to education. The actions of wealthy and influential Parsis who aimed to assist their co-religionists in Iran were seminal and will be examined in Chapter 1, as will the significance of the growth in the Iranian Zoroastrian community in India, members of which were also able to use their position to support Zoroastrians in Iran.

Not only were there stronger connections between the Zoroastrian communities of India and Iran but Parsis were also increasingly referencing their ancient Persian heritage and their imperial history. During the last decades of the nineteenth century, a small group of early nationalists in Iran were similarly looking back to the pre-Islamic period as a golden age. Chapter 2 will examine sentiments of 'Persianness' amongst Parsis, in relation to both the development of early nationalist thought in Iran and the rising interest in ancient Iran expressed by Zoroastrians in the context of colonial India. As well as interactions that took place between individuals in Iran, the relations between Iranian diplomats and Zoroastrians in India will be analysed. By the early twentieth century, Parsis were discussing the possibility of establishing a colony in or near their ancient 'homeland' of Iran, and Parsi feelings of patriotism towards Iran were encouraged by the British.

Strategic reasons for the emphasis placed by the British on Parsis being Persians will be addressed in Chapter 3, with specific regard to British concerns about Russian influence in southern Iran in the years leading up to the Iranian Constitutional Revolution. From the mid-nineteenth century, a growing number of Iranian Zoroastrians became involved in trade, and some were amongst the most successful merchants and bankers in Iran. This affected British attitudes towards the community, leading the British to regard the nurturing of positive relations with Iranian Zoroastrians, both directly and through the Parsi community, as being of potential tactical importance. Thus, the British were also keen to support efforts to improve the social standing of members of the Iranian Zoroastrian community, including through the promotion of education.

The political changes that were precipitated by the Constitutional Revolution of 1906–11 further impacted the position of Zoroastrians in Iranian society, and Zoroastrians were the first non-Muslims to be represented in the Iranian Parliament, the Majles. Whilst relations with the British and the Parsis contributed to the ability of Zoroastrians in Iran to take advantage of the events of the Constitutional Revolution, the outcome was an improvement in their sociopolitical position, paving the way for further change. The involvement of Zoroastrians in the early months of the revolution will be addressed in Chapter 4, as will the reaction to the revolution amongst Zoroastrians in India, in the context of Parsi concerns regarding their future political position in India.

Although the revolution appeared to mark a positive development for Zoroastrians, the murders of two prominent Zoroastrian merchants in 1907 and 1908 called into question whether there had been any real improvements for the community. Taking into consideration concurrent debates that were taking place in Iran regarding the rights of recognized non-Muslim communities, Chapter 5 will examine the reaction to these murders in relation to the question as to what extent Zoroastrians were considered Iranian nationals.

Following the Lesser Despotism, a period when the Majles was dissolved and Mohammad 'Ali Shah briefly re-established autocratic rule, the constitution was restored in 1909 which led to renewed hope in Iran and India regarding the position of Zoroastrians. The political and societal position of Zoroastrians in Iran at this time will be addressed in Chapter 6. In addition, the impact of the restoration of the constitution on Parsi views towards Iran will be analysed, as will the degree to which Parsis maintained an interest in Iranian events following the dissolution of constitutional rule in 1911, and the First World War, a time when Iranian Zoroastrian relations with the British were weakening.

The final chapter will cover the period from the end of the First World War to the mid-1930s. These years saw the rise of Reza Khan, who founded the Pahlavi dynasty in 1926. Under the rule of Reza Shah, there was greater centralization of power in Iran, and a push for modernization and secularization. The pre-Islamic imperial past was key to Pahlavi nationalist rhetoric, and the elevation of ancient Iran was further encouraged by members of the Zoroastrian community. With the political situation in India in mind, links between Zoroastrians in India and their co-religionists in Iran will be examined, as will broader links between Zoroastrians in India and the Iranian nation.

1

Zoroastrian Philanthropy and Iran

Parsi philanthropy

As a community, Parsis have an enduring reputation for their philanthropic works. The significance of charity to Parsis is such that it has been described by Jesse Palsetia as a 'potent symbolic marker of identity'.[1] In religious terms, it is noteworthy that rather than praising asceticism, the creation of wealth is encouraged in Zoroastrianism, with the understanding that with prosperity comes the responsibility to help others.[2] Good deeds are believed to contribute to the fight against evil, and, at an individual level, they are thought to help secure a positive outcome when the soul is judged after death.[3]

These ideas can be traced back to Zoroastrian religious texts and have historically had an impact on the distribution of wealth amongst Zoroastrians. Maria Macuch has discussed the role of Zoroastrian charitable foundations during the Sasanian period (224–651 CE). As well as being established to safeguard the soul of the deceased, they could also provide a source of income for the descendants of the individual who had died. Endowments were often set up to aid religious practice, for example, to pay for rituals and the maintenance of fire temples. However, resources were also directed towards broader issues, including supporting poorer members of the community and conducting public works.[4] After the fall of the Sasanian Empire and the establishment of Islamic rule, Zoroastrians in Iran were able to use endowments as a way of safeguarding community properties and funds. It was common for seasonal religious festivals, *gahambar*s, to be paid for in this manner. In addition to a meal that was prepared for local Zoroastrians, on the day of a *gahambar*, unconsecrated food would be offered to disadvantaged members of the Muslim community.[5]

The distribution of food and clothing is also referenced as a key part of Parsi religious practice in the sixteen Sanskrit *Shlokas*, a text often dated to the twelfth or thirteenth century.[6] Similar to Zoroastrians in Iran, Parsis used their resources to assist poorer members of the community, as well as to pay for rituals and the upkeep of buildings such as fire temples.[7] The *Qesse-ye Sanjan* recounts the generosity of Changa Asa, a Parsi layman who lived in Navsari during the fifteenth–sixteenth centuries,[8] and Europeans who travelled in India in the seventeenth century also highlighted Parsi charity.[9] With greater numbers of Parsis becoming involved in trade, the economic success enjoyed by some individuals enabled them to undertake large-scale philanthropic acts. For instance, a merchant from Surat called Rustam Manek (*c.*1635–1721) paid for various projects, such as the building of roads and public wells. Following Manek's lead, his descendants helped facilitate the settlement of Parsis in Bombay through their own charitable works.[10] Although philanthropy was not a new aspect of community life, David White has described how the 'mechanics' of Parsi gifting adapted to suit the environment of eighteenth-century Bombay, where the priority was the establishment of a religious infrastructure to 'permit Parsis to *be* Parsis'.[11] Fire temples and *dakhmeh*s, funerary towers, were built, and funds were also used to provide housing for Parsis arriving in the city.

The decisions that Parsis made regarding the distribution of funds helped define group boundaries and, in White's words, resulted in a 'sense of unity and belonging to a separate and supportive community'.[12] Rusheed Wadia has suggested that Parsi charitable institutions, such as the Parsi Benevolent Institution (PBI), also served to strengthen Parsi commercial networks.[13] The PBI was established in 1849 by Sir Jamsetjee Jejeebhoy (1783–1859), and it was the largest Parsi charitable foundation in existence at the time.[14] One of the factors that had led the wealthy merchant to set up the foundation was the conversion to Christianity in 1839 of two Parsi boys who had been pupils at the school of the missionary John Wilson. Significantly, the funding that the PBI directed towards the creation of new Parsi schools enabled Parsis to gain access to a Western-style education, without having to attend Christian missionary schools.[15]

In addition to this emphasis on education, the PBI aimed from the outset to assist Parsis who were experiencing poverty. Food and clothes were provided for children, and payments were made for religious ceremonies, including marriages.[16] Due to the overlap in the individuals involved, the PBI effectively merged with the Bombay Parsi Panchayat (BPP). This was an organization that had been formed in the eighteenth century to manage the religious and social affairs of the Parsi community in Bombay.[17] By the mid-nineteenth century the authority of the BPP over legal matters had decreased, partly due to Parsis increasingly using British courts to settle disputes, and its role as a charitable institution subsequently became more prominent.[18] The charitable work of the BPP focused on receiving and administering funds, and managing community properties.[19]

Philanthropic acts were also conducted by Parsis who lived outside Bombay, for example in Poona (Pune) and Surat.[20] Although supporting other Parsis was a key concern, Jesse Palsetia has described how 'Parsi liberality became a duty towards the greater community'.[21] Parsis acted to help the wider population, for example during periods of famine and drought, and they offered humanitarian assistance to those who were affected by major fires that broke out in Bombay and Surat, in 1803 and 1837 respectively.[22] The aid given by Parsis at such critical times strengthened their relations with members of other religious communities.[23] Influential Parsis were also able to use their links with the British to encourage them to back these relief efforts, for instance during the 1837 famine in Gujarat.[24]

According to Palsetia, Parsi charity took on 'a greater political significance under imperialism as it became an expression of the social and political power of philanthropic Parsi elites in British Indian society'.[25] Palsetia has highlighted how the influence of British values prompted 'Western-style charity' amongst Parsis, with funds increasingly being used to establish hospitals and schools.[26] The prospect of public recognition may also have been a factor impacting these choices, as some Parsi philanthropists were given titles by the British; indeed, Jamsetjee Jejeebhoy was awarded both a knighthood and a baronetcy.[27] Figures such as Jamsetjee Jejeebhoy are prominent in discussions of Parsi charity, but acts of giving were not solely carried out by the wealthiest individuals in the community. John Hinnells has pointed out that charity was often private and was 'a feature of a broad spectrum of Parsi society', with many women also offering donations.[28]

Whilst Parsis focused their efforts on causes in India, Parsi philanthropy did reach further afield. Funds were sent to Britain, for instance, to hospitals in London and to striking workers from cotton mills in Lancashire. Support was also given to people in Ireland who suffered the effects of famine during the early and mid-nineteenth century.[29] Additionally, Zoroastrians in Iran benefitted from Parsi charity; for example, in the eighteenth century, the construction and maintenance of a fire temple in Yazd was funded by Nasarvanji Kohiyar, a merchant who worked as an agent for the Dutch in Surat.[30] In the mid-nineteenth century, Zoroastrians in India began to direct aid towards their co-religionists in Iran in a systematic manner; this development was to have a substantial impact on the future of the Iranian Zoroastrian community.

The Society for the Amelioration of the Conditions of the Zoroastrians in Persia

The Society for the Amelioration of the Conditions of the Zoroastrians in Persia (Amelioration Society) was founded in 1853, due to the growing concern of Zoroastrians in India regarding the position of their co-religionists in Iran.[31] Awareness of the situation in Iran had been raised through increased contact between Parsis and Iranian Zoroastrians who had emigrated to India in recent years.[32] Amongst these individuals was a girl called Golestan, who left Iran with her father in 1796, to escape being forcibly married to a wealthy Muslim merchant.[33] Significantly, it was due to Golestan that her husband, the Parsi merchant Framji Bhikaji Panday (d.1876), was inspired to assist other Iranian Zoroastrians who had arrived in India.[34] In the 1830s, their eldest son, Burjorji Framji Panday, established a fund for Iranian Zoroastrians in Bombay, and his brother, Mehrwanji Framji Panday (1812–76), was a founding member of the Amelioration Society.[35] The couple also had a daughter called Sakarbai (1826–90), who married Sir Dinshaw Maneckji Petit, 1st Baronet (1823–1901), another Parsi who was heavily involved in the organization.[36] Thus, many of the individuals closely associated with the Amelioration Society had direct family ties to Iran.[37]

A provocative article by the Danish scholar, Niels Ludvig Westergaard, was another factor that encouraged the Parsis to take action.[38] Following his travels in Iran in the early 1840s, Westergaard wrote to John Wilson, a vociferous critic of the Zoroastrian religion, and described the poverty experienced by Zoroastrians living in Iran. In 1848, an extract of this letter was reprinted in the *Oriental Christian Spectator*, a journal that had been established by Wilson.[39] Westergaard questioned why 'the opulent Parsis of Bombay don't send a mission of inquiry to their brethren in Yazd and Kerman', whom he claimed knew 'nothing whatever' about their religion and were 'by degrees becoming

Musalmans'.[40] According to Daniel Sheffield, the article 'must have caused a shock'.[41] Later in the same year, a petition from Zoroastrians in Kerman was printed in a Parsi newspaper; the details of instances of violence against members of the community led an unnamed Parsi to express the hope that the British conquer Iran, in the belief that this might benefit Zoroastrians.[42] In addition to concerns about safety, the account by Westergaard had also stoked arguments between Parsis regarding the dates of the ritual calendar, and whether or not Iranian Zoroastrians, as the 'original' community, held religious authority over the Parsis.[43] Although the article had implications for communal disputes, Parsis who opposed one another on these issues were united in the view that their co-religionists ought to be supported.[44]

Consequently, members of the Amelioration Society decided to send an emissary to assess the conditions of the Zoroastrians in Iran, and they appointed Manekji Limji Hataria (1813–90) to take on this role. Donations that had been sent to Yazd in earlier years had allegedly been mishandled, and it was hoped that this issue would be resolved if the society had a representative in Iran. With his prior experiences of managing accounts, Hataria was well-suited to the position.[45] Hataria was descended from Zoroastrians who had left Iran during the Safavid period, and not only was he fluent in Persian, but he had been hoping to travel to the country for some time.[46] The journey had been too dangerous in the past, but security on the roads had improved following the reforms of Mirza Taqi Khan Farahani (1807–52), who held the position of Amir Kabir, chief minister, from 1848 to 1851.[47] Hataria also benefited from his status as a British subject, and he set out on his journey in 1854 with letters of recommendation from British officials in Bombay.[48]

On the basis of the initial reports that Hataria sent back to the Amelioration Society, the group agreed that Iranian Zoroastrians should be given financial support and that funds ought to be raised to pay for schools, fire temples and *dakhmehs*.[49] Despite restrictions on the repair and construction of Zoroastrian religious buildings, Hataria was able to organize for fire temples to be restored in Yazd and Kerman in 1855 and 1857, and for *dakhmehs* to also be built and restored.[50] Substantial funds were directed towards education. This was viewed as a priority, as Hataria had stated that nearly all Iranian Zoroastrians were illiterate when he arrived in the country.[51] In addition, the Amelioration Society helped pay for food, clothes and medical care.[52] Hataria attempted to reform the organizational structure of Zoroastrian communities in Yazd and Kerman by founding Zoroastrian *anjomans* (councils), modelled on the Bombay Parsi Panchayat.[53] The *anjomans* were responsible for dealing with internal matters, including the administration of religious endowments, as well as relations between Zoroastrians and wider society. This role had previously been undertaken by councils of elders, or by an officially recognized individual from the local Zoroastrian community who was appointed as their *kalantar*, mayor.[54]

In 1863, Hataria returned to Bombay for almost two years. During this time, he raised awareness about his mission and gathered donations to help pay for the various projects he had instigated, as well as for the *jezya*, a tax paid by non-Muslim communities. The economic burden of this tax incentivized conversion to Islam, as did the law that allowed Zoroastrian converts to Islam to become the sole inheritors of their family's wealth.[55] Hataria confirmed Parsi concerns about the dwindling size of the Iranian Zoroastrian population, estimating that there were only 7,123 members of the faith living in the country.[56] One issue that indirectly contributed to population decline was the expense of dowries. Thus, some of the donations from India were used to cover costs linked to weddings.[57]

Hataria and the other members of the Amelioration Society worked to improve the lives of Zoroastrians in Iran. However, at the same time, Zoroastrians continued to leave Iran for India, where conditions appeared to be safer and there seemed to be better opportunities in terms of work. Recognizing the challenges Zoroastrians faced in Yazd and Kerman, Hataria wrote to the Iranian prime minister in the late 1850s, stating that he was willing to support Zoroastrians who wanted to leave 'our fatherland'.[58] The number of Zoroastrians emigrating to India rose during the early 1870s, when a period of drought in Iran resulted in widespread famine.

Zoroastrian networks and famine relief

Between 1869 and 1873 there was a catastrophic famine in Iran. Estimated figures vary, but it has been suggested that around 1.5 million people died, a figure that may have represented as much as a fifth of the population.[59] The area surrounding Yazd was badly affected, in part due to the integration of Iran into the wider world economy. This had led to an increase in the cultivation of cash crops, such as opium, meaning that grain had to be brought in from other regions.[60] In a letter sent to Bombay from Tehran, Hataria suggested that high taxes had made the situation even worse.[61] Although the famine had begun to be felt earlier, it was in 1871 that it was widely reported abroad, including in India.[62]

In May 1871, the desperate plight of Iranian Zoroastrians was highlighted in an article printed in the Parsi newspaper, *Jam-e Jamshed*, which stated that unless Zoroastrians in Bombay took swift action, Iranian Zoroastrians were 'in danger of being exterminated'.[63] Not only were Zoroastrians reported to be starving and vulnerable to robbery, but the newspaper claimed that they were also victims of cannibalism.[64] An appeal for funds was made by the Amelioration Society, which had been trying from its foundation to reverse the declining numbers of Zoroastrians in Iran, and a special committee was appointed in June 1871, which 'promptly transmitted' 8,000 rupees to be distributed by Hataria 'amongst their casteman'.[65] Wealthy individuals were approached for donations, such as the businessman and philanthropist, Cowasjee Jehangir Readymoney, who 'at once' subscribed 11,000 rupees towards famine relief and the payment of the *jezya*.[66]

Alongside the action taken by the Amelioration Society, a separate organization was founded with the specific purpose of providing aid for victims of the famine. This was the Persian Famine Relief Fund, which was spearheaded by members of the Iranian Zoroastrian Mehrban family.[67] The secretaries of the fund were two brothers, Godrez and Ardeshir, who lived in Bombay. They were successful merchants who had established the firm, Messrs. Godrez Mehrban & Co., an import-export business that traded tea from India and asafoetida from Iran.[68] During the famine, their network of contacts enabled them to successfully transfer funds and provisions to Iran, and to assist Zoroastrians who were attempting to emigrate to India. Amongst those involved was another of the Mehrban brothers, Khosrow, who was based in Bandar Abbas.[69] British officials in Iran also cooperated with the Persian Famine Relief Fund and the Amelioration Society, helping distribute grain in Tehran and southern Iran.[70]

Despite the efforts of the Persian Famine Relief Fund and the Amelioration Society, the situation in Yazd had worsened by October 1871, with the effects of the famine intensified by an outbreak of cholera. Rising numbers of Zoroastrians planned to leave Iran; around two hundred individuals were reportedly preparing to travel to Bombay at this time, with another five hundred hoping to make the journey in the following months.[71] The Iranian authorities tried to prevent Zoroastrians from leaving Bandar Abbas by boat, but the agents of Mehrban & Co. were determined to help them.[72] Pleas were made to Zoroastrians in India for further donations, and Parsis were requested to prepare food and shelter for individuals arriving from Iran.[73] Both the Amelioration Society and the Persian Famine Relief Fund were striving to help Iranian Zoroastrians, but, at one point, the Amelioration Society was criticized for only transferring 2,000 rupees to the Famine Relief Fund, despite having surplus funds.[74] In defence of their actions, members of the society stated that the money they raised was specifically for their co-religionists in Iran, rather than for Zoroastrians who had left the country, or who were preparing to do so.[75]

Whilst different views were expressed regarding the distribution of funds, there was widespread agreement that Zoroastrians in India held a certain responsibility towards their Iranian co-religionists, including in relation to the provision of housing and employment for those who reached India.[76] This view was also promoted in the *Times of India*, which suggested that wealthy Parsis could find work for Iranian Zoroastrians on their land, with six estates near Bombay listed as potential sites.[77] Simin Patel has highlighted that the Mehrban brothers effectively made use of the Bombay press to encourage donations, arranging for articles about the famine to be published.[78] Newspaper coverage did have an impact, with personal accounts fuelling sympathy for the refugees. After reading the 'painful narrative' of the journey of Zoroastrians from Iran to Bombay, the Parsi businessman Byramjee Jeejeebhoy agreed to pay 'a fixed monthly stipend to the poorest of them', and allowed them to make use of some of his land.[79]

Emigration to India was not the only route taken to escape the famine in Yazd. According to a report in the *Times of India*, approximately five hundred Zoroastrians left Yazd and Kerman and travelled to Tehran, where they hoped to find better conditions. Fifty of these individuals were paid by the British to construct a road, and permission was obtained for them to build a new *dakhmeh*, 'with the view of giving work to the people'.[80] Not only did this intervention provide employment, but it also enabled Zoroastrians to practice their religion in the capital.

However, the number of Iranian Zoroastrians arriving in Bombay still exceeded expectations. Parsis discussed how to best respond, with some questioning whether further immigration ought to be encouraged. The idea was raised that 'the whole tribe' could move to Bombay, leading to a debate between those who viewed this as 'impracticable', and others who believed it might help prevent the 'evident gradual extinction of the race'.[81] Significantly, not all of the Zoroastrians who arrived in

Bombay considered themselves to have been poor in Iran, a detail that counters the dominant narrative regarding the position of Iranian Zoroastrians during the Qajar period.[82] The *Rast Goftar* reported that the Amelioration Society opposed the proposal that all Zoroastrians should relocate to India; as well as the cost, the society pointed out that Iranian Zoroastrians 'dislike the idea of abandoning their mother country, where some of them have large properties and fields'.[83] In light of this, the recommendation was made that only the poorest should leave.[84]

An additional criticism was raised by the editor of the *Times of India* regarding the suggested 'wholesale removal . . . of the remnant of their race'. Alongside practical concerns,

> There are also arrayed against such an entire deportation, all the sentiments of race and religious traditions. Shall the sacred fire of the Magi cease to be reflected in the skies of Iran: shall every one of the priests of Ormazd flee from before the merciless sons of the false Prophet?[85]

Although Iranians of all religious backgrounds suffered during the famine, the *Times of India* framed the question of Zoroastrian emigration in terms of religious discrimination against a community that was regarded as being bound to Iran. This emphasis on Iran as the true homeland of all Zoroastrians is found in other articles in the *Times of India*, including one that exhorted Parsis to offer 'patriotic assistance' to Iranian Zoroastrians, their 'fellow-countrymen'.[86]

Support offered to Zoroastrians in Iran during the famine was facilitated by the links that had been forged between India and Iran in the preceding years by Hataria and other individuals involved in the work of the Amelioration Society. The network of the Mehrban company was also vital to relief efforts. Indeed, Sheriar Behram, one of the Zoroastrians who had been helped, exclaimed that had it not been for the brothers, 'we all would have been lost'.[87] Whilst Iranian Zoroastrians who settled in India during this period did not always fully assimilate into the Parsi community,[88] greater contact between Parsis and Zoroastrians who had recently arrived from Iran did heighten Parsi concern for their co-religionists who were still living in the country.

Parsi political pressure: Justice and the *jezya*

In the years following the famine, members of the Amelioration Society continued with their mission to assist their co-religionists in Iran. A significant challenge faced by Zoroastrians in Iran was the annual payment of the *jezya*. Consequently, the long campaign that resulted in Zoroastrians being granted exemption from the tax in 1882 is often regarded as the society's greatest achievement.[89]

Earlier efforts had been made to lessen the burden of the tax on the Zoroastrian community. Indeed, Daniel Sheffield has pointed out that it is 'almost universally forgotten' that whilst Karim Khan Zand was in power (r.1751–79), Zoroastrians had successfully petitioned for the *jezya* to be recalculated to reflect current population figures.[90] However, by the mid-nineteenth century, there were fewer Zoroastrians in

Iran, so the level of tax was again disproportionately high, with only a fifth of families reportedly able to pay the *jezya* without it causing severe financial hardship.[91] Local governors and tax collectors in Yazd and Kerman also disregarded orders from the shah and frequently demanded that Zoroastrians pay more than the agreed sum, and the process of tax collection could be a threatening and humiliating experience for Zoroastrians.[92]

When Hataria arrived in Iran in 1854, Armenian Christians living in the northern provinces no longer had to pay the *jezya*. The crown prince, Abbas Mirza (1789–1833), had anticipated that by abolishing the tax for Armenians in this region, relations between Iran and Russia might be improved. This set a precedent, giving hope to non-Muslim communities from whom the tax continued to be levied.[93] Aiming to secure the cancellation of the *jezya* for Zoroastrians, Hataria moved to Tehran in 1856; here he was better placed to establish positive relationships with members of the Iranian ruling class, as well as with foreign diplomats posted in Iran.[94] The fact that Hataria was both a British subject and a Freemason was helpful in this respect.[95] Hataria also tried to establish relations with members of the ulama, and, hoping for their assistance regarding the mistreatment of Zoroastrians, he made reference to the legal terms of the *jezya* and to the importance of the concept of justice in Islam. Although his efforts were not always positively received, Hataria did have some success; for example, he gained the support of the cleric responsible for Friday prayers in Kerman.[96]

Despite his connections, it was not until 1860 that Hataria eventually gained an audience with Naser al-Din Shah, in a meeting facilitated by the British ambassador Henry Rawlinson. On this occasion, Hataria successfully negotiated for the annual payment demanded from Zoroastrians to be decreased.[97] To overcome the issue of regional governors collecting more than the officially agreed sum, Hataria organized for the *jezya* to be paid to the Iranian authorities by the Amelioration Society, via the British legation. According to Hataria, this arrangement would dissuade Zoroastrians from emigrating.[98] By 1882, when the *jezya* was abolished, Zoroastrians in India had donated 109,564 rupees to pay for the tax, thereby alleviating one of the pressures felt by Zoroastrians in Iran and removing an economic motivation for conversion to Islam.[99]

Parsi networks in Europe had also been utilized by Hataria and the Amelioration Society to supplement the steps being taken in Iran. For instance, in November 1858, Hataria wrote to the Iranian diplomat and Freemason, Farrokh Khan, who had just returned from the court of Napoleon III. Hataria reminded Farrokh Khan that whilst in Paris, he had promised Sir Mancherji Hormusji Cama that he would offer his support to the Amelioration Society's campaign.[100] This was a strategic move, as reform-minded Farrokh Khan was soon appointed minister of the interior.[101]

Hataria was in contact with members of the small but influential Parsi community in Britain, including Dadabhai Naoroji, who had shown a strong interest in the work of the Amelioration Society from its inception.[102] Naoroji had moved to Britain in 1855, initially as a business partner of Mancherji Hormusji Cama.[103] Over the following decades, he spent time in both India and Britain, where, in 1892, he was elected as a member of Parliament. Whilst he is remembered as a leading figure in the Indian nationalist movement, Naoroji also engaged with issues that specifically affected the Zoroastrian community. In 1873,

Naoroji was one of a group of four Parsis who met with Naser al-Din Shah when he visited London as part of his tour of Europe. The Parsi deputation presented the shah with an address that requested the end to discriminatory practices against Zoroastrians; this had been signed by over 1,500 individuals.[104] This meeting had been planned with the assistance from both Rawlinson and Edward Eastwick, an Orientalist and diplomat who had also worked in Iran.[105] Similar to the Parsis, the Alliance Israélite Universelle and the Anglo-Jewish Association petitioned the shah on behalf of Iranian Jews.[106]

One factor prompting the shah's first tour of Europe in 1873 was the opportunity it gave him to show himself to be the ruler of a modern nation, whose independence and self-determination ought to be respected.[107] Before leaving Iran, the shah had issued a decree within which he declared various changes that would be made to the state administration. This decree had been influenced by the Ottoman Tanzimat reforms.[108] Significantly, the Tanzimat reforms of 1856 had included the abolition of the *jezya* in the Ottoman Empire. In 1858, Hataria had referred to the global reputation of the shah and had stated that if the shah reduced or cancelled the *jezya*, his name would 'shine among the names of the Emperors of the world'.[109] Likewise, in another letter written in the same year, Hataria had explicitly contrasted the situation in Iran to that in Constantinople, where the *jezya* was no longer collected.[110] Thus, in view of the announcement made by the shah before he travelled to Europe, it is not surprising that this was regarded as a favourable time to raise the issue of the rights of Zoroastrians in Iran, and to push the shah to prove his commitment to reform.

Despite the shah stating that he would give his 'best attention' to the position of Zoroastrians in Iran, the meeting between the shah and the Parsi deputation did not result in any immediate improvements.[111] The shah's dismissal of his reformist chief minister, Mirza Hosayn Khan (1827/8–81), soon after his return from Europe was unlikely to have helped. Mirza Hosayn Khan, also known by his title, Sepahsalar, had encouraged the shah to travel to Europe and was heavily involved in efforts to reform the state, partly influenced by his experiences as a diplomat in the Ottoman Empire.[112] When Sepahsalar lost his position, the drive for reform was weakened. In addition, the attempt made by the shah to present himself as a liberal and enlightened leader may have led to increased animosity against Zoroastrians and other non-Muslims, who were perceived as having profited from the influence of foreign powers in Iran and from the 'European' stance taken by the shah.[113]

The murder of Rasheed Mehrban in November 1874 may have been linked to the anger provoked by the prospect of changes to the status of non-Muslims. Together with his brothers, Rasheed had helped coordinate aid for Zoroastrians during the famine, and he had also distributed money and food amongst Muslims.[114] A prominent member of his community, Rasheed was described as the 'leading Zoroastrian inhabitant of Yazd', who even 'enjoyed the confidence of the Shah'.[115] According to the *Times of India*, the motive for the murder was jealousy. Local Muslims were reportedly 'scandalised', as the shah had given Rasheed 'magisterial rights over the Parsee quarter of Yezd', and had granted him permission to use a carriage.[116] The reaction this triggered should be viewed in the context of humiliating and discriminatory conditions imposed on Zoroastrians, which included the rule that they were not to ride horses in the presence of Muslims.[117]

Following the murder, Rasheed's two brothers, who lived in India, used their position as naturalized British subjects to garner support from the British authorities.[118] Despite their attempts to secure justice for Rasheed at any expense, four years passed before an agent of Mehrban & Co. discovered the suspected murderer, Rajab Ali, whilst he was in the port of Bushehr on his way to Mecca.[119] Iranian officials in Shiraz and Tehran were contacted to ensure that Rajab Ali was not released. However, there was 'no sign' of them taking up the matter, so Zoroastrians in India were urged: 'Use all your influence with the British Government to insist upon justice.'[120] The *Times of India* expected that the Parsis would send an appeal to the government:

> Of course the Government of India have no direct connection with the Parsee inhabitants of Persia, but some influence has been repeatedly exerted indirectly to protect them from an almost normal condition of oppression.[121]

In 1881, another petition from Zoroastrians in India was presented to the shah by Ronald Ferguson Thomson, the British representative in Tehran, following requests made by Dinshaw Petit to the viceroy of India.[122] Here it was highlighted that Rajab Ali was allowed to go free, 'although several petitions were presented to obtain justice'.[123] This incident was later referenced by Lieutenant Vaughan as an illustration of the limitations of the power of the shah; despite the shah ordering that he be punished, Rajab Ali had escaped justice by taking refuge at religious sites.[124] Although Rajab Ali was not convicted, it is noteworthy that Iranian Zoroastrians drew on the strength of relations between the Parsis and the British in order to exert pressure on the Iranian government. A similar approach would be taken numerous times in the following years.

The 1881 petition had also drawn attention to instances of forced conversion, especially of Zoroastrian girls.[125] To counter this, it was suggested that 'all those who wish to embrace Mahomedanism should present an application . . . to the Court of Justice at Teheran'.[126] Particular reference was also made to the *jezya*, and the petition implied that one possible reason why injustices such as these were allowed to continue was that the shah was unaware of them.[127] By framing the petition in these terms, Zoroastrians in India did not criticize the shah, but rather they encouraged him to use this opportunity to demonstrate that he was a just and modern sovereign. According to Tsadik, over the course of several days, Thomson was able to persuade the minister of foreign affairs, Mirza Sa'id Khan, to instigate several, albeit limited, changes.[128] Subsequently, the Amelioration Society received a reply from the shah, via the Government of India, announcing that *farmans*, decrees, would be issued to ensure that Zoroastrians would be granted some of the privileges previously denied them, such as permission to build new homes.[129]

Just a few months later, celebrations were held in Tehran to mark the news that Zoroastrians were to be relieved of the annual payment of the *jezya*.[130] This momentous change was communicated in a *farman* issued by the shah, within which Zoroastrians were referred to as descendants of the 'ancient and noble population of Persia'.[131] The *farman* of 1882 also stated that Zoroastrians should not be treated differently in regard to 'trades and custom duties' or 'tribute of the land and water and real-estate tax'.[132] Mitra

Sharafi has described the abolition of the *jezya* as the most famous accomplishment of Parsi lobbying, which worked 'across Eurasian polities – from the British to the Persian – as well as within them'.[133] Effectively making use of their political influence and their relations with the British, Zoroastrians in India had pressurized the shah into issuing orders that benefitted their co-religionists in Iran.

Over the following years, Parsis continued to publicly remind Naser al-Din Shah of his responsibility towards Zoroastrians. On hearing that the shah was going to be in England in the summer of 1889, 'A Zoroastrian' wrote to the *Times of India* to suggest that Parsis should welcome him during his visit, as they had done in the past.[134] The shah travelled up the River Thames on a steamship and arrived in London on 1 July, accompanied by several ministers, military officers and chamberlains, including his own dentist. Acting as his interpreter was Sir Henry Rawlinson, who, almost thirty years earlier, had helped organize the shah's initial meeting with Hataria about the *jezya*.[135] The hopes expressed by the correspondent to the *Times of India* were fulfilled, and Dadabhai Naoroji was given the opportunity to present the shah with a message from the Parsi community. This address thanked Naser al-Din Shah, principally for the abolition of the *jezya*; in response, the shah emphasized his role as 'protector of the Zoroastrians', and made clear that he 'greatly liked them'.[136]

The petition had been written by Naoroji with the assistance of a young scholar, Edward Browne, who had travelled around Iran in 1887–8, and had shown an interest in the Iranian Zoroastrian community.[137] Following his return to Britain, Browne contacted the politician Sir Matthew White Ridley, calling for greater attention to be paid to the dangers faced by Zoroastrians, and he had asked that the British representative in Tehran intervene on their behalf.[138] Although Browne acknowledged that the status of Zoroastrians had improved in recent years, he noted that they were still often regarded 'coldly' by Muslims.[139] Browne also expressed his concern that if the shah were to die, the community might be persecuted, as anti-Zoroastrian feelings had been enflamed by the recent *farmans* issued by the monarch.[140] Whilst there was a danger of a backlash due to the steps being taken towards greater equality, Colonel Ross, the British Resident in Bushehr, was optimistic about the impact of the 1889 meeting between the shah and the Parsi deputation. Ross stated that, 'Doubtless when the Shah returns from Europe, H.M. will be particularly well disposed to attend to any representations which may be considered advisable to make on behalf of the Zoroastrians'.[141] The meeting between the Parsis and the shah that took place in London was viewed as a positive event in terms of the potential success of future appeals made in Iran.

Although the *jezya* had been cancelled, similar to Browne, members of the Amelioration Society believed that more could be done to help their co-religionists. Thus, after the death of Hataria in 1890, another emissary was sent to Iran. The individual appointed to the role was Kaykhosrow Khansaheb, an Iranian Zoroastrian who had moved to India as a boy and had gone on to study at the University of Bombay.[142] Khansaheb was described as holding great influence in the shah's court,[143] and he received the honorary title 'Khan' from the prime minister, 'Ali Asghar Khan Amin al-Soltan, who referred to him as a friend.[144] With permission from the authorities in Tehran and from the governor of Yazd, in addition to the support of local members of the ulama, Khansaheb was able to re-establish local Zoroastrian councils, *anjoman*s, in Kerman and Yazd. These had initially been founded by Hataria but had ceased functioning in the intervening years.[145] One issue prompting Khansaheb to revive the *anjoman*s was the lack of cooperation within the Zoroastrian community. The *anjoman*s were to have authority over both civil and religious matters, and all members had to be approved by the emissary of the Amelioration Society.[146] Whilst the *anjoman*s posed a threat to the religious authority of Iranian Zoroastrian priests, they did provide a channel through which members of the community could communicate their concerns to local authorities and to officials in Tehran.[147] The Amelioration Society tried to strengthen relations with influential individuals, so when Khansaheb visited India in 1892, he returned to Iran with numerous gifts from the society for the shah and other dignitaries.[148]

Ultimately, these gifts had to be distributed by Khansaheb's successor, Ardeshir Edulji Reporter (1865–1933), as Khansaheb died soon after his journey back from India.[149] Reporter settled in Iran; he married an Iranian Zoroastrian called Shirin and held the position of emissary from 1894 until his death, almost forty years later. He maintained close relations with British officials in Iran, and he was issued a British diplomatic passport. An article published in India in 1905 described Reporter as 'one of those Parsis who have a lingering love for the Fatherland of Persia', and it highlighted that his efforts to help Iranian Zoroastrians had been recognized by the government of Iran.[150] In addition to his role as emissary, Reporter took on other work; for example, he taught for a time at a college in Tehran, and he was a news correspondent for the London *Times*. He took an interest in broader political and social issues, and, as well as arguing in favour of schools for Zoroastrian girls, he supported wider efforts being made by Iranian women to gain greater rights and access to education. During the decades he spent in Iran, Reporter witnessed substantial political change, and within just two years of his arrival, Naser al-Din Shah was assassinated, bringing his long reign to a violent end.

Similar to his father, Mozaffar al-Din Shah (r. 1896–1907) also travelled to Europe, providing Parsis with opportunities to impress upon him the responsibilities he held towards his Zoroastrian subjects. Mozaffar al-Din Shah was keen to secure foreign loans, including from the British government, and Malcolm Deboo has argued that due to the political influence of Parsis, the shah could not afford to ignore their petitions.[151] During the shah's trip to Ostend in 1900, he received several illuminated addresses from Zoroastrians; these were bound together and presented to him by a deputation of Parsis. The individuals making up this group included the politicians Dadabhai Naoroji and Sir Mancherjee Bhownaggree.[152] On this occasion, it was with the assistance of the Aqa Khan, the leader of the Nizari Isma'ili Muslims, that the Parsis were granted access to the shah. The involvement of the Aqa Khan was deemed to be significant, as his friendship with Bhownaggree was said to have illustrated to the shah that the Parsis were 'an honoured community in a powerful Empire'.[153] The shah seems to have been keen to show his respect for the Parsis, as he decorated Bhownaggree with the Order of the Lion and the Sun.[154]

When Mozaffar al-Din Shah returned to Europe a couple of years later, he was presented with two more addresses from Zoroastrians. One was from Parsis in Bombay, and the other from Zoroastrians in Iran. This suggests that requests made to the shah in the presence of a European audience were believed to be more effective than those delivered in Tehran.[155] The arrangements for the meeting between the Zoroastrians and the shah had been made by Sir Arthur Hardinge, the British minister in Tehran, and by the secretary of the Persian legation, Hosayn Qoli Khan, who was a close friend of Edward Browne.[156] Bhownaggree played a prominent role in the proceedings and expressed to the shah

> the sentiments of gratitude felt by them for your Majesty's kind and considerate treatment of their co-religionists who, living under your Majesty's protection, keep alive that fire of love for his ancient fatherland which glows in every Parsee heart.[157]

The address from the Amelioration Society similarly highlighted the Persian heritage of the Zoroastrians and their roots in Iran.

As 'descendants of the Ancient Iranians', Parsis were 'concerned and connected with their kindreds' in Iran and were 'still attached to the native land of our ancestors'.[158] Mozaffar al-Din Shah was also described in relation to the pre-Islamic past, and was referred to as the 'successor to the imperial throne of the Great Jamshed, Faridun and other celebrated Iranian Kings'.[159] The improvements that Zoroastrians in Iran had experienced in recent years were noted, and the shah emphasized that Zoroastrians would be 'treated with fairness and justice' by his officials. This may have been in part a reference to an order issued by Mozaffar al-Din Shah in 1898, that reaffirmed the content of his father's *firman*, as, despite the 1882 rulings regarding the *jezya*, in the intervening years there had been instances of the tax being demanded from Zoroastrians in Yazd and Kerman.[160] The Parsi address stressed that the shah would be sure to enjoy a valuable reward in return for his actions – the loyalty of his Zoroastrian subjects. It seems likely that this was an allusion to the reputation held by Parsis for their loyalty to the British, exemplified by the figure of Sir Jamsetjee Jejeebhoy, who had travelled to London to represent the Parsis at the coronation of Edward VII, and who was introduced to the shah as 'the head of all the Parsees'.[161]

The political standing of the Parsis enabled them to meet with both Naser al-Din Shah and Mozaffar al-Din Shah. Not only did the status of individual Parsis make an impression on the Iranian monarchs, but an awareness of the power held by Parsis contributed to the issuing of decrees that improved the legal status of Zoroastrians in Iran. Alongside wider developments taking place in Iran, the actions of members of the Amelioration Society also affected the Zoroastrian community in Iran in other ways, for instance in relation to education and religious reform.

The Amelioration Society and social change in Iran

Mirroring the priorities of the Parsis in India, the provision of education was a major aspect of the work of the Amelioration Society.[162] In 1860, Hataria founded a boarding school for boys in Tehran. Following this, Zoroastrian schools were established in and around Yazd and Kerman. A report from 1893 stated there were twelve schools in operation, which had already educated 481 pupils.[163] According to Mary Ellen 'Nellie' Brighty, who worked for the Church Missionary Society (CMS), the Zoroastrian schools in Yazd had 'lofty and good buildings', surpassing those attended by Muslims. Brighty also noted that their upkeep was paid for by Bombay Parsis.[164] One such individual was the 'well-known philanthropist' Byramjee Jeejeebhoy, who, after his death in 1890, was described in the *Times of India* as having promoted education in India and as having made large donations to support the Amelioration Society, including 5,000 rupees towards the maintenance of a school.[165]

Lessons at the Amelioration Society schools were conducted in Persian, rather than Zoroastrian Dari, thereby weakening the linguistic divide between local Muslims and Zoroastrians.[166] Books were shipped from Bombay, and Hataria emphasized that the curriculum at the boarding school was 'job-oriented', covering science, mathematics and technical crafts, as well as religious education.[167] Some of the individuals who attended these schools went on to establish Zoroastrian businesses, the success of which had a positive impact on the wider community.[168] According to Nile Green, through the Amelioration Society, Parsis in Bombay sowed 'some of the earliest seeds of modernization in provincial Iran'; in time, this led to the transformation of their co-religionists from 'forgotten village peasants into educated urban merchants and, ultimately, technocrats'.[169] However, not all Iranian Zoroastrians welcomed this drive to increase educational opportunities, as it disrupted internal class divisions.[170]

Whilst the main beneficiaries of the new Zoroastrian schools were boys, by the early twentieth century, some girls were also able to access education. A school for girls was founded in Yazd by Sohrab Kayanian, a prominent member of the Iranian Zoroastrian community, and girls' schools were later established in Kerman and Tehran.[171] There was also a CMS school for Zoroastrian girls in Yazd, which had been set up by Brighty in 1902.[172]

Although the outreach of the CMS in Yazd resulted in several conversions, overall, relations between Zoroastrians and the missionaries do not seem to have suffered. This may have been in part because the CMS offered medical care.[173] Significantly, conversion to Christianity did not have the same economic implications as conversion to Islam, and Christian converts could continue to live within the Zoroastrian community. Good relations between Zoroastrians and the missionaries appear to be reflected in the invitation to a Bombay Parsi, 'Noruzgi', to deliver the opening speech at the CMS school.[174]

Whereas members of the Parsi community in India had directed funds towards the education of girls for several decades, the education of girls was very unusual in Iran at this time. Noruzgi addressed this in his speech; he encouraged the pupils to attend their lessons, even when people 'spoke against the school'.[175] Amongst those who opposed the education of girls were a number of Iranian Zoroastrian priests, who argued with Ardeshir Reporter about the issue. These debates took place in 1902, which suggests that they may have been related to the establishment of the CMS school in Yazd. Reporter later founded a school for girls in Khurramshah and described how he had lectured in the Yazd fire temple about the value of education for girls over the course of two years; this apparently inspired Kaykhosrow Shahjahan to start a school for girls in Yazd.[176]

Tension between the emissaries of the Amelioration Society and Zoroastrian priests in Iran had also been inflamed by the promotion of Parsi views regarding 'authentic' religious practice.[177] Comparable to the efforts of reformist Parsis in India, who discouraged practices that they believed reflected the influence of Hinduism, Hataria criticized various customs of Zoroastrians in Iran, such as animal sacrifice, which he thought had emerged due to the impact of Islam.[178] Another example Hataria cited to illustrate his argument that priests in Yazd held erroneous views, was their refusal to use the new *dakhmeh* that had been built using funds from the Amelioration Society, as it was made of stone rather than mud.[179]

Likewise, the idea that Parsis held greater religious authority was expressed by the Parsi historian and magistrate, Dosabhai Framji Karaka. He referred to the observations made by Westergaard, and stated that 'instead of being in a position to impart knowledge, the Zoroastrians of the fatherland needed advice and instruction from those in India'.[180] According to the American scholar, Abraham Valentine Williams Jackson, Parsi views had influenced the opinions and religious practices of Zoroastrians in Iran by the early twentieth century.[181] Jackson had travelled in Iran, and he enthusiastically reported that a number of Iranian Zoroastrian priests had studied in India, and were 'bringing back the seed of knowledge to sow once again in the Zoroastrian soil which originally produced it'.[182] Thus, links between Zoroastrians in Iran and India were resulting in changes to the education and religious practice of both Iranian Zoroastrian priests and members of the laity. Nile Green has situated the work of the Amelioration Society in the wider context of nineteenth-century Bombay, which was becoming an important centre for Iranians in 'social and religious terms'.[183] The strengthening of ties between the city and Iran was not only significant for Zoroastrianism but also had an impact on Islam in Iran, and on the new Bahá'í faith.[184]

The rise of the Bahá'í faith affected the internal dynamics of the Iranian Zoroastrian community, as well as external attitudes towards Zoroastrians. This was a new religion that had developed from Babism, a Shi'i messianic movement that emerged in Iraq and Iran during the 1840s. The Babi leader, Sayyed 'Ali Mohammad Shirazi (1819–50), had pronounced that he was the '*bab*', the 'gate', who was to prepare the way for the Twelfth, or Hidden, Imam, whose return would herald the end of time.[185] However, in 1846, Qorrat al-'Ayn, a prominent female follower of the Bab, stated that in a letter she had received, the Bab had pronounced that Islam was to be abrogated.[186] Two years later, the Bab confirmed this in another letter, within which he also claimed to be the Imam.[187] This was a threat to both the religious and political status quo in Iran, as the authority of the retuned Twelfth Imam would supersede that of the Shi'i clerics and the shah.[188]

In 1850, following a series of violent clashes between Babis and provincial and state forces, the Bab was executed under orders of the government, bringing the political force of the movement to an end. One of the followers of the Bab, Mirza Yahya Nuri, known as Sobh-e Azal (c.1830–1912), emerged as his successor. However, Sobh-e Azal's position was contested by his half-brother, Mirza Hosayn 'Ali Nuri, 'Bahá'u'lláh' (1817–92), who, in the 1860s, declared himself to be the messianic figure that the Bab had referred to in his teachings.[189] This led to a split amongst the Babis, resulting in two factions: a smaller group of Azali Babis, who viewed Sobh-e Azal as their leader, and the Bahá'ís, who followed Bahá'u'lláh.[190]

Whereas Judaism, Christianity and Zoroastrianism were accepted as 'recognized' religions by Shi'i religious authorities, Azali Babism and the Bahá'í faith were regarded as heresies. Consequently, those perceived to be linked to either group sometimes faced persecution on religious grounds. The two factions were often viewed as one movement, and in addition to being seen as 'unbelievers', the earlier militancy of the Babis meant that even though the Bahá'ís adopted a pacifist stance, they too were regarded with suspicion.[191] Despite the dangers of being associated with the Bahá'í faith, some Muslims were attracted to the new religion, as were members of other religions.[192]

Zoroastrians were amongst those who joined the Bahá'í faith. However, the number of Zoroastrian converts is difficult to ascertain, in part because they could remain active members of the Zoroastrian community whilst also belonging to a network of Bahá'ís from different religious backgrounds.[193] According to the Christian missionary Napier Malcolm, the appeals made by Bahá'ís for 'religious liberty and toleration' led Zoroastrians to regard the spread of the Bahá'í faith as beneficial to their own community.[194] Furthermore, Bahá'u'lláh viewed Zarathustra and other religious figures as manifestations of God, and, significantly for Zoroastrians, he claimed to be a descendant of the last Zoroastrian ruler of Iran, Yazdegird III.[195] Susan Stiles has proposed that the new religion was particularly attractive to educated Zoroastrian merchants, who had been positively impacted by social and economic reforms initiated by the Amelioration Society, but had found that reform in the religious sphere had not accelerated to the same degree.[196] This argument appears to be supported by the account given by N. Shetalov, a Russian doctor based in Yazd in 1898–9, who claimed that many Zoroastrians had converted as they had a low opinion of the Zoroastrian priesthood.[197]

Close relations between Hataria and members of the Bahá'í faith were another factor that may have encouraged positive attitudes towards the religion amongst Zoroastrians. Bahá'u'lláh corresponded with Hataria, whom he had met in Baghdad, as well as with Zoroastrians who had joined the Bahá'í faith.[198] Additionally, Hataria employed a member of the religion, Abu'l-Fazl Golpayegani, as his secretary.[199] Golpayegani taught at the Zoroastrian school in Tehran, and some of his students were reportedly early Zoroastrian converts.[200] Similarly, Stiles has outlined how another convert, Ostad Javanmard, was the principal of the Zoroastrian school in Yazd.[201] Molla Bahram, who had also converted to the Bahá'í faith, wrote in his memoirs that many members of the Zoroastrian Anjoman of Yazd professed to be Bahá'ís, and the majority were at the very least sympathetic towards the new religion.[202] Indeed, Janet Amighi has noted that the *anjomans* were dominated by merchants, who were predominantly in favour of reform, whereas the priests, *mowbeds*, held more conservative views and disapproved of liberal attitudes towards Bahá'ís.[203]

Though the spread of the Bahá'í faith augmented fractures within the Zoroastrian community in Iran, it also facilitated the building of relations between Zoroastrians and individuals from outside the community. Meanwhile, Zoroastrians in India were considering the strength of their links with the Zoroastrian community in Iran, a question that had implications for the scope of Parsi philanthropy.

A broader Zoroastrian community

Vital financial support for the work of the Amelioration Society was provided by Iranian Zoroastrians who had settled in India, and by their extended families and descendants.[204] For instance, following the death of Nusserwanji Maneckji Petit, it was noted that he had been involved in the management of the Amelioration Society and that he had donated 25,000 rupees towards the Zoroastrian boarding school in Iran.[205] Similarly, when Dinshaw Maneckji Petit was knighted in 1887, references were made to the large sums he had given to help Zoroastrians in Iran and to his involvement in the campaign for the abolition of the *jezya*.[206] Other benefactors with direct ties to Iran included one of the Mehrban brothers, Kaykhosrow, 'a well-known merchant of Bombay', whose substantial donations included 10,000 rupees for the establishment of a library for Zoroastrians in Yazd and 5,000 rupees towards a school.[207] Likewise, Hormizdiar Sheriar Boman Irani donated 2,700 rupees to found a school in his home-town, 'Kuchabiog', and a further 3,000 rupees to the Amelioration Society.[208] Many of these philanthropic acts were publicly announced in the *Times of India*. In addition to raising awareness of these gifts, such reports may have encouraged further donations from the wider Parsi community, particularly as British commentators praised the efforts being made by Zoroastrians in India to assist their co-religionists in Iran.[209]

Framjee Naserwanjee Patel (1804–92) was one of the individuals whose actions were highlighted by the *Times of India*. His obituary described how he had donated 'large sums' to causes that helped Zoroastrians in Iran, whilst also paying annual subscriptions to both the Amelioration Society and the fund for destitute Iranian Zoroastrians in Bombay.[210] Patel was a merchant and a prominent member of the Parsi Law Association. He also appears to have been interested in pre-Islamic Iran, and he cited customs believed to have been current at that time to add weight to his proposals regarding female inheritance in the Parsi community.[211]

The emphasis placed by some Parsis on their Persian heritage and the strengthening of relations between Zoroastrians in India and Iran were connected. This can be seen in an explanation given in 1902 by N. M. Wadia, concerning a charitable trust that he had established:

> I shall now give you another illustration of the difficulty I foresaw in the restriction of the charity to India and India alone. Supposing a famine, or a disastrous flood or fire, were to occur in Persia – my fatherland for which I have such a great regard – and that my co-religionists – however small their number – suffered from the effects of these calamities, would it be prudent on my part to deprive the trustees of the power of contributing towards the relief of such sufferers because they were not residing in India but in Persia?[212]

The comments made by Wadia suggest that he regarded Iran as his ancestral home, and that he felt a degree of responsibility towards the Zoroastrians living there.

Donations directed towards Zoroastrians in Iran were only a small proportion of the total sum given to charity by Zoroastrians in India, but without these funds, the Amelioration Society would not have been able to function. A broader view of who was included within the 'Parsi' community encouraged gifts to causes that helped Iranian Zoroastrians, who were referred to by Hataria as Parsis of Iran.[213] The rekindling of links with Iran did not just have an impact on the Zoroastrians in Iran but also encouraged Parsis to place a greater emphasis on their identity as Persians.

2

Parsis and pre-Islamic Iran

A confluence of interests

Manekji Limji Hataria and nationalism in Iran

During their campaign to improve conditions for Zoroastrians in Iran, members of the Amelioration Society highlighted that they were 'descendants of the Ancient Iranians', and made reference to their imperial history, thereby creating a link between their own community and the contemporary shahs of Iran whom they were trying to influence.[1] The first emissary of the Amelioration Society, Manekji Limji Hataria, had a near mythical view of the ancient Iranian past. During his time in Iran, Hataria associated with several individuals who also elevated the pre-Islamic era and who referenced the past to illustrate that Iran had the potential to become a modern state. Alongside the practical measures he enacted to support Iranian Zoroastrians and encourage reform within their community, Hataria contributed to the development of these early nationalistic ideas in Iran.[2]

Military losses to European powers heightened concerns felt amongst members of the Iranian ruling class that Iran was less developed than Europe in military and economic terms.[3] In the first decades of the nineteenth century, the Russo-Persian Wars of 1804–13 and 1826–8 resulted in Iran conceding territory to Russia, prompting the crown prince, Abbas Mirza (1789–1833), who had been involved in both conflicts, to implement military reforms.[4] This desire to strengthen the military also led to the establishment of Dar al-Fonun, a college founded in 1851 to provide army officers with a modern education, and to the formation of the Russian-backed Cossack Brigade in 1879.[5] Other recommendations regarding the modernization of the state included suggestions by Mirza Malkam Khan (1833–1908), who argued that Iran would benefit if laws were introduced to regulate the power of the shah.[6]

In addition to these pragmatic interventions and proposals, Reza Zia-Ebrahimi has described how there was also a 'discursive' response to the 'intellectual crisis' that had been precipitated by the perceived inferiority of Iran in relation to Europe.[7] This was a form of nationalism that elevated the pre-Islamic period and, conversely, held Islam and the Arabs responsible for the current problems faced by Iran. Archaism was popular in Iran at the time, with the ancient past referenced in a variety of different contexts, for example, to reinforce the legitimacy of the monarchy.[8] In the case of emerging nationalistic ideas, the argument was made that the restoration of the purity of the authentic Iranian past would lead to future national success.[9] Key figures who contributed to this discourse included one of the many Qajar princes, Jalal al-Din Mirza (1827–72),[10] and the Azerbaijani playwright Mirza Fath-'Ali Akhundzadeh (1812–78).[11]

Both Jalal al-Din Mirza and Akhundzadeh were in contact with Hataria, who similarly looked back to the pre-Islamic period, when Zoroastrianism was the dominant religion, as a golden age.[12] According to Zia-Ebrahimi, Hataria was regarded by Jalal al-Din Mirza and Akhundzadeh as a representative of this glorious past.[13] Hataria anticipated that a growing appreciation of ancient Iran would lead to increased respect for Zoroastrians in the present.[14] Taking a broader view, Jalal al-Din Mirza and Akhundzadeh also hoped for a new national identity that would help regenerate Iran.[15] Although Akhundzadeh was critical of religion, Hamid Algar has stated that the 'outspoken atheist' did not look down on Zoroastrianism, as his 'sense of Iranian identity along with his hostility to Islam produced in him a hatred for the Arabs and a nostalgia for pre-Islamic Iran'.[16] Writing to his 'dear friend' Hataria, Akhundzadeh described Iranians as the children of the Parsis and referred to Zoroastrians as the 'living memory of their glorious forefathers'.[17] Akhundzadeh did not have a detailed understanding of the Zoroastrian faith, but he did express an interest in the religion. Similarly, Jalal al-Din Mirza included a text by Hataria about the history of Zoroastrianism as an appendix to the first volume of his *Nameh-ye Khosrovan*, 'Book of Sovereigns', which he wrote in 1868–70.[18]

Keen for his *Nameh-ye Khosrovan* to be an educational text, Jalal al-Din Mirza wrote in an accessible style of Persian.[19] In contrast to earlier historiography, which tended to highlight events relevant to the history of Islam, Jalal al-Din Mirza focused on the national history of Iran; thus, Zia-Ebrahimi has argued that it was in this work that Jalal al-Din Mirza 'introduced the idea of Iran as a continuous historical entity'.[20] *Nameh-ye Khosrovan* has been described by Afshin Marashi as a 'hybrid' text. As well as being inspired by his interactions with Hataria, Jalal al-Din Mirza was also influenced by 'traditional myth narratives', and contemporary European thought.[21] Amongst the sources he used for information about the pre-Islamic period were the neo-Zoroastrian *Dasatiri* texts, dating from the sixteenth and seventeenth centuries. Jalal al-Din Mirza also consulted European histories of Iran. He would have encountered European scholarship at Dar al-Fonun, and through his association with Europeans who taught at the college.[22]

European views of the civilization of ancient Iran not only influenced emerging nationalistic thought in Iran but were also likely to have been advantageous for Hataria in terms of garnering support for his work for the Amelioration Society. For instance, during his time working in Tehran for the French diplomatic service (1855–8 and 1862–3), Joseph Arthur de Gobineau (1816–82) became increasingly interested in Iran's Zoroastrian past.[23] Talinn Grigor has highlighted that Gobineau was likely to have been a Freemason; this may have further inspired both his fascination with ancient Iran and his efforts to help Hataria, who had been initiated into a Masonic lodge in Bombay.[24] After becoming acquainted with Hataria, Gobineau praised him to members of the Persian court.[25] Similarly, Hataria's first meeting with Naser al-Din

Shah was facilitated by the British minister in Iran, Sir Henry Rawlinson (1810–95), who had conducted research about ancient Persian cuneiform inscriptions.[26]

The high regard in which foreigners held the pre-Islamic period also appears to have influenced the views of Iranians who spent time in Europe. According to Gobineau, it was during his time in France that an Iranian student, Hosayn Qoli Aqa, developed a strong aversion to Islam. In contrast, Gobineau outlined how 'all his love was for the creed of the [Zoroastrians], under whom Persia had been so great'.[27] As well as encouraging negative views of Islam, the glorification of the pre-Islamic past led to the related denigration of the Arabic language.

Akhundzadeh, Jalal al-Din Mirza and Hataria were all in favour of the removal of Arabic vocabulary from the Persian language, with Akhundzadeh also recommending that the Arabic script be replaced with the Latin script.[28] The opinions these individuals held regarding 'pure' Persian were connected to their positive views of the pre-Islamic period.[29] This can similarly be seen in the work of Mohammad-Esma'il Khan Zand Tuyserkani, who referred to himself as a Zoroastrian and was encouraged by Hataria to write a mythical history of Iran in 'pure' Persian. Hataria shared relevant literature with Tuyserkani, which probably included *Dasatiri* texts.[30] In addition to finding inspiration in the content of *Dasatiri* texts, these works were used as sources of 'pure' Persian vocabulary since they were believed to date from the pre-Islamic period, although they were actually composed in the sixteenth and seventeenth centuries.[31] *Dasatiri* texts were promoted by Hataria, who also disseminated and published other works written in 'pure' Persian, some of which he had commissioned and others that he had authored.[32]

This castigation of Arabic was influenced by contemporary, and now discredited, European racialist theories. In the late eighteenth century, the Orientalist and philologist Sir William Jones had argued that due to similarities between various languages, including Sanskrit, Persian, Latin and Greek, one could speak of an Indo-European linguistic family group. Spurred by Darwinian ideas relating to evolution and progress, different linguistic groups were subsequently tied to the concept of race, leading to the belief that humankind was made up of a hierarchy of different racial groups. The Indo-European language group was held to be linked to the Aryan race, which was viewed as superior to the Semitic race.[33] Early nationalists in Iran were aware of these ideas; for example, Akhundzadeh referenced the work of Ernest Renan (1823–92),[34] who popularized the Aryan theory and had argued that Islam represented 'the dreadful simplicity of the Semitic mind'.[35] Gobineau was another prominent proponent of the Aryan theory, and he believed that 'racial purity' was necessary for 'Aryan societies' to flourish.[36]

The impact of such ideas on individuals in Iran has been traced by Zia-Ebrahimi, who has highlighted that although the term Aryan was derived from the word *ariya*, which was used as an ethnic epithet in ancient Iran, the racialized use of the word 'Aryan' first appeared in Iran in the 1890s. This was in the work of another early nationalist, Mirza Aqa Khan Kermani (1854–96), who described the Zoroastrians of pre-Islamic Iran as the 'noble Aryan nation'.[37] Kermani made a clear distinction in racial terms between ancient Iranians and Semitic Arabs, whose 'invasion' of Iran was regarded as the root cause of current challenges facing the country. Conversely,

Iranians and Europeans were regarded as belonging to a larger Aryan racial group.[38] Due to these supposed racial links, early Iranian nationalists believed that through a process of 'purification', Iran had the potential to become a modern state, similar to European powers.[39] The term 'dislocative nationalism' has been used by Zia-Ebrahimi to describe these views, as an emphasis is placed on the presumed disconnect between Iran and the people and culture in the surrounding region.[40]

According to Zia-Ebrahimi, the opinions expressed by individuals such as Akhundzadeh and Kermani remained 'marginal' in their lifetimes, and only started to become more popular during the 1910s.[41] However, in contrast, the views of Hataria encouraged the contemporary trend seen amongst Parsis in India to emphasize their Persian heritage. Whilst the glorification of the pre-Islamic period can be seen in relation to the emergence of dislocative nationalism in Iran, the elevation of the ancient past by Parsis fed into a sense of separation from neighbouring communities in India.

Pre-Islamic Iran through an Indian lens

Expressing his passion for the ancient Iran, Hataria proclaimed that it was the 'duty' of individuals within the community to increase their knowledge of their past and to spread the findings of their research more widely.[42] This was linked to his concerns that Parsis were reliant on the work of Western scholars for information about the history of their religion. Therefore, during his visit to India in 1863–5, Hataria urged Zoroastrians to study 'the ancient Parsis', having himself built up a collection of relevant documents and objects that he believed could be used as the basis for research.[43] In 1865, Hataria also published a travelogue, which Daniel Sheffield has suggested can be seen as marking a shift in Parsi attitudes towards Iran.[44] Although ancient Iran had always held a significant place in 'Parsi communal identity', Hataria's text was important as it presented a different interpretation of Zoroastrian history.[45] Rather than linking the current position of Iranian Zoroastrians to the negative impact of unrest in recent years, Sheffield describes how Hataria,

> was the first to posit the 'continuous decline' model of post-Sasanian Zoroastrianism history that became very important in the development of Iranian nationalism in the nineteenth and twentieth centuries, and almost paradigmatic among Parsi and even many Western historians of Zoroastrianism.[46]

Sheffield argues that whilst this change in perspective was 'related to the great hardships Iranian Zoroastrians faced', it must also be seen in terms of 'changing social currents within the Parsi community'.[47] In particular, Sheffield highlights both the calendar dispute, which had led many Parsis to reject the religious authority of their Iranian co-religionists, as well as the status that Parsi reformers accorded to ancient Iran.[48]

Influenced by Western scholarship and also reacting to the criticisms of Christian missionaries, Parsis looked to ancient Iran in search of the true 'essence' of Zoroastrianism. The tenets of Zoroastrianism, in its supposedly 'pure' and 'authentic' ancient form, were cited by Parsi reformers to illustrate that Zoroastrians did not have to copy Christian beliefs and adopt Western values in order to access modernity.[49] Dosabhai Framji Karaka (1829–1902) was an early proponent of Parsi reformist views, and, similar to Hataria, he had a high opinion of the civilization of pre-Islamic Iran.[50] Targeted towards a non-Parsi readership, in his 1858 book, *The Parsees: Their History, Manners, Customs, and Religion*, Karaka differentiated Parsis from other communities in India and stressed that Parsis were 'descendants of the ancient Persians'.[51] According to Ringer, Karaka believed that there was a 'profound connection between race, religion, civilization and progress', and thus saw a direct link between the ancient glories of Iran and the success of Parsis in India.[52] The Parsi priest and scholar Jivanji Jamshedji Modi (1854–1933), or J. J. Modi, is described by Ringer as having 'a foot in both the Reformist and Orthodox camps'.[53] However, he too argued that modern values were visible in ancient Zoroastrian texts. In the paper he presented in Chicago for the 1893 World's Parliament of Religions, Modi spoke about the moral and spiritual aspects of Zoroastrianism, including the promotion of equal rights for women. Modi held that Zoroastrian views regarding women were key to the 'progress' of both ancient Persians and contemporary Parsis.[54]

Within this address, Modi referenced several Western scholars who had translated and analysed Zoroastrian texts. Amongst them was James Darmesteter (1849–94), who had been assisted by Modi and other Parsis whilst he conducted research in India in 1887.[55] During his time in Bombay, Darmesteter delivered a talk in which he outlined that he held Zoroastrianism in higher regard than either Hinduism or Islam. Similar to the arguments of Parsi reformers, he pointed to early Zoroastrian texts as a 'triumph of morality'.[56] Darmesteter claimed that Parsis enjoyed economic success because their religion was not fatalistic, like Islam, but full of 'action and hope'.[57] Another of the scholars cited by Modi was the philologist Martin Haug, who emphasized that Zoroastrianism was the earliest monotheistic religion.[58] Likewise, George Birdwood, who lived in India for many years and was well known to the Parsi community, described ancient Persians as 'the Protestants of antiquity', an opinion that chimed with the views expressed by Parsi reformers.[59]

Echoing earlier proposals made by Hataria, individuals outside the community also advised Parsis to direct greater attention towards locating and studying historical sources. In his 1901 lecture 'Modern Researches in Ancient Zoroastrianism', which was delivered to a large audience of Parsis at the Framjee Cowasjee Hall in Bombay, the American scholar A. V. Williams Jackson suggested that they organize a research expedition to Iran.[60] Thanking Jackson for his talk, the prominent Parsi scholar K. R. Cama urged young Parsis to gather funds for this venture.[61] Similarly, in 1905, Colonel Henry Steel Olcott, a leading figure in the Theosophical movement, exhorted members of the community to start a search in Iran and Central Asia for 'the lost remnants of their ancient literature'.[62]

Parsis were also encouraged to finance archaeological projects. In an article published in the *Parsi*, J. J. Vimadalal, a lawyer and later a promotor of Parsi eugenics, expressed support for the views of the archaeologist Flinders Petrie:

> if there is one way superior to all others in which modern Parsis might prove themselves worthy descendants of those devoted souls who over twelve hundred

years ago sacrificed everything for the sake of their religion ... that channel is archaeological research in their motherland.[63]

Vimadalal argued that since his community spent thousands of rupees on charities annually, a proportion ought to be allocated to this important cause:

> Shall the work of archaeological research promising a revival of religion and a harvest of testimony to our ancient greatness remain unheeded? Or shall we prove ourselves worthy descendants of our forefathers in Persia by setting about this noble task in right earnest?[64]

Thus, efforts were made to inspire Parsis to reconnect with Iran and their ancient Iranian past in order to elevate their status in the present.

Iran was referred to as the land of the Parsis, and, as Monica Ringer has highlighted, the 'trope of exile' was used to reinforce the idea that Parsis were 'authentically Iranian'.[65] For instance, Monier Monier-Williams referred to Iran as the 'fatherland' and 'holy land' of the Parsis, and he argued that, similar to Jews, they had been forced to renounce their ancestral lands.[66] In reference to the architectural style of fire temples in Bombay, Talinn Grigor has described how, by the late nineteenth century, Parsis 'began to cling to the idea of being true, yet displaced Persians: a diasporic community that found its home in the ancient land of Iran and the grandeur of the Achaemenid civilization'.[67] Indeed, in 1881, the *Satya Mitra*, a weekly Gujarati Parsi-run newspaper, pointed out that a new history of Persia, by Clements R. Markham, would be useful and interesting to the community, as 'A study of such works engenders love of their country among Parsis'.[68] Whilst the rediscovery of the ancient past was strongly tied to religious reform and the search for the essential Zoroastrian religion, Eckehard Kulke has argued that Parsi interest in Iran was also a reaction against some elements of emerging Indian nationalism, which emphasized that the heritage of India was rooted in Hinduism.[69] With this in mind, it is not surprising that aspects of Parsi identification with Iran echo nationalistic ideas, such as the concept of a national language.

Whereas early nationalists in Iran proposed that the Persian language needed to be reformed, some Parsis were concerned that their community's knowledge of their 'mother-tongue' had substantially declined. Parsis had used both Persian and Gujarati in the past, but by the mid-nineteenth century, although an educated Parsi elite still learnt Persian, the number of Parsis who understood the language had diminished.[70] From 1837, Persian was no longer the administrative language of India, with English and Urdu taking its place, and there was also a shift towards a more secular and Anglophone education in the Parsi community.[71] Daniel Sheffield has argued that 'the Parsi encounter with colonial modernity' led to 'the loss of an Indo-Persianate identity', with a 'constructed ancient Iranian identity' taking its place.[72] Indeed, during the last decades of the century, efforts appear to have been made to revive the use of Persian. For instance, a society called the *Anjuman-e Elmi-e Farsi* was established to encourage 'the study of Persian language and literature'.[73] The founder of the society, J. J. Modi, later described how, 'like many other Orientalists', the Hungarian scholar and traveller

Ármin Vámbéry had recommended that Parsis learn Persian,[74] an example of Western attitudes fortifying Parsi interest in their Iranian heritage.

Parsi enthusiasm for the Persian language continued to be expressed in the following years. Nationalistic in its tone, an article from the *Parsi* lamented that Persian was no longer widely used by the community:

> We can never cease regretting that we ever forgot the sweet native tongue of our fatherland and adopted by circumstance an uninteresting Indian language. . . . We wish we had retained our Persian mother-tongue, to constantly remind us of our great past, of our ancient home, of the achievements of our ancestors.[75]

The use of Gujarati had been listed in the sixteenth-century Parsi poem the *Qesse-ye Sanjan* as one of the conditions that needed to be fulfilled for Parsis to be accepted in India. Comparable to the rejection by Parsi reformers of various customs that were perceived to be inauthentic, such as polygamy,[76] by the early twentieth century, Gujarati was also being denigrated by some Parsis. In contrast, the Persian language was praised and was regarded as a way of reconnecting Parsis with their imperial history.

Similarly, the *Shahnameh*, the 'Book of Kings', was held in high regard by the Parsi community, who celebrated its stories of heroes from the pre-Islamic era. This Persian epic was composed during the early eleventh century by Abol-Qasem Ferdowsi Tusi, often known as Ferdowsi, who had drawn on earlier sources for the content of his own poem. Although the *Shahnameh* provides an insight into the mythological traditions of Iran, Philip Kreyenbroek has argued that prior to the nineteenth century, it was unlikely to have held a prominent place in Parsi culture.[77] According to Kreyenbroek, an important factor leading to the rise in its popularity was the dissemination of lithographed editions of the poem, which were produced in Bombay from the mid-nineteenth century. Additionally, Kreyenbroek describes how the *Shahnameh* may have been seen as helpful in terms of raising the prestige of the community, particularly as the British placed an emphasis on the importance of 'past achievements and cultural heritage'.[78] By the early twentieth century, the *Shahnameh* appears to have been a significant element in Parsi religious life, as is reflected in the following description of its use, dating from 1900:

> Next to their Avesta only they rank the Shahnameh; and readings of portions of their epics either in private gatherings, in family houses, or on the public platform are still very popular, especially during their great religious festival [i.e. New Year].[79]

A few years earlier, Darmesteter had described the *Shahnameh* as 'a poetical commentary upon the epical fragments of the Avesta', thereby linking it directly to Zoroastrian sacred texts.[80]

A clear connection was made between the protagonists of the poem and the Parsi community by a reviewer of Pallonjee Burjorjee Desai's *Sassanian Shahnameh*, published in 1900. The reviewer considered this translation of the 'historical' section of the poem to be 'very acceptable to the Parsis'.[81] Rather than describing the characters of the epic as Persians, the reviewer referred to them as 'Parsee', thus tying the Parsis in India to the heroes described by Ferdowsi. Parsi respect for Ferdowsi was deemed 'natural', and the observation was made that they 'cherish his poem as almost a sacred book'.[82] Whilst acknowledging that Ferdowsi was a Muslim, the reviewer stated that it was clear that the poet 'glories in the glory and success of the Parsee kings and heroes'.[83] This is comparable to views expressed by Akhundzadeh, who had used selective quotes to argue that the *Shahnameh* was anti-Arab.[84]

The epic was referenced by other early Iranian nationalists: Jalal al-Din Mirza had likened his own use of 'pure Persian' to the language of the *Shahnameh*,[85] and Mirza Aqa Khan Kermani presented the *Shahnameh* as a revival of the ancient heritage of Iran, stating that Ferdowsi had helped keep 'national pride' alive.[86] Similarities between the views of Kermani and those of the French Orientalist Ernest Renan have been highlighted by Zia-Ebrahimi, and Marashi has also noted the influence that European thought had on attitudes towards the *Shahnameh* in Iran, in particular the idea that a national epic was a marker of nationhood.[87] The *Shahnameh* had retained a position of cultural significance in the Persianate world since its composition, but its popularity increased during the nineteenth century, facilitated by the use of printing technologies.[88]

As well as the greater availability of printed editions of the *Shahnameh* in Iran and India, stories from the epic were recited in public spaces, and, in Bombay, the *Shahnameh* was brought to the stage.[89] In 1853, when the Amelioration Society was just beginning its work, the newly established Parsi Theatrical Committee provided support for a series of performances based on the *Shahnameh*. In David Willmer's opinion, this was probably 'the first time the Parsi community's Iranian heritage had been represented in such a public way in India'.[90] The following year, another theatrical programme included scenes from the *Shahnameh*, followed by a satire about doctors in contemporary Bombay that portrayed the Parsis as a progressive community.[91] In reference to similar events, Rashna Nicholson has argued that,

> The stage . . . became part of a larger socio-political apparatus for the formulation of a liberal, rationalised Zoroastrianism that would raise Parsis in status and esteem.[92]

Nicholson outlines how it was hoped that the farcical elements might prompt changes in behaviour within the Parsi community. Thus, overall, this combination of the *Shahnameh* and the satire created a link between the glorious past of the Parsis and their route to modernity.[93]

In 1882, the *Shahnameh* story of Rostam and Sohrab was dramatized by the Parsi playwright and journalist Kaikhosro Kabraji (c.1842–1904) to a different end.[94] According to Nicholson, Kabraji's interpretation, which included references to 'racial blood', can be seen as the 'articulation of a new racial character for Zoroastrianism'.[95] Kabraji and other orthodox Parsis were critical of the lifestyles of reformist members of their community, believing that the adoption of Western habits was causing damage to the physical and moral state of Parsis. One reaction to this was that a greater emphasis was placed on the maintenance of strong community boundaries, including in relation to race.[96] Whilst contextualizing this preoccupation with race in terms of broader global trends, Mitra Sharafi also argues that in the case of the Parsi community, this idea of racial purity was an alternative marker of Parsi identity following the relaxation of rules regarding ritual purity. This had occurred in part to facilitate Parsi engagement with professional and educational opportunities.[97]

Divergent views regarding race came to the fore in the legal sphere, notably during the *Petit v. Jijibhai* case of 1908, also known as the Parsi Panchayat case. This case addressed the question of whether non-Parsis, *juddins*, could be initiated into the faith by taking part in the *navjote* ceremony. Suzanne Brière, the French wife of the Parsi businessman Ratanji Dadabhoy Tata, was the individual concerned. Prior to the *Petit v. Jijibhai* case reaching court, an article in the *Times*, 'Parsee Exclusiveness', stated that contemporary Parsis, the 'vanguard of the army of civilisation and progress', were 'against the mingling of their blood with that of strangers', and were 'as much a foreigner to the great mass of the Indian population as was his predecessor of the eighth'.[98] Sharafi has described how, in contrast to the views of reformist Parsis concerning conversion, orthodox Parsis were 'adamantly opposed to the idea on economic and racial grounds'.[99] Not only were they critical of the access converts would gain to community funds,[100] but they also believed that 'converts of any ethnicity would dilute Parsi racial purity'.[101] In his ruling, the orthodox Parsi judge Dinshaw D. Davar concluded that there was a distinction between the term 'Zoroastrian', which he stated was linked to religion, and the term 'Parsi', which was related to ethnicity; previously, the two terms had been used interchangeably.[102]

Encouraged by the conclusions reached by Davar, the idea that Parsis were an ethnic as well as religious community gained further traction. For instance, Davar was referenced during the *Saklat v. Bella* case of 1925, which dealt with the status of a girl who had been adopted by Parsis. According to Sharafi, although 'Persian heritage was notably absent in determining the content of Parsi law . . . it lay at the core of how many Parsis saw themselves as a group', and, whilst a minority of Parsis regarded themselves primarily as Indians, many 'worked to fortify their separateness through law'.[103] Interestingly, whilst being cross-examined by the orthodox Parsi J. J. Vimadalal, a defendant in the *Saklat v. Bella* case, J. D. Nadirshaw, claimed that the view held by Vimadalal and others, that Parsis were pure Persians, was a new phenomenon dating from the 1870s. Nadirshaw also specifically linked Parsi pride in ancient Iran to the printing of Gujarati translations of the *Shahnameh*.[104]

At times, this 'pure Persian' ancestry was referenced in relation to the success of the Parsi community. An article in *Men and Women of India*, printed in 1905, stated that Parsis were the 'remnant of the race which flourished in Persia', now regarded as the 'Salt of India' due to their 'aptitude for reform, progress, and advancement', and their 'fine qualities'.[105] Similarly, in a speech given in 1897 to mark the Diamond Jubilee of Queen Victoria, Sir Jamsetjee Jejeebhoy argued that out of all the communities in India, Parsis had prospered the most under British rule; he proposed that reasons for this included their 'good religion' and their 'pure Kyanian blood', a reference to legendary kings of ancient Iran.[106] Jejeebhoy quoted a former governor of Bombay, who had described the Parsis as 'a handful of persons among the teeming millions of India . . . who not only have preserved their ancient race with the utmost purity, but also their religion absolutely unimpaired by contact with others'.[107] Likewise, an article published in the *Parsi* in 1905 emphasized both religion and race. Here, Parsis were said to be 'Aryan Jews', who were 'good subjects' cherished by 'all Governments'.[108] In addition to the impact that Western racial theories had on contemporary European thought, the idea of a supposedly superior Aryan race influenced views held by individuals in Iran and India.[109] Whilst some similarities were drawn between Parsis and Jews in this article, anti-Semitic attitudes were also displayed.

Copies of contemporary travelogues written by Westerners who had visited Iran were held in libraries frequented by Parsis. In many of these accounts, elevated views of the pre-Islamic period were linked to the supposed racial characteristics of ancient Persians.[110] For instance, Ella Sykes, who travelled in Iran with her brother Percy, believed it was 'an irony of Fate that the followers of the pure religion of Zoroaster should have been forcibly "converted" by a race that had only just turned from the grossest idolatry, and that was on a far lower plane of civilisation than the Persians'.[111] As well as reflecting hierarchical views of race, these comments can be seen in relation to the evolutionary theories of religion that had also influenced Parsi reformers.[112]

Physical attributes were referenced by authors who aimed to highlight the connection between ancient Persians and present-day Zoroastrians in Iran. Writing in the mid-nineteenth century, the Parsi writer, Karaka, stated that, 'Centuries of oppression have not been able to destroy the strong, muscular and hardy appearance of the Zoroastrians'.[113] Using similar words, Arnold Henry Savage Landor (1865–1924) described the Zoroastrians he had met during his travels in Iran as 'manly fellows, sound in body and brain, instead of lascivious, demoralised, effeminate creatures like their tyrants'.[114] In his opinion, Zoroastrians were 'still as hardy and proud as when the whole country belonged to them', and he went on to pronounce that neither had the 'demoralising contact of the present race, to whom they are subject, had any marked effect on their industry, which was the most remarkable characteristic in the ancient Zoroastrians'.[115] Negative perceptions of the 'Arab invasion' of Iran, and more broadly of Islam, were pervasive in Orientalist texts, and can be linked to contemporary European ideas concerning race.[116]

Indeed, whilst the theory of a hierarchy of races was referenced to justify European colonialism, Zia-Ebrahimi has pointed out that even Edward Browne, who forcefully opposed British interventionist policies in Iran, 'fully subscribed to a racial reading of Iranian history as a clash between Iranian Aryans and Semitic Arabs'.[117] Likewise, a preoccupation with race is seen in the writings of Jackson, who stated that Persians are of 'Aryan stock', but 'show an admixture of foreign blood introduced by conquest or due to contact with border nations'. Jackson went on to say that, 'Purest of all . . . are the Zoroastrians, who have maintained the old Iranian religion and have never intermarried with alien races'.[118] This opinion was further expounded in the description Jackson gave of his guide:

> a bright, intelligent fellow, straightforward and honest, manly in his bearing, and agreeable in his manners. I could picture from him what might have been the type of youth in Zoroaster's day, since blood of the ancient faith flowed in his veins by direct descent.[119]

Similarly, Jackson stated that another Zoroastrian he met reminded him of 'the types in the Old Persian and Sasanian sculptures at Behistan and Tak-i Bostan'.[120]

On some occasions, individuals who displayed a bias towards Zoroastrians specifically applauded their religion. The CMS missionary, Napier Malcolm, argued that Zoroastrian converts to Islam 'often develop all the Mussulman characteristics in a few generations, without the slightest admixture of race'.[121] Malcolm viewed religions in hierarchical terms, and, being a missionary, it seems likely that he believed that conversion to a different faith would impact the character of a convert. This is reflected in his claim that the 'strong moral character' exhibited by Zoroastrians was eroded over a few generations if a family converted to Islam.[122]

Although Zoroastrians in India and Iran were regarded as being members of the same race, alleged differences between the communities were highlighted. The presence of Iranian Zoroastrians in India prompted such comparisons. For instance, in 1895, the *Times of India* stated that one of the ways to distinguish one of the 1,500 Iranian Zoroastrians in Bombay from the wider Parsi community was by their 'better physical development'.[123] The article pointed out that 'all the Parsees of Bombay are Iranees by descent, and that the only constitutional difference between the Irani and modern Parsee is that the latter has become very much mixed up with his environment'; this was in part a reference to the influence of Hindu superstitions, thoughts, and customs.[124] On an earlier occasion, the *Times of India* had contrasted the Iranian Zoroastrians with the Parsis, noting that most were agriculturalists and 'far superior' in physical terms to the Parsis.[125]

Reflecting on his experiences in Iran during the 1890s and 1900s, Percy Sykes suggested that Zoroastrians were 'a finer and healthier race than their Mohamedan fellow-countrymen', because they were 'pure Iranians'.[126] Having praised the strength of Iranian Zoroastrians, Sykes stated that 'their co-religionists at Bombay are an example of the physical deterioration which India so surely produces'.[127] Gendered terms were used to describe the supposed effect of the climate on Zoroastrians; Parsis in India were said to have become effeminate and weak, whereas life in Iran was believed to have sustained the virility of Iranian Zoroastrians. This emphasis on the impact of the environment of India echoes certain ideas used to justify colonialism; these have been summarized by John Marriott:

> Civilization . . . had attained its heights in Europe because its temperate climate produced a vigorous and virile race, while tropical countries were inhabited by carnal and indolent peoples, incapable of improvement.[128]

Alongside such views regarding the negative influence of the Indian climate, additional issues compounded anxiety within the Parsi community regarding their physical strength.

Following the 1857 Indian Rebellion, or 'Mutiny', a rise in communal tensions between Parsis and Muslims led Parsis to question whether their community would be able to defend itself if necessary. According to Nicholson, Parsi economic losses, caused by a financial crisis in Bombay in 1865, added to feelings of 'lost glory', prompting concerns that Parsis were 'weak in bodily strength, cowardly and effeminate'.[129]

In response, gymnasiums were established, and the ancient Kayanian kings were promoted as models for Parsis to emulate.[130] Similarly, in a speech marking the opening of a new *dakhmeh* in Navsari in 1878, the governor of Bombay, Sir Richard Temple, made reference to the *Shahnameh* whilst urging Parsis to undertake more physical activity as protection against the danger of 'national decadence'.[131] A review of Sykes' *Ten Thousand Miles in Persia*, printed in the *Parsi*, suggested Parsis ought to consider remarks made by Sykes regarding their physical decline,[132] and another issue included an article by the famous bodybuilder Eugene Sandow: 'The Physical Deterioration of the Parsis: A Word of Warning'.[133] Sandow raised the following question to his Parsi readers:

> Surely they have not forgotten that they are the descendants of one of the mighty warrior races, and that with them it ought to be as it were a point of honour to develop their bodies.[134]

In this instance, the physical state of members of the community in the present was seen in direct relation to their heroic past.[135]

Thus, the connection between the contemporary Parsis and their ancient past was highlighted in various contexts, both by Parsis and by individuals outside the community. The elevation of the pre-Islamic period was strongly linked to the search by Parsi reformers for an authentic Zoroastrian tradition. Alongside a growing emphasis on the belief that Parsis were pure Persians, which was influenced by Western racial theories, the idea of Iran as the true homeland of Parsis intensified. Meanwhile, in Iran, Hataria's interactions with individuals such as Jamal al-Din Mirza had contributed to a current of nationalist thought that looked to the pre-Islamic past as a golden age, and which had potentially positive implications for Zoroastrians in Iran. Towards the end of the nineteenth century, further relations were forged between Parsis and non-Zoroastrian Iranians, this time in Bombay.

Parties and politics: Persian diplomats in Bombay

A rise in the volume of trade between India and Iran during the nineteenth century resulted in greater numbers of Iranians travelling to Bombay.[136] According to Nile Green, these individuals 'took a strange pride in their non-Muslim overseas Persian ("Parsi") compatriots'.[137] In addition to the commercial success of Parsis, another factor that is likely to have contributed to these positive views of the community was the connection between Zoroastrianism and Iran's pre-Islamic past. Whilst they were in Bombay, some Iranians became Freemasons; amongst them were merchants and diplomats who joined Lodge of the Rising Star, a Masonic lodge established by Parsis in 1843.[138] According to Grigor, the glorification of ancient Iran was prominent amongst Parsi Freemasons, and, alongside religious reform, this was another arena where the Persian Revival could be used to challenge European claims of authenticity and superiority.[139]

Interactions between Iranian diplomats and Parsis in India reinforced Parsi interest in their Iranian heritage. This is particularly clear in reports printed in the *Times of India* about various gatherings that took place towards the end of the nineteenth century.[140] For instance, to reciprocate the 'good feelings' shown by the consul-general, Mirza Hosayn Qoli Khan, Parsis organized a concert in his honour in May 1886.[141] During the interval, an address was given by Jamsetjee Cursetjee Cama, who stated that through his friendship and the 'expressions of good will made by the command of his Majesty the Shah', the consul-general had 'revived the remembrance of their past and drawn attention to a country which had for the community a fascination which neither time nor distance could efface'.[142] These words were endorsed by 'Loud and prolonged cheers' from the audience.[143]

Speaking on behalf of the Parsi community, Cama thanked Naser al-Din Shah for his 1882 decree, which had cancelled the *jezya* for Zoroastrians, and he welcomed the new 'mark of civilisation' now visible in Iran.[144] Having mentioned Parsi loyalty to the British monarchy, Cama was also keen to stress that Parsis were 'willing to interest themselves in a country in which still dwelled the relics of a race which had a history of its own and of which one might well feel proud'.[145] Hosayn Qoli Khan was the first consul-general to be 'so cordially received' by Parsis, and the diplomat claimed to have been 'specially commanded' by the shah 'to be on terms of amity and friendship with the community'.[146] He reassured his Parsi audience that the shah held them in high esteem, evidenced by the title he had received in recognition of his own efforts to strengthen ties with their community in Bombay.[147] In 1873, Naser al-Din Shah had met with a Parsi deputation in London, and he would have seen the potential political and economic benefits of promoting good relations with the community. As well as pointing out improvements in the position of Zoroastrians in Iran, the consul-general described how the shah was 'following in the footsteps of the ancient kings of Persia', citing his recent bestowal of a 'purely Persian' title on his daughter 'Aftekhar-ud-Dowla', who had governed the eastern provinces on her brother's behalf.[148] This reference to a powerful female ruler may also have aimed to highlight the resurgence of supposed pre-Islamic values, which some argued included equality between women and men.[149]

Iranian diplomats in Bombay regarded Parsis as co-heirs of Iran's pre-Islamic heritage; consequently, Parsis were viewed as belonging of the city's 'Persian' community. In November 1886, the consul-general invited 'a large number of the leading members of the Parsee community and a few Moguls [Iranian Muslims]' to events marking the birthday of the shah.[150] Birthday celebrations for the shah had been introduced in Tehran in the 1860s,[151] and the custom was now replicated abroad, presumably to heighten the international prestige of the monarch.

Two parties were held at the consulate on consecutive nights. Guests were treated to a 'pretty spectacle' of Chinese lanterns hanging from the flagstaff, which illuminated the bungalow and its 'spacious compound'.[152] This was the first time that Parsis had been asked to such events, and in an address delivered at one of the parties, Jamsetjee Cursetjee Cama praised 'the great change which has come over the Persian people'. Cama suggested that the shah's trips to Europe in 1873 and 1878 had led him to 'introduce into his country the civilisation of the West', an allusion to the recent abolition of the *jezya*.[153] Due to this momentous transformation, Cama proposed that educated Parsis keen on 'a political or military career' would happily work for the government of Iran, if the opportunity arose in 'the land of their ancestors'.[154] The following evening, Parsi ties to Iran were reiterated in another address, which referred to the 'gracious messages' that Parsis had received from the shah in the preceding year and to their feelings of 'patriotic pride in being so well thought of by the ruler of our Fatherland'.[155]

Similar parties were held the next year, by which time a Parsi called D. Rustomji Banaji had been appointed Persian vice-consul in Bombay.[156] This was seen as 'tangible proof' of the 'goodwill' of the shah towards the community.[157] During the celebrations, the consul-general praised the Parsis profusely:

> They are a proof as to what a nation naturally intelligent might become under the protection and fostering care of such a liberal, just and tolerant Government as the English; and it is my earnest prayer that their co-religionists who are subjects of my august master may also be able to reach an equal degree of prosperity and become as useful citizens in the ancient land of their sires.[158]

This comparison between British and Iranian governance was made on other occasions, with the recurrent theme being that the modernization of Iran would result in conditions that would enable the Iranian Zoroastrian community to flourish. Not only would they contribute to the wealth of Iran but the implication was that they would prove to be loyal subjects of the shah.[159]

Whilst many Parsis stressed their loyalty to the British crown, expressions of allegiance were also made to the shah.[160] At one of the parties celebrating the shah's birthday, the playwright Kaikhosro Kabraji proclaimed that with the arrival of the consul-general in Bombay,

> our ancient native land of Persia and the glories of its monarch have been brought very prominently to our notice by being reminded in these halls on many occasions of his Majesty's attachment to our country and our race, and his kind treatment of our co-religionists who have still clung to the land of their Kayanian ancestors, and of the justice and mercy with which the Persian Sovereign of to-day rules over them.[161]

Kabraji articulated the love that Parsis had for their 'ancient Fatherland' and stated that although they were loyal to the British, they had 'not forgotten the past glories of our forefathers in ancient Iran'.[162] According to the Kabraji, Parsi love for Persia was previously subdued, but had 'found vent' due to their contact with the consul-general in Bombay.[163]

Prior to Hosayn Qoli Khan's departure from Bombay in 1888, Parsis made efforts to show their warm feelings towards him. A dinner was organized in his honour at the Elphinstone Club, and the club's president, the reformer and writer, Dosabhai Framji Karaka, who was also a Freemason, reflected that this was the first time the club had welcomed someone who was not an 'Indo-Parsee'.[164] However, Karaka highlighted that their guest was someone with whom they shared 'through the golden ages of the Sassanide Empires, a common ancestry and a common kinship'.[165] Various gifts were presented to the consul-general before he left, including a silver tea and coffee from the Amelioration Society.[166]

The founder of the Amelioration Society, Sir D. M. Petit, outlined how Hosayn Qoli Khan had 'tried to bring Persia to the prominent notice of the Parsees'.[167] In addition to the possibility of Parsis expanding their trade into Iran,[168] this may have encouraged greater Parsi support for the Amelioration Society. A prominent figure in Bombay, Petit also directly asked the consul-general to help their cause, and requested that he try to secure state funding for Zoroastrian schools. Similar tactics were used in 1894, when Parsis met with the then consul-general to raise their concerns about the welfare of Zoroastrians in Yazd. On this occasion, 'desirous of standing well with the powerful Parsi community in Bombay', the consul-general contacted Zel al-Soltan, the governor of Isfahan, who responded with reassurances that Zoroastrians would be protected.[169]

As well as being advantageous for Zoroastrians in Iran, relations between Zoroastrians in India and Iranian diplomats were regarded as potentially beneficial for the Iranian state. After receiving a title from the shah in 1893, the consul-general Mirza Hosayn Khan thanked the Parsis for their warm congratulations and suggested to his 'Zoroastrian brethren' that it was 'the coursing of pure Persian blood in their veins that had brought about this display of affection towards him'.[170] Two addresses were then delivered in Persian, one from the Amelioration Society, and the other on behalf of the *Anjuman-e Elmi-e Farsi*, which had appointed the consul-general as its president.[171] This reveals that efforts made to revive the use of the Persian language amongst Parsis were not only backed by European scholars but were also supported by Iranian officials. Similarly, during the 1890 prizegiving at the Mulla Feroze Madressa, a seminary for Parsi priests, the consul-general had urged Parsis, 'his own brethren', to focus on learning Persian and to consider settling in Persia.[172]

Towards the end of the nineteenth century, several Parsis received Persian honours. This appears to have been motivated by the aim of nurturing positive relations with Parsis. In 1892, the shah gave Sir Dinshaw Petit the title 'Siro Khurshid', the Order of Lion and Sun, for his work helping Iranian Zoroastrians.[173] The Parsi politician Sir Mancherjee Bhownaggree also received this decoration, and the playwright Kaikhosro Kabraji was awarded a gold medal from the shah 'for his services to his community'.[174] The titles received by Parsis may have added weight to the view articulated in the *Parsi* that, although there were not many Parsis in the British consular service, 'it will be readily admitted that the Parsis are eminently fitted to fill the subordinate posts of vice-consuls in the East – and nowhere more so than in Persia'.[175] Bolstered by the respect they enjoyed from the Iranian political elite, by the early twentieth century there was a growing enthusiasm felt by some Parsis towards Iran, their 'ancient fatherland'.[176]

The Parsi colony scheme: Resettlement in the ancient homeland

The idea that Iran was the true home of Parsis influenced proposals regarding a Parsi colony either within, or near, Iran. Some of the first references to this idea appeared in 1888, when the consul-general Mirza Hosayn Qoli Khan was preparing to depart from Bombay.[177]

According to the editor of the *Jam-e Jamshed*, the consul-general had stated that the shah wished to be in closer contact with the Parsis. Whilst the 'sensible few' were not overwhelmed, the editor described how other Parsis 'lost their heads completely and spoke of returning to Persia *en masse* and forming a colony under the protection of his Excellency Hajee Mirza Coolikhan'.[178] Enthusiasm dissipated when the *Jam-e Jamshed* asked to see evidence of the shah's interest in the community, and the consul-general had nothing specific to show. Furthermore, several months after Hosayn Qoli Khan's departure, disappointment was felt amongst Parsis as promises he had made were yet to be fulfilled. In reaction to this, the *Jam-e Jamshed* printed a satirical article that described 'an imaginary Durbar [court] in which the Shah promises to form a protectorate to be placed in charge of the Parsees of Bombay'. This was reprinted in translation in the *Times of India*, having been interpreted as a serious news report.[179]

The initial excitement sparked by the words of the consul-general can be seen in the context of the growing interest expressed by some Parsis in their ancient Iranian heritage. This was also linked to conflicting views held by Parsis regarding their prospects in India, including in relation to the rise of Indian nationalism and the establishment of the Indian National Congress (INC), which held its first meeting in Bombay in 1885. Members of the INC hoped that the resolutions passed at their annual sessions would, in time, result in greater Indian involvement in governance.[180] For two decades, the INC advocated action within the existing political framework, but, even during this period, often termed the INC's 'moderate phase', the INC was only supported by a minority within the Parsi community.[181]

However, a small number of Parsis did play a significant role in the INC; in particular Dadabhai Naoroji (1825–1917), Sir Pherozeshah Mehta (1845–1915) and Sir Dinshaw Wacha (1844–1936), who, between 1886 and 1906, were all elected at least once to preside over the annual meeting of the INC. Believing that Parsis should see themselves foremost as Indians, then as Parsis, they stressed that members of the community should work alongside other Indians for the benefit of the wider population.[182] According to Mehta, joining the nationalist movement was in the self-interest of Parsis, in contrast to the alternative 'almost . . . suicidal policy' of isolation from the rest of Indian society.[183] Prior to the formation of the INC, in addition to advocating for reforms within the Parsi community, Naoroji had addressed broader issues, and he came to be known as 'The Grand Old Man of India'. For instance, he argued that changes ought to be made to the exams for the Indian civil service to facilitate the success of Indian candidates, so that funds would not be directed towards the salaries of Britons in the Indian civil service. The demands made by Naoroji were linked to his 'drain of wealth' theory: that there was a direct correlation between British rule and poverty in India. Naoroji spent time in both India and England, and, as well as presiding over the INC in 1886, 1893 and 1906, he pursued a career in Parliament in Westminster, using his position as a Liberal MP to campaign for changes to British policy regarding India.[184]

Whilst Parsis were proud of the achievements of Mehta, Wacha and Naoroji, this did not translate into widespread support for the INC.[185] In 1888, the *Rast*

Goftar advised Parsis not to attend the fourth INC session, and amongst those who criticized the movement was the wealthy industrialist and philanthropist Sir D. M. Petit, who had founded the Amelioration Society. Hoped-for financial backing from Parsis did not materialize, and the 1889 session of the INC was almost relocated due to the negative reaction amongst Parsis and Muslims in Bombay.[186] Comparable to the concerns voiced by some Muslims in India,[187] Parsis worried that the INC was at its core a Hindu movement, and, in view of their position as a numerically small community, they feared that the success of the INC would bring about an end to their political influence.[188]

Another issue raised was the impact that Parsi involvement in the INC might have on their relations with the British. In the run-up to the 1890 session, over which Mehta was to preside, Nusserwanji Sheriarji Ginwalla wrote a letter to the *Times of India*, 'The Parsees and the Congress'.[189] Ginwalla criticized his co-religionists who wanted increased Indian self-governance, arguing that the success of the INC would not benefit the Parsi community. He questioned whether the Parsis really loved India and 'its people', and stated his belief that their sympathies were 'all English', thereby drawing a clear distinction between Parsis and the rest of the population of India.[190]

Rather than participating in the INC, Ginwalla exhorted Parsis to 'take the example of the Jews', who were also 'wanderers from father-land', and who 'steered clear of politics'.[191] It is noteworthy that Ginwalla cited Kabraji, whose plays popularized the pre-Islamic period of Iranian history, and who used his position as editor and publisher of the *Rast Goftar* to warn Parsis against involvement in the nationalist movement.[192] As well as referencing loyalty to the British, Parsis who did not favour political change appear to have emphasized their Persian, rather than Indian, identity.

Prompted by a recent article in the *Times of India*, which had suggested that Parsis open commercial centres in Iran, Ginwalla argued that members of his community should revive their enterprising spirit and focus on trade. However, Ginwalla also clarified that he did see a future political role for Parsis, not in India, but in Iran:

> There will be time enough for us to play a part in politics when the British will have taken Persia – as they must in time – only we wish it were sooner. We may then return to Persia with them, in which country our interest yet remains as fresh as ever.[193]

Likewise, Jamshedji Dorabji Khandalwala hoped that his book on the *Shahnameh* would lead to a resurgence of the sentiments held in 'the good old days' when

> Every Parsee, young and old, was well posted in the history of the Shah-nameh, and never lost his interest in the ancient father-land to which he fondly hoped to be restored some day by the all-powerful arm of the British whose great mission it is to carry civilisation and justice to long suffering nations.[194]

Thus, alongside the idea that Iranians might invite Parsis to live and work in Iran, references were also made to the prospect of Parsis 'returning' to Iran, under British rule.

The possibility of Parsis returning to Iran was a topic of debate in 1905, when the idea of a Parsi territory was raised again. The key proponent was Khan Bahadur Burjorjee Dorabjee Patel, a wealthy Parsi who lived in Quetta, a city with a Parsi population of about 150 individuals.[195] Patel spent several months 'agitating' in the *Rast Goftar* 'the necessity of establishing a colony for the Parsee community'.[196] Whilst visiting Bombay for business, Patel addressed the 'Parsee Association' and outlined his view that greater competition from Hindus and Muslims was leading to a decrease in Parsi influence. Rather than struggling to maintain their position in India, he suggested that Parsis find 'fresh fields and pastures anew', for example in Sistan and Makran, 'where they would be in the neighbourhood of their ancient Fatherland and where they might be able, under the protection of the British, to establish a colony for those who find it difficult to make ends meet'.[197] Patel believed that the climate and mineral wealth of these areas would lead to future prosperity for the Parsis, mirroring the glory of their ancient past. Following Patel's speech, some members of the association pointed to potential challenges, but others were keen to conduct further investigations.[198]

By December, the *Parsi* described how 'wise men, who shook their heads ... when the subject was first mooted, are now discussing it soberly, and are evincing a certain amount of respect for it'.[199] A factor prompting changes in attitudes regarding the plausibility of a Parsi territory may have been the partition of the Bengal Presidency in October 1905; this resulted in the formation of a predominantly Hindu western region and a majority Muslim eastern region. Indian nationalists criticized the partition, viewing it as an example of British 'divide and rule' policies. In addition to petitions and protests, opposition was expressed through the establishment of the *swadeshi* movement, which called for the boycotting of British goods.[200] The unrest provoked by the partition may have compounded concerns felt by members of the Parsi community regarding their future in India.

Some advocates of the colony plan favoured a territory under British rule in India, but others argued that due to economic factors, 'fresh fields' were preferable.[201] The activities of the Zionist Organization, which had been established in 1897, seem to have inspired the recommendation made in the *Samachar*, a Parsi newspaper, for a site in present-day Kenya that had earlier been considered as the location of a Zionist colony.[202] However, the *Parsi* argued that 'the one great feature of a Parsi colony should be its location either in our fatherland of Iran of somewhere near it'.[203] This was for practical as well as sentimental reasons, and the suggestion was made that Iranian Zoroastrians could relocate to the colony:

> a large number of Zoroastrian agriculturalists and farmers can easily be secured from Yezd and Kerman, where, with a few exceptions, the bulk of the Zoroastrians are and always have been tillers of the soil. . . . They would be only too happy to move about in Persia or near Persia, in any place where their lot could be bettered.[204]

Thus, Iranian Zoroastrians would live in greater safety, but they would be expected to take on physically demanding roles.

Although in certain respects Parsis differentiated themselves from their co-religionists in Iran, the discussions about the colony scheme reveal that some Parsis viewed themselves as Iranians who were entitled to return to their homeland. The *Parsi* raised the question as to why Parsi capitalists were working in Australia and China instead of Iran. Not only were there opportunities for enterprise, for example, in the oil industry, but 'as the true sons of the Persian soil the Parsis have a double claim on the country'.[205] Linked to the colony proposal was the idea that Parsis were Persians in a foreign land, despite their presence in India for hundreds of years. Khan Bahadur Burjorjee Dorabjee Patel argued that Parsis were 'descendants of a handful of Zoroastrian refugees', who had never been regarded as 'natives' of India, and would 'still be looked upon as aliens' if the British were to leave.[206] The hope was expressed that the colony scheme might 'lay the germs for the fertilisation of a new national self-consciousness', an illustration of the notion that Parsis were not true Indian nationals.[207]

Supposed differences between the Parsis and other communities in India were highlighted to support the view that Parsis were 'precisely suited to the purpose of colonisation', and would consequently be able to restore Iran to its former glory.[208] In the July 1905 edition of the *Parsi*, it was outlined that:

> If once again Persia chances to number among its inhabitants an energetic and enterprising race like the Parsis, – the direct descendants of the once powerful rulers of the soil, – it might attain to a height of undreamt of prosperity and power.[209]

Despite this display of confidence, the same journal occasionally expressed the more pessimistic opinion that life in India had precipitated physical decline within the Parsi community.

In reference to trade opportunities in Iran, an article in the *Parsi* described it as pitiable that Parsis, 'softened by the mild and temperate climate of Western India think only of clinging fast to a city accidentally connected with their birth'.[210] However, it was noted that once Parsis left India, for example, for China or England, they rarely returned. This did not surprise the author, who stated that 'there is no country which the Parsis can call their own, unless it be Persia'. They went on to explain that:

> Parsis still call Persia their fatherland, and there is a faint, lingering tradition of a prophecy that some day the Parsis will lift Persia out of the slough of barbarism and bad government into which it has sunk.[211]

Thus, echoing arguments made to justify the British Empire, by the early twentieth century there were expressions of the view that Parsis were pure Persians, who might return to their ancient homeland on a civilizing mission.[212] Similarly, Kulke has described how Parsi proposals were inspired by the context of the concurrent 'climax of European imperialistic expansion', which led members of the community to 'imitate' this fervour for colonization.[213]

The Parsi colony proposals were endorsed by the Hungarian scholar, Ármin Vámbéry, who had also given his support to Theodor Herzl, the founder of political

Zionism.[214] Vámbéry had travelled in Iran, and, in an article in the *Parsi*, he noted the improvements for Zoroastrians brought about by the work of Hataria, which had been enhanced by a 'national revival'. This had led to some relief being offered to Zoroastrians, 'the poor remnants' of the glorious past. He pointed out that in Iran it had become fashionable 'to mention with pride and enthusiasm' the Sasanian period, and the 'pure' Persian used by Ferdowsi.[215] In Vámbéry's opinion, due to the power of the ulama, these ideas were not yet widespread, but he believed they would be strengthened if the Parsis established a colony.[216] Vámbéry welcomed Parsi attendance of Persian-language classes in Bombay, perhaps believing that this would ease the relocation of Parsis to Iran.

A staunch Anglophile, Vámbéry thought that in order for the Parsi colony to succeed, the British would have to play a key role. Referring to what he regarded as the 'salutary influence' of the British Empire, Vámbéry argued that the rejuvenation of Persia could 'only be effectuated by the civilising efforts of the English, if the latter are duly assisted by their Parsi pupils'.[217] Vámbéry, who viewed Parsis as Persians, believed that their reputation for being loyal, and their adoption of British values, meant that they were ideally suited to playing a leading role in this enterprise.[218] Confident that the British would back a Parsi colony scheme in south-eastern Iran, Vámbéry hoped that the plan would go ahead, believing that 'the interest of Great Britain's imperialism and of the sacred cause of humanity coincide here in every respect'.[219] Ultimately, the plans were not enacted. Even so, the consideration of a Parsi colony in the early twentieth century highlights a growing anxiety within the community regarding their future in India, an increased association with their Persian past, and the significance of their relations with the British in the present.

3

Zoroastrians and the 'Great Game'

The 'Great Game' and trade

Expectations of British support for a Zoroastrian colony in Sistan must be viewed in the context of Anglo-Russian rivalry in Iran and Central Asia. Concerned by a possible Russian attack on India, the British were anxious to strengthen border regions and regarded Iran as an important 'buffer state'. The term commonly used to refer to Russian and British imperial intrigue and ambition, the 'Great Game', conjures an image of Iran as a passive geographical board. However, on various levels, Iranians were also active players.[1] When the position of the Zoroastrian community is brought into focus, the complexity of the interplay between the British, Russians and Zoroastrians is revealed. In addition to being affected by the competition between the two foreign powers, members of the Zoroastrian community were at times able to use this rivalry to their own advantage.[2]

Both Britain and Russia had long-standing relations with Iran; Russia as a neighbour and Britain through trade and diplomacy. In the early years of Qajar rule, wars between Russia and Iran resulted in Iranian territorial losses in the Caucasus, detailed in the treaties of Golestan (1813) and Turkmenchay (1828).[3] Fearing Russia's expansionist policies and Russian influence at the Qajar court, the British resisted Iranian efforts to secure control over western Afghanistan. Consequently, when the city of Herat was captured by Iran in 1856, diplomatic relations between Iran and Britain temporarily broke down and Britain took military action, leading to the Anglo-Iranian War of 1856–7. This ended with the Iranians relinquishing control over Herat, and the British agreeing to withdraw troops from southern Iran.[4] Maintaining Iran as a barrier to protect India from Russian advances was a British priority, but, although military force was sometimes used, the British were keen to keep expenditure as low as possible.[5]

Towards the end of the nineteenth century, Anglo-Russian rivalry was increasingly played out in the economic sphere, with the two powers competing over trade and concessions. In 1872, a wide-ranging concession was granted to the British entrepreneur, Baron Julius de Reuter. This included rights for the exploitation of many natural resources, as well as control over numerous infrastructure projects, such as the building of roads, bridges and railways. Before any measures were enacted, the Reuter Concession was cancelled. Not only had it faced criticism in Iran but neither had it received backing from the British government.[6] According to Vanessa Martin, British reluctance to support the concession was linked to fears about the economic disruption that the development of Iran might cause.[7] However, attitudes amongst British officials soon changed, and concessions were seen as a way of strengthening Iran, which would in turn increase Iran's effectiveness as a buffer state.[8]

A number of more focused concessions were subsequently granted by the shah and his ministers to individuals and to foreign governments, principally Britain and Russia. Some were linked to specific resources and others to particular services, such as the telegraph network. On occasion, there was public reaction against concessions, most notably seen in the protests that led to the cancellation of the Tobacco Concession in 1892. The Iranian government did make immediate financial gains by granting concessions, but the terms on which they were agreed were restrictive. Due to Anglo-Russian rivalry, an equilibrium also had to be maintained between the two powers. This is reflected in the granting of two banking concessions, resulting in the establishment of the British Imperial Bank of Persia and the Russian Loan Bank.[9] Mansoureh Ettehadieh has outlined that

> Taken as a whole, Persian concessions encouraged foreign trade, commercialization of agriculture, contacts with the West, and gradual incorporation of the country into the world economy.[10]

The intensification in the farming of cash crops for a global market resulted in a decrease in the export of manufactured goods, with raw materials taking their place. Although Iran did remain independent, this trading pattern has been compared to patterns usually seen in colonized countries.[11]

Whilst mercantile links between India and Iran were well-established, Nile Green has described how new technologies in steamship production led to an increase in the volume of this trade during the nineteenth century. As a result, Bombay became the 'commercial focus for the traditional trading towns of central and southern Iran'.[12] Writing in 1849, Keith Edward Abbott, the British consul in Tabriz, stated that the city of Yazd was 'very favourably situated for trade', and was 'well suited to become an emporium for the commerce between India and Central Asia'.[13] Abbott suggested that opium from the area could be exported, especially as it was deemed to be of 'esteemed' quality.[14] During the 1850s, techniques facilitating the large-scale production of opium were introduced to Iran by a merchant from Isfahan, who had apparently learnt the methods from Parsis in India.[15] This led to a surge in the production of opium, which soon dominated the export market.[16] By the late nineteenth century, other exports from Yazd included: nuts, carpets, silk, wool, felt, dyes, walnut wood and tobacco. Machine-made cotton, spices, tea, jewellery, arms and sugar were amongst the goods imported.[17] Cotton manufactured in Manchester and Bombay became the principal import commodity, leading to a decrease in Iranian cotton production, with opium taking its place.[18]

Due to trade links with India as well as British geopolitical concerns regarding border regions, H. Lyman Stebbins has argued that the southern provinces of Iran were 'the real focus of British power and influence', rather than Tehran.[19] The decentralized nature of Qajar rule meant that relations with local governors and elites, such as tribal leaders, were of importance to the British, and vice versa.[20] Attention was also paid to the position of Zoroastrians, who lived predominantly towards the south of the country. After visiting Yazd, Abbott had pointed out that Zoroastrians were the 'principal cultivators' of the opium poppy, yet many had emigrated to India because of the hardships they faced, and others were keen to follow.[21] Conditions in Iran remained difficult for Zoroastrians, but from the mid-nineteenth century, there was an increase in the number of Zoroastrians who became wealthy through their involvement in trade. They were seen as profitable trading partners by the British, particularly in light of their links with Zoroastrians in India. However, it was not purely for commercial reasons that the British showed an interest in the community, as the strengthening of relations with Zoroastrians also tied in with wider British strategies. Although by the end of the century the British Foreign Office was increasingly worried about the rising power of Germany, the Government of India continued to fear a Russian advance.[22] Encouraging positive relations with Iranian Zoroastrians was viewed as one method that might help weaken Russian influence in central and southern Iran.

The rise of a Zoroastrian mercantile class

Without this improvement in the socio-economic position of some Iranian Zoroastrians, from a British perspective, the commercial and strategic significance of strengthening relations with the community would have been negligible. There were a number of wealthy Zoroastrians living in Yazd during the early nineteenth century, but Nasser Mohajer and Kaveh Yazdani have highlighted that an outbreak of cholera in the 1840s had a devastating impact on the community.[23] However, Zoroastrians and other non-Muslims benefitted when Mirza Taqi Khan Farahani was appointed chief minister, Amir Kabir, in 1848. Aiming to strengthen the state, Amir Kabir tried to remove factors that might lead non-Muslims to seek foreign protection.[24] He also encouraged commercial links with Parsis and attempted to entice Iranian Zoroastrians who had emigrated to India to return.[25] Amir Kabir was dismissed from his post in 1852, but just two years later, Manekji Limji Hataria, emissary for the Amelioration Society, arrived in Iran. The impact of the Amelioration Society was also significant in relation to the emergence of wealthy Zoroastrian merchants. Indeed, Joseph Arthur de Gobineau stated that Zoroastrians in Tehran had been too impoverished to undertake any 'speculations' in 1857, but due to the efforts made by Hataria, their circumstances changed in just a few years.[26]

The number of Zoroastrians involved in trade grew steadily, particularly in Yazd. By 1863, Lieutenant Colonel Lewis Pelly reported that Zoroastrians were the 'principal merchants' of Yazd, 'one of the wealthiest and most enterprising towns in Persia'.[27] In spite of the famine in the early 1870s, this trend continued; A. V. Williams Jackson noted in 1903 that Zoroastrians in Yazd were 'largely occupied in trading', a 'privilege' that 'was not accorded them until about fifty years ago'.[28] Around the same time, Napier Malcolm, a missionary based in Yazd, described Zoroastrians as a 'wealthy community', who were permitted to trade in the 'caravanserais' but not in the bazaars.[29] Zoroastrians were still subjected to certain discriminatory rules, but the emergence of affluent merchants marked an important shift for the community. The 1882 *farman* that abolished the *jezya* had an additional benefit for merchants, insofar as the *farman* was implemented, as it stipulated that Zoroastrians were to pay the same 'trading dues' as Muslims.[30]

Zoroastrian merchants contributed to the rising trade between southern Iran and India, and profited from their involvement in these commercial activities.[31] Writing in 1917, M. M. Murzban described changes that had occurred since the late 1860s:

> Some of the Guebres [Zoroastrians] are naturalized English subjects, and, thanks to them, for the last fifty years, the trade of Yezd has grown by their intercourse with India. Their *rôle* is similar to that performed in the open ports of Japan by the *compradores* and the Chinese agents, into whose hands nearly all business passes. This activity is due to the efforts of their co-religionists in India.[32]

Links with India are also reflected in a report dating from 1881, which recorded that a 'large number' of Zoroastrians from Ardakan, a town near Yazd, had travelled to India.[33] Similarly, in the 1890s, Lieutenant-General T. E. Gordon stated that Iranian Zoroastrians were 'rich and prosperous merchants, who have close personal and commercial relations with the prosperous Parsee community in Bombay, and they own a large share of the import and export trade of Yezd'.[34] Stronger ties between Zoroastrians in Iran and India led to a higher level of British interest in the Iranian Zoroastrian community, especially as some had become British subjects. Although the British were primarily concerned with trade in southern Iran, the growing number of Zoroastrians in Tehran must also be examined, as this had an influence on the socio-economic position of the wider Zoroastrian community.

During the nineteenth century, migration from the provinces led to a rapid rise in the population of Tehran, with new arrivals in the city including individuals from various ethnic and religious backgrounds.[35] Hataria encouraged Zoroastrians to move to the capital; in addition to establishing a boarding school and a hostel, he organized for the *dakhmeh* to be rebuilt.[36] In the early years of the twentieth century, a fire temple was constructed, a contrast to the situation in the mid-nineteenth century, when the only place for communal worship was a shrine built *c.* 1830 by Zoroastrians who worked in Tehran during the summer months.[37]

Attitudes towards Zoroastrians appear to have been more positive in the capital than in the provinces, and Hataria described how he received 'kindness and love' from Muslims in the city.[38] Having examined the records of two *shari'a* courts,[39] Nobuaki Kondo argues that Hataria and other non-Muslims in Tehran successfully made use of these courts to protect their rights, for instance, in respect to financial affairs. Kondo highlights that Hataria did complain about some discrimination, but, after gaining the support of a high-ranking cleric, he seems to have been treated fairly and in accordance with the law.[40]

Foreigners also noted that there was less hostility towards Zoroastrians in Tehran, with Jackson referring to the 'more liberal conditions that prevail in general at the capital'.[41] In addition to the diversity of Tehran, other suggested explanations for the greater tolerance experienced in the capital include the proximity to the shah, as well as the presence of foreign diplomats who expressed an interest in the welfare of non-Muslims.[42] Similar observations were made in the late 1880s by Edward Browne, who stated that it was only in and around Yazd and Kerman that Zoroastrians were still expected to wear yellow clothes that marked them out as non-Muslims.[43]

Zoroastrians in Tehran had a reputation for their work as gardeners, and some were employed in this capacity by the British legation.[44] However, in the 1890s, George Nathaniel Curzon reported that the majority of the 'several hundred' Zoroastrians in the city, were 'engaged in correspondence with their mercantile head-quarters at Yezd and Kerman'.[45] Their rising success is reflected in the presence of Zoroastrian traders in the Grand Bazaar by 1899.[46] The growth of the Zoroastrian community in Tehran, albeit gradual at first, and its commercial focus, must in part be credited to the expansion of the trading house of Arbab Jamshid Jamshidian (c.1850–1932).

Born in Yazd c. 1850, Arbab Jamshid began his career trading textiles in southern Iran, before moving to Tehran c. 1873.[47] His business grew, and in the late 1880s his Jamshidian firm diversified and started offering money-changing services. Branches were established across Iran, and the firm also had representatives in Baghdad, Bombay, Calcutta and Paris.[48] The emergence of Iranian Zoroastrian trading houses such as the Jamshidian firm and Mehrban & Co. led to greater employment opportunities for Zoroastrians in Iran.[49] By the early twentieth century, Arbab Jamshid employed around 100–150 Zoroastrians. He also gave practical support to the poorer members of his community and established a primary school in Tehran.[50]

Another major Zoroastrian trading company that emerged in the late nineteenth century was the Jahanian firm. This company also had agents in several Iranian cities, as well as in London, Bombay and New York. The firm was founded c. 1890, by Khosrow Shahjahan and his brothers: Parviz, Gudarz, Rostam and Bahram, who were Zoroastrian landowners from Yazd.[51] By 1897, Khosrow Shahjahan was counted amongst the most influential merchants in Fars province.[52]

Wealthy Iranian Zoroastrians such as Arbab Jamshid and Khosrow Shahjahan were members of a broader social class of 'big merchants' who had benefitted from rising international trade and from the sale of state land, which had been encouraged by the government to increase revenue.[53] Indeed, the title 'Arbab' denoted Jamshid's status as a large-scale landowner; he had bought properties in and around Tehran, and in the provinces of Khorasan and Fars, where cash crops were grown.[54] According to Ann Lambton, as well as being profitable, landownership was significant as it increased a person's social prestige and political power.[55]

Arbab Jamshid was held in high esteem by members of the ruling class, and Jackson described how his 'recognition at Court' benefitted Zoroastrians 'considerably', as appeals to the shah could be voiced through him. Not only did Arbab Jamshid have a fortune 'in the hundreds of thousands of tomans' but he was also said to have been respected for his honesty.[56] The British were well-aware of his position, and he was one of the twenty-eight Tehran merchants included in the 'Biographical Notices' of 1897, a confidential compilation of descriptions of influential individuals.[57] In this document, the following entry was given for Arbab Jamshid:

Sarraf [money changer] of Teheran. Has a capital of 10,000 tomans at his disposal, but has large amounts to receive from Government Officials etc. Is very trustworthy and merits confidence. Receives deposits from Persians. Is a Zoroastrian or Parsi.[58]

Mozaffar al-Din Shah used both the Jamshidian and Jahanian firms, and they processed his foreign loans.[59] Although Amighi states that Arbab Jamshid was not fully accepted into the inner circle of the elite,[60] a reference to a lavish banquet that Arbab Jamshid organized in honour of Mozaffar al-Din Shah reflects his social standing.[61] Additionally, Arbab Jamshid was given an honorary title by Mozaffar al-Din Shah,[62] and he was also close to the influential minister, Mirza ʿAli Asghar Khan Amin al-Soltan, often known by his title Atabak-e Aʿzam.[63] By the turn of the century, Malcolm believed that requests on behalf of the Zoroastrian community made by Arbab Jamshid were likely to have a greater effect on the government than petitions from the Parsis.[64] Similarly, Rashid Shahmardan has argued that by lending money to influential individuals in the provinces, Arbab Jamshid and other Zoroastrian merchant-bankers secured some protection for members of their community.[65]

Due to the decentralized rule of the Qajar shahs, the attitudes of local governors had a significant impact on the lives of Muslims and non-Muslims alike. Consequently, the situation for Zoroastrians in Yazd and Kerman could fluctuate, depending on who was governor, and whether or not they were present and able to exert their authority.[66] For instance, Zoroastrians appear to have had good relations with ʿAbd al-Hosayn Mirza Farmanfarma, who was intermittently governor of Kerman in the 1890s and early 1900s.[67] Likewise, according to Malcolm, during the late 1890s and early 1900s, most governors of Yazd had been 'stronger' and were 'friendly' towards Zoroastrians; this was apparently particularly true in the case of Jalal al-Dowleh.[68] Indeed, in an address Bhownaggree presented to the shah in 1900 on behalf of the Zoroastrian community, the hope was expressed that Jalal al-Dowleh would retain his position for many years.[69] Daniel Tsadik has described an incident from the mid-1880s when Jalal al-Dowleh's father, Zel al-Soltan, who was governor of Isfahan, ordered the execution of a Muslim who had killed a Zoroastrian.[70] The action taken by Zel al-Soltan appears to have been influenced by pressure from Zoroastrians in Bombay, whose concerns had been communicated via the Persian consul-general.[71] Zel al-Soltan also intervened to help the Jewish community at times, but, as Tsadik has pointed out, he was inconsistent, and there are negative reports of his governorship, including in relation to non-Muslim communities.[72]

Zoroastrians and other non-Muslims were also affected by the varying stances adopted by local members of the ulama.[73] Ordering attacks on non-Muslim communities was a method used by some clerics to assert their authority, and to test the power of local governors. On occasion, non-Muslims were targeted to express anger at foreign interference and influence in Iran, as members of these communities often had support from European states.[74]

However, affluent Zoroastrians were able to use their wealth to promote positive perceptions of their community. Analogous to the Parsis in India, Zoroastrian philanthropy in Iran helped negate some of the resentment that may have arisen due to Zoroastrian success. The charitable works of Arbab Jamshid were sometimes specifically for his community, such as the *dakhmeh* he built in Cham, but other acts benefitted the wider population; these included the provision of meals for people in Tehran and the building of fountains.[75] In 1898, Gudarz (also known as Godrez) Mehrban donated a caravanserai in Yazd to the Church Missionary Society, which was to be used as a hospital where people of all religions were to be treated.[76] According to Delphine Menant, this helped integrate the Zoroastrian community into the wider society of Yazd.[77]

The success of the Bahá'í faith may also have been beneficial to Zoroastrians, including individuals involved in trade. Amighi has pointed out that 'monetary incentives' prompted conversions, as wealthy Bahá'ís looked after those who joined the faith.[78] In contrast to conversion to Islam, Zoroastrians who joined the Bahá'í faith could also keep their Zoroastrian religious identity.[79] Similar to Hataria, Arbab Jamshid closely associated with Zoroastrian converts to the Bahá'í faith, and Susan Stiles has argued that this increased the 'prestige' of the Bahá'í faith amongst Zoroastrians.[80] Not only did Bahá'í ideas about religious equality and reform reportedly have a positive effect on attitudes towards Zoroastrians,[81] but its popularity amongst merchants may also have opened up commercial opportunities for Zoroastrian converts.[82]

Native agents and consulates

From the mid-nineteenth century, mutually beneficial relations between the British and Parsis had a positive impact on Zoroastrians in Iran. For instance, Parsis had support from the British during the campaign against the *jezya*. Humanitarian concerns may have been another reason prompting the British to try to improve conditions for Zoroastrians, but Tsadik has argued that there were other factors motivating British assistance towards non-Muslims, including the possibility of increasing their political reach in the Qajar state.[83] Offering support to religious minorities was a method used by colonial powers to the same effect elsewhere; for example, Anaïs Massot has examined how this approach was taken by consuls in Damascus.[84] However, it was not only by protecting religious minorities that the British could strengthen their influence in Iran. Commercial ties with non-Muslims were also significant. In 1890, Lieutenant Henry Bathurst Vaughan described how the Russians had successfully used their links with Armenians, who were fellow-Christians, to widen their trade network.[85] This led him to argue that, in view of positive and well-established relations between the British and the Parsis, similar relations could be forged with Zoroastrians in Iran to the benefit of British trade.[86]

Following his travels in Iran in 1888–9, Vaughan suggested that a British or native agent should be appointed in Yazd, where a large proportion of the Iranian Zoroastrian population lived.[87] Vaughan believed that if Zoroastrians were protected by the British, trade with India would increase, and so too would British economic and political influence in the city.[88] Most of the trade between Yazd and Bombay passed through the hands of fifteen naturalized British subjects in Yazd, some of whom were Zoroastrians.[89] Vaughan pointed out that due to a lack of security, these merchants invested no more than a quarter of their 'fortune'; this was particularly the case for Zoroastrians, through whose hands over half of the trade passed, and who were in the greatest danger.[90] With the appointment of an agent, 'the effect on British trade would be astonishing', and 'Parsis of Yezd would form companies and firms', leading to an increase in the import of English-manufactured items.[91] Raising the possibility of the subsequent expansion of British trade across Iran, Vaughan suggested that mills and mines might be built, which would then encourage Parsis to relocate to Iran.[92]

Whilst trade with Iran was not economically significant when seen in the context of the volume of British trade on a global scale, it was important in terms of rivalry with Russia.[93] Thus, the idea of capitalizing on relations with Zoroastrians in order to strengthen the position of the British in Iran was taken seriously. A year after Vaughan wrote his report, discussions took place between the Foreign Office and the Government of India, as to whether or not a Zoroastrian should be appointed as the native agent in Yazd.[94] The man suggested for the post was Ardeshir Mehrban, an agent of the recently established British-owned New Oriental Bank,[95] and one of the brothers who had organized famine relief in 1871. Apparently, Ardeshir had already made 'indirect overtures' to the British legation in Tehran about taking on the role, as he believed it would be helpful for his community.[96] Ardeshir may have been partly motivated by his family's experiences of injustice; his brother Rasheed had been murdered in Yazd in 1874, and the perpetrator had not been punishment.

Not only did Ardeshir have 'great influence' within his community, but Vaughan also pointed out that he was 'friends' with leading Muslim merchants, who were 'tolerant as regards other creeds'.[97] As a Zoroastrian, Ardeshir did face certain challenges, but Vaughan was confident these would be overcome as Ardeshir would gain a certain level of prestige as a native agent. Furthermore, Vaughan commented that a Muslim agent might not 'give the Parsis fair play'; this would be problematic, as it was through links with Zoroastrians that British trade was likely to develop.[98]

Colonel Edward Charles Ross, who was at the time the British Political Resident in Bushehr and consul-general for South Persia, also favoured the appointment of a native agent who could protect trade with India, 'nearly the whole of which' was in the hands of Zoroastrians.[99] A report cited by Ross stated that out of 6,737 Zoroastrians living in the region of Yazd, 704 were now involved in trade. Although Ross regarded Ardeshir as a 'very respectable merchant' with a 'good financial position', and he believed there was 'no doubt' that the position of Zoroastrians had improved, he described how the community was viewed with 'mingled contempt and jealousy', so he was not sure that it would be wise to appoint a Zoroastrian.[100]

In addition to the implications of Ardeshir's religion, another issue raised was the question of who would be responsible for paying his salary: the Foreign Office, or the Government of India. The suggestion was made that Ardeshir could be offered an unpaid honorary position for a year, after which a decision would be made. Ardeshir accepted this arrangement. He had since travelled to Bombay, so he organized for his agents in Yazd to undertake his 'political duties' until he returned.[101] However, the year passed, and although Ardeshir was addressed as 'Native Agent' in correspondence, his appointment had not been formally announced.[102]

Writing to Sir Frank Lascelles, the British minister in Tehran, Ardeshir emphasized that he was willing to continue to work unpaid, as long as his position was officially acknowledged.[103] To persuade Lascelles of his suitability for the role, Ardeshir outlined his background, giving an insight into his life. Ardeshir had moved to Bombay as a boy and had passed his university matriculation exams in 1866; he had studied at the prestigious Elphinstone College for a year and a half but had to stop due to ill-health. For the next twenty years, he worked as a merchant in India, before returning to Yazd *c.* 1878.[104] During this time, Ardeshir had become a wealthy landowner, with 75,000 rupees worth of land in Bombay and Poona (Pune), and a further 60,000 rupees worth of land in Yazd. In 1869, Ardeshir had become a naturalized British subject, and he was keen to assist the British. He stated that his own 'personal interests' and those of the Zoroastrian community were 'entirely wound up in those of the British Government, to whose enlightened and beneficial rule we owe so much'.[105] With his links to Bombay, his Anglophone education and his expressions of loyalty, Ardeshir seemed to be the ideal candidate for the position of native agent. Thus, in view of the 'importance, commercial and political' of securing official British representation at Yazd, his appointment was endorsed by the India Office.[106]

However, despite this, in light of the attitudes of Muslims in Yazd, Ardeshir's appointment was deemed to be too provocative.[107] A report by the British military attaché in Tehran, General Thomas Edward Gordon, was the impetus leading to this change in plan.[108] Gordon described the Zoroastrians of Yazd as a 'rich and prosperous' community, who had 'close personal and commercial relations' with the Parsis of Bombay, and a large share in the import and export trade of Yazd.[109] In contrast to the 'comparatively poor' Jewish community, 'well to do' Zoroastrians were able through the 'judicious use of money to secure for themselves better treatment', thereby becoming 'a source of permanent profit' for local officials.[110] Yet, even after the abolition of the *jezya*, Zoroastrians were still subject to discriminatory rules; for example, they were 'condemned to wear a distinctive dress as a mark of degradation and public proof of being "outcasts"'.[111] Ardeshir was one of a number of Iranian Zoroastrians who had spent time in India and had become naturalized British subjects,[112] a position that gave him some protection.[113] Zoroastrian merchants in Yazd who were British subjects could legitimately disregard clothing regulations, but Gordon observed that they accepted them to help maintain a peaceful atmosphere in Yazd for the sake of the wider Zoroastrian community.[114] Gordon suggested that if Ardeshir was officially appointed, he would 'necessarily consider it highly derogatory' to follow these rules and would be subject to insults and worse for not conforming. This could lead to a dangerous situation. Thus, Gordon argued that it was 'inexpedient and impolitic' to proceed any further.[115]

Although Ardeshir did not receive his official appointment, its consideration reflects the strategic importance Zoroastrians were believed to hold. Writing in the early 1890s, Curzon described how naturalized Zoroastrians were 'proud' of their connection to India. He pointed out that, due to Zoroastrians, trade between Yazd and India had reached 'considerable dimensions' over the past fifty years, adding to the 'great commercial reputation of the city'.[116] Curzon referred to Ardeshir Mehrban as the 'leading merchant' of the Zoroastrians in Yazd, and a 'man of high repute'.[117] Not only was Ardeshir a successful businessman, but he was also head of the Zoroastrian Anjoman of Yazd, revealing the high status of merchants, comparable to the position of Parsi merchants in Bombay.[118] The rising socio-economic position of some Iranian

Zoroastrians is apparent in the case of Ardeshir, who counted Muslims as well as Zoroastrians amongst his employees.[119]

The potential benefits of relations with the Zoroastrian community were not only recognized by the British but also by their rivals, the Russians. Elena Andreeva has argued that Russian interest in the community represents a 'typical colonial reaction' to the supposed 'threat of Islam', which led Russian officers to secure the support of religious and ethnic minorities against the Shi'i majority, in order to 'divide and rule'.[120] Due to religious and geographical factors, the Russians had long-standing ties with Armenian Christians in Iran. However, they also viewed Zoroastrians in a positive light; for example, N. Shetalov, a Russian doctor who lived in Yazd in 1898–9, wrote that Zoroastrians possessed 'many attractive features when compared to the Muslim population'.[121] In addition to their links with the pre-Islamic past, Zoroastrians had a reputation for being honest and were therefore viewed as attractive business partners.[122] Russian reports from the late nineteenth century noted that Zoroastrians in Yazd and Kerman were friendly, keen to do business, and enthusiastic about learning Russian.[123] This engagement with Russians in Iran facilitated the growth of Zoroastrian trading houses, as loans from the Russian Loan Bank enabled Zoroastrian firms to expand.[124] In spite of Parsi loyalty to the British, and the fact that some Iranian Zoroastrians were British subjects, Zoroastrians took advantage of opportunities offered by the Russians.

Closely linked to competition over trade and the appointment of local agents, the establishment of consulates was another method used by the British and the Russians to further their influence.[125] In 1892, General Gordon suggested that vice-consuls should be appointed in Yazd and Kerman, as this would increase the confidence of Bombay Parsis to trade with Iran. Due to a rise in commerce between Yazd and India in the preceding two years, he believed that 'Politically and commercially the place is becoming of importance'.[126] Indeed, Ali Modarres has outlined how the bazaar in Yazd became politicized, and subject to 'regional, national, and international dynamics'.[127] The same applied to Kerman, which Nile Green has described as having been 'brought into Bombay's commercial hinterland' in the 1860s.[128] According to James Gustafson, the growing Russian presence in southern Iran meant that Kerman became 'an important geo-political space'; consequently, in 1894, plans went ahead to establish a British consulate.[129] Reflecting concerns over Russian advances towards India, the new consulates were staffed by individuals appointed by the Government of India rather than the Foreign Office, and those in key positions were often men with a military background.[130] The prospect of a British invasion was discussed by Arnold Henry Savage Landor, who had travelled in Iran in 1902; he was in favour of Iran retaining independence but argued that 'it would not be unwise to prepare for emergencies in case the country – already half spoiled by European ways – should one day collapse and make interference necessary'.[131] In his view, the creation of consulates was therefore a matter of great importance.[132]

The establishment of the consulate in Kerman enabled the British to become more involved in the social and political affairs of the area,[133] and it is noteworthy that the location chosen was in the east of Kerman, close to the Zoroastrian quarter.[134] Major Percy Sykes was appointed as consul in 1895, a position he held until 1905, with some interruptions.[135] Sykes attempted to strengthen British influence in southern Iran by encouraging Zoroastrians and Indian merchants from Shikarpur in Sindh to trade in carpets from Kerman, a business that was dominated by merchants from Tabriz.[136] By protecting Zoroastrian merchants and appointing them as agents for British firms, the British gained greater control over trade without substantially increasing the number of British merchants based in Iran.[137]

Iranian Zoroastrians appear to have profited from the presence of the British consul in Kerman. With hints of a self-congratulatory tone, Sykes described how,

> Mainly owing to the establishment of this Consulate, the Parsees of Kerman have made immense progress. Formerly they hardly dared engage in trade, whereas they are now among the most prosperous shopkeepers and merchants.[138]

Before leaving his post in 1905, Sykes reiterated his view that the establishment of the consulate had 'perhaps benefitted this community [the Zoroastrians] more than any other'.[139] Sykes described how a couple of years prior to his appointment, two young Zoroastrians had been murdered by the *kalantar*, the local mayor, and 'no attempt at redress was possible'.[140] In contrast, Sykes claimed he had been able to intervene on behalf of the community. For instance, he had asked the governor of Kerman to arrest a Muslim cleric who had been threatening Zoroastrians because they were outside in rainy weather. The actions of the cleric can be seen in relation to the belief that non-Muslims were physically impure and that impurities could be spread via raindrops into the ground.[141]

Relations between the British and Zoroastrians in Iran were neither purely altruistic nor solely based on commercial gain. The broader tactical significance of the Zoroastrian population for the British was noted by the missionary Napier Malcolm, who considered the possibility of greater foreign involvement in the government of Iran. Malcolm believed that if this occurred, potential difficulties in establishing order in the south would be alleviated by good relations with Zoroastrians.[142]

Opportunities in the homeland: Parsis and Persia

It was not exclusively in regions of Iran with existing Zoroastrian communities that the British thought their relations with Zoroastrians might prove to be beneficial. On several occasions, the British tried to encourage Parsis to become more directly involved in trade in parts of Iran that did not have a Zoroastrian population, highlighting their Persian heritage to spark their enthusiasm. For instance, in the 1888 trade report for South Persia and the Persian Gulf, Colonel Ross emphatically stated that 'Here, in the country from which they came, there should be a good opening for Parsee pioneers, Parsee merchants, and Parsee capital'.[143] Parsis were urged to seize opportunities that would arise in the province of Khuzestan, in south-western Iran, following the Karun River Concession and the opening of the river for navigation; this was an area of strategic interest to the British that did not have an established Iranian Zoroastrian community.[144]

A few years later, the topic of Parsi trade with Iran was raised again in an open letter from Major Chenevix-Trench, the British consul in Sistan. Addressed to Sir Jamsetjee Jejeebhoy (4th Baronet) and published in the *Times of India*, the letter focused on the overland trade route between India and Iran via Quetta.[145] Russian incursions into eastern Iran in the early 1880s had raised British concerns over the possibility of a Russian attack on British-ruled Baluchistan from Sistan, so the British constructed an overland trade route to Sistan to strengthen links with India.[146] The suggestion was made by Chenevix-Trench, that wealthy Indian merchants might be encouraged to expand their ventures into Iran, and he expressed the hope that Sir Jejeebhoy might agree to the following:

> communicate my information by any means in your power to that enterprising community the head of which you have the honour to be. If there is any class of people likely to establish themselves in Persia, it is the Parsees of India, and I would be willing to afford every information and render every assistance to any member of the community who may be tempted to trade in Persia by the Seistan route.[147]

Chenevix-Trench anticipated that the Parsis would help develop Iran, 'their own country'.[148] This description reveals that the emphasis on Parsis being Persians was sometimes directly linked to the colonial concerns of British officials.

The following day, an article commenting on the letter was published. This was likely to have dampened Chenevix-Trench's expectations. In addition to expressing concerns as to whether Parsis would be welcomed in Iran, the argument was made that Parsis had lost their position as 'pioneers' of trade and that prosperity and their lifestyle in India had led to 'racial deterioration'; consequently, the correspondent believed that 'other races will have to do the rough pioneer work'.[149] However, despite this negative forecast, in January 1901, Chenevix-Trench recorded in his diary that Sir Jejeebhoy was 'very kind in assisting to encourage his community', with the result that several Parsis had enquired further about the trade route.[150] It seems likely that these discussions informed the 1905 proposals for a Parsi colony near Sistan.

Sykes was an advocate for the use of the overland trade route and also promoted stronger commercial relations between Parsis and Iran.[151] In 1903, he suggested that there was 'a good opening' in Kerman for a 'general Parsee shop', like those found in India, and he stressed that the position of Iranian Zoroastrians would be further improved if Parsis took a more active interest in their co-religionists.[152] Although concerns for the safety of Zoroastrians played a part in British interest in the community, the prospect of increasing trade, in conjunction with wider geopolitical factors, also pushed the British to emphasize the ties between Parsis and Zoroastrians in Iran.

The Commercial Mission

The reports linked to the Commercial Mission of 1904 similarly reflect the hope that British relations with Zoroastrians, as well as relations between Zoroastrians in Iran and India, would benefit the British. Plans for the mission were drawn up after Sykes and the British Resident in Bushehr both pointed out that a trade report from the previous year had concentrated on northern and western Iran.[153] Sykes was adamant that attention be paid to the south, arguing that in contrast to other regions where 'British trade and influence are waning', in Kerman and Iranian Baluchistan, British 'ascendancy' was 'at its zenith'.[154] The significance of trade was emphasized by the businessman who was to head the mission, Arthur H. Gleadowe-Newcomen, who stated that trade and politics were 'nearly one'.[155] When the decision was made to proceed with the plan, Sykes suggested that 'a Parsi might be attached with advantage, in view of the special efforts which I am making to unite the Kerman Parsis to their Bombay co-religionists'.[156] His intention to reinforce relations between Zoroastrian communities in India and Iran was clearly aligned with the aim of strengthening the position of the British in southern Iran.

Initially, two Parsis, D. M. Kapadia and R. P. Masani, were nominated to join the mission by the Bombay Chamber of Commerce and the Millowners' Association, which were helping to manage the project.[157] Sir Dinshaw Maneckji Petit (2nd Baronet), who was involved in the Amelioration Society, was keen for Masani to be included, as Masani had a scholarly as well as a commercial interest in Iran.[158] However, it was decided that because of the expense and the dangers they might face, the Parsis would not participate.[159] Disappointment was expressed by the *Parsi* on behalf of the community, and the journal presented its readers with an open question:

> If the reconquest of our lost country is possible by any means, it is only by the means of two weapons, trade and commerce. Will the Parsis gird their loins?[160]

Parsis were called to show their virility by taking part in the battle for their homeland, not with conventional arms but through the use of more familiar means, mercantile activity.

The *Parsi* linked its coverage of the Commercial Mission to the discussions taking place at the time about the proposed Parsi colony. These topics overlapped as one of the locations suggested for the colony was Sistan, an area of tactical importance to the British.[161] Contemporary lectures and articles referenced the danger of Russian advances in Sistan, as well as opportunities for agriculture and trade in the region.[162] The paper 'Seistan: Past and Present' was delivered in 1906 by Sir Arthur Henry McMahon, to an audience that included prominent Parsis such as Sir Bhownaggree, as well as British officials who had worked in India, for example, Sir George Birdwood and Sir Curzon Wyllie.[163] McMahon argued that 'Seistan might be made one of the richest grain-producing districts in the world', and, similar to Parsi descriptions of ancient Iran, he outlined how ancient ruins 'testified to a time when Seistan was far more populous, prosperous and civilised than now'.[164] Thus, the hopes held by some Parsis regarding the possibility of a Parsi territory in this area dovetailed neatly into British concerns over the weakness of frontier regions.

Accompanying the Commercial Mission was a correspondent for the *Indian Daily Telegraph* who spoke to 'a Parsi gentleman' about the plans for a Zoroastrian colony.[165] This unnamed Parsi was said to be connected to the Amelioration Society and the Persian Foreign Office, and was presumably Ardeshir Reporter, emissary of the

Amelioration Society.[166] In reference to the Quetta-Sistan trade route, he presented his community as reformers on a civilizing mission, stating that

> The Parsi people would realise that in themselves depended principally the regeneration of Iran. The long banished sons of Iran would return to their fatherland and would teach their countrymen how to live. As a preliminary they meant to ask the British Indian Government for a tract of territory somewhere in the neighbourhood of the Seistan Road, which they would colonize and erect into a semi-independent State. There they would develop themselves, spread their influence and do good on all sides.[167]

As well as suggesting an awareness of the colony plans amongst Zoroastrians based in Iran, this extract highlights the contemporary view of Parsis as a progressive community living in exile.

Members of the Commercial Mission approached merchants from the Iranian Zoroastrian community, as they were keen to gather information about the Russians and to ascertain how trade with India could be increased. Lists were made of influential merchants in the towns that were visited and in relation to their small population, the number of Zoroastrians was high; for example, out of the ten principal merchants listed in Bahramabad, the provincial capital of Rafsanjan, three were Zoroastrians.[168] One was Mulla Gudarz, a partner in the Jahanian firm, and the other two were agents of Arbab Jamshid, reflecting the prominence of these two merchant-houses. Mulla Gudarz was keen to promote trade with the British, and he sent samples of tea brought by the mission to other branches of the Jahanian firm.[169] Similarly, when they were in Bam, Sykes recorded that they were 'Visited by Ardeshir agent of Arbab Jamshid of Tehran and by the other Parsis. The former is a most intelligent man and gave the Mission valuable information'.[170] The Jamshidian firm predominantly traded in Russian goods at the time, but Gleadowe-Newcomen thought it would be straightforward to encourage Ardeshir to switch to British merchandise instead.[171] Zoroastrians were a useful source of intelligence, and the Zoroastrian Anjoman of Kerman offered the mission advice regarding commercial matters. The Anjoman made it known that Iranian merchants were keen to trade in 'woollens', and pointed out that Zoroastrians had started drinking tea, which was likely to become a profitable import commodity.[172]

Although relations between Zoroastrians in Iran and the British were not as strong as those between the Parsis and the British,[173] at the time of the mission, members of the Zoroastrian Anjoman of Kerman appear to have regarded the British in positive light.[174] This is likely to have been due to the high proportion of Anjoman members who were merchants and who would have seen advantages in developing their trade with India. Furthermore, there were strong links between the India-based Amelioration Society and the Anjoman, with Ardeshir Reporter acting as 'spokesman' for the Anjoman, which Gleadowe-Newcomen claimed 'might be called the Chamber of Commerce of Kerman'.[175] Gleadowe-Newcomen discussed various schemes with Reporter, as well as with the Kerman Anjoman, whose members helped the mission and 'instructed the Parsees at Yazd, a great Parsee centre, to give us [the mission] every information and assistance'.[176] The pro-British attitude of Ardeshir Reporter is apparent; he declined to meet with the Russian consul, Alexander Miller, and he emphasized to other Zoroastrians 'the mistake of having any dealings with him'.[177] In addition, the Kerman Anjoman suggested that the British government ought to lower the price of British merchandise in order to instigate a trade war with the Russians. Whilst this recommendation could potentially have helped the British, it can also be seen as an instance of Zoroastrians using the competition between the two powers to their own benefit.[178]

The possible wider strategic aims of the Commercial Mission were not overlooked by Indian newspapers that were critical of British imperialism. Indeed, the Native Press Report for 1904 described how the mission was seen as having 'secret political motives', with the *Oriental Review* regarding it as a 'feeler' for political ends.[179] In contrast, the hope was expressed in *Men and Women of India* that the expedition had achieved its purpose of proving to the Iranians that they had no need to be suspicious of the Government of India.[180] Similarly, the *Times of India* supported the mission and encouraged Parsi involvement in Iran, noting that there was potential for the volume of trade between Zoroastrians in Kerman and India to increase.[181] The 'marked' improvement in the 'prosperity and position' of the Zoroastrians of Iran in recent times was pointed out, in effect presenting Iranian Zoroastrians as good trading partners.[182]

Concern was expressed in the *Bombay Guardian* about the spread of Russian influence, especially as 'Russian bounty-fed trade threatened to stifle competition',[183] and there continued to be reports of Russian mercantile activities in southern Iran after the British mission returned to India. The new consul in Kerman, Lionel Haworth, described how the Russian consul had invited Zoroastrians to his home to show them samples of cloth patterns and tea, and he recorded that Zoroastrians in Kerman ordered chintz worth 20,000 tomans from a Russian merchant.[184] Following the British mission, the Russians became more vigorous in their efforts to increase their trade in the area and also established a Commercial Mission, led by Prince Anatouni.[185]

The prominence of trade in 'Great Game' machinations fuelled British interest in the small Zoroastrian community of Iran. Due to their strong relations with the Parsis, the British were keen to win the loyalty of Zoroastrians in Iran and to promote links between the two Zoroastrian communities. Although a number of Iranian Zoroastrians were naturalized British subjects and displayed a pro-British attitude, other members of the community were more than happy to establish commercial ties with Russian merchants. Relations between Russians and Zoroastrians in Iran were of concern to the British, and, in 1904, a British report noted that the Russian legation in Tehran had sent one hundred books and two maps to the Zoroastrian school in Kerman.[186] This brings to light another arena where Anglo-Russian rivalries were played out: education.

British foreign policy and Zoroastrian education in Iran

Supporting the education of Zoroastrians was suggested as a low-cost initiative that would bolster British influence in Iran. Sykes was a proponent of this idea and he argued that by collaborating with the Amelioration Society, which regarded education as one of its fundamental concerns, the British could ensure that Zoroastrians learn

English. In view of the strategic importance of southern Iran, Sykes aimed to foster loyalty to the British amongst Zoroastrians in Iran that would mirror the loyalty displayed by Parsis to the British Raj.

The action taken by Sykes was viewed positively by Iranian Zoroastrians in Bombay. In 1902, when Sykes stopped off at the city on his way to Iran, he was warmly welcomed by the 'Irani Parsees', who expressed their gratitude for his work in Iran and presented him with an address. The group referenced the efforts Sykes had made to improve trade and their belief that his endeavours would lead to 'highly beneficent results in the future'.[187] As consul in Kerman, Sykes was described as being 'in a position to do much good, and render valuable help in time of need'.[188] These individuals from the Iranian Zoroastrian community correlated the achievements of Parsis in India with their education and their good relations with the British. They hoped that Sykes would help improve opportunities for Iranian Zoroastrians and they requested that he relay a message to the shah via the British minister in Tehran. This included an appeal that Zoroastrians be included in a group of Iranian youths who were to be sent to Europe 'for western training'.[189]

Thanking the Zoroastrians for their address, Sykes emphasized that throughout the ten years he had spent in southern Iran he had taken the 'keenest interest' in the welfare of the Zoroastrian community. Not only did he respect the 'high ideals' and the 'antiquity' of their religion, but he also anticipated that Iranian Zoroastrians might be 'stimulated' to follow the example of the Parsis.[190] It is clear that the influential position of the Parsis in India shaped Sykes' attitude towards Iranian Zoroastrians, as he stated that, 'considering their numbers . . . no race has ever played such a large part on the stage of Asia, and it is on this fact that I base my hopes for the future'.[191] Sykes believed that education was crucial:

> We all know that bread rises by being leavened with yeast, and in the same way I trust that the Parsees of Persia may be raised both by education and also by intercourse with India.[192]

According to Sykes, Mozaffar al-Din Shah was keen to improve the situation of Zoroastrians, as were the British, and it now remained for Zoroastrians to fortify the mutually beneficial bond between 'both sections' of their community.[193]

Echoing Sykes, whose visit to Bombay appears to have reignited wider interest in the position of Zoroastrians in Iran, the *Times of India* stated the hope that Parsis would 'keep in touch with their brethren in Kerman'.[194] The impetus of 'racial pride' was used to encourage Parsis to assist in the 'distinctly patriotic work' of educating Iranian Zoroastrians.[195] Meanwhile, Sykes remained in 'constant correspondence' with Sir Dinshaw Petit and underlined to him that, 'apart from sentiment, it is to the advantage of the Parsees in Bombay to increase their trade relations and interests in Southern Persia'.[196] With their shared goals, the two men worked together on a plan to bring a number of Iranian Zoroastrian boys to Bombay for their education; this idea was subsequently supported by Gleadowe-Newcomen, head of the 1904 Commercial Mission.[197]

Members of the Zoroastrian Anjoman of Kerman were also eager for the plan to be enacted and Sykes argued that the Government of India ought to endorse the scheme, as it would strengthen Parsi links with Iran 'without any cost to Imperial funds'.[198] Sykes emphasized that

> Trade, too, will undoubtedly increase to the benefit of both countries, and, finally, we shall gradually forge the Parsees of Persia into a political weapon that will, I anticipate, help us to baffle Russian intrigues in South-East Persia.[199]

Thus, although there were potential advantages for Zoroastrians in Iran and in India, Sykes appears to have had British strategic concerns at the forefront of his mind.

Sykes also tried to encourage loyalty to the British amongst Zoroastrians in Iran through the annual award of a gold medal to a Zoroastrian pupil in Kerman who had made good progress in learning English.[200] The 1904 prize-giving at the Zoroastrian school in Kerman was reported with enthusiasm in India, with the *Parsi* noting that the large gathering was presided over by Sykes,

> whose sympathy for our co-religionists is well known, and who exerted himself to induce the Bombay Parsis to turn their kindly glances to their fatherland, and settle there under British protection as traders and merchants.[201]

Local dignitaries were invited to the event, including the governor of Kerman, 'Abd al-Hosayn Mirza Farmanfarma,[202] who was on good terms with Sykes.[203]

Kaykhosrow Shahrokh, the headmaster of the Zoroastrian school in Kerman, also facilitated relations between Zoroastrians and the governor, as he was the personal secretary of Farmanfarma and taught him English.[204] Shahrokh was born in Kerman in 1874; he experienced poverty as a child but, with the support of his wider family, he was able to access educational opportunities. After attending the American Presbyterian Missionary school in Tehran, Shahrokh went to Bombay where he studied at the Sir Jamsetjee Jejeebhoy School. He gained a place at the latter school due to the assistance of Sir Dinshaw Petit, who had married his great-aunt.[205] On his return to Kerman c. 1893, Shahrokh worked for the Amelioration Society as a teacher and was appointed as secretary of the Zoroastrian Anjoman of Kerman.[206] Shahrokh took a stand against the discrimination faced by members of the Zoroastrian community; for example, he rode on horseback and introduced uniforms for pupils at the Zoroastrian school.[207] In 1904, Sykes requested an additional medal for the annual prizegiving which was to be given to Shahrokh, apparently in recognition of the efforts he had made to warn Zoroastrians not to have any dealings with the Russians.[208] As well as receiving a gold medal of the King's Order, an Iranian official presented Shahrokh with the gold Order of the Lion and the Sun. This was the first time an Iranian Zoroastrian was honoured by both the British government and the shah of Iran.[209]

However, in contrast to the Parsis, who largely expressed loyalty to the British and were a minority living under colonial rule, members of the Zoroastrian community in Iran were able to use Anglo-Russian rivalry to their advantage. Just months after he was decorated by the British, Shahrokh abandoned his teaching position and started working for the Russians.[210] Shahrokh was believed to have been persuaded to do so by the new Russian consul in Kerman, Alexander Miller, who was trying to increase anti-British agitation.²¹¹ Miller had previously been the Russian vice-consul in the strategically significant region of Sistan, and in 1901 he had reported that Zoroastrians were warm towards him, as they were keen to participate in Russian trade.²¹² Records from 1902 reveal that Shahrokh was in contact with Miller, and that Shahrokh was consequently viewed with suspicion by Major Phillott, who was British consul in Kerman at the time. Despite being wary of Shahrokh, Phillott grudgingly acknowledged his position within the Zoroastrian community:

> on account of a certain knowledge of English has much influence with the Parsi Anjuman. He is sly, untrustworthy and cringing. . . . He studies Russian as well as English, and corresponds with the Russian Vice-Consul of Seistan and with a Russian 'doctor' formerly in Kerman.²¹³

Ardeshir Reporter surmised that Miller had appointed Shahrokh as the Russian agent in Odessa in order to prevent English being taught at the Zoroastrian school.²¹⁴ Reporter's disapproval of Shahrokh in this instance hints at personal differences between the two individuals which occasionally resurfaced in later years.²¹⁵

Secretive night-time gatherings at Miller's home were attended by Zoroastrians.²¹⁶ The consular summary for January 1905 gave the following interpretation:

> One of Mr. Miller's objects in Kerman is undoubtedly to create a Russian, or rather anti-British party among the Parsees of Southern and Eastern Persia, and, through them, among their co-religionists in India.²¹⁷

This highlights that the British were anxious about the possibility that Zoroastrians might become a vehicle for the spread of Russian influence within Iran, which could subsequently impact the reputation of the British in India.²¹⁸

Perhaps in order to reassure his superiors, Sykes presented the departure of Shahrokh as an opportunity for a more qualified English teacher from Bombay to be appointed in his place.²¹⁹ Sykes claimed this would be beneficial to the education of the Zoroastrians in the long-run, and requested that the Government of India send a 'first rate' teacher, as a Parsi 'gifted with tact' would, 'in a few months time, absolutely sway the entire community' towards the British.²²⁰ He explained that this was 'by far the best method of influencing the Parsis [meaning Zoroastrians in Iran] at small cost', and he argued that the Government of India should contribute to the salary of the teacher, as he believed that one 'could not possibly expend such a sum to better advantage'.²²¹ In the same correspondence, Sykes stated that he had also raised his concerns to Petit regarding clandestine meetings that had taken place between Shahrokh and Miller.²²²

Shahrokh was later a leading figure in the community and was elected as the Zoroastrian representative in the Majles, the Iranian Parliament, for many years. However, when he left for Odessa, he does not seem to have had been held in such high regard by all of the Zoroastrian community in Kerman, and accusations were made that he had taken with him the seal and accounts of the Zoroastrian Anjoman of Kerman.²²³ Only a couple of months later, Reporter told Sykes that 'the runaway schoolmaster was bitterly repenting of his act, as his post at Odessa has proved to be so badly paid that he cannot make ends meet'.[224] Shahrokh gave up the post and wrote to Sykes to say that he would give 'full details as to Russian plans of action for defeating British supremacy in commerce'.[225] A different account was given by Shahrokh in his memoirs, where he stated that he left Odessa due to the unrest in the city.[226]

The incident of Miller and Shahrokh reveals the perceived importance of the Zoroastrians to both the Russians and the British. It also clarifies that British support for the education of Zoroastrians in Iran was linked to the encouragement of Zoroastrian trade with India, and that both were viewed as effective ways of strengthening British influence. In a bid to gain support for the plans he had drawn up with Sykes, Petit emphasized to the Government of India that the 'main object' of his scheme, which would involve assistance being given to Iranian Zoroastrians educated in India when they returned to Iran, was 'to raise in Persia a class of educated and trained Persian Zoroastrians who would be the medium of increasing British prestige and influence in that quarter'.[227] The Persian consul-general in India also saw potential in the community, and wanted to organize a meeting with the Iranian Zoroastrians of Bombay to see what action could be taken to 'promote the education of their children'.[228] He suggested that wealthy Iranian Zoroastrian merchants and other individuals in Bombay donate a voluntary monthly sum to pay for promising young Zoroastrian men to study in Europe.[229] It is clear that the success of the Parsis in India led both British officials as well as some Iranians to view Zoroastrians in Iran in positive light. The education of Iranian Zoroastrians was one of the fundamental aims of the Amelioration Society from its establishment in the mid-nineteenth century; by the early twentieth century, this mission was also supported by some members of the Iranian political elite, as well as by Sykes and others who were keen to secure British influence in southern Iran.[230]

Sykes' lecture: A call to action

In May 1906, Sykes delivered a lecture on the 'Parsis of Persia' to the Indian Section of the Society of Arts in London.[231] Beginning with an historical overview, as 'Antiquity appeals strongly to mankind', Sykes then discussed contemporary Zoroastrians, 'a virile remnant of adherents to this venerable faith . . . now setting its footsteps on the stony tracks of progress'.[232] The education of Iranian Zoroastrians was stressed to be of paramount importance. Whilst congratulating the Amelioration Society on its achievements, Sykes pointed out that only £40 was allotted to the school in Kerman per year, and he hinted that an insufficient wage had precipitated Shahrokh's recent departure. Sykes referred to the attempt he had made in 1902 to enlist Parsi support for the plans he had drawn up with Sir Dinshaw Petit, and he concluded his lecture with a renewed appeal, proposing that all that was required were 'the crumbs from some rich Parsi's table'.[233]

Sykes argued that wealthy Parsis had become physically 'less vigorous' due to the 'enervating climate' in India, whereas Iranian Zoroastrians were 'finer in physique' but in contrast to the Parsis, were 'backward in all that makes for progress'.[234] Playing on the anxieties of the Parsis, he suggested that if links with Zoroastrians in southern Iran were strengthened through trade, greater numbers of Parsis would travel there, enabling them to benefit from 'the glorious climate of Irán'. In turn, this would 'revitalise' their whole community, which he stated was 'threatened with extinction'.[235] Sykes emphasized the significance of relations between Zoroastrians in India and Iran, going so far as to proclaim:

> I foresee that the destiny of the Zoroastrians is bound to their ancient home of Irán with links of steel, and that the Parsi who assists to fulfil that destiny will outshine in lustre that of all the merchant princes of Bombay.[236]

At a time when some Parsis questioned their prospects in India, this may have sounded enticing.

Both the lecture and the discussion that followed it were published, providing an insight into some British views of Zoroastrians. George Birdwood linked Parsi success to the virtues they shared with ancient Persians, and Colonel C. E. Yate, who had worked in Indian Baluchistan, applauded the Parsis for their work ethic and enterprise. Yate expressed his disappointment that the Parsi colony scheme had not yet come to fruition, asserting that he would have 'gladly assigned land' if the Parsis had pushed forward with the plan.[237] Chairing the event was Curzon, who praised Iranian Zoroastrians for preserving 'with extraordinary success, the purity not only of their religion but of their race'.[238] Curzon agreed with Sykes, that the British were to some extent responsible for the welfare of Zoroastrians in Iran; not only were 'many' now British subjects but they were also connected 'by blood' to the Parsis.[239] Although Curzon had not used Government of India funds to support Zoroastrians in Iran when he was viceroy (1898–1905), he had agreed to back the proposal made by Petit and Sykes for some Iranian Zoroastrians to be educated in India.[240]

Similar to Sykes, Curzon believed that the two Zoroastrian communities belonged to the same race, and he argued that this ought to encourage Parsi benevolence:

> In the spirit prevailing now-a-days, when race feeling was so strong that people were always looking up and enquiring about those who had the same origin as themselves, in all parts of the world, when one saw the wealthy Jewish community in England, presenting certain features of resemblance to the Parsi community in Bombay, exerting themselves by organisation and co-operation and by large gifts of money, to improve the condition of their miserable Jewish brethren in Jerusalem and other distant parts of the world, were the Parsis of Bombay to lag behind? They would only be conforming to the spirit of the age, and would be satisfying the dictates of their own naturally noble nature if they listened to the appeal.[241]

There were a number of Parsis attending the talk, including the politician Sir Mancherjee Bhownaggree. For a community that was proud to be famed for philanthropic acts, the statement made by Sykes which was reiterated by Curzon, that the Parsis could do more to help their co-religionists, was a painful sting. In defence, Bhownaggree stressed that Parsis would gladly offer money to help their 'compatriots in their ancient fatherland'.[242]

Not only did the lecture spark a reaction amongst Parsis in London, but it was also reported in India, where it stoked the interest of Parsis in their co-religionists, and encouraged charitable donations, including £500 from the philanthropist Ratan Tata.[243] Cartoons in the *Hindi Punch* illustrated a plea for help from Iranian Zoroastrians and a call for Parsis in Bombay to act with 'sympathy', particularly as a stronger connection with southern Iran was seen to be to their 'obvious advantage'.[244] The point was also made that although it was laudable that a proportion of Parsi charity was not sectarian, recognizing 'no class, creed or soil',

> The Parsi prosperous has of late, it seems, not cast his eyes Iranwards and not measured properly the condition of his fellow-religionists there. . . . *Hindi Punch* will be glad to hear soon that the opulent Parsi too now knows and will act and strive to improve the lot of his few countrymen languishing in the land of their birth.[245]

The response to Sykes' talk reveals that the Parsis did not like to be criticized by the British, particularly regarding their charitable reputation. Writing to the secretary of the Government of India a couple of months later, Sykes noted that the 'strong support' he had received from Curzon had increased the impact of his talk, and Sykes stated his hope that the funds collected could be used to implement new plans that he had drawn up with Sir Dinshaw Petit.[246]

Donations were gathered by the Amelioration Society, which had launched an appeal directed at Zoroastrians in India and China.[247] The fund was opened in July 1906 and in a related report, reference was made to the 'stirring' lecture given by Sykes, which had already resulted in over 21,000 rupees being subscribed by the 'Irani Parsee residents of Bombay'.[248] In a meeting he convened, Sir Jamsetjee Jejeebhoy explicitly stated that the interest shown by Sykes and Curzon in the Zoroastrians in Iran was of 'vital importance to the future generations of Parsees not only of Persia but of India', and he encouraged his community to 'uphold the traditions of generosity' for which they were known.[249] The Parsi scholar K. R. Cama spoke at length about the importance of education, including for girls, and argued that

> Persia afforded a great field for the development of trade and commerce, and if the Persian Parsees were educated they would by their industry, enterprise and honesty soon become wealthy and if they were made fit by education, they might in the near future obtain not only freedom but political rights.[250]

At the time that Cama was made these comments, the events that would come to be known as the Constitutional Revolution were unfolding in Iran. Although it seems that the revolution eclipsed the proposed education scheme, greater political rights for Zoroastrians in Iran that Cama had envisaged were just months away from realization.

4

Arbab Jamshid and the Revolution

A new era

The Iranian Constitutional Revolution

By 1906, widespread discontent had prompted individuals from various groups in Iranian society to come together, forming a movement that would ultimately call for the establishment of a constitution and an end to arbitrary rule.[1] The initial phase of what came to be known as the Constitutional Revolution resulted in the creation of a National Consultative Assembly (*Majles-e Shura-ye Melli*), the Majles. There was only one non-Muslim deputy in the First Majles, the Zoroastrian merchant Arbab Jamshid Jamshidian. In the years preceding the revolution, the socio-economic position of Iranian Zoroastrians had improved, partly due to their relations with the Parsis and the British. Although these links continued to be important, the revolution brought about a substantial development for the Zoroastrian community in Iran, the inclusion of Zoroastrians in the Iranian nation at a political level.

Demands for constitutional rule should be seen in the context of earlier attempts at reform. In addition to efforts that were made to modernize the military following the Russo-Persian Wars of the early nineteenth century, some ministers had tried to reorganize the administration of the state. Prominent in this regard were two individuals; Mirza Taqi Khan Farahani, who was Amir Kabir, chief minister, from 1848 to 1851, and Mirza Hosayn Khan, who was chief minister and commander in chief, Sepahsalar, from 1871 to 1873. Mirza Hosayn Khan had worked as an ambassador in Constantinople (1859–71), where he had witnessed the Ottoman Tanzimat reforms; this experience informed his plans to strengthen central government control in Iran.[2] However, the shah had the power to dismiss ministers such as Amir Kabir and Sepahsalar at will, and consequently many of their strategies to modernize the state only had a short-term impact. According to Mangol Bayat, the military academy Dar al-Fonun was an exception; this had been established by Amir Kabir in 1851 and it provided young men with a European-style education, often in preparation for diplomatic and political careers.[3]

One of the tutors at Dar al-Fonun was Mirza Malkam Khan (1834–1908). The legal terms that he introduced to a Persian-speaking audience in his writings, including 'constitution', were prevalent during the revolution.[4] Malkam Khan was born into an

Armenian Christian family, but later professed his belief in Islam.[5] He spent some time in Paris where he was initiated into a Masonic lodge,[6] and, in 1859, he founded a Masonic-style society in Iran, the *Faramushkhaneh*, 'House of Oblivion'. Due to concerns that Malkam Khan was encouraging republicanism amongst its members, Naser al-Din Shah removed him from his teaching position at Dar al-Fonun in 1861. Malkam Khan was exiled to Baghdad and he then moved to Constantinople, where Mirza Hosayn Khan helped him re-enter political life.[7] Despite his earlier suspicions, the shah appointed Malkam Khan as the Persian minister in London, a position he held from 1872 until his dismissal in 1889, following a scandal over a planned lottery concession.[8] Malkam Khan remained in London and established *Qanun* (*Law*), one of a handful of Persian-language newspapers published abroad during this period.[9] *Qanun* was also secretly distributed in Iran.[10]

In the pages of *Qanun*, Malkam Khan proposed that legislative reform ought to be carried out by a national consultative assembly.[11] Malkam Khan was keen to stress that these laws would be compatible with Islamic law, and he outlined the need for collaboration with the ulama. A comparable approach was also favoured by Mirza Yusef Khan Mostashar al-Dowleh, a reformist minister who associated with Malkam Khan and Mirza Hosayn Khan.[12] Both Malkam Khan and Mostashar al-Dowleh admired European ideas and institutions, but opposed foreign interference in Iran.[13] Similar concerns were held by other Iranian intellectuals, including the activist Sayyed Jamal al-Din Asadabadi, often known as 'al-Afghani' (1838/39–97), who was an ardent critic of British imperialism. Jamal al-Din Asadabadi travelled widely and lived in several countries, including India, Egypt and England.[14] During his stay in London in 1891–2, Jamal al-Din Asadabadi contributed to *Qanun*, and both he and Malkam Khan expressed their discontent with the Iranian state, particularly in relation to the events surrounding the Tobacco Revolt, which was unfolding in Iran at the time.[15]

The Tobacco Revolt was a reaction to a monopoly granted by the shah and his government to a British subject, Major Gerald F. Talbot, which gave Talbot control over the entire Iranian tobacco industry for fifty years.[16] Concerned by the negative impact this would have on their economic interests, Iranian merchants opposed the concession and gained the support of members of the ulama, some of whom were similarly anxious about the financial implications of the concession.[17] Petitions were drawn up, people demonstrated, and, from December 1891, a boycott on tobacco was observed across much of Iran. The boycott began after a ruling prohibiting the use of tobacco, which was likely to have been forged, was purportedly issued by Mirza Hasan Shirazi, a leading Shi'i cleric.[18]

Yielding to pressure, the shah cancelled the concession in January 1892. According to Homa Katouzian, the public protests that had pushed the arbitrary state into changing its position on this issue can be seen as the first 'political act' in Iran.[19] Similarly, the impact of 'public opinion' led Ann Lambton to describe the Tobacco Revolt as a 'prelude' to the Constitutional Revolution, when merchants and clerics united again to elicit change.[20] Although members of the ulama had initially been reluctant to become involved in the Tobacco Revolt, Fatema Soudavar Farmanfarmaian has observed that they were 'unexpectedly empowered by a newfound awareness of their ability to influence events'.[21] Both Malkam Khan and Jamal al-Din Asadabadi hoped that the clerical force could be harnessed to bring about reform.[22]

Non-Muslims also observed the boycott,[23] but the religious importance of maintaining the purity of fire meant that Zoroastrians did not usually smoke, so the order not to use tobacco may not have had such an impact the community.[24] Additionally, Janet Amighi has argued that most Zoroastrians did not actively participate in the revolt, perhaps because they viewed a neutral stance as being safer.[25] However, there were exceptions, and Michael Fischer has highlighted that Gudarz Mehrban 'refused' to follow orders to give his caravanserai in Yazd to Talbot's company.[26] Despite Mehrban's solidarity with the protesters, Zoroastrians in Yazd suffered in the aftermath of the revolt. There was a decrease in central government control and Zoroastrians were the target of attacks, a factor that resulted in about five hundred members of the community deciding to emigrate to India.[27]

Financial repercussions linked to the cancellation of the concession had a negative impact on the Iranian economy, which was concurrently affected by other issues such as the global fall in the price of silver. These problems continued into the reign of Mozaffar al-Din Shah, who succeeded his father in 1896.[28] Attempts were made by the grand vizier, Mirza 'Ali Khan Amin al-Dowleh, to organize state finances, and, in 1898, a group of Belgian officials led by Joseph Naus was tasked with reforming customs duties.[29] State revenue increased but the changes were not favourable for Iranian merchants. By the turn of the century demonstrations were taking place in cities across Iran.[30] Angered by the humiliating terms of foreign loans that the shah used to fund his trips to Europe, as well as by European involvement in Iranian affairs, merchants formed alliances and called for greater economic control; non-Muslims also participated, amongst them Zoroastrians from the Jahanian and Jamshidian firms.[31] Keen to limit the power of the shah and his government regarding economic affairs, merchants were to play a central role in the protests that developed into the constitutionalist movement. Thus, the emergence of wealthy Zoroastrian merchants during the nineteenth century was a key factor leading to Zoroastrian support for the movement that developed into the Constitutional Revolution.

However, negative attitudes towards non-Muslims that were encouraged by some members of the ulama lead one to question why Zoroastrians would join a movement in which Shi'i clerics played a prominent role. Individuals from the religious classes protested against the state for a variety of reasons. Similar to merchants, some were motivated by the economic situation and by concerns over increased foreign interference in Iranian affairs. Additionally, there were clerics who hoped that their own power would increase through the introduction of new legislation which they presumed would be based on Islamic law.[32]

Greater power in the hands of conservative clerics would not have been beneficial to members of non-Muslim communities in Iran. However, Janet Afary has highlighted that one must be wary of treating the religious class as a homogenous block:

many of the leaders of the revolution who seemed to be conventional clerics, called *mujtahids, sayyids, 'ulama,* and *shaikhs,* were in fact Azali Babis, pan-Islamists, Freemasons, and freethinkers.[33]

The practice of using Islamic terminology to disguise radical ideas, seen in the work of Malkam Khan, was an approach that was also taken in the early twentieth century by the preachers Malek al-Motakallemin (1861–1908) and Sayyed Jamal al-Din Va'ez Esfahani (1862–1908). This gave the preachers a degree of protection from other members of the ulama who held more conservative views, and was also an effective way of attracting supporters.[34] Malek al-Motakallemin was one of a number of constitutionalists who were said to have been Babis.[35] This may be relevant in regard to Zoroastrian involvement in the revolution, as some Zoroastrians had converted to the Bahá'í faith and others were sympathetic towards Babis and Bahá'ís. However, D. M. MacEoin has argued that the controversial opinions of individuals such as Malek al-Motakallemin regarding the rights of non-Muslims may have been due to their secular outlook, rather than any possible affiliation with Babism.[36] Positive views of the pre-Islamic period were expressed by Malek al-Motakallemin, and it is noteworthy that he had good relations with Zoroastrians prior to the revolution.

Malek al-Motakallemin had spent a couple of years in Bombay during the 1880s. Not only did he meet Zoroastrians in the city but the financial support he received from Parsi merchants enabled him to publish his polemical essay, *Min al Khalq ila al-Haqq*.[37] In this text, Malek al-Motakallemin glorified the pre-Islamic period and he also expressed a critical view of contemporary social conditions in Iran.[38] According to Mehdi Malekzadeh, the encounters his father had with Parsis in India led Malek al-Motakallemin to advocate for greater rights for Iranian Zoroastrians, and to propose that Parsis, 'the pure children of Iran', ought to be invited to 'return' to help with the 'advancement' of Iran.[39] Malek al-Motakallemin also used his position as a preacher to spread his views.[40] This was significant because in the period before the Constitutional Revolution, sermons were the most effective method of mass communication in Iran.[41] Recognizing their impact, Zoroastrians funded preachers who spoke in favour of religious equality.[42]

In the first few years of the twentieth century, reform-minded individuals, including Malek al-Motakallemin, gathered together in semi-secret societies, such as the Tehran-based Revolutionary Committee, formed in 1904, and the Secret Society, founded in February 1905.[43] Although both groups stressed the compatibility of their demands with Islam, neither limited their membership to Muslims.[44] According to Mangol Bayat these societies were influenced by European Masonic lodges, and Bayat argues that this is reflected in their views regarding the secularization of education and the judiciary, and the calls they made for equality for people from different religious communities.[45] Those who joined the Revolutionary Committee reportedly included members of the ulama, merchants, guildsmen, Azali Babis and two Zoroastrians.[46] The preachers Malek al-Motakallemin and Sayyed Jamal al-Din Va'ez and the journalist Mirza Jahangir Khan were amongst those involved who are said to have been influenced by Babism, and the two Zoroastrians listed were Arbab Guiv and Ardeshir Reporter, the emissary of the Amelioration Society.[47] Alongside the emphasis that was placed on education, both the Revolutionary Committee and Secret Society held the establishment of a rule of law to be a key goal.[48] One method used by members of the societies to spread their ideas was the distribution of leaflets known as *shabnameh*s, which had a significant impact in Tehran.[49]

Awareness of pro-reform and anti-imperialistic movements abroad, for example in India and in the Ottoman Empire, intensified the belief that the introduction of a legal code would benefit Iran.[50] Also of significance was the outcome of the 1904–5 Russo-Japanese War: the victory of Japan, a country that had recently established constitutional rule, over autocratic Imperial Russia. The Russian Revolution of 1905 and the convening of the first Duma, an elected assembly, gave weight to the opinion that popular political struggle could effectively bring about change.[51] Additionally, there was an influx of revolutionary ideas from Russia, particularly via Iranians who were seasonal workers in Transcaucasia.[52]

Both the Russo-Japanese War and the Russian Revolution had a detrimental effect on trade between Russia and Iran, leading to drastic increases in the price of wheat, sugar and other goods.[53] In reaction to this situation, Tehran merchants went on strike in March 1905. Protesters were further enraged when the high-ranking cleric, *mojtahed*, Sayyed 'Abdollah Behbahani shared an image of Joseph Naus dressed up as a member of the ulama; this led to calls for Naus's dismissal.[54] The strike concluded after the crown prince guaranteed that Naus would be fired when the shah returned from his trip to Europe.[55] However, Naus retained his position and the Tehran bazaar went on strike again in December, after the governor of Tehran gave orders that two sugar merchants be beaten for refusing to lower their prices.[56] Demands were made for the governor to be removed, and, by this stage, another prominent cleric had joined the movement, the pro-reform *mojtahed*, Sayyed Mohammad Tabataba'i.[57] Backed by a varied group of donors, about 2,000 people took sanctuary at the shrine of Shah 'Abd al-'Azim, just south of Tehran.[58] Sykes wrote to the Government of India predicting that 'the end of Persia is approaching', and he advised that troops be prepared to occupy Iranian Baluchistan and Sistan.[59] However, by January 1906, the *bast* and the strikes ended, as the shah agreed to dismiss both the governor and Naus, and also promised that a vaguely defined 'house of justice' would be established.[60]

Months passed with little progress being made, so the campaigning continued and support was garnered from influential individuals, including wealthy Zoroastrians.[61] Following the death of a theology student during a protest in July 1906, tension rose again in the capital. Led by Behbahani and Tabataba'i, members of the ulama and other protesters sought sanctuary at a mosque in Tehran, before travelling south to the city of Qom. The popular *mojtahed* and rival to Behbahani, Shaikh Fazlallah Nuri, joined the movement, adding to its legitimacy.[62] Prompted by Behbehani, merchants also went on strike at this time, and they organized a *bast* in the British legation.[63] By early August, there were about 14,000 people camping in the legation grounds.[64] Both commercial and religious affairs in Tehran were thus severely disrupted.

Financial backing from merchants, including Arbab Jamshid, enabled the *bast* in the legation to continue for weeks.[65] Arbab Jamshid was not the only Zoroastrian who supported the *bast*; in particular, Malekzadeh described how 'Ardeshirji' (Ardeshir Reporter), a 'freedom-seeking Zoroastrian', helped facilitate the *bast* by using his position as a British national to mediate between the merchants and British officials.[66] In his account, Malekzadeh stated that Reporter had explained that he believed constitutional rule would help liberate Zoroastrians in Iran.[67] Alongside his work for the Amelioration Society, Reporter was a tutor at the School of Political Science.

According to Farhang Mehr, Reporter had outlined the benefits of democracy to his students, some of whom participated in the constitutional movement.[68] Indeed, Bayat has argued that members of secret societies encouraged students from both Dar al-Fonun and the School of Political Sciences to participate in, and popularize, protests.[69] In view of his teaching position, and his involvement in secret societies, it seems likely that Reporter was amongst them.

The establishment of constitutional rule had not been one of the initial aims of the merchants.[70] Significantly, it was during the *bast* that members of the secret societies discussed constitutionalism with those camping in the legation grounds.[71] Consequently, appeals for the promised 'house of justice' were superseded by calls for a 'national consultative assembly'.[72] Mangol Bayat has argued that a reason why protesters in the legation insisted on the use of the word 'national', rather than 'Islamic', was to enable recognized non-Muslim communities to be represented in the assembly.[73] On 9 August 1906, the shah agreed to the demands that had been made, bringing the *bast* to an end.[74]

Arbab Jamshid and the First Majles

Following the swift ratification and implementation of electoral laws, the First Majles convened in October 1906, and the elected deputies promptly started to draft a constitution.[75] This document was signed by Mozaffar al-Din Shah on 30 December 1906, just days before his death on 6 January 1907. The Majles was stated to have authority over legislative, diplomatic and financial affairs, and thus reflected the aims of merchants who had been keen to increase their control over economic matters. Influenced by the Belgian constitution, details were set out regarding the role of the senate, but this body was not actually formed until many years later.[76] Elections for the Majles were to take place bi-annually and although women were actively involved in the constitutionalist movement, the right to vote was only granted to men who fulfilled the conditions set out in the electoral laws.[77]

Of the 156 deputies in the First Majles, Arbab Jamshid was the only non-Muslim. He was also one of just sixteen men specifically described as 'Reformers' in a British Foreign Office document from December 1906.[78] However, as a wealthy merchant living in Tehran, Arbab Jamshid was in some respects similar to many other deputies. Only about 3 per cent of the total population of Iran lived in the capital, yet the city was over-represented in the First Majles and was allocated sixty seats.[79] Additionally, a significant proportion of the deputies in the Majles were involved in trade. Whilst Arbab Jamshid may have had similar hopes for the economy as other merchants, it is striking that out of the recognized non-Muslim communities, only the Zoroastrians had a deputy in the First Majles.

Initially it had been agreed that recognized non-Muslim communities would be represented in the Majles, and a group of prominent individuals from these communities had even greeted leading members of the ulama as they returned from Qom in August 1906, thanking them for bringing about increased unity between different religious groups.[80] However, just a few months later, under the threat of persecution, the Jewish and Christian communities were pressurized into accepting the *mojtahed*s Behbahani and Tabataba'i to act on their behalf.[81] The justification given by Tabataba'i for this change was that the presence of non-Muslims in the Majles would anger the ulama in both Isfahan and the 'Atabat, the Shi'i shrine cities in Iraq, and would weaken the constitutional movement.[82] In contrast, Kaykhosrow Shahrokh, who represented Zoroastrians in the Majles from 1909 to 1940, described how Zoroastrians successfully negotiated with members of the ulama to guarantee Arbab Jamshid's seat in the First Majles.[83] Other accounts explicitly describe how in order to secure his place as a deputy, Arbab Jamshid paid a large sum of money to Behbahani, who then publicly praised Zoroastrians during the election period, describing them as '"honorable," "reasonable," well-educated children of Iran'.[84] Interestingly, statements made in the Majles give the impression that rather than being a representative for Zoroastrians, Arbab Jamshid's election was linked to his status as a leading merchant,[85] although this does not appear to be how the Zoroastrian community viewed his position in the assembly.

Support for the inclusion of Arbab Jamshid in the Majles was expressed by the wider Zoroastrian community. Shahrokh recalled how in order to keep the 'momentum' going, 'some thirty or forty Zoroastrians signed a declaration' outlining that Arbab Jamshid was to represent them, with others sending telegrams from Yazd and Kerman to the same effect.[86] Reflecting their enthusiasm for the reforms that were taking place on a national scale, members of the recently re-established Tehran Zoroastrian Anjoman (TZA), mirrored the actions of the Majles representatives and drafted their own constitution.[87]

Zoroastrian *anjoman*s were not a new phenomenon, having initially been set up during the nineteenth century by the Amelioration Society. However, the revival of the TZA at this time can be seen in the context of the revolution, when many *anjoman*s were established. In addition to official *anjoman*s founded across Iran to support the running of the Majles elections, popular *anjoman*s also proliferated. Some, like the TZA, were linked to specific groups, whereas others had broader memberships. In Azerbaijan and Gilan, radical social democratic ideas from Transcaucasia had taken root, and the involvement of non-Muslims in provincial councils was encouraged.[88] Shahrokh associated the restoration of the TZA with this surge in the formation of *anjoman*s during the early months of the revolution, when 'words such as "equality" and "brotherhood" filled people's minds'.[89] Alongside Shahrokh, other founding members of the TZA included Ardeshir Reporter, emissary of the Amelioration Society, as well as Arbab Khosrow Shahjahan, one of the brothers who directed the Jahanian merchant house, who also backed the constitutionalist cause.[90]

The financial assistance that wealthy Zoroastrian merchants were able to provide made Zoroastrian representation in the Majles more likely. However, it was also significant that in contrast to members of the Christian and Jewish communities, Zoroastrians were sometimes viewed as having a greater right to inclusion in the 'National' Assembly due to the prominence of Zoroastrianism in the pre-Islamic period, and the idea that Zoroastrianism was an inherently Iranian religion.[91] For instance, the *Habl al-Matin* newspaper printed a list of Majles deputies and described Arbab Jamshid as the 'deputy of the noble Persian community of Zoroastrians'.[92] Whilst it is true that both the language used by constitutionalists and the central role played by members of the ulama underline the importance of Islam to the revolutionary movement,[93] the wording in the *Habl al-Matin* hints at positive perceptions of the pre-Islamic past. The *Revue du Monde Musulman* regarded the inclusion of a Zoroastrian in the Majles as a reflection of substantial changes in attitudes towards the community, commenting that 'the age-old antagonism between Muslims and Zoroastrians seems to have ended today'.[94] Similarly, in a later edition of the journal, Delphine Menant referred to the election of Arbab Jamshid as a 'real event' that had brought the Zoroastrian community out of the shadows.[95]

Greater freedom of the press resulted in a dramatic increase in the number of newspapers printed in Iran,[96] and references to Zoroastrians in these publications would have raised awareness of the community, particularly amongst educated members of the public in cities such as Tehran.[97] Various publications also displayed an interest in the Parsis; for example, the newly established constitutionalist newspaper, *Neda-ye Vatan*, reprinted articles from the *Parsi*, a Parsi journal that favoured stronger ties with Iran.[98] Likewise, in October 1906, *Tarbiyat* highlighted the Iranian ancestry of the Parsis, and included an article from the *Parsi* which described how political developments in Iran were greeted 'with joy' and 'confidence' in India.[99] The reputation of the Parsis, who were regarded as a wealthy community with political influence, may have affected views towards Iranian Zoroastrians. Indeed, in relation to Zoroastrian representation in the Majles, Behbahani is quoted by Mehr as having said that

> Zoroastrians have an inherent right to the air, land and water of Iran. They are prudent and patriotic. Their co-religionists abroad are highly educated and have a seat in the British Parliament. Zoroastrians of Iran should be allowed to have a representative in the Majles.[100]

In another issue of *Tarbiyat*, positive contributions made by Iranian Zoroastrians were emphasized, and it was stated that the patriotism and benevolence of Arbab Jamshid created a connection between Iranians and Parsis, 'ancient fellow citizens', who ought to be invited to settle in Iran to help with projects that Iranians would not be able to undertake alone.[101] Ardeshir Reporter was later named in *Tarbiyat* as a Parsi already living in Iran, whose knowledge and experiences could be drawn upon,[102] and in *Habl al-Matin* the suggestion was made that Parsis, who were said to be Persians, would be able to help invigorate the Iranian economy.[103]

Parsis expressed their support for the constitution and although Mozaffar al-Din Shah had been pressurized into agreeing to the new laws, he was personally praised by Parsis for Arbab Jamshid's inclusion in the Majles. The revolution had not aimed to overthrow the shah, and he was still regarded as being influential in terms of the overall security of the Zoroastrian community. Sir Mancherjee Bhownaggree had contacted the shah to stress the importance of Zoroastrian representation in parliament,[104] and, immediately after receiving news of the election of Arbab Jamshid, Parsis in England sent a telegram to the shah, followed by a letter of thanks.[105] A 'Special General Meeting' of the Zoroastrian Funds of Europe (ZFE) was held on 15 October 1906. At this gathering, a resolution to write to the shah was proposed by Dadabhai Naoroji, seconded by Bhownaggree, and 'unanimously passed' by the attendees.[106] The letter was sent via the Persian chargé d'affaires in London, Mirza Mohammad 'Ali Khan, who sent a reply on 8 December 1906 within which he claimed that

> it will be gratifying to His Imperial Majesty to see that his endeavours to further the well-being of his Zoroastrian subjects, whose welfare He has so much at heart, are appreciated by their co-religionists in this country.[107]

The letter from the ZFE referred to the Parsi deputations that both the current shah and his predecessor had received in earlier years.[108] This gives the impression that Zoroastrian representation in the Majles was regarded by Parsis as a major stage in Iran's modernization, comparable to the abolition of the *jezya* in 1882. The enthusiastic response from London was noted in India, where the news regarding Arbab Jamshid had also generated excitement in the Zoroastrian community.[109]

Indeed, articles marking the Parsi New Year in September 1907 viewed the election of Arbab Jamshid as exemplifying the progress made by Zoroastrians in the past twelve months.[110] However, criticisms were raised in the *Rast Goftar* over the initial delay in thanks being sent to the shah from Zoroastrians in India, in contrast to the prompt action taken in London. The *Rast Goftar* emphasized that Parsis had a responsibility to use their influence to support their co-religionists:

> The significance of such a message would not be lost upon the Shah, and it will be an incentive to him and to his ministers to take greater interest in future for the communal welfare of the small but faithful band of their Zoroastrian subjects.[111]

Although the inclusion of Arbab Jamshid in the Majles was believed to be an important step towards greater equality, Parsis recognized that Zoroastrians in Iran still faced challenges. Iran was viewed as being 'on the dawn of a great political movement',[112] an opportune moment for Parsis to act to help reinforce the changes that were taking place.

Parsi enterprise and Iran

Not only were events in Iran regarded by Parsis as being beneficial for their co-religionists, but the developments were also seen as positive for their own community, particularly in relation to trade. Having visited Iran just months before the revolution, Naoroz Parveez, a Parsi rail contractor and businessman, was filled with optimism following the news of the election of Arbab Jamshid. This outlook was reflected in his lecture, 'Indo-British Trade with Persia', which he delivered on 6 November 1906 at a gathering organized by the East India Association.[113] The talk was presided over by Sir Lepel Griffin, who had worked in India and Afghanistan, and others present included Sir George Birdwood and Mohandas Gandhi. An article about the event was published by the *Parsi* in Bombay, which was then translated into Persian and reprinted in *Neda-ye Vatan*,[114] revealing that although it took place in London, the lecture had piqued the interest of Zoroastrians in India, and of constitutionalists in Iran.

Echoing views that had been expressed on earlier occasions, for instance by Sykes, Parveez reiterated that the British ought to do more to capitalize on their relations with Zoroastrians. He stated that

> there is one circumstance which I have for years past regarded as most favourable to British interests. I refer to the presence in Persia of a hardy remnant of the enlightened race and faith which held sway there for so many centuries until the Sassanian dynasty was swept away by the sword of Islam.[115]

Reflecting contemporary discussions concerning Zoroastrianism and pre-Islamic Iran, Parveez highlighted the imperial history of the Zoroastrian community and made reference to their supposed superior religion and race. Parveez argued that it was under British rule that the Parsis had made 'such progress in enlightenment and wealth'. He also believed that the British had been instrumental in improving conditions for Zoroastrians in Iran, and hinted that with further support, Iranian Zoroastrians might emulate the successes of their co-religionists in India.[116] Hoping to galvanize his audience into action, Parveez claimed that the Russians had recognized the 'sterling characteristics' of Iranian Zoroastrians, and were planning to induce them to colonize areas in northern Iran.[117]

To counter Russian influence, Parveez advocated the establishment of the proposed Zoroastrian colony in Sistan, arguing that it would regenerate the region and enhance trade. This would be to the benefit of the British, the Zoroastrians and the Iranian nation.[118] However, whilst Birdwood was pleased that Parsis were beginning to 'appreciate their glorious past', he questioned whether the colony, which he imagined would be inhabited predominantly by Iranian Zoroastrians, would result in financial gain.[119] This doubt was contested by Parveez, who was adamant that the venture would not merely be philanthropic.[120] Another optimistic member of the audience was the Parsi newspaper editor and publisher Nasarvanji Maneckji Cooper, who listed a number of wealthy Parsis who could 'easily' supply the necessary capital to support the scheme in its initial stages.[121]

Parveez described how he had 'the honour to belong to a race which shows men of Iranian blood to be capable still of high achievement, both in business and in civic life'.[122] Yet, coupled with his belief in Parsi potential, Parveez held that life in India had weakened the community. Displaying the anxieties felt by some Parsis regarding the physical state of their community, Cooper was pleased that Parveez had penetrated 'desolate parts of Persia', showing 'what a Parsi can do when once he makes up his mind to achieve an object'.[123] Similarly, Birdwood viewed Parveez's travels as a reflection of

> the most hopeful of present-day signs of the renaissance of national consciousness and of those ancient Parsi characteristics of courage and personal hardiness which had been somewhat lost sight of and neglected under the Pax Britannica.[124]

The spirit of adventure that Parveez had exemplified filled Birdwood with the 'highest hopes for their future'.[125] Birdwood interpreted the journey undertaken by Parveez as a demonstration that, despite their love of a 'safe, and quiet, and comfortable life', Bombay Parsis were 'worthy of their heroical forefathers . . . when put to the trial'.[126] Although Birdwood doubted the colony would be economically significant, he believed the idea ought to be 'welcomed by all students of the history of ancient Persia', as it indicated that Parsis were 'taking a pride in the reassertion of their great historical personality'.[127] This endorsement was happily received by Parveez, who, referencing the *Shahnameh*, hoped that the opportunity would arise for Parsis to develop the economic and industrial resources of the 'land of Jamshid and Rustam', as they had done in India.[128] Many of the ideas proposed were similar to those outlined in the *Parsi* in 1905, but a substantial difference was emphasized by Parveez and by the individuals commenting on his lecture: the establishment of constitutional rule in Iran.

The founding of the Majles was widely regarded as marking a turning point in the history of Iran. In an article about Parveez's lecture, the London correspondent for the *Times of India* spoke of this being a 'critical stage in the history of modern Persia'.[129] As well as being seen as the harbinger of benefits to the country as a whole, the specific impact of the constitution on the Zoroastrian community was applauded. Cooper viewed the election of Arbab Jamshid as signifying great change, announcing that 'The East always moves so slowly, but the East also is awakening'.[130] He argued that the success of the Majles would not only guarantee the 'future prosperity and independence' of Iran but that it would also be advantageous for Zoroastrians.[131] Parveez praised Arbab Jamshid, whose guest he had been in Tehran, and he described him as

> the most influential and enlightened of the Iranian Parsis, whose election to represent that community on the National Council is a thoroughly well-deserved honour.[132]

Taking a broader view, Parveez claimed that Zoroastrians in Iran now enjoyed a 'national reputation for enterprise, intelligence, and integrity'.[133]

Thus, the Constitutional Revolution was regarded as the start of a new era, for Iran and for the whole Zoroastrian community. Commenting on the lecture delivered by Sykes in May 1906, and relating the issues raised to more recent events in Iran, an article in *The Men and Women of India* stated that Sykes's suggestion that Parsis increase trade with Iran was 'no feeble appeal'; rather, 'Its echo resounded and reverberated in Bombay from all directions'.[134] It was noted that Sykes was 'not unaware of the anxiety of the Parsis for emigration', and the point was made that 'Renewed attachment to the fatherland and a revival of interest in its affairs mark the special features of the past Parsi year'.[135] Reflecting on the movement for political reform, a photograph of Arbab Jamshid with his employees was printed with the following comment:

> it is good for the Parsi community that this remnant has clung so tenaciously to its ancient home of Iran which in course of time might give the shelter and protection of an enlightened government to a large section of the Parsis of India now hemmed in on all sides by fearful competition.[136]

The implication was that Parsis would be wise to consider taking advantage of emerging opportunities in Iran.

Links were made between the 'awakening' of Iran and an expected increase in Parsi engagement with Iranian affairs, with some observers positing that the 'return' of Parsis to the land of their ancestors would enable Iran to rise again as a great nation. Addressing Parsis, Birdwood stated his desire that

> the regenerated race of Parsis shall make up their minds to restore the Persian Empire, just as the Jews dream of restoring the Kingdom of Judaea. That ideal should be the lode star of your ethnical revival, the light of which should irradiate every generous Parsi heart.[137]

This idea of the Parsis contributing to the elevation of Iran was also found in the words of M. A. R. Seoharvi, who envisioned 'Persia reviving her ancient glories'.[138] In an article in *East & West*, Seoharvi described how 'Up to this time the unanimous verdict of the politicians had been that Persia was doomed for ever, but recent events have changed that opinion appreciably'.[139] Regarding the arrival of modernity in Iran as a renewal of an heroic past, Seoharvi held the view that a vital aspect of the new order would be the homecoming of the Parsis, whom he regarded as living in exile:

> the Parsees, by the grant of free admittance and other concessions, should be persuaded to return back to their Holy Land. The Parsees, when they return to Persia, will return with immense wealth and many industries in their hands, which will greatly increase the capital of the country and the general prosperity of the people. They will present themselves as examples to be followed by other Persians.[140]

Seoharvi thought Bahá'ís also ought to be welcomed, and that to encourage both groups 'a *firman* should be issued by the Shah and the new constitution declaring all the subjects of the Shah, whether Shia, Parsee or Behai, to have equality of rights'.[141] It is noteworthy that Jews and Christians were not included in this list, perhaps reflecting a distinction being made between religions Seoharvi regarded as 'Iranian' and those seen as 'non-Iranian'.[142]

However, although Parsis were paying greater attention to Iranian affairs and references were made to their Persian identity, as in 1905, the proposed Parsi 'return' to Iran, or to regions bordering Iran, was not embraced by the whole community. A cartoon in the *Hindi Punch* ridiculed the idea, using an image based on the *Shahnameh* story of the flying throne of Kay Kavus to illustrate that it was doomed to fail (Plate 1).[143] Doubts were also raised by Lepel Griffin as to whether the climate in Sistan would suit the Parsi temperament.[144]

In contrast, Parveez had argued that Sistan was particularly attractive to Zoroastrians, as 'it was the home of the great heroes and kings of their race'.[145] He proclaimed that Zoroastrians were 'better fitted than any other Persian race to restore to Seistan something, at least, of its ancient populousness, wealth, and prosperity'.[146] When one of the members of his audience, Sir William Wedderburn, questioned whether other Iranians might not be equally suited to the regeneration of this area, Parveez explained that this was not the case, as Parsis possess the confidence and trust of the two Powers which have most to gain from the success of any such experiment – the Persian and the Indo-British Governments.[147]

Thus, Parveez believed Zoroastrians had an advantage due to the respect in which they were held in India as well as in Iran, where Arbab Jamshid's position in the Majles was seen as confirmation of positive changes to their sociopolitical status.

Plate 1 A Picture from the Shah Nameh: Shah Kaekaoos Flying for a Kingdom in Heaven!

(With apologies to Claude Cooper: – Presented without permission to the Parsi Association and those of its members who crave for a Parsi Colony and Parsi Raj!)

'The wily Iblis, Spirit of Evil, pondered for long how he could take advantage of the ambition and vanity of the King, and one day sent a Demon to him, disguised as a servant, who persuaded him to fly in order to explore the secrets of the heavens. The magicians, after much consultation, hit upon a novel plan of flying ... They fixed four javelins in an upright position at the corners of a light raft, and put pieces of meat on the point of each javelin and the monarch sat in the middle. Four strong and hungry eagles were then tethered to the corners, and, as each bird flew upwards to seize the meat, the Persian King was carried higher and higher into the air ... At last, however, the poor eagles became exhausted, and King, birds, and raft all fell down together.' – *Legends of Old Persia*

NB 'Parsi Association' is written on the raft, 'Scheme for Parsi Colony' is on the king, the four eagles are labelled 'Claptrap', 'Jargon', 'Gas', and 'Talk', and the pieces of meat are labelled 'Bunkum', 'Hypocrisy', 'Rant', and 'Humbug'.

© British Library Board (Asia, Pacific & Africa SV 576, *Hindi Punch*, 15 September 1907, 23).

A question of loyalty: The shah of Persia and the amir of Afghanistan

Parsi connections to Iran were brought into focus in January 1907, as the death of Mozaffar al-Din Shah of Iran coincided with the visit to India of the amir of Afghanistan, Habibollah Khan (r.1901–19). This led to heated debates between Parsis over where their allegiances ought to be placed, as some were keen to welcome the amir with a special address on behalf of the community. Similar to the colony scheme, this was an instance where potential commercial gains converged with historical ties. Alongside references to their ancient links with Afghanistan, future trade opportunities, including the possibility of Parsi merchants settling in Afghanistan, were used to justify the address by its proponents.[148]

Vehemently criticized in the 'majority' of Parsi newspapers, accusations were made that those who backed the address had the wrong priorities, and that their plans for trade with Afghanistan were fanciful, especially since a previous attempt made by Parsi merchants to settle in Kabul had failed.[149] Rather than focus on the amir, the overwhelming feeling was that Parsis should reaffirm their loyalty to Iran. The *Rast Goftar* argued that instead of offering a separate address to the amir, Parsis ought to welcome him alongside the other residents of Bombay.[150] The newspaper criticized the 'silence' of the community following the death of Mozaffar al-Din Shah, and outlined how they should 'first redeem the sacred duty they owe to themselves and to their co-religionists in Persia' by composing a communal message for his successor.[151] Parsis had a 'debt of obligation' to the Iranian government and were thus, in terms of loyalty, linked to Iran.[152] This responsibility was explicitly tied to the position of their co-religionists, as the article viewed the plan to give a special welcome to the amir as potentially 'supremely injurious' to Zoroastrians in Iran,[153] perhaps due to recent disagreements between Iran and Afghanistan over the location of their shared border in Helmand.[154]

A meeting was held by the 'Parsi Association', an organization 'founded with the object of bettering the social and economic condition of the race', where it was agreed that a separate address should be presented to the amir. However, only forty of four hundred members were in attendance.[155] The *Hindi Punch* mocked them, describing how 'Some busybodies . . . have made the discovery that the Parsees are more Afghans than Persians and that it behoves them, therefore, to present a separate address on the name of the community' (Plate 2).[156] Conversely, the *Jam-e Jamshed* stated that 'the Parsis have had a good deal to do with Afghanistan in the past and will have much to do with that country in the future'.[157] Indeed, the Parsi scholar and priest J. J. Modi linked the proposed address to opportunities for scholarship, and reportedly argued that

> it was in the interests of the commercial advancement of his coreligionists and of literary research regarding their ancient history and religion that they should cultivate friendly relations with Afghanistan by paying their respects to the Amir whose dominions once formed a part of the ancient Iranian Empire.[158]

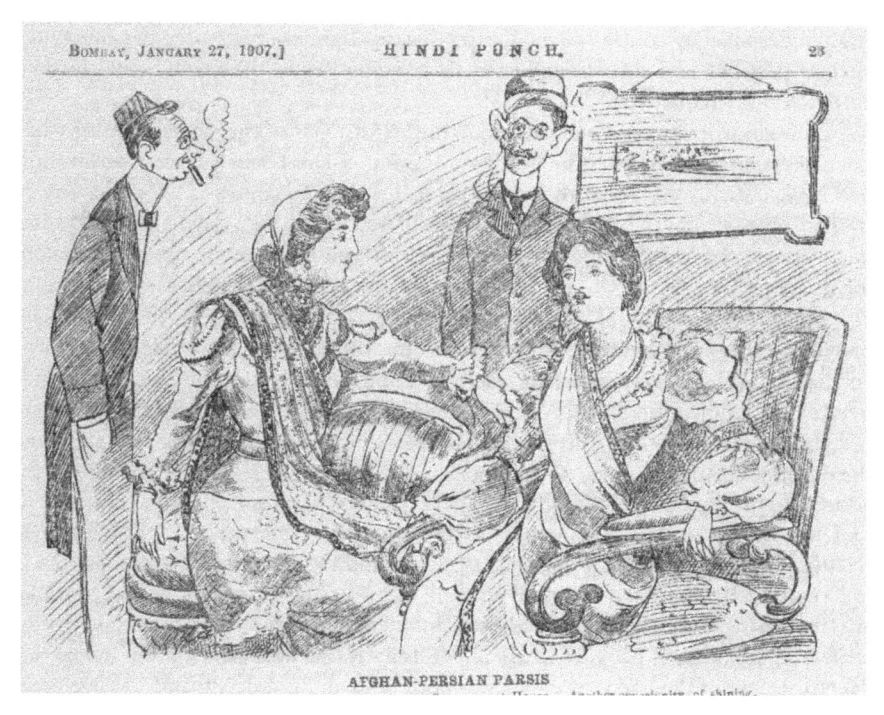

Plate 2 Afghan-Persian Parsis.

Dina – The Amir is coming and there will be a reception at Government House. Another opportunity of shining.
Goolcher – Or of cooling heels at the door-stop. There will be such a crush.
Dina – But we'll claim priority as *Afghan* Parsis! The Zoroastrian Association will vouch for us!

© British Library Board (Asia, Pacific & Africa SV 576, *Hindi Punch*, 27 January 1907, 23).

In addition to speaking at the meeting, Modi also expressed his views in an article titled, 'The Afghanistan of the Amir and the Ancient Mazdayaçnâns', within which he pointed out that Afghanistan had been 'the seat of their Mazdayaçnân religion and of their ancient Iranian civilisation'.[159] Modi linked Parsi interest in Afghanistan to the *Shahnameh*, as those living in the land had 'cherished, up to a late period, the ancient traditions of Irân which supplied to Firdousi a great part of the materials for his Shâhnâmeh'.[160] Thus, Modi aimed to harness Parsi interest in the pre-Islamic past to rally support for an address that he hoped would be beneficial to both Parsi trade and scholarly research.

Ultimately, the request made by this group of Parsis to address the amir was not granted, much to the relief of the *Hindi Punch*. The journal declared that the 'large body of the Parsis' were 'proud of calling themselves Persians' but did not consider themselves to be Afghans.[161] Whilst there were prospects for trade in Afghanistan, this was not enough of an incentive for the majority of Parsis to openly proclaim an

Afghan heritage. By contrast, Parsi loyalty towards Iran was partly due to pride in the ancient past but was also strengthened by ongoing ties to the country and to their co-religionists living there.

Although worries had been expressed in the *Rast Goftar* that the community had not acted appropriately after the death of Mozaffar al-Din Shah, Zoroastrians in India had in fact swiftly conveyed their respects to his son. To express their condolences, Iranian Zoroastrians in Bombay had 'closed all their shops' for a day, causing 'no small inconvenience' as they owned and managed 'most of the tea shops and dining salons for natives'.[162] A meeting was held with around five hundred members of the Iranian Zoroastrian community of Bombay in attendance. They agreed to send a message of sympathy to Mohammad 'Ali Shah regarding the death of his father, as well as a congratulatory message for his accession to the throne.[163] This meeting was chaired by the 'well-known merchant' Ardeshir Mehrban, and the Persian consul, Mirza 'Ali Akbar, was also present.[164] The speakers were not limited to Iranian Zoroastrians and the prominent Parsi scholars, K. R. Cama and J. J. Modi, who had been in favour of the address to the amir of Afghanistan, also paid tribute to the shah.[165]

During this meeting, the actions of the late shah were praised, particularly in relation to the establishment of the constitution and the inclusion of a Zoroastrian in the Majles.[166] The position of Arbab Jamshid was described as evidence that Mozaffar al-Din Shah was 'as just as he was liberal minded, and showed his solicitude for the welfare of the original people of the soil'.[167] Similarly, the *Rast Goftar* pronounced that 'His treatment of the Parsis of Persia was both kind and indulgent, and he gave proof of his regard for his Zoroastrian subjects by assigning to them a seat in the Parliament recently created'.[168] The death of the shah was depicted by the *Hindi Punch* as the death of the protector of the constitution (Plate 3),[169] and by the *Rast Goftar* as the death of the guardian of the Zoroastrian community in Iran:

> The Parsi residents of Persia have suffered a great loss in the death of the Monarch, who has shown them more leniency than any of his predecessors, and they may look forward with anxious expectation that his successor may be inspired with the same ideal of religious tolerance which marked the policy of the deceased Shah.[170]

In the same vein, the *Times of India* optimistically asserted that there was consolation in the fact that Mohammad 'Ali Shah had promised to uphold the new constitution.[171]

The messages sent from Bombay aimed to secure the good will of the new shah. Following the meeting, the Persian consul was left 'touched by the feelings of loyalty expressed by the Zoroastrian community towards their Persian monarch'.[172] Through their actions, Zoroastrians in India hoped to gain assurances that the new shah would protect their co-religionists. Just a few days after the initial meeting, Ardeshir Mehrban received a reply from the Iranian foreign minister that Mohammad 'Ali Shah was 'exceedingly well pleased at receiving such a grateful tribute of good will from the Zoroastrians in Bombay, and has expressed for them his kindliness'.[173] Zoroastrians in India clearly thought they were in a position to influence how their co-religionists in Iran were treated; this belief is reflected in the reaction to the proposed address to the

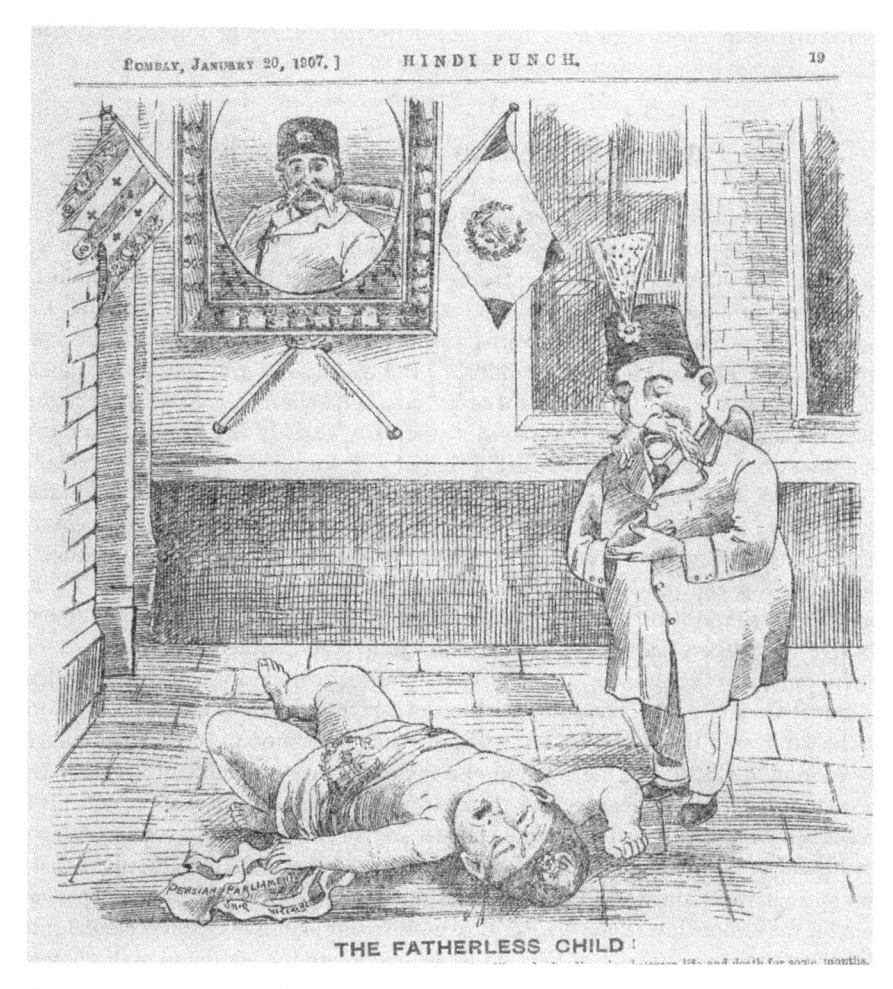

Plate 3 The Fatherless Child!

The poor babe was no sooner born then the father was taken ill, and after lingering between life and death for some months, crossed the bar at last.

[His Majesty Muzafferuddin, the Shah of Persia, the first Oriental Potentate to grant Constitutional Parliamentary Government to his subjects, died at Tehran at 11 p.m. on the 8th January, 1907.]

NB 'Persian Parliament' is written on the cloth worn by the baby.

© British Library Board (Asia, Pacific & Africa SV 576, *Hindi Punch*, 20 January 1907, 19).

amir of Afghanistan, and in their actions following the death of Mozaffar al-Din Shah. Expressions of loyalty had been used by the Parsis to help safeguard their community under Hindu, Muslim and British rule.[174] By emphasizing this reputation for loyalty,

Zoroastrians in India appear to have hoped to defend recent improvements for Zoroastrians in Iran at a time of political change.

Patriotic Persians or Indian nationalists?

Debates over public displays of Parsi loyalty towards the rulers of Iran and Afghanistan must also be seen in relation to Parsi concerns about the future of their community in India, and differing attitudes regarding the strength of their ties to the country. According to Eckehard Kulke, by the early twentieth century, the 'cultural and national frame of reference' of the Parsis was divided between India, Britain and Iran, prompting a 'permanent loyalty conflict'.[175] The question of whether Parsis should view themselves primarily as Persians or as Indians had been discussed in preceding decades, and it continued to be raised in the early years of the twentieth century, at a time when events in Iran were being viewed with considerable interest in India.[176]

News of the Iranian constitution added fuel to fervent hopes held by Indian nationalists. An article in the *Phoenix* stated that Iran was proving to be 'fit to govern her own affairs', and went on to enquire why India was not yet in a similar position.[177] Similarly, *Kal* contrasted Iran's 'happy news' with ongoing British rule.[178] In the annual press report for 1905–6, Syed Shamsuddin Kadri described how the tone of 'Native' newspapers had 'greatly increased in wildness and virulence'.[179] He linked this development to the situation in India, highlighting growing divisions in the Indian National Congress (INC) and the partition of Bengal, as well as to external factors, such as unrest in Egypt, the Zulu uprising in Natal, revolution in Russia, the political awakening in China and 'the creation of a Representative Assembly in Persia'.[180] The revolution in Iran was regarded by the newspapers *Kesari* and *Kal* as an optimistic event, which strengthened the argument that British rule was incompatible with the well-being of the population of India.[181] However, Syed Shamsuddin Kadri noted that a few journals maintained a 'moderate' stance; these viewed Indian self-government as an aim for the remote future and were critical of the rising agitation against colonial rule. Amongst the publications that 'refused to be drawn into the whirlpool of discontent' were the Parsi journals *Jam-e Jamshed* and *Rast Goftar*.[182]

Parsis greeted the news of a Zoroastrian representative in the Majles with joy, but not all within the community shared the ambitions of Indian nationalists, who had likewise welcomed the events taking place in Iran. Whereas the establishment of the Iranian constitution was seen as being positive for Zoroastrians, the prospect of political change in India was viewed by many Parsis with trepidation due to the potential impact on the community. By the early twentieth century, some Parsis feared that their political power was in decline,[183] and John Hinnells has pinpointed 1906 as having been a crucial year in this respect.[184] In the 1906 British general elections, Bhownaggree lost the seat he had held since 1895, and Naoroji was also unsuccessful in his electoral campaign. Adding to this, back in Bombay, the compiler of the Native Press Report remarked that the Parsi community was 'conspicuous by its absence' from the 1907 New Year Honours list.[185]

Although the activities of Naoroji and other Parsis involved in the INC have since been referenced as examples of the community's loyalty to the Indian nation, at the time, Parsi views towards Indian nationalism were complex.[186] In 1905, Curzon had ordered the partition of Bengal into two regions, one had a Muslim majority and the other was predominantly Hindu; this division remained in place until 1911. The partition provoked anger amongst Indian nationalists and prompted the beginning of the *swadeshi* movement, the boycott of British-manufactured goods. This was met with press censorship and the heavy-handed suppression of nationalists.[187] In 1905, Bal Gangadhar Tilak (1856–1920), a prominent nationalist, launched the *swadeshi* movement in Maharashtra. According to Shabnum Tejani, 'support from Gujaratis and Parsis, who together dominated Bombay's commercial life, was negligible'.[188] Alongside economic factors, the reluctance of Parsis to back the movement may have been linked to their concerns regarding Tilak. In contrast to the Parsi presidents of the INC, described by Palsetia as proponents of 'secular nationalism', Tilak placed a greater emphasis on Hindu religious traditions and cultural identity.[189] Within the INC, there was a growing divide between followers of Tilak, and others who favoured a more moderate approach. Naoroji was invited to preside over the December 1906 meeting of the INC in Calcutta, as he was respected by both factions.[190] Just days before the INC meeting, Mozaffar al-Din Shah signed the constitution in Iran. Naoroji used his presidential address to make the demand for *swaraj*, self-government, explicitly contrasting the 'awakening' of Persia to the 'despotism' experienced in India.[191] This address by Naoroji has been regarded as marking the end of the moderate phase of the INC.[192]

Together with the rising apprehension felt by Parsis over the trajectory of Indian nationalism, demands being made by the All-India Muslim League also impacted Parsi views about their possible future political status. The Muslim League was established in December 1906, following a meeting between a group of Muslims, including the Aqa Khan, and the new viceroy, Lord Minto. This had been arranged after Viscount John Morley, the secretary of state for India, had made references to the possibility of greater Indian representation on legislative councils. The individuals who met with Minto emphasized their loyalty to the British and requested that Muslims be treated as a distinct electoral category, in order to guarantee fair representation.[193] Supporters of the Muslim League viewed the partition of Bengal as a positive step, as it had led to greater political influence for Muslims in the region, and, similar to some Parsis, they did not believe their interests were being served by the INC. However, it is important to note that the Muslim League did have critics amongst Muslims in India.[194]

Likewise, Parsis disagreed over whether they ought to try to secure recognition as a distinct community in political terms. This is reflected in discussions that took place in 1907 regarding Parsi representation on legislative councils. The *Rast Goftar* referred to a memorandum drafted by the Zoroastrian Association of Bombay, which described their community as a 'pioneer race',[195] and stated that they fulfilled the requisite conditions to be treated as an influential minority. The proposal was made that Parsis should be granted the same privileges as Muslims and have a certain number of seats reserved for them, particularly in view of the loyalty they had shown towards the British and the role they played in the success of Bombay.[196]

A contrasting view was outlined in another Parsi-edited journal, the *Oriental Review*. Here, the community was warned not to act in ways that would enable the British to gain from their 'divide and rule' tactics.[197] Reference was made to the favours granted to Muslims by the British, and it was argued that the idea of asking for similar treatment was a 'retrograde' act that diverged from the previous stance held by Parsis, who had been, until now, 'in the vanguard of progress in all matters'.[198] Dadabhai Naoroji and Sir Pherozeshah Mehta were named as Parsis who had identified primarily as Indians; Naoroji was described as having 'first instilled into the minds of the Indian people a passion for nationality', and Mehta as someone who 'fought for India as an Indian'.[199] Thus, the *Oriental Review* urged Parsis to treat India as their 'mother-land', and stressed that this was the community's route to 'progress and advancement' in the future.[200]

Emphatic declarations to the same effect had previously been made in the *Indian Sociologist*, an 'organ of freedom, and of political, social, and religious reform'.[201] The journal was first published in London in 1905, under the editorship of Shyamji Krishnavarma (1857–1930), who also established India House as a hostel for Indian students in London, and the Indian Home Rule Society, which campaigned for Indian political freedom.[202] One of the contributors to the *Indian Sociologist* was Manchershah Barjorji Godrej, a Parsi businessman based in Paris and a vice president of the Indian Home Rule Society.[203] In March 1906, Godrej addressed the question of Parsi identity in a letter to the editor, 'Is the Parsi an Indian or a foreigner?'[204] Godrej was adamant that the answer was obvious:

> When a man speaks of his *own native* land or his *home*, the idea conveyed to the mind is that he attaches importance to the rights and obligations appertaining to his *birth, domicile* and possessions.[205]

As residents of India for over a thousand years, Godrej stated that the Parsis were Indians. They had been successful in India, which had treated them as a 'true mother', and Godrej argued that every Parsi should therefore feel a sense of duty and gratitude towards the land 'that has given him *birth*'.[206]

Godrej believed contemporary Parsis had been 'Indianized'. He described how members of the community had been affected by their environment:

> His habits, manners and customs, his language, character and ways of thinking, his superstitions, and even the very blood in his veins – for how many Parsis are children of intermarriages with Hindus![207]

This reference to mixed marriages grated with the discourse of a pure Persian heritage favoured by some Parsis. Godrej argued that despite assertions of loyalty to Iran, Parsis who lived in India had 'nothing to do with the Shahan-Shah of Teheran'.[208] The letter ended with a direct question from Godrej to his 'Parsi friends':

> If they consider Persia their home, why don't they charter a boat and leave India *en masse* singing 'Home, Sweet Home,' or 'Haihat, az Iran Zamin.' . . . Will they tell me how long they intend to call themselves homeless strangers in a foreign land?[209]

A clear link was made by Godrej between Parsi pronouncements regarding their ties to Iran and Parsi attitudes towards their situation in India.

Similar themes are found in another article from the *Indian Sociologist*, published the following year, 'The Political Attitude of the Parsis in India'.[210] The author described how Parsis in London welcomed remarks made by Lord Reay, former governor of Bombay, that the fortunes of India and Great Britain were interrelated. This was interpreted as proof that, 'with the exception of an infinitesimal minority', Parsis favoured British rule.[211] The *Indian Sociologist* questioned why Parsis preferred to live under 'an oppressive foreign yoke', and concluded that it was due to a loss of their sense of duty and gratitude.[212] The 'self-interest' of the Parsis was appealed to, and the argument was made that if they aligned themselves with those who called for independence, they would benefit in the future when India broke free from British rule.[213] To allay Parsi fears about a decrease in their political power post-independence, the article highlighted that 65 per cent of Parsis were literate, in comparison to the national average of 10 per cent, and pointed out that although 'it is well known that the Parsi community as a whole is opposed to the Indian National Congress', with 'barely half-a-dozen Parsis who openly side with that body', three Parsis had held the position of president.[214] Although this low estimate of Parsi support may be an exaggeration, many Parsis were wary of the INC and were concerned by the possible implications of independence for their community.

Bhikaji Rustom Cama (1861–1936), also known as 'Madame Cama' and as 'India's Joan of Arc', was a notable exception.[215] Born into a wealthy family, she married Rustom Kharshedji Cama, the son of the Parsi scholar K. R. Cama. The couple separated and in 1902, Madame Cama left India for London. During this time, she became involved in political activism alongside Krishnavarma, before moving to Paris in 1909, where she associated with other anti-colonial expatriates living in the city.[216] Cama was passionate in her struggle against colonialism and believed that all Indians had to unite against British imperialism. She expressed these views in, 'An Open Letter to the People of India from an Indian Lady in Paris', which was published in the *Indian Sociologist*.[217] Responding to the arrest of the pro-independence activist Lala Lajpat Rai in May 1907, Cama referenced Naoroji's presidential address and urged Indians of all faiths to work together towards the goal of liberty and equality under *swaraj*, proclaiming: 'Hindus, Mahomedans, Parsis, Christians, we are all as much Indians as Lajpatrai. Let us all make his cause and his sufferings as our own.'[218] This emphasis on combined action was also displayed in a weekly Indian paper, the *Patriot*, which praised Madame Cama and contrasted her to other Parsis: 'some silly members of that community refuse to admit that they are natives of India.'[219] Although she was adamant that Parsis were Indians, Cama did also draw on Parsi links with Iran in her efforts to drive political change; for example, she represented both India and Iran at the International Women's Congress in Paris in 1913, and she campaigned against the involvement of foreign powers in Iranian affairs.[220]

Whilst Cama and Godrej urged fellow-Parsis to stand together with Indians of all religious backgrounds in the campaign for independence, there was a simultaneous hope held by some nationalists in Iran that wealthy Zoroastrians in India would view themselves as patriotic Persians. Thus, they might choose to offer economic assistance to the Majles, including via subscriptions to the National Bank.

Finances were a major concern for the newly formed Majles. In order to raise funds without resorting to foreign loans, the establishment of a National Bank was prioritized.[221] Edward Browne described how preachers such as Sayyed Jamal al-Din Va'ez encouraged people to back the bank, and 'students sold their books and women their ornaments' to this end.[222] The project did not succeed, partly due to the actions of the British and Russian banks,[223] but nonetheless, Zoroastrian involvement should be highlighted.

As a founding member of the National Bank, Arbab Jamshid expressed his support for the initiative,[224] and the offices of his firm were amongst the few designated places where people could deposit funds.[225] According to the Persian correspondent of the *Pioneer*, the board of directors consisted of one hundred individuals, referred to as founders, who each pledged to subscribe between 5,000 and 50,000 tomans to the bank, equivalent to approximately £900–£9,000 at the time.[226] Farhang Mehr has described how Arbab Jamshid personally donated 20,000 tomans to support the constitutionalist cause, and collected a further 20,000 tomans from other Zoroastrian merchants.[227] Although no date is given, both the amount raised and the reference to Arbab Jamshid gathering the funds suggest that these donations may have been linked to the National Bank.

Conversely, consideration should be given to the argument made by Janet Afary that although 'big merchants' publicly endorsed the scheme, not all of them wanted it to succeed, as the National Bank would be detrimental to their own money-lending activities.[228] British Foreign Office records do describe competition between the Jamshidian firm and the National Bank, noting that criticisms were made in the Iranian press about people who chose to invest in the well-established Jamshidian firm rather than the nascent National Bank.[229]

Taking a broader view, given their position in Iran during the nineteenth century, it is significant that Zoroastrians were involved in the National Bank at all. The economic challenges faced by the Majles may have made the inclusion of wealthy non-Muslims such as Arbab Jamshid and the Armenian Tumanian brothers more likely.[230] However, it also indicates that there was some acceptance of the idea that non-Muslims were Iranian nationals. Contributions were offered by members of the Jewish community as well,[231] and it is possible that non-Muslims hoped that they could demonstrate their patriotism by engaging with the scheme.

The National Bank was categorically not open to foreigners,[232] but attempts were made to attract funds from Iranians living abroad, including from Parsis. An agent was appointed in Bombay to receive deposits, and the *Bombay Gazette* reported that 'From India, England, and other parts of the world, the Persians are purchasing the bank shares'.[233] The *Habl al-Matin*, a Persian newspaper published in Calcutta but also read in Iran, took an anti-British stance and described the promoters of the National Bank as the 'saviours of Persia'.[234] Commenting from Tehran, Spring-Rice stated that the newspaper 'talks as if, by a stroke of pen, Persia had now been restored to all her ancient glories'.[235] This reference to the pre-Islamic past can be linked to changing attitudes towards Zoroastrians, similarly reflected in the acceptance of Parsis as eligible depositors. The reputation of Parsis as a wealthy community likely played a part in this, but it must also have been the case that they were considered to be Iranians.[236]

Parsis were initially keen to back the National Bank. British records outline how they were 'anxious to assist the popular movement', so they 'instructed their agent to make all necessary inquiries'.[237] The 'agent' is likely to have been the emissary of the Amelioration Society, Ardeshir Reporter, and the 'Parsees' would have included Iranian Zoroastrians, as well as the largely wealthier Parsi community. However, the agent cautioned that 'the National Bank was not worthy of confidence, and that the Parsee community would act wisely in withholding its assistance'.[238] Enthusiasm also subsided following news of the murder of a prominent Iranian Zoroastrian merchant, Arbab Parviz Shahjahan, in February 1907. In his account of the revolution, Browne made a direct link between the murder and the reluctance of Parsis to subscribe to the bank.[239]

Although the National Bank ultimately failed, the initial interest it generated amongst the wider Zoroastrian community reveals that Parsis were supportive of the constitutionalist movement. In addition, the encouragement of Parsi contributions highlights that some Iranians were willing to view Parsis as compatriots. The early months of the Constitutional Revolution had resulted in Zoroastrian representation in the Majles, an event welcomed by Zoroastrians in Iran and beyond. Further positive developments were anticipated by Parsis who were increasingly emphasizing their Persian credentials. This was prompted by several factors, including the political situation in India and the hope held by some Parsis that they might capitalize on opportunities in Iran. However, with the murder of Parviz Shahjahan, this buoyant mood came to an end, and the position of Zoroastrians in the Iranian nation was called into question.

5

Struggles for justice

Zoroastrians and the law

The murder of Parviz Shahjahan

If the inclusion of Arbab Jamshid in the Majles appeared to signify changing attitudes towards Zoroastrians, the murder of the merchant Arbab Parviz Shahjahan soon challenged such ideas. Parviz, one of the brothers who ran the Jahanian trading firm, was shot in Yazd on the evening of 13 February 1907, as he was returning home from the bazaar, and died the following day.[1] The murder followed several months of growing hostility and incitement to violence against non-Muslims in Yazd.[2] This had reportedly included the offer of a fifty-toman reward for the death of Parviz, which had resulted in him being attacked and wounded in November.[3] Fearing further unrest, the Zoroastrian Anjoman of Yazd telegraphed the authorities in Tehran for assistance.[4] Anti-Zoroastrian feelings had been stoked by a preacher called 'Hadji Mirza Aqa', who, as a result of pressure from the capital, was forced to retract his words. This provided some immediate relief, and agitation decreased somewhat by December, but it was not enough to save Parviz.[5]

As well as situating the attack in the broader context of the recent encouragement of hostile attitudes towards Zoroastrians, there are reasons that may explain the specific targeting of Parviz. One suggestion, made by Farhang Mehr and others, links the murder to the role played by the Jahanian firm in transporting weapons to constitutionalists.[6] However, this argument is weakened by the fact that constitutionalists were not engaged in fighting at this time. In addition, Touraj Amini has pointed out that one cannot assume that the involvement of Zoroastrians in trading arms was necessarily indicative of their active support for constitutionalism.[7] Given Parviz's prominent position in the community and the international links of the Jahanian firm, the motive may have been to discourage financial assistance from Parsis for the National Bank, as a way of sabotaging the venture.[8] Edward Browne described the murder as an unprovoked attack,[9] but another possibility is that disagreements at a local level played a role. The British vice-consul at Yazd, H. Baggaley, reported that a 'stony interview' had taken place between Parviz and the acting governor, Moshir al-Mamalek, who had borrowed money from Parviz. According to Baggaley, this could have led Moshir al-Mamalek to instigate the murder.[10]

The time of year may also have been significant, as the murder occurred early in the month of Moharram. Shi'i Muslims would have been taking part in rituals building up to the commemoration of the martyrdom of the Imam Hosayn on 'Ashura, the tenth day of the month. This was a period when people gathered in large numbers and religious feelings were heightened, which had led to tension with non-Muslim communities in previous years.[11] Nellie Brighty, who worked for the Church Missionary Society (CMS), mentioned this in her diary and also made reference to political instability in the region:

> Heard tonight that another bill has been put up in town threatening the life of Dr White, Sheikh Mohammed Jafar & others. Poor Mrs W. is very nervous I hear & no wonder as this is a most trying time of year – one can't help wishing the 10th of Muharram (Sat.) the most fanatical day in the whole year were over – as this is the time when the people get in a perfect frenzy & we have no governor in Yezd! Then the death of Parviz just now does not allay ones fears.[12]

A few days later, a Zoroastrian unfamiliar with local customs was beaten for wearing a 'qaba', a type of coat, leading Brighty to reflect on the differences between Yazd and other regions:

> Parsees not allowed to wear them, but he has been away from Yezd & only just returned to find he cannot wear in Yezd what wd [sic] be allowed in Is. [Isfahan] & Tehran.[13]

On the very same day that this beating took place, Brighty noted that a football match had been organized between a Zoroastrian team and a team of Armenians and Europeans; the Zoroastrian team won, one-nil. Although Zoroastrians in Yazd were subjected to discriminatory measures and faced ongoing difficulties, it is important to recognize that this was not the totality of their lives.

Responding to rumours of further attacks on the community, measures were taken to prevent an escalation of violence.[14] Advances in technology, principally the establishment of the telegraph system, enabled more efficient communication between Zoroastrians across Iran. In Kerman, Zoroastrians disrupted trade by going on strike, only agreeing to re-open their shops when an investigation into the murder was confirmed.[15] Meanwhile, in Shiraz, Parviz's brother implored the British consul, George Grahame, to request that the British minister in Tehran, Sir Cecil Spring-Rice, use his influence on the Iranian government to ensure the 'atrocity should not go unpunished'.[16] Rather than relying solely on direct appeals to the authorities in Tehran to deal with the situation, Zoroastrians in Yazd also called on established networks of support: the British and the wider Zoroastrian community, both within and beyond Iran.

News of Parviz's murder reportedly 'caused a great sensation' amongst Iranian Zoroastrians in India.[17] Using their links with the Persian consul in Bombay, they relayed a message to the foreign minister, 'Ala' al-Saltaneh, who had worked as a diplomat in Bombay during the 1860s, and in London in 1889–1906.[18] Remembered primarily for its role in the campaign leading to the abolition of the *jezya* in 1882, the Amelioration Society continued to operate into the early twentieth century. The Zoroastrian Anjoman of Yazd appealed to the organization, and its president, Sir Dinshaw Petit, sent a telegram to the Sadr-e A'zam (prime minister), Mirza Nasrollah Khan Moshir al-Dowleh, emphasizing the role of the shah as the protector of Zoroastrians.[19] Quick to answer, the Sadr-e A'zam reassured him: 'Strict orders given. Justice will be done.'[20] Alongside these exchanges, Petit cabled Spring-Rice, requesting that he intervene to guarantee safety for members of the community and the 'arrest and punishment' of the perpetrator.[21] A swift reply was sent by Spring-Rice, who stated that he had 'reason to know that energetic steps are being taken by both civil and religious authorities',[22] a reflection of the ongoing influence exerted by the ulama.

Zoroastrians in London were also promptly contacted. Due to his political standing, Sir Mancherjee Bhownaggree received telegrams from Ardeshir Reporter, the Amelioration Society emissary in Iran and from the Zoroastrian community in Yazd.[23] Bhownaggree approached the Persian legation, resulting in the chargé d'affaires agreeing to take the matter further, and he alerted the India Office, believing that in this instance British involvement would more likely 'see justice done'.[24] Although uncertain as to whether or not Parviz was a British subject, Bhownaggree pointed out that the British had assisted Iranian Zoroastrians in the past. Even if they were not obliged to intervene, he argued that men of Parviz's 'race and class' frequently travelled between Iran and India, so issues concerning 'such individuals' should be of concern to the British.[25] This clearly implies that the level of attention paid to an individual Zoroastrian was directly linked to their wealth and social class. The attitude in the India Office was as Bhownaggree had hoped; although Parviz Shahjahan was not a British subject, the situation was deemed to be one in which the British were 'bound to take an interest'.[26]

Indeed, Spring-Rice had in fact anticipated the appeals by Bhownaggree and others. Gauging the political and symbolic significance of the murder, he had written in confidence to the foreign minister, 'Ala' al-Saltaneh, and to one of the leading *mojtahed*s, Mohammad Tabataba'i. Spring-Rice warned 'Ala' al-Saltaneh that care should be taken not to alienate the Parsis, who not only enjoyed 'considerable business relations' but were also 'able to exercise a considerable amount of influence in the English press'.[27] Similar to descriptions of the Parsis in constitutionalist newspapers, Spring-Rice outlined that they were the 'natural' friends and supporters of the Iranians.[28] He pointed out that whilst Jews and Armenians were emigrating, the Zoroastrian population in Iran was growing, partly due to the sympathy of powerful Parsis 'in exile',[29] but he raised the possibility that the murder of Parviz might change this.[30] In his correspondence with Tabataba'i, Spring-Rice referred to a speech the cleric had given in the Majles, within which he had spoken about religious equality; the British minister argued that in light of these comments, Tabataba'i must ensure the crime be punished.[31]

Positioning himself as a friend of Iran, who wished to see a restoration of the country's 'old glories', Spring-Rice emphasized that the Parsis looked to Iran as 'their mother' and would 'do all in their power to help her'.[32] Bombay Parsis were at that very moment 'consulting as to what they can do to help Persia in her present difficulties', perhaps a reference to potential contributions to the National Bank. However, he warned that Parsi support might wane due to the murder.[33] In response to his letters, Spring-Rice was asked to remain in the background but was reassured that the importance of safeguarding Zoroastrians was acknowledged, as was the related concern of encouraging links with the Parsis.[34] These points were presumably also impressed upon the authorities by 'prominent' Zoroastrians in Tehran, whom Spring-Rice noted had been taking their own 'private steps' following the murder.[35] Tabataba'i made it clear that he understood the 'unfortunate consequences' if a similar event were to happen again or if the perpetrator was not punished. As well as ordering the ulama in Yazd not to hinder the administration of justice, he asked the Sadr-e A'zam to insist on the capture of the murderer.[36]

The British wrote to Parsis in Britain, India and China, reassuring them that the authorities in Tehran recognized that Zoroastrians must be protected, especially in view of the funds that 'powerful' Parsis motivated by 'race patriotism' might direct towards the Majles.[37] Similarly, the Persian legation in London informed Bhownaggree that a 'searching investigation' was being made, and there was 'no cause for Parsees in Persia to be anxious as regards their safety', as they were 'liked and respected'.[38] Reporting on the story, the *Times of India* claimed that thanks to 'energetic representations' from Bombay and London, 'further trouble in Yezd has been averted'.[39] The economic status of the community was highlighted, and an emphasis was placed on positive changes linked to the revolution:

> The leading mullahs, who have taken the most prominent part in bringing about the constitutional experiment which is now being carried out in Teheran, have taken energetic steps to ensure that justice shall be done, and they have shown an intelligent appreciation of the necessity for affording protection to a community which, small though it be, contributes very largely to the commercial prosperity of Yezd.[40]

This reaction was explicitly contrasted by the correspondent to that which had followed the murder of Rasheed Mehrban in 1874.[41]

However, Brighty's diary entries for March document that Zoroastrians in Yazd remained 'v. frightened'.[42] Bhownaggree was contacted again by the community, with palpable urgency: 'Parviz still unavenged. Many more lives threatened. Danger imminent. Reign of terror prevails.'[43] Concerned, Bhownaggree considered advising Zoroastrians to take refuge in British properties in Yazd or Tehran.[44] The British vice-consul in Yazd was aware of the danger and listed prominent Zoroastrians who might be targeted. Baggaley described how few Zoroastrians were out on the streets, as they were 'afraid to leave their houses', but he pointed out that they had 'many' Muslim friends who could warn them of planned attacks.[45] Whilst crowds could be roused against non-Muslims, at a personal level there were friendships between members of the different religious communities. Yet, in contrast to the views expressed in the *Times of India*, Baggaley highlighted the similarity between the murders of Rasheed Mehrban and Parviz Shahjahan; he stated that Zoroastrians in Yazd were only treated well when they 'allow themselves to be oppressed', noting that both Rasheed and Parviz had taken a stand against the discriminatory practices implemented in the city.[46]

Orders were sent from Tehran directing the ulama in Yazd to 'preach from the pulpit in favour of Zoroastrians', in the hope that this would improve the situation and persuade Zoroastrians to end their strike.[47] Additionally, in response to the calls for justice, Cossack soldiers were sent from the capital to support an inquiry into the murder. According to Brighty, this approach did not ease the tension in Yazd but only made matters worse. On 16 March she wrote, 'One rumour today was to the effect that the Moslems were going en masse into the Parsee quarter to kill like they did at the time of the Babi massacre'.[48] Similarly, the Tehran correspondent for the *Daily Mail* reported the prevalence in Yazd of a 'strong anti-Parsee and anti-Christian movement', leading many to leave the district.[49] In April, a Zoroastrian woman with a baby was 'severely beaten' by a mob, and a number of Zoroastrians planned to emigrate to Quetta, which was under British rule.[50] Anti-Zoroastrian sentiments were also mentioned by the British consul in Shiraz, who decided not to notify local authorities when shots were fired from the garden of a wealthy Zoroastrian, as he feared they would have 'fleeced the whole Zardushti community without punishing the actual offenders'.[51] Clearly, central government interventions had not negated the dangers faced by Zoroastrians in the provinces.

Two men suspected of being involved in the murder were tracked down by April. However, after being tried in 'burlesque fashion',[52] they took *bast* in a mosque in Yazd, leading Zoroastrians to worry that if they were arrested, there would be a violent backlash against the community.[53] The British report from Yazd for April 1907 described how the governor was 'powerless' to punish those responsible, but highlighted that 'The principal Mujteheds at Tehran have urged their colleagues at Yazd to see that justice is done in this matter'.[54] Indeed, Tabataba'i had earlier instructed members of the ulama in Yazd not to protect anyone involved in the crime.[55] According to Bayat, this reflected a 'radical departure from judiciary norms' in cases relating to non-Muslims.[56] Commenting at the time, Bhownaggree also believed that the steps taken were significant. Although the murderers were not punished, Bhownaggree had heard from 'several correspondents' in Iran, including one of Parviz's brothers, that 'what has been done so far, and especially the interest evinced by our Minister at Teheran, has tended in the direction of securing the fraternity at present against the imminent danger of similar attacks'.[57]

The attention given to the murder of Parviz must be seen in the context of concurrent debates over proposed Supplementary Fundamental Laws, especially Article 8, which was concerned with the legal position of non-Muslims.

The Supplementary Fundamental Laws and religious equality

Due to Mozaffar al-Din Shah's ill-health, the Majles deputies quickly drew up an initial constitution for the shah to sign before his expected death. Following the ratification of this constitution in December 1906, the Majles elected a committee to prepare a supplement.[58] According to Eric Massie and Janet Afary, this document was the result of 'critical engagement' with existing texts, particularly the Belgian, Ottoman and Bulgarian constitutions,[59] and Afary has described these new articles as the 'heart and soul of the Iranian constitution'.[60] Although the supplement was drafted by the end of March 1907, it was not until October, after months of debate, that the additional articles were accepted by the new shah, Mohammad 'Ali.[61]

Individuals with disparate views had united during the initial stages of the revolution, but ruptures soon emerged. This was apparent during the drafting of the supplement, a process that raised questions about the role of the ulama in society and the authority of Islamic law. Some secular constitutionalists, such as Hasan Taqizadeh, favoured the inclusion of liberal laws that would address issues such as freedom of the press and a government-run education system and that would enhance the reputation of Iran as a modern nation. Laws that were more secular in tone were contentious as they threatened the power of the ulama, who had played a critical role in the revolution.[62] The majority of constitutionalist clerics assumed that they would retain control over matters that fell under the remit of *shari'a* law, and that the constitution would only cover issues traditionally dealt with by *'urf*, customary, courts, which were under the control of the state.[63] However, there were constitutionalists who favoured a new legal system that would dispense with this division between *shari'a* and *'urf* jurisdiction.[64] In view of these different positions, it is not surprising that there were intense debates over the proposal that members of recognized non-Muslim religions should have the same legal status as Muslims. Arguments over the issue of the position of non-Muslims were fraught, and Charles Marling, the new British chargé d'affaires in Tehran, stated that these disagreements almost 'wrecked' the National Assembly.[65]

A key individual who opposed this proposed law, and the constitution more broadly, was the *mojtahed* Shaikh Fazlallah Nuri. According to Nuri, Islam was not compatible with the idea of legal equality, as non-Muslims were not equal to Muslims.[66] Other prominent members of the ulama were more willing to compromise; for instance, the *mojtahed* Tabataba'i hoped that the ulama would retain some authority in legal matters but saw reform as a necessity in order to protect Iran.[67] Opinions were also divided in the influential Shi'i centres in Iraq; Nuri gained the backing of the prominent cleric Mohammed Kazem Yazdi, whilst others gave vital support to the constitutionalists. Amongst them was Mohammad Kazem Khorasani, who was based in Najaf and who believed that the constitution would not impinge on *shari'a* law.[68]

To reassure members of the ulama, amendments were made to the draft supplement, resulting in a document that was less secular than the constitution that had been signed in 1906. Additionally, the draft supplement affirmed the central position of Shi'i Islam in Iran.[69] Article 1 identified the Twelver branch of Shi'i Islam as the official religion of Iran, whilst Article 2 granted a council of clerics the power to approve legislation and specified that laws enacted by the Majles must not contravene the principles of Islam. The traditional division between *shari'a* and *'urf* courts was maintained, and only Muslims were permitted to hold ministerial positions.[70] Non-Muslims were thus still disadvantaged, but the wording of Article 8 in the draft agreed by the Majles in June 1907 was significant, as this stated that 'The people of the Persian Empire are to enjoy equal rights before the Law'.[71] Even though Article 8 concerned equality before state law, rather than religious law, Afary has argued that it did make it more difficult for legal differences on religious grounds to be upheld.[72]

The inclusion of Article 8 was in part due to the efforts made by Zoroastrians who had campaigned for the law and had also used their financial status to try to win the support of Muslim merchants and constitutionalist clerics.[73] In May 1907, Spring-Rice noted that Zoroastrians had been 'pressing for equality before the law of all persons irrespective of religion' and had been reassured by the 'chief leaders' and by Tabataba'i that the supplement would have an article to this effect.[74] The ex-headmaster of the Zoroastrian school in Kerman, Kaykhosrow Shahrokh, who later represented Zoroastrians in the Majles, described how he had gone with a group of his co-religionists to raise the matter with the speaker of the Majles and other deputies.[75] According to Shahrokh, Arbab Jamshid did not have time for his parliamentary duties due to his business concerns. Thus, Shahrokh took the lead in pressing for the wording of the article to be changed from that of an earlier version, which had just stipulated that 'all Muslims' were equal, thereby excluding non-Muslims.[76] Shahrokh also outlined how he had also been in communication with individuals from the Jewish and Armenian communities.[77] Although Spring-Rice reported that it seemed as if the Zoroastrians had been acting alone, with the Armenian and Jewish communities 'kept in the background', he did report that the Armenians had said that they would 'do their worst' if the clause was excluded,[78] apparently threatening to take sanctuary in foreign legations.[79]

Despite attempts to appease the ulama with laws such as Article 2, the idea of increased rights for non-Muslims was not accepted by Nuri, who continued to oppose the draft of the supplement that had been agreed in June.[80] Between June and September 1907, Nuri and his supporters took sanctuary, *bast*, at the shrine of Shah 'Abd al-'Azim.[81] From the shrine, Nuri wrote a series of open letters criticizing the constitution, stressing that it contained foreign political concepts and that those who backed it were Baha'is and atheists.[82] Nuri argued that the Majles should only include Shi'is, that all legislation should conform to Islamic law, and that freedom of the press should be curtailed. The *bast* was partly paid for by the shah, who initially resisted agreeing to the supplementary laws.[83] Mohammad 'Ali Shah was concerned that his authority would be diminished by the new laws, and realized that an effective way to damage the Majles would be to voice his agreement with Nuri and others who argued that the supplement was incompatible with Islamic law.[84] However, the shah did eventually sign the document in October 1907, following the assassination of the prime minister, and protests in cities across Iran.[85] In terms of the role of the shah, the supplement explicitly stated that the power of the ruler was bestowed upon him by the nation.[86]

The debates that had taken place in the preceding months regarding Article 8 can be seen in relation to contrasting opinions that were held on the topics of equality and the constitutional position of Islamic law, as well as the more specific subject of the status of Zoroastrianism. Whereas Nuri viewed Zoroastrians and members of other non-Muslim communities, as well as Sunni Muslims, as inferior to Shi'i Muslims, one alternative perspective elevated members of the Zoroastrian community. For instance, the newspaper *Sur-e Esrafil* stated that Zoroastrians had preserved the spirit of ancient Iran, which was now being manifested in the constitution and the promotion of equal rights.[87] These opposing views were apparent when attempts were made to secure justice for Parviz, as the murder prompted questions about how matters should be dealt with when Muslims were found guilty of crimes against non-Muslims. Traditionally, a Muslim would only pay a fine for murdering a non-Muslim, but Zoroastrians and others who pushed for Article 8 hoped that the law would lead to changes in the administration of justice in Iran.

In order to gain wider support for Article 8, Zoroastrians had given funds to the editors of constitutionalist newspapers. Letters from Zoroastrians were printed in these papers, for instance, from the Zoroastrian Anjoman of Kerman and Ardeshir Reporter, as were articles that highlighted the strong ties binding Zoroastrians to Iran.[88] There was also extensive coverage of Parviz's case; for example, a letter about Parviz was published in *Sur-e Esrafil* a few weeks before the supplementary laws were signed.[89] Not only was Parviz praised for his charitable works but he was specifically compared to the fifth-century figure of Mazdak, who was remembered for his message of social reform. Indeed, in the late nineteenth century, Mazdak had been described by Mirza Aqa Khan Kermani as having 'laid the foundations of republicanism and égalité'.[90] Articles about Parviz were also printed in *Neda-ye Vatan*, and Evan Siegel has pointed out that in addition to referencing Islamic values to back his calls for equality, the editor Shaikh Ahmad Majd al-Eslam Kermani expressed concern about international opinion, and also raised the possibility that Parsis might be inspired to assist Iran.[91]

Similar themes are found in petitions sent by Zoroastrians to the Majles, within which they appealed for equality and adequate protection and stated that the Parsis, 'proud Iranians', were considering returning to serve their homeland after 1256 years in exile.[92] In response, Taqizadeh underlined that the rights of Zoroastrians must be secured, clearly recognizing the potential benefit of positive relations between the Majles and Zoroastrians, both within and beyond Iran. Taqizadeh also believed that the inclusion of Article 8 would result in international recognition of Iran as a constitutional state, and a decrease in foreign intervention in Iranian affairs. This can be seen in relation to Zoroastrians, who still drew on their links with the British for protection.[93] Additionally, as the Zoroastrian petition highlighted, improved conditions might encourage Parsis to return to their 'original homeland',[94] an idea also referenced in the journal *Majalleh-ye Estebdad*.[95] Zoroastrians were described by members of the Majles as 'noble', 'national brothers' and as 'children of Iran',[96] and were reassured that they had equal political rights with Muslims,[97] even though this was not yet ratified in the law.

Whilst Article 8 did not explicitly refer to the recognized non-Muslim communities or differentiate between them, in discussions regarding the rights of non-Muslims, Zoroastrians and Muslims were sometimes grouped together and described as Iranians, in contradistinction to Christians and Jews. The *Habl al-Matin* suggested that it was due to their shared heritage with Iranian Muslims that a Zoroastrian petition to the Majles was read out, whereas a message from the Armenians was not.[98] Referring to the Zoroastrians, the newspaper stated:

> Brothers of the Muslims, belonging to the same race as them and having a glorious past, they will have, in Persia, the place to which they are entitled. But foreigners living in Persia must not be placed on the same footing. The example of Turkey, whose autonomy is always threatened and which constantly sees foreign powers

intervening in its internal affairs, should not be forgotten. Jews and Armenians are foreigners.[99]

Likewise, in response to the murder of Parviz, the *Habl al-Matin* emphasized that Zoroastrians were part of the nation and proclaimed that 'there is every reason to believe that the unity of the two religions of the Persians will not suffer any damage as a result of this deplorable event'.[100] Abdulrahim Talbof, who lived in the Russian Caucasus, expressed his support for Article 8 and outlined that Christians and Jews in Iran should be represented in the Majles. However, he appears to have found the idea that Zoroastrians, 'our ancestors', might not be granted full rights as being particularly problematic.[101] The acceptance of Zoroastrians as Iranians also had economic implications, especially in relation to potential assistance from Parsis.

The hope that wealthy Parsis might direct funds towards the Majles had been expressed in relation to the National Bank and was also reflected in interactions between Iranians and Parsis in London. Positive accounts of the experiences of Zoroastrians in Iran were given by members of the Persian legation, despite the backdrop of the murder of Parviz and the heated debates over Article 8. In April 1907, whilst he reassured Bhownaggree that an investigation into the murder had begun, the chargé d'affaires, Mirza Mehdi Khan, declared:

> Zoroastrians in Persia have rights and privileges that no other non-Mahomedan community possesses. The Persian Government have had their welfare and their well-being so much at heart that they have given them even the right of having a representative in the new National Assembly.[102]

Aiming to gain the confidence of Zoroastrians beyond Iran, reference was made to the distinct political position of the community.

Mehdi Khan reportedly enjoyed 'cordial' relations with Parsis, and, in March 1907, he was guest of honour at the Jamshedji Nowruz celebrations hosted by the Zoroastrian Funds of Europe (ZFE), which took place at the Café Royal in central London.[103] Addressing the attendees, Mehdi Khan expressed his pleasure at the improved status of Zoroastrians in Iran. He reiterated in his speech that they were not seen in the same light as Christians and Jews, and he emphasized the 'strong link' between Iranians and Parsis that his 'countrymen' wished to reinforce.[104] In his view, the Nowruz celebration itself 'proved, if proof were needed, that they were one people', and he urged that there be 'no misapprehension as to the Persian Zoroastrians being looked upon as aliens of different race'.[105] As evidence of the respect held for Zoroastrians, and the 'connexion between the two peoples', Mehdi Khan referred to the movement taking place in Iran to remove Arabic words from the language, and to 'write and speak the pure Persian – in other words the Parsi tongue'.[106] This reveals that negative assessments of the impact of 'Arabization' in Iran were sometimes explicitly related to positive views of Zoroastrians. Considering the success of the Parsis in India, and the fact that Zoroastrians were amongst the wealthiest bankers and merchants in Iran, Mehdi Khan was confident that Zoroastrians would 'play a useful part in the development of the institutions and resources of the country'.[107] The Persian heritage of the Parsis had been cited in earlier years, for example, by Persian consuls in Bombay, and it was now being underlined by Iranian officials at a time of heightened economic pressure.

Parsis in London were also keen to display their ties to Iran, and this was reflected in the Nowruz menu, which included 'pilao a la Jamshid' and 'Persian drinks'.[108] Not only were toasts made to the British royal family but they were also made to the shah, 'whose name was received with loud cheers'.[109] Bhownaggree expressed gratitude towards the late shah for improving the position of Zoroastrians in Iran, and he voiced the hope that this trend would continue. Echoing points that had been raised when the amir of Afghanistan visited Bombay earlier in 1907, Parsi loyalty to the shah was outlined:

> At all events, the Parsis, wherever they might be still cherished the traditions and ancient memories of their Fatherland and felt as if they still owed direct allegiance to the Shah.[110]

Indeed, at the request of their co-religionists in Iran, Zoroastrians in London seized another opportunity to pay their respects to Mohammad 'Ali Shah, when a Special Mission travelled to London in June 1907, to formally announce his accession.[111]

A lavish reception at the Criterion Restaurant at Piccadilly Circus was organized for this mission by the ZFE.[112] There were approximately seventy Parsis in attendance, and, as on other recent occasions that had brought together Parsis and Iranians, reference was made to the constitution. Addresses were read by Bhownaggree, who spoke about Parsi hopes for a 'bright future for their compatriots in their ancient land', and by Sir Dinshaw Petit, who, on behalf of the Amelioration Society, predicted that the kindness and protection of the shah would result in greater loyalty to the monarch amongst Iranian Zoroastrians.[113] This may have been an allusion to the reputation the Parsis had for loyalty to the British, and to the perceived benefits for both parties. The Persian minister avowed that his government would continue to promote the welfare of Zoroastrians, who enjoyed 'special claims on his [the shah's] protection and regard'.[114] Wishing for the prosperity and influence of Zoroastrians worldwide, he promised to do all that he could 'to promote the well-being of those of them in the Fatherland. (Loud cheers.)'[115] An emphasis was placed throughout on Iran being the true home of Zoroastrians, and assurances were given to the Parsis that their co-religionists were treated especially well, thus differentiating them from other non-Muslim communities.

Just weeks before these optimistic claims were made in London, Zoroastrians in Iran had been raising concerns about the dangers they faced. According to Siegel, Zoroastrians 'felt compelled to couch their appeal in terms of expedience as well as justice'.[116] A letter from the community printed in the newspaper *Sobh-e Sadeq*, which referred to Zoroastrians making use of their relations with the British for protection, proposed two alternative routes forward.[117] Either the Iranian government could grant Zoroastrians equal rights and safeguard the community, an act that would be indicative of their status as Iranian nationals, or else Zoroastrians would continue to resort to foreign support. This was a provocative suggestion as constitutionalists hoped to decrease the interference of imperial powers in Iranian affairs.[118]

The letter can also be seen in light of discussions about the possible emigration of Zoroastrians from Yazd to Quetta, which took place following the murder of Parviz. The British Foreign Office corresponded with Bhownaggree on this matter; Bhownaggree was unaware of earlier debates about the Parsi colony scheme, but he thought the idea was 'worth considering confidentially among a few rich leading Parsees', even though it would result in loss of property and a 'final severance from their ancient Fatherland'.[119] The Foreign Office also contacted officials in Bombay to see if they knew of this 'alleged offer' that Parsis had made to their 'countrymen in Persia',[120] and the foreign secretary, Edward Grey, was advised by Spring-Rice to take Zoroastrian plans to relocate seriously.[121]

On the one hand, positive relations between the British and the Parsis had been referenced to add weight to the argument that Iranian Zoroastrians were also loyal and valuable citizens, yet, on the other hand, these same relations led to questions being raised as to whether or not it was in the interest of Zoroastrians to leave Iran and become British subjects. Links between the British and Zoroastrians in Iran during this period should also be considered in view of the Anglo-Russian Convention.

The Anglo-Russian Convention

Despite Anglo-Russian rivalry, in August 1907 an agreement was signed between the two governments that detailed their policies towards Iran, Afghanistan and Tibet. According to Firuz Kazemzadeh, this treaty was prompted by the domestic situation in Russia following the Russo-Japanese War and the 1905 revolution, and by British fears over the rising power of Germany.[122] The Anglo-Russian Convention outlined how Iran was to be divided into a Russian zone, a British zone and a neutral zone. Concessions could be sought by the British and the Russians in their respective spheres of influence, and revenue from Iranian customs and other sources would be used to pay off loans previously made to Iran.[123] Although it claimed to 'respect the integrity and independence of Persia', the agreement had been drawn up without any Iranian input.[124] When the implications of the convention became clear, anger was expressed by Iranian nationalists, who regarded the agreement as a betrayal by the British.[125] Indeed, the scholar Edward Browne stated that constitutionalists no longer felt that they could count on Britain as a friend.[126]

Similarly, the lack of respect shown to the independence of Iran provoked widespread condemnation of the convention in India.[127] The *Rast Goftar* noted that these frustrations were felt by some Parsis, and the *Hindi Punch* printed a cartoon illustrating this view (Plate 4).[128] Conversely, the previous year, Naoroz Parveez had set out his hope that an agreement might be reached between Britain and Russia, as he believed that this would lead to greater trade opportunities.[129] Mansour Bonakdarian has suggested that some Parsi merchants may have been disappointed with the convention because a number of major trading cities, including Yazd, remained outside the British zone; this objection was also made by the Government of India.[130] In addition to highlighting Parsi reactions to the treaty, the possibility that it affected

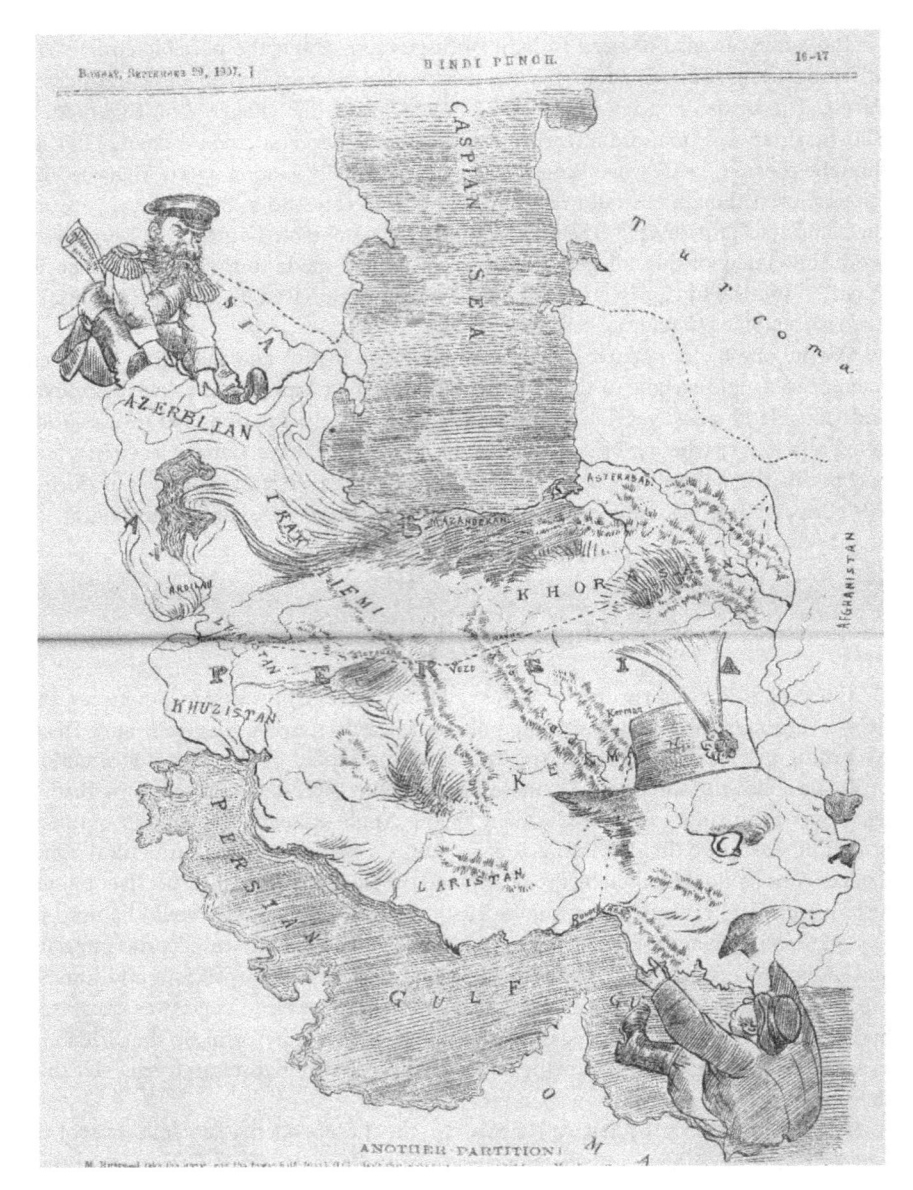

Plate 4 Another Partition!

M. Russe – I take the upper, you the lower half, friend Bull. Isn't that right? Are you satisfied?
Mr John Bull – Oh yes, quite! Just the right division!
The Persian Cat (aside) – Sport to you, but death to me! A plague on both your houses!

© British Library Board (Asia, Pacific & Africa SV 576, *Hindi Punch*, 29 September 1907, 16-7).

British relations with Zoroastrians in Iran should be explored, especially since Anglo-Russian competition had heightened British interest in the community in earlier years.

Even though attempts were made by constitutionalists to improve the situation for Zoroastrians following the murder of Parviz, in July 1907, another Zoroastrian was killed, this time in Taft.[131] The Zoroastrian Anjoman of Yazd demanded the Majles secure justice for both murders. In response, Taqizadeh and other Majles deputies criticized the Interior Ministry and Ministry of Justice for not having fully resolved the cases.[132] Just weeks later, Fariborz Namdar, a Zoroastrian landowner from Khalilabad, near Yazd, was also murdered. Dinshaw Petit described how Parsis expressed their 'great consternation' following the death of Fariborz Namdar, and there was 'almost a panic' amongst Iranian Zoroastrians in Bombay.[133] From Tehran, Ardeshir Reporter reassured Petit that the authorities had acted decisively:

Government most sympathetic. Due steps promptly taken. Governor dismissed. Culprits unknown.[134]

Petit had also contacted the Atabak-e A'zam (prime minister), Mirza 'Ali Asghar Khan Amin al-Soltan, who sent him the following reply: 'I deeply sympathise and am doing all I can. Full particulars later on.'[135] However, on the 31 August, the day that news of this message reached Bombay, the unpopular prime minister was himself assassinated.

This was also the day that the Anglo-Russian Convention was signed. One outcome of the treaty was that the British government was reluctant either to openly side with the constitutionalists or to criticize the shah, as the shah had the backing of the Russians.[136] For this reason, Pierre Oberling has proposed that the convention had an immediate detrimental effect on the position of Zoroastrians in Iran, due to a decrease in British concern both for the Zoroastrian community, and for the broader constitutionalist cause.[137]

However, a close examination of records, including those related to the murder of Fariborz Namdar, counters this view.[138] As well as a feeling of responsibility towards Iranian Zoroastrians prompted by their relations with the Parsis, another factor contributing to ongoing British interest in the community may have been that many Zoroastrians lived in Yazd, which was in the 'neutral' zone. According to H. Lyman Stebbins, as the regions bordering India were now within their sphere of influence, the British could 'devote their resources to consolidating their hold on the neutral zone',[139] which consequently became 'more British than was the British sphere'.[140] Continuity in British engagement with Zoroastrians in this region can be seen in the reaction to the murder of the merchant Behram Gushtasp, which occurred in Yazd on 14 November 1907.[141] After consulting Ardeshir Reporter, Spring-Rice made 'unofficial representations to the Persian Government' regarding the case.[142]

The Amelioration Society was also quick to respond and Petit contacted the shah directly: 'Another Zoroastrian murdered at Yezd. We humbly supplicate your Majesty's gracious protection.'[143] Petit received a reply from the minister of foreign affairs, Hasan Pirniya, also known by his title Moshir al-Dowleh:

Prompt, energetic measures are taken by Government to punish the culprit and to ensure quiet and protection for Parsi community. Special Commissioner despatched for this purpose.[144]

Gratitude to the shah was expressed by the Amelioration Society, but the *Rast Goftar* doubted the impact this would have, and pointed out that 'Unless the Government is determined to mete out justice and to deal with the case with a firm hand, it is bound to suffer the fate of the previous cases'.[145] The newspaper outlined how the violence experienced in Iran was driving a growing number of Zoroastrians to leave their 'motherland' for India.[146] Furthermore, the rule of Mohammad 'Ali Shah was contrasted to that of his father, who had been 'benevolently inclined' towards Zoroastrians.[147] No reason was suggested to explain this difference, but it may have been linked to Mohammad 'Ali Shah's alliance with Nuri.

Rather than marking an abrupt end to British support for the Zoroastrian community, with instantaneous negative consequences, the Anglo-Russian Convention can be seen alongside other factors that impacted the position of Zoroastrians in Iran, such as the actions of the new shah, and the debates over Article 8. Despite the ratification of the supplementary laws in October 1907, Zoroastrians continued to make use of their relations with the British, and, with the encouragement of the Amelioration Society, there were times when the British put pressure on the Iranian government to protect Zoroastrians, even after the Anglo-Russian Convention had been signed. Early in 1908, the issue of the safety of the community and the rights of non-Muslims came to the fore again.

The murder of Arbab Fereydun

On the night of 7 January 1908, a number of armed men broke into the Tehran home of Arbab Fereydun Khosrow.[148] According to Jahangir Oshidari, in an attempt to protect her husband, Sorur Vakil grasped the sword of one of the intruders with her bare hands, but this did not stop the masked men from killing the Zoroastrian merchant.[149]

The attack took place in the aftermath of a period of major unrest in the capital, provoked by the shah's attempt to dissolve the Majles. In mid-December 1907, Mohammad 'Ali Shah ordered the arrest of the prime minister, and supporters of the shah, including Nuri and his followers, gathered in Tupkhaneh Square, not far from the Majles. Meanwhile, over three thousand members of constitutionalist *anjoman*s assembled and prepared to defend the Majles buildings. A prominent role was played by members of the *Anjoman-e Azerbaijan*, an organization led by Taqizadeh that represented the interests of the province of Azerbaijan. The strength of the constitutionalists, alongside pressure from the Russians and the British, pushed the shah to reach a compromise. The immediate crisis was over by late December; the shah swore to uphold the constitution and Majles deputies reaffirmed their loyalty to the shah.[150]

Just days later, Fereydun was killed. A prominent member of the Zoroastrian community, Fereydun managed the Tehran branch of the Jahanian firm, and was a founding member of the Tehran Zoroastrian Anjoman.[151] Charles Marling, the British chargé d'affaires, was adamant that there was 'no doubt that crime had political motive', to 'frighten' Zoroastrians 'from whom Popular party have received warm support'.[152] Fereydun was an obvious target, as he had 'assisted the Popular cause with money and arms'.[153] Similarly, in a later analysis, Mehr described how Zoroastrian merchants hid arms in bales of cotton and smuggled them from Bushehr to Tehran, and he argued that the shah's agents had killed Fereydun because he had been distributing weapons for the *Anjoman-e Azerbaijan*, whose meetings he had attended and sometimes hosted.[154] A number of Zoroastrians were reportedly involved in the *Anjoman-e Azerbaijan*, including Reporter.[155] Zoroastrian backing for the constitutionalists was also referenced in the memoirs of Yahya Dowlatabadi, who stated that Fereydun and Arbab Jamshid had both given money and guns to the people who had protected the Majles in December 1907.[156] In Mehr's opinion, Fereydun's murder was ordered by the shah and then implemented by Sani Hazrat and several other men.[157] Contemporary British records describe Sani Hazrat as one of the 'leaders of the roughs' who gathered in Tupkhaneh Square, but do not mention him in relation to the murder of Fereydun.[158] Instead, Marling viewed the murder as the work of one of the shah's 'trusted Chamberlains', Mojallel al-Soltan.[159] Despite discrepancies in these accounts, it is clear that from the time it occurred, the murder was seen in association with the recent tension between constitutionalists and the shah.[160]

Supporters of the constitution went out on the streets, shouting slogans that compared the death of Fereydun to an episode in the *Shahnameh* where the hero, Siavash, is executed at the command of the emperor, Afrasiab.[161] Malekzadeh described how the murder roused 'strong emotions', leading to a 'sense of brotherhood' amongst Zoroastrians and Muslims.[162] Zoroastrians went on strike,[163] and they used their political and economic standing to push for justice. A petition sent to the Majles by the Tehran Zoroastrian Anjoman emphasized their 'Iranian essence and national blood'. Similar to earlier instances, it was stated that Zoroastrians would have to leave their 'dear homeland' if the situation did not improve.[164] Several other *anjoman*s wrote to the Majles, including one that represented the guilds, and Taqizadeh called for the cabinet to become involved in the matter. Deputies described Zoroastrians as 'noble Iranians', and expressed regret that some considered emigrating.[165] The president of the Majles underlined that Zoroastrians were 'national brothers' and highlighted that two suspects had been caught within days of the murder.[166] According to Marling, the shah had permitted the arrest of two of Mojallel al-Soltan's servants who were implicated in the murder, but he continued to protect the 'prime mover in the crime'.[167]

Constitutionalist newspapers also expressed solidarity with the Zoroastrian community, as they had done after the murder of Parviz. For instance, in *Mosavat*, a newspaper that received financial backing from Zoroastrians, demands were made for the perpetrators to be punished.[168] The *Anjoman-e Azerbaijan* printed an announcement in *Sur-e Esrafil* and referred to Zoroastrian involvement in their organization. In this statement, Zoroastrians were described as the 'ancestral heirloom of Iran', and as the country's 'ancient people', who ought to be respected.[169]

Whilst men are prominent in accounts of the constitutionalist struggle, some studies have highlighted the role played by women during the revolution; for example, Janet Afary has pointed out that many women helped to raise funds for the National Bank.[170] Afary argues that the period was significant in terms of the emergence of modern Iranian feminism. Women organized their own *anjoman*s, and they also established schools and campaigned for greater educational opportunities.[171] Muslim women sometimes contrasted their position to that of Zoroastrian women and women from other non-Muslim communities, who had greater access to education.[172] However, although they may have been at an advantage in educational terms, non-Muslim women faced additional discrimination because of their religion. Despite these challenges, Sorur Vakil was actively involved in the attempts to secure justice for her late husband, and she collaborated with the *Anjoman-e Azerbaijan* to this end.[173]

Action was also taken by the wider Zoroastrian community. Within days of the murder, the Amelioration Society appealed to both the shah and the Majles. An emphatic reply was received from the foreign minister, Moshir al-Dowleh:

No efforts spared to redress murder of Arbab Faraidoon. Prompt measures already taken to bring culprits to justice and inflict severe exemplary punishment.[174]

Similarly, the president of the Majles reassured the Amelioration Society:

Government taking stringent measures to redress Faraidoon's murder. Two culprits already arrested. Parliament's great sympathy with Parsi community.[175]

The Iranian authorities were evidently keen to impress upon the Parsis that justice would be administered.

British officials in Iran also intervened. Thus, despite the Anglo-Russian Convention, there was a level of continuity in British relations with Zoroastrians in Iran. Marling contacted the new prime minister, Nezam al-Saltaneh, who promised he would do his best to secure the arrest of the perpetrators.[176] In addition, after receiving reports from Yazd in early 1908 that local Zoroastrians were being bribed and were living in fear, Marling raised the matter with Moshir al-Dowleh.[177] Members of the Zoroastrian Anjoman in Kerman also drew on their relations with the British. When a Zoroastrian was attacked in Rafsanjan in February 1908, they approached the consul, Claude Ducat. Writing to the deputy-governor, Ducat emphasized that although they were not British subjects, Zoroastrians had 'always enjoyed our quasi-protection'.[178] The level of interest in the welfare of Zoroastrians is reflected in the notes Marling added to Ducat's weekly report; Marling expressed his frustration that this urgent message had been sent to Tehran by post rather than telegram.

Meanwhile, in Shiraz, shots had been fired at the garden house of Rostam Shahjahan, one of the managers of the Jahanian firm. Rostam had already received threatening letters that said he would be killed unless he paid a sum of 6,000 tomans. These were apparently similar to a letter Fereydun received before his death.[179] Concerned for Rostam's safety, the British consul, Thomas Grahame, let him stay in the consulate whilst he 'privately' contacted local authorities, including the governor-general of Fars, and asked Marling to raise the matter with the Iranian government.[180] To add weight to his request, Grahame forwarded a petition signed by CMS missionaries and other members of the British community in Shiraz.[181] The signatories stated that the cause of their concern was 'common humanity coupled with the fact that the Parsees are closely allied to us as British subjects and large representatives of our commerce'.[182] Marling promptly wrote to Moshir al-Dowleh and received the reply that 'local authorities instructed to take measures';[183] subsequently, the situation for the small Zoroastrian community in Shiraz improved, and local authorities were reported to be more friendly towards them.[184]

The commercial ties referenced in the petition proved to be significant. The Jahanian company acted as the agent for a British firm, Dixon & Company, and, in a letter to the Foreign Office, representatives of Dixon & Co. argued that Zoroastrians must be assisted, especially since 'during the recent troubles in Persia these people have been singled out for attack on account of their religion, position, and wealth'.[185] In addition to a feeling of responsibility towards the wider Zoroastrian community prompted by their relations with the Parsis, the British had financial reasons to be worried about the safety of Zoroastrian merchants. This reveals the ongoing importance of trade links, which had been fostered during the late nineteenth century.

Although the affluence of some Zoroastrians may have been a factor leading to targeted attacks on members of the community, their wealth also gave them a certain amount of influence. Following the murder of Fereydun, one of the Shahjahan brothers requested that Marling publicize British concern for Zoroastrians, stating that the economic role played by the community ought to be considered.[186] Marling agreed to write to Moshir al-Dowleh and asked that the content of his letter be communicated to the Majles.[187] This request was carried out, and Moshir al-Dowleh gave a copy to the shah as well, as 'a hint in that quarter was of more consequence than in the Assembly'.[188] Marling made it clear to Moshir al-Dowleh that the British took 'a very warm interest' in the welfare of Zoroastrians.[189] He stressed that the community would be more confident if the killers of Fereydun were punished, and that without greater safety, Zoroastrians would continue to emigrate, echoing points raised by Zoroastrians to the Majles.[190] Noting the benefits brought about by Zoroastrians, Marling stated:

> The Imperial Government cannot fail to recognize what a serious loss would be entailed upon Persia by the disappearance of an industrial mercantile community.[191]

Moshir al-Dowleh offered assurances that the government would continue to pay Zoroastrians 'special attention'. He described the community as the 'ancient subjects of Persia', perhaps reflecting his own positive views of the pre-Islamic period.[192] Marling later wrote that he had 'on many occasions, both verbally and in writing, reminded the Persian Government of the deep interest which His Majesty's Government take in the Parsee community in this country', but he feared that even if the Majles intended to safeguard Zoroastrians, it would not be able to do so.[193]

Aside from the limited power of the Majles, there were divisions within the assembly regarding the legal position of non-Muslims; these were brought into focus over the specific question of what punishment ought to be given for the murder of a Zoroastrian.[194] In contrast to the case of Parviz, the murder of Fereydun occurred after the supplementary laws had been ratified. As all Iranians were now supposedly equal under state law, some constitutionalists called for punishments to be meted out that went beyond the traditional 'blood-money' fine which was paid when a Muslim killed a non-Muslim.[195] Amongst those who wanted the new law to be put into practice in this manner were the preachers Malek al-Motakallemin and Jamal al-Din Va'ez, who helped bring Fereydun's case to the Ministry of Justice.[196] Crowds also gathered outside the Majles, calling for the perpetrators to be executed. These demands had the support of some Majles deputies, but there was strong opposition from a group led by the *mojtahed* Behbahani, who argued that executing the men would contravene the principles of Islam.[197] As Daniel Tsadik has highlighted, although Article 8 declared that there was equality before the law in matters relating to the state, other articles in the supplement outlined that *mojtahed*s held power to pass judgement over matters that fell within the boundaries of religious laws. A case concerning the punishment of Muslims for a crime against a non-Muslim could be seen as being within this parameter.[198]

Despite these conflicting interpretations of the constitution, Hadi Enayat has argued that the trial of the murderers of Fereydun was one of very few cases where constitutionalists managed to successfully press for equality before the law. After weeks of 'political battle' an agreement was reached; in early May, a group of *mojtahed*s pronounced sentences of between 100 and 1,350 lashes, and up to fifteen years in prison, for the nine men who had been found guilty of murder.[199] According to Majd al-Eslam Kermani, Behbahani and his supporters only accepted this sentence after being heavily bribed by Zoroastrians.[200] In keeping with contemporary custom, the accused men were whipped in public.[201] About three thousand people gathered to watch, including Sorur Vakil and other Zoroastrians,[202] and the Jahanian firm paid for celebrations afterwards.[203]

Several days later, two of the men were reported to have escaped.[204] Rumours spread that they may even have been released by the shah.[205] After hearing the news, Marling contacted the Iranian government and expressed his grave concern that the murderers were free in Tehran, explicitly citing the significance of British trade links with Zoroastrians.[206] Dixon & Co. had also alerted the Foreign Office about this worrying development and offered to pay for the protection of their Zoroastrian agents.[207] Dissatisfied by claims made by 'Ala' al-Saltaneh that the murderers had either died or were still in prison,[208] Marling emphasized the 'unfortunate impression' that would be created if any more Zoroastrians were harmed. He hinted that 'Ala' al-Saltaneh would do well to spread this message to 'influential quarters where it may perhaps be insufficiently understood', most likely a barbed reference to the shah.[209] In September, Marling wrote again to 'Ala' al-Saltaneh and mentioned a petition from Sorur Vakil. Thus, it seems that she continued to press for justice after hearing that the men accused of Fereydun's murder had escaped.[210]

Guarantees were made by the Iranian government, but these did not assuage the fears of Khosrow, one of the Shahjahan brothers. In the summer of 1908, Khosrow was in Manchester for business, and he asked to be issued with a British passport before embarking on his journey back to Iran. Although his status as an Iranian national meant that he was not given a passport, the British did offer him some assistance.[211] However, over the following months, Khosrow and other members of the Jahanian firm continued to face danger. In June 1909, the consul in Kerman reported that shots had been fired at Khosrow, leading him to suggest that the British should 'extend the good offices of the Legation to the Parsee firm of Khosrow Shahjahan'.[212] According to Mehr, Khosrow was being threatened by the shah's followers and he subsequently left Iran for Bombay.[213]

During a period in which questions regarding equality and the position of Zoroastrians in Iranian society were being debated, pressure was still applied on the British to support the community, and the British had their own economic reasons for doing so. This continued to be the case in the year-long Lesser Despotism, which saw a temporary break in constitutionalist rule.

Zoroastrians during the Lesser Despotism

Animosity towards Mohammad 'Ali Shah did not dissipate following the events of December 1907, and a couple of months later he survived an assassination attempt. Rising tension between the shah and the constitutionalists led members of the Qajar family to try to persuade him to cooperate with the Majles. Concerned that his position as shah was threatened, in June, Mohammad 'Ali instigated another attack on the Majles.[214] Although *anjoman*s mobilized to defend the Majles, they were not fully supported by the Majles deputies, who were initially in favour of negotiating with the shah.[215] In addition to being weakened by factionalism, the constitutionalists did not have the funds needed to sustain actions that had been impactful in the past, such as closing the Tehran bazaar.[216] Indeed, after the murder of Fereydun, Arbab Jamshid was apparently wary of offering financial backing to the constitutionalists, particularly as the Majles did not appear to have the power to safeguard the public.[217]

These fears were well-founded. Before long the Majles was shut down after the shah ordered the Russian-backed Cossack Brigade to seize control over Tehran.[218] A number of prominent constitutionalists were killed, including the preachers Malek al-Motakallemin and Jamal al-Din Va'ez, as well as Jahangir Khan, the editor of *Sur-e Esrafil*, all three of whom were accused of being Babis.[219] Other influential individuals were arrested, amongst them the *mojtahed*s Behbahani and Tabataba'i. Encouraged by the success of the shah, Nuri continued his attack of constitutionalism.[220] Nuri derided the view that non-Muslims ought to be equal to Muslims before the law,[221] and he implied that the destruction of the Majles was divine punishment for the implementation of Article 8 following the murderer of Fereydun.[222]

Despite the closure of the Majles, during the period known as the Lesser Despotism (June 1908–July 1909), the struggle for constitutionalism continued. Tabriz became the centre of opposition against the shah, with the Tabriz Anjoman playing a vital role in maintaining momentum for the constitutionalist cause. The inhabitants of Tabriz, including women, fought to protect their city from reactionary forces and endured a lengthy siege.[223] Individuals from Transcaucasia also came to fight for the reinstatement of constitutionalist rule in Iran. Amongst them were Armenians, who anticipated that their involvement would lead to greater rights for Armenians in Iran in the future.[224]

Support for the constitutionalist cause was also sought by exiled Iranians who approached potential allies, such as members of the pro-reform Young Turk movement. A number of constitutionalists went to Europe, including to Britain, where they were welcomed by Edward Browne.[225] Amongst those who took refuge in Britain was Hasan Taqizadeh, who had been a Majles representative for Tabriz and who had helped to bring the murderers of Fereydun to justice. In order to raise awareness of the situation in Iran, Taqizadeh and another former deputy, Mo'azed al-Saltaneh, published a manifesto in the *Times*. They stated that Russia had played a critical role in the destruction of the Majles, and they exhorted European powers not to assist the shah.[226] Soon after the manifesto was published, Taqizadeh and Mo'azed al-Saltaneh were introduced to sympathetic British politicians by the MP Henry Finnis Blosse Lynch; this meeting led to the establishment of the Persia Committee. Members of the Persia Committee criticized the policies of the foreign secretary, Edward Grey, and they played a significant role in stopping the British government from granting a loan to Mohammad 'Ali Shah.[227]

The manifesto in the *Times* emphasized the positive outcomes of the revolution. Divisions between the *anjoman*s and the Majles deputies were downplayed, and, as Bonakdarian has noted, reference was made to the greater equality brought about by the constitution.[228] Indeed, the second of its three major points was that,

> contrary to the practice of former times, all Persian subjects, irrespective of race or creed, were placed on an equal footing, and the Mejliss included a member of the Zoroastrian community.[229]

According to Bonakdarian, the constitutionalists were keen to gain the backing of wealthy Parsis.[230] Furthermore, they may have hoped that Parsis could influence British policy towards Iran.

Similarly, the aim of heightening Parsi interest in Iran is reflected in comments made by Taqizadeh in November 1908, following a lecture by Browne.[231] Taqizadeh took to the floor and, in agreement with Browne, stated that if protected from Russian intervention, constitutional rule would flourish and Iran 'could work out her own salvation'.[232] He stressed that the new laws had led to measurable improvements in Iran:

> One thing established by the Constitution was religious equality – (Loud cheers) – a real religious equality, and not a theoretical one. Before that non-Mussulmans had been treated as not on the same plane in the matter of liberty of observance as the followers of the Prophet. The unjust differentiation fell most heavily on the Zoroastrians.[233]

The 'Loud cheers' that followed the statement regarding religious equality points to the presence of Parsis at the lecture, also hinted at by references Taqizadeh made to the arrest and 'exemplary punishment' of the murderers of Fereydun.[234] By underlining the discrimination endured by Zoroastrians in earlier years, Taqizadeh accentuated the positive impact of the constitution. Taqizadeh also referred to the pre-Islamic period as the high point of Iranian civilization, in contrast to the situation in recent years: 'Her [Persia's] decline in the last century was as great as her progress in the days of the Achaemenian dynasty.'[235] This description of ancient Iran would have been welcomed by Parsis in the audience.

However, although Taqizadeh stated to members of the Parsi community that constitutional rule had resulted in religious equality, Zoroastrians in Iran continued to face challenges during the period of the First Majles. Due to the lack of central control, this was particularly true for those living outside Tehran. After the dissolution of the Majles, the situation appears to have worsened. Robberies in the provinces of Yazd and Kerman affected Muslims and non-Muslims,[236] but Zoroastrians were at a greater risk. British reports for 1909 describe how the road between Yazd and Kerman was unsafe, noting that 'Parsees are frequently interfered with and appear generally never to be free from the fear of molestation'.[237] Rather than being solely due to discrimination on religious grounds, the targeting of Zoroastrians was likely to have been the result of a combination of factors, including the wealth of some Zoroastrian merchants, and the knowledge that crimes against Zoroastrians were less likely to be punished, especially after the shah's coup.

Indeed, British records reveal that Zoroastrians were wary of demanding justice. In December 1908, a young Zoroastrian man was approached by robbers who ordered him to guide them to the house of a rich Zoroastrian; when he refused, they attacked him and slashed his arm.[238] Despite his injuries, he was unwilling to make a complaint to the authorities, 'for fear of worse consequences'.[239] A few months later, two Zoroastrian employees of Arbab Rostam Shahjahan were stabbed in Shiraz by a drunken servant of the governor-general. Their attacker was arrested, but 'a large crowd besieged the house of the Parsee employer of the wounded men'. Thus, Zoroastrians were pressurized into going to the palace of the governor-general to ask for the immediate release of the offender.[240]

Even when Zoroastrians did attempt to secure support from sympathetic ministers in Tehran, this did not always translate into tangible results for the community. Zoroastrians who lived in the area around Yazd were particularly at risk of attack by armed bandits from Taft. The region was described as being 'infested with bands of robbers' who stole from the houses of 'wealthy Parsees'.[241] Although it was not until 1911 that the bandits were suppressed,[242] the situation appears to have been at its worst during the Lesser Despotism, with Zoroastrians targeted by 'roughs' from Taft numerous times.[243] In January 1909, the houses of six Zoroastrians in Taft were ransacked, and three Zoroastrians were held hostage.[244] The community in Yazd contacted Ardeshir Reporter and sent a petition to the authorities in Tehran.[245] However, neither guarantees from the capital nor the arrival of a new governor provided alleviation from their state of 'constant fear'.[246]

In addition to appealing to Tehran, Zoroastrians continued to make use of their relations with the British. Although British policy was ostensibly 'strict non-intervention' in Iranian politics, the vice-consul in Yazd, E. Blackman, was reminded that he should offer 'unofficial help' to Zoroastrians because of 'the interest taken in this community'.[247] This approach led British officials in Iran to place pressure on the

Iranian prime minister, and it also resulted in Zoroastrians being permitted to take refuge in British properties. Early in 1909, fearing further attacks from the bandits, Zoroastrian villagers from the area around Taft left their homes and took *bast* in the British-operated telegraph office in Yazd.[248] This occurred during the month of Moharram, which was likely to have been another factor provoking fear amongst Zoroastrians.[249] Local authorities did express some concern at the situation, and in mid-February, the governor launched an attack on the bandits; this resulted in most of the Zoroastrian villagers returning to their homes by late March.[250] Despite this intervention, Zoroastrians continued to be blackmailed by the bandits, and some considered leaving Iran for India.[251] Those who made the decision to emigrate faced a dangerous journey, and one group of ten families making their way to India was robbed at least three times.[252]

There were several instances where hostility against Zoroastrians appears to have been particularly linked to their status as non-Muslims. In December 1908, a Zoroastrian in Yazd, Bahrami Faraidan Bamas, had his *abbas*, cloak, and his silk shawl taken from him because a member of the ulama had issued the order that Zoroastrians must not wear cloaks.[253] Likewise, a man tried to pull a Zoroastrian called Dinyar off his donkey, giving the explanation that Zoroastrians have 'no business to ride'.[254] These actions reflect discriminatory regulations regarding the clothes Zoroastrians were permitted to wear, and the rule that Zoroastrians must not ride in the presence of Muslims.[255]

Another issue was that of forced conversion to Islam, predominantly of Zoroastrian girls who were abducted and made to marry Muslim men. Whilst by no means a new problem, it became more prevalent during this period of insecurity.[256] A rise in cases is implied in a British report, which described it as the 'newest form of tyranny' against Zoroastrians.[257] Occasionally, Zoroastrians managed to escape being forcibly converted; for example, in June 1909, a quick-thinking girl 'started doing nonsensical things', and was subsequently freed by her captors.[258] The threat of conversion was of great concern to the community. Following the forced conversion of a girl in Yazd in July 1909, other girls stayed at home, resulting in the closure of their school.[259]

However, it is important to note that individuals within the Zoroastrian community held different views, and some Zoroastrians voluntarily chose to convert to Islam.[260] This was apparently the case when a young man from Yazd converted to Islam in October 1908, after arguing with his friends. Described as being wealthy, the actions of the man resulted in turmoil within the community, in likelihood due to the financial implications of his decision.[261] Blackman noted that the conversion of this man 'of fairly well to do parentage' caused 'some little stir', in contrast to the conversion of a villager, which 'did not excite much attention'.[262] Besides highlighting class divisions in the community, British reports also bring to light disagreements over religious reform. For instance, there had been 'bickering' amongst Zoroastrians in Yazd over the question of which of two brothers ought to succeed their father as *dastur*, high priest; one had studied in Bombay and was pro-reform, and the other had a more traditional outlook and was backed by the Zoroastrian Anjoman of Yazd.[263]

Not only were internal dynamics complex but so too were Zoroastrian relations with external groups and individuals. The revolution had brought together people with different aims and opinions, not all of whom favoured greater rights for non-Muslims. In April 1909, forces from Lar who described themselves as 'Constitutionalist' arrived at the town of Darab; they gave the Jewish community the choice of converting to Islam or death. On hearing the news, Zoroastrians and other non-Muslims in Yazd were extremely worried for their own safety.[264] Similarly, the Tafti bandits, who caused so much trouble for Zoroastrians, also claimed to be in favour of the constitution.[265] This should be seen in relation to the local context, where the ruling elite, who tried to suppress the Taftis, were predominantly reactionary and were only 'edging' towards the constitutionalist side in March 1909, when the outlook for the shah was bleak.[266] Whilst Mehr has emphasized the wholehearted and unambiguous support from Zoroastrians for the constitutionalist cause, there were times when Zoroastrians were accused of siding with the royalists. In the spring of 1909, Bakhtiyari khans claimed that the Jamshidian firm had transported arms to the shah, an assertion interpreted by the British as a ploy used by the khans to clear their debts with the company.[267] Zoroastrians were clearly in a vulnerable position during the Lesser Despotism, facing threats from some so-called constitutionalists as well as their opponents.

After a year of sustained resistance, the period of the Lesser Despotism concluded with the deposition of the shah. The siege of Tabriz had already ended in April 1909, when Russian troops entered the city, supposedly to safeguard Europeans who were living there. Revolutionaries in Tabriz were angered by this act of foreign intervention, which resulted in a stronger Russian presence in northern Iran.[268] Meanwhile, constitutionalist forces were gaining ground in other areas of the country, including Gilan, Mashad and Isfahan. Armenians were heavily involved in the constitutionalist activities during this period,[269] and in Rasht, a revolutionary government was established by the Armenian Yeprem Khan, who brought the area around Qazvin under constitutionalist control in May 1909. Yeprem Khan's forces were joined by fighters from Tabriz, and together they advanced towards Tehran. Concurrently, Bakhtiyari tribesmen approached from the south, under the leadership of Samsam al-Saltaneh, who had declared his sympathy for the constitutionalists. Attempts at compromise between the shah and the constitutionalists failed, and the constitutionalists entered Tehran on 13 July 1909. The shah, who had taken refuge in the Russian embassy, was deposed on 16 July and exiled to Russia. Constitutional rule was restored, reigniting the hopes held by Zoroastrians in India and Iran regarding their prospects in Iran.

6

Constitutional rule is restored

Nationalism in Iran and Parsi dreams of 'return'

Kaykhosrow Shahrokh and the Second Majles

Zoroastrians were quick to express their gratitude when the Second Majles convened in November 1909, sending congratulatory telegrams to the assembly from a number of cities and towns across Iran.[1] Constitutionalist forces had gained control over Tehran a few months earlier, and with the deposition of Mohammad ʿAli Shah, the Lesser Despotism was brought to an end.[2] His son Ahmad became shah, but as he was only twelve years old, a senior member of the Qajar tribe was appointed regent. In a symbolically significant move, the leading anti-constitutionalist cleric, Shaikh Fazlallah Nuri, was tried and executed.[3] The most prominent reactionary figures were thus removed from the scene. New electoral laws had resulted in changes being made to electoral categories; due to these revisions, there were fewer merchants and guildsmen in the Second Majles, and delegates were on average wealthier than those elected to the First Majles.[4] There was increased tribal and provincial representation,[5] and the recognized religious minorities (Zoroastrians, Jews and Armenian and Assyrian Christians) were to have their own deputies. This was partly in response to the Armenian contribution towards the restoration of constitutional rule.[6] Whilst the amendment secured representation for recognized non-Muslim communities, the allocation of seats on the basis of religion reinforced societal boundaries.[7]

The former headmaster of the Zoroastrian school in Kerman, Arbab Kaykhosrow Shahrokh, was elected to represent Zoroastrians. Following his brief employment as a Russian agent in Odessa in 1904, Shahrokh had settled in Tehran, where he undertook administrative work for Arbab Jamshid.[8] In his new position as a deputy in the Majles, Shahrokh was particularly involved in financial affairs, and was held in high esteem for his work in the Audit Office.[9] During the period of the First Majles, Shahrokh had participated in the campaign for Article 8,[10] and had written articles for *Neda-ye Vatan*.[11] He had also helped to re-establish the Tehran Zoroastrian Anjoman (TZA), and he was its president until his death in 1940.[12]

Aiming to spread knowledge of Zoroastrianism both within the community and beyond, Shahrokh wrote two books and distributed the first editions of both free of charge. These texts were written at a time when, in Shahrokh's words, Muslim attitudes towards Zoroastrians were 'most unhelpful'.[13] His first book, *A'ineh-ye A'in-e Mazdayasna* (*Mirror of the Faith of the Mazda Religion*), was published in 1907, with expenses paid by Arbab Jamshid,[14] and was referred to in the *Parsi* as the first Zoroastrian 'catechism' in Persian.[15] Two years later, Shahrokh published *Forugh-e Mazdayasna* (*The Illumination of the Mazda Religion*), which Afshin Marashi has described as an essay that reveals his 'modernist, universalist, and ecumenical understanding of Zoroastrianism'.[16] According to Marashi, these texts were amongst the 'foundational sources' for what was to become the 'ideology of twentieth-century Iranian nationalism'.[17] Shahrokh presented Zoroastrianism as a modern religion, and, similar to Parsi reformers in India, he emphasized that Zoroastrianism was a monotheistic faith. In his second book, he also referenced Western opinions of Zoroastrianism that he anticipated would lead to a greater appreciation of the religion in Iran.[18] According to Marashi, Shahrokh's 'racialized' view of the pure Persian heritage of Zoroastrians and his negative opinion of 'Arab-Islamic culture', sit in unresolved tension alongside his enthusiasm for greater 'unity and brotherhood' between Iranians of different religions, which he believed had gained momentum with the ratification of the constitution and the supplementary laws.[19]

The emphasis placed on 'brotherhood' can also be seen in relation to Shahrokh's involvement in Freemasonry. Shahrokh was a founding member of *Réveil de l'Iran*, or *Bidari-ye Iran* (Awakening of Iran), a Masonic lodge established in 1907, which was linked to the Grand Orient de France.[20] Other individuals involved included constitutionalists such as Jamal al-Din Va'ez (d. 1908), Tabataba'i and Taqizadeh.[21] Members were expected to promote Masonic values such as tolerance and universalism,[22] and, according to Talinn Grigor, they shared a high opinion of the civilization of ancient Iran.[23] For instance, a Masonic poem by Abib al-Mamalek Farahani praised Zarathustra,[24] and Grigor has highlighted that members of the lodge were inspired by *'Asar-e 'Ajam*, a nineteenth-century text about ancient Iranian monuments.[25] Many of the deputies in the Second Majles were Freemasons, and respect for the pre-Islamic heritage of Iran was reflected in some of their goals, such as the establishment of a national museum.[26]

Just when the deputies of the Second Majles were preparing to convene, an article concerning the Zoroastrian community was printed in Yazd, in the newspaper *Ma'rifat*. Zoroastrians were described as heirlooms from the age of the legendary Kayanian kings, true Iranians and sons of the nation.[27] The author argued that Zoroastrians must be treated well, and that wealthy Parsis ought to be encouraged to return to Iran. As well as praising Zoroastrians for their honesty, their significant economic contribution to the province was underlined.[28]

The financial success achieved by some Zoroastrians was important for the community, as money could be used to secure protection. In one case, in return for the cancellation of a 3,000-toman debt with the Jamshidian firm, a leader of the Bakhtiyari tribe, Samsam al-Saltaneh, safeguarded a Zoroastrian who had apparently drunkenly accidentally shot a Muslim.[29] However, despite the economic status of some Zoroastrian merchants, the situation for Zoroastrians in the provinces was difficult, and at the time when the article was published in *Ma'rifat*, seventy-one Zoroastrians from Yazd were making their way to India, and others had sought refuge in the British vice-consulate.[30]

Discrimination on religious grounds continued to be experienced by Zoroastrians. For instance, in September 1909, accusations were made that a new Zoroastrian school was too tall.[31] This indicates that the rule that Zoroastrian buildings must not be higher than those constructed by Muslims was still sometimes enforced.[32] Concerns were also raised by Zoroastrians that candidates for the Majles seats for Yazd did not accept that Muslims should be punished for crimes against non-Muslims, despite the inclusion of Article 8 in the supplementary laws.[33] Additionally, the community was refused a seat in the provincial *anjoman*, even though stipulations had been made that Zoroastrians and other regional constituencies should be represented at a local level.[34] An explanation given in a British report was that the two Zoroastrian men nominated for the *anjoman* were excluded because they were British nationals, thereby contravening orders from Tehran that all *anjoman* members had to be Persian subjects.[35] Shahrokh raised the issue in the Majles in February 1910, and he also referenced the difficulties confronted by Zoroastrians in Yazd in previous months.[36] Whilst Shahrokh did use his political position to advocate for the rights of Zoroastrians as Iranian citizens,[37] he was keen to emphasize that he was a representative for the whole nation.[38]

Thus, Shahrokh adopted a neutral position when divisions hardened in the Majles between members of the two most prominent of the newly formed political parties, the Moderates and the Democrats, who were more openly in favour of secular laws.[39] In contrast to Shahrokh, who did not align himself to either party, other members of the Zoroastrian community in Tehran helped finance the influential pro-Democrat newspaper *Sharq*.[40] According to Reza Zia-Ebrahimi the promotion of laws relating to all citizens, 'irrespective of ethnicity or religion', can be regarded as an expression of civic, rather than ethnic, nationalism.[41] An editorial in the Democrat newspaper *Iran-e Now*, titled 'We Are One Nation', proposed that this type of inclusive nationalism was the antidote to autocracy and communalism:

> The constitutional movement united the many communities, and thus brought down the despotic regime. To ensure that no such regime will appear again, Iran must treat all its citizens – Muslims and Jews, Christians and Zoroastrians, Persians and Turkic speakers – as equal, free, and full Iranians.[42]

Opinions expressed in *Iran-e Now* regarding Islamic law prompted criticism from some clerics, including the *mojtahed* Behbahani, who unsuccessfully called for the newspaper to be shut down.[43]

Concerns about *Iran-e Now* had also been raised by Mohammad Kazem Khorasani, a leading *mojtahed* in Najaf, who had contacted Behbahani regarding the necessity of ensuring adherence to Islamic law.[44] On another occasion, Khorasani cited Islamic law in order to help protect non-Muslims who were being abused in Kerman.[45] In response to the situation, Khorasani issued a decree within which he stated: 'To vex and humiliate the Zoroastrian Community or other non-Muslims who are under the protection of Islam is unlawful.'[46] Khorasani was an important constitutionalist cleric, and whilst he spoke out to improve the position of non-Muslims, in contrast to secular reformers, he did not envisage that the constitution would remove the social distinction between Muslims and non-Muslims.[47]

Indeed, the idea that Zoroastrians and other non-Muslims ought to be treated as equal members of the Iranian nation remained provocative. In April 1910, there was unrest in Yazd after the *Nazmieh*, the local police, encouraged Zoroastrians 'to wear Persian costume as a mark of equality'.[48] Members of the ulama reacted against this, and the son of a *mojtahed* removed the clothing from a Zoroastrian in the bazaar. The incident was reported, and the *Nazmieh* seized the man responsible. Clerics then 'joined in closing bazaars'; this situation lasted several days, as 'most of the people of the town' were 'much disgusted' with the *Nazmieh* for detaining a member of the ulama. Messages were sent to Tehran asking for the man's release, 'especially' from Zoroastrians who feared further repercussions.[49]

The position of non-Muslims as Iranian nationals was debated in the Majles, including in relation to proposals regarding the establishment of a standing army. In the neighbouring Ottoman Empire, the Young Turk Revolution of 1908 had resulted in the introduction of universal conscription; this was theoretically linked to the idea that all citizens were equal, regardless of their religious affiliation.[50] Echoing this approach, when conscription was discussed in the Majles in February 1911, the Armenian representative, Mirza Yanes, argued that non-Muslims and Muslims should be treated the same. Shahrokh was not so enthusiastic. Whilst affirming that the constitution ensured equality before the law, Shahrokh did not think that this should be related to the issue of conscription, and he added that Zoroastrians were not used to fighting.[51] Over a decade would pass before non-Muslims were conscripted to the army, but at this stage, it was agreed that they could volunteer to join.

Deviating from the views expressed by Shahrokh, Zoroastrians in Kerman chose to enlist in a short-lived local force of 'national volunteers'. This group mobilized towards the end of 1911, when Russian activity in northern Iran provoked 'considerable excitement'.[52] British reports noted that Zoroastrians regarded their participation as 'implied recognition of citizenship'.[53] Symbolically, Zoroastrian involvement can be seen in contradistinction to the conditions of the long-endured *jezya*, a tax on non-Muslims that exempted them from military service.

Whilst keen to be regarded as fellow nationals, Zoroastrians still took advantage of British protection, and British officials continued to make representations to the Iranian government on their behalf.[54] Agitation against Zoroastrians in Yazd led twenty-four members of the community to take *bast* in the British vice-consulate in March 1911.[55] Likewise, following the murder of two Zoroastrians in July 1911, around one hundred Zoroastrians took *bast* in the consulate in Kerman.[56]

Thomas Wolseley Haig, British consul in Kerman, believed that these murders were linked to local power struggles. He suspected that the acting governor, Sardar-e Nosrat, had instigated the first murder to tarnish the reputation of the governor-general, Jalal al-Dowleh.[57] Prior to these murders, another Zoroastrian had been attacked, and Jalal al-Dowleh had been 'severely censured' for not offering the community adequate protection. Haig suggested that the murder of a Zoroastrian would 'commend itself to an enemy of the Prince as the most certain means of ensuring his dismissal'.[58] Indeed, Shahrokh referred to his own involvement in the removal of Jalal al-Dowleh in his memoirs.[59] This points to subtle yet important changes in the sociopolitical position of Zoroastrians, principally that the murder of a Zoroastrian was seen as an issue that could sabotage the career of a high-ranking statesman. Despite this, Haig was not hopeful that the perpetrators would be arrested, as the influence of the constitutionalist ulama in Tehran did not extend to the provinces.[60]

Although views expressed in Tehran did not always have a positive impact on the lives of Zoroastrians further afield, there were other instances when Shahrokh used his own political power to benefit Zoroastrians living outside the capital. Towards the end of 1911, Shahrokh intervened on behalf of Zoroastrians in Yazd, who were being targeted by bandits from Taft.[61] Having previously helped the politician Amir A'zam re-enter public life after Amir A'zam was accused of colluding with the deposed shah, Shahrokh now requested that Amir A'zam repay the favour; Shahrokh asked him to restore order in Yazd, before taking up his new position as governor of Kerman.[62] Referencing a conversation he had with an eye-witness, Ali Modarres has described how Amir A'zam also went to Taft, where he made threats to return if Zoroastrians continued to be attacked.[63]

In addition to disorder in the provinces, the deputies in the Second Majles faced numerous challenges, including lack of funds and the continued presence of the Russian army in northern Iran. From the summer of 1910, divisions within the Majles deepened following the assassination of the *mojtahed* Behbahani, which had sparked protests in the capital.[64] Later that year, the British threatened to post troops in the south, which some feared would lead to the partition of Iran.[65] With a worsening financial situation and weak central control, the Majles turned to neutral countries for assistance. Swedish military officers were employed to help organize the Government Gendarmerie, which was tasked with increasing security to facilitate trade, and, in May 1911, an American lawyer and civil servant, William Morgan Shuster, arrived in Iran to take on the role of treasurer-general, with a brief to reform the economy.[66] Shuster developed close relations with Zoroastrians in Iran; he was based at Atabak Park, the palatial Tehran residence of Arbab Jamshid, whom he described as 'very patriotic', and he also spoke highly of Shahrokh, who offered him assistance with his work.[67]

Sympathetic to the aims of the Democrats, Shuster was critical of Anglo-Russian interference in Iran.[68] However, his attempts to instigate reforms to strengthen the Iranian economy provoked anger amongst the political elite, who would face increased taxation as a result. Shuster also faced accusations from the Russians that he was intruding into their sphere of influence.[69] In July 1911, the Russians backed an attempt made by the deposed shah to regain the throne, and in November, they asserted their power again, issuing an ultimatum which included the demand that Shuster be dismissed.[70] The British did not intervene in support of constitutional rule, leading Bayat to point to the Anglo-Russian Convention of 1907 as the most significant factor that sealed the fate of the Second Majles.[71] In response to the Majles' rejection of their ultimatum, the Russians sent troops towards Tehran. Attempting to protect national sovereignty, the cabinet accepted the ultimatum and dissolved the Second Majles, an event that is often regarded as marking the end of the Constitutional Revolution.

Renewed hopes: Parsis and the Second Majles

The restoration of constitutional rule in 1909 and the election of Shahrokh to the Second Majles had been viewed with optimism by Zoroastrians abroad and had reinvigorated their interest in Iran (Plate 5).[72] Amongst the Parsis who hoped for stronger ties between their community and Iran was Nasarvanji Maneckji Cooper, the London-based publisher and writer.[73] Cooper had prior relations with Iranians in London,[74] and he also seems to have been in contact with Zoroastrians in Iran.

Plate 5 Under Protecting Wings.

(The New Boy-Shah of Persia, Sultan Ahmed Mirza)

© British Library Board (Asia, Pacific & Africa SV 576, *Hindi Punch*, 25 July 1909, 13).

Indeed, early in 1909, Arbab Jamshid bought one hundred copies of Cooper's edition of Lawrence Heyworth Mills' translation of the *Gathas*.[75]

Greatly affected by Zoroastrian representation in the First Majles, Cooper dedicated his 1910 publication, *The Imitation of Zoroaster: Quotations from Zoroastrian Literature*, to Arbab Jamshid. This short book contained extracts from Zoroastrian texts set out like proverbs, reflecting the emphasis placed on ethics by Parsi reformers. In the dedication, Cooper suggested that, as well as following the example of the founder of their faith, Zoroastrians might be inspired by the contemporary figure of Arbab Jamshid, whose 'high probity, untiring philanthropy and public spirit' he praised:

> Your election to the first Majliss as representative of the Parsee community was hailed with satisfaction by our co-religionists in India. The future progress and welfare of the Persian Zoroastrians cannot be in doubt if they follow the example you have set.[76]

The previous year, Cooper had published *The Zoroastrian Code of Gentlehood*, within which he had expressed support for Parsi efforts to help Zoroastrians in the 'Fatherland'.[77] Distributed in India and Britain,[78] this was dedicated to Hormusji Cowasji Dinshaw, who was later involved in the Iran League, an organization that promoted relations between India and Iran. The work was also translated into Persian and it was published in Tehran by Kaykhosrow Shahrokh in 1909.[79] Thus, through the medium of print, Cooper encouraged links between Zoroastrians in Iran, India and Britain. Alongside his publications, Cooper organized events where talks were delivered on topics related to Zoroastrianism and Iran. Due to reports of these gatherings that were published in India, news of these London-based discussions had an impact much further afield.

In July 1910, the opulent Holborn Restaurant was chosen as the location for one of these events.[80] Cooper had invited three guest speakers: the Reverend James Hope Moulton, Professor Lawrence Heyworth Mills and Sir George Birdwood.[81] The latter gave a rousing account of Zoroastrian history, and he described Parsis as 'remnants of a race now scattered abroad ... once a mighty nation'.[82] Linking the past to the present, Birdwood compared the 'character and deeds' of famous Parsis, such as Sir Jamsetjee Jeejeebhoy, to the 'ancient Persians'. Birdwood ended by proclaiming his hope that Parsis would 'everlastingly uphold the glory of their race', and that of their 'yet to be restored nation, in the future, even as did their most famed of famous forefathers in their renowned past'.[83] These words were followed by 'loud and long continued applause', clearly striking a chord with the Parsi audience, whose interest in Iran had been heightened following the establishment of the Second Majles.

Cooper published these speeches in a booklet dedicated to Shahrokh, whom he viewed as an embodiment of Zoroastrian values. Shahrokh had recently published his own books about Zoroastrianism, and he was seen by Cooper to be taking Zoroastrian ideals into the political sphere:

> The Parsees outside the Fatherland have the fullest confidence that you will do all that lies in your power to cement more closely the ties of a common patriotism existing between Zoroastrians and their Persian fellow-subjects, and that you

will consistently uphold those great principles of toleration and religious liberty and equality which are among the fundamental liberties it is essential for the new Constitutional Government to firmly establish and maintain.[84]

Rather than referencing the power of the shah to protect Zoroastrians, Cooper believed the rule of law could safeguard his co-religionists. Similar to statements made by exiled constitutionalists who had tried to gain Parsi support during the Lesser Despotism, Cooper emphasized the bonds that linked all Zoroastrians to Iran.

Patriotism towards Iran was expressed by other members of the Parsi community. For instance, to commemorate the life of the editor of *Sur-e Esrafil*, Mirza Jahangir Khan, who had been killed after the 1908 coup and was regarded as a constitutionalist martyr, Zoroastrian traders in Shanghai raised money for the population of Ardabil, a city in north-western Iran that had been the location of heavy fighting during the Lesser Despotism.[85] In addition to this donation of 320 tomans, the *Revue du Monde Musulman* reported that in order to keep the memory of Mirza Jahangir Khan alive, 'they saw no better way than to give his name to a school, for the foundation of which about 420 tomans had been gathered'.[86] When the plan was announced, the newspaper *Iran-e Now* was apparently touched by this initiative, which saw Parsis in China celebrating the life of an Iranian who was not a Zoroastrian and raising funds for a cause that was not solely directed towards their co-religionists.[87]

The responsibility Parsis held in regard to their 'homeland' was a theme expounded at an event arranged by Cooper in September 1910, 'Persia and the Parsees of India'.[88] The speakers included Birdwood and Mirza Mehdi Khan, the Persian minister in London. Cooper outlined that, due to greater opportunities for Zoroastrians in Iran, some Parsis were 'thinking of once more making Persia their home'.[89] This idea, which had been discussed before the Constitutional Revolution and in the early months of the First Majles, regained traction again after the constitution was restored. The strengthening of ties between Parsis and Iran was similarly emphasized by Mehdi Khan.[90] Echoing a speech he had delivered in 1907, Mehdi Khan pointed out that 'many of the influential bankers' in Iran were Zoroastrians. Even though there were other non-Muslim deputies in the Second Majles, he referred to Zoroastrian representation as 'a privilege which no other nation enjoyed'. Mehdi Khan highlighted the status of Zoroastrians to encourage Parsis to become more involved in Iran, reiterating that 'Parsees were not considered a foreign community, but as one of themselves'.[91]

According to Mehdi Khan, the low number of Parsi visitors to Iran was pitiable. He underlined that closer relations between Parsis and Iran would be of 'mutual advantage', and argued that if Parsis went to Iran, they would see the 'respect and admiration that was felt for the Zoroastrians'.[92] Similar sentiments were expressed by Pheroze Kershasp, a Parsi civil servant who had written about ancient Iran.[93] Kershasp had travelled to Iran, which he described as 'completely transformed', and he urged his co-religionists to follow his example.[94] Yet, in private letters to Browne, Kershasp was not so optimistic about the outlook for the Majles.[95] Mansour Bonakdarian has noted that Kershasp corresponded with Iranian nationalists,[96] and it is possible that, along with Browne and Taqizadeh, he hoped wealthy Parsis might alleviate the economic challenges being faced in Iran. Mehdi Khan also claimed that there were opportunities for enterprising Parsis, 'whom the country would welcome',[97] and his colleague, Mirza Ghaffar Khan, expressed admiration for the community. However, Ghaffar Khan raised two criticisms: Parsis had not done enough to improve the welfare of their co-religionists, and they had 'given up their own national, beautiful, and ancient language'.[98] Ghaffar Khan thought this was 'surprising' in the current climate, 'when people were clinging to everything that was distinctly national'.[99] There were possible economic benefits for the Majles if members of the Parsi community chose to identify with this Persian heritage and strengthen their ties with contemporary Iran.

Indeed, Mangol Bayat has referred to discussions that took place in 1910 regarding a potential Parsi loan.[100] Negotiations were initiated with the help of Browne, who advised Taqizadeh against accepting loans from European governments and pointed out that Parsis were keen to help develop Iran. Furthermore, Browne's assistant in Cambridge, Shaikh Hasan Tabrizi, clarified that Parsis were Iranians and were thus not constrained by the terms of the Anglo-Russian Convention. Shaikh Hasan Tabrizi consulted with Parsis in Bombay, and a proposal was drawn up; in return for a £500,000 loan, Parsis would be granted several concessions. However, Shaikh Hasan Tabrizi was unable to persuade Samad Khan Momtaz al-Saltaneh, the Iranian ambassador in Paris, to agree to the deal, and consequently, no loan was secured. Bayat has noted that the terms set out by the Parsis were 'financially exorbitant', and that Samad Khan Momtaz al-Saltaneh may also have had concerns regarding the impact on relations with France.[101]

Although the terms of the loan were not accepted, the related discussions reflect a certain level of Parsi interest in Iranian affairs. Whilst some Indian nationalists referred to events in Iran to support the argument that Asian countries were ready for constitutional rule,[102] Parsis focused their attention more closely on the benefits for Zoroastrians. Writing to the *Times of India*, an anonymous Parsi, 'J', had 'a few suggestions on a question that is agitating them [Parsis]': how to 'improve' their 'race' through opportunities currently offered in Iran.[103] Reflecting wider concerns, 'J' referred to the supposed physical degeneration of Parsis, and recommended that life in Iran would make them 'rough and hardy'.[104] The notion that the Indian climate had negatively impacted the Parsis was not new, but with the establishment of the Second Majles, there was a revival of the idea that 'returning' to Iran could be the solution.

The *Hindi Punch* suggested that Parsis who had kept their faith alive in a 'foreign land' could now take advantage of this 'opening' and 'return to their fatherland' (Plate 6).[105] To mark the 1910 Parsi New Year, the journal printed a series of cartoons illustrating key issues from the preceding year. The first cartoon, 'To Iran', depicted the ghosts of Yazdegerd, the last Sasanian king, and Naser al-Din Shah, who had abolished the *jezya*. They were shown to be discussing the return of Parsis, who would work 'hand in hand' with Iranians to help Iran rise to its 'former glory and power'.[106] Thus, it was recommended that investigations be conducted into the 'fields of commerce and industry that may be open to Parsee enterprise and Parsee capital'.[107] However, there was an assumption that the British would provide some protection, perhaps betraying a sense of trepidation,[108] and the Amelioration Society decided to appoint a committee to conduct preliminary inquiries, rather than immediately organizing a full Commercial Mission.[109]

Plate 6 Mr Punch's Pateti Pictures – No. 1.

To Iran!

Shade of Shah Nasruddin (to Shade of Yezdezard Shehriar) – After thirteen hundred years of residence in Ind, your posterity are thinking of entering the service of my heirs in Iran!
Shade of Yezdezard – Yes, the old love of country still burns bright, as in the past. May your children and mine work hand in hand and shoulder to shoulder for the peace and betterment of our Ancient Land! And may Iran rise to its former glory and power through their joint peaceful co-operation!
Shade of Shah Nasruddin – Amen! Amen! May the Parsee New Year inaugurate a new era in Iran!

[The sub-committee of the Parsi Association has suggested to send a few Parsees to Persia under the protection of the British Consul there to make investigations on the spot as to the fields of commerce and industry that may be open to Parsee enterprise and Parsee capital. Mr Jeejeebhai Pestonjee Mistry, the Secretary of the Association for ameliorating the condition of Zoroastrians residing in Persia, has publicly asked for applications from Parsee candidates willing to serve the Persian Government for the posts in the Revenue, Customs, Municipal Police, Post and Telegraph Departments. About fifteen such posts are open.]

© British Library Board (Asia, Pacific & Africa SV 576, *Hindi Punch*, 11 September 1910, 10).

These plans were ridiculed in the *Jam-e Jamshed*, but the *Times of India* argued that 'level headed practical men' supported the idea, including the scholar R. P. Masani, who had almost joined the 1904 Commercial Mission to Iran, as well as Sir Dinshaw Petit, and the scholar and priest J. J. Modi.[110] In addition to economic opportunities, the secretary of the Amelioration Society, Jeejeebhoy Pestonji Mistry, optimistically claimed that there were about fifteen posts available in the Iranian government, which had 'publicly asked for applications from Parsee candidates willing to serve'.[111] Relations between the Iranian government and the Amelioration Society were seemingly inverted, with Iranians now appealing to Zoroastrians for help. Similar themes are reflected in another picture in the same edition, 'Mr Punch welcomed in the Ancient Land of the Parsees'.[112] Despite acknowledging that difficulties encountered might temper the 'popular cry' of 'To Iran',[113] Parsis, 'modern descendants of Zal and Rustom', were encouraged to emulate the legendary heroes of the *Shahnameh*, thereby reclaiming their ancient Persian past and forging a future in Iran.[114]

In the past, the Amelioration Society had primarily been concerned with the position of Zoroastrians in Iran, but, by 1910, Parsis were increasingly worried about the outlook for their community in India.[115] Thus, the prospect of government positions in Iran may have seemed appealing to Parsis, who were feeling marginalized in Indian politics, particularly after the 1909 Morley-Minto Reforms. Also known as the Indian Councils Act, these reforms were regarded by many Parsis as having privileged Muslims, as Muslims were granted separate electorates, which guaranteed Muslim representation on legislative councils, whereas Parsis were not.[116]

Whilst there were critics of communalism within the Parsi community, Sharafi has highlighted that during the 1910s, orthodox Parsis increasingly emphasized strong community boundaries and the idea of racial purity. In addition, there was a 'new nostalgia' for Persia.[117] This is also reflected in the emergence of a Parsi esoteric movement, *Ilm-e Khshnoom*, 'Path of Knowledge', in 1909. Its founder, Behramshah Naoroji Shroff (1858–1927), claimed to have been instructed by a group of Zoroastrian spiritual masters who lived on Mount Damavand in Iran, in a secret colony named Firdaus, 'Paradise'.[118] In light of Parsi interest in ancient Iran and their perceptions of the political situation in both Iran and India, Hinnells has argued that 'Shroff's teaching met the mood of the times for many'.[119]

Bearing this context in mind, it is not surprising that the content of the talks organized by Cooper fed into discussions in Bombay. In a front-page article, 'Parsis and Persia', the *Rast Goftar* referred to 'strongly divided' opinions over economic prospects for Parsis in 'their fatherland' during this 'transitional period'.[120] The writer exclaimed, 'If there was any moment facile to the establishment of Parsi influence in Persia it is the present.' However, despite supporting Parsi plans for commerce, caution was advised, and it was doubted that many Parsis would leave 'their adopted land'.[121] Judging from the 'acerbity' of discussions on the topic of Parsi relocation to Iran, the writer commented that one would expect there to be enough Parsis ready to set sail to form a colony. Although this was not the case, it was suggested that young Parsis might consider working for Zoroastrian trading houses in Iran. Overall, the author agreed with the recommendations made in London, and hoped that with greater numbers of Parsis visiting Iran, Iranians would have a greater awareness of the community and would 'welcome, even more cordially than now, social and business intercourse with the Parsis'.[122]

Having pointed out the challenges of undertaking economic activities in Iran, the *Times of India* reinforced the idea that Parsis were Persian, stating that 'Everyone with a spark of patriotism' would praise 'the increased interest that the Parsis are manifesting in the land from whence they sprang'.[123] Parsis were said to have 'natural advantages' in terms of developing trade with Iran; both the geographical position of Bombay and their 'racial affinity' with Iran would help them succeed.[124] The impact that business might have on Parsi influence in Iran was highlighted in an article in the *Rast Goftar*, which proposed that

> Parsis may find a good parallel in the history of the advent and growth of the power of Englishmen in India, who came to the country for trade, and are now its masters. Parsis may not likewise become rulers of Persia, but if they seek a revival of their power and prestige in the land of their forefathers their foundation should be laid on commercial grounds.[125]

In a later edition, the argument was made that Parsis were regarded by Iranians as 'long lost brothers', and as the 'ancient race of Persia'; therefore, 'At such a juncture, it is befitting Parsis should come to the rescue of their fatherland, and acquire immortal renown, stamping their name on history and civilisation'.[126] The situation in Iran was regarded as unprecedented: 'such an opportunity has occurred after 1,300 years, and if it is let slip will never recur.'[127] Thus, action was encouraged with exhortations that fused the credentials of the Parsis as the direct descendants of ancient Iranians together with their reputation as a modern community.

The *Rast Goftar* postulated that the warmth shown by Mehdi Khan towards Parsis in London had been stoked by a growing recognition amongst Iranians of 'the philanthropic and progressive work of Parsis in India'.[128] Parsi charity in Iran was also noted to have indirectly positively impacted trade and industry. Additionally, the *Rast Goftar* argued that the support directed towards the education of Iranian Zoroastrians could benefit Parsis, as it might result in a higher number of intermarriages between the two communities and a stronger Zoroastrian population. Although Parsis were keen to improve the position of their co-religionists in Iran, their interest in the country also appears to have been linked to the perceived decrease in the virility of their community, and the belief that their influence in India was diminishing.[129]

A critique of the view that a better life could be built in Iran was given by 'a Parsi' who wrote to the *Times of India*.[130] Tellingly, they chose to remain anonymous. Reflecting on the 'lurking affection' that Parsis felt towards their 'ancient fatherland', despite the hardships endured by their co-religionists, the author expressed their bemusement at the 'strange forms' taken by Parsi enthusiasm for Iran, such as the proposed Parsi colony 'gravely mooted' a few years earlier. Although some continued to 'hug the idea', the new scheme 'discussed with great interest' was related to trade. The author explicitly linked the suggestions being aired to contemporary political events: 'Persian affairs are being keenly watched by the Parsis, and the recent revolution there has had curious effects on many among them.'[131] These 'signs of awakening' led to 'visions of new fields opening out before them in that country'.[132] However, the article's author disagreed, asserting that the revolution had resulted in 'lawlessness . . . which has wellnigh killed trade altogether'.[133] They dismissed the notion that Parsis had been encouraged to apply for government posts in Iran, offering instead the explanation that after reading that Europeans might be appointed to administrative positions, some Parsis mistakenly assumed that they would be welcomed to take on these roles.[134] Linked to these hopes were concerns that Parsi influence in India had waned:

> The future of their people, according to many pessimists among them, is gloomy in this country; but they can have a bright future in Persia if only they resume their connection with their former fatherland, and seize the opportunities that present themselves under the new popular regime.[135]

Thus, Parsi plans for trade with Iran were bolstered by negative views regarding their position in India combined with positive perceptions of political change in Iran.

In November 1910, the Parsi Authors' Society and Writers' Association addressed Parsi-Persia relations, 'the question much canvassed of late', at a well-attended lecture delivered by the writer, Rustom P. Karkaria (1869–1919).[136] The society aimed to provide an arena for discussion on current community issues in the hope that, following the 'interchange of views' amongst members, the opinions of the wider Parsi public might be moulded along the 'right lines'.[137] Although Karkaria stated his support for any scheme beneficial to the community, he raised concerns about safety in Iran. In contrast to the rosy view that 'Persia had awakened' and was ready to embrace the original 'children of her soil', Karkaria stressed that there was ongoing lawlessness and argued that Parsis were still considered 'aliens' rather than compatriots.[138]

Passionate debate followed and contributions were made by Masani and Modi, who both supported the proposal of stronger trade links with Iran. Modi argued that religious fanaticism in Iran had decreased, partly due to the impact of the Bahá'í faith, and he viewed it as imperative that Parsis act before Muslims and Hindus seized commercial opportunities.[139] Likewise, Masani was keen to point out that there were openings for Parsis, and that the Majles was 'very friendly' towards them; he also regarded it as the 'duty' of Parsis 'to help in the present regeneration of Persia'.[140] Similar views were expressed in the *Habl al-Matin*, which printed a letter emphasizing that benefits would ensue for all parties.[141] Arguing that Parsis ought to cooperate to aid Iranian economic development, the suggestion was made that Zoroastrians could fund and staff a railroad to connect Yazd to Bandar Abbas.[142] The idea that this was a favourable moment for Parsi action was also emphasized in the title of a lecture delivered in Bombay by Syed Mohammad Bakir, 'Parsis to Persia – Now or Never'.[143] As well as being motivated by possible economic and political gains, some Parsis appear to have believed that they should take part in the development of Iran due to a sense of responsibility towards the whole of Iran, not just to their co-religionists living there.

The ancient heritage of the Parsis was sometimes explicitly cited to inspire involvement in Iran. This approach was taken by the Parsi legal historian and Iranist P. B. Watcha.[144] Originally printed in the *Parsi* between October and December 1910, articles by Watcha about the poet Ferdowsi were published as a booklet in 1911.

Funding was provided by Khan Bahadur B. D. Patel, who had promoted the Parsi colony scheme in 1904. The Preface stressed that the articles were written 'when efforts were made in many quarters to rouse the Parsis to take an active interest in their old, forgotten, far-off, father-land', a reference to the proposed trade deputation.[145] Watcha hoped to fuel Parsi pride in their glorious past, as described in the *Shahnameh*, and thus instill loyalty towards present-day Iran.[146] The articles were 'addressed primarily to Parsis' and supported an appeal to 'raise a memorial to Ferdowsi' in Tus, where he had been buried.[147] A memorial to Ferdowsi was later erected in Tus during the reign of Reza Shah, but it is noteworthy that Parsis were already discussing the idea in 1911.[148]

According to Watcha, Parsis were indebted to Ferdowsi, as his *Shahnameh* enabled them 'among the myriad races of India, to hold our heads up, as a remnant of the imperial and magnificent race' at a time of 'competition and racial conflicts'.[149] Critical of Parsis who spoke 'feeble' and 'foreign' Gujarati and did not know Persian,[150] Watcha argued that the loss of their ancestral language had contributed to Parsis becoming 'degenerate and denationalised'.[151] Watcha drew on an idealized vision of the pre-Islamic era; he argued that there was equality between women and men in ancient Iran, and that 'the subjugation and degradation of women is *essentially un-Iranian and un-Zoroastrian*'.[152] Despite being in India for more than a thousand years, Watcha asserted that Parsis could not 'pretend to share the nationalism which inspires the heart of the genuine Indian', as they had 'remained essentially *un-Indian*'.[153] The reaction of some Parsis to the suggestion that members of the community ought to go to Iran disappointed Watcha:

> What is more disheartening is that if some ardent spirits succeed in infusing into us some enthusiasm for the past we have forgotten, and the father-land we are exiles from, there are not wanting persons among ourselves, who are not ashamed to ridicule a sentiment they are not fit to share. No people who are thus denationalised can achieve anything. We are denationalised; we have not, with all our vaulted claims, achieved anything worthy of a great nation in these 1300 years; and we shall not while we continue thus.[154]

Watcha connected appreciation of the *Shahnameh* to 'a strong sentiment for our living, though bleeding, mother-country, Iran',[155] a reflection of where he believed the allegiance of the Parsi community ought to lie.

Lectures delivered by Professor A. V. W. Jackson touched on similar themes. Jackson regarded Ferdowsi as the Parsis' 'own national poet',[156] and his own work on Zoroastrianism is described by Monica Ringer as being nationalistic in tone.[157] In April 1911, a prizegiving was organized for students of the Sir Jamsetjee Madressa in honour of Jackson's return to Bombay after a long absence.[158] After reading a report on the school, J. J. Modi offered Jackson a selection of books that reportedly highlighted 'the great advancement the Parsis had been steadily making in the cultivation of their own ancient Iranian literature'.[159] As well as encouraging research into the ancient past, Modi was interested in exploring economic opportunities in Iran. Thus, he made plans to travel to Iran with Jackson so that he might assess the situation. In view of his intentions, Parsis presented Modi with an address that made reference to the 'controversy raging . . . as to the desirability or otherwise of their going to Persia'. The hope was expressed that Modi would use his experiences to 'enable them to form an enlightened opinion on the subject'.[160] Modi thanked the community for the honour granted to him, and stated his wish that his travels would lead other Parsis to 'renew their interest in the Fatherland'.[161]

Discussions regarding the trade deputation continued into 1911, but advice from the British legation in Tehran swayed Masani and many others against the idea.[162] At a time when the British were increasingly concerned about safety along trade routes,[163] there was widespread agreement amongst Parsis that it would be wise to postpone action. However, despite the risks, some remained hopeful.[164] Khan Bahadur B. D. Patel continued to promote both the colony scheme and commercial involvement in Iran, particularly as he believed Parsis faced growing competition with Hindus and Muslims in India.[165] At the root of the opposing stances were contrasting opinions regarding the position of Parsis in India. Whereas Patel had a pessimistic outlook, Karkaria was adamant that India was their home. Karkaria argued that Parsis 'could participate in the great future which awaits that country if they only proved true to themselves and to India, and did not think of running away to Persia'.[166] Questions were also raised about the status of Zoroastrians in Iran; Parsis in Bombay were in correspondence with Cooper, and some expressed doubts over the extent to which attitudes towards Zoroastrians had changed.[167]

Despite the turbulent conditions in Iran, Cooper appeared to remain optimistic. In June 1911, he organized another reception and invited Edward Browne to be the guest speaker. Browne was a supporter of the constitutionalist cause, and had campaigned against the policies of the British foreign secretary, Edward Grey, vis-à-vis Iran.[168] Addressing his audience on 'The Duty of the Zoroastrian Community towards Regenerate Persia',[169] Browne reinforced the view held by some Parsis that, as Persians, they ought to contribute to the success of Iran. There were almost one hundred guests, including seventeen Parsi women, Sir Jamsetjee Jejeebhoy and three prominent Iranian constitutionalists: Yahya Dowlatabadi, Mirza Hasan Khan Sa'ed al-Vozara and Sayyed Zia' al-Din Tabataba'i, who had edited *Sharq*, a newspaper funded in part by Iranian Zoroastrians.[170] Cooper emphasized that Iranians wanted Parsis to return, not because the Majles was in financial need but because they 'had among them men with brains, able to organise movements, to develop commerce, and to establish great industrial undertakings'.[171] By taking part in this renaissance, Parsis would prevent the interference of 'Western speculators', and would help safeguard the independence of Iran.[172] Urging his audience to put aside 'stupid notions' that Parsis would not reach high administrative positions in Iran, Cooper encouraged them to use their resources and expertise to preserve the Iranian 'customs, manners and language' from Western influence.[173] Parsis would thus contribute to the modernization of Iran, and lessen the likelihood of European intervention.

After Cooper's introductory remarks, Browne delivered his speech. He claimed that Iranians recognized the inherent qualities of the Parsis, which he believed had been enhanced by the education they had received under British rule.[174] Suggesting that Parsis could play a leading role in the industrial regeneration of Iran, Browne stated that they should cooperate for 'the good of the Fatherland'.[175] By comparing the significance of Iran for Parsis with that of Palestine for Jews, Browne gave a 'vigorous and earnest appeal to the Parsis to look upon Persia as their real home'.[176] Additionally, he pointed out that although Iranians were suspicious of foreign influence, they regarded the Parsis as 'belonging to themselves'.[177] Indeed, a few months later, the suggestion was made in the Majles that employing Parsis to teach at Dar al-Fonun would help end the reliance on foreign instructors.[178] In support of the points made by Browne, Yahya Dowlatabadi highlighted that Zoroastrians were protected by the new constitution. Dowlatabadi spoke in Persian, and it was reported that 'the cheers with which some of his remarks were greeted showed that many of the Parsis present were able to follow him', reflecting that a proportion of the Parsi community were familiar with the language.[179]

However, towards the end of 1911, Parsi enthusiasm for greater involvement in Iran was affected by news of widespread insecurity, and specific reports that Zoroastrians in Kerman were being threatened.[180] Momentum was also lost after the death of Cooper by suicide in August 1911.[181] Speculations were made that one factor leading Cooper to take his own life was the outcome of a legal case against Sir Mancherjee Bhownaggree, which was apparently related to an argument between the two men about a proposed £1,000,000 loan to Iran.[182] Details remain unclear, and Bhownaggree dismissed all the allegations,[183] but it is possible that the sum referenced was linked to the earlier attempt to secure a loan from the Parsis.

Although commercial plans were paused, there was ongoing Parsi interest in Iranian affairs, and despite their reputation for loyalty to the British,[184] members of the community expressed their disapproval of both British policies and Russian aggression (Plate 7).[185] In this respect, Bonakdarian has highlighted Parsi involvement in the Calcutta-based Persia's Defence Society, which was active from 1910, if not before. The society claimed to represent 50,000 Persians living in India, many of whom would have been Parsis, and Bonakdarian has noted that J. J. Modi may have been its president.[186] The threat to Iranian independence from the Russian advance on Tehran in late 1911 angered the Zoroastrian community in India, as well as Iranian Muslim expatriates, and an article in *East & West* suggested that this had brought the different communities closer together.[187] Action was also taken by Madame Cama, who arranged for telegrams to be sent from Iranians in Paris in opposition to Russo-British policies.[188]

Iranian Zoroastrians in India contributed to the criticisms made of the British at this time, and may have influenced the broader Zoroastrian community. Anxiety about the situation in Iran was expressed in the *Parsi*, a journal that encouraged relations with Iran but was largely loyal to the British.[189] The *Parsi* reported that Iranian Zoroastrians in Bombay urged the British government to act; they had sent a resolution to the prime minister, Henry Asquith, and the foreign secretary, Edward Grey, to this effect.[190] Indeed, the second point made in the resolution was that

> this meeting humbly craves the sympathies of civilised nations for the cause of liberty in Persia and earnestly appeals to them and the British Government to use their moral influence in supporting Persia in her attempts to safeguard her liberty and integrity for which she has been striving with patience.[191]

Constitutional rule is restored 139

| 20 | HINDI PUNCH. | [BOMBAY, DECEMBER 31, 1911. |

THE BOA CONSTRICTOR.
(POOR CAT!)

Plate 7 The Boa Constrictor

(Poor cat!)

The perversity of the Persian Parliament has given to Russia its wished-for opportunity to pounce upon the whole of North Persia, which is now virtually in its whole hands.

NB the cat wears a sash with 'Persia' written on it, and the snake has 'Russia' written on its body.

© British Library Board (Asia, Pacific & Africa SV 576, *Hindi Punch*, 31 December 1911, 20).

Whilst the resolution did not succeed in securing British support for the Majles, it does reflect how Zoroastrians in India tried to utilize their good relations with the British to protect the gains of the Constitutional Revolution.

Post-constitutional 'chaos' and World War

Attempts to save the Second Majles failed, and in December 1911, the assembly was dissolved in the face of Russian demands.[192] The self-determination of Iran was threatened; Russian troops occupied areas in the north, the British used relations with local power bases to consolidate their control in the south, and there was a high level of foreign involvement in military and economic affairs.[193] Martial law was declared and nearly three years passed before the Majles briefly reconvened.[194] Seemingly a time of chaos, the years between the Second Majles and the coup of Reza Khan in 1921 have often been regarded as a time of 'disintegration'.[195]

This assessment has been critiqued by Oliver Bast, who has argued that when the period is dismissed as a caesura, elements of continuity from previous years are overlooked. As well as being utilized to legitimize Reza Khan's rise to power, Bast has suggested that due to its 'historiographical usefulness', the 'discourse of disintegration' has also been promoted by individuals who have been critical of the Pahlavi shahs, as it serves to create a clean break between the Constitutional Revolution and the Pahlavi era.[196] Stephanie Cronin has also questioned the 'catastrophic perspective', pointing out that institutions established during the revolution did not all come to an end in 1911. Although the Majles did not convene regularly between 1911 and 1921, it did survive in the long term.[197] Additionally, Marashi has highlighted that rather than being a time of stagnation, these were the years when the type of nationalism that was later propagated by the Pahlavi shahs gained ground, and the 'new nationalist model' emerged.[198] Conceptually linked to the views of nineteenth-century nationalists such as Akhundzadeh, this form of nationalism glorified pre-Islamic Iran, a development that was therefore of relevance to the Zoroastrian community in Iran.

Nationalists were keen to limit foreign interference in Iran, but Zoroastrians initially continued to draw on long-standing relations with the British, principally when the community faced danger.[199] Fearing that government control did not stretch to Yazd, in June 1912, the Zoroastrian Anjoman wrote to Bhownaggree, hoping that his political standing in London could be used to their advantage.[200] Bhownaggree swiftly alerted the Foreign Office and stated that his co-religionists desired 'immediate British protection or naturalisation'. According to Bhownaggree, this revealed the severity of the situation, as Zoroastrians usually expressed loyalty to the Iranian government. The British agreed to safeguard the community, 'whose welfare His Majesty's Government take a special interest', but could not offer naturalization to Zoroastrians who were residents of Iran.[201] Despite reassurances from the British, conditions in Yazd remained challenging, and 'Naib Hossein', a 'notorious ex-outlaw', seized control of the city soon after.[202] Even after order was restored in 1913, there were further outbreaks of violence against Zoroastrians.[203]

Although the British offered some assistance to Zoroastrians, the strength of relations between the British and Zoroastrians in Iran was tested at this time. Not only did the British reproach the Jamshidian company for negatively impacting regional security by trading in arms,[204] but the demands made by the British and Russian banks for the repayment of loans contributed to both the Jahanian and Jamshidian firms going bankrupt.[205] Early in 1913, the office of the Jamshidian firm in Kerman was forcibly closed by the Russian consul and a group of Cossack soldiers.[206] The firm played a significant role in the economy of Kerman, and local authorities were angered by the measures taken by the consul and appealed to Tehran.[207] Arbab Jamshid took refuge in the home of the prime minister, whilst Kaykhosrow Shahrokh negotiated a reduction in the sum to be repaid to the Russians.[208] The Zoroastrian firms also owed money to the British, which led to tension between the British and the Zoroastrian community. Dissatisfied by the slow pace at which Zoroastrians were settling their debts, in February 1913, the new consul in Kerman refused to satisfy the Zoroastrian Anjoman of Kerman's requests for written confirmation of British protection.[209]

As well as weakening Zoroastrian relations with the British and the Russians, the collapse of these companies consolidated Kaykhosrow Shahrokh's position as a leading figure in the community.[210] Shahrokh also continued to be involved in broader political issues after the suspension of the Majles and he had kept his position in the Audit Office.[211] This role was unpaid, and Shahrokh later described how he had felt it was his duty as an Iranian to undertake the work.[212] In 1914, Shahrokh was chosen to represent Zoroastrians in the Third Majles, and he was subsequently involved in organizing the coronation of Ahmad Shah.[213] Elections for the Third Majles had been prompted by the young shah coming of age, as the constitution directed that the formal accession of the monarch had to be legitimized by the assembly.[214]

Beyond Iran, the constitution upheld its status as a symbol of positive change for Zoroastrians, notwithstanding the dissolution of the Second Majles. In an early issue of the *Journal of the Iranian Association*, Khodayar Dastur Sheriar Irani accepted that conditions in Iran were currently difficult but emphasized that a 'bright future' lay ahead.[215] Established in 1911, the Iranian Association countered the opinions of orthodox Parsis and Theosophists, and aimed to maintain the 'purity' of Zoroastrianism and to promote the welfare of Parsis.[216] The article by Irani focused on the position of Zoroastrians in Iran. Irani argued that 'modern education and civilization' had led some Iranians to regard Zoroastrians as a

> constructive and not a destructive element in the formation and preservation of the Persian Government. They knew that if there was any true sympathiser who would help them in preserving the power, integrity, independence and splendour of their beloved fatherland, it was the Zoroastrian community alone.[217]

Muslims were beginning 'to court' the 'friendship and help' of Zoroastrians, particularly in Tehran,[218] and Zoroastrians were viewed by some as 'the only true and faithful sons of the soil', and as 'descendants of the old famous Persians' who had 'pure Iranian blood running through their veins'.[219] Irani claimed that there were even Muslims who were 'inclined to embrace the Zoroastrian faith'.[220] Evidently, he believed that Zoroastrians had benefitted from the events of recent years.

Echoing views aired during the period of the Second Majles, in another article, Irani encouraged Parsis to do everything possible to support this 'new era of progress and prosperity',[221] particularly as Iranians looked to them as 'men capable of rendering all sorts of valuable service to their country, to which they consider us legitimately to belong'.²²² Similar to earlier appeals, Irani hoped that more Parsis would learn Persian, for practical as well as sentimental reasons, as some might consider 'sharing in the national regeneration of Persia'.²²³ Significantly, although Irani acknowledged the need to help Zoroastrians, he believed that Parsis, who were respected in Iran for their philanthropic works, ought to extend the reach of their charity to benefit all Iranians.²²⁴

Prioritizing education, Irani outlined that schools should be open to children of all faiths, as this would 'promote the work of national regeneration by scattering the seeds of a common culture in the minds of the rising generation and moulding their character'.²²⁵ These opinions were shared by other Zoroastrians in India; for example, in addition to leaving over 15,000 rupees to Zoroastrians in Iran in his will, Sheheriar Aspandiar Irani, a trader of musical instruments, also chose to fund the education of poor Persians, 'without distinction of caste and creed'.²²⁶ The drive for Zoroastrian-run schools to be non-sectarian was in part based on the hope that this inclusive philanthropy would further the integration of Zoroastrians in Iranian society.

Improvements in the status of Zoroastrians in Iran were also highlighted by some Muslims in India. Speaking at a public lecture chaired by J. J. Modi, H. M. Qasem Irani, professor of Persian at Aligarh College, exclaimed that a Muslim had laid the foundation stone for a fire temple in Tehran, providing 'proof positive of the good feelings' towards Zoroastrians.²²⁷ Describing Parsis as descendants of ancient Persians, he proposed that they ought to visit Iran, learn Persian to strengthen their 'solidarity', and have a 'national uniform dress', so that they could be recognized as 'remnants of a mighty glorious nation' amongst the inhabitants of India.²²⁸ After the lecture, the Parsi scholar Gushtaspshah Kaikhushro (G. K.) Nariman added that the history of the Persian kings, as described in the *Shahnameh*, should be taught in schools.²²⁹

In London, members of the Persia Society also advocated greater Parsi engagement with Iran. This society was founded in 1911 and was nominally a cultural organization. However, similar to the overtly political Persia Committee, with which it had an overlapping membership, it did sometimes criticize the policies of the British government.²³⁰ One member, Arthur Campbell Yate, reiterated that southern Iran was open to Parsi enterprise and urged Parsis to work together with Muslims in defence of Iranian independence.²³¹ In support of his appeal for united action, Yate referenced a comment made by Bhownaggree that Muslims, Christians and Zoroastrians all worshipped the same God.²³² Bhownaggree had attended the Persia Society's first dinner,²³³ and its members socialized with Parsis at other events, including the Nowruz celebrations in 1914. On this occasion, the president of the Persia Society, Lord Lamington, remarked that he was pleased to hear that Parsis were giving more funds to help Zoroastrians in Iran than they had when he was governor of Bombay (1903–7). He referred to the 10,000 rupees collected after a deputation of Iranian Zoroastrians recently travelled to India to place before the Parsis 'the needs of the community in the fatherland'. Sykes was also present at the Nowruz party; he exhorted Parsis to take an interest in Iranian affairs and recommended that Zoroastrians in Britain join the Persia Society.²³⁴ However, with the onset of the First World War (1914–18), hopes for a strong and independent Iran seemed further out of reach, and fewer criticisms of the policies of Edward Grey were voiced in Britain.²³⁵

The shah declared Iranian neutrality in November 1914, but this did not prevent foreign troops from fighting in Iran during the war.[236] Due to anger at British and Russian actions in the past, members of the Democrat party tended to adopt a pro-German position.[237] Consequently, when Russian soldiers advanced towards Tehran in November 1915, there were disagreements amongst Majles deputies as to how they should react, and a significant number left the city to form an alternative provisional government.[238] Shahrokh was asked by the premier, Mostowfi al-Mamalek, to negotiate between the factions, reflecting the respect in which he was held.[239] However, no agreement could be reached and the Third Majles came to a premature end.

Ottoman and Russian forces invaded and occupied areas in western and northern Iran, whilst the Germans focused their efforts on the southern provinces, hoping to open a land route to Afghanistan to facilitate an attack on India. The German commander Wilhelm Wassmuss, known as the 'German Lawrence', collaborated with anti-British Iranians, including tribal leaders, Democrats and some members of the ulama,[240] and encouraged Iranians to attack British forces and consulates.[241] In response, the British formed a militia, the South Persia Rifles (SPR). This was headed by the ex-consul of Kerman Percy Sykes, who strengthened existing ties with tribes in the region. Despite these alliances, the force was widely unpopular and became a target for anti-British resistance.[242] The south of Iran was strategically significant for the British, partly due to the oil installations of the Anglo-Persian Oil Company. These were effectively under British government control and were critically important in terms of fuelling the British navy.[243] By 1917, the Allies had occupied most of Iran, but the Russian Revolution that year resulted in the withdrawal of Russian troops and the cancellation of imperial treaties, including the 1907 Anglo-Russian Convention. Subsequently, the British maintained a military presence in Iran, partly to prevent the spread of Bolshevism.[244] Iranians suffered greatly during this period; as well as the direct effects of war, poor harvests led to widespread famine, the impact of which was exacerbated by the spread of diseases, including influenza and cholera.[245] Regarded as being fair and honest, Shahrokh was appointed by the prime minister to oversee the distribution of grain and to prevent hoarding.[246]

According to Jamsheed Choksy, political and economic instability during the war was particularly unfavourable for minorities.[247] This is reflected in reports of Iranian Zoroastrians emigrating to India.[248] However, although some Zoroastrians sought safety under British rule, the tension felt following the bankruptcy of the Jamshidian and Jahanian firms does not appear to have fully dissipated. In 1915, the British consul in Kerman attempted to remove the local *kargozar*, the official responsible for overseeing relations with foreigners, as he was 'politically active in the German interests' and 'anti-English'.[249] The *kargozar* was apparently helping people avoid repaying their debts to the British; amongst these individuals was a Zoroastrian, who had been encouraged by the *kargozar* to take *bast* in 'the house of a Persian Mulla'.[250] Not only were Zoroastrians seemingly on good terms with some Muslims in Kerman, but they also sent a telegram to Tehran asking that the *kargozar* retain his position. This led the consul to question in exasperation: 'Am I to continue to protect a community which work actively to upset my plans?'[251] Relations were clearly strained. Furthermore, Choksy has described how Zoroastrians were pleased when a German-led tribal revolt forced the British to leave

Kerman, as they anticipated this would lead to greater national autonomy.[252] When Sykes regained control over Kerman in 1916, local Zoroastrians were punished for their dealings with German agents, and two 'leading' Zoroastrian merchant-houses, 'Surushiyan and Kayanian', were fined for buying British items that had been seized by the Germans.[253] There were also several instances where Zoroastrians were arrested because of suspected links with Wassmuss.[254]

The British were not solely concerned about the weakening of relations with Zoroastrians in Iran. Echoing earlier worries about the spread of pro-Russian views, the possibility was raised that through their links with their co-religionists, Iranian Zoroastrian merchants might influence attitudes further afield, for instance in Bombay.[255] Although Iranian Zoroastrians were more likely than Parsis to hold anti-British views, Foreign Office records about 'C. Hormusji (alias Hasan, Ali Khan)', a Parsi who was arrested in Iran in 1916, highlight British concerns regarding transnational anti-British cooperation. Hormusji was found to be carrying bombs 'intended for the murder of British Officers', as well as 'seditious literature in connection with the Ghadar, "mutiny", party'.[256] Founded in 1913 by Indians in San Francisco, the Ghadar party was a revolutionary anti-colonial organization with a predominantly Sikh membership.[257] Ghadar members were also involved in the Indian Independence Committee (IIC), which was established in Germany at the beginning of the war and which had German and Ottoman support. The IIC brought together groups that opposed British imperialism, and amongst the individuals who contributed to its activities was the former Majles deputy Hasan Taqizadeh.[258] Additionally, Taqizadeh was part of the 'Iranian Committee for Cooperation with Germany', which assisted Wassmuss and other German agents active in Iran.[259]

Between 1916 and 1922, Taqizadeh edited a newspaper called *Kaveh*. This was named after the legendary blacksmith and hero of the *Shahnameh*, who led an uprising to overthrow the tyrannical rule of Zahak. According to Marashi, the name chosen for the journal can be seen as representing the 'combination of a popularizing tone and a new nationalist sentiment'.[260] *Kaveh* received financial backing from the German government during the war; as well as criticizing Allied activity in Iran, the paper encouraged the Iranian government to offer support to the Ottomans, emphasizing that they were fellow-Muslims.[261] Articles were primarily about political events, but some discussed Iranian history and literature. These themes became more pronounced in the post-war editions of *Kaveh*, which were more focused on the glories of ancient Iran.[262] Other Iranian expatriates, such as Ebrahim Purdavud, worked in collaboration with Taqizadeh to promote similar views. Just before the war broke out, Purdavud had published a short-lived nationalistic newspaper called *Iranshahr*, and he then contributed to *Rastakhiz* (*Resurrection*), a newspaper first printed in 1915 in Baghdad. However, in 1916, the Ottomans ordered the closure of *Rastakhiz* because rather than encouraging pan-Islamism, the newspaper was promoting nationalistic ideas that drew on the pre-Islamic period of Iranian history.[263]

By the end of the war, the ancient past was becoming more prominent in nationalist discourse. In his 1918 pamphlet, 'Researches about Zoroaster', Hosayn Danesh, an Iranian expatriate in Constantinople, wrote the following:

Knowest thou why after thousands of years the modern Persian is seeking Zoroastrian medicine for the cure of his spiritual ailments? This is the reason, that when Persia's star was in the ascendant . . . the rule was the rule of the Zoroastrians.[264]

Not only was Zoroastrianism referenced in discussions regarding reform on a national scale, but Zoroastrian projects were also given support from Iranian politicians. For instance, a Zoroastrian school was established in Tehran 'under Government auspices', and in 1917, a fire temple was consecrated by Ebrahim Hakimi, a prominent politician and Freemason, in the presence of members of the ulama.[265] The Tehran fire temple had been funded by two Parsi sisters, Zarbai and Sunabai Dubash, and Talinn Grigor has pointed out that due to improvements in the position of Zoroastrians following the revolution, it was safe enough for the building to be constructed along the lines of the Parsi 'open plan' temples.[266] As president of the Tehran Zoroastrian Anjoman, Shahrokh had been involved in the project. In Grigor's opinion, his 'commitment to Iran's modernization through the promotion of Zoroastrian heritage' explains the architectural style, which was influenced by Shahrokh's appreciation of Parsi designs that drew on the ancient past.[267]

The elevation of the pre-Islamic period by nationalists was also reflected in the drive to 'purify' Persian, which, out of the numerous languages spoken in Iran, had been declared in the constitution to be the official national language.[268] In 1916, *Nameh-ye Parsi*, a journal written in 'pure Persian', was founded by Abu al-Qasem Azad Maraghah'i. Fearing the possible colonization of Iran and the impact this would have on the Persian language, he emphasized the urgency of language reform and the purification of the language from foreign words.[269] The journal included correspondence from Zoroastrians and positive references to members of the community, who were viewed as true Persians. Shahrokh was praised for his work in the Majles and was mentioned in the context of discussions about the Persian language.[270] Echoing views expressed by Hataria in the nineteenth century, Shahrokh criticized the use of 'foreign' vocabulary, and was proud of having introduced 'pure Persian words in the Majles'.[271] In February 1911, he had asked deputies to protect the 'national language' by refraining from using 'foreign words',[272] and he had also promoted the use of 'pure' Persian in his writing, for example in his articles for *Neda-ye Vatan*.[273]

Utilizing his position in the Majles, Shahrokh worked to improve relations between Zoroastrians and Muslims in Iran. When a Zoroastrian was killed by a servant of the governor of Kerman, Shahrokh successfully insisted that the governor implement laws regarding religious equality, without calling on the British or Parsis for support.[274] Relations with Parsis were sometimes tense, for instance when Ardeshir Reporter interfered in the 1917 elections for the Zoroastrian Anjoman of Yazd.[275] Shahrokh had been influenced by Parsi ideas concerning religious reform, but now Iranian Zoroastrians were now asserting their independence from their co-religionists, in this instance in the political sphere. The matter of Reporter's meddling in the elections was taken by Shahrokh to the Iranian prime minister, 'Ala' al-Saltaneh, resulting in cooler relations between Shahrokh and the British, who had supported Reporter during the dispute.[276]

Although there were exceptions, Zoroastrians in India were predominantly loyal to the British during the war. In 1914, the Iranian Zoroastrian community in Bombay donated 5,000 rupees to the War and Relief Fund, and Dinshah J. Irani expressed their allegiance to British rule.[277] Similar declarations were made by Parsis and some members of the community fought in the British army.[278] Burjor Rustamji Karanjia was a Parsi soldier who was posted in Iran and was effusively praised by Jehangir Barjorji Sanjana for

> infusing into the Iranian youths his great selfless love for the old land and his overabundant enthusiasm to see Iran integral and independent, and multitudes of them followed at his call.[279]

This later account by Sanjana highlights the continued significance of ancient and contemporary Iran for some Parsis.[280]

Indeed, lectures about the history of Iran were delivered by Parsis during the war, for example, by J. J. Modi and S. H. Jhabvala.[281] The *Shahnameh* continued to be celebrated,[282] and a guide to learning Persian was published by Hormasji Tehmulji Dadachanji.[283] References to the Persian heritage of the Parsis were sometimes linked to claims of racial superiority; according to David Mellor, these views had grown stronger due to rising Parsi concerns about their future in India.[284] Following celebrations held in 1916 to mark the 1,200-year anniversary of the arrival of the 'religious exiles' in India, it was noted that, although this was a 'sufficiently long period to make them Indians', Parsis were a distinct group because of their 'strict solicitude for their religion and race'.[285] There was a concurrent solidifying of an Iranian Zoroastrian, or Irani, identity, and in 1918 the Iranian Zoroastrian Anjoman of Bombay was founded. This organization later helped establish schools and orphanages in Yazd, and shared information with Parsis about the Zoroastrian community in Iran.[286]

Whilst Parsis largely continued to express loyalty towards the British, the Second Majles had reignited their interest in Iran and in their Persian heritage; this continued after the Majles was dissolved and during the turbulent years of war. In Iran, the pre-Islamic period was increasingly being cited by nationalists, a trend that was set to become even more pronounced in the following years.

7

The 'Awakening' of Pahlavi Iran

Zoroastrians and the post-war political landscape

Anger at foreign interference in Iran had been exacerbated by the events of the First World War. Hoping for greater independence, Iranian nationalists looked back to the powerful empires of the pre-Islamic period as a source of inspiration.[1] The glorification of ancient Iran, which was potentially positive for Zoroastrians, occurred at a time when the British, who had offered some support to Zoroastrians in the past, faced growing criticism from Iranian nationalists.

One reason for this animosity was that, in contrast to other foreign powers, Britain had maintained a military presence in Iran, even after peace was declared.[2] Another factor was the proposed Anglo-Persian Agreement of 1919. This was the outcome of secret negotiations between a small group of individuals, including the British foreign secretary, Lord Curzon, the British minister in Tehran, Sir Percy Cox, and the new prime minister of Iran, Vosuq al-Dowleh. Mansour Bonakdarian has stated that the treaty was 'tantamount to the establishment of a virtual British protectorate over Persia'.[3] Whilst the agreement maintained that Iran would be independent, it permitted wide-ranging British involvement in financial and military matters in exchange for a £2,000,000 loan.[4] The treaty was not ratified by the Majles, which was a constitutional requirement, and it was subsequently suspended when Vosuq al-Dowleh was removed from office in June 1920.[5]

Vosuq al-Dowleh has often been viewed as a traitor for his role in drawing up the agreement, but Philip Henning Grobien has argued that he was a nationalist who believed that British intervention was necessary for the successful implementation of reforms in post-war Iran.[6] Similarly, Oliver Bast has argued that the negative assessment of the years between the Constitutional Revolution and the rise of Reza Khan has impacted views of the agreement, contributing to the widespread vilification of Vosuq al-Dowleh.[7] Ali Ansari has pointed out that elements of the treaty corresponded to some of the aims of the Iranian delegates who attended the 1919 Paris Peace Conference. However, the Anglo-Persian Agreement was just between Britain and Iran rather than a group of nations, and this was an issue that prompted international criticism, particularly from France and the United States of America.[8] In contrast to the approach taken by Vosuq al-Dowleh, the Iranian delegation at the peace talks believed that modernization was possible without British involvement, a claim that had popular appeal in Iran.[9] Thus, the Anglo-Persian Agreement faced opposition from Iranians.[10]

Indeed, Shahrokh, who was in the United States of America in August 1919, reportedly filed a protest against it with the US secretary of state, Robert Lansing.[11] Later British records describe Shahrokh as a staunch nationalist, who had never shown a great affection towards the British,[12] and the position he took in 1919 can also be seen in relation to his earlier frustration at British officials.

Criticisms of the Anglo-Persian Agreement were also voiced in private by the Government of India. As well as concerns over the financial implications, Bonakdarian has noted that there were fears that the agreement would strengthen opposition to British rule in India, particularly amongst Muslims.[13] The cancellation of the partition of Bengal in 1911 and the fact that Britain and the Ottoman Empire were on opposite sides during the war had already weakened the loyalty of Muslims towards the British. In 1916, the 'Lucknow Pact' was signed by the Muslim League and the Indian National Congress (INC), whereby both groups agreed to push for self-governance within the British Empire after the end of the war.[14] Over one million Indian soldiers were posted overseas during the war, of whom 50,000–70,000 died.[15] Even though Indians had made this vital contribution to the Allied war effort, British oppression in India was only further enforced when peace was declared. In 1919, the 'Rowlatt Acts' was passed, which permitted the imprisonment of Indians without trial.[16] Soon after, Mohandas Gandhi, who was becoming increasingly involved in the Indian nationalist movement, led a campaign of non-violent resistance, *satyagraha*, against the new laws.[17] Calls for the end of British rule intensified after April 1919, when, under the orders of Reginald Dyer, hundreds of peaceful protesters and attendees of a religious festival were massacred at Jallianwala Bagh in Amritsar.[18] By the end of 1920, there was a degree of unity between Hindus and Muslims in terms of support for Gandhi's proposed strategy of non-violent non-cooperation.[19] This included the boycotting of foreign-made goods and British institutions, marking a shift in the tactics used by the INC, which had previously encouraged reform via constitutional methods.

Despite Gandhi's hopes for Parsi participation in the Non-Cooperation Movement, there was little support from the community.[20] One reason for this was the economic impact it would have on Parsis, for example, on merchants who benefitted from importing and exporting goods. In addition, the majority of Parsis had been wary of the INC for years, even when Dadabhai Naoroji, Pherozeshah Mehta and Dinshaw Wacha were heavily involved, and they were now increasingly concerned by the direction it was taking, especially as the growing nationalist movement appeared to be more closely tied to Hinduism.[21] Recent reforms had affirmed that Muslims would be treated as a separate electorate, and, although Sir Jamsetjee Jejeebhoy had asked for similar concessions, Parsis had not been granted communal representation.[22] According to Kulke, the anxiety felt by Parsis over the loss of their political power led to the strengthening of group boundaries, reflected in the establishment of communalist associations.[23] Likewise, Dinyar Patel has described how Parsis emphasized their loyalty to the British and also distanced themselves from their surroundings:

> in a curious process of mental gymnastics with their ancient Persian ancestry, Parsis even started to argue that they were themselves foreigners, more Iranian than Indian.[24]

The view that Parsis were pure Persians was not new, but developments in India resulted in this idea rising to prominence.

The Persian heritage of the community was referenced by a Parsi who wrote to the *Times of India* and suggested that, due to their relations with the British, the Anglo-Persian Agreement gave Parsis the chance to fulfil their duty to 'assist in the development of the ancient land of Iran'.[25] Ardeshir Reporter also tried to stimulate such sentiments when he visited Bombay in 1919; he highlighted post-war openings for Parsis and emphasized that Iranian Muslims held the culture of the pre-Islamic era in high esteem.[26] Schemes proposed by Reporter to strengthen ties with Iran were welcomed by some members of the community, although 'G. K. N.', likely to be G. K. Nariman, pointed out that these claims of 'attachment' to Iran did not even inspire a single Parsi to travel back with Reporter in May 1919.[27]

Concern about the 'unsettled state' of Iran was expressed by the president of the Iranian Association, H. J. Bhabha, but despite this, he cautiously anticipated closer relations between Parsis and Iranians in the future.[28] The idea of a Parsi colony resurfaced in the association's journal, and Iran was described as the true home of the Parsis.[29] This notion that Parsis were disconnected from their environment in India is also seen in the hope articulated by the author, S. H. Jhabvala, for a revival of Parsi 'nationalism'.[30] Likewise, the *Times of India* observed that a group of Parsis were keen for the community to have its own national flag, reminiscent of the standard of the legendary blacksmith, Kaveh, a hero in the *Shahnameh*.[31] There was also talk of funding a memorial to Ferdowsi, which a Parsi correspondent to the *Times of India* linked to a rise in 'nationalism' in the community.[32]

Positive views of contemporary Iran were expressed by Parsis who met with Ahmad Shah when he visited London in November 1919.[33] On handing the shah an illuminated address signed by over one hundred individuals, including 'many Parsee ladies', Bhownaggree mentioned the 'peaceful and prosperous existence' awaiting Zoroastrians in Iran.[34] Reference was made to the 'equality of opportunity and treatment' under his 'constitutional reign', highlighting the perceived significance of the revolution.[35] Having encountered strong opposition to the Anglo-Persian Agreement in Paris, Ahmad Shah did not officially endorse the treaty whilst in London,[36] but Parsis spoke of their enthusiasm for the treaty, particularly in terms of Parsi loyalty to both Britain and Iran. In turn, the shah voiced his pleasure at receiving the Parsis, who reminded him of 'the glorious traditions of the Fatherland', and he praised the Zoroastrian community in Iran:

> I admire their particular qualities of love for the Fatherland, intelligence, probity, perseverance, laboriousness – all of which fit them to contribute very effectively to the common task of increasing the prosperity of the country.[37]

Echoing the words of the Parsi address, Ahmad Shah reassured his audience that Zoroastrians had 'full rights as Persian citizens', which were guaranteed by the constitution.[38]

However, attempts made to weaken divisions between Zoroastrians and Muslims in Iran were not always welcomed. According to British records, the ulama in

Yazd initiated a boycott of Zoroastrian businesses in October 1920, because 'Parsi [Zoroastrian] schoolboys were dressed in khaki drill clothing and Persian hats instead of the usual Parsi costume'.[39] This reaction should be seen in light of historic discriminatory rules regarding the clothes worn by Zoroastrians,[40] as well as the status of hats, described by Sivan Balslev as 'Iranian men's most important item of clothing'.[41] The hostility towards Zoroastrians highlights that their position in society continued to be contested and that clothing was significant as a visible marker of national identity.

In his memoirs, Shahrokh described how he had instigated the change in uniform that triggered this 'commotion'.[42] Shahrokh explicitly linked this incident to the issue of equality:

> I argued that we Zoroastrians were protecting our rights. They responded that this act would result in bloodshed. I maintained throughout this inquisition that we would pay with our blood to buy our rights.[43]

Members of the ulama tried to pressurize Shahrokh to revoke his decision, as did Zoroastrians in Yazd, who were 'tired of the situation' because Muslims had stopped selling them food and doctors were prevented from visiting them. However, Shahrokh was supported by members of the cabinet, who threatened to send troops to restore order.[44] British officials do not appear to have intervened, but they reported that by late November,

> The differences between the Mussalmans and Zoroastrians have been amicably settled. The boycott of the latter has been withdrawn, and several of the leading notables of Yezd proceeded to the Zoroastrian Anjuman and conducted the Parsi merchants to the bazaar.[45]

Following this denouement, Shahrokh stressed that Zoroastrians and Muslims were from the same 'land and water and blood', and he thanked the officials who had helped improve relations between the two communities.[46]

The connection between Zoroastrianism and Iran was referenced by nationalists who underlined that under Sasanian rule, Iran had been an independent power with a strong and centralized state.[47] After the war, contributors to *Kaveh*, such as Hasan Taqizadeh, used the journal to spread knowledge about ancient Iran in order to bolster national pride, believing that a greater awareness of the past would facilitate reform in the present.[48] According to Afshin Marashi, during the Constitutional Revolution, an 'ideologically ecumenical' nationalism had been encouraged, partly due to the importance of retaining the support of the ulama; in contrast, *Kaveh* promoted a secular nationalism 'grounded in mythic antiquity'.[49] In this respect, Marashi has described how both *Kaveh*, which was printed in Berlin between 1916 and 1922, and the journal *Iranshahr*, which was published a few years later, created a link between the nationalistic views articulated by a few individuals in the nineteenth century, and the 'statist project' of Reza Khan, later Reza Shah, whose approach to the modernization of Iran included secularization and the glorification of the pre-Islamic period.[50]

Reza Khan's rise to power, 1921–5

Writing in 1936, Pestanji Phirozshah Balsara, a young Parsi lawyer with a passion for Iranian history, stated that Iran had been left to 'degenerate' under the 'foreign-minded' Qajars. Balsara argued that in 1921, Reza Khan, a 'powerful leader and patriot' began to reverse this situation.[51] An officer in the Persian Cossack Brigade, Reza Khan emerged in the political sphere following the success of the military coup that he had planned with the journalist Sayyed Zia' al-Din Tabataba'i. In February 1921, Reza Khan led approximately 2,500 soldiers from Qazvin to Tehran. After gaining control over the city, he arrested around sixty politicians, prompting Ahmad Shah to agree to the formation of a new government. Sayyed Zia' al-Din Tabataba'i was appointed prime minister, and Reza Khan took the new role of commander of the army.[52] Reza Khan formed strategic alliances with influential individuals and was soon appointed minister of war; in contrast, Sayyed Zia' al-Din Tabataba'i was removed from office after just three months.[53]

The level of British involvement in the coup has been contested, and critics of Reza Khan, later Reza Shah, have argued that the British were responsible for his rise to power, thus questioning the legitimacy of his Pahlavi dynasty.[54] According to Mansour Bonakdarian, whilst British officials in London do not appear to have been aware of Reza Khan's plans, he was assisted by individuals based in Iran, including Major-General Sir Edward Ironside, the commander of the British North Persia Force.[55] The two men had apparently been introduced by Ardeshir Reporter, who admired the patriotism of Reza Khan.[56] However, despite this link with Reporter, Bonakdarian has argued that there is no evidence to back later claims that Parsis helped organize the coup.[57] Whereas British officials in Britain and India were ambivalent about the coup, Stephanie Cronin has suggested that British officers in Iran may have regarded it as a way of fulfilling the objectives of the failed Anglo-Persian Agreement, which was formally annulled in June 1921 by the Fourth Majles (1921–3).[58] For instance, Reza Khan strengthened central government control, and he soon suppressed the Jangali movement, a separatist group in the northern province of Gilan that was backed by the Bolsheviks.[59]

By the end of 1923, Reza Khan had been appointed prime minister. He enjoyed a strong support base in the Fifth Majles (1924–6), partly a consequence of the manipulation of elections.[60] Ali Ansari has described how Reza Khan 'cultivated the myth of the saviour', and was seen as such by nationalists, who thought that through his strong leadership, the aims of the Constitutional Revolution might be realized.[61] Influenced by the establishment of the republic of Turkey by Mustafa Kemal Ataturk, Reza Khan attempted to encourage support for republicanism in Iran. The prospect of Iran becoming a republic was viewed by some intellectuals and army officers as a move towards modernization, but there was resistance to the idea, particularly from the ulama. Thus, Reza Khan changed his approach and pushed instead for the replacement of the Qajar dynasty. In October 1925, the Majles voted to depose Ahmad Shah and to appoint Reza Khan as head of state.[62] Reza Khan was crowned in April 1926, in a ceremony that emphasized his supposedly 'pure' Iranian descent to differentiate him from the 'Turkish' Qajar dynasty.[63] The name chosen for his dynasty, Pahlavi, was a reference to the pre-Islamic era, being the name of a form of the Middle Persian language widely used during the Sasanian period.[64]

Throughout the years of Reza Khan's rise to power, Kaykhosrow Shahrokh was elected to represent Zoroastrians in the Majles, a position he held until his death in 1940.[65] In conjunction with his political duties, Shahrokh continued to disseminate knowledge about Zoroastrianism. A new edition of his 1907 book was printed in 1921, with costs covered by sponsors from the Zoroastrian communities in India and Iran. In addition to being read by Zoroastrians and being used as educational resources in Zoroastrian schools, Shahrokh's books were also read by non-Zoroastrian Iranians, who, in Marashi's words, 'were reevaluating Iran's cultural, religious, and political heritage'.[66] Indeed, when Shahrokh was praised by members of the Fourth Majles for his honesty, the deputy Soleyman Mirza revealed his own high opinion of the ancient period, stating that Shahrokh exemplified the values of pre-Islamic Iran.[67]

From the early 1920s, references to Iran's pre-Islamic culture became more prominent in national life, in part due to the influence of Shahrokh. During the period of the Fifth Majles, Shahrokh advised Reza Khan on the issue of calendar reform, resulting in the use of Zoroastrian names for the months.[68] This has been cited by Michael Stausberg as an example of 'an element of minority religion becoming part of mainstream civic culture'.[69] Another instance of this is seen in the introduction of national holidays linked to Zoroastrian festivals.[70] Shahrokh was also a founding member of the *Anjoman-e Asar-e Melli* (The Society for National Heritage), which was established in 1922 to protect the heritage of Iran and to raise public awareness of Iran's cultural history. According to Talinn Grigor, Shahrokh was an active member of the group and was influential in promoting a 'neo-Achaemenid' architectural style.[71]

Alongside the elevation of Iran's pre-Islamic heritage, the steps taken by Reza Khan to centralize the power of the state were also significant for Zoroastrians. Having urged Reza Khan to end discrimination against Zoroastrians, Shahrokh described how Reza Khan was keen to implement rulings to this effect, as a way of asserting his authority over the ulama.[72] The rising influence of Reza Khan also impacted the position of the British. According to H. Lyman Stebbins, for British consuls in southern Iran, 'Riza Khan's supremacy confirmed the end of their own local ascendancy'.[73] Thus, although the British military attaché in Yazd, M. Saunders, reported 'increasing friction' between Muslims and Zoroastrians in 1923, rather than asking for British assistance, Zoroastrians 'appealed to the Central Government for protection', and Reza Khan placed Yazd under martial law until a new governor arrived.[74] In 1924, Zoroastrians in Tehran visibly demonstrated their support for Reza Khan by participating in 'anti-Qajar agitation', after which they presented the prime minister with a memorial.[75] The following year, Shahrokh encouraged Zoroastrians to take *bast* to show their allegiance to Reza Khan, despite earlier recommending to members of the Tehran Zoroastrian Anjoman that they ask the wider community to abstain from politics. This change in approach is viewed by Manouchehr Kasheff as being linked to Shahrokh's own political ambitions; by gaining greater recognition for the Tehran Zoroastrian Anjoman, Shahrokh was able to bolster his own reputation.[76]

Military reform was a crucial element in Reza Khan's plan to increase central government control, and, in June 1925, a conscription bill was ratified by the Fifth Majles.[77] In addition to increasing the power of the army, it was believed that conscription would weaken regional ties and heighten loyalty to the nation.[78] Stephanie Cronin has argued that the act was inspired by the ideology of modern nationalism, and although exemptions were made for religious students, 'no concession was made to traditional Muslim sentiment' regarding non-Muslims.[79] In disagreement with the conservative Majles deputy and cleric, Sayyed Hasan Modarres, who argued that military service was a religious duty for Muslims, Shahrokh expressed support for the bill, maintaining that Zoroastrians ought to share the responsibilities of citizenship.[80] This was one of several instances where Shahrokh spoke in favour of equality; for example, he also argued for the amendment of Article 58 of the constitution, as it barred non-Muslims from holding ministerial positions. Shahrokh raised the point that Zoroastrians living abroad were observing events in Iran and might decide to return with their wealth and knowledge if conditions changed.[81] Whilst Article 58 was not revised, Cronin has stated that the inclusion of non-Muslims in the conscription bill 'symbolised the triumph of nationalism over religious and communal identity'.[82] Although the bill did mark a turning point, it can also be seen as the realization of plans that had been proposed during the period of the Constitutional Revolution.

Continuities can also be seen in the elevation of the pre-Islamic era. Reza Shah's coronation ceremony aimed to show how he differed from his Qajar predecessors, and motifs echoing the heritage of ancient Iran were used to emphasize that Reza Shah was a 'true' Iranian.[83] However, during the years of Reza Khan's rise to power, members of the Qajar family also drew on the pre-Islamic period for political purposes. Just a few months after Reza Khan's coup, the crown prince and brother of Ahmad Shah, Mohammad Hasan Mirza (1899–1943), travelled to Bombay, where he was warmly welcomed by the Zoroastrian community. Dinshah Jijibhoy Irani (1881–1938), the president of the Iranian Zoroastrian Anjoman (IZA), delivered an address to the prince; he spoke of the 'fire of love' Zoroastrians in India felt for their 'ancient fatherland', and he requested that the prince show 'gracious interest' in the welfare of Zoroastrians, as the Qajars had done in previous years.[84] In response, the prince emphasized that there was 'absolute equality' in Iran, presumably an indirect reference to the constitution; he went on to pronounce his pride in Zoroastrians, 'the original children of Iran', and stated that 'the ancient history of Persia with its glorious past was the pride of every true Persian'.[85]

A group of Parsis also met with the prince. Not only did they describe how their hearts constantly turned to Iran, for centuries 'the centre of a world-wide Empire', but they also hoped for a day 'when they might once more renew their connection with Persia and play their part, however humble, in the regeneration, development and glorification of their fatherland'.[86] Proclaiming that 'Blood is thicker than water', Mohammad Hasan Mirza encouraged them to visit Iran and establish permanent relations with the country.[87] He also referred to the pre-Islamic era as a time when Iran was a great 'civilising force', and, having highlighted the heroism described in the *Shahnameh*, he went on to express the wish that Parsis would turn their, 'great intellectual, moral and material resources to achieve the greatness and prosperity' of their 'common Fatherland'.[88] These words, which aimed to encourage stronger relations between Parsis and Iran, echo earlier exchanges between Iranian dignitaries and Parsis, and relate to themes found in the form of nationalism that was later seen as a hallmark of the Pahlavi era.

The Qajar prince was not the only prince who visited Bombay in 1921; in November, Edward, Prince of Wales, arrived in the city. The Prince of Wales had a very different reception, as Gandhi had called for a boycott of his trip to India.[89] Although there had been increase in Parsi support for the Non-Cooperation Movement in the months leading up to this visit, when the prince arrived in Bombay on 17 November, members of the Bombay Parsi Panchayat disregarded the boycott and welcomed him.[90] In reaction to this, riots broke out in the city. Dinyar Patel has described how, over the following days, these 'took on a decisively communal colour, with lines clearly drawn between Hindus and Muslims on one side and Parsis and Anglo-Indians on the other'.[91] Gandhi went on a hunger strike in order to bring an end to the violence, which resulted in over fifty people being killed and many being wounded.[92] According to Patel, Gandhi was keen to restore his relations with the Parsi community, so he explicitly criticized the violence that had been directed towards Parsis but outlined that Parsi acts of violence could be justified.[93] Following the riots, Gandhi stressed that minority communities must be protected by majority communities, meaning Hindus and Muslims. Patel has argued that by placing the responsibility in the hands of the majority communities, Gandhi aimed to reassure Parsis of their place in India, and guard against communal tensions in the future.[94]

Whereas Gandhi was keen to regain the confidence of Parsis and thus made reassurances to the community that they were safe in India, the Iranian crown prince encouraged Parsis to view themselves as patriotic Iranians and as potential investors in Iran's future. Likewise, Kashef al-Saltaneh, who had served as consul-general in India, stated that Parsis, 'old Persians', might 'turn their attention to Persia and help her in developing her industries by their acumen and generosity'.[95] Writing in 1922, Major B. Temple, the British commercial secretary in Iran, observed that Iranian Zoroastrians viewed Parsi visits to Iran as being potentially significant in economic terms, and he noted a sharp rise in the number of Parsis exploring business opportunities.[96] Indeed, in the same year, R. K. Dadachanji described a 'wave of the intensest [sic] nationalism' passing over members of his community, who were 'almost feverishly eager and keen to revive their ancient glories', not only in India but also 'amongst their Islamic brethren in Persia'.[97] Mirroring the suggestions made by Kashef al-Saltaneh, Dadachanji urged Parsis to play a role in the construction of railways in Iran, and he also proposed the formation of 'The Parsee-Persia Trading Company'.[98] Dadachanji listed a number of Zoroastrians who could be involved in the company, some of whom had apparently already agreed to take part; the group included Sir D. M. Petit, J. J. Vimadalal and Dinshah Irani, a lawyer, philanthropist and scholar, who played a prominent role in forging links between Zoroastrians in India and Iran.[99]

Similar points were raised in an article about 'Parsi Zionism', printed in the *Advocate of India*. Inspired by recent Zionist activity, some Parsis reportedly wanted to strengthen their economic relations with Iran, although they did not go so far as to advocate 'wholesale emigration'.[100] Fears of religious intolerance were said to be unfounded, and reference was made both to the constitution, which ensured that Zoroastrians had a 'position of equality in the eye of the law', and to the centralized government of Reza Khan, which had broken the power of the 'fanatic' members of the ulama.[101] Despite widespread 'hatred for all aliens', Iranians were said to 'profess a warm preference for the Parsis to any other community in the world with whom to join hands for the uplift of the country'.[102] Another article, 'Parsis and Persia: An Appeal', cited an Iranian newspaper that had exhorted Parsis, the 'purest of Persia's progeny', to return.[103] Parsis were encouraged to contribute to the national effort, as 'Persia yearns that all those having Persian blood should now foregather in Persia, join hands and serve the common cause of the country', including the 'old owners' of Iran, who were invited to 'come over as new guests'.[104]

The author of 'A Call to the Fatherland', an article printed in the *Times of India* in 1923, claimed that 'a section of the educated Persians is now pining to embrace the descendants of the old persecuted Zoroastrians after that long separation'. Reference was made to the Persian newspaper *Farohar*, which requested a 'public invitation' be extended to the Parsi community, to entice them to help regenerate Iran.[105] Not for the first time, comparisons were made between Parsis and Jews, with the *Farohar* article exclaiming:

O! Ye Sons of Iran! The Jews all over the world consider it a shame to live under foreign rule and are now rallying round Jerusalem to make Palestine once more a prosperous country. Is it not a pity that when your countrymen here are ready to welcome you back to your fatherland you should live far away from it?[106]

Although the proposal was viewed with amusement by a correspondent to the *Times of India*, who doubted the offer would be taken up,[107] the idea of Parsis settling in Iran did have advocates in India and Iran. Indeed, in a talk delivered in the same year, Baman Banaji highlighted that Parsis were 'invited' by Reza Khan to assist in raising Iran to its 'former glory'; by doing so, they would 'prove themselves to be true "Kiyanis"', descendants of the legendary kings of ancient Iran.[108]

One Parsi who was inspired to relocate to Iran was Maneck Dady, who reportedly changed his name to the 'purely Persian' Minocher. With the 'moral support' of Dinshah Irani, and financial backing from 'patriotic Persian merchants' in Bombay, Dady set out for Iran, where he planned to practice as a doctor.[109] Dady had fought in Iran during the war,[110] and had subsequently founded the 'Society for the Prosperity of Iran', an organization that had 'members of all religions'.[111] His decision to return to Iran in 1922 was described as being connected to 'the desire of a large number of the Parsee community in India to settle in Persia'.[112] Keen to impress upon Parsis that conditions were favourable, Dady underlined that Bombay firms already trading in Iran had no worries regarding safety.[113] Dady was welcomed by Muslims and Zoroastrians in Yazd and Kerman, and he was urged to invite fellow-Parsis to visit the 'old country', where they might found mills, repair ancient dams and 'turn hundreds of acres of arid land into smiling fields of Sasanian times'.[114] Bearing a resemblance to earlier utopian descriptions of the proposed Parsi colony, Iran was presented as being on the threshold of a renewed period of glory that would mirror the pre-Islamic past.

The governor-general of Fars was amongst those wanted other Parsis to follow Dady's example, proposing that it was 'high time that these old sons of the country should return'.[115] Implicitly referring to the constitution, he told Dady to 'assure the Parsis that there is no religious persecution: they have equal rights of citizenship'.[116] In a public speech, Dady stated that despite a thousand years in India, Parsis took great pride in their 'Persian blood', and he anticipated that they 'would make their mother country the greatest in the world', replicating their impact in western India.[117] Dady met with a group of Iranians in Kerman who told him that Parsis would be welcomed, as long as they 'came as Persians and not as emissaries of the British', a reflection of hardening anti-British sentiments.[118]

In Dady's case, enthusiasm for Iran was linked to a critical view of British involvement in the country. During his time in Tehran, Dady enjoyed the hospitality of Shahrokh, whose attitude was described by Major B. Temple as the '"Gott strafe England [God punish England]" type'.[119] Temple reported that 'Pro-Persianism has modernly become so identified with anti-Britishism', and confirmed Dady had 'already begun to qualify in this respect'.[120] It was not only the British that Dady castigated. When he visited Mr Chick, the British consul in Shiraz, Dady disclosed that Parsis considered moving to Iran, as they did not feel 'wanted or liked' in India, and were 'dissatisfied with their recent treatment by the Hindu population'. This is probably a reference to the 1921 riots in Bombay.[121]

However, the commissioner of police in Bombay brushed aside the notion that Parsis seriously considered emigration.[122] Describing their commercial plans as 'castles in the air', he doubted Parsis would risk their funds without British backing,[123] and reported that only a handful of 'enthusiasts' were keen on greater involvement in Iran, with the Parsi newspaper *Jam-e Jamshed* expressing scepticism about such schemes.[124] The commissioner also pointed out that Dady lacked legitimacy within the community. Although he claimed to have been sent by the 'Iran Mandal' and 'Jashan Committee', the former was 'still under contemplation', and the latter was 'only a nominal body'; in addition, Dady did not have the support of the Bombay Parsi Panchayat.[125]

Whilst very few Zoroastrians seriously considered moving from India to Iran, the strengthening of connections with Iran had a wider appeal, and this led to the foundation of the Iran League in 1922.[126] The 'Iran Mandal', which had backed Dady's mission, was probably a precursor to the Iran League, an organization that aimed to promote positive relations between India and Iran as well as to improve opportunities for Zoroastrians in Iran. Individuals who were involved included the well-connected industrialist and philanthropist Sir Hormusji Cowasji Dinshaw Adenwalla, who was elected as president, Dinshah Irani, Sir Cowasji Jehangir and Sir Rustom Masani. Although the Iran League was created after the coup of Reza Khan, many of its members, such as the Parsi scholar G. K. Nariman, had been encouraging Parsi interest in Iran prior to this date.[127] As well as exploring possible economic links with Iran, the Iran League strengthened cultural ties; for example, Parsis in Bombay were offered Persian classes.[128]

A key objective of the Iran League was to help raise the socio-economic standing of Iranian Zoroastrians, for instance, through education. In this respect, its aims were closely aligned with those of the Amelioration Society and the Bombay-based

Iranian Zoroastrian Anjoman, and there was an overlap in membership between all three.[129] Their shared concerns are reflected in the presence of members of both the Iran League and the Iranian Zoroastrian Anjoman at a reception to welcome Ahmad Shah to Bombay in 1922. At this event, Adenwalla referred to the 'change of times, the happy future of Persia and the liberalising principles which actuated the modern constitutional Government of the ruler of the country', and he expressed the hope that there would be an increase in the educational opportunities available to Zoroastrians in Yazd.[130]

Attitudes towards Zoroastrians in Iran may have improved in the years following the Constitutional Revolution, but the community continued to ask for financial assistance from their co-religionists. In addition to the direct effects of war, Iranians had experienced famine and disease, and these difficult conditions had led Shahrokh, as president of the Tehran Zoroastrian Anjoman, to contact Sir Mancherjee Bhownaggree in 1919 to ask for help.[131] The appeal made by Shahrokh to Zoroastrians abroad, particularly those living in Bombay, seems to have prompted action. A new medical hall was opened in Yazd in November 1922; this was named after the principal benefactor, Sir Ratan Tata, and was backed by the Iranian Zoroastrian Anjoman.[132] An extensive report about Zoroastrian institutions in Yazd compiled by the acting British vice-consul, C. E. Treadwell, reveals the involvement of the Zoroastrian community outside Iran; for instance, fourteen schools in the area were under the auspices of the Amelioration Society.[133]

New educational projects were also initiated, as Zoroastrians in India regarded education as key to improving the status of Zoroastrians in Iran.[134] Having read about Hataria's work in Iran during the nineteenth century, the Parsi businessman Peshotanji D. Marker (1871–1965) was inspired to provide funds for an orphanage; this was established in Yazd in 1923.[135] The following year, Marker, who was a member of the Iran League, toured Iran with a small group of Zoroastrians from India, and, for the rest of his life, he maintained links with Iran and supported various philanthropic projects.[136] Boys at the orphanage were taught skills such as carpentry. This can be contrasted to the situation at the turn of the century, when animosity from Muslim craftsmen in Yazd pushed a Parsi carpenter to give up his attempt to offer training to Zoroastrians in the city.[137] Plans were also made for a new technical school; this was to be directed by the Amelioration Society and housed in a large building offered by Arbab Dinyar, a wealthy Zoroastrian from Yazd.[138]

Many Zoroastrian institutions in Iran were accessible to non-Zoroastrians, although Zoroastrians were the main beneficiaries. Dinshah Irani stated that the new medical hall would be open to all communities free of charge,[139] and in 1923, T. C. Tasker, the Parsi superintendent at the Kaikhasṛawi High School in Yazd, reported that Zoroastrian schools also had Muslim and Bahá'í pupils.[140] According to Marashi, Parsis hoped that this approach would encourage the emergence of a more 'ecumenical and pluralistic political culture', and help remove the barriers that Zoroastrians continued to face.[141] Indeed, K. K. Khosrawy described witnessing first-hand how non-sectarian medical aid led to an improvement in relations in Yazd between the 'two sister communities' of Zoroastrians and Muslims,[142] and Dady noted that the philanthropy of Iranian Zoroastrians gave a good impression in Iran.[143] Viewing the maintenance of good relations with non-Zoroastrians as a priority, Tasker complained that members of the Zoroastrian Anjoman of Yazd were causing tension with local Muslims.[144] The fostering of positive cross-community relations also motivated Marker, who hoped to strengthen 'the ties of fraternity' between religious groups in India and Iran, 'especially between the Moslems and the Zoroastrians'.[145] In order to achieve this goal, he funded a series of books on the history, literature and philosophy of Iran.

One of the contributors to Marker's series was Ebrahim Purdavud (1885–1968), an Iranian scholar who had a long-standing interest in ancient Iran and Zoroastrianism.[146] Purdavud had been inspired by Shahrokh's books,[147] as well as by his friendship with Madame Cama, whom he had met in Paris.[148] Whilst he was living in Berlin in the early 1920s, Purdavud published two articles about texts related to Zoroastrianism and ancient Iran in *Iranshahr*, a nationalistic journal that was rumoured to have received funding from Parsis.[149] According to Marashi, Iranian nationalists saw Parsis as 'representing the core of Iranian authenticity'.[150] This was reflected in the interest they took in the social position of Parsi women, which was seen as echoing the status of women in Iran during the pre-Islamic period. A letter written by the Parsi lawyer, Zarbanu Dinshah Molla, was printed in *Iranshahr*. Here, she linked the level of education and successes of Parsi women, such as herself, to the 'blood which they have brought with them from Iran', and to their continued adherence to the values of ancient Iran. The letter was translated from Gujarati into Persian by Purdavud.[151]

Aware of Purdavud's linguistic skills and his interest in Zoroastrianism, Dinshah Irani, the vice president of the Iran League, invited him to Bombay in 1925, and commissioned him to translate the *Gatha*s and other Zoroastrian texts into Persian.[152] These were published as part of the Marker literary series. Copies were distributed in Iran in the hope that perceptions of Zoroastrianism and Zoroastrians would improve, an instance of what Marashi has described as Parsi 'textual philanthropy'.[153] In Marashi's opinion, Iranian nationalists and Zoroastrians in India recognized that making Zoroastrian texts such as the *Gatha*s accessible to 'modern Iranian readers' was a vital element in the promotion of 'a broader revaluation of Iran's classical heritage'.[154] Books about Zoroastrianism were also sent to the library of the Majles, and to the library of the Tehran Zoroastrian Anjoman.[155]

Another individual who was involved in the Marker series was G. K. Nariman, who wrote extensively about Zoroastrianism and Iranian history.[156] In the preface to his 1925 book, *The Ahad Nameh*, Nariman described how 'patriotic' Muslims were stretching out 'the kindly hand of fraternity to their Zoroastrian compatriots and the Parsis of India'.[157] The book itself was tied to this idea, as it included translations of two charters that Nariman had selected to illustrate religious tolerance during the early years of Islam.[158] Although Nariman's work can be seen in the context of the wider aims of the Iran League, Dinyar Patel has outlined that in some respects Nariman went against popular opinion, as he did not subscribe to the 'anti-Arab' narrative seen in many Zoroastrians accounts of the history of Iran, which was also utilized by some Iranian nationalists.[159]

This shared elevation of the pre-Islamic past was also reflected in various instances of cultural collaboration and exchange. Ferdowsi's *Shahnameh* continued to be popular amongst Parsis, and the Iran League contributed funds towards a statue of Ferdowsi, which was to be displayed in the grounds of the Majles.[160] Extracts from the *Shahnameh* were recited to Zoroastrian boy scouts to create a 'Parsee spirit',[161] and, in 1924, passages were read to an organ accompaniment during Parsi Nowruz celebrations. At the same event, there were readings from *Rastakhiz-e Shahriyaran-e Iran* (*Resurrection of the Kings of Iran*), an operetta about ancient Iran by the Iranian writer and poet Mirzadeh 'Eshqi.[162] Later that year, a play based on 'Eshqi's operetta was staged to a large audience in Bombay. According to 'Prof. Abbas' the event illustrated the 'chain of friendship between the two communities', and the *Times of India* described how it reminded Parsis 'of their ancient Iranian glory and creates love of Iran in the present generation'.[163]

Historic ties to Iran motivated some Parsi travellers who were keen to visit archaeological sites, particularly the rock reliefs at Taq-e Bostan, which included a figure that was said to be a representation of Zarathustra.[164] According to Sir Percy Loraine, the British minister in Tehran, Parsis made the journey to Iran, 'partly for sentimental and partly for business reasons'.[165] British records noted that Dr N. H. Bamboat, who visited Iran in 1923, considered 'numerous schemes', such as generating electricity from the River Kor.[166] Likewise, the following year, a group aiming 'to promote Parsi interests in Persia' discussed irrigation and engineering projects in Kerman; they also crossed paths with Lieutenant Nariman Karkaria, who was collecting material for a book.[167] In 1924, three Zoroastrians from the firm of Ardeshir Khadabaksh Irani arrived in Bushehr, bringing with them a twelve-seater car to be used to provide a motor service between Bushehr and Shiraz,[168] and Rustam Mistry, a Parsi merchant who was reportedly involved in the opium trade, also visited the country.[169] Murali Ranganathan has analysed four travelogues by Parsis who went to Iran during the early 1920s. Ranganathan has argued that these texts, written in Gujarati for a Parsi audience, acted as 'community manuals', which, both explicitly and implicitly, addressed questions regarding future Parsi economic engagement in Iran, as well as the possible relocation of Parsis to the country.[170]

A group from the Iran League, who visited Iran in 1924, were amongst a number of Parsis who gained an audience with Reza Khan whilst they were in the country.[171] Reflecting on their experiences, G. K. Nariman described how they had been 'cordially and sympathetically' received by the premier.[172] Nariman believed the expectations of Iranian Zoroastrians and Muslims, who 'were looking forward to substantial financial help from Bombay Parsis', were exaggerated, but he stated that he had been 'more than satisfied' with the 'social position' of his co-religionists, who were 'free to live as Zoroastrians in every town throughout the country'.[173] He was also 'struck with the pride the Moslem Persian took in the Zoroastrian monumental remains of antiquity',[174] an indication of the rise of nationalistic sentiments focused on the pre-Islamic era. Reza Khan had taken steps to increase security in Iran, and safety on the roads had improved. However, reservations were still felt by Parsis; Karkaria did not endorse the commercial plans discussed by some members of his community in Bombay, and the scholar and priest J. J. Modi, who travelled in Iran with his family in 1925, was cautious, suggesting that 'a few brave Parsis' could try their luck.[175]

Whereas in the past, the British had recommended that Parsis invest in southern Iran, hoping that this would indirectly increase British influence in the region, by the early

1920s, a greater impetus came from Iranians and from the Zoroastrian community.[176] In 1925, Adenwalla, the president of the Iran League, headed an expedition to Iran, which British officials believed was linked to the possible 'repatriation of Parsees'.[177] The party was welcomed with military honours,[178] and the British consul in Shiraz, H. G. Chick, noted that when they arrived in the city, 'By orders of the Persian Government they were paid exceptional consideration by the provincial authorities'.[179] There had been a 'movement in the press of Shiraz for the enlistment of Parsee capital for the development of Persia', and it was hoped that the warm reception would influence the visitors.[180] However, 'apart from the stressing of sentimental ties of a common origin', no definite plans were made.[181] It is striking that the 'small and poor Zoroastrian colony at Shiraz', were reportedly 'disgusted with their rich co-religionists from India, who expect hospitality on their sight-seeing journeys and make no donations to local funds'.[182] This counters the dominant narrative of the positive impact of charity from India, and appears to confirm that in this instance, rather than specifically setting out to support Iranian Zoroastrians, the primary motive of the Parsi travellers was to strengthen broader links with Iran.

Zealous calls for Parsis to become more involved in Iran were sometimes criticized for being overly idealistic or even insincere. An anonymous correspondent to the *Times of India* interpreted suggestions of 'repatriation' as threats to the Bombay government,[183] which presumably aimed to guarantee benefits for Parsis in the event of future political reform. In another letter about the 'Iran Movement', 'E. A. C.' argued that due to the hardships they would face, Parsis were unlikely to want to relocate. As a warning to the community, reference was made to the unsuccessful outcome of the *hijrat*, the recent emigration of several thousand Indian Muslims to Afghanistan.[184] The 'impracticability' of Parsi proposals was stressed, and the author also criticized 'jingoistic' methods used to encourage donations from poor Parsis for causes in Iran, arguing that funds ought to be spent closer to home.[185] This was to become an often-repeated lament over the coming years.

However, the Iran League continued to nurture relations with Iran. Thus, when an Iranian general and other high-ranking officers arrived in Bombay in December 1925, Adenwalla entertained them at his home.[186] Members of the Iranian Muslim community of Bombay were also invited, and during the party, one of the guests, a solicitor called Mirza Ali Akberkhan, 'testified to the sincere love for Iran which abided in the hearts of Parsis'. In support of this statement, J. J. Vimadalal suggested to his fellow-Parsis that, 'instead of merely visiting Persia as sightseers', they ought to enact 'measures for contributing to its concrete prosperity'.[187] The general stressed that due to the actions of Reza Khan, soon to be shah, Zoroastrians were safe in Iran,[188] and he emphasized that 'Parsis were cordially invited and would be received with open arms by their former country'.[189] Some Parsis seem to have viewed the coronation with great anticipation, and a cartoon from the 1925 Parsi New Year edition of *Hindi Punch* depicted Sir Jamsetjee Jejeebhoy, a leading figure in the Parsi community, seated on the Iranian throne.[190] Echoing rumours from the period of the Second Majles about government positions being available to Parsis, reference was made to political opportunities for Parsis in Iran and to the possibility that they might be included in the cabinet of the new shah.[191]

The allure of the Pahlavi state

'Jubilant' Parsis celebrated the coronation of Reza Shah at a reception in Bombay, and hopes were expressed that he would 'rejuvenate' Iran.[192] In a tribute to the shah, G. K. Nariman highlighted his key achievements to date: the reorganization of the army and the end to laws that imposed 'civil disabilities' on non-Muslims.[193] Mirroring assertions made in Iran, the Persian consul described Reza Shah as being of the 'purest Iranian lineage', and claimed that this was the first time, since the pre-Islamic era, that the whole of their 'ancient land' was under Iranian rule.[194] In London, the Persian chargé d'affaires spoke of the Parsis returning to Iran,[195] and similar sentiments were expressed in India, where Dr J. J. Modi encouraged Parsis to accept the shah's invitation to their 'old motherland'.[196] The coronation spurred calls for the 'Persianisation' of Parsi education,[197] and an article in the *Times of India*, 'A Parsi Dream', described how the idea of relocating to Iran was 'gaining ground', outlining that Parsis were motivated by business opportunities and by the desire to help with the reconstruction of Iran, with the aim of supporting their co-religionists mentioned as a third factor.[198]

The Iran League was represented at the coronation,[199] and in Bombay, the Aqa Khan, who was the organization's honorary patron, stated his desire that Parsis 'play their part' in the development of their 'Fatherland'.[200] The Aqa Khan was adamant that this would be mutually beneficial, as he doubted that any new 'purely Parsi enterprise' would succeed in India, due to the 'awakening on the part of the Hindus and Moslems'.[201] With sectarianism described in the *Times of India* as being 'glaringly prominent' in the 1926 Bombay municipal elections, the future political influence of the Parsis seemed uncertain, and stronger ties to Iran may have appealed to members of the community.[202]

An example of closer connections with Iran is seen in Zoroastrian involvement in the *Anjoman-e Mavaddat*. Based in India, this organization had a predominantly Iranian Muslim membership, and, similar to the Iran League, it aimed to strengthen relations between both countries.[203] Following the publication of articles in *Habl al-Matin* that were critical of the Parsi community, the *Anjoman-e Mavaddat* circulated a resolution in their defence, stressing their 'spirit of enterprise, charity, and industry', and their support for Iran. This document was sent to the Ministry of Foreign Affairs in Tehran, as well as to newspapers in Iran and India, and to Iranian diplomats in India.[204] Reference was made to the growth in 'brotherly feelings' between Iranian Muslims and Parsis, and to their cooperation in working towards the 'uplift of Iran on its entering upon a beneficent era of progress, justice and tolerance', thus emphasizing that Zoroastrians could play a valuable role in the success of the Pahlavi state.[205]

In the eyes of his supporters, the large-scale infrastructural projects instigated by Reza Shah demonstrated that he was Iran's modernizing saviour.[206] Alongside his role as the representative for Zoroastrians in the Majles, Kaykhosrow Shahrokh was involved in a number of these schemes; for example, he established a company that provided electricity to areas of northern Iran, and he helped manage the national telephone company and railway network.[207] Ali Ansari has noted that the reach of the Trans-Iranian railway into south-western Iran may have had been linked to the military concerns of the shah, principally his campaign against the tribal confederacies, which he viewed as a threat to his own position and as an obstruction to modernization.[208]

In addition to the use of military force to suppress groups within Iranian society, the constitution was also violated during Reza Shah's reign; freedom of speech was compromised, elections were manipulated, and political opposition was oppressed.[209] As Reza Shah's rule became increasingly autocratic, he attempted to control the private as well as public lives of Iranians, including in relation to clothing. Dress codes were widely unpopular, and Ansari has outlined how the Pahlavi cap, introduced in 1928, was seen as an attempt to 'encourage irreligiousness'.[210] This military-style cap was superseded by European-style hats in 1935, and the following year, a controversial decree banned women from wearing the veil.[211] One outcome of these laws was there was no longer such a visible difference between the clothing of Muslims and non-Muslims.[212]

Under Reza Shah, there was increased secularization of both education and law, resulting in a decrease in the power of the ulama. The education system was used as a tool to promote the Pahlavi state's view of Iranian national culture, which was founded on an appreciation of the pre-Islamic era.[213] One aspect of educational reform was the imposition of a standardized version of Persian as the national language of Iran, and, echoing the emphasis Shahrokh had placed on 'pure' Persian in earlier years, the use of 'foreign' words was discouraged.[214] Reforms were also enacted in the legal sphere, and in 1928–35, a new civil code was introduced. When this was announced, the newly established *Iran League Bulletin*, the journal of the Iran League, enthusiastically proclaimed that 'The prerogatives of the Mullahs will be minimised'.[215] However, Islamic law was used as the basis for many of the new regulations. Therefore, following the recommendations made by Shahrokh, as well as by the Jewish and Armenian Majles deputies, recognized non-Muslim communities were permitted to determine their own laws regarding personal issues, such as divorce.[216] Despite these reforms and the efforts made by Reza Shah to create a secular state, non-Muslims continued to face discrimination. There were instances of the abduction and forced conversion of Zoroastrian girls, and non-Muslims were still disadvantaged at a constitutional level; for example, they were excluded from holding ministerial positions.[217]

The introduction of universal conscription in 1926 can be seen as an instance where barriers between Muslims and non-Muslims were removed. However, the new law was not welcomed by all Zoroastrians in Iran. In 1929, the British noted that conscription was 'extremely unpopular' in Kerman, and the previous year, Zoroastrians had paid to avoid it. Perhaps in reaction to this, in 1928–9 Zoroastrians were enlisted 'regardless of any claim to exemption'.[218] Indeed, Stephanie Cronin has highlighted that Zoroastrians were targeted by the committee sent to Kerman that year to gather recruits for the army.[219] Interestingly, rather than expressing sympathy for their co-religionists, the *Iran League Bulletin* criticized Zoroastrians in Iran for not showing 'their appreciation of religious equality' by complying with this 'patriotic law'.[220]

Positive views of Pahlavi Iran were augmented by the unease felt by Parsis regarding their position in India.[221] Some Parsis argued that they risked 'political extinction' unless they made 'common cause' with nationalists who called for *swaraj*, self-government,[222] but others wanted to distance themselves from such activities. In 1928, members of the 'Simon Commission' arrived in India; this was a committee of seven British MPs tasked with reporting on constitutional reform. The commission faced heavy criticism, particularly as it had no Indian members, and the INC encouraged Indians to demonstrate and to boycott the commission.[223] According to one contemporary Parsi commentator, M. K. Patel, many Zoroastrians participated in the boycott.[224] However, there was a group of Parsis willing to cooperate with the commission. They proposed that the commission consider separate electorates for Zoroastrians to counter the 'bare numerical strength' of the 'vast masses' who had not yet attained 'education and political experience'.[225] In contrast to Muslims, Zoroastrians could not cite the size of their population to justify their requests; instead, their recommendations were linked to the idea that, as a progressive community, they should hold a greater proportion of power.[226]

The strength of the reaction against the Simon Commission pushed the viceroy, Lord Irwin, to declare that India would gain 'Dominion' status.[227] A group of representatives from India were subsequently invited to London for a series of three 'Round Table Conferences', which took place between 1930–2. The British hoped that these discussions would lead to an agreed course of action regarding constitutional reform in India.[228] During the talks, one of the three Parsi participants, Sir Cowasji Jehangir, proposed that franchise ought to be tied to levels of education, an outcome that would be advantageous to his community. Another of the Parsis present, Sir Pheroze Sethna, spoke out against the idea of separate electorates for Parsis, as he was confident that Parsis would continue to have a political presence without such measures.[229]

Writing to the *Times of India* in February 1930, J. M. Desai stated that it was 'ludicrous' to think that Parsi success was reliant on British rule. Desai recommended that 'it may prove beneficial to the community if some of its members champion the new movement' and support Gandhi.[230] According to Rashna Writer, there was an increase in Parsi support for the nationalist movement around this time. One reason for this was the arrest of the Parsi politician, Khurshed Nariman, who had helped organize mass meetings in Bombay in April 1930, linked to the Salt March initiated by Gandhi.[231] However, concerns about nationalist activities continued to be raised, with an anonymous Parsi describing the 1921 riots as 'the foretaste of "swaraj"'.[232] As in the past, Parsis, who took a more cautious approach towards Indian nationalism, tended to stress beneficial relations between their community and the British, as well as their links to Iran.[233]

Political uncertainty compounded the apprehension felt by some Parsis about their economic prospects in India.[234] According to an article that marked the Parsi New Year in September 1927, the high level of unemployment in the community was the 'all absorbing topic' that had dominated discussions over the past year.[235] Financial concerns contributed to acrimonious debates regarding the suggestion aired in 1929, that Parsis should fund a girls' school in Tehran. The idea was backed by Shahrokh and other Zoroastrians in Iran, but criticisms of the proposal were printed in Parsi newspapers, and in letters sent to the *Times of India*.[236] A. E. Bengali, vice president of the *Anjoman-e Mavaddat*, was a frequent correspondent. He disapproved of the plan, partly because he thought the Iranian government was financially irresponsible.[237] Additionally, he argued:

Our own Parsi needs here, nearer home, are so very pressing that we would be making an exhibition of ourselves if we started philanthropic operations in foreign lands and attempted to play Providence to half the world.[238]

The situation in India led to questions being raised regarding the sagacity of funding projects in Iran, even by members of organizations that aimed to forge links with the country. Furthermore, the point was made that Parsi philanthropy directed towards Iran would not specifically benefit Zoroastrians, as Zoroastrian schools were open to members of other religious communities.[239] In this instance, it was believed that the majority of the pupils would be Muslim.[240] Whilst the Iran League encouraged donations towards educational schemes,[241] and noted that non-sectarian philanthropy had led to 'more cordial relations' between Muslims and Zoroastrians,[242] not all Parsis were convinced of the urgency to fund schools in Iran.

Discussions about the school were closely linked to perceptions of the economic position of the Parsis. F. K. Bativala exclaimed: 'I do not pretend to be *au courant* with all the affairs of Persia, but I do know the growing poverty of my community'.[243] Bativala argued that it was 'unreasonable' to send money to a foreign country, disloyal to donate funds to 'non-Parsis', and 'the height of foolish extravagance' to pay for a school for Muslim girls.[244] Conversely, others were adamant that Iranian finances were 'thoroughly well organised', and pointed out that Parsis only sent around 30,000 rupees to Iran annually.[245] K. K. Khosrawy, who had worked at a dispensary in Yazd from 1919–20, noted that Parsis had helped fund a university in China; he maintained it would therefore be 'out of taste' for them to 'postpone doing a little bit for our Fatherland'.[246] In contrast, having criticized the donations made by the Wadia Trust to an INC-backed hospital, a case of 'glorified blackmail', Jehangir R. P. Mody reasoned that at least India was their 'real home', whereas 'the drain of Parsi wealth to foreign countries', meaning Iran, could not be justified.[247] One example he gave was of funds sent to provide relief for the victims of a recent earthquake. In this instance, Shahrokh had appealed to Zoroastrians in India for donations, even though most Zoroastrians lived far from the affected area.[248]

Towards the end of 1930, rumours about Zoroastrian converts in Iran exacerbated these debates.[249] The issue of whether converts should be permitted to join the community was a divisive one and had already led to heated legal disputes amongst Parsis in recent years.[250] Accusations made in the *Times of India* concerning a 'missionary' who lectured about the '*necessity* of propagating Zoroastrianism in Persia', prompted Merwanji Cursetji to express his concerns. Rather than seeking converts in Iran or contemplating emigration to the country, Cursetji argued that Parsis needed to look after their own community.[251] Allegations were made that the Iran League was encouraging conversions. These were contested by M. P. Madan, who also dismissed reports of a planned colony as 'fiction'.[252] Likewise, A. M. Bomanji said talk of 'religious propaganda and proselytising' was 'twaddle'.[253]

Despite these protestations, K. K. Lalkaka maintained that without converts, Ardeshir Reporter's forecast of an 'immense increase' in the Iranian Zoroastrian population in 'the near future' was inexplicable.[254] Whilst visiting India in 1930, Reporter secured financial support for the girls' school in Tehran from Ratanbanu

Bamji Tata, the sister of the successful industrialist Jamsetji Tata. Reporter had been collaborating on the school project with a number of individuals, including Shahrokh and Dinshah Irani.[255] During this trip, Reporter had also emphasized the importance of encouraging the growth of the Zoroastrian population of Tehran.[256]

Similar to Lalkaka, Merwanji Cursetji believed that a 'conversion scheme' was being promoted. Cursetji argued that the reality of life in Iran was not being reported, and he stated that:

> This incessant cry of 'Iran' is harming Parsi businessmen and the Parsi community as a whole. The Congressites ask the Parsi merchants with some justification either to join them or clear out of India to their 'motherland of Iran' to sell there their European liquors and Chinese silks.[257]

Criticisms were also raised by S. N. Tarapore, who urged the Bombay Parsi Panchayat to enquire into the 'lakhs of rupees' sent to Iran.[258] He enclosed a newspaper cutting with his letter to the *Times of India*, 'evidencing the jubilations at Teheran over the Parsi "patriotic" munificence!' Tarapore was also concerned by Parsi communalism and the impact it would have on the future of the Parsis in India. He highlighted the 'outrageous scenes and references' in a contemporary play about ancient Iran, 'Yazdegard Sheriar', also known as 'Yad-e Vatan (memory of the fatherland)', and condemned the 'extreme views' of Parsis who promoted 'their "Iran propaganda"' and created 'bad blood' with 'sister communities' in India.[259]

This 'propaganda' was likely to have included the *Iran League Bulletin*.[260] Although the journal expressed pride in Parsi participation in Indian politics,[261] it also supported Zoroastrian involvement in the development of Iran.[262] The June 1928 edition cited an article from a Tehran newspaper that referred to Parsis as Persians, and suggestions were made as to how Parsis could take advantage of opportunities in the country.[263] Positive accounts were given of Pahlavi rule,[264] and readers were introduced to the work of contemporary Iranian poets, such as Mirzadeh 'Eshqi and 'Aref Qazvini, who were inspired by the pre-Islamic era.[265] The journal also celebrated the work of Ebrahim Purdavud, who had been commissioned by the Iran League to translate the *Gathas* into Persian. Reports about the translations being read in Iran may have fed speculations about converts.[266]

There was a growing interest in Zoroastrianism amongst non-Zoroastrian Iranians, reflected in the distribution of the *Iran League Bulletin* in Iran, and the decision made by some Iranians to travel to India to study and work with members of the Zoroastrian community.[267] One of these individuals was Abdolhossein Sepanta (1907–69), who had been educated at the Zoroastrian school in Tehran and was then encouraged to go to India by a number of people, including Ardeshir Reporter.[268] His arrival in India in the late 1920s was not welcomed by all Parsis. K. K. Lalkaka disapproved of 'Abdul Husain Wahi', a Muslim from Isfahan who had been given the Zoroastrian name 'Spenta'. Lalkaka questioned how much he was being paid, believing that community funds ought to be spent in other ways.[269]

During his time in Bombay, Sepanta worked for a whilst as an assistant to Dinshah Irani,[270] and he also collaborated with the Zoroastrian director, Ardeshir

Irani (1886–1969). The two men produced the first Persian-language sound film, *Dokhtar-e Lor* (*Lor Girl*).[271] Released in India in 1933, *Dokhtar-e Lor* told the story of a couple who fled from Iran to Bombay whilst the Qajar dynasty was still in power, and who then returned to Iran after the coronation of Reza Shah.[272] The film has usually been analysed in reference to Iranian nationalism, but Laura Fish argues that the depiction of Bombay as a site of modernity is also significant. Indeed, Fish suggests that the production aimed for the 'transnational expansion' of the Parsi community's influence and prestige, with the involvement of Sepanta adding a level of 'Persian' authenticity that it was hoped would facilitate the film's success in Iran.[273] When it was released in Iran, the film was advertised with the title, *Iran of Yesterday and Iran of Today*, emphasizing the progressive rule of Reza Shah.[274] In one review, Ardeshir Irani was praised for his patriotism, and the suggestion was made that his company release further films with 'national' themes, including stories from the *Shahnameh*.[275]

By the 1930s, Zoroastrians in India were broadening their reach into Iran and raising the profile of their community through the export of cultural products, such as translated texts, journals and films. Writing in 1931, the Parsi scholar, Jamshedji Maneckji Unvala, referred to the contemporary 'Iranian movement', and the greater attention being paid to ancient Iranian languages and texts by Iranian intellectuals. Unvala stated that these individuals wanted to see a resurgence of Zoroastrian ethics,[276] believing that 'the moral and material regeneration of Persia is only possible, if the teachings of Persia itself become the dominant factor moulding the thoughts of Persians'.[277] In addition to noting that the religious practices of Zoroastrians in India and Iran differed, Unvala highlighted that intellectuals in Iran were critical of some Zoroastrian practices, particularly the use of *dakhmehs*.[278]

Shahrokh was also in favour of replacing *dakhmehs* with cemeteries. Not only was he concerned by the desecration of the *dakhmeh* in Tehran, but he also thought *dakhmehs* were unhygienic and contrary to Zoroastrian doctrine.[279] As president of the Tehran Zoroastrian Anjoman, Shahrokh was in a position to influence reform in Iran, and, with the support from the Iranian Zoroastrian community, a site was secured for a cemetery in Tehran in 1935.[280] This assertion of independence in terms of religious practice was criticized by some Parsis, whom Shahrokh described as having become increasingly 'autocratic' following the death of Reporter in 1933.[281] Despite objections raised by orthodox Parsis, the cemetery plans went ahead. In Shahrokh's view, this was a return to 'authentic' Zoroastrian doctrine, which was well-suited to the modern day.[282] Taking place on a larger scale, some of the reforms of the Pahlavi state were also said to be reviving the values of pre-Islamic Iran.

Although the nationalism promoted by the Pahlavi state was secular, and therefore accessible to all Iranians, as members of the dominant religion of the pre-Islamic period, Zoroastrians were in a distinct position in comparison to other religious communities. According to Ringer,

> Modernity was mapped onto a reimagined past, and the Zoroastrians held special status as the 'authentic' Iranians unsullied by intervening years of decline, conversion, and distance from cultural origins.[283]

Likewise, the *Iran League Quarterly* presented Pahlavi reforms as a return to pre-Islamic customs; for example, the compulsory unveiling of women was said to be a revival of the freedoms enjoyed by women in the past.[284] These claims reflected the arguments made by Parsi reformers during the nineteenth century. The *Iran League Quarterly* recommended Parsi women travel to Iran, 'to encourage their Persian sisters there to follow them in desirable modern and progressive ways'.[285] This was a sentiment shared by Fakhrozzaman Jabbar Vaziri, who had moved from Iran to Bombay, where she played a leading role in several films directed by Sepanta. Writing in the *Iran League Quarterly*, she urged Parsi women to support the reforms being enacted in Iran, arguing that Parsis had safeguarded Iranian values regarding women's rights, which were now being restored by Reza Shah.[286]

Linked to this elevation of pre-Islamic Iran were concurrent efforts being made by the Pahlavi state to promote the idea of a broader ancient Indo-Iranian heritage.[287] Afshin Marashi has outlined that, 'The connection between Iranian national authenticity and the classical heritage of India was a common and consistent theme of Iranian nationalism during this period'.[288] This was demonstrated in 1932, when the Bengali writer, artist, and activist, Rabindranath Tagore (1861–1941), was invited to tour Iran for four weeks, during which time the Nobel Prize winner delivered lectures and visited cultural sites.[289] According to Marashi, Tagore was presented as a symbol of a shared Indo-Iranian heritage, which provided the Iranian nation with a 'civilizational genealogy'.[290] Although, as Marashi has discussed, there was a degree of tension between the more 'narrowly conceived' nationalism of the Pahlavi state, and Tagore's inclusive 'pan-Asian solidarity',[291] Tagore did make references to a supposed shared Indo-Iranian Aryan ancestry.[292] Due to the ancient roots of their religion, Zoroastrians were seen to embody the Indo-Iranian heritage that was highlighted throughout Tagore's tour.

Zoroastrians in India and Iran played a significant role in the preparation and execution of Tagore's visit. Dinshah Irani and Hormusji Adenwalla helped to plan the trip, working in collaboration with Jalal al-Din Kayhan, the Persian consul-general in Bombay.[293] On his arrival in Shiraz, Tagore was greeted by Shahrokh, who had also been involved in organizing the tour, and whilst in Tehran, he was granted the honour of laying the foundation stone for the Firuz Bahman Zoroastrian school.[294] A number of Zoroastrians from India travelled with Tagore, including Dinshah Irani. According to Marashi, Irani had been a key influence on Tagore in regards to his views of a shared Indo-Iranian civilization.[295] During the trip, Irani delivered several lectures; he referred to Iran as 'our beloved country', and he displayed his support for Reza Shah by wearing a Pahlavi hat.[296] Also travelling with the group was Rustom Masani, managing director of the recently established 'Persia Industrial and Trading Company', which aimed to generate economic links between India and Iran.[297]

In his report of Tagore's tour, Reginald Hoare, the British minister in Tehran, stressed the significance of the group of Zoroastrians accompanying him. Hoare interpreted the invitation to Tagore as a way 'to add réclame to the party of Persians [Parsis] with whom he travelled'.[298] He stated that Masani had a low opinion of Tagore's poetry, and that 'the main object of the party was to ascertain for themselves whether the state of the country would justify their investing capital in it'.[299] Discussions about

Parsi involvement in the development of Iran were ongoing, and the *Times of India* noted that Iranian newspapers were 'full of Parsi Commercial projects'.[300]

Concerns were expressed by Parsis about their economic position in India, but there were mixed feelings as to whether or not stronger ties with Pahlavi Iran might provide a solution.[301] Merwanji Cursetji argued that Parsis were Indian and that individuals such as Masani, who thought they could succeed in Iran, were overly optimistic.[302] Ultimately, although Masani was 'favourably impressed' by security in Iran, and by the 'great decrease of anti-Zoroastrian feeling', he concluded that large-scale Parsi investment was not yet advisable.[303] However, he believed conditions had improved significantly since 1910, when there had been talk of a Parsi commercial mission to Iran,[304] and he considered plans for the establishment of wool, cotton and tile factories, as well as a flour mill.[305] Textile production was a growing industry in Iran,[306] and the *Iran League Quarterly* encouraged Parsis to enter this field, particularly in view of the unsettled political and economic situation in India.[307] In contrast, the journal noted positive changes in Iran, and a poem printed in 1934 exclaimed:

O Ye Iranian Exile!' – 'You were wronged' – 'Return home, the wrong is righted,
And the home restored and ready to receive you!'[308]

A number of Parsis did move to Iran.[309] Some were employed by the national railway company,[310] and Phiroz Saklatvala, honorary Persian consul-general in New York, urged his fellow-Parsis to take advantage of openings in Iran, especially in the oil industry.[311] As well as claims made regarding opportunities for Parsis in Iran, there were also occasions when the idea of a Parsi colony was raised again.[312]

Parsi interest in Iran was reciprocated by Reza Shah who, as Marashi has observed, took note of members of the community, partly because of their wealth, but also due to the belief that Zoroastrians were an 'embodiment of Iranian authenticity'.[313] Whilst travelling in Sistan in 1930, Reza Shah asked after a group of Parsis who had applied for permission to live there. The individuals were 'produced from the crowd, and he [Reza Shah] congratulated them on their good sense in returning to the country of their origin'.[314] Similarly, Masani later recollected Reza Shah's message to him and the other Parsis who had toured Iran with Tagore:

He expressed his regret that the descendants of the ancient Iranians had very little contact with their fatherland. He wished to see more of them. He did not ask that they should take their money with them from Hindustan to Iran, although he was anxious to see the resources of Iran developed and the Parsis taking a hand in it.[315]

Economic incentives may have been downplayed by Reza Shah, but they were certainly a factor contributing to the nurturing of relations with the Parsi community during the earlier years of his reign.

Despite the enthusiastic reception that Parsis were given by Reza Shah there were concerns raised within the Parsi community about the direction being taken by nationalism in Pahlavi Iran. Farzin Vejdani has highlighted how some individuals expressed fears regarding the effect of the 'glorification of a shared "Aryan" past' linking

Iran to India, particularly in relation to attitudes towards Indian Muslims. This issue was a topic discussed by the Parsi scholar, G. K. Nariman, and Mohammad Iqbal, an Indian Muslim poet and political activist. Both men opposed the promotion of a narrative that described the 'decline' of Iran as being linked to the introduction of Islam, a view that was popular amongst Parsis and Iranian nationalists.[316] Nariman was also critical of the Iranian journalist 'Abdulrahman Saif Azad, as he believed Saif Azad was spreading rumours to bolster the hope held by some Parsis that Pahlavi rule would lead to a resurgence of Zoroastrianism in the country.[317]

According to British reports, Saif Azad claimed to have been 'personally instructed' by Reza Shah to 'induce wealthy Parsees to return to Persia'.[318] Described in the *Iran League Quarterly* as a friend of Ardeshir Reporter,[319] Saif Azad also had links with prominent Zoroastrians in Bombay,[320] through whom he hoped to encourage Parsi involvement in Iran.[321] Indeed, when Saif Azad visited the city in 1931, he was welcomed by the Iran League and Iranian Zoroastrian Anjoman, and a dinner held in his honour was attended by about one hundred 'leading Parsis'.[322] Hoare outlined that the Iran League had relations with 'a nebulous organisation' that Saif Azad had founded in Tehran.[323] This was his cultural centre, 'Kanun-e Iran-e Bastan', towards which some Parsis had donated funds.[324]

In addition to the centre, in 1933, Saif Azad established an illustrated weekly journal, *Nameh-ye Iran-e Bastan*. The title page included the following statement detailing its aims:

> Partisan of the present policy of Persian Empire to uplift Persia to grandeur of ancient Iran. To encourage fraternal sentiments between the Parsees of India and Persians, to stimulate commercial relations, industrial enterprises and to encourage Parsees to visit Iran frequently.[325]

The first issue sold out in five hours, and the journal was positively reviewed in the *Iran League Quarterly*, a publication with which it shared some similar goals.[326] Emphasizing race as a factor that linked the Parsis to Iran,[327] Saif Azad argued that the Parsis had a greater right to live in Iran than the Jews had in Palestine.[328] British officials in Iran believed the journal to be 'subsidised by the Persian Government to attract Parsi capital, by painting modern Persia in glowing colours and running down British rule in India'.[329] This is exemplified by an early article titled, 'An example of the dark and chaotic state of India'.[330] The journal continued to be published until late in 1935, but Parsis had distanced themselves from Saif Azad by late 1933, due to the anti-British sentiments and increasingly pro-Nazi views expressed in his journal.[331]

Whilst Saif Azad may have fallen out of favour, the elevation of ancient Iran by the Pahlavi state was still of interest to Zoroastrians in India. This is evident in the extensive coverage in the *Iran League Quarterly* of the celebrations held in Iran in 1934 to mark the millenary of the poet Ferdowsi, whose *Shahnameh* was viewed as Iran's national epic.[332] Funds were raised by the Iran League for a bronze statue of Ferdowsi to be sent to Iran, and the poet was described by the society's secretary, Kaikhosrow Fitter, as 'Persia's greatest patriot' who had kept the spirit of pre-Islamic Iran alive.[333] The Ferdowsi millenary was a critical element in the wider project of Pahlavi state nationalism and was the result of years of planning. As a key member of the *Anjoman-e Asar-e Melli*, Shahrokh had helped organize the event, and he was particularly involved in the construction of Ferdowsi's mausoleum in Tus.[334] Celebrations took place for almost a month and, in addition to a ceremony at the mausoleum, scholars travelled from across the world to participate in a congress in Tehran.[335] Under the auspices of the Iran League, a group of Zoroastrians from India attended the celebrations, also taking the opportunity to recognize the impact of the philanthropic work of Peshotanji Marker in Yazd.[336]

The funding of projects in Iran continued to be an issue that attracted the disapproval of some Parsis. Writing anonymously to the *Times of India*, a 'Parsi Traveller' drew attention to the numbers of Parsis 'acutely suffering economical distress', whilst a 'steady flow' of money was sent to Iran. The author, who had visited Iran, argued that Iranians should finance their own education system and 'relieve Parsis of what they consider (wrongly in my opinion) to be their duty towards a foreign land'.[337] Specifically, the point was made that since the Iranian government was able to fund a chair in Persian culture at Tagore's institution in India, it was clear that Parsi philanthropy was not needed.[338] Instead, the author proposed that for five years charity be restricted to the 'poor Parsi community of India alone', as Parsis needed to think 'more of their own interests than of aliens'.[339] In addition to the effect of worldwide recession, the involvement of Parsis in the production and sale of alcohol meant that Gandhi's advocacy for temperance was negatively impacting members of the community.[340] Indeed, boycotts of the industry, and the introduction of prohibition in Gujarat in 1937, prompted some Parsi farmers to sell their properties and move to Bombay.[341]

Unemployment remained a cause of anxiety for Parsis throughout the 1930s, and concerns were raised regarding their future economic and political position in India.[342] Alongside worries about the economic outlook, the 1935 Government of India Act heightened the fears held by some Parsis that, due to their population size, the political influence of the community would soon be negligible. In contrast to Muslims and several other minority groups, Parsis had not been granted separate representation in the act. Some Parsis tried to gain British support, whilst others suggested an independent Parsi state might be established within India in order to preserve their presence on the political stage.[343] Combined with a critical outlook of the economic policies of the INC, this situation resulted in more vocal opposition to the INC in the pages of the *Iran League Quarterly*, and increasingly hyperbolic praise for Pahlavi Iran.[344]

Even so, Parsis remained cautious about relocating to Iran or investing in the country. Parsi involvement in the Khosravi Spinning and Weaving Mills company in Mashad was one exception. This was a joint venture between the Iranian government and a group of Parsis, who provided 40 per cent of the capital.[345] The mill opened in 1938 and was the outcome of discussions that had been taking place between Shahrokh and Bombay Parsis for about a decade; those involved included Rustom Masani, who had travelled to Iran with Tagore in 1932.[346] Despite limited Parsi economic engagement in the country, in the late 1930s Iran was still presented as a land of opportunity. Speaking to an audience of young Parsis, Sir Jehangir Coyajee said that it was 'necessary to establish a sort of a liaison between the community and Iran', so that Parsis could go there to pursue commercial activities.[347] Whilst Coyajee did suggest Parsis try their luck in Iran, he cautioned his audience: 'Do not be under the impression . . . that Iran is thirsting for our wealth. That country has wealth of its own.'[348] Likewise, Murali Ranganathan has noted that by the late 1930s, Reza Shah no longer had economic motivations to build relations with Parsis,[349] and the Iranian consul-general reported that as Parsis were British subjects, 'their capital would not therefore be acceptable to Iran'.[350] Indeed, Marashi has highlighted how restrictions on foreign investment had prevented Parsis from owning a larger share of the Khosravi mills.[351]

Rather than turning to their ancient homeland, the priest and scholar, Dastur M. N. Dhalla, who had travelled to Iran with his family in 1921, exhorted Parsis to direct their energies towards the future of the country in which they resided. Viewing communalism as 'the greatest hindrance to India's becoming a homogeneous nation',[352] Dhalla believed that Parsis had a 'bright future' in India if only they would 'adapt' and 'move with the times'.[353] A similar view was expressed by A. P. Sabavala in a lecture about 'the communal problem', delivered to an audience of Parsi students. Sabavala described Parsis as 'all Indians first and last', being 'part and parcel' of India, as they had been living in the country for hundreds of years.[354] The fact that Parsis had not taken up Reza Shah's earlier invitation to settle in Iran was highlighted in 1938 at the Parsi New Year party in London by the high commissioner for India, Sir Feroz Khan Noon. He stated that by acting in this way, Parsis had 'paid a great compliment to India, which was their motherland'.[355]

Although links between Zoroastrians in India and Iran had been more visible after Reza Khan rose to power and established the Pahlavi dynasty, by the late 1930s, the increasing likelihood of war discouraged Parsis from taking risks in Iran. In addition, the death of Shahrokh in 1940 shocked the community, particularly as it seemed likely that he had been assassinated under the orders of Reza Shah due to the involvement of his son, Bahram Shahrokh, in pro-Nazi activities in Berlin.[356] Adding to this, in 1941 Reza Shah was forced to abdicate by the British and the Russians, whose forces occupied Iran during the Second World War (1939–45). Ultimately, despite the concerns that had been voiced by Parsis regarding the end of British rule, in 1947, members of the community participated in celebrations marking Indian independence.[357]

Conclusion

Before setting off in October 1947 to take up his post as the first ambassador of independent India to Iran, Syed Ali Zaheer met with members of both the Iran League and the Iranian Zoroastrian Anjoman (IZA). A Shi'i Muslim and a supporter of the nationalist movement in India, Zaheer had joined the INC at a young age and was, in his own words, a 'staunch believer in Hindu-Muslim unity'.[1] On behalf of the IZA, Dinshaw Irani described Zaheer as a representation of the 'real spirit of Islam', a spirit of tolerance and equality, and he stated that Zaheer's appointment as ambassador reflected the 'spirit of new India', a country where individuals of any religious background had the opportunity to succeed in the political sphere.[2]

Speaking just months after the partition of the Indian subcontinent into independent India and Pakistan, a time of mass communal violence and loss of life, Zaheer praised Zoroastrians, whom he viewed as 'ideal citizens' in their 'adopted' country.[3] He proposed that they set an example that other minorities ought to emulate, outlining that if their lead was followed, 'there would be no question of minority communities at all in India'.[4] The words of Zaheer can be seen in light of the fact that Parsis had not been granted communal representation in independent India, so they did not form a distinct group in political terms. In contrast, following the Constitutional Revolution in Iran, Zoroastrians and other recognized non-Muslim communities were granted reserved seats in the Majles; this remains the case to this day.

The political rights of Zoroastrians in Iran were implicitly referenced by the Iranian consul in Bombay, who was also present at the meeting between Zaheer and the Iran League. Reminiscent of interactions between Parsis and Iranian diplomats during the late nineteenth century, the consul reiterated the reassurances that had been given since the time of the Constitutional Revolution: Zoroastrian interests in Iran were protected 'because Iran did not make any differentiation between any of its citizens'.[5] During the revolution, the inclusion of Article 8 in the supplementary laws was a contentious issue, as it outlined that all Iranians were equal before the law. Under Reza Shah, further measures were implemented to increase national unity, such as universal conscription. By the time Zaheer was preparing to take up his post in Iran, Reza Shah had been succeeded by his son Mohammad Reza, who became shah after his father was forced to abdicate in 1941. Similar to his father, Mohammad Reza Shah continued to promote the nationalism of the Pahlavi state, which elevated the pre-Islamic era and which viewed Zoroastrianism in a positive light.

Echoing the narrative propagated by the Pahlavi state, during the reign of Reza Shah, Parsis had proclaimed that the beginning of his rule was the start of a 'Renaissance', and the dawn of a new age for Zoroastrians in Iran.[6] Indeed, Phiroz D. Saklatvala stated that with his accession to the throne, 'almost like the waving of a magic wand the awakening of Persia became a fact'.[7] A clear demarcation was made between the Qajar period, described as a dark age when Iran was ruled over by a foreign Turkic tribe, and the 'purely Iranian movement', initiated by Reza Shah.[8] Claims were made that Reza Shah had 'elevated the Parsis [Zoroastrians], almost a depressed class under the Kajars, to equality with Muslims'.[9] The shared Iranian heritage of the Parsis and the shah was highlighted; Reza Shah was the 'embodiment of Iranian genius, Iranian power and Iranian character', and the Parsis were 'inheritors of the light of Iran and Iranian character'.[10] Therefore, it was natural that at this time, 'Dear Persia' was 'opening her arms wide to welcome back her parted children'.[11]

However, although Reza Shah emphasized how his dynasty differed from that of the Qajars, the idea of Iran 'awakening' and the possibility of Parsis 'returning' to their homeland had been raised in earlier years. Likewise, references had been made by Zoroastrians and by non-Zoroastrian Iranians to the glories of their shared ancient heritage, including by members of the Qajar family. The Constitutional Revolution had been viewed as the birth of a new era for Iran and, more specifically, for the Zoroastrian community. Whilst acknowledging the impact of Pahlavi policies promoting secularization, as well as the use of ancient Iran in nationalist discourse, benefits felt by Zoroastrians in the years following the coup of Reza Khan must also be seen in light of the gains made during the Constitutional Revolution, which, in turn, were facilitated by developments that had taken place from the mid-nineteenth century.

Iran had always retained the status of the original homeland of the Zoroastrian religion, but from the mid-nineteenth century, weakened links between the Zoroastrian communities in India and Iran were revived, in large part due to the emigration of Iranian Zoroastrians to India. Increased awareness of the difficulties faced by Zoroastrians in Iran prompted the foundation of the Amelioration Society. Alongside the society's efforts to support the religious life of the community and increase access to education, its members were able to use their political influence to push for improvements in the legal status of Zoroastrians in Iran. Questions were raised regarding the extent to which Parsis ought to feel responsible for their co-religionists in Iran, particularly during the famine in the early 1870s, when Parsis were urged to offer their 'patriotic' assistance.

This patriotic sentiment tied in with an increased interest amongst Parsis concerning the history of Iran, their ancient homeland. The pre-Islamic period of Iranian history was elevated by Zoroastrians in India, partly due to Parsi engagement with contemporary Western scholarship and the movement for religious reform within the Parsi community. Similarly, the use of the past as a template for present-day reform was a theme discussed in Iran by early nationalists. These two strands overlapped in several ways: through Hataria, the Amelioration Society's emissary in Iran, as well as in Bombay, where Iranian diplomats socialized with members of the Zoroastrian community, whose political and economic success in the city they admired. The idea that the Parsis were an exilic community gained ground, and, in conjunction with Parsi concerns over their future political and economic position in India, some members of the community raised the possibility of a Parsi colony in or near Iran.

Parsi ties with Iran were perceived to have broader geopolitical implications and were encouraged by the British. Stronger links between Zoroastrians in India and Zoroastrians in Iran were in alignment with British strategic aims and imperial ambitions. By the latter half of the nineteenth century, the socio-economic standing of some members of the Iranian Zoroastrian community had improved considerably. Thus, they were considered by the British to be potentially useful trade partners and allies in the ongoing competition between the British and the Russians in Iran. Consequently, trade with Zoroastrians in Iran was encouraged, and the British also tried to win the loyalty of the Iranian Zoroastrian community through education.

The tripartite relationship between the British and Zoroastrian communities in both India and Iran continued to be of importance during the years of the Iranian Constitutional Revolution. As well as calling on the Parsis and the British to intervene to help protect members of the community, the point was made that if Zoroastrians were granted equal rights, they would no longer need British protection and foreign interference in Iranian affairs would decrease. Whilst the position of Zoroastrians in the nation was being contested in Iran, in India the Parsis were questioning whether their ties to India were stronger than those to their Iranian 'homeland', where the situation for their co-religionists seemed to be improving.

A significant event in this respect was the election of Arbab Jamshid to the First Majles. In contrast to other recognized non-Muslim communities, the Zoroastrians had a representative in the new political apparatus. The economic success and influence of Arbab Jamshid helped to secure his acceptance in the parliament, but there were also instances of positive attitudes towards Zoroastrians because of their status as members of the ancient religion of Iran. Although the Iranian constitution divided the population between Muslims and non-Muslims, with greater opportunities open to Muslims, the invitation to Parsis to contribute to the National Bank of Iran reveals that all Zoroastrians were considered to be Iranian, even if this view was influenced by economic factors. The restoration of constitutional rule with the Second Majles led to a heightened interest in a possible 'return' amongst Parsis, for example, as is seen in the work of Nasarvanji Maneckji Cooper in London. References were made to the glories of the ancient past, and calls were made for Parsis to act patriotically and to do their duty in assisting with the development of Iran.

Despite the end of constitutional rule following the Russian ultimatum in 1911, the gains that had been made by the Zoroastrian community were substantial, and the revolution marked a watershed for Zoroastrians in Iran. Zoroastrians had been included from the start in the Majles, and members of the community had played a key role in the campaign for the inclusion of the highly controversial Article 8 in the supplementary laws and for its implementation following the murder of Fereydun. Pressure exerted on the Iranian government by Zoroastrians in India, particularly via the Amelioration Society, was also significant at this time, as the Majles regarded them as possible financial backers of the constitutionalist project. Thus, during periods of unrest, links with the British and with the Parsis continued to be vital. Even though the Anglo-Russian Convention of 1907 led to a change in British priorities in Iran, the British still had trade relations with Iranian Zoroastrians and continued to act as if they held a level of responsibility towards the community. This was in part due to the pressure placed on them by influential Parsis.

However, broader political currents affected the strength of relations between Zoroastrians in Iran and the British. The conditions of the Anglo-Russian Convention,

British actions in Iran during the First World War, and the 1919 Agreement cumulated in widespread anger at British interference in Iranian affairs. Additionally, the bankruptcy of the two major Zoroastrian trading houses, the Jamshidian and Jahanian firms, also had a negative impact on relations between the British and the Zoroastrian community in Iran. Despite having benefitted from British protection in the past, Iranian Zoroastrians increasingly looked towards Tehran for assistance and to their representative in the Majles, Kaykhosrow Shahrokh, who held the position from 1909 to 1940. In India, Parsis and Iranis continued to be keen on maintaining relations with Zoroastrians in Iran, and, with the rise of Reza Khan in the 1920s, hopes for opportunities in the country for Zoroastrians were augmented.

Although explicit connections between Zoroastrians in India and the Iranian nation were more obvious during the reign of Reza Shah, suggestions of greater involvement in Iran were opposed on both political and economic grounds. The argument was made that Parsis ought to align themselves with nationalists in India, rather than turning to a 'foreign' country. Whereas in the mid-nineteenth century, the idea of directing funds towards the Zoroastrian community in Iran was not contentious, by the early 1930s, criticisms were voiced by Parsis regarding donations being made to causes in Iran, especially since the secularization of Iranian society meant that these funds were less likely to solely benefit the Iranian Zoroastrian community. In Iran, although members of the community still faced discrimination, there was greater integration of Iranian Zoroastrians into the nation than in the past, particularly at a discursive level, leading to a clearer distinction between the Zoroastrian communities of India and Iran in terms of nationality. With Indian independence on the horizon and at a time when Parsis faced economic challenges, many within the Parsi community looked inwards rather than further afield, positioning themselves as members of the Indian rather than Iranian nation. Indeed, whilst agreeing with the hopes expressed by Zaheer for closer links between India and Iran, Sir Jehangir Cowasji, president of the Iran League, was emphatic that Zoroastrians in newly independent India were happy to stay in 'what is today our motherland'.[12]

Notes

Note on the text

1 Available online at https://www.iranchamber.com/calendar/converter/iranian_alendar_converter.php (accessed 18 March 2023).

Introduction

1 *Neda-ye Vatan* 10, 28 Zu al-Hijja 1324 (12 February 1907), 5–6.
2 The census also records that Aimai and Nasarvanji employed a servant, Emily Horsnail. In 1916, Aimai returned to Bombay, where she died in 1938 (*Times of India* [*ToI*], 21 July 1938, 2). I am very grateful to Gerard Greene, manager of the Redbridge Museum and Heritage Centre, for generously sharing with me the research that was conducted by the Redbridge Museum about the life of Aimai Cooper.
3 *ToI*, 17 August 1911, 7.
4 Although Zoroastrianism and Iran appear to have been of particular interest to Cooper, he did write about a variety of topics; for example, he wrote a booklet titled *Curries, and How to Prepare Them*, and an article, 'Prospects of Indian Labour in British and Foreign Fields', which drew on his experiences of travelling to British Guiana, present-day Guyana (*Imperial and Asiatic Quarterly Review and Oriental and Colonial Record* [*IAQROCR*] 23 [April 1907]: 315ff).
5 Jenny Rose, *Zoroastrianism: An Introduction* (London and New York: I.B. Tauris, 2011), xix.
6 Ibid., 9. During the sixth or seventh century CE these texts were written down, and a new alphabet was created for this specific purpose (ibid.).
7 Ibid., 9–11.
8 Ibid., xvii–xx.
9 Ibid., Chapters Two, Three, and Four.
10 Ibid., Chapter Five (in particular, pages 152–8).
11 Ibid., Chapter Four (in particular, pages 99–103, and 107–8), and Michael Stausberg, 'From Power to Powerlessness: Zoroastrianism in Iranian History', in *Religious Minorities in the Middle East: Domination, Self-Empowerment, Accommodation*, ed. Anh Nga Longva and Anne Sofie Roald (Leiden and Boston: Brill, 2012), 173–5.
12 Richard Foltz, 'Zoroastrians in Iran: What Future in the Homeland?', *The Middle East Journal* 65, no. 1 (2011): 73–4, and Rose, *Zoroastrianism*, 170–3.
13 Foltz, 'Zoroastrians in Iran', 73–4. See also Jamsheed Choksy, 'Zoroastrians in Muslim Iran: Selected Problems of Coexistence and Interaction during the Early Medieval Period', *Iranian Studies* 20, no. 1 (1987): 17–30.

14 Rose, *Zoroastrianism*, 163, and Eliz Sanasarian, *Religious Minorities in Iran* (Cambridge: Cambridge University Press, 2000), 20–1.
15 Vera B. Moreen, 'Jezya', http://www.iranicaonline.org/articles/jezya (accessed on 18 March 2023).
16 John R. Hinnells, 'Parsi Communities i. Early History', https://iranicaonline.org/articles/parsi-communities-i-early-history (accessed on 18 March 2023).
17 Alan Williams, *The Zoroastrian Myth of Migration from Iran and Settlement in the Indian Diaspora: Text, Translation and Analysis of the 16th Century Qesse-ye Sanjān 'The Story of Sanjan'* (Leiden and Boston: Brill, 2009), 205, and Rose, *Zoroastrianism*, 190–2.
18 See Williams, *The Zoroastrian Myth of Migration from Iran and Settlement in the Indian Diaspora*, for analysis of the significance of the epic, as well as an English translation of the text.
19 For further discussion, see Eckehard Kulke, *The Parsees in India: A Minority as Agent of Social Change* (Munich: Welforum-Verlag, 1974), 25ff. See also Hinnells, 'Parsi Communities i. Early History', and Paul Axelrod, 'Myth and Identity in the Indian Zoroastrian Community', *Journal of Mithraic Studies* 3, no. 1–2 (1980): 150–65.
20 Williams, *The Zoroastrian Myth of Migration from Iran and Settlement in the Indian Diaspora*, 229–37.
21 Hinnells, 'Parsi Communities i. Early History'.
22 Kulke, *The Parsees in India*, 30–1.
23 Mary Boyce, *Zoroastrians: Their Religious Beliefs and Customs* (Abingdon: Routledge, 2001), 171, and Hinnells, 'Parsi Communities i. Early History'.
24 Hinnells, 'Parsi Communities i. Early History'.
25 Kulke, *The Parsees in India*, 31, and Monica M. Ringer, *Pious Citizens: Reforming Zoroastrianism in India and Iran* (Syracuse, New York: Syracuse University Press, 2011), 27.
26 Juan R. I. Cole, 'Iranian Culture and South Asia, 1500-1900', in *Iran and the Surrounding World: Interactions in Culture and Cultural Politics*, ed. Nikki R. Keddie and Rudi Matthee (Seattle: University of Washington Press. 2002), 16–18.
27 Rose, *Zoroastrianism*, 194.
28 H. Corbin, 'Āzar Kayvān', https://iranicaonline.org/articles/azar-kayvan-priest (accessed on 18 March 2023).
29 Kioumars Ghereghlou, 'On the Margins of Minority Life: Zoroastrians and the State in Safavid Iran', *Bulletin of the School of Oriental and African Studies* 80, no. 1 (2017): 50–1. NB the overland trade route from Gujarat to Kerman became too dangerous in the late seventeenth century (ibid., 68).
30 Hinnells, 'Parsi Communities i. Early History'.
31 Monica M. Ringer, 'Reform Transplanted: Parsi Agents of Change amongst Zoroastrians in Nineteenth-Century Iran', *Iranian Studies* 42, no. 4 (2009): 549–50.
32 NB during the period of the *Revayat*s additional manuscripts were brought to India (Rose, *Zoroastrianism*, 193).
33 Hinnells, 'Parsi Communities i. Early History', and Shahrokh R. Vafadari, 'A Note on Kerman and Dustur Jamasb', in *Ātaš-e Dorun, The Fire Within: Jamshid Soroush Soroushian Memorial Volume II*, ed. Carlo G. Cereti and Farrokh Vajifdar and co-ordinated by Mehrborzin Soroushian (United States: 1st Books, 2003), 452.
34 Daniel J. Sheffield, 'Iran, the Mark of Paradise or the Land of Ruin?: Historical Approaches to Reading two Parsi Zoroastrian Travelogues', in *On the Wonders of Land and Sea: Persianate Travel Writing*, ed. Roberta Micallef and Sunil Sharma

(Cambridge, MA: Harvard University Press, 2013), 19–20. NB in the early twentieth century a third calendar was suggested by the newly formed Fasli group (Rose, *Zoroastrianism*, 209).
35 Rose, *Zoroastrianism*, 201.
36 Jesse S. Palsetia, *The Parsis of India: Preservation of Identity in Bombay City* (Leiden: Brill, 2001), 24–5.
37 Sheffield, 'Iran, the Mark of Paradise or the Land of Ruin?', 20–1.
38 Kulke, *The Parsees in India*, 32, and Hinnells, 'Parsi Communities i. Early History'.
39 John R. Hinnells, 'Bombay, Persian Communities of. i. The Zoroastrian Community', https://www.iranicaonline.org/articles/bombay-persian-communities-of#pt1 (accessed on 18 March 2023), and Boyce, *Zoroastrians*, 187.
40 Kulke, *The Parsees in India*, 33–4.
41 Ibid., 36.
42 Dinyar Patel, *Naoroji: Pioneer of Indian Nationalism* (Cambridge, MA: Harvard University Press, 2020), 17.
43 Boyce, *Zoroastrians*, 192, and Ringer, *Pious Citizens*, 33. See also John R. Hinnells, 'Bombay Parsi Panchayat', https://www.iranicaonline.org/articles/bombay-parsi-panchayat-the-largest-zoroastrian-institution-in-modern-history (accessed on 18 March 2023).
44 Hinnells, 'Bombay, Persian Communities of. i. The Zoroastrian Community', and Rose, *Zoroastrianism*, 198.
45 David Willmer, 'Parsis and Public Space in 19th Century Bombay: A Different Formulation of "The Political" in a Non-European Context', *Critical Horizons* 3, no. 2, (2002): 286.
46 Hinnells, 'Bombay, Persian Communities of. i. The Zoroastrian Community'. See also Kejia Yan, 'Parsis in the Opium Trade in China', Shanghai Academy of Social Sciences, https://asianscholarship.org/publications/ (accessed on 3 November 2023).
47 Kulke, *The Parsees in India*, 78–9, and 239–40.
48 Ringer, *Pious Citizens*, 37–8, and Jesse S. Palsetia, 'Parsi and Hindu Traditional and Nontraditional Responses to Christian Conversion in Bombay, 1839–45'. *Journal of the American Academy of Religion* 74, no. 3 (2006): 621–9. See also Ian Copland, 'The Limits of Hegemony: Elite Responses to Nineteenth-Century Imperial and Missionary Acculturation Strategies in India', *Comparative Studies in Society and History* 49, no. 3 (July 2007): 648–56.
49 Ringer, *Pious Citizens*, 38, and Mridula Ramanna, 'Social Background of the Educated in Bombay City: 1824-58', *Economic and Political Weekly* 24, no. 4 (1989): 203–7.
50 Patel, *Naoroji*, 23–6.
51 Rose, *Zoroastrianism*, 204–7, and Ringer, *Pious Citizens*, 52–6. Having been assisted in India by a Parsi priest, Darab Kumana, the French scholar A. H. Anquetil-Duperron (1731–1805), published his translation of the *Avesta* in 1771. Other scholars subsequently translated Zoroastrian texts into other European languages (Boyce, *Zoroastrians*, 194–5, and Jacques Duchesne-Guillemin, 'Anquetil-Duperron', https://iranicaonline.org/articles/anquetil-duperron-abraham [accessed on 18 March 2023]).
52 Rose, *Zoroastrianism*, 205.
53 Kulke, *The Parsees in India*, 95ff, and Ringer, *Pious Citizens*, 75.
54 James R. Russell, 'Cama, Kharshedji Rustamh', https://iranicaonline.org/articles/cama-kharshedji-rustamh-b (accessed on 18 March 2023).

55 Patel, *Naoroji*, 34–5.
56 Kulke, *The Parsees in India*, 115.
57 Ringer, *Pious Citizens*, 73.
58 Tanya M. Luhrmann, 'Evil in the Sands of Time: Theology and Identity Politics among the Zoroastrian Parsis', *The Journal of Asiatic Studies* 61, no. 3 (2002): 867.
59 Ringer, *Pious Citizens*, 84.
60 For detailed analysis, see Ringer, *Pious Citizens*, Chapter Four. For example, see Dosabhai Framji Karaka, *The Parsees: Their History, Manners, Customs, and Religion* (London: Smith, Elder and Co.; Bombay: Smith, Taylor and Co., 1858), 258ff, where Karaka quotes a number of Western scholars to support his argument that Zoroastrianism is a monotheistic faith.
61 Ringer, *Pious Citizens*, 56–7.
62 Ibid., 73ff, and 139.
63 Mitra Sharafi, *Law and Identity in Colonial South Asia: Parsi Legal Culture, 1772-1947* (New York: Cambridge University Press, 2014), 21.
64 Kulke, *The Parsees in India*, 78–9.
65 Luhrmann, 'Evil in the Sands of Time', 868, and 865.
66 Ringer, *Pious Citizens*, 42–3.
67 Kulke, *The Parsees in India*, 104–5. For example, see Karaka, *The Parsees*, 73.
68 Ringer, *Pious Citizens*, 42–5.
69 Rose, *Zoroastrianism*, 213.
70 John R. Hinnells, 'Social Change and Religious Transformation among Bombay Parsis in the Early 20th Century', in *Traditions in Contact and Change*, ed. Peter Slater and Donald Wiebe (Waterloo, ON: Wilfrid Laurier University Press, 1983), 106.
71 Hinnells, 'Bombay, Persian Communities of. i. The Zoroastrian Community', and Willmer, 'Parsis and Public Space in 19th Century Bombay', 278.
72 Willmer, 'Parsis and Public Space in 19th Century Bombay', 289ff.
73 Kulke, *The Parsees in India*, 134. An example of this can be found in the *Parsi*, where the statement was made that 'The Parsi's loyalty to his rulers is proverbial' (*Parsi*, July 1905, 258).
74 Sharafi, *Law and Identity in Colonial South Asia*, 19, and Kulke, *The Parsees in India*, 50ff.
75 John R. Hinnells, *Zoroastrian and Parsi Studies: Selected Works of John R. Hinnells* (Aldershot: Ashgate, 2000), 142.
76 Sharafi, *Law and Identity in Colonial South Asia*, 19.
77 Hinnells, 'Parsi Communities i. Early History', and Jesse S. Palsetia, 'Parsi Communities ii. In Calcutta', https://iranicaonline.org/articles/parsi-communities-ii-in-calcutta (accessed on 18 March 2023).
78 Stausberg, 'From Power to Powerlessness', 175–6.
79 Touraj Daryaee, 'Zoroastrianism under Islamic Rule', in *The Wiley Blackwell Companion to Zoroastrianism*, ed. Michael Stausberg and Yuhan Sohrab-Dinshaw Vevaina (Chichester: Wiley Blackwell, 2015), 115.
80 Aptin Khanbaghi quoted in Stausberg, 'From Power to Powerlessness', 176.
81 Daryaee, 'Zoroastrianism under Islamic Rule', 116–17. See also Kiyan Foroutan, 'Yazd and Its Zoroastrians: A Review Paper of Ali Akbar Tashakori's *A Social History of the Zoroastrians of Yazd* (2019)', *Iranian Studies* 56, no. 4 (2023): 815.
82 John R. Hinnells, Mary Boyce, and Shahrokh Shahrokh, 'Charitable Foundations ii. Among Zoroastrians in Islamic times', https://www.iranicaonline.org/articles/charitable-foundations-mpers#pt2 (accessed on 18 March 2023).

83 Ghereghlou, 'On the Margins of Minority Life', 48, and 64.
84 Stausberg, 'From Power to Powerlessness', 176–7.
85 Jamsheed Choksy, 'Despite Shāhs and Mollās: Minority Sociopolitics in Premodern and Modern Iran', *Journal of Asian History* 40, no. 2 (2006): 136–7.
86 Ibid., 136.
87 Daryaee, 'Zoroastrianism under Islamic Rule', 117–18, and Sanasarian, *Religious Minorities in Iran*, 23–4. NB Daryaee has pointed out that some of the details in a text by Majlesi appear to reflect the content of earlier Zoroastrian texts, for example, the rule that nails must not be clipped at night. See also Daniel Tsadik, 'The Legal Status of Religious Minorities: Imāmī Shīʿī Law and Iran's Constitutional Revolution', *Islamic Law and Society* 10, no. 3 (2003): 381–5, which focuses in particular on the position of Iranian Jews.
88 Daryaee, 'Zoroastrianism under Islamic Rule', 117.
89 Choksy, 'Despite Shāhs and Mollās', 138.
90 Daryaee, 'Zoroastrianism under Islamic Rule', 117–18; Choksy, 'Despite Shāhs and Mollās', 139–41; and, Vafadari, 'A Note on Kerman and Dustur Jamasb', 451. See also Ghereghlou, 'On the Margins of Minority Life', 69.
91 Choksy, 'Despite Shāhs and Mollās', 141. NB Kiyan Foroutan has argued that there is no evidence linking later attitudes towards Zoroastrians to anger at their support for the Afghans (Foroutan, 'Yazd and its Zoroastrians', 817–18).
92 Ernest Tucker, 'Nāder Shah', https://www.iranicaonline.org/articles/nader-shah (accessed on 18 March 2023).
93 Foroutan, 'Yazd and its Zoroastrians', 818.
94 Ferdinand Méchin, *Lettres d'un voyageur en Perse: Djoulfa, Yesd, les Guèbres* (Bourges: A. Jollet, 1867), 7, and Karaka, *The Parsees*, 35.
95 John R. Perry, 'Karim Khan Zand', https://www.iranicaonline.org/articles/karim-khan-zand/ (accessed on 18 March 2023).
96 Boyce, *Zoroastrians*, 190–1, and Sheffield, 'Iran, the Mark of Paradise or the Land of Ruin?', 20ff.
97 Ringer, 'Reform Transplanted', 550–1.
98 Daryaee, 'Zoroastrianism under Islamic Rule', 118.
99 Hinnells, 'Bombay, Persian Communities of. i. The Zoroastrian Community'.
100 Fatḥ-Allāh Mojtabaʾī, 'Dasātīr', https://iranicaonline.org/articles/dasatir (accessed on 18 March 2023).
101 Hinnells, 'Bombay, Persian Communities of. i. The Zoroastrian Community'.
102 John R. Perry, 'Zand Dynasty', http://www.iranicaonline.org/articles/zand-dynasty (accessed on 18 March 2023).
103 *Oriental Christian Spectator* (*OCS*) 2, no. 9 (May 1848): 175.
104 Rose, *Zoroastrianism*, 180.
105 Other languages spoken in Iran include Kurdish, Luri, Arabic, Turkish, Baluchi and Armenian (Sanasarian, *Religious Minorities in Iran*, 9). Estimated population figures for Zoroastrians and for the whole of Iran vary. The approximation that during the nineteenth century, Zoroastrians comprised around 0.1 per cent of the total population is based on estimates that there were roughly 10,000 Zoroastrians in a population of around 10,000,000 (Farhang Mehr, 'Zoroastrians in Twentieth Century Iran', in *A Zoroastrian Tapestry: Art, Religion and Culture*, ed. Pheroza J. Godrej and Firoza Punthakey Mistree [Ahmedabad: Mapin Publishing, 2002], 279, and Ahmad Seyf, 'Population and Agricultural Development in Iran, 1800-1906', *Middle Eastern Studies* 45, no. 3 [2009]: 449).

106 Said Amir Arjomand, *Turban for the Crown: The Islamic Revolution in Iran* (New York: Oxford University Press, 1988), 14.
107 By the early twentieth century, there were approximately 50,000 Jews, 44,000 Assyrians and 65,000 Armenians in Iran (Pierre Oberling, 'The Role of Religious Minorities in the Persian Revolution, 1906-1912', *Journal of Asian History* 12, no. 1 [1978]: 5, 21, and 24). See Sanasarian, *Religious Minorities in Iran*, Chapter One, for an overview of non-Muslim communities in Iran.
108 Stausberg, 'From Power to Powerlessness', 176. For example, although both Jews and Zoroastrians were regarded as *dhimmi*s, Malcolm notes that the Jews in Yazd, who were, on the whole, poorer than Zoroastrians, were 'in some ways less restricted' (Napier Malcolm, *Five Years in a Persian Town* [London: John Murray, 1908], 44).
109 Malcolm, *Five Years in a Persian Town*, 44–8. See also Keikhosrow Shahrokh, *The Memoirs of Keikhosrow Shahrokh*, ed. and trans. Shahrokh Shahrokh and Rashna Writer (Lewiston, NY; Lampeter: Edwin Mellen Press, 1994), 33.
110 Daniel Tsadik, *Between Foreigners and Shi'is: Nineteenth-Century Iran and its Jewish Minority* (Stanford, California: Stanford University Press, 2007), 52.
111 For an analysis of the concept, see Benjamin Thomas White, *The Emergence of Minorities in the Middle East: The Politics of Community in French Mandate Syria* (Edinburgh: Edinburgh University Press, 2011), Chapter One.
112 Stausberg, 'From Power to Powerlessness', 173–4.
113 Ibid., 172–3.
114 Anh Nga Longva, 'Introduction: Domination, Self-Empowerment, Accommodation', in *Religious Minorities in the Middle East: Domination, Self-Empowerment, Accommodation*, ed. Anh Nga Longva and Anne Sofie Roald (Leiden and Boston: Brill, 2012), 5.
115 Sharafi, *Law and Identity in Colonial South Asia*, 31. For discussion about the census, see R. B. Bhagat, 'Census and the Construction of Communalism in India', *Economic and Political Weekly* 36, no. 46/47 (24–30 November 2001): 4352–6.
116 Henry Waterfield, *Memorandum on the Census of British India of 1871-72* (London: Eyre and Spottiswoode for H.M. Stationery Office, 1875), 28.
117 Rashna Darius Nicholson, 'The Picture, the Parable, the Performance and the Sword: Secularism's Demographic Imperatives', *Ethnic and Racial Studies* 41, no. 12 (2018): 2207–8.
118 Simin Patel, 'Cultural Intermediaries in a Colonial City: The Parsis of Bombay, c. 1860-1921' (DPhil Thesis, University of Oxford, Oxford, 2015), 74–5.
119 Afshin Marashi, *Exile and the Nation: The Parsi Community of India and the Making of Modern Iran*, (Austin, TX: University of Texas Press, 2020).
120 Afshin Marashi, *Nationalizing Iran: Culture, Power, and the State, 1870–1940* (Seattle and London: University of Washington Press, 2008).
121 Reza Zia-Ebrahimi, 'An Emissary of the Golden Age: Manekji Limji Hataria and the Charisma of the Archaic in Pre-Nationalist Iran', *Studies in Ethnicity and Nationalism* 10, no. 3 (2010): 377–90, and Michael Stausberg, 'Manekji Limji Hatāriā and the Rediscovery of Ancient Iran', in *Ātaš-e Dorun, The Fire Within: Jamshid Soroush Soroushian Memorial Volume II*, ed. Carlo G. Cereti and Farrokh Vajifdar and co-ordinated by Mehrborzin Soroushian (United States: 1st Books, 2003).
122 Shervin Farridnejad, 'The Royal Farmān and the Abolition of Zoroastrian Poll Tax in Qajar Iran', *Himalayan and Central Asian Studies* 25, no. 1–3 (2021): 105–31, and Dinyar Patel, 'Power and Philanthropy: The Imperial Dimensions of Parsi Amelioration of the Iranian Zoroastrians', *Iranian Studies* 56, no. 2 (2023): 205–29.

123 Dinyar Patel, 'Caught Between Two Nationalisms: The Iran League of Bombay and the Political Anxieties of an Indian Minority', *Modern Asian Studies* 55, no. 3 (2021): 764–800.
124 Afshin Marashi, '"Rich Fields in Persia": Parsi Capital and the Origins of Economic Development in Pahlavi Iran, 1925–1941', *Iranian Studies* 56, no. 1 (2023): 61–83, and Murali Ranganathan, 'Back to the Motherland? Parsi Gujarati Travelogues of Iran in the Qajar-Pahlavi Interregnum, 1921–1925', *Iranian Studies* 56, no. 1 (2023): 37–59.
125 Ringer, *Pious Citizens*.
126 For example, Talinn Grigor, 'Parsi Patronage of the *Urheimat*', *Getty Research Journal*, no. 2 (2010): 53–68.
127 Janet Kestenberg Amighi, *The Zoroastrians of Iran: Conversion, Assimilation, or Persistence* (New York: AMS Press, 1990), 143. This is a theme that has also been addressed in works by Monica Ringer and Michael Stausberg.
128 Mansour Bonakdarian, 'India ix, Relations: Qajar Period, Early 20th Century', https://www.iranicaonline.org/articles/india-ix-relations-qajar-period-early-20th-century (accessed on 18 March 2023).

Chapter 1

1 Jesse S. Palsetia, 'Parsi Charity: A Historical Perspective on Religion, Community, and Donor-Patron Relations among the Parsis of India', in *Holy Wealth: Accounting for this World and the Next in Religious Belief and Practice. Festschrift for John R. Hinnells*, ed. Almut Hintze and Alan Williams (Wiesbaden: Harrassowitz Verlag, 2017), 190.
2 Hinnells, *Zoroastrian and Parsi Studies*, 209–10.
3 See Sarah Stewart, 'The Politics of Zoroastrian Philanthropy and the Case of Qasr-e Firuzeh', *Iranian Studies* 45, no. 1 (2012): 60–1, and Rashna Writer, 'Charity as a Means of Zoroastrian Self-Preservation', *Iranian Studies* 49, no. 1 (2016): 117–20.
4 Maria Macuch, 'Charitable Foundations i. In the Sasanian Period', https://www.iranicaonline.org/articles/charitable-foundations-mpers#pt1 (accessed on 18 March 2023).
5 Hinnells, Boyce, and Shahrokh. 'Charitable Foundations ii. Among Zoroastrians in Islamic Times'.
6 Williams, *The Zoroastrian Myth of Migration from Iran and Settlement in the Indian Diaspora*, 234, and Rose, *Zoroastrianism*, 195.
7 Hinnells, 'Parsi Communities i. Early History'.
8 Mary Boyce and Firoze M. Kotwal, 'Chāngā Āsā', https://www.iranicaonline.org/articles/changa-asa-an-eminent-parsi-layman-who-lived-in-the-15th-16th-centuries-a (accessed on 18 March 2023), and Williams, *The Zoroastrian Myth of Migration from Iran and Settlement in the Indian Diaspora*, 200.
9 Palsetia, 'Parsi Charity', 177.
10 Boyce, *Zoroastrians*, 187. For a detailed analysis of Parsi gifting in the eighteenth century, with a focus on Rustam Manek and his family, see David L. White, 'From Crisis to Community Definition: The Dynamics of Eighteenth-Century Parsi Philanthropy', *Modern Asian Studies* 25, no. 2 (1991): 303–20. See also Palsetia, 'Parsi Charity', 180–1, and 183.
11 White, 'From Crisis to Community Definition', 316–17.

12 Ibid., 317.
13 Rusheed Wadia, 'Bombay Parsi Merchants in the Eighteenth and Nineteenth Centuries', in *Parsis in India and the Diaspora*, ed. John R. Hinnells and Alan Williams (London: Routledge, 2007), 130.
14 Hinnells, Boyce and Shahrokh, 'Charitable Foundations ii. Among Zoroastrians in Islamic Times'. See also Palsetia, 'Parsi Charity', 187–8.
15 Hinnells, *Zoroastrian and Parsi Studies*, 222.
16 Hinnells, Boyce and Shahrokh, 'Charitable Foundations ii. Among Zoroastrians in Islamic Times'.
17 Hinnells, 'Bombay Parsi Panchayat'.
18 Ringer, *Pious Citizens*, 35–6.
19 For further details, see Hinnells, *Zoroastrian and Parsi Studies*, 219–21.
20 Hinnells, 'Parsi Communities i. Early History'.
21 Palsetia, 'Parsi Charity', 183.
22 For examples, see ibid., 183–4, and Hinnells, *Zoroastrian and Parsi Studies*, 235.
23 Hinnells, *Zoroastrian and Parsi Studies*, 211, and Palsetia, 'Parsi Charity', 184–5.
24 Palsetia, 'Parsi Charity', 186.
25 Ibid., 185. See also pages 186–8, and Hinnells, *Zoroastrian and Parsi Studies*, 235. On one instance when a Parsi gave a large donation and wanted to remain anonymous, the point was made that anonymous donations had been frequent in the past, and that habits had changed due to 'European example and taste' (*ToI*, 5 June 1871, 2).
26 Palsetia, 'Parsi Charity', 186. For an overview of Parsi charity in the medical field, see Hinnells, *Zoroastrian and Parsi Studies*, 224–7.
27 Hinnells, Boyce, and Shahrokh, 'Charitable Foundations ii. Among Zoroastrians in Islamic Times'.
28 Hinnells, *Zoroastrian and Parsi Studies*, 212, 219, and 224. Charitable acts were sometimes later made public when details were printed in obituaries. For example, the philanthropic works of Bai Awabai Framji Petit are outlined in the announcement of her death (*ToI*, 5 October 1907, 7).
29 Palsetia, *The Parsis of India*, 44, and Hinnells, *Zoroastrian and Parsi Studies*, 226, and 236.
30 Dosabhai Framji Karaka, *History of the Parsis: Including Their Manners, Customs, Religion and Present Position*, vol. 2 (London: MacMillan, 1884), 38–9. See also Palsetia, 'Parsi Charity', 184.
31 The organization was also known as the 'Society of the noble Parsis' (*Anjoman-e Akabar-e Parsiyan*).
32 Arnavaz S. Mama, 'Manekji Limji Hataria: Redeeming a Community', *Parsiana* 12, no. 11 (1990): 26, and Patel, 'Cultural Intermediaries in a Colonial City', 62. NB Muslims also fled to India during this period (Sheffield, 'Iran, the Mark of Paradise or the Land of Ruin?', 28).
33 Boyce, *Zoroastrians*, 209, and Mama, 'Manekji Limji Hataria', 26.
34 Boyce, *Zoroastrians*, 209.
35 Ibid., and Mama, 'Manekji Limji Hataria', 26.
36 See S. M. Edwardes, *Memoir of Sir Dinshaw Manockjee Petit, First Baronet (1823–1901)* (Oxford: Oxford University Press, 1923), 9. For details of D. M. Petit's work related to the Amelioration Society, and the role played by his father, see pages 5–7, and 52–5.
37 This is clear from the list of the individuals who were part of the Managing Committee in 1858 (Typescript of 'A Report on the work of the Charitable Institution

set up to Ameliorate the Condition of poor Zoroastrians in Iran', held at the K. R. Cama Oriental Institute Library [henceforth, 'Amelioration Society Typescript'], 1–2).
38 For biographical details, see Rüdiger Schmitt, 'Westergaard, Niels Ludvig', http://www.iranicaonline.org/articles/westergaard-niels-ludvig (accessed on 18 March 2023).
39 *OCS* 2, no. 9 (May 1848): 171ff.
40 Ibid., 171–2, and 175.
41 Sheffield, 'Iran, the Mark of Paradise or the Land of Ruin?', 28.
42 Ibid., 30–1.
43 *OCS* 2, no. 10 (June 1848): 228. See also Ringer, 'Reform Transplanted', 551–2.
44 Palsetia, *The Parsis of India*, 169–70, and 289.
45 Firoze M. Kotwal, Jamsheed K. Choksy, Christopher J. Brunner, and Mahnaz Moazami, 'Hataria, Manekji Limji', http://www.iranicaonline.org/articles/hataria-manekji-limji (accessed on 18 March 2023), and M. Kasheff, 'Anjoman-e Zartoštīān', http://www.iranicaonline.org/articles/anjoman-e-zartostian (accessed on 18 March 2023).
46 Kotwal et al., 'Hataria, Manekji Limji', and Kasheff, 'Anjoman-e Zartoštīān'. See also Rashid Shahmardan, *Farzanegan-e Zartoshti* (Tehran: Sazman-e Javanan-e Zartoshti-ye Bamba'i, 1330/1961–2), 617–42.
47 Touraj Amini, *Asnadi az Zartoshtiyan-e Moʿaser-e Iran* (Tehran: Entesharat-e Sazman-e Asnad-e Melli-ye Iran, 1380/2001), 2, and Kasheff, 'Anjoman-e Zartoštīān'.
48 Kasheff, 'Anjoman-e Zartoštīān'.
49 Kotwal et al., 'Hataria, Manekji Limji'. See also 'Amelioration Society Typescript', 1, which refers to a detailed report from October 1855 to September 1858. This was published in Bombay in 1859, and was 'distributed free to the people here and all over the country'.
50 Kotwal et al., 'Hataria, Manekji Limji'.
51 Ibid.
52 For examples of the projects supported by Parsi charity, see Manekji Limji Hataria, 'Support from the *Sethias*: Travels in Iran: 5', *Parsiana* 13, no. 6 (1990): 29–32.
53 Kasheff, 'Anjoman-e Zartoštīān'. *Anjoman*s were founded in Yazd in 1854, and Kerman in 1855. However, Hataria's successor, Kaykhosrow Khansaheb, had to re-establish the *anjoman*s in 1890, as those started by Hataria had ceased to function effectively.
54 Kasheff, 'Anjoman-e Zartoštīān'.
55 For discussion of factors leading Zoroastrians to convert to Islam, see Janet Kestenberg Amighi, 'Zoroastrians of 19th Century Yazd and Kerman', http://www.iranicaonline.org/articles/kerman-13-zoroastrians (accessed on 18 March 2023).
56 Kotwal et al., 'Hataria, Manekji Limji'. NB estimates made during this period of the total number of Zoroastrians in Iran varied (see Farridnejad, 'The Royal *Farmān* and the Abolition of Zoroastrian Poll Tax in Qajar Iran' 113, and 116).
57 Manekji Limji Hataria, 'Rites of Passage: Travels in Iran: 3', *Parsiana* 13, no. 4 (1990): 39. Between 1856 and 1865, the Amelioration Society helped pay for almost one hundred dowries (M. M. Murzban, *The Parsis in India: Being an Enlarged and Copiously Annotated, Up to Date English Edition of Mlle. Delphine Menant's 'Les Parsis'*, vol. 1 [Bombay: Published by M. M. Murzban, 1917], 136).
58 'Amelioration Society Typescript', 13–14. In another letter, Hataria pointed out that the Sadr-e A'zam, the prime minister, 'wished that those Zoroastrians who had left the country and went away to other places be called back to live here as faithful

subjects'. Hataria argued that if the *jezya* was abolished, Zoroastrians might be tempted to return to 'their Motherland' ('Amelioration Society Typescript', 25).
59 Tsadik, *Between Foreigners and Shi'is*, 83. Mohammad Gholi Majd has proposed an even greater population decline from seventeen to six million people (Mohammad Gholi Majd, *A Victorian Holocaust: Iran in the Great Famine of 1869–1873* [Lanham; BO; New York; Toronto; Plymouth: Hamilton Books, 2017], 123).
60 Majd, *A Victorian Holocaust*, 7, and Xavier de Planhol, 'Famines', https://iranicaonline.org/articles/famines (accessed on 18 March 2023).
61 *ToI*, 24 June 1871, 2.
62 Majd, *A Victorian Holocaust*, 15.
63 *Jam-e Jamshed*, quoted in *ToI*, 9 May 1871, 3.
64 *ToI*, 9 May 1871, 3. For references to similar reports regarding the Jewish community, see Tsadik, *Between Foreigners and Shi'is*, 82–3. NB see the following pages for discussion about the assistance given by Jewish communities outside Iran to their co-religionists during this period.
65 *ToI*, 6 June 1871, 2. A list of donors was printed, which included several women (*ToI*, 9 June 1871, 3). For details about the role played by D. N. Petit, see Edwardes, *Memoir of Sir Dinshaw Manockjee Petit*, 52–3.
66 *ToI*, 5 June 1871, 2. For further details about Cowasjee Jehangir Readymoney, who was knighted in 1872, see Palsetia, *The Parsis in India*, 133–4.
67 See also, Simin Patel, 'The Great Persian Famine of 1871, Parsi Refugees and the Making of Irani Identity in Bombay', in *Bombay Before Mumbai: Essays in Honour of Jim Masselos*, ed. Prashant Kidambi, Manjiri Kamat, and Rachel Dwyer (New York: Oxford University Press, 2019). For further details about the Mehrban family, see Nasser Mohajer and Kaveh Yazdani, 'From Yazd to Bombay —Ardeshir Mehrabān "Irani" and the Rise of Persia's Nineteenth-Century Zoroastrian Merchants', *Journal of the Royal Asiatic Society* 34, no. 1 (2024): 1–25. This article was published when I was preparing my manuscript for submission, so its findings have not been fully addressed in this text.
68 *ToI*, 12 December 1874, 2, and Mehr, 'Zoroastrians in Twentieth Century Iran', 285.
69 See *ToI*, 2 August 1871, 2, for a report of the positive impact these funds had for Zoroastrians in Yazd.
70 For example, see *ToI*, 7 September 1871, 2; *ToI*, 12 January 1872, 2; and, Edwardes, *Memoir of Sir Dinshaw Manockjee Petit*, 53.
71 *ToI*, 19 October 1871, 2.
72 *ToI*, 19 January 1872, 2.
73 *ToI*, 19 October 1871, 2.
74 *Rast Goftar* (*RG*), cited in *ToI*, 7 November 1871, 4.
75 Ibid.
76 In addition to donations from Parsis in Bombay, donations were also made to the Persian Famine Relief Fund by Parsis living elsewhere in India, including Poona (Pune), Surat, and Calcutta (Kolkata), as well as by Parsis living in Amoy (Xiamen) in China (Patel, 'Cultural Intermediaries in a Colonial City', 71). The Persian Famine Relief Fund did not only receive donations from Zoroastrians; for example, funds were offered by the Muslim prime minister of Hyderabad, H. E. Sir Salar Jung (*ToI*, 11 April 1872, 3).
77 *ToI*, 30 January 1872, 2.
78 Patel, 'Cultural Intermediaries in a Colonial City', 68.
79 *ToI*, 25 February 1871, 3.

80 *ToI*, 5 February 1872, 3.
81 *ToI*, 6 June 1871, 2. See also Patel, 'Cultural Intermediaries in a Colonial City', 73–4.
82 For instance, one individual stated that he owned properties worth 3,500 rupees. He also mentioned that he had a son who had been in Bombay for some time, revealing how family ties connected Zoroastrians in Iran and India (*ToI*, 19 January 1872, 2).
83 *RG*, cited in *ToI*, 22 September 1871, 3. Indeed, in his 1878 travelogue, Grattan Geary noted that some Zoroastrian families returned to Yazd when the famine ended (Grattan Geary, *Through Asiatic Turkey: Narrative of a Journey from Bombay to the Bosphorus*, vol. 1 [London: Sampson Low, 1878], 81).
84 *RG*, cited in *ToI*, 22 September 1871, 3.
85 *ToI*, 26 June 1871, 2.
86 *ToI*, 5 June 1871, 2. For example, the following year, the *Times of India* emphasized Zoroastrian attachment to Iran, describing Iranian Zoroastrians as 'descendants of a once powerful race', and 'the oldest inhabitants' of Persia (*ToI*, 19 January 1872, 2).
87 *ToI*, 19 January 1872, 2.
88 Patel, 'Cultural Intermediaries in a Colonial City', 73–4.
89 For a detailed account of the process leading to the abolition of the *jezya*, see Farridnejad, 'The Royal *Farmān* and the Abolition of Zoroastrian Poll Tax in Qajar Iran'.
90 Sheffield, 'Iran, the Mark of Paradise or the Land of Ruin?', 27n26.
91 Karaka, *History of the Parsis*, 1:61–2, and Farridnejad, 'The Royal *Farmān* and the Abolition of Zoroastrian Poll Tax in Qajar Iran', 110. Hataria noted that Zoroastrians who could afford to pay the tax were fearful of paying it promptly, as they worried that it would then be increased, on the assumption that they could afford to pay more ('Amelioration Society Typescript', 10).
92 Karaka, *History of the Parsis*, 1:62, and Malcolm, *Five Years in a Persian Town*, 47. NB in 1849 efforts were made by Zoroastrians in Iran to ensure that they were not made to pay more than the agreed sum; however, despite orders from the shah, local governors continued to demand larger sums (Farridnejad, 'The Royal *Farmān* and the Abolition of Zoroastrian Poll Tax in Qajar Iran', 108–9). The tax had reportedly been raised in Yazd because of the enmity of the local tax collector towards a prominent figure in the community called Marzban ('Amelioration Society Typescript', 21). Hataria also noted that the amount being collected in Kerman was greater than the agreed sum of 35 tomans per person ('Amelioration Society Typescript', 26).
93 Farridnejad, 'The Royal *Farmān* and the Abolition of Zoroastrian Poll Tax in Qajar Iran', 116.
94 Ibid., 117, and Kotwal et al., 'Hataria, Manekji Limji'. See also 'Amelioration Society Typescript', 15–17.
95 Sheffield, 'Iran, the Mark of Paradise or the Land of Ruin?', 32. See also Talinn Grigor, 'Freemasonry and the Architecture of the Persian Revival, 1843–1933', in *Freemasonry and the Visual Arts from the Eighteenth Century Forward: Historical and Global Perspectives*, ed. Reva Wolf and Alisa Luxenberg (London: Bloomsbury, 2019), 163.
96 Farridnejad, 'The Royal *Farmān* and the Abolition of Zoroastrian Poll Tax in Qajar Iran', 117; Michael M. J. Fischer, 'Zoroastrian Iran Between Myth and Praxis' (PhD Thesis, University of Chicago, Chicago, 1973), 98–9; and, Amini, *Asnadi az Zartoshtiyan-e Mo'aser-e Iran*, 10.

97 Farridnejad, 'The Royal *Farmān* and the Abolition of Zoroastrian Poll Tax in Qajar Iran', 117–18. Hataria also contacted other British officials (for examples, see 'Amelioration Society Typescript', 19–22).
98 'Amelioration Society Typescript', 25; and Fischer, 'Zoroastrian Iran Between Myth and Praxis', 97.
99 Karaka, *History of the Parsis*, 1:81.
100 'Amelioration Society Typescript', 25. NB M. H. Cama had requested and paid for a translation of the 1854 commentary on the *Avesta* by Friedrich Spiegel, and had collaborated with Hataria on this project (Grigor, 'Parsi Patronage of the *Urheimat*', 57–8). For references to Farrokh Khan being initiated as a Freemason, see Hamid Algar, 'Freemasonry ii. In the Qajar Period', https://www.iranicaonline.org/articles/freemasonry-ii-in-the-qajar-period (accessed on 18 March 2023), and Mangol Bayat, *Iran's Experiment with Parliamentary Governance: The Second Majles, 1909-1911* (Syracuse, New York: Syracuse University Press, 2020), 19.
101 F. Gaffary, 'Amīn-al-dawla, Farrok͟h Khan Ḡaffārī', http://www.iranicaonline.org/articles/amin-al-dawla-farrok-khan-gaffari (accessed on 18 March 2023).
102 R. P. Masani, *Dadabhai Naoroji: 'The Grand Old Man of India'* (London: George Allen & Unwin, 1939), 68, and Patel, *Naoroji*, 304n36.
103 Patel, *Naoroji*, 43, and 50.
104 *Times*, 26 June 1873, 7–8, and *Times*, 28 June 1873, 5.
105 Karaka, *History of the Parsis*, 1:75–6, and Parvin Loloi, 'Eastwick, Edward Backhouse', https://www.iranicaonline.org/articles/eastwick-edward-backhouse- (accessed on 18 March 2023). NB Eastwick had translated various texts from Persian to English, including the *Qesse-ye Sanjan*.
106 For an account of appeals to the shah made by Jewish groups, see Tsadik, *Between Foreigners and Shi'is*, 90–4.
107 Marashi, *Nationalizing Iran*, 22–3.
108 Ibid., 22. For an overview of the attempts made to reform the state administration in the early 1870s, see Shaul Bakhash, 'The Evolution of Qajar Bureaucracy: 1779-1879', *Middle Eastern Studies* 7, no. 2 (1971): 155–60.
109 Hataria made this comment in a petition that was presented to the shah, via the British minister in Iran, Charles Murray ('Amelioration Society Typescript', 20–1).
110 Ibid., 24.
111 Karaka, *History of the Parsis*, 1:76–7.
112 NB Sepahsalar had also been consul in Bombay in 1851 (Tsadik, *Between Foreigners and Shi'is*, 88–90).
113 See ibid., 95, where Tsadik makes this point in relation to the Jewish community in Iran.
114 *ToI*, 12 December 1874, 2.
115 *ToI*, 17 February 1875, 2.
116 *ToI*, 12 December 1874, 2 (NB the article notes that there had been a previous attempt to kill Rasheed).
117 Malcolm, *Five Years in a Persian Town*, 46.
118 *ToI*, 31 October 1878, 2.
119 Ibid., 2, and 3.
120 Ibid., 2.
121 Ibid. See also Geary, *Through Asiatic Turkey*, 1:81, for reference to the action taken by Parsis and members of the British legation in Tehran.
122 Kotwal et al., 'Hataria, Manekji Limji'.

123 *ToI*, 3 November 1881, 5. NB initially hopes had been expressed that the murderer would be punished (see *ToI*, 14 November 1878, 2).
124 Lieutenant H. B. Vaughan, Memorandum on the Parsis of Yezd, July 1889, IOR/L/PWD/7/1097. See also Karaka, *History of the Parsis*, 1:66–7.
125 *Times*, 12 October 1881, 9. See also *ToI*, 3 November 1881, 5.
126 *Times*, 12 October 1881, 9.
127 Ibid.
128 Tsadik, *Between Foreigners and Shi'is*, 114–15.
129 *ToI*, 14 January 1882, 5.
130 For a description of the celebrations, see Fischer, 'Zoroastrian Iran Between Myth and Praxis', 100, and for examples of invitations to the celebration in Tehran, see Amini, *Asnadi az Zartoshtiyan-e Mo'aser-e Iran*, 60–2.
131 For the text of the *farman* and discussion concerning the wording and the extant copies, see Farridnejad, 'The Royal *Farmān* and the Abolition of Zoroastrian Poll Tax in Qajar Iran', 118ff.
132 Ibid., 121.
133 Sharafi, *Law and Identity in Colonial South Asia*, 88.
134 *ToI*, 27 June 1889, 4. The correspondent also suggested that the community should invite the shah to visit India, 'where the Parsee community will willingly defray his expenses', as this would result in closer relations between Parsis and Iran, and an increase in trade.
135 *ToI*, 23 July 1889, 6.
136 Ibid.
137 Dinyar Patel, 'Our Own Religion in Ancient Persia: Dadabhai Naoroji and Orientalist Scholarship on Zoroastrianism', *Global Intellectual History* 2, no. 3 (2017): 13, and Foreign Office to Sir H. D. Wolff, 19 April 1889, FO 60/499:69. For details of Browne's life and work, see G. Michael Wickens, Juan Cole, and Kamran Ekbal, 'Browne, Edward Granville', http://www.iranicaonline.org/articles/browne-edward-granville (accessed on 18 March 2023).
138 Foreign Office to Sir H. D. Wolff, 19 April 1889, FO 60/499:69.
139 Ibid.
140 Ibid.
141 Ross to Kennedy, 13 June 1889, FO 60/539.
142 Murzban, *The Parsis in India*, 1:135. For further information about Khansaheb, see Shahmardan, *Farzanegan-e Zartoshti*, 552–8.
143 *ToI*, 21 February 1893, 3. See also Shahrokh, *The Memoirs of Keikhosrow Shahrokh*, 17, and 48n12.
144 Kasheff, 'Anjoman-e Zartoštīān'. See also see Shahmardan, *Farzanegan-e Zartoshti*, 553–5.
145 Kasheff, 'Anjoman-e Zartoštīān'. These *anjoman*s were known as *Anjoman-e Naseri*, after Naser al-Din Shah, a name they retained until the end of the Qajar period.
146 Ibid.
147 Foroutan, 'Yazd and its Zoroastrians', 825.
148 Shahmardan, *Farzanegan-e Zartoshti*, 557–8.
149 Ibid., 557–8, and 360.
150 *Parsi*, July 1905, 257. For further details about Reporter's life and work, see Shahmardan, *Farzanegan-e Zartoshti*, 360–7.
151 Malcolm M. Deboo, 'The Amelioration of the Condition of Zoroastrians in Qajar Iran' (Unpublished paper), 12.

152 *Times*, 25 August 1900, 8. See also *ToI*, 3 September 1900, 5; *ToI*, 10 September 1900, 5; and, ZTFE minutes, 16 January 1901.
153 *ToI*, 6 November 1901, 5. Indeed, the Zoroastrian Anjoman of Yazd sent an address to thank the Aqa Khan (*ToI*, 12 April 1901, 4).
154 *ToI*, 3 September 1900, 5.
155 *ToI*, 6 September 1902, 5. See also John R. Hinnells, *Zoroastrians in Britain: The Ratanbai Katrak Lectures, University of Oxford, 1985* (Oxford: Clarendon Press, 1996), 111.
156 NB in later years, Hosayn Qoli Khan associated with radical constitutionalists (Mansour Bonakdarian, *Britain and the Iranian Constitutional Revolution of 1906-1911: Foreign Policy, Imperialism, and Dissent* [New York: Syracuse University Press in association with Iran Heritage Foundation, 2006], 200, and 451n11).
157 *ToI*, 6 September 1902, 5.
158 Ibid.
159 Ibid.
160 Farridnejad, 'The Royal *Farmān* and the Abolition of Zoroastrian Poll Tax in Qajar Iran', 124–5.
161 Ibid. See also *ToI*, 21 July 1906, 5.
162 For examples of Parsi philanthropy directed towards education, see Hinnells, *Zoroastrian and Parsi Studies*, 222–4.
163 Murzban, *The Parsis in India*, 1:111, and Kotwal et al., 'Hataria, Manekji Limji'. See also Shahmardan, *Farzanegan-e Zartoshti*, 238–9, and 555–6. The building for the boarding school was donated by a Zoroastrian in Tehran (Hataria, 'Education for Amelioration: Travels in Iran: 6', *Parsiana* 13, no. 7 (1991): 15). It seems likely that there were priestly schools for Iranian Zoroastrians prior to the arrival of Hataria, but the intake would have been limited (Fischer, 'Zoroastrian Iran Between Myth and Praxis', 97n1).
164 Brighty, 1899, CMS/ACC/113/F1. See also *Church Missionary Gleaner* (*CMG*) 271, no. 23 (1896): 103.
165 *ToI*, 13 September 1890, 4.
166 Amighi, *The Zoroastrians of Iran*, 112.
167 Hataria, 'Education for Amelioration', 17, and 15.
168 *Iran League Quarterly* (*ILQ*) 1, no. 1–2 (April–July 1930): 75.
169 Nile Green, *Bombay Islam: The Religious Economy of the West Indian Ocean, 1840-1915* (New York: Cambridge University Press, 2011), 121.
170 Fischer, 'Zoroastrian Iran Between Myth and Praxis', 99.
171 Kasheff, 'Anjoman-e Zartoštīān'; Shahrokh, *The Memoirs of Keikhosrow Shahrokh*, 19ff; and, *ILQ* 1, no. 1–2 (April–July 1930): 77.
172 *Mercy and Truth* (*MT*) 8, no. 88 (1904): 115. For information about British schools in Iran, see Gulnar E. Francis-Dehqani, 'Great Britain xv. British Schools in Persia', https://www.iranicaonline.org/articles/great-britain-xv (accessed on 18 March 2023).
173 Delphine Menant, in *Revue du Monde Musulman* (*RMM*) 3, no. 11–12 (1907): 448–9. A missionary report from 1890 noted that 'Mr Carless' received the 'warmest welcome' from Zoroastrians in Yazd, who were described as the 'remains of the old ruling people in Persia', and who were regarded as being 'open to receive the Gospel' (*Church Missionary Intelligencer and Record* [*CMIR*]15 [October 1890]: 718). For references to Zoroastrian converts to Christianity, and to friendly relations between Zoroastrians and members of the CMS (albeit from a possibly biased CMS perspective), see: *MT* 2, no. 21 (September 1898): 210; *MT* 2, no. 24 (December

1898): 287; *MT* 7, no. 77 (May 1903): 133; *MT* 9, no. 99 (March 1905): 71; *MT* 9 no. 101 (May 1905): 134; and, *MT* 18, no. 209 (May 1914): 137.
174   4 October 1902, CMS/ACC/133/F3.
175   Ibid.
176   *ILQ* 1, no. 1–2 (April–July 1930): 77. NB in 1897, Edward Browne, Joachim Menant, and B. Malabari had suggested paying for a 'lady doctor' to help Zoroastrians in Yazd. Similar attitudes to those experienced by Reporter prevented the plan from going ahead. Indeed, Ardeshir Mehrban, a leading figure in the community, explained that it would not be acceptable to many Zoroastrians (*RMM* 3, no. 11–12 [1907]: 436).
177   Ringer, *Pious Citizens*, 150–4. Ardeshir Reporter described how his attempts to decrease superstitious beliefs 'made him a little unpopular in Yezd' (*ILQ* 4, no. 2–3 [January–April 1934]: 121). For a reference to Zoroastrian priests in Yazd opposing 'progress', see Sykes' account of his transfer from Kerman to Meshed (Mashad), March 1905, FO248/853. See also Foroutan, 'Yazd and its Zoroastrians', 824–5.
178   For example, see Hataria, 'Rites of Passage', 40, and Hataria, 'Support from the *Sethias*', 32. See also, Murzban, *The Parsis in India*, 1:137, and Marzban Giara, Ramiyar P. Karanjia, and Michael Stausberg, 'Manekji on the Religious/Ritual Practices of the Iranian Zoroastrians: An English Translation of a Passage from His Travel Report in Gujarati (1865)', in *Zoroastrian Rituals in Context*, ed. Michael Stausberg (Leiden and Boston: Brill, 2004).
179   Hataria, 'Education for Amelioration', 14.
180   Karaka, *History of the Parsis*, 1:59–60.
181   A. V. Williams Jackson, *Persia Past and Present: A Book of Travel and Research* (New York and London: MacMillan, 1906), 363, 370–2, and 380–1.
182   Jackson, *Persia Past and Present*, 380. See CMS/ACC/133/F2 for the view that animal sacrifice was dying out as a practice amongst Zoroastrians in Iran. However, in contrast, for a reference to Zoroastrian women sacrificing fowl when the British consulate was built in Kerman, see *Men and Women of India* (*MWI*) 2 (August 1906): 475.
183   Green, *Bombay Islam*, 119.
184   Ibid., Chapter Four.
185   D. M. MacEoin, 'Babism', http://www.iranicaonline.org/articles/babism-index (accessed on 18 March 2023), and Juan R. I. Cole, 'Bahaism i. The Faith', http://www.iranicaonline.org/articles/bahaism-i (accessed on 18 March 2023).
186   MacEoin, 'Babism'.
187   Ibid.
188   Margit Warburg, 'Baha'is of Iran: Power, Prejudices and Persecutions', in *Religious Minorities in the Middle East: Domination, Self-Empowerment, Accommodation*, ed. Anh Nga Longva and Anne Sofie Roald (Leiden and Boston: Brill, 2012), 196.
189   MacEoin, 'Babism'.
190   Ibid., and Cole, 'Bahaism i. The Faith.'
191   D. M. MacEoin, 'Bahaism vii. Bahai Persecutions', https://www.iranicaonline.org/articles/bahaism-vii (accessed on 18 March 2023). For analysis of anti-Bahá'í riots, see Fischer, 'Zoroastrian Iran Between Myth and Praxis', 409–18.
192   For an overview of the expansion of the Bahá'í faith, see P. Smith, 'Bahaism iv. The Bahai Communities', https://iranicaonline.org/articles/bahaism-iv (accessed on 23 March 2023).
193   Amighi, *The Zoroastrians of Iran*, 123; Susan Judith Stiles, 'Zoroastrian Conversions to the Bahá'í Faith in Yazd, Iran' (MA Thesis, University of Arizona, 1983), vii;

and, Juan R. I. Cole, 'Conversion v. To Babism and the Bahai Faith', https://www.iranicaonline.org/articles/conversion-v (accessed on 18 March 2023). NB Browne reported that some Zoroastrians in Yazd had become Babis (Edward Granville Browne, *A Year Amongst the Persians* [London: Adam and Charles Black, 1893], 173). For more detailed discussion as to why Zoroastrians were attracted to the Bahá'í faith, see Fereydun Vahman, 'The Conversion of Zoroastrians to the Baha'i Faith', in *The Baha'is of Iran: Socio-Historical Studies*, ed. Dominic Parviz Brookshaw and Seena B. Fazel (London and New York: Routledge, 2008). NB Foroutan has discussed the impact of the 'ideological perspectives' of the scholars who have addressed this topic; for example, Foroutan highlights that Susan Stiles (Maneck) is a member of the Bahá'í faith (Foroutan, 'Yazd and its Zoroastrians', 826).

194 Malcolm, *Five Years in a Persian Town*, 52.
195 Stiles, 'Zoroastrian Conversions to the Bahá'í Faith in Yazd, Iran', 21.
196 Ibid., vii, and 30–1.
197 Elena Andreeva, *Russia and the Great Game: Travelogues and Orientalism* (London and New York: Routledge, 2007), 173.
198 Fischer, 'Zoroastrian Iran Between Myth and Praxis', 353, and M. Momen and B. T. Lawson, 'Lawḥ', https://iranicaonline.org/articles/lawh (accessed on 18 March 2023). It is likely that Hataria also contributed to the Babi historical account, the *Kitab-e jadid* (Mangol Bayat, *Mysticism and Dissent: Socioreligious Thought in Qajar Iran* [Syracuse: Syracuse University Press, 1982], 171).
199 M. Momen, 'Abu'l-Fażl Golpāyegānī', http://www.iranicaonline.org/articles/abul-fazl-or-abul-fazael-golpayegani-mirza-mohammad-prominent-bahai-scholar-and-apologist (accessed on 18 March 2023). For a contemporary account that highlights the status of women in Babism, and compares their position to that of women in the pre-Islamic era, as well as in the Zoroastrian community in the nineteenth century, see Thomas Edward Gordon, *Persia Revisited, 1895, With Remarks on M.I.M. Mozuffer-Ed-Din Shah, and the Present Situation, 1896* (London and New York: Edward Arnold, 1896), 91.
200 Stiles, 'Zoroastrian Conversions to the Bahá'í Faith in Yazd, Iran', 19.
201 Ibid., 20.
202 Ibid., 41.
203 Amighi, 'Zoroastrians of 19th Century Yazd and Kerman'. NB Amighi has highlighted that the aim of Bahá'u'lláh to improve trade regulations would have been of particular interest to merchants, including Zoroastrians.
204 Records of the Amelioration Society imply that during its first few years, donations were primarily from those with family ties to Iran. The committee expressed the hope that 'all Zoroastrians' would read their report and that they would be convinced that 'this charitable institution needs the support of our Indian Zoroastrians' ('Amelioration Society Typescript', 1). Reference is made to it being 'the duty of all Zoroastrians in India to donate to this fund . . . ' (ibid., 5), and the late Sir Jamsetjee Jejeebhoy was praised for donating 25,000 rupees for the payment of the *jezya*.
205 *ToI*, 23 November 1891, 5. NB the Petit family had become wealthy through their involvement in the cotton trade (Palsetia, *The Parsis of India*, 58–9).
206 *ToI*, 7 March 1887, 6. See also Edwardes, *Memoir of Sir Dinshaw Manockjee Petit*, 52–4. For earlier references to donations from members of the Petit family towards causes in Iran, see *Bombay Times and Journal of Commerce* (*BTJC*), 23 February 1859, 124, and *BTJC*, 25 May 1859, 332.

207 *ToI*, 28 August 1890, 5. For further details about the life and charitable works of Kaykhosrow Mehrban, see Shahmardan, *Farzanegan-e Zartoshti*, 576–80.
208 *ToI*, 28 August 1890, 5. See also Shahmardan, *Farzanegan-e Zartoshti*, 555. Another Iranian Zoroastrian, Dinshaw Merwan, founded a boarding school, which was also supported by other Iranis 'for the benefit of their class' (*Parsi*, April 1905, 137).
209 *ToI*, 1 April 1890, 5.
210 *ToI*, 23 March 1892, 5.
211 Palsetia, *The Parsis of India*, 212–13.
212 *ToI*, 22 October 1902, 5.
213 According to Rastin Mehri, 'For Hataria, the prevailing cultural and ethnic differences between Iranian and Parsi communities in Iran and India were irrelevant', and instead he looked to 'an authentic community perhaps existing in a timeless state' (Rastin Mehri, 'A Zoroastrian Historical Imaginary in India', in *Time, History and the Religious Imaginary in South Asia*, ed. Anne Murphy [Routledge: Abingdon, 2011], 77).

Chapter 2

1 For example, see the wording of an address delivered in 1902 (*ToI*, 6 September 1902, 5). Likewise, an inscription on the restored fire temple in Kerman stated that the work had been funded by Zoroastrians in India, who were 'of the race of the ancient Persians of Iran' (quoted in Mehri, 'A Zoroastrian Historical Imaginary in India', 75).
2 For more detailed discussion see Zia-Ebrahimi, 'An Emissary of the Golden Age', and Stausberg, 'Manekji Limji Hatāriā and the Rediscovery of Ancient Iran' .
3 Zia-Ebrahimi, 'An Emissary of the Golden Age', 379–80.
4 H. Busse, 'Abbās Mīrzā Qajar', http://www.iranicaonline.org/articles/abbas-mirza-qajar (accessed on 18 March 2023). NB Abbas Mirza predeceased his father Fath-'Ali Shah so never became shah.
5 John Gurney and Negin Nabavi, 'Dār al-Fonūn', https://www.iranicaonline.org/articles/dar-al-fonun-lit (accessed on 18 March 2023), and Muriel Atkin, 'Cossack Brigade', https://www.iranicaonline.org/articles/cossack-brigade (accessed on 18 March 2023).
6 See Reza Zia-Ebrahimi, *The Emergence of Iranian Nationalism: Race and the Politics of Dislocation* (New York: Columbia University Press, 2016), 26–7. For detailed analysis of the life of Malkam Khan, see Hamid Algar, *Mirza Malkum Khan: A Biographical Study in Iranian Modernism* (Berkeley and London: University of California Press, 1973).
7 Zia-Ebrahimi, 'An Emissary of the Golden Age', 379–80.
8 Ibid, 380.
9 Zia-Ebrahimi, *The Emergence of Iranian Nationalism*, 38.
10 Abbas Amanat and Farzin Vejdani, 'Jalāl-al-Din Mīrzā', https://www.iranicaonline.org/articles/jalal-al-din-mirza (accessed on 18 March 2023).
11 Hamid Algar, 'Āḵundzāda', http://www.iranicaonline.org/articles/akundzada-playwright (accessed on 18 March 2023).
12 For examples of correspondence between Akhundzadeh, Hataria, Jalal al-Din Mirza and other individuals, covering topics including pre-Islamic Iran, the Persian language and Zoroastrianism, see Hamid Mohammadzadeh and Hamid Arasli (eds),

Mirza Fath 'ali Akhundov: Alefba-ye Jadid va Maktubat (Baku: Izdatel'stvo Akademii Nauk Azerbaidzhanskoi SSR, 1963), 170–3, 220–4, 249–51, 336–40, 387–8, 395–7, 402–7, 423–4, and 429–35.

13 Zia-Ebrahimi, 'An Emissary of the Golden Age', 384, and 387.
14 Zia-Ebrahimi, *The Emergence of Iranian Nationalism*, 83.
15 Zia-Ebrahimi, 'An Emissary of the Golden Age', 383–4, and 387. For analysis of the views of Akhundzadeh, see also Juan R. I. Cole, 'Marking Boundaries, Marking Time: The Iranian Past and the Construction of the Self by Qajar Thinkers'. *Iranian Studies* 29, no. 1 (1996): 37–43.
16 Algar, 'Āḵūndzāda'.
17 Mohammadzadeh and Arasli, *Mirza Fath 'ali Akhundov*, 249, and Zia-Ebrahimi, *The Emergence of Iranian Nationalism*, 53.
18 Zia-Ebrahimi, 'An Emissary of the Golden Age', 383–4.
19 Zia-Ebrahimi, *The Emergence of Iranian Nationalism*, 38.
20 Ibid., 36.
21 Marashi, *Nationalizing Iran*. 63.
22 Ibid., 58–60. See also Amanat and Vejdani, 'Jalāl-al-Din Mirzā', and Gurney and Nabavi, 'Dār al-Fonūn'.
23 Jean Calmard, 'Gobineau, Joseph Arthur de', https://www.iranicaonline.org/articles/gobineau (accessed on 18 March 2023).
24 Grigor, 'Freemasonry and the Architecture of the Persian Revival, 1843–1933', 166–7.
25 Kotwal et al., 'Manekji Limji Hataria'.
26 Ibid., and Peter T. Daniels, 'Rawlinson, Henry ii. Contributions to Assyriology and Iranian Studies', https://iranicaonline.org/articles/rawlinson-ii (accessed on 18 March 2023).
27 Gobineau, quoted in Reza Zia-Ebrahimi, '"Arab Invasion" and Decline, or the Import of European Racial Thought by Iranian Nationalists', *Ethnic and Racial Studies* 37, no. 6 (2014): 1053.
28 Mehrdad Kia, 'Persian Nationalism and the Campaign for Language Purification', *Middle Eastern Studies* 34, no. 2 (1998): 12–13.
29 Ibid., 10–13.
30 Kotwal et al., 'Manekji Limji Hataria'.
31 Kia, 'Persian Nationalism and the Campaign for Language Purification', 12, and Mojtaba'ī, 'Dasātīr'.
32 Zia-Ebrahimi, 'An Emissary of the Golden Age', 386–7. For details of texts written and promoted by Hataria, see Marashi, *Nationalizing Iran*, 61–5. For discussion on the significance of the *Dasatir* (and *Shahnameh*) in the re-imagining of Iranian history, see Mohamad Tavakoli-Targhi, *Refashioning Iran: Orientalism, Occidentalism and Historiography* (New York: Palgrave, 2001), Chapters Five and Six, and 'Historiography and Crafting Iranian National Identity', in *Iran in the Twentieth Century: Historiography and Political Culture*, ed. Touraj Atabaki (London: I.B. Tauris, 2009).
33 Marashi, *Nationalizing Iran*, 73. See also, Zia-Ebrahimi, '"Arab Invasion" and Decline, or the Import of European Racial Thought by Iranian Nationalists', 1048ff.
34 Marashi, *Nationalizing Iran*, 73.
35 Renan, quoted in Zia-Ebrahimi, '"Arab Invasion" and Decline, or the Import of European Racial Thought by Iranian Nationalists', 1050.
36 Stausberg, 'Manekji Limji Hatūriā and the Rediscovery of Ancient Iran', 444. See also Peter van der Veer, *Imperial Encounters: Religion and Modernity in India and Britain* (Princeton and Oxford: Princeton University Press, 2001), 139–40.

37 Kermani, quoted in Reza Zia-Ebrahimi, 'Self-Orientalization and Dislocation: The Uses and Abuses of the "Aryan" Discourse in Iran', *Iranian Studies* 44, no. 4 (2010): 454. Despite holding positive views of Zoroastrians, Kermani did not think highly of Hataria (ibid., 59, and 82). For biographical information see Mangol Bayat, 'Āqā Khan Kermānī', http://www.iranicaonline.org/articles/aqa-khan-kermani (accessed on 18 March 2023).
38 Zia-Ebrahimi, 'Self-Orientalization and Dislocation', 464, and 467–8.
39 Marashi, *Nationalizing Iran*, 75.
40 Zia-Ebrahimi, *The Emergence of Iranian Nationalism*, 6–7.
41 Ibid., 10.
42 Kotwal et al., 'Manekji Limji Hataria'.
43 Stausberg, 'Manekji Limji Hatāriā and the Rediscovery of Ancient Iran', 443–4, and Hataria, 'Education for Amelioration', 18.
44 Sheffield specifically contrasts Hataria's text with an account written in 1786 by Mulla Firuz about his time in Iran, which Sheffield situates within an Indo-Persianate literary tradition (Sheffield, 'Iran, the Mark of Paradise or the Land of Ruin?', 15–16, and 31ff). NB Hataria's account, originally in Gujarati, was also published in an abridged Persian version for the Iranian Zoroastrian community in Bombay, and for distribution in Iran (ibid., 33).
45 Ibid., 15, and 31ff.
46 Sheffield, 'Iran, the Mark of Paradise or the Land of Ruin?', 33. For example, see Manekji Limji Hataria, 'A Millennium of Misery: Travels in Iran: 2', *Parsiana* 13, no. 3 (1990): 34, for his description of the Arab conquest of Iran.
47 Sheffield, 'Iran, the Mark of Paradise or the Land of Ruin?', 15–16.
48 Ibid., 33.
49 Ringer, *Pious Citizens*, 83–5 (see the rest of Chapter Three for related discussion and analysis). See also Mehri, 'A Zoroastrian Historical Imaginary in India', 72–4.
50 Ringer, *Pious Citizens*, 76–8. For references to ancient Iran, see Karaka, *The Parsees*, 1–4. NB Ringer highlights that although Karaka praised the civilization of ancient Iran, he did not go as far as Hataria, who mythologized the pre-Islamic period (Ringer, *Pious Citizens*, 159).
51 Karaka, *The Parsees*, ix–x.
52 Ringer, *Pious Citizens*, 155ff.
53 Ibid., 116.
54 Jivanji Jamshedji Modi, 'Belief and Ceremonies of the Followers of Zoroaster', in *The World's Congress of Religions*, ed. J. W. Hanson (Chicago: Monarch Book Co., 1894), 461–2, and 464. See also Ringer, *Pious Citizens*, 99–100, for analysis of the World's Parliament of Religions. For biographical details for Modi, see Michael Stausberg and Ramiyar P. Karanjia. 'Modi, Jivanji Jamshedji', http://www.iranicaonline.org/articles/modi-jivanji-jamshedji (accessed on 18 March 2023).
55 Mary Boyce and D. N. MacKenzie, 'Darmesteter, James', https://iranicaonline.org/articles/darmesteter (accessed on 18 March 2023).
56 Darmesteter quoted in *ToI*, 4 February 1887, 6.
57 Ibid.
58 See Ringer, *Pious Citizens*, 56–7, regarding the impact of Haug's views on the Zoroastrian community in India.
59 *Journal of the Society of Arts* (*JSA*) 54, no. 2794 (8 June 1906), 765.
60 *ToI*, 11 March 1901, 9.
61 Ibid.

62 *Parsi*, June 1905, 202.
63 *Parsi*, April 1905, 141 (NB for information about Vimadalal, see Sharafi, *Law and Identity in Colonial South Asia*, 251–2, 297–9, 301 and 304–5, and Rashna Writer, *Contemporary Zoroastrians: An Unstructured Nation* [Lanham, Maryland: University Press of America, 1994], 122).
64 *Parsi*, April 1905, 142.
65 Ringer, *Pious Citizens*, 154–5. NB there were alternative opinions. For an example of the argument that Parsis should not be viewed as foreigners in India, see *RG* quoted in *ToI*, 26 June 1888, 5.
66 Monier-Williams quoted in *ToI*, 23 March 1881, 3.
67 Grigor, 'Parsi Patronage of the *Urheimat*', 61–3. See also Sharafi, *Law and Identity in Colonial South Asia*, 310.
68 *Satya Mitra* referenced in *ToI*, 2 November 1881, 3.
69 Kulke, *The Parsees in India*, 142.
70 See Jamsheed Choksy, 'Persian Literature of the Parsis in India', in *Persian Literature from Outside Iran: The Indian Subcontinent, Anatolia, Central Asia, and in Judeo-Persian*, ed. J. R. Perry (London: I.B. Tauris, 2018), particularly pages 171–2, for analysis of the decline in the use of Persian by Parsis. For a reference to the knowledge of Persian amongst educated Parsis, see for example *BTJC*, 23 February 1859, 123. Likewise, in 1889, 337 of the 401 Parsis who took university matriculation examinations in Bombay chose Persian as their second language (Writer, *Contemporary Zoroastrians*, 103n79). See also *MWI* 2, no. 3 (March 1906): 138, for a reference to Sir J. Jejeebhoy (4th Baronet) having studied Persian as a second language in the early 1870s, and to a comment about his father also having been 'very fond' of Persian.
71 Choksy, 'Persian Literature of the Parsis in India', 171–2, and Farzin Vejdani, 'Indo-Iranian Linguistic, Literary, and Religious Entanglements: Between Nationalism and Cosmopolitanism, ca. 1900–1940', *Comparative Studies of South Asia, Africa and the Middle East* 36, no. 3 (2016): 436.
72 Sheffield, 'Iran, the Mark of Paradise or the Land of Ruin?', 16.
73 *ToI*, 30 November 1891, 3. See also *ToI*, 14 April 1892, 3; *ToI*, 6 August 1892, 3; and, *ToI*, 20 August 1892, 3.
74 *ToI*, 22 September 1913, 6.
75 *Parsi*, September 1905, 351. See also *Parsi*, June 1905, 212.
76 Ringer, *Pious Citizens*, 72.
77 Philip G. Kreyenbroek, 'The Role of the *Shāhnāme* in the Culture of the Parsi Community', Unpublished paper, 2, http://misc.ilexfoundation.org/pdf/ferdowsi_2/kreyenbroek300.pdf (accessed on 19 June 2016).
78 Ibid., 5. The British also encouraged Parsis to seek inspiration from the *Shahnameh*. In the early nineteenth century, Mulla Firuz was commissioned by the British to write the *George-nameh*, a poetic account in Persian of British campaigns in India, based on the style of the *Shahnameh* (Hinnells, 'Bombay, Persian Communities of. i. The Zoroastrian Community').
79 *ToI*, 13 October 1900, 8. NB the *Shahnameh* was also included in the curriculum at Parsi priestly schools, which Kreyenbroek suggests 'furthered its acceptance in the community' (Kreyenbroek, 'The Role of the *Shāhnāme* in the Culture of the Parsi Community', 6).
80 Darmesteter, quoted in *ToI*, 4 February 1887, 6.
81 *ToI*, 13 October 1900, 8.

82 Ibid.
83 Ibid.
84 Zia-Ebrahimi, *The Emergence of Iranian Nationalism*, 50.
85 Marashi, *Nationalizing Iran*, 64.
86 Kermani, quoted in Zia-Ebrahimi, '"Arab Invasion" and Decline, or the Import of European Racial Thought by Iranian Nationalists', 1051.
87 Ibid., and Marashi, *Nationalizing Iran*, 60.
88 Marashi, *Nationalizing Iran*, 60, and Tavakoli-Targhi, 'Historiography and Crafting Iranian National Identity', 7ff.
89 See Dinsha Edulji Wacha, *Shells from the Sands of Bombay: Being my Recollections and Reminiscences, 1860-1875* (Bombay: K. T. Anklesaria, 1920), 85-6, for a description of open-air *Shahnameh* readings that took place in the mid-nineteenth century. See also *ToI*, 31 January 1891, 3. Additionally, in the early twentieth century, R. P. Masani wrote a novel based on the *Shahnameh* (*ToI*, 3 December 1904, 10).
90 Willmer, 'Parsis and Public Space in 19th Century Bombay', 280.
91 Ibid., 280-1.
92 Rashna Darius Nicholson, 'Corporeality, Aryanism, Race: The Theatre and Social Reform of the Parsis of Western India', *South Asia Journal of South Asian Studies* 38, no. 4 (2015): 617.
93 Ibid. NB some actors were Iranian Zoroastrians, who added a certain 'authenticity' to productions (Patel, 'Cultural Intermediaries in a Colonial City', 65).
94 Nicholson, 'Corporeality, Aryanism, Race', 627. For a description of a performance, see *ToI*, 18 January 1906, 3. For discussion about Kabraji and Parsi plays based on the *Shahnameh*, see also Kathryn Hansen, 'Languages on Stage: Linguistic Pluralism and Community Formation in the Nineteenth-Century Parsi Theatre', *Modern Asian Studies* 37, no. 2 (2003), 389-91. For further details about Kabraji, including his support for social reform and his opposition to Parsi involvement in nationalist politics, see Dinkar J. Bhojak, 'Kaikhushro Navroji Kabraji', in *The Oxford Companion to Indian Theatre*, ed. Ananda Lal (New Delhi: Oxford University Press, 2004), 177-8; Delphine Menant, *The Parsis*, vol. 3, trans. Anthony D. Mango (Bombay: Danai, 1996), 255; *ToI*, 26 March 1891, 8; and, Palsetia, *The Parsis of India*, 193-4, and 305-7.
95 Nicholson, 'Corporeality, Aryanism, Race', 627.
96 Ibid.
97 Sharafi, *Law and Identity in Colonial South Asia*, 31ff, and 311.
98 *Times*, 23 May 1905, 4.
99 Sharafi, *Law and Identity in Colonial South Asia*, 22.
100 Ibid., 21-2. See also Palsetia, *The Parsis of India*, 226-51.
101 Sharafi, *Law and Identity in Colonial South Asia*, 22.
102 Ibid.
103 Ibid., 313.
104 Ibid., 304.
105 *MWI* 1, no. 1 (1905): 39, and 33. See also *MWI* 1, no. 11 (1905): 610, and *MWI* 2, no. 1 (1906): 38. Similarly, the linguist Monier Monier-Williams regarded the Parsis as especially suited to 'intellectual development', partly due to their supposed inherent racial characteristics (Monier Monier-Williams, 'The Pārsīs', *The Nineteenth Century*, 49 [March 1881]: 516).
106 *ToI*, 26 April 1897, 3.
107 Ibid.

108 *Parsi*, May 1905, 175.
109 Zia-Ebrahimi, 'Self-Orientalization and Dislocation', 453. For analysis of the impact of the Aryan myth in India, see Chapter Six of Veer, *Imperial Encounters*.
110 Whilst conducting research in Mumbai, I noted that in the libraries I visited, there were copies of many nineteenth-century and early twentieth-century travelogues describing journeys in Iran; for example in the collection of the J. N. Petit Library, which was established by Parsis. For a list of books about Iran that were held in the Elphinstone College Library, see Grigor, 'Parsi Patronage of the *Urheimat*', 61–3.
111 Ella C. Sykes, *Persia and Its People* (London: Methuen, 1910), 28. See also, for example, Eliot Crawshay-Williams, *Across Persia* (London: Edward Arnold, 1907), 53.
112 See Ringer, *Pious Citizens*, particularly Chapter Four.
113 Karaka, *The Parsees*, 47.
114 Arnold Henry Savage Landor, *Across Coveted Lands or a Journey from Flushing (Holland) to Calcutta, overland*, vol. 1 (London: MacMillan, 1902), 398. See also Sykes, *Persia and its People*, 126.
115 Landor, *Across Coveted Lands*, 1:398.
116 Zia-Ebrahimi, '"Arab Invasion" and Decline, or the Import of European Racial Thought by Iranian Nationalists', 1048–9.
117 Ibid., 1049.
118 Jackson, *Persia Past and Present*, 25.
119 Ibid., 377.
120 Ibid., 274–5. Similarly, after delivering a lecture about ancient Iranian inscriptions, Jackson described how Parsis had the 'blood of Iran' flowing in their veins (*ToI*, 2 March 1901, 7).
121 Malcolm, *Five Years in a Persian Town*, 62.
122 Ibid., 113.
123 *ToI*, 21 December 1895, 4.
124 Ibid.
125 *ToI*, 31 October 1878, 2.
126 Percy Molesworth Sykes, *Ten Thousand Miles in Persia or Eight Years in Iran* (London: John Murray, 1902), 198.
127 Ibid.
128 John Marriott, *The Other Empire: Metropolis, India and Progress in the Colonial Imagination* (Manchester and New York: Manchester University Press, 2003), 145.
129 Nicholson, 'Corporeality, Aryanism, Race', 618–19.
130 Ibid.
131 *ToI*, 6 March 1878, 2.
132 *Parsi*, July 1905, 277.
133 *Parsi*, January 1905, 15.
134 Ibid.
135 NB suggestions were made by some individuals that physical decline in the Parsi community was linked to the practice of endogamy. This view countered the arguments made by J. J. Vimadalal and others, that endogamy was beneficial as it resulted in racial purity (Sharafi, *Law and Identity in Colonial South Asia*, 297–305).
136 Green, *Bombay Islam*, 118–19.
137 Ibid., 120.
138 For references to Iranians joining lodges in India, and for analysis of Freemasonry in India and Iran, particularly in relation to the elevation of the pre-Islamic past and the

Persian Revival architectural style in India and Iran, see Grigor, 'Freemasonry and the Architecture of the Persian Revival, 1843–1933'. See also, Algar, 'Freemasonry ii. In the Qajar Period'; Palsetia, *The Parsis of India*, 150; and, Kulke, *The Parsees in India*, 99 n33. See *ToI*, 20 May 1913, 5, for a reprint of an article from the Masonic Record of Western India, January 1865, detailing why Parsis were considered eligible for admission to Masonic lodges, whilst caution was advised regarding the admission of Hindus. K. R. Cama, a reformist Parsi and Freemason, claimed that Zarathustra was the first Freemason (see K. R. Cama, *A Discourse on Zoroastrians and Freemasonry* [Bombay: Times of India Steam Press, 1876]).
139 See Grigor, 'Freemasonry and the Architecture of the Persian Revival, 1843–1933'.
140 NB Iranian diplomats had been posted to Bombay in earlier years; for example, see *BTJC*, 16 August 1851, 536, and *Bombay Times and Standard* (*BTS*), 15 April 1861, 4.
141 *ToI*, 10 May 1886, 3. The performers at the concert were the Gayan Utejak Mandali, described in the *ToI* as the 'Native Philharmonic Society'. For further information about the Gayan Utejak Mandali and its cultural context, see Rashna Darius Nicholson, '"A Christy Minstrel, a Harlequin, or an Ancient Persian"?: Opera, Hindustani Classical Music, and the Origins of the Popular South Asian "Musical"', *Theatre Survey* 61, no. 3 (2020): 338–40. For biographical information about Hosayn Qoli Khan, see Hossein Kamaly, 'Ḥāji Vāšangtonʼ, https://www.iranicaonline.org/articles/haji-vasangton (accessed on 18 March 2023).
142 *ToI*, 10 May 1886, 3.
143 Ibid.
144 Ibid.
145 Ibid.
146 Ibid.
147 Ibid. Similarly, before leaving Bombay, Hosayn Qoli Khan claimed that the shah would not have appointed him to his new ministerial position in Tehran, were it not for the good relations he had fostered with Parsis (*ToI*, 20 March, 1888, 5, and *ToI*, 15 October 1888, 5).
148 *ToI*, 10 May 1886, 3.
149 Zia-Ebrahimi, *The Emergence of Iranian Nationalism*, 56, and Palsetia, *The Parsis of India*, 213. For example, see Darab Dastur Peshotan Sanjana, *The Position of Zoroastrian Women in Remote Antiquity, as Illustrated in the Avesta, the Sacred Books of the Parsees* (Bombay: Education Society's Steam Press, 1892).
150 *ToI*, 4 November 1886, 5.
151 Marashi, *Nationalizing Iran*, 37.
152 *ToI*, 4 November 1886, 5.
153 Ibid.
154 Ibid.
155 Ibid.
156 *ToI*, 25 October 1887, 3. See *ToI*, 15 March 1890, 3, for D. R. Banaji's obituary. Other members of the Banaji family also held positions in the Persian diplomatic service (see *ToI*, 20 November 1902, 4; *ToI*, 25 November 1902, 3; *ToI*, 9 May 1904, 4; and, Wacha, *Shells from the Sands of Bombay*, 280). See also Dinyar Patel, 'The Banaji and Mehta Families: Forging the Parsi Community in Calcutta', in Hintze and Williams, *Holy Wealth*, 222–3, regarding the rivalry between the Banaji and Mehta families, including the 'Consul Defamation Case' between Cowasji Dadabhoy Banaji, vice-consul in Bombay, and R. D. Mehta, Persian consul in Calcutta. For an overview of this case, see *ToI*, 8 March 1901, 3.

200   *Notes*

157 Jamsetjee Cursetjee Jamsetjee, quoted in *ToI*, 25 October 1887, 3. Similar points were made in *ToI*, 29 March 1888, 3, and *ToI*, 31 May 1893, 3. For references to Parsis taking part in birthday celebrations for the shah in later years see *ToI*, 15 October 1888, 5, and *Parsi*, September 1905, 351.
158 *ToI*, 25 October 1887, 3.
159 *ToI*, 20 March 1888, 5.
160 *ToI*, 4 November 1886, 5; *ToI*, 25 October 1887, 3; and, *ToI*, 20 March 1888, 5. Expressions of loyalty to the shah were regarded as being compatible with loyalty to Queen Victoria, and good relations between the two rulers were cited to support this idea (*ToI*, 15 October 1888, 5).
161 *ToI*, 5 November 1886, 3.
162 Ibid.
163 Ibid.
164 *ToI*, 20 March 1888, 5, and Kulke, *The Parsees in India*, 99 n33.
165 *ToI*, 20 March 1888, 5.
166 *ToI*, 29 March 1888, 3. Over 1,500 rupees were donated towards the gifts (*ToI*, 24 March 1888, 5).
167 *ToI*, 29 March 1888, 3.
168 Ibid.
169 *Times*, 11 September 1894, 6. The previous year, reports in Parsi newspapers about Zoroastrians being mistreated in parts of Iran prompted the consul-general to contact the Iranian prime minister (*ToI*, 31 May 1893, 3). See Chapter Three, for references to an instance where Zel al-Soltan intervened on behalf of Zoroastrians in Yazd, perhaps due to Parsi petitions.
170 *ToI*, 31 May 1893, 3. Similarly, in 1888, the consul-general stated that the 'blue blood of Persia flowed in their [the Parsis'] veins' (*ToI*, 15 October 1888, 5).
171 *ToI*, 31 May 1893, 3.
172 *Jam-e Jamshed* referenced in *ToI*, 12 February 1890, 3.
173 Edwardes, *Memoir of Sir Dinshaw Manockjee Petit*, 50. By the 1880s, the Order of the Lion and the Sun was for the Persians 'an inexpensive and possibly profitable way of winning friends' (Denis Wright, *Britain and Iran, 1790–1980: Collected Essays of Sir Denis Wright*, ed. Sarah Searight [London: Iran Society, 2003], 14). The shah had wanted to decorate Dadabhai Naoroji, but Naoroji declined, as he did not want to accept personal decorations (Masani, *Dadabhai Naoroji*, 373).
174 *ToI*, 26 March 1891, 8.
175 *Parsi*, June 1905, 213.
176 For example, see Jamsetjee Cursetjee Jamsetjee, quoted in *ToI*, 25 October 1887, 3.
177 *ToI*, 21 June 1888, 4. Another reference to the idea of a Parsi colony was made on 21 March 1886 (the date of Nowruz, Persian New Year) in the *Indian Spectator* (Kulke, *The Parsees in India*, 144).
178 *ToI*, 21 June 1888, 4.
179 Ibid.
180 Kulke, *The Parsees in India*, 165. See also Peter Heehs *India's Freedom Struggle 1857–1947: A Short History* (Delhi: Oxford University Press, 1991), 54ff.
181 Kulke, *The Parsees in India*, 166–7.
182 Palsetia, *The Parsis of India*, 303, and 318–19.
183 Kulke, *The Parsees in India*, 167–8.
184 For detailed analysis of the life and work of Naoroji, see Patel, *Naoroji*.
185 Kulke, *The Parsees in India*, 173, and 189.

186 Ibid., 182, and Anil Seal, *The Emergence of Indian Nationalism: Competition and Collaboration in the Later Nineteenth Century* (Cambridge: Cambridge University Press, 1971), 293.
187 Seal, *The Emergence of Indian Nationalism*, 324ff.
188 Kulke, *The Parsees in India*, 183-4.
189 *ToI*, 14 November 1890, 4.
190 Ibid.
191 Ibid.
192 Ibid., and Palsetia, *The Parsis of India*, 306, and 312.
193 *ToI*, 14 November 1890, 4.
194 Jamshedji Dorabji Khandalwala, *An Introduction to the Shah-Nameh of Firdousi from the French of Jules Mohl* (Veerkshetra Mudralay, 1898), Preface. The Trustees of the Bombay Parsi Panchayat subscribed to the book, reflecting that it was deemed to be worthy of community support and attention.
195 *RMM* 5, no. 5 (May 1908): 137.
196 *ToI*, 28 January 1905, 7.
197 Ibid.
198 Ibid. See also *Parsi*, February 1905, 43, and *Parsi*, April 1905, 141.
199 *Parsi*, December 1905, 525. See also *Parsi*, March 1905, 105, and *Parsi*, July 1905, 241.
200 Barbara D. Metcalf and Thomas R. Metcalf, *A Concise History of Modern India* (Cambridge: Cambridge University Press, 2006), 155ff. For analysis of the *swadeshi* movement in Maharashtra, see Shabnum Tejani, *Indian Secularism: A Social and Intellectual History 1890–1950* (Bloomington and Indianapolis: Indiana University Press, 2008), 85ff.
201 *Parsi*, December 1905, 525.
202 Ibid.
203 Ibid.
204 Ibid.
205 *Parsi*, October 1905, 414. This recommendation was made four years after an oil concession had been granted to the English financier and entrepreneur, William Knox D'Arcy, but three years before commercially viable quantities of oil were discovered in Iran [for further details, see Parviz Mina, 'Oil Agreements in Iran', https://iranicaonline.org/articles/oil-agreements-in-iran (accessed on 18 March 2023)].
206 *Parsi*, June 1905, 209.
207 *Parsi*, July 1905, 242.
208 Ibid.
209 Ibid., 278.
210 *Parsi*, August 1905, 286.
211 *Parsi*, January 1905, 23.
212 See also Marashi, *Exile and the Nation*, 5.
213 Kulke, *The Parsees in India*, 145-6. Similarly, Kershaw D. Khambatta proposed that a Parsi Military Training School be established (*Parsi*, August 1905, 307).
214 Vámbéry facilitated a meeting between Herzl and the Ottoman sultan in 1901 (Jacob M. Landau, 'Arminius Vambéry: Traveller, Scholar, Politician', *Middle Eastern Studies* 50, no. 6 [2014]: 864–5, and Walter Laqueur, *The History of Zionism* [London: I.B. Tauris, 2003], 114–15).
215 *Parsi*, September 1905, 346.
216 Ibid., 346-7.

217 Ibid., 347.
218 Ibid.
219 Ibid.

Chapter 3

1. See James M. Gustafson, 'Qajar Ambitions in the Great Game: Notes on the Embassy of 'Abbas Qoli Khan to the Amir of Bokhara, 1844', *Iranian Studies* 46, no. 4 (2013): 535–52, and Abbas Amanat, 'Great Britain iii. British Influence in Persia in the 19th Century', https://iranicaonline.org/articles/great-britain-iii (accessed on 18 March 2023).
2. For further discussion about Zoroastrians and the 'Great Game', see Patel, 'Power and Philanthropy', which focuses on the period from the mid-nineteenth century to 1906. Patel's article was published when I was in the final stages of writing this book, so although the themes addressed overlap and are highly relevant, I have not fully integrated the points made by Patel into this text.
3. Rudolph P. Matthee, 'Facing a Rude and Barbarous Neighbor: Iranian Perceptions of Russia and the Russians from the Safavids to the Qajars', in *Iran Facing Others: Identity Boundaries in a Historical Perspective*, ed. Abbas Amanat and Farzin Vejdani (New York: Palgrave Macmillan, 2012), 107–8.
4. Jean Calmard, 'Anglo-Persian War (1856–57)', http://www.iranicaonline.org/articles/anglo persian war 1856 57 (accessed on 18 March 2023).
5. For discussion regarding the significance of concerns over expenses, see Vanessa Martin, 'British Policy Towards Iran 1809-1914: The Question of Cost', *British Journal of Middle Eastern Studies* 48, no. 5 (2021): 1000–15.
6. Mansoureh Ettehadieh, 'Concessions ii. In the Qajar Period', https://www.iranicaonline.org/articles/concessions#pt2 (accessed on 18 March 2023).
7. Martin, 'British Policy Towards Iran, 1809-1914', 1007.
8. Ibid., 1008.
9. Ettehadieh, 'Concessions ii. In the Qajar Period'.
10. Ibid.
11. Janet Afary, *The Iranian Constitutional Revolution, 1906–1911: Grassroots Democracy, Social Democracy, and the Origins of Feminism* (New York: Columbia University Press, 1996), 19–22, and Hassan Hakimian, 'Economy viii. In the Qajar Period', https://www.iranicaonline.org/articles/economy-viii-in-the-qajar-period (accessed on 18 March 2023). NB Iran is sometimes described as having been in a 'semicolonial' state during the nineteenth century (e.g. Ettehadieh, 'Concessions ii. In the Qajar Period').
12. Green, *Bombay Islam*, 105, and 118.
13. Abbas Amanat (ed.), *Cities and Trade: Consul Abbott on the Economy and Society of Iran, 1847–1866* (London: Ithaca Press, 1983), 80–1.
14. Ibid., 81, and 104–5.
15. Shoko Okazaki, 'The Great Persian Famine of 1870-71', *Bulletin of the School of Oriental and African Studies* 49, no. 1 (1986): 187–8.
16. Shabaz Shahnavaz, 'Afyūn', http://www.iranicaonline.org/articles/afyun-opium (accessed on 18 March 2023), and Green, *Bombay Islam*, 139.
17. Landor, *Across Coveted Lands*, 1:152–3, and 384–5.

18 Green, *Bombay Islam*, 139.
19 H. Lyman Stebbins, *British Imperialism in Qajar Iran: Consuls, Agents and Influence in the Middle East* (London and New York: I.B. Tauris, 2016), 2.
20 H. Lyman Stebbins, 'British Imperialism, Regionalism, and Nationalism in Iran, 1890-1919', in Amanat and Vejdani, *Iran Facing Others*, 156-7.
21 Amanat, *Cities and Trade*, 105 and 137.
22 Mansour Bonakdarian, 'Great Britain iv. British Influence in Persia, 1900-21', https://www.iranicaonline.org/articles/great-britain-iv (accessed on 18 March 2023).
23 Mohajer and Yazdani, 'From Yazd to Bombay—Ardeshir Mehrabān "Irani" and the Rise of Persia's Nineteenth-Century Zoroastrian Merchants', 2-3. NB Foroutan has pointed out that in the early years of the nineteenth century, French travellers had noted the position of Yazd as a trade centre, including in regards to trade with India, and had highlighted Zoroastrian involvement in the production of cotton and silk (Foroutan, 'Yazd and its Zoroastrians', 820-1).
24 Hamid Algar, 'Amīr Kabīr, Mīrzā Taqī Khan', http://www.iranicaonline.org/articles/amir-e-kabir-mirza-taqi-khan (accessed on 18 March 2023). Amongst the issues addressed by Amir Kabir were inheritance laws that favoured converts to Islam over non-Muslim family members (Tsadik, *Between Foreigners and Shi'is*, 42-6). See also Foroutan, 'Yazd and its Zoroastrians', 822.
25 Amighi, *The Zoroastrians of Iran*, 140n6. See also Jahangir Oshidari, *Tarikh-e Pahlavi va Zartoshtiyan* (Tehran: Hukht, 2535/1976), 231-3.
26 Gobineau quoted in Charles Issawi, *The Economic History of Iran, 1800-1914* (Chicago: University of Chicago Press, 1971), 23n23.
27 Report No. 67 of 1863 detailing the tribes, trades and resources of the Gulf Littoral, Mss Eur F126/48:17. This can be contrasted to the figures cited in the 1854 Amelioration Society report (Karaka, *History of the Parsis*, 1:55).
28 Jackson, *Persia Past and Present*, 374.
29 Malcolm, *Five Years in a Persian Town*, 51, and 47.
30 Karaka, *History of the Parsis*, 1:80-1.
31 Ali Modarres, *Modernizing Yazd: Selective Historical Memory and the Fate of Vernacular Architecture* (Costa Mesa: Mazda Publishers, 2006), 59.
32 Murzban, *The Parsis in India*, 1:115.
33 Lieutenant-Colonel Charles Edward Stewart, 'Report on the North-Eastern Frontier of Persia and the Tekeh Turkomans', 4 July 1881, IOR/L/PS/18/C32:5. See also the Appendix of Lieutenant H. B. Vaughan, Memorandum on the Parsis of Yezd, July 1889, IOR/L/PWD/7/1097.
34 Lieutenant-General T. E. Gordon, enclosed in Sir F. Lascelles to the Marquess of Salisbury, 27 July 1892, FO 539/58.
35 See Nobuaki Kondo, 'Migration and Multiethnic Coexistence in Qajar Tehran', in *Human Mobility and Multiethnic Coexistence in Middle Eastern Urban Societies 1: Tehran, Aleppo, Istanbul, and Beirut*, ed. Hidemitsu Kuroki (Tokyo: Research Institute for Languages and Cultures of Asia and Africa, 2014).
36 Kasheff, 'Anjoman-e Zartoštīān'. See Stewart, 'The Politics of Zoroastrian Philanthropy and the Case of Qasr-e Firuzeh', 67-8, regarding the rebuilding of the *dakhmeh*.
37 Kasheff, 'Anjoman-e Zartoštīān', and Boyce, *Zoroastrians*, 218-19, who describes how prior to the establishment of the fire temple, a *Dadgah* fire, a lower grade of fire, was maintained by the wealthy merchant, Arbab Jamshid Jamshidian.

38 Mama, 'Manekji Limji Hataria', 27. In contrast, the situation for Iranian Jews was not always better in Tehran (Tsadik, *Between Foreigners and Shi'is*, 118ff).
39 For discussion regarding the two types of law that regulated Qajar society, *shari'a*, religious law, and *'urf*, customary law, see Janet Afary, 'Performance of Justice in Qajar Society', *International Journal of Humanities* 26, no. 1 (2019): 74–5.
40 Nobuaki Kondo, 'Non-Muslims at the Shari'a Court in Qajar Tehran', in *Human Mobility and Multiethnic Coexistence in Middle Eastern Urban Societies 2: Tehran, Cairo, Istanbul, Aleppo, and Beirut*, ed. Hidemitsu Kuroki (Tokyo: Research Institute for Languages and Cultures of Asia and Africa, 2018), 13–18.
41 Jackson, *Persia Past and Present*, 426. See also Gordon, in Sir F. Lascelles to the Marquess of Salisbury, 27 July 1892, FO 539/58.
42 Gordon, *Persia Revisited*, 80–1, and Murzban, *The Parsis in India*, 1:131n140.
43 Browne, *A Year Amongst the Persians*, 361.
44 George Nathaniel Curzon, *Persia and the Persian Question*, vol. 1 (London: Longmans, Green and Co., 1892), 334. In the 1860s, some Zoroastrians lived in the garden house in the British legation (Edward B. Eastwick, *Journal of a Diplomate's Three Years' Residence in Persia* (London: Smith, Elder and Co., 1864), 1:230–1). See also, John Piggot, *Persia – Ancient and Modern* (London: Henry S. King, 1874), 131–2, and Ella R. Durand, *An Autumn Tour in Western Persia* (Westminster, London: A. Constable and Co., 1902), 44.
45 Curzon, *Persia and the Persian Question*, 1:333. An Iranian gazette from 1877 counted 400 Zoroastrians in Tehran (Kondo, 'Migration and Multiethnic Coexistence in Qajar Tehran', 20), and in 1904 there were reportedly 423 Zoroastrians in the capital (Murzban, *The Parsis in India*, 1:109 n106). Amighi has suggested that the emigration of poor Zoroastrians to India may have slowed the growth of the Tehran community (Amighi, *The Zoroastrians of Iran*, 148).
46 Kondo, 'Migration and Multiethnic Coexistence in Qajar Tehran', 21.
47 For further biographical details, see Shahmardan, *Farzanegan-e Zartoshti*, 432–45, and Khosrow Mehrfar, 'Jamshid Bahman Jamshidian', *Chehrehnama* 167 (2013): 7–11.
48 Farhang Mehr, *Sahm-e Zartoshtiyan dar Enqelab-e Mashrutiyat-e Iran* (Tehran: Hukht, 1348/1969), 7–8.
49 Mehr, 'Zoroastrians in Twentieth Century Iran', 285.
50 Janet Kestenberg Amighi, 'Zoroastrians in Iran iv. Between the Constitutional and the Islamic Revolutions', http://www.iranicaonline.org/articles/zoroastrians-in-iran-parent (accessed on 18 March 2023), and Shahmardan, *Farzanegan-e Zartoshti*, 432–4; and, Mehrfar, 'Jamshid Bahman Jamshidian', 8–9.
51 For information about the Jahanian firm, and Khosrow Shahjahan and his brothers, see Shahmardan, *Farzanegan-e Zartoshti*, 467–73.
52 Colonel H. Picot, Biographical Notices of members of royal family, notables, merchants and clergy, December 1897. FO 60/592.
53 Afary, *The Iranian Constitutional Revolution*, 17–19; Ahmad Ashraf and Ali Banuazizi, 'Class System v. Classes in the Qajar Period', https://iranicaonline.org/articles/class-system-v (accessed on 18 March 2023); and, Gad G. Gilbar, 'Qajar Dynasty viii. "Big Merchants" in the Late Qajar Period', http://www.iranicaonline.org/articles/qajar-big-merchants (accessed on 18 March 2023).
54 Abdullaev quoted in Issawi, *The Economic History of Iran*, 46.
55 Ann K. S. Lambton, *Landlord and Peasant in Persia: A Study of Land Tenure and Land Revenue Administration* (Oxford: Oxford University Press, 1953), 140, and 151–2.

56 Jackson, *Persia Past and Present*, 426. According to Sykes, Zoroastrians were known for their 'integrity', and were consequently appointed to 'positions of trust' by 'Persian noblemen' (*JSA* 54, no. 2794 [8 June 1906]: 760).
57 For information about the Biographical Notices, see Lyman Stebbins, *British Imperialism in Qajar Iran*, 23.
58 Colonel H. Picot, Biographical Notices of members of royal family, notables, merchants and clergy, December 1897, FO 60/592. A similar description appeared in the updated 1904 Biographical Notices, which also included a print of Arbab Jamshid's seal (George Percy Churchill, Biographical Notes, 1904, IOR/R/15/1/746).
59 Mozhgan Haji Akbari, 'Naqsh-e Zartoshtiyan dar Eqtesad-e Dowreh-ye Qajari-ye ba Ta'kid bar Tojaratkhaneha-ye Zartoshti', *Tarikh-e Now* 11 (Tabestan 1394/2015): 13, and Sir M. Durand to Marquess of Salisbury, 27 July 1899, FO 416/1.
60 Amighi, *The Zoroastrians of Iran*, 156.
61 *ILQ* 3, no. 2 (January 1933): 62.
62 Mehr, *Sahm-e Zartoshtiyan dar Enqelab-e Mashrutiyat-e Iran*, 9.
63 Shahrokh, *The Memoirs of Keikhosrow Shahrokh*, 57.
64 Malcolm, *Five Years in a Persian Town*, 51–2.
65 Shahmardan, *Farzanegan-e Zartoshti*, 434. For example, the vizier of Fars borrowed 50,000 tomans from the Jamshidian firm (Shiraz diary, 30 May 1907, FO 248/912). In addition, both the Jahanian and Jamshidian firms had good relations with nomadic tribes in the province of Fars (Mehr, *Sahm-e Zartoshtiyan dar Enqelab-e Mashrutiyat-e Iran*, 12).
66 For example, see Shahrokh, *The Memoirs of Keikhosrow Shahrokh*, 36ff. For references to continued discrimination against Zoroastrians, see extracts from Browne's diary in 'Report of a Journey through Persia', Lieutenant Henry Bathurst Vaughan, 1890, IOR/L/PS/20/91:30. Writing in June 1889, Colonel Ross described how the situation for Zoroastrians in Kerman was perceived to be better than in Yazd, as the local governor was strong enough to support them (Ross to Kennedy, 13 June 1889, FO 60/539). Indeed, it was at this time that Ardeshir Mehrban feared that the absence of a governor would leave him vulnerable to extortion or robbery, prompting Lieutenant Vaughan to extend his stay in Yazd (Vaughan to Ross, 19 June 1889, FO 60/539).
67 Marashi, *Exile and the Nation*, 31–2, and Kasheff, 'Anjoman-e Zartoštiān'. See also G. D. Ogilvie, 1 September 1906, FO 248/878, where reference is made to Zoroastrians in Bam telegraphing Farmanfarma for assistance in settling a local dispute.
68 Malcolm, *Five Years in a Persian Town*, 51–2. See also Browne, *A Year Amongst the Persians*, 368–9, and *ToI*, 12 February 1890, 3. According to Gordon, Zoroastrians may have been protected during the 1891 massacre of Babis in Yazd because of payments made to Jalal al-Dowleh (General Gordon, 30 June 1892, FO 60/539). NB the term Babi was often also used in reference to Bahá'ís.
69 *ToI*, 3 September 1900, 5.
70 Tsadik, *Between Foreigners and Shi'is*, 123.
71 See *Times*, 11 September 1894, 6, and Chapter Two.
72 Tsadik, *Between Foreigners and Shi'is*, 116. Kaykhosrow Shahrokh also described Zel al-Soltan as 'Tyrannical' (Shahrokh, *The Memoirs of Keikhosrow Shahrokh*, 40).
73 Tsadik, *Between Foreigners and Shi'is*, 125ff. See also CMS ACC 113 F1.
74 Tsadik, *Between Foreigners and Shi'is*, 53–4, and 176–7, and Fischer, 'Zoroastrian Iran Between Myth and Praxis', ix, and 412–13.

75 Shahmardan, *Farzanegan-e Zartoshti*, 432ff; Amighi, *The Zoroastrians of Iran*, 156; and, Mehrfar, 'Jamshid Bahman Jamshidian', 8–9.
76 *MT* 10, no. 117 (September 1906): 257–8; *MT* 11, no. 122 (February 1907): 49; *MT* 11, no. 130 (October 1907): 293; and, *MT* 18, no. 207 (March 1914): 91. NB Gudarz Mehrban's sons later gave c.£350 towards a new hospital (*Preaching and Healing* [*PH*], 1905–6, 61). See also Hinnells, Boyce, and Shahrokh, 'Charitable Foundations ii. Among Zoroastrians in Islamic Times'.
77 *RMM* 3, no. 11–12 (1907): 449.
78 Amighi, 'Zoroastrians of 19th Century Yazd and Kerman'.
79 Ibid.
80 Stiles, 'Zoroastrian Conversions to the Bahá'í Faith in Yazd, Iran', 55.
81 Malcolm, *Five Years in a Persian Town*, 52.
82 Indeed, the Russian Native Agent in Yazd was reportedly a Babi merchant (the term Babi was sometimes used interchangeably for Bahá'í), who was married to the daughter of Bahá'u'lláh (Gordon, 30 June 1892, FO 60/539).
83 Tsadik, *Between Foreigners and Shi'is*, 41–2. See also Afary, 'Performance of Justice in Qajar Society', 88–90.
84 Anaïs Massot, 'Ottoman Damascus during the Tanzimat: The New Visibility of Religious Distinctions', in *Modernity, Minority, and the Public Sphere: Jews and Christians in the Middle East*, ed. S. R. Goldstein-Sabbah and H. L. Murre-van den Berg (Leiden: Brill, 2016), 163.
85 Vaughan, Report of a Journey through Persia, 1890, IOR/L/PS/20/91:28–9.
86 Ibid.
87 Ibid. The appointment of a British agent in Yazd had been proposed in 1870. However, due to the famine discussions were put on hold (IOR/L/PS/5/268).
88 Vaughan, Report of a Journey through Persia, 1890, IOR/L/PS/20/91:29.
89 Ibid. Vaughan noted in his report that there were 973 Zoroastrians from Yazd resident in Bombay, and that there were 28 Zoroastrians living in Yazd who had been born in Bombay.
90 Ibid.
91 Ibid.
92 Ibid.
93 Lyman Stebbins, *British Imperialism in Qajar Iran*, 38–9. In 1905, British exports to Asia were valued at £87,379,894, with exports to Iran only totalling £473,026 (*IAQROCR* 48 [October 1906]: 261).
94 'Yezd and Kerman Agencies', FO 60/539.
95 P. Basseer, 'Banking in Iran i. History of Banking in Iran', https://www.iranicaonline.org/articles/banking-in-iran (accessed on 18 March 2023). For detailed discussion about Ardeshir and the Mehrban firm, see Mohajer and Yazdani, 'From Yazd to Bombay—Ardeshir Mehrabān "Irani" and the Rise of Persia's Nineteenth-Century Zoroastrian Merchants'. This article was printed when I was in the final stages of completing my manuscript, so I was not able to fully integrate the points raised into this book.
96 Colonel Ross, enclosed in Kennedy to the Marquess of Salisbury, 9 July 1889, FO 60/539. See also Browne, *A Year Amongst the Persians*, 381.
97 Vaughan to Ross, 19 June 1889, FO 60/539.
98 Ibid. NB Edward Browne was cited as agreeing with Vaughan regarding British protection for Zoroastrians.
99 Colonel Ross, enclosed in Kennedy to Marquess of Salisbury, 9 July 1889, FO 60/539.

100 Ibid.
101 Mehrban to Lascelles, 17 January 1892, FO 60/539.
102 Mehrban to Lascelles, 22 September 1891, and Mehrban to Lascelles, 17 January 1892, FO 60/539.
103 Mehrban to Lascelles, 22 September 1891, FO 60/539.
104 Ardeshir appears to have returned to Iran to search for his brother's murderer (*ToI*, 31 October 1878, 2).
105 Mehrban to Lascelles, 22 September 1891, FO 60/539.
106 Horace Walpole, India Office to the Secretary of State, Foreign Office, 30 April 1892, FO 60/539.
107 Memorandum by General T. E. Gordon, 30 June 1892, enclosed in Lascelles to Marquess of Salisbury, 3 July 1892, FO 60/539.
108 Ibid.
109 Ibid.
110 Ibid.
111 Ibid.
112 For references to Iranian Zoroastrians who were naturalized British subjects, see *ToI*, 31 October 1878, 2, and *ToI*, 15 May 1897, 3.
113 NB Landor suggested that more could be done to help naturalized Zoroastrians (Landor, *Across Coveted Lands*, 1:404–6).
114 Memorandum by General T. E. Gordon, 30 June 1892, enclosed in Lascelles to Marquess of Salisbury, 3 July 1892, FO 60/539. Bishop Stuart of Persia also described how Ardeshir dismounted his 'fine horse', and rode instead the 'humbler equipage of a donkey', so as not to provoke hostility (*CMG* 271, no. 23 [July 1896]: 103).
115 Memorandum by General T. E. Gordon, 30 June 1892, enclosed in Lascelles to Marquess of Salisbury, 3 July 1892, FO 60/539.
116 Curzon, *Persia and the Persian Question*, 2:241.
117 Ibid. See also extracts from Browne's diary in Lieutenant Henry Bathurst Vaughan, Report of a Journey through Persia, 1890, IOR/L/PS/20/91:30.
118 Landor, *Across Coveted Lands*, 1:405. See also Browne, *A Year Amongst the Persians*, 340. NB Ardeshir's brother Gudarz was also a member of the Anjoman in Yazd (Mehr, 'Zoroastrians in Twentieth Century Iran', 281).
119 Notes on the Leading Notables, Officials, Merchants, and Clergy of Khorasan, Seistan, Kain, and Kerman, Mss Eur F111/352:5.
120 Andreeva, *Russia and the Great Game*, 5.
121 Shetalov, quoted in Andreeva, *Russia and the Great Game*, 173.
122 See extracts from travelogues by S. Lomnitskii, Pavel Ogorodnikov, and A. Miller (Andreeva, *Russia and the Great Game*, 174–5).
123 Andreeva, *Russia and the Great Game*, 193, and P. A. Rittikh, quoted on page 173.
124 Amighi, *The Zoroastrians of Iran*, 146, and Shahmardan, *Farzanegan-e Zartoshti*, 433.
125 Durand to Marquess of Salisbury, 12 February 1899, FO 60/648. Between 1889 and 1921, the number of British consulates in Iran increased from four to twenty-three (Lyman Stebbins, *British Imperialism in Qajar Iran*, 2).
126 Lascelles to Marquess of Salisbury, 20 July 1892, and Gordon to Chapman, 1 August 1892, FO 60/539.
127 Ali Modarres, 'Form and Function: On Politics and the Morphology of the Bazaar in Yazd', in *The Bazaar in the Islamic City: Design, Culture, and History*, ed. Mohammad Gharipour (Cairo: London: American University in Cairo Press, 2012), 259.
128 Green, *Bombay Islam*, 139.

129 James M. Gustafson, 'Opium, Carpets and Constitutionalists: A Social History of the Elite Households of Kirman, 1859–1914' (PhD Thesis, University of Washington, Washington, 2010), 207. See also Wright, *Britain and Iran, 1790–1980*, 56–7, and 82.
130 Lyman Stebbins, 'British Imperialism, Regionalism, and Nationalism in Iran, 1890–1919', 154–5.
131 Landor, *Across Coveted Lands*, 1:168.
132 Ibid., 162.
133 Gustafson, 'Opium, Carpets and Constitutionalists', 209.
134 Choksy, 'Despite Shāhs and Mollās', 145.
135 Sykes was temporarily consul in Sistan. See Antony Wynn, *Persia in the Great Game: Sir Percy Sykes - Explorer, Consul, Soldier, Spy* (London: John Murray, 2004), for a biography of Sykes.
136 Gustafson, 'Opium, Carpets and Constitutionalists', 200, and 209.
137 Ibid., 215. Despite increased trade, the number of Europeans living in Iran remained low during the Qajar era (approximately 150 in 1850s, and 1,000 in 1901) (Gad G. Gilbar, 'The Opening up of Qajar Iran: Some Economic and Social Aspects', *Bulletin of the School of Oriental and African Studies* 49, no. 1 [1986]: 76).
138 *ToI*, 20 August 1903, 5. See also *JSA* 54, no. 2794 (8 June 1906): 760, where Sykes, speaking in 1906, outlined the changes that had taken place: 'whereas a decade ago few of them dared to engage in trade, they are now monopolising various branches of it'.
139 Sykes, 24 March 1905, FO 248/846.
140 *JSA* 54, no. 2794 (8 June 1906): 759.
141 Ibid., 760. See also *Iran League Bulletin* (*ILB*) 1, no. 1 (March 1928): 4.
142 Malcolm, *Five Years in a Persian Town*, 114.
143 *ToI*, 26 September 1889, 4. Ginwalla, whose views regarding Parsi involvement in the INC are noted in Chapter Two, did not expect Parsi merchants to take advantage of the opening of the Karun River. He argued that their 'enterprise and energy' had decreased in the previous thirty years (*ToI*, 14 November 1890, 4).
144 For details about the concession, see Shabaz Shahnavaz, 'Karun River iii. The Opening of the Karun', https://www.iranicaonline.org/articles/karun_3 (accessed on 18 March 2023).
145 *ToI*, 30 November 1900, 6.
146 Lyman Stebbins, *British Imperialism in Qajar Iran*, 61–2. See also Rose L. Greaves, 'Sīstān in British Indian Frontier Policy', *Bulletin of the School of Oriental and African Studies* 49, no. 1 (1986): 90–102.
147 *ToI*, 30 November 1900, 6. The possibility that Parsis could be encouraged to expand their trade networks into Afghanistan and Sistan had also been raised in 1888 (Memorandum in regard to British and Indian trade in Central Asia, China and Persia, FO 65/1348).
148 *ToI*, 30 November 1900, 6. See also Diary of Major G. Chenevix-Trench, 16–30 September 1900, Mss Eur F111/355.
149 *ToI*, 1 December 1900, 6.
150 Diary of Major G. Chenevix-Trench, 1–15 January 1901, Mss Eur F111/355.
151 Sykes supported the efforts of Chenevix-Trench; in 1900 he encouraged Iranian Zoroastrians to export carpets to India via Quetta. Although there were initial profits, the expense and the difficulties of the route meant it was later abandoned (Gustafson, 'Opium, Carpets and Constitutionalists', 214).

152 *ToI*, 20 August 1903, 5. See also *ToI*, 12 May 1903, 4. During the nineteenth century, Parsis established shops for British troops who were on military campaigns, with one firm reaching as far as Kabul during the 1838–42 Afghan Wars (Palsetia, *The Parsis of India*, 50). It is possible that this is the type of shop that Sykes had in mind.
153 *MWI* 1, no. 10 (1905): 533–4.
154 Sykes to the Government of India, 9 April 1903, FO 416/15.
155 Gleadowe-Newcomen to the Secretary of the Upper India Chamber of Commerce, 1 January 1905, FO 248/852.
156 Sykes to the Government of India, 9 April 1903, FO 416/15.
157 *ToI*, 18 October 1904, 5. For Masani's recollections, see *ToI*, 17 June 1932, 6.
158 C. H. A. Hill, Secretary to the Government of Bombay to the Foreign Secretary, Simla, 3 October 1904, FO 248/852.
159 *ToI*, 2 March 1905, 8.
160 *Parsi*, January 1905, 4.
161 Lyman Stebbins, *British Imperialism in Qajar Iran*, 61. See also Firuz Kazemzadeh, *Russia and Britain in Persia, 1864–1914: A Study in Imperialism* (New Haven: Yale University Press, 1968), Chapter Six.
162 For example, C. E. D. Black, 'Baluchistan and its Possibilities', *IAQROCR* 20 (July 1905): 10–18, and C. E. Yate, 'Baluchistan', *IAQROCR* 43 (July 1906): 15–35.
163 *Indian Magazine and Review* (*IMR*) 425 (May 1906): 118.
164 Ibid., 118–19. For example, see Manekji Limji Hataria, 'The Land that Time Forgot: Travels in Iran: 1', *Parsiana* 13, no. 2 (1990): 60–4.
165 *ToI*, 11 April 1905, 6.
166 *Parsi*, April 1905, 136.
167 Ibid.
168 Gleadowe-Newcomen to the Secretary of the Upper India Chamber of Commerce, 20 December 1904, FO 248/852.
169 Ibid.
170 Sykes, 15 January 1905, FO 248/846.
171 Gleadowe-Newcomen to Secretary of the Upper India Chamber of Commerce, 20 January 1905, FO 248/852.
172 Gleadowe-Newcomen to Secretary of the Upper India Chamber of Commerce, 1 January 1905, FO 248/852.
173 Choksy, 'Despite Shahs and Mollas', 144–5.
174 Gleadowe-Newcomen to the Private Secretary to the Viceroy, 29 December 1904, FO 248/852.
175 6th Report from Gleadowe-Newcomen, March 1905, FO 248/853.
176 Ibid. See also Sykes, 28 February 1905, FO 248/846.
177 Sykes, 21 March 1905, FO 248/846.
178 6th Report from Gleadowe-Newcomen, March 1905, FO 248/853.
179 Mirza Abbas Ali Baig, Report on Native Press for 1904, IOR/L/PS/7/316.
180 *MWI* 2, no. 1 (1906): 38.
181 *ToI*, 13 June 1905, 6. See also *MWI* 1, no. 11 (1905): 609, regarding the potential regeneration of Kerman, and *MWI* 2, no. 1 (1906): 35, for the significance of Yazd, 'the Iranian "Clapham Junction"'.
182 *ToI*, 13 June 1905, 6.
183 *Bombay Guardian*, 20 May 1905, 5.
184 Kerman diary, 10 June, and 30 June 1905, FO 248/846.

185 *ToI*, 29 August 1906, 4. See Colonel Stewart, Kerman diary, 3 February 1906, FO 248/878, regarding Prince Anatouni going to Bam to try to encourage trade.
186 Memorandum regarding external affairs other than those relating to the North-West Frontier and Afghanistan, March 1904, FO 106/8:4.
187 *ToI*, 27 November 1902, 3.
188 Ibid.
189 Ibid. Iranian Zoroastrians in Bombay also used their relations with Iranian diplomats posted in Bombay to pass on their requests to the shah. In May 1905 they 'entrusted' the Persian consul-general, who was about to accompany the shah on his tour of Europe, 'with a small but important mission': to secure the shah's patronage for their new school (*Parsi*, June 1905, 212).
190 *ToI*, 27 November 1902, 3.
191 Ibid.
192 Ibid.
193 Ibid.
194 *ToI*, 12 May 1903, 4.
195 Ibid. See also the article 'Advance Iranians!: An Echo from the Fatherland', which criticized the Parsis for not doing more to help their 'kith and kin' in Iran (*Parsi*, February 1905, 49).
196 Sykes to Kemball, 14 May 1904, FO 416/19.
197 Gleadowe-Newcomen to the Private Secretary to the Viceroy, 29 December 1904, FO 248/852. See also Sykes, 28 February 1905, FO 248/846, where Sykes refers to a meeting with Ardeshir Reporter, who was worried that Sykes' imminent move from Kerman 'may upset Sir Dinshaw Petit's plan'. Sykes also noted that Reporter was discussing 'various schemes' with Gleadowe-Newcomen.
198 Sykes to Kemball, 14 May 1904, FO 416/19.
199 Ibid.
200 Gleadowe-Newcomen to the Private Secretary to the Viceroy, 29 December 1904, FO 248/852.
201 *Parsi*, February 1905, 49–50. Sykes later explained that not all the medals were metal; some were made of paper and represented 'a hundred congratulations for a hundred attendances' (*ToI*, 9 June 1906, 7).
202 NB there were also instances where local officials were invited to Zoroastrian events in Yazd; for example, after the death of Sir Dinshaw Maneckji Petit (1st Baronet) in 1901, Zoroastrians held a ceremony in Yazd which was attended by the governor of the province (Edwardes, *Memoir of Sir Dinshaw Manockjee Petit*, 88–9).
203 Denis Wright, 'Prince 'Abd ul-Husayn Mirza Farman-Farma. Notes from British Sources', *Iran* 38 (2000): 108.
204 Shahrokh, *The Memoirs of Keikhosrow Shahrokh*, 19.
205 Ibid., 1–3.
206 Ringer, *Pious Citizens*, 185, and Shahrokh, *The Memoirs of Keikhosrow Shahrokh*, 28. See also the image on the front cover, a postcard of Kaykhosrow Shahrokh with pupils from the Zoroastrian school at Kerman.
207 Shahrokh, *The Memoirs of Keikhosrow Shahrokh*, 34–6.
208 Sykes to Kemball, 14 May 1904, FO 416/19.
209 *Parsi*, February 1905, 50. See also Shahrokh, *The Memoirs of Keikhosrow Shahrokh*, 54.
210 Sykes, 12 January 1905, FO 248/846.
211 Hardinge to the Marquess of Lansdowne, 10 June 1904, FO 416/19.

212 Miller, quoted in Andreeva, *Russia and the Great Game*, 193.
213 Major D. C. Phillott, 'List of Kerman Officials', 15 June 1902, Mss Eur F111/352. See also Shahrokh, *The Memoirs of Keikhosrow Shahrokh*, 55.
214 Sykes, 12 January 1905, and 23 February 1905, FO 248/846.
215 For example, see Shahrokh, *The Memoirs of Keikhosrow Shahrokh*, 18.
216 Sykes, 23 February 1905, FO 248/846.
217 Hardinge to the Marquess of Lansdowne, 8 February 1905, FO 416/22.
218 The perceived threat of 'rumour' spreading in India and the 'nightmare' of the 'loss of British prestige' has also been highlighted by B. D. Hopkins (*The Making of Modern Afghanistan* [New York: Palgrave Macmillan, 2008], 59).
219 Sykes, 12 January 1905, and 23 February 1905, FO 248/846.
220 Correspondence from Sykes, 17 January 1905, GI Foreign Department, Secret E (Proceedings of June 1905, 497).
221 Ibid.
222 Ibid.
223 Sykes, 12 January 1905, FO 248/846.
224 Sykes, Kerman diary, 21 March 1905, FO 248/846.
225 Sykes, Meshed diary, 27 May 1905, FO 248/853.
226 Shahrokh, *The Memoirs of Keikhosrow Shahrokh*, 55.
227 Letter from Sir Dinshaw Petit, 24 March 1905, enclosed in C. H. A. Hill (Acting Secretary to Government of Bombay, Political Department) to Secretary to the Government of India, Foreign Department, 6 April 1905, GI Foreign Department, Secret E (Proceedings of June 1905, 498).
228 *Parsi*, February 1905, 58.
229 Ibid.
230 Sykes' efforts did not go unnoticed by the *Habl al-Matin* newspaper, which published an article stating that Sykes had turned the inhabitants of Kerman towards the British government (Sykes, 24 June 1905, FO 248/853).
231 NB Sykes was now consul-general in Mashad. For the lecture and following discussion, see *JSA* 54, no. 2794 (8 June 1906): 753–67.
232 Ibid., 754.
233 Ibid., 761–2.
234 Ibid. Sykes had earlier praised the Parsis for being 'in the vanguard in all that makes for progress and civilisation' (Ibid., 754).
235 Ibid. 762.
236 Ibid.
237 Ibid., 764–6.
238 Ibid., 762. Sykes made similar comments and also highlighted the supposedly 'Aryan head' of Iranian Zoroastrians (ibid., 760), a reflection of contemporary pseudoscientific and racist phrenological theories (see Veer, *Imperial Encounters*, 145ff).
239 *JSA* 54, no. 2794 (8 June 1906): 762–3.
240 Ibid., 763.
241 Ibid.
242 Ibid., 766.
243 For example, see: *MWI* 2, no. 6 (1906): 339–43; *Pickings from Hindi Punch*, July 1906, 24–5, and 32; *Parsi Prakash* 4–5, 156; and, *ToI*, 9 June 1906, 7. The talk was also referred to in a later article by Delphine Menant (*RMM* 3, no. 11–12 [1907]: 450–2).
244 *Pickings from Hindi Punch*, July 1906, 25, and 32.

245 Ibid., 24–5. The encouragement given to Parsis to help Zoroastrians in Iran was linked to concurrent discussions about a possible Parsi colony. On the same page it was stated that 'The Parsi has often thought of Seistan and Makran and Penang as places to colonize and live independently in' (ibid., 24).
246 Sykes to Sir Louis Dane, Secretary to the Government of India, Foreign Department, 5 July 1906, GI Foreign Department, Secret E (Proceedings of November 1906, 376–9).
247 Sykes to Sir D. Petit, 4 July 1906, and Sykes to Sir Louis Dane, Secretary to the Government of India, Foreign Department, 5 July 1906, GI Foreign Department, Secret E (Proceedings of November 1906, 376–9), and *ToI*, 21 July 1906, 5.
248 *ToI*, 21 July 1906, 5. See also *Parsi*, July 1905, 277, where the reviewer of Sykes' 1902 book *Ten Thousand Miles in Persia* stated that 'one of the best ways in which the Parsis can employ their money for charitable purposes would be to devote it towards the education of their ignorant co-religionists in Persia. A movement has already been set on foot for that purpose, and it requires to be strongly backed and supported'.
249 *ToI*, 21 July 1906, 5.
250 Ibid.

Chapter 4

1 Afary, *The Iranian Constitutional Revolution*, 22–3, and Abbas Amanat, 'Constitutional Revolution i. Intellectual Background', https://www.iranicaonline.org/articles/constitutional-revolution-i (accessed on 18 March 2023).
2 Bayat, *Iran's Experiment with Parliamentary Governance*, 22. For a detailed account of the work of Mirza Hosayn Khan, see Guity Nashat, *The Origins of Modern Reform in Iran* (Urbana; Chicago; London: University of Illinois Press, 1981).
3 Bayat, *Iran's Experiment with Parliamentary Governance*, 25–6. See also Gurney and Nabavi, 'Dār al-Fonūn'.
4 Amanat, 'Constitutional Revolution i. Intellectual Background'. For a detailed account of the life of Malkam Khan, see Algar, *Mirza Malkum Khan*. NB although his ideas influenced supporters of the constitution, there is little information about his views of the revolution (Algar, *Mirza Malkum Khan*, 247–8).
5 Algar, *Mirza Malkum Khan*, 9ff.
6 Ibid., 24–5.
7 Nashat, *The Origins of Modern Reform in Iran*, 23.
8 Ann K. S. Lambton, *Qajar Persia: Eleven Studies* (London: I.B. Tauris, 1987), 303.
9 ʿAlī-Akabr Saʿīdī Sīrjānī, 'Constitutional Revolution vi. The Press', https://www.iranicaonline.org/articles/constitutional-revolution-vi (accessed on 18 March 2023).
10 Afary, *The Iranian Constitutional Revolution*, 26.
11 Amanat, 'Constitutional Revolution i. Intellectual Background'.
12 Hadi Enayat, *Law, State, and Society in Modern Iran: Constitutionalism, Autocracy, and Legal Reform, 1906–1941* (New York: Palgrave Macmillan, 2013), 54 (and all of Chapter Two for related discussion), and Bayat, *Iran's Experiment with Parliamentary Governance*, 21.
13 Afary, *The Iranian Constitutional Revolution*, 26; Hassan Bashir, '*Qanun* and the Modernisation of Political thought in Iran', *Global Media Journal* 8, no. 14 (2009):

1–39; and, Mehrdad Kia, 'Constitutionalism, Economic Modernization and Islam in the Writings of Mirza Yusef Khan Mostashar od-Dowle', *Middle Eastern Studies* 30, no. 4 (1994): 751–77.
14 N. R. Keddie, 'Afḡānī, Jamāl-al-Dīn', http://www.iranicaonline.org/articles/afgani-jamal-al-din (accessed on 18 March 2023).
15 Lambton, *Qajar Persia*, 305, and Algar, *Mirza Malkum Khan*, 210–13.
16 For the terms of the treaty, which was signed in 1890, see J. C. Hurewitz, *Diplomacy in the Near and Middle East: A Documentary Record*, vol. 1 (Princeton: Van Nostrand, 1956), 205–6. For detailed analysis of the concession and the opposition it faced, see Nikki R. Keddie, *Religion and Rebellion in Iran: The Iranian Tobacco Protest of 1891–1982* (London: Cass, 1966); Ann K. S. Lambton, 'The Tobacco Regie: Prelude to Revolution', in *Qajar Persia: Eleven Studies* (London: I.B. Tauris, 1987); and, Fatema Soudavar Farmanfarmaian, 'Revisiting and Revising the Tobacco Rebellion', *Iranian Studies* 47, no. 4 (2014): 595–625.
17 Soudavar Farmanfarmaian, 'Revisiting and Revising the Tobacco Rebellion', 598, and Afary, *The Iranian Constitutional Revolution*, 32.
18 Soudavar Farmanfarmaian, 'Revisiting and Revising the Tobacco Rebellion', 609ff. For information about Shirazi, see Hamid Algar, 'Ḥasan Šīrāzī', http://www.iranicaonline.org/articles/hasan-sirazi-mirza-mohammad (accessed on 30 December 2012).
19 Homa Katouzian, 'The Revolution for Law: A Chronographic Analysis of the Constitutional Revolution of Iran', *Middle Eastern Studies* 47, no. 5 (2011): 759.
20 Lambton, *Qajar Persia*, 275–6.
21 Soudavar Farmanfarmaian, 'Revisiting and Revising the Tobacco Rebellion', 625.
22 Algar, *Mirza Malkum Khan*, 211–13.
23 See references in Soudavar Farmanfarmaian, 'Revisiting and Revising the Tobacco Rebellion', 596n4.
24 Speaking in the early twentieth century, P. M. Sykes noted that Zoroastrians were prohibited from smoking both tobacco and opium for religious reasons (*JSA* 54, no. 2794 [8 June 1906]: 760). However, in the mid-nineteenth century, Westergaard had stated that Iranian Zoroastrians did smoke (*OCS* 2, no. 10 [June 1848]: 228). It seems that the changes in practice were linked to reforms promoted by Hataria (Fischer, 'Zoroastrian Iran Between Myth and Praxis', 100). I would like to thank Jenny Rose who, during my PhD viva, raised the question of Zoroastrian respect for fire in relation to the tobacco boycott.
25 Amighi, *The Zoroastrians of Iran*, 157.
26 Fischer, 'Zoroastrian Iran Between Myth and Praxis', 436. NB Gudarz Mehrban later donated this building to the CMS to be used as a hospital.
27 Tsadik, *Between Foreigners and Shiʿis*, 154.
28 NB Naser al-Din Shah was assassinated by Mirza Reza Khan, a follower of Jamal al-Din Asadabadi (Afary, *The Iranian Constitutional Revolution*, 33, and Vanessa Martin, 'Constitutional Revolution ii. Events', https://iranicaonline.org/articles/constitutional-revolution-ii [accessed on 18 March 2023)].
29 For further details, see Annette Destrée, 'Belgian-Iranian Relations', https://www.iranicaonline.org/articles/belgian-iranian-relations (accessed on 18 March 2023), and H. F. Farmayan, 'Amīn-al-Dawla, Mīrzā ʿAlī Khan', http://www.iranicaonline.org/articles/amin-al-dawla-mirza-ali-khan (accessed on 18 March 2023).
30 Martin, 'Constitutional Revolution: ii. Events'.
31 Ibid.; Lambton, *Qajar Persia*, 310; and, Afary, *The Iranian Constitutional Revolution*, 34, and 39. See also Gilbar, 'Qajar Dynasty viii. "Big Merchants" in the Late Qajar

Period', for discussion regarding the economic, political and social significance of 'big merchants'.

32 Afary, *The Iranian Constitutional Revolution*, 23. See also, Vanessa Martin, 'Aqa Najafi, Haj Aqa Nurullah, and the Emergence of Islamism in Isfahan 1889-1908', *Iranian Studies* 41, no. 2 (2008): 155–72.
33 Afary, *The Iranian Constitutional Revolution*, 23.
34 Ibid., 23–4.
35 For example, see Afary, *The Iranian Constitutional Revolution*, 23.
36 D. M. MacEoin, 'Azali Babism', http://www.iranicaonline.org/articles/azali-babism (accessed on 18 March 2023). See also Sohrab Yazdani, 'Heterodox Intellectuals of the Iranian Constitutional Revolution', in *Religion and Society in Qajar Iran*, ed. Robert Gleave (Abingdon: Routledge Curzon, 2005).
37 Bayat, *Iran's First Revolution*, 61. See also Ali-Asghar Seyed-Gohrab and Sen McGlinn (eds), *The True Dream: Indictment of the Shiite Clerics of Isfahan, an English Translation with Facing Persian Text* (London and New York: Routledge, 2017), 15. NB Malek al-Motakallemin was influenced by reforms that he witnessed in India (Abdul-Hadi Hairi, 'European and Asian Influences on the Persian Revolution of 1906', *Asian Affairs* 6, no. 2 [1975]: 159).
38 Bayat, *Iran's First Revolution*, 61. The positive views Malek al-Motakallemin held regarding the pre-Islamic era are apparent in a speech he made at the opening of a school established by the Society of Learning, of which he was a leading member. During his speech, he stated that education would 'enable Iran . . . to retain its ancient glory' (Malek al-Motakallemin, quoted in Ervand Abrahamian, *Iran Between Two Revolutions* [Princeton: Princeton University Press, 1982], 76).
39 Hossein Hasheminiasari, 'The Newspaper and the Pulpit: Media, Religious Anxieties, and the Revolutionary Crowd Prior to Iran's Constitutional Revolution of 1905-1911' (MA Thesis, University of Colorado, Boulder, 2018), 12.
40 Bayat, *Iran's First Revolution*, 62, and 145.
41 Saʿīdī Sīrjānī, 'Constitutional Revolution vi. The Press'.
42 Bayat, *Iran's First Revolution*, 49. For examples of positive references to Zoroastrians in the sermons of Sayyed Jamal al-Din Va'ez Esfahani, see Yazdani, 'Heterodox Intellectuals of the Iranian Constitutional Revolution', 184.
43 See Lambton, *Qajar Persia*, 301–18, for further discussion about the secret societies.
44 Ibid., 311–14.
45 Bayat, *Iran's Experiment with Parliamentary Governance*, 36.
46 Abrahamian, *Iran Between Two Revolutions*, 78 (see also pages 76–80 for further information about the societies).
47 Mehdi Malekzadeh, *Tarikh-e Enqelab-e Mashrutiyat-e Iran* (Tehran: Ketabkhaneh Soqrat, 1949), 2:10, and Amanat, 'Constitutional Revolution i. Intellectual Background'. Arbab Guiv may have been Arbab Shahpur Guiv, an older brother of Rostam Guiv, who later represented Zoroastrians in the Majles (for biographical details, see Jamshid Pavri, 'Arbab Rustam Bahman Guiv', http://www.zoroastrian.org.uk/vohuman/Article/Rustam%20Guiv.htm (accessed on 18 March 2023). For further discussion about Jamal-al-Din Va'ez, see Asghar Fathi, 'Seyyed Jamal Vaez and the "Ajmal" Newspaper in Iran', *Middle Eastern Studies* 33, no. 2 (1997): 216–25.
48 Lambton, *Qajar Persia*, 311, and 313. See also Afary, *The Iranian Constitutional Revolution*, 42–3. Adolphe Back de Surany referred to a society called the 'Anjoman of Brothers' which also counted Zoroastrians amongst its members (Adolphe Back de Surany, *Essai sur la Constitution Persane* [Paris: A. Pedone, 1914], 102).

49 Afary, *The Iranian Constitutional Revolution*, 53.
50 Hairi, 'European and Asian Influences on the Persian Revolution of 1906', 158–62.
51 Afary, *The Iranian Constitutional Revolution*, 37. See also Grant Duff to Grey, 19 March 1906, IOR L/PS/20 FO 23.
52 Afary, *The Iranian Constitutional Revolution*, 22. Indeed, the formation of the Secret Society seems to have been directly linked to events taking place in Russia (ibid., 42).
53 Martin, 'Constitutional Revolution: ii. Events', and Afary, *The Iranian Constitutional Revolution*, 50–1.
54 Afary, *The Iranian Constitutional Revolution*, 51.
55 Ibid.
56 Ibid.
57 Martin, 'Constitutional Revolution: ii. Events'.
58 Ibid., and Katouzian, 'The Revolution for Law', 763.
59 Sykes to the Government of India, 19 January 1906, IOR L/PS/20 FO 23.
60 Afary, *The Iranian Constitutional Revolution*, 52, and Bayat, *Iran's First Revolution*, 115–16.
61 Bayat, *Iran's First Revolution*, 124.
62 Afary, *The Iranian Constitutional Revolution*, 54–5; Martin, 'Constitutional Revolution: ii. Events'; and, Vanessa Martin, 'Nuri, Fażl-Allāh', http://www.iranicaonline.org/articles/nuri-fazl-allah (accessed on 18 March 2023).
63 Martin, 'Constitutional Revolution: ii. Events'.
64 Ibid.
65 Ibid.
66 Malekzadeh, *Tarikh-e Enqelab-e Mashrutiyat-e Iran*, 2:168.
67 Ibid.
68 Mehr, 'Zoroastrians in Twentieth Century Iran', 298. See also Touraj Amini, *Ta'amol Aqalliyyatha-ye Mazhabi va Enqelab-e Mashrutiyat-e Iran* (Los Angeles: Ketab Corp, 1387/2008), 62–3. For information about the School of Political Science, see Bayat, *Iran's Experiment with Parliamentary Governance*, 25–6, and Ahmad Ashraf, 'Faculties of the University of Tehran iii. Faculty of Law and Political Science', https://iranicaonline.org/articles/faculties-iii (accessed on 18 March 2023).
69 Bayat, *Iran's Experiment with Parliamentary Governance*, 37.
70 Vanessa Martin, *Islam and Modernism: The Iranian Revolution of 1906* (London: I.B. Tauris, 1989), 55.
71 Grant Duff to Grey, 13 August 1906, IOR L/P&S/20 FO 23:29707.
72 Martin, 'Constitutional Revolution: ii. Events'.
73 Bayat, *Iran's First Revolution*, 137.
74 Afary, *The Iranian Constitutional Revolution*, 57–8.
75 For further details, see Said Amir Arjomand, 'Constitutional Revolution iii. The Constitution', https://iranicaonline.org/articles/constitutional-revolution-iii (accessed on 18 March 2023).
76 NB the senate did not convene until 1950.
77 Edward Granville Browne, *The Persian Revolution of 1905–1909* (Cambridge: Cambridge University Press, 1910), 355ff; Martin, 'Constitutional Revolution: ii. Events'; and, Afary, *The Iranian Constitutional Revolution*, 64ff. For analysis of the role played by women during the Constitutional Revolution, see Afary, *The Iranian Constitutional Revolution*, Chapter Seven. NB women did not gain suffrage in Iran until 1963.
78 Spring-Rice to Grey, 7 December 1906, IOR L/PS/20 FO 23:42982.

79 Arjomand, 'Constitutional Revolution iii. The Constitution'.
80 Bayat, *Iran's First Revolution*, 139.
81 Afary, *The Iranian Constitutional Revolution*, 70.
82 Ibid.
83 Shahrokh, *The Memoirs of Keikhosrow Shahrokh*, 57.
84 Nezam al-Eslam Kermani, referenced in Bayat, *Iran's First Revolution*, 145. Similarly, Mahdi Bamdad refers to a conversation he had with Arbab Jamshid who mentioned that he had paid a large sum of money to Behbahani (Mahdi Bamdad, *Sharh-e Hal-e Rejal-e Iran*, vol. 1. [Tehran: Zuvvar, 1347/1968], 280).
85 Majles 1:255.
86 Shahrokh, *The Memoirs of Keikhosrow Shahrokh*, 57.
87 Ibid., 29. See also Amighi, *The Zoroastrians of Iran*, 162.
88 Afary, *The Iranian Constitutional Revolution*, 73–81.
89 Shahrokh, *The Memoirs of Keikhosrow Shahrokh*, 29. See also Amighi, *The Zoroastrians of Iran*, 162.
90 Amini, *Asnadi az Zartoshtiyan-e Moʿaser-e Iran*, 285; Mehr, *Sahm-e Zartoshtiyan dar Enqelab-e Mashrutiyat-e Iran*, 10–11; Mehr, 'Zoroastrians in Twentieth Century Iran', 281; and Oshidari, *Tarikh-e Pahlavi va Zartoshtiyan*, 241, and 243.
91 Afary, *The Iranian Constitutional Revolution*, 70.
92 *Habl al-Matin*, 12 November 1906, quoted in *RMM* 1 no. 3 (January 1907): 416. For further information about *Habl al-Matin*, see Nassereddin Parvin, 'Ḥabl al-matin', https://www.iranicaonline.org/articles/habl-al-matin (accessed on 18 March 2023).
93 Zia-Ebrahimi, *The Emergence of Iranian Nationalism*, 173–4.
94 *RMM* 1, no. 2 (December 1906): 262.
95 *RMM* 3, no. 10 (October 1907): 193. Delphine Menant included in this article a photograph of Arbab Jamshid that he had sent to her, perhaps revealing that Arbab Jamshid was keen to use links with European scholars to encourage positive publicity abroad.
96 For an overview of the press during this period, see Saʿīdī Sīrjānī, 'Constitutional Revolution vi. The Press'.
97 Bayat, *Iran's First Revolution*, 145.
98 For example, *Neda-ye Vatan* 7, 14 Zu al-Hijja 1324 (29 January 1907), 7–8, and *Neda-ye Vatan* 8, 21 Zu al-Hijja 1324 (5 February 1907), 8.
99 *Tarbiyat*, 15 Shaʿban 1324 (4 October 1906), referenced in *RMM* 1, no. 2 (December 1906): 263. On the same page of the *RMM*, it was noted that the Persian minister in India had attended Parsi festivals at which the name of the shah was cheered.
100 Mehr, 'Zoroastrians in Twentieth Century Iran', 281.
101 *Tarbiyat*, 29 Shaʿban 1324 (18 October 1906), quoted in Shahmardan, *Farzanegan-e Zartoshti*, 438–9.
102 *Tarbiyat*, 2 Zu al-Hijja 1324 (17 January 1907), referenced in Shahmardan, *Farzanegan-e Zartoshti*, 367.
103 *RMM* 1, no. 2 (December 1906): 263.
104 John R. Hinnells, 'Bombay Parsis and the Diaspora in the 18th and 19th Centuries', in Godrej and Mistree, *A Zoroastrian Tapestry*, 476.
105 ZTFE (file with correspondence relating to Persia). See also *Times*, 11 October 1906, 3. A reply sent by the prime minister, Moshir al-Dowleh stated that, 'His Imperial Majesty is much pleased with your telegram, and thanks Zoroastrian community for their kind wishes' (*Pickings from Hindi Punch*, July 1906-July 1907, 264).

106 ZTFE (file with correspondence relating to Persia).
107 Ibid.
108 Ibid.
109 ToI, 27 October 1906, 8; ToI, 5 November 1906, 7; ToI, 10 November 1906, 9; *Rast Goftar* (*RG*), 28 October 1906, quoted in *Parsi Prakash* 4–5, 166; and, *Pickings from Hindi Punch*, July 1906-July 1907, 264, which has a cartoon of Arbab Jamshid holding a scroll that says 'The First Parsi Member of the Persian Government'.
110 ToI, 14 September 1907, 6.
111 *RG*, quoted in *Bombay Gazette*, 4 January 1907, 6.
112 Ibid.
113 *IAQROCR* 23 (January 1907): 12–29 (lecture), 106–18 (discussion following the lecture). The East India Association was established in 1866 and Dadabhai Naoroji was one of the founding members (Palsetia, *The Parsis of India*, 284–5).
114 *Neda-ye Vatan* 3, 25 Zu al-Qa'dah 1324 (10 January 1907), 4–5.
115 *IAQROCR* 23 (January 1907): 27.
116 Ibid.
117 Ibid. NB this claim may have been inspired by Shahrokh's brief employment as a Russian agent in Odessa.
118 Ibid. Parveez also pointed out that Russian diplomats protected Armenian merchants, many of whom traded with Russia (ibid., 21–2).
119 Ibid., 110.
120 Ibid., 116.
121 Ibid., 108.
122 Ibid., 13.
123 Ibid., 107.
124 *ToI*, 26 November 1906, 6.
125 *IAQROCR* 23 (January 1907): 110.
126 Ibid.
127 Ibid.
128 Ibid., 115.
129 *ToI*, 26 November 1906, 6. See also *ToI*, 5 November 1906, 7, and Syed Shamsuddin Kadri, Annual Report of the Press (1905–6), IOR/L/PS/7/317. The *Bombay Gazette* exclaimed that, 'Books on Persia are multiplying fast, and now that the land is showing unmistakeable signs of an awakening in common with other lands of the East, and the interest of the Western world is increasing proportionately, we may expect the stream of new books on that old country to flow stronger in the near future'. Reference was also made to Jackson's 'very high' opinion of Zoroastrians in Iran (*Bombay Gazette*, 12 January 1907, 4).
130 *IAQROCR* 23 (January 1907): 108.
131 Ibid., 109.
132 Ibid., 14–15.
133 Ibid., 27.
134 *MWI* 2, no. 8 (August 1906): 430.
135 Ibid.
136 Ibid, 432.
137 *RG*, 14 April 1907, 10.
138 *Bombay Gazette*, 26 January 1907, 4.
139 M. A. R. Seoharvi, 'Proposed Reforms in Persia', *East & West* (*EW*) 6, no. 1 (January-June 1907): 56.

140 Ibid., 59. See also the description of Seoharvi's article in the *Bombay Gazette*, 26 January 1907, 4.
141 Seoharvi, 'Proposed Reforms in Persia', 59.
142 Given the views expressed, it is possible that Seoharvi was a member of the Bahá'í faith and that he was Abdurrahman Seoharvi, author of 'Bahaism', an article published in the *Calcutta Review* 124, July 1907, 409–27.
143 *Hindi Punch* (*HP*), 15 September 1907, 23 (Plate 1).
144 *IAQROCR* 23 (January 1907): 112.
145 *ToI*, 26 November 1906, 6.
146 *IAQROCR* 23 (January 1907): 27.
147 Ibid., 116.
148 *Bombay Gazette*, 17 January 1907, 5; *Bombay Gazette*, 21 January 1907, 7; *RG*, 27 January 1907, 2; and, Native Press Report, 19 January 1907, IOR L/R/5/162.
149 Native Press Report, 26 January 1907, IOR/L/R/5/162; *RG*, 27 January 1907, 2; and, *Bombay Gazette*, 17 January 1907, 5.
150 *RG*, 20 January 1907, 3.
151 Ibid.
152 Ibid.
153 Ibid.
154 A. H. H. Abidi, 'Irano-Afghan Dispute over the Helmand Waters', *International Studies 16*, no. 3 (1977): 362–4.
155 *Bombay Gazette*, 31 January 1907.
156 *HP*, 27 January 1907, 14. See also *HP*, 27 January 1907, 23 (Plate 2).
157 Native Press Report, 26 January 1907, IOR L/R/5/162.
158 Ibid.
159 Jivanji Jamshedji Modi, 'The Afghanistan of the Amir and the Ancient Mazdayaçnâns', *East & West* 6, no. 1 (February 1907): 114.
160 Ibid.
161 *HP*, 3 February 1907, 19.
162 *ToI*, 17 January 1907, 10.
163 *Bombay Gazette*, 30 January 1907, 3, and *Bombay Gazette*, 17 January 1907.
164 *Bombay Gazette*, 17 January 1907.
165 Ibid. See also *ToI*, 17 January 1907, 10, and Native Press Report, 26 January 1907, IOR L/R/5/162.
166 *Bombay Gazette*, 17 January 1907.
167 *ToI*, 17 January 1907, 10. See also *Bombay Gazette*, 10 January 1907, 4.
168 *RG*, 13 January 1907, 2.
169 *HP*, 20 January 1907, 19 (Plate 3).
170 *RG*, 13 January 1907, 2.
171 *ToI*, 17 January 1907, 10.
172 Ibid. The loyalty of Iranian Zoroastrians to the shah was also noted in the *Bombay Gazette*, 30 January 1907, 3.
173 *ToI*, 30 January 1907, 5.
174 Kulke, *The Parsees in India*, 133.
175 Ibid., 144.
176 Regarding Indian interest in the Iranian revolution, see Bonakdarian, 'India ix, Relations: Qajar Period, Early 20th Century'.
177 Native Press Report, 13 April 1907, IOR L/R/5/162.
178 Native Press Report, 22 September 1906, IOR L/R/5/161.

179 Syed Shamsuddin Kadri, Annual Report of the Press (1905-6), IOR/L/PS/7/317.
180 Ibid.
181 Ibid. An article in the *Modern Review*, '"Swaraj" or Self-Rule in Oriental Countries', praised the revolution in Iran, and, referencing the pre-Islamic period, predicted that the establishment of the Majles would 'lead the people of that country to that position of eminence which they once occupied in days of yore and which made it possible for a Zoroaster to appear in that land' (*Modern Review* 1, no. 6 [1907]: 540).
182 Syed Shamsuddin Kadri, Annual Report of the Press (1905-6), IOR/L/PS/7/317.
183 In October 1905, the *Hindi Punch* highlighted that Parsi charity had almost halved in a decade (*Pickings from Hindi Punch*, July 1905-July 1906, 160). These figures may have been interpreted as a sign of economic decline.
184 Hinnells, 'Bombay, Persian communities of. i. The Zoroastrian community'.
185 Native Press Report, 5 January 1907, IOR L/R/5/162. The following year, there was only one Parsi on the list (Native Press Report, 4 January 1908, IOR L/R/5/163).
186 Writer, *Contemporary Zoroastrians*, 97, and Kulke, *The Parsees in India*, 189.
187 Bonakdarian, 'India ix, Relations: Qajar Period, Early 20th Century'.
188 Tejani, *Indian Secularism*, 87.
189 Palsetia, *The Parsis of India*, 300-1, and Tejani, *Indian Secularism*, 95.
190 Palsetia, *The Parsis of India*, 302.
191 Dadabhai Naoroji, 'Twenty-second Congress - Calcutta - 1906', in *Congress Presidential Addresses: From the Foundation to the Silver Jubilee*, ed. G. A. Natesan (Madras: G. A. Natesan, 1935), 729. For contextualized analysis of Naoroji's presidential address, see Patel, *Naoroji*, Chapter Seven.
192 Kulke, *The Parsees in India*, 178-9. For example, see Naoroji, in Natesan, *Congress Presidential Addresses*, 724.
193 Metcalf and Metcalf, *A Concise History of Modern India*, 157-60, and Heehs, *India's Freedom Struggle 1857-1947*, 73-5.
194 Bonakdarian, 'India ix, Relations: Qajar Period, Early 20th Century'.
195 *RG*, quoted in *ToI*, 27 November 1907, 8.
196 *RG*, quoted in *Bombay Gazette*, 4 September 1907, 6. See also *RG*, 1 September 1907, 1-2; *RG*, 10 November 1907, 2; and, *RG*, 24 November 1907, 1. Articles from the *RG* were also reprinted in the *ToI*; for example, see *ToI*, 13 November 1907, 8.
197 Native Press Report, 5 October 1907, IOR L/R/5/162. In the 1904 Report on the Native Press by Mirza Abbas Ali Baig, the *Oriental Review* and *Kaisar-i Hind* were described as reflecting 'the views of the extreme wing of the Congress Party'. Both were run by Parsis (IOR/L/PS/7/316).
198 Native Press Report, 5 October 1907, IOR L/R/5/162.
199 Ibid.
200 Ibid.
201 This subtitle was included on the cover page of the *Indian Sociologist (IS)*.
202 See Alex Tickell, 'Scholarship Terrorists: The India House Hostel and the "Student Problem" in Edwardian London', in *South Asian Resistances in Britain, 1858-1947*, ed. Sumita Mukherjee and Rehana Ahmed (London: Bloomsbury, 2012), 29-32.
203 *IS* 1, no. 3 (March 1905): 10.
204 *IS* 2, no. 3 (March 1906): 11.
205 Ibid.
206 Ibid.
207 Ibid.
208 Ibid.

209 Ibid.
210 *IS* 3 no. 5 (May 1907): 17.
211 Ibid.
212 Ibid.
213 Ibid.
214 Ibid., 18.
215 Marashi, *Exile and the Nation*, 136. For further information about Cama see Nawaz B. Mody, 'Madame Bhikhaiji Rustam Cama', in *The Parsis in Western India: 1818–1920*, ed. Nawaz B. Mody (Bombay: Allied Publishers Limited, 1998), and Ole Birk Laursen, '"I Have Only One Country, It Is the World": Madame Cama, Anticolonialism, and Indian-Russian Revolutionary Networks in Paris, 1907–17', *History Workshop Journal* 90 (2021): 96–114.
216 Marashi, *Exile and the Nation*, 136–7, and Laursen, '"I Have Only One Country, It Is the World"', 100–1.
217 *IS* 3, no. 6 (June 1907): 22.
218 Ibid., 22–3.
219 Native Press Report, 29 June 1907, IOR L/R/5/162.
220 Bonakdarian, 'India ix, Relations: Qajar Period, Early 20th Century'.
221 Martin, 'Constitutional Revolution: ii. Events'.
222 Browne, *The Persian Revolution of 1905–1909*, 137, and Edward Granville Browne, *A Brief Narrative of Recent Events in Persia* (London: Luzac and Co., 1909), 19.
223 Browne, *A Brief Narrative of Recent Events in Persia*, 19. For later discussions about the challenges faced by the bank, see Majles 1:235.
224 Imperial Bank of Persia to Foreign Office, 21 March 1907, Enclosure 2, Mr Rabino to Imperial Bank of Persia, 19 March 1907, FO 371/305; Majles 1:5; and, Ahmad Kasravi, *Tarikh-e Mashruteh-ye Iran*, vol. 1, trans. Evan Siegel (Costa Mesa: Mazda Publishers, 2006), 208.
225 Majles 1:5 (NB there only seem to have been four other companies taking deposits). For references to funds being received by Arbab Jamshid, see Majles 1:7, and Majles 1:26.
226 *Pioneer*, referenced in *Bombay Gazette*, 22 February 1907, 3. The exchange rate between tomans and pounds is based on figures cited in Hooshang Amirahmadi, *The Political Economy of Iran under the Qajars: Society, Politics, Economics and Foreign Relations, 1796 to 1926* (London: I.B. Tauris, 2012), 68. Similar exchange rates are referenced by Gilbar, 'Qajar Dynasty viii. "Big Merchants" in the Late Qajar Period'.
227 Mehr, *Sahm-e Zartoshtiyan dar Enqelab-e Mashrutiyat-e Iran*, 10. See also Shahmardan, *Farzanegan-e Zartoshti*, 469, who notes that the National Bank was supported by the Jahanian firm.
228 Afary, *The Iranian Constitutional Revolution*, 72.
229 Barnham to Spring-Rice, 29 January 1907, FO 248/905.
230 Majles 1:5, and Imperial Bank of Persia to Foreign Office, 21 March 1907, Inclosure 2, Mr Rabino to Imperial Bank of Persia, 19 March 1907, FO 371/305. In 1899, the Tumanian brothers and other Iranian merchant-bankers had unsuccessfully tried to establish a company to compete with the British Imperial Bank (Basseer, 'Banking in Iran i. History of Banking in Iran').
231 Fischer, 'Zoroastrian Iran Between Myth and Praxis', 436.
232 *ToI*, 23 February 1907, 9, and *IAQROCR* 23 (April 1907): 435.

233 *Bombay Gazette*, 22 February 1907, 3. See also *Bombay Gazette*, 26 January 1907, 4, for a positive assessment of the potential of the bank to free Iran from reliance on foreign loans.
234 Spring-Rice to Grey, Monthly Summary, 27 February 1907, FO 371/304.
235 Ibid.
236 See also *Neda-ye Vatan* 3, 25 Zu al-Qa'dah 1324 (10 January 1907), 4–5, where Naoroz Parveez is referred to as an Iranian, and Parsi investment in Iran is encouraged, for example in the cotton industry.
237 Spring-Rice to Grey, Report for the first nine months of 1907, FO 371/498.
238 Ibid.
239 Browne, *The Persian Revolution of 1905–1909*, 137. See also Mehr, *Sahm-e Zartoshtiyan dar Enqelab-e Mashrutiyat-e Iran*, 14–15. An examination of contemporary Bombay newspapers supports this conclusion, as articles concerning the bank and the murder were printed in close proximity in the pages of some publications; for example, *Bombay Gazette*, 22 February 1907, 3.

Chapter 5

1 Baggaley to Barnham, 17 February 1907, FO 248/905.
2 Barnham to Spring-Rice, 9 October 1906, FO 248/877.
3 Telegram from Yazd to Barnham, Isfahan, 17 November 1906, FO 248/877.
4 Barnham to Spring-Rice, 'Yezd News', 15 December 1906, FO 248/877, and the reference made to a telegram from 16 November 1906, concerning an attack on Parviz Shahjahan (Baggaley to Barnham, 17 February 1907, FO 248/905).
5 Barnham to Spring-Rice, 'Yezd News', 15 December 1906, FO 248/877, and Spring-Rice to Grey, Monthly Summary (Yezd), 4 January 1907, FO 371/304. See also *Majles* 1:6.
6 Mehr, *Sahm-e Zartoshtiyan dar Enqelab-e Mashrutiyat-e Iran*, 12–14. The documentary *Shahjahan* describes a similar version of events (*Shahjahan*, directed by Hassan Naghashi [1392/2013]). See also Oshidari, *Tarikh-e Pahlavi va Zartoshtiyan*, 245.
7 Amini, *Ta'amol Aqalliyyatha-ye Mazhabi va Enqelab-e Mashrutiyat-e Iran*, 54–5.
8 Ibid., 55, and Shahmardan, *Farzanegan-e Zartoshti*, 469.
9 Browne, *The Persian Revolution of 1905–1909*, 137.
10 Spring-Rice to Grey, 28 March 1907, FO 416/32. See also Baggaley to Barnham, 17 February 1907, FO 248/905.
11 For example, see Tsadik, *Between Foreigners and Shi'is*, 169. See also Vanessa Martin, *The Qajar Pact: Bargaining, Protest and the State in Nineteenth-Century Persia* (London: I.B. Tauris, 2005), 127.
12 Brighty, Diary entry for 18 February 1907, CMS/ACC/113/F3. Baggaley suggested that these bills were linked to a local preacher, as well as to Moshir al-Mamalek (Baggaley to Barnham, 17 February 1907, FO 248/905).
13 Brighty, Diary entry for 22 February 1907, CMS/ACC/113/F3.
14 Those living in fear included Mr Mehrban, the CMS teacher (Baggaley to Barnham, 17 February 1907, FO 248/905).
15 Kerman diary, 27 February 1907, FO 248/906. See also *Habl al-Matin*, 24 June 1907, quoted in *RMM* 3, no. 9 (September 1907): 144, which reported that Zoroastrians

closed their shops, and that they used the telegraph system to contact various people, including the shah.
16 Grahame to Spring-Rice, 22 February 1907, FO 248/911.
17 *ToI*, 18 February 1907, 6.
18 Ibid., and Bāqer Āqeli, "'Alā'-al-Salṭana", http://www.iranicaonline.org/articles/ala-al-saltana-mohammad-ali-1 (accessed on 18 March 2023).
19 *ToI*, 18 February 1907, 6, and *Bombay Gazette*, 22 February 1907, 3. See *Bombay Gazette*, 25 February 1907, 3, for the reply Petit received to his second message to the Sadr-e A'zam. In the *Bombay Gazette*, 6 March 1907, 6, there is a riposte to the accusation made in the *Rast Goftar*, 3 March 1907, that the Amelioration Society did not act swiftly following the news of the murder. The *Rast Goftar* issued an apology on 10 March 1907, 3.
20 *Bombay Gazette*, 22 February 1907, 3.
21 Ibid. See also *ToI*, 21 February 1907, 9.
22 *Bombay Gazette*, 22 February 1907, 3.
23 Ardeshir Reporter to Bhownaggree, 18 February 1907, enclosed in Bhownaggree to Montgomery, 19 February 1907, FO 371/307, and *ToI*, 18 February 1907, 6.
24 Bhownaggree to Montgomery, 19 February 1907, FO 371/307. See also *RG*, 7 April 1907, 1. Interestingly, an article in the *Times* indicates that not all Zoroastrians in London were enthusiastic about Bhownaggree's approach (13 April 1907, 16).
25 Bhownaggree to Montgomery, 19 February 1907, FO 371/307.
26 Sir A. Godley to the Foreign Office, 18 February 1907, FO 371/307.
27 Spring-Rice to Ala es Sultaneh ['Ala' al-Saltaneh], 16 February 1907, FO 371/307.
28 Ibid.
29 Ibid.
30 Spring-Rice to Grey, 27 February 1907, FO 371/304. NB in this report, it was noted that members of the Armenian community were choosing to stay in Iran, rather than emigrate.
31 Spring-Rice to Agha Seyed Mahomed [Tabataba'i], 17 February 1907, FO 371/307.
32 Ibid.
33 Ibid. See also Spring-Rice to Grey, 24 February 1907, FO 371/307.
34 Spring-Rice to the Foreign Office, 21 February 1907, and 22 February 1907, FO 371/307.
35 Spring-Rice to the Foreign Office, 21 February 1907, FO 371/307.
36 Spring-Rice to Grey, 27 February 1907, FO 371/304.
37 Spring-Rice to Grey, 24 February 1907, FO 371/307. See also, 'Message to be relayed to Zoroastrians in India and China', Bhownaggree to Sir Kidon Gorst, Under Secretary of State, Foreign Office, 3 April 1907, and, 'Viceroy to inform Parsis', Secretary of State to the Viceroy, 9 April 1907, FO 371/307.
38 *ToI*, 15 March 1907, 7.
39 Ibid.
40 *ToI*, 18 March 1907, 6. See also Baggaley to Barnham, 22 March 1907, FO 371/307, where Baggaley describes Zoroastrians in Yazd as the, 'life and soul of business enterprise'. Similarly, in a later report, Spring-Rice noted that the central government recognized the significance of ensuring Zoroastrians were protected, and had a 'firm intention' to do so (Spring-Rice to Grey, 24 April 1907, FO 371/307).
41 *ToI*, 18 March 1907, 6.

42 Brighty, Diary entry for 12 March 1907, CMS/ACC/113/F3. Brighty highlighted that the Zoroastrian schoolmaster 'begged to be excused from giving lessons in the mission as he is afraid of being out'.
43 Details of this telegram are given in Bhownaggree to Montgomery, 7 March 1907, FO 371/307.
44 Bhownaggree to Montgomery, 7 March 1907, FO 371/307. See also the direct appeal for help: Anjoman-e Naseri-e Zartoshtiian-e Yezd [Zoroastrian Anjoman of Yazd] to Baggaley, 7 March 1907, FO 248/905.
45 Baggaley to Barnham, 11 March 1907, FO 248/905.
46 Spring-Rice to Grey, 24 April 1907, FO 371/307. NB this includes a report by Baggaley, 22 March 1907.
47 Baggaley to Barnham, 22 March 1907, FO 371/307.
48 Brighty, Diary entry for 16 March 1907, CMS/ACC/113/F3. NB this massacre occurred in 1903, and resulted in the death of around 100 Bahá'ís (Fischer, 'Zoroastrian Iran Between Myth and Praxis', 409–15).
49 *ToI*, 2 April 1907, 8. Rather than improving conditions for minorities, the correspondent believed that the revolution had resulted in 'rabble-rule' and a lack of centralized control, making the situation more dangerous.
50 Spring-Rice to Grey, Monthly Summary (Yezd), 23 May 1907, FO 416/32. Spring-Rice also wrote to 'Ala' al-Saltaneh regarding this matter (11 April, FO 250/34). See also the report by Baggaley, 22 March 1907, in Spring-Rice to Grey, 24 April 1907, FO 371/307.
51 Grahame to Spring-Rice, 16 April 1907, FO 248/911.
52 *ToI*, 20 July 1907, 8.
53 Spring-Rice to Grey, 19 May 1907, FO 371/307. NB this report also contains a description of the trial.
54 Spring-Rice to Grey, 24 April 1907, FO 416/32. See also Baggaley to Barnham, 29 April 1907, FO 248/905, which includes a translation of a telegram dated 19 April 1907, from Tabataba'i to the most prominent cleric in Yazd, requesting that he do all he can to 'secure peace for the people at large and the Parsis especially'. In his report, Baggaley describes the trial as farcical and notes that Zoroastrians were still in a 'state of great anxiety'.
55 Spring-Rice to Grey, 24 February 1907, FO 371/307. It seems that Mohammad Behbahani, son of the constitutionalist leader Sayyed 'Abdollah Behbahani, also urged the ulama in Yazd not to oppose the execution of the murderer (Hamid Algar, 'Behbahānī, Moḥammad', http://www.iranicaonline.org/articles/behbahani-ayatollah-mohammad [accessed on 18 March 2023]).
56 Bayat, *Iran's First Revolution*, 190.
57 Bhownaggree to the Under Secretary of State, Foreign Office, 27 June 1907, FO 371/307.
58 Arjomand, 'Constitutional Revolution iii. The Constitution'. For a translation of the supplementary laws, see Browne, *The Persian Revolution of 1905–1909*, 372–84.
59 Eric Massie and Janet Afary, 'Iran's 1907 Constitution and Its Sources: A Critical Comparison', *British Journal of Middle Eastern Studies* 46, no. 3 (2019): 466.
60 Janet Afary, 'Civil Liberties and the Making of Iran's First Constitution', *Comparative Studies of South Asia, Africa and the Middle East* 25, no. 2 (2005): 347.
61 Arjomand, 'Constitutional Revolution iii. The Constitution'.
62 Afary, *The Iranian Constitutional Revolution*, 104–5.
63 Janet Afary, 'The Place of *Shi'i* Clerics in the First Iranian Constitution', *Critical Research on Religion* 1, no. 3 (2013): 329.

64 Afary, 'Civil Liberties and the Making of Iran's First Constitution', 355.
65 Marling to Grey, 7 November 1907, FO 371/111.
66 Afary, *The Iranian Constitutional Revolution*, 110.
67 Enayat, *Law, State, and Society in Modern Iran*, 58 (see pages 57–60, for a summary of the different views held by members of the ulama). See also Afary, 'The Place of *Shi'i* Clerics in the First Iranian Constitution'.
68 Said Amir Arjomand, 'The Ulama's Traditionalist Opposition to Parliamentarianism: 1907-1909', *Middle Eastern Studies* 17, no. 2 (1981): 181, and Afary, 'The Place of *Shi'i* Clerics in the First Iranian Constitution', 328, and 333. For analysis of the views of Mohammad Hosayn Na'ini Gharavi, a student of Khorasani, see Fereshte M. Nouraie, 'The Constitutional Ideas of a Shi'ite Mujtahid: Muhammad Husayn Na'ini', *Iranian Studies* 8, no. 4 (1975): 234–47.
69 Arjomand, 'Constitutional Revolution iii. The Constitution', and Afary, 'The Place of *Shi'i* Clerics in the First Iranian Constitution', 330.
70 Browne, *The Persian Revolution of 1905–1909*, 372–3, 376, and 379.
71 Ibid., 374.
72 Afary, 'Civil Liberties and the Making of Iran's First Constitution', 356–7. For example, see Article 97, which was concerned with taxation (Browne, *The Persian Revolution of 1905–1909*, 383).
73 Bayat, *Iran's First Revolution*, 190. Farhang Mehr refers to a debate that took place amongst TZA members, over whether or not the community should fight for constitutionalism. Although no date is given, it seems likely that the debate took place during this period. One member argued that it was a bad idea for Zoroastrians to be involved in fighting, as the community was so small and could not afford to lose any Zoroastrian lives, whereas another member disagreed, and said that they ought to trust in the Zoroastrian belief that truth will win a final victory over falsehood, and should therefore continue to support the constitutionalists (*Sahm-e Zartoshtiyan dar Enqelab-e Mashrutiyat-e Iran*, 15).
74 Spring-Rice to Grey, 23 May 1907, FO 416/32. According to Abdul-Hadi Hairi, an eye-witness described how Behbahani only conceded to the inclusion of Article 8 after being threatened with violence (Abdul-Hadi Hairi, *Shi'ism and Constitutionalism in Iran: A Study of the Role Played by the Persian Residents of Iraq in Iranian Politics* [Leiden: E. J. Brill, 1977,] 233).
75 Shahrokh, *The Memoirs of Keikhosrow Shahrokh*, 58.
76 Ibid.
77 Ibid.
78 Spring-Rice to Grey, 23 May 1907, FO 416/32. See also Hairi, *Shi'ism and Constitutionalism in Iran*, 234.
79 Afary, 'Performance of Justice in Qajar Iran', 88. For a reference to a petition from the Armenian community, see *Manchester Guardian* (*MG*), 24 May 1907, 6.
80 Enayat, *Law, State, and Society in Modern Iran*, 63.
81 Martin, 'Constitutional Revolution ii. Events'.
82 For example, see Mohammad Torkman (ed.), *Rasa 'el, e 'lamiyeh-ha, maktubat va ruznameh-ye Shaikh Shahid Fazl Allah Nuri*, vol. 1 (Tehran: Rasa, 1983), 260–9, and 278–81.
83 Martin, 'Constitutional Revolution ii. Events' (NB Martin suggests that Nuri may have left the shrine in September because the shah stopped giving him financial support).
84 Afary, *The Iranian Constitutional Revolution*, 93–4.

85 Abrahamian, *Iran Between Two Revolutions*, 91.
86 See Article 35, and Articles 36–57, for details about the position of the monarch (Browne, *The Persian Revolution of 1905–1909*, 377–9).
87 Bayat, *Iran's First Revolution*, 171. For example, see *Sur-e Esrafil* 1, 17 Rabi' al-Thani 1325 (30 May 1907), 6–7.
88 Bayat, *Iran's First Revolution*, 190, and 262.
89 *Sur-e Esrafil* 14, 10 Sha'ban 1325 (18 September 1907), 6–7.
90 Boyce, *Zoroastrians*, 130–1, and Kermani, quoted in Mangol Bayat-Philipp, 'Mīrzā Āqā Khān Kirmānī: A Nineteenth Century Persian Nationalist', *Middle Eastern Studies* 10, no. 1 (1974): 48.
91 Evan Siegel, 'Shariatism versus Constitutionalism in the Iranian Constitutional Revolution', *Asiatische Studien* 59, no. 3 (2005): 887. For coverage of the murder of Parviz in *Neda-ye Vatan*, and other references to Zoroastrians during this period, including letters from and to Ardeshir Reporter and a letter from the Zoroastrian Anjoman of Kerman, see the following issues: 12, 13 Moharram 1325 (26 February 1907), 2–3; 14, 20 Moharram 1325 (5 March 1907), 6–7; 15, 24 Moharram 1325 (9 March 1907), 5–6; 16, 1 Safar 1325 (16 March 1907), 7; 19, 15 Safar 1325 (30 March 1907), 2; 20, 18 Safar 1325 (2 April 1907), 4–5; 21, 25 Safar 1325 (9 April 1907), 4–5; 32, 15 Rabi' al-Thani 1325 (28 May 1907), 1–5; 38, 10 Jumada al-Awwal 1325 (21 June 1907), 1–2; and, 42, 27 Jumada al-Awwal 1325 (8 July 1907), 2–3.
92 Majles 1:86, and Majles 1:104. The murder of Parviz continued to be discussed periodically in the Majles; for example, it was raised again in October, just after the supplementary laws were passed. The case was made for a new investigation but it was stated that those accused had been acquitted (Majles 1:165).
93 Afary, 'Performance of Justice in Qajar Iran', 89–90, and Afary, 'The Place of *Shi'i* Clerics in the First Iranian Constitution', 337. See also Majles 1:86, and Majles 1:104.
94 Majles 1:104. See also Bayat, *Iran's First Revolution*, 190–1.
95 *Majalleh-ye Estebdad*, 21 Shawwal 1325 (28 November 1907), quoted in Ali Gheissari, 'Despots of the World Unite! Satire in the Iranian Constitutional Press: The *Majalleh-ye Estebdad*, 1907-1908', *Comparative Studies of South Asia, Africa and the Middle East* 25, no. 2 (2005): 374.
96 Majles 1:86, and Majles 1:104.
97 Spring-Rice to Grey, 21 June 1907, FO 371/301.
98 It is worth mentioning that when letters of thanks were sent by the Zoroastrian and Armenian communities to the Majles following the ratification of the supplement, the message from the Armenians was not read out. The president of the Majles explained that this was to save time, as both messages were similar (Majles 1:171).
99 *Habl al-Matin*, 15 July 1907, quoted in *RMM* 3, no. 9 (September 1907): 144. See also Cosroe Chaqueri, 'The Armenian-Iranian Intelligentsia and Non-Armenian-Iranian Elites in Modern Times: Reciprocal Outlooks', in *The Armenians of Iran: The Paradoxical Role of a Minority in a Dominant Culture: Articles and Documents*, ed. Cosroe Chaqueri (Cambridge, MA: Harvard University Press, 1998), 122.
100 *Habl al-Matin*, 24 June 1907, quoted in *RMM* 3, no. 9 (September 1907): 144.
101 Abdulrahim Talbof, quoted in Afary, 'The Place of *Shi'i* Clerics in the First Iranian Constitution', 338.
102 *ToI*, 2 April 1907, 7. See also *Bombay Gazette*, 15 March 1907, 5.
103 *ToI*, 2 April 1907, 7. NB Mehdi Khan supported the constitutional cause. He was the son of the previous Iranian minister in London, Mirza Mohammad 'Ali Khan,

also known by his title, 'Ala' al-Saltaneh (Bonakdarian, *Britain and the Iranian Constitutional Revolution of 1906–1911*, 193, and 450n121).
104 *ToI*, 6 April 1907, 9.
105 Ibid.
106 Ibid.
107 Ibid.
108 Ibid.
109 Ibid.
110 Ibid.
111 ZTFE minutes, June 1907.
112 *ToI*, 13 July 1907, 9.
113 *Times*, 27 June 1907, 10.
114 Ibid. See also *Bombay Gazette*, 13 July 1907, 6, and *RG*, 21 July 1907, 3.
115 *ToI*, 13 July 1907, 9.
116 Siegel, 'Shariatism versus Constitutionalism in the Iranian Constitutional Revolution', 889.
117 *Sobh-e Sadeq* 1, no. 42 (13 Rabi' al-Thani 1325/ 26 May 1907).
118 Similarly, an article in the *Habl al-Matin* pointed out that non-Muslims would be better protected in Iran if they became foreign citizens (Afary, *The Iranian Constitutional Revolution*, 104). The issue of citizenship had been contentious in the past; for example, in 1905, Zoroastrian landowners were threatened with the confiscation of their land if they did not give up their status as British subjects (Hardinge to Mushir ed-Dowleh, 6 February 1905, FO 248/856).
119 Bhownaggree to the Under Secretary of State, Foreign Office, 27 June 1907, FO 371/307.
120 Secretary to the Government of India, Foreign Department to the Secretary to the Governor of Bombay, Political Department, 16 July 1907, FO 371/307.
121 Spring-Rice to Grey, 19 May 1907, FO 371/307. Spring-Rice had already notified Grey that if the Persian government was unable to protect Zoroastrians, 'it would become my painful duty to recommend the Zoroastrians who came to me for advice to take advantage of the liberal offers made by the Parsee inhabitants of India who had promised to provide them with a refuge in British territory' (Spring-Rice to Grey, 24 April 1907, FO 371/307).
122 Firuz Kazemzadeh, 'Anglo-Russian Convention of 1907', http://www.iranicaonline.org/articles/anglo-russian-convention-of-1907-an-agreement-relating-to-persia-afghanistan-and-tibet (accessed on 18 March 2023). NB An alternative theory is proposed by Christopher Clark, who has argued that the British wanted to appease the Russians (referenced in Bayat, *Iran's Experiment with Parliamentary Governance*, 383).
123 For the text of the treaty, see Hurewitz, *Diplomacy in the Near and Middle East*, 1:265–7.
124 Kazemzadeh, 'Anglo-Russian Convention of 1907'.
125 Bonakdarian, *Britain and the Iranian Constitutional Revolution of 1906–1911*, 77–80, and 'Great Britain iv. British Influence in Persia, 1900-21'.
126 Browne, *A Brief Narrative of Recent Events in Persia*, 27.
127 Bonakdarian, 'Great Britain iv. British Influence in Persia, 1900-21'.
128 *RG*, 29 September 1907, 2, and *HP*, 29 September 1907, 16–17 (Plate 4). See also *Oriental Review*, 25 September 1907, quoted in Native Press Report, 28 September 1907, IOR/L/R/5/162. In this report, reference was also made to the possibility that the Anglo-Russian Convention might provoke unrest in India.

129 *IAQROCR* 23 (January 1907): 29.
130 Bonakdarian, 'India ix, Relations: Qajar Period, Early 20th Century'. See also *Bombay Gazette*, 26 September 1907, where the criticism was made that Indian merchants had lost the right to push trade north of Isfahan.
131 Brighty, 31 July 1907, CMS/ACC/113/F3.
132 Majles 1:124.
133 Sir D. Petit, enclosed in H. O. Quin, Acting Secretary to Government of Bombay, Political Department, to the Government of India, 17 September 1907, Government of India Foreign Department, Secret E (Proceedings of December 1907, 143–8).
134 *ToI*, 5 September 1907, 8.
135 Ibid.
136 Bonakdarian, 'Great Britain iv. British Influence in Persia, 1900-21'. NB Bonakdarian does point out that some members of the British consular staff did not always follow the official line.
137 Oberling, 'The Role of Religious Minorities in the Persian Revolution, 1906-1912', 20–1.
138 Government of India Foreign Department, Secret E (Proceedings of December 1907, 143–8), and Sir D. N. Petit to Spring-Rice, 5 September 1907, FO 371/307.
139 Lyman Stebbins, *British Imperialism in Qajar Iran*, 73.
140 Ibid., 92.
141 As in previous instances, the news was reported in India; for example, see *ToI*, 21 November 1907, 7. For reports of anti-Zoroastrian attitudes amongst members of the ulama in Yazd, exacerbated by the inclusion of Article 8 in the supplementary laws, see *Sur-e Esrafil* 17, 14 Shawwal 1325 (20 November 1907), 3–5.
142 Marling to Grey, 4 December 1907, FO 371/301. See also Evans to Barnham, 16 November 1907, FO 248/905.
143 *ToI*, 21 November 1907, 7.
144 Ibid.
145 *RG*, 24 November 1907, 2.
146 Ibid.
147 Ibid.
148 Marling to Grey, 30 January 1908, FO 416/35, and Mehr, *Sahm-e Zartoshtiyan dar Enqelab-e Mashrutiyat-e Iran*, 15–17.
149 Oshidari, *Tarikh-e Pahlavi va Zartoshtiyan*, 247.
150 Afary, *The Iranian Constitutional Revolution*, 133–5, and 75, and Martin, 'Constitutional Revolution ii. Events'.
151 Mehr, *Sahm-e Zartoshtiyan dar Enqelab-e Mashrutiyat-e Iran*, 15.
152 Marling to Grey, 11 January 1908, FO 416/35. NB it was later suggested that the motive may have been 'common robbery' (Marling to Grey, 23 April 1908, FO 416/36).
153 Marling to Grey, 29 January 1908, FO 416/35. According to Mehr, Fereydun had angered the shah as he had spread the news that the monarch had tried to pawn the crown jewels (Mehr, *Sahm-e Zartoshtiyan dar Enqelab-e Mashrutiyat-e Iran*, 16). For references to the shah trying to use the crown jewels to secure a loan with Russia, see Marling to Grey, 7 November 1907, FO 371/313.
154 Mehr, *Sahm-e Zartoshtiyan dar Enqelab-e Mashrutiyat-e Iran*, 13 and 15–16. See also, Bayat, *Iran's First Revolution*, 211.
155 Oshidari, *Tarikh-e Pahlavi va Zartoshtiyan*, 249.

156 Yahya Dowlatabadi, *Tarikh-e Moʻaser, ya Hayat-e Yahya*, vol. 2 (Tehran, 1331 [1952/3]), 187 and 274.
157 Mehr, *Sahm-e Zartoshtiyan dar Enqelab-e Mashrutiyat-e Iran*, 18. NB Dowlatabadi also refers to Sani Hazrat (*Tarikh-e Moʻaser-e ya Hayat-e Yahya*, 2:188).
158 Marling to Grey, 29 January 1908, FO 416/35.
159 Marling to Grey, 30 January 1908, FO 416/35.
160 For discussion about the different accounts, see Amini, *Taʻamol Aqalliyyatha-ye Mazhabi va Enqelab-e Mashrutiyat-e Iran*, 56ff.
161 Mehr, *Sahm-e Zartoshtiyan dar Enqelab-e Mashrutiyat-e Iran*, 18.
162 Malekzadeh, *Tarikh-e Enqelab-e Mashrutiyat-e Iran*, 3:74.
163 *MG*, 11 January 1908, 9, and *MG*, 15 January 1908, 7.
164 Majles 1:213.
165 Ibid.
166 Majles 1:215, and Amini, *Taʻamol Aqalliyyatha-ye Mazhabi va Enqelab-e Mashrutiyat-e Iran*, 56.
167 Marling to Grey, 29 January 1908, FO 416/35.
168 Afary, *The Iranian Constitutional Revolution*, 118, and 138. Judicial punishment was also demanded in *Habl al-Matin* (ibid.).
169 *Sur-e Esrafil* 23, 17 Moharram 1326 (20 February 1908), 8.
170 See Afary, *The Iranian Constitutional Revolution*, Chapter Seven. See also Mangol Bayat, 'Women and Revolution in Iran, 1905-1911', in *Women in the Muslim World*, ed. Lois Beck and Nikki Keddie (Cambridge, MA: Harvard University Press, 1978).
171 Afary, *The Iranian Constitutional Revolution*, 178–9. NB in 1910, a play was staged at Arbab Jamshid's residence, Atabak Park, to raise funds for the education of girls and women, and for healthcare. The event was organized by the Anjoman of Ladies of the Homeland (ibid., 196).
172 Ibid., 200.
173 *Sur-e Esrafil* 22, 25 Zu al-Hijja 1325 (29 January 1908), 3, where there is a reference to a petition from the *Anjoman-e Azerbaijan* that was written together with the wife of Fereydun.
174 *ToI*, 23 January 1908, 8.
175 Ibid.
176 Marling to Grey, 11 January 1908, FO 416/35, and Marling to Grey, 29 January 1908, FO 416/35.
177 See reports from Yazd in FO 248/937 concerning the first few months of 1908. Brighty also recorded that Zoroastrians were scared to travel to their *dakhmeh* to celebrate the festival of Isfand (Esfand) in February 1908, and she noted in March that *luti*s went to the boys' school and threatened to start a massacre in the Zoroastrian *mahalleh* (quarter) (CMS ACC113/F3/2). For discussion about *luti*s in Qajar Iran, see Martin, *The Qajar Pact*, Chapter Six, and for information about the festival, see Habib Borjian, 'Kashan vi. The Esbandi Festival', http://www.iranicaonline.org/articles/kashan-vi-the-esbandi-festival (accessed on 18 March 2023).
178 Kerman Diary, 7–11 February 1908, FO 248/938.
179 Grahame to Marling, 15 January 1908, FO 248/942. For further details of the insecurities faced by Zoroastrians in Shiraz, see Marling to Grey, 26 February 1908, FO 416/35.
180 Grahame to Marling, 15 January 1908, FO 248/942. See also Marling to Grey, 28 February 1908, FO 371/499.

181 Letter dated 16 January 1908, enclosed in Grahame to Marling, 18 January 1908, FO 248/942.
182 Ibid.
183 Marling to Moshir al-Dowleh, 17 January 1908, and Moshir al-Dowleh to Marling, 21 January 1908, FO 250/34.
184 Marling to Grey, 26 February 1908, FO 371/504.
185 H. C. Dixon & Co. to the Secretary for Foreign Affairs, Foreign Office, 1 March 1908, FO 371/503. The letter describes how Dixon & Co. also contacted the British Resident at Bushehr, who had promised to do all he could to help.
186 Marling to Grey, 26 February 1908, FO 416/35.
187 Ibid.
188 Marling to Grey, 26 February 1908, FO 371/504.
189 Marling to Moshir al-Dowleh, 5 February 1908, FO 416/35.
190 Marling to Grey, 26 February 1908, FO 371/504, and Majles 1:213.
191 Marling to Moshir al-Dowleh, 5 February 1908, FO 416/35.
192 Moshir al-Dowleh to Marling, 5 February 1908, enclosed in Marling to Grey, 26 February 1908, FO 371/504. NB Moshir al-Dowleh was the title given to Hasan Pirniya. Pirniya was influenced by contemporary theories concerning Aryanism and was responsible for writing history textbooks during the Pahlavi era (Zia-Ebrahimi, 'Self-Orientalization and Dislocation', 455–7); the views that he held may have made him more sympathetic towards Zoroastrians.
193 Marling to Grey, 14 April 1908, FO 371/503.
194 See Majles 1:217, Majles 1:222, and Majles 1:224.
195 For a brief account of some nineteenth-century legal writings on this topic, see Tsadik, 'The Legal Status of Religious Minorities', 392–4.
196 Bayat, *Iran's First Revolution*, 217, and Dowlatabadi, *Tarikh-e Mo'aser-e, ya Hayat-e Yahya*, 2:242. NB Jamal al-Din Va'ez was reported to have explicitly linked Islam with liberty and equality (Spring-Rice to Grey, 23 May 1907, FO 416/32).
197 Afary, *The Iranian Constitutional Revolution*, 137–8. This was the first of three instances when Behbahani led attempts to prevent the implementation of aspects of the supplementary laws that limited clerical power (ibid.).
198 See Tsadik, 'The Legal Status of Religious Minorities', in particular 392–4, and 407. See also articles 27 ii. and 71 of the supplementary laws (Browne, *The Persian Revolution*, 376, and 381).
199 Enayat, *Law, State, and Society in Modern Iran*, 74–5; Amini, *Ta'amol Aqalliyyatha-ye Mazhabi va Enqelab-e Mashrutiyat-e Iran*, 60; and, Majles 1:267. See also Majles 1:229; Majles 1:230; Majles 1:244; and, Majles 1:245.
200 Kermani, referenced in Bayat, *Iran's First Revolution*, 217.
201 Afary, 'Performance of Justice in Qajar Society', 75.
202 Enayat, *Law, State, and Society in Modern Iran*, 75; Amini, *Ta'amol Aqalliyyatha-ye Mazhabi va Enqelab-e Mashrutiyat-e Iran*, 61; and, Oshidari, *Tarikh-e Pahlavi va Zartoshtiyan*, 248.
203 Dowlatabadi, *Tarikh-e Mo'aser-e, ya Hayat-e Yahya*, 2:242.
204 Marling to Grey, 21 May 1908, FO 371/499.
205 Grey to Marling, 24 July 1908, Government of India Foreign Department, Secret E (Proceedings of October 1908, 867).
206 Grey to Marling, 24 July 1908, Government of India Foreign Department, Secret E (Proceedings of October 1908, 867), and Marling to Grey, 23 August 1908 (with Marling to 'Ala' al-Saltaneh, 23 August 1908 also enclosed), FO 371/503.

207 H. C. Dixon & Co. to the Secretary for Foreign Affairs, 20 July 1908, FO 371/503.
208 Marling to Grey, 23 August 1908, FO 371/503.
209 Marling to 'Ala' al-Saltaneh, 23 August 1908, FO 371/503.
210 Marling to 'Ala' al-Saltaneh, 7 September 1908, FO 250/34.
211 H. C. Dixon & Co. to the Under Secretary for Foreign Affairs, 6 July 1908, FO 371/503. See also 'Protection of the firm of Khusrow Shahjehan in Kerman', 18 August 1908, FO 248/938.
212 Bill to Tehran, 21 June 1909, FO 248/972. See also Jahanian to Barclay, 24 June 1909, and Barclay to Sad ud Dowleh [Sa'd al-Dowleh], 2 July 1909, FO 250/34.
213 Mehr, *Sahm-e Zartoshtiyan dar Enqelab-e Mashrutiyat-e Iran*, 19, and 22. According to Shahmardan, Khosrow Shahjahan spent some time in London and he alerted Dadabhai Naoroji to the situation of Zoroastrians in Iran. No dates are mentioned by Shahmardan. However, Naoroji left London for the last time in October 1907, so whatever was discussed between them cannot have been related to the events surrounding the murder of Fereydun (Shahmardan, *Farzanegan-e Zartoshti*, 471, and 473).
214 Martin, 'Constitutional Revolution ii. Events'.
215 Afary, *The Iranian Constitutional Revolution*, 140–1.
216 Bayat, *Iran's First Revolution*, 229.
217 Dowlatabadi, *Tarikh-e Mo'aser-e, ya Hayat-e Yahya*, 2:274, and Bayat, *Iran's First Revolution*, 229.
218 Martin, 'Constitutional Revolution ii. Events'.
219 Bayat, *Iran's Experiment with Parliamentary Governance*, 111.
220 Abdul-Hadi Hairi, 'Shaykh Faẓl Allāh Nūrī's Refutation of the Idea of Constitutionalism', *Middle Eastern Studies* 13, no. 3 (1977): 329, and Torkman, *Rasa'el, e'lamiyeh-ha, maktubat va ruznameh-ye Shaikh Shahid Fazl Allah Nuri*, 1:56–75, and 101–14.
221 Torkman, *Rasa'el, e'lamiyeh-ha, maktubat va ruznameh-ye Shaikh Shahid Fazl Allah Nuri*, 1:107–8.
222 Ibid., 106.
223 Afary, *The Iranian Constitutional Revolution*, 211–12 (see the rest of this chapter for further details).
224 Bayat, *Iran's Experiment with Parliamentary Governance*, 153.
225 Ibid., 41ff. See also Afary, *The Iranian Constitutional Revolution*, Chapter Nine. NB some constitutionalists took refuge in Calcutta where Iranians had already expressed their anger at the coup. The Persian consul-general in Calcutta had received protestations from Iranians in Calcutta and Burma, who declared that they would no longer retain their status as subjects of the shah (*RMM* 6 no. 9 [September 1908]: 191–2).
226 *Times*, 15 October 1908, 8.
227 Afary, *The Iranian Constitutional Revolution*, 230. See also Mansour Bonakdarian, 'The Persia Committee and the Constitutional Revolution in Iran', *British Journal of Middle Eastern Studies* 18, no. 2 (1991): 186–207, and, 'Iranian Constitutional Exiles and British Foreign-Policy Dissenters, 1908–9', *International Journal of Middle East Studies* 27, no. 2 (1995): 175–91.
228 Bonakdarian, 'India ix, Relations: Qajar Period, Early 20th Century'.
229 *Times*, 15 October 1908, 8.
230 Bonakdarian, 'India ix, Relations: Qajar Period, Early 20th Century'.

231 *Times*, 12 November 1908, 7, and Edward Granville Browne, 'The Persian Constitutionalists: An Address', in *Proceedings of the Central Asian Society* (London, 1909).
232 *Times*, 12 November 1908, 7.
233 Browne, 'The Persian Constitutionalists', 10.
234 Ibid.
235 Ibid.
236 *RMM* 8, no. 7–8 (July-August 1909): 484.
237 Barclay to Grey, 25 February 1909, FO 371/713. See also Barclay to Grey, 18 June 1909, FO 416/41.
238 Barclay to Grey, 31 December 1908, FO 371/713.
239 Blackman to Aganoor, 4 November 1908, FO 248/937. See also Blackman to Aganoor, 5 December 1908, FO 248/937.
240 Barclay to Grey, 25 March 1909, FO 371/713, and Bill to Tehran, 24 February 1909, FO 248/972.
241 Barclay to Grey, 31 December 1908, FO 371/713.
242 *Encyclopædia Iranica* (based on an article submitted by Ali Modarres), 'Taft', https://www.iranicaonline.org/articles/taft (accessed on 18 March 2023).
243 Blackman to Aganoor, 4 November 1908, and 5 December 1908, FO 248/937. The latter report describes how thirty armed men forced their way into the home of Gushtaseb, an elder from Qasemabad. Gushtaseb was attacked and his belongings were stolen, as were valuables he had been safe-keeping on behalf of other Zoroastrians. Although members of the community knew the identities of the perpetrators, they felt it was too dangerous to make any accusations.
244 The writing is unclear but this message seems to have been sent by Zoroastrians in Taft to the Director of the Telegraph Department in Yazd, January 1909, FO 248/965.
245 Zoroastrian Anjoman of Yazd to Ardeshir Reporter, 27 January 1909, and Blackman to Grahame, 3 January 1909, FO 248/965. See also Blackman to Grahame, 30 January 1909, FO 248/965.
246 Barclay to Grey, 25 February 1909, FO 371/713.
247 Barclay to Blackman, 18 February 1908, FO 248/937. For an example of unofficial action taken by the British during the Lesser Despotism, see the handwritten notes in the file, 'Persecution of Taft Parsees', in FO 248/965, which includes a note from January 1909 stating that the prime minister, Sa'd al-Dowleh, had 'promised to do the needful' (see also Grahame to Tehran, 5 February 1909, FO 248/965). In May 1909, Brighty reported that a Zoroastrian man was stabbed in Yazd, 'only as the people say to raise a "shubuk" in town' (CMS ACC113/F3/3). The assault was also noted in Foreign Office records, as was the murder of a Zoroastrian wine-seller. Following these events, the British minister made 'strong representations' to Sa'd al-Dowleh, who replied that a new governor would go to the town with sufficient forces to maintain order (see records for May 1909, FO 248/966).
248 Barclay to Grey, 25 February 1909, FO 371/713.
249 Blackman to Grahame, 13 February 1909, FO 248/965.
250 Blackman to Grahame, 24 March 1909, FO 248/966.
251 Blackman to Grahame, 13 February 1909, FO 248/965.
252 Blackman to Grahame, 7 April 1909, FO 248/966.
253 Blackman to Aganoor, 5 and 12 December 1908, FO 248/937.
254 Blackman to Grahame, 26 December 1908, FO 248/965. See also Blackman to Grahame, 30 May 1909, FO 248/966.

255 For example, see Malcolm, *Five Years in a Persian Town*, 45–6.
256 For example, see Blackman to Aganoor, 9 August 1908, FO 248/937; Marling to Moshir al-Dowleh, 15 August 1908 and 27 August 1908, FO 250/34; and, Barclay to Grey, 13 August 1909, FO 371/713.
257 Barclay to Grey, 13 August 1909, FO 371/713.
258 Blackman to Grahame, 20 June 1909, FO 248/966.
259 Blackman to Grahame, 4 July 1909, FO 248/966, and Barclay to Grey, 13 August 1909, FO 371/713.
260 Baggaley to Aganoor, 16 December 1908, FO 248/937.
261 Blackman to Aganoor, 11 October 1908, FO 248/937.
262 Ibid.
263 Blackman to Grahame, 4 July 1909, FO 248/966, and Barclay to Grey, 13 August 1909, FO 371/713. A short-lived rival Anjoman was also established during this period (Blackman to Grahame, 25 July 1909, and Blackman to Grahame, 1 August 1909, FO 248/967).
264 Blackman to Grahame, 14 April 1909, FO 248/966.
265 Barclay to Grey, 25 February 1909, FO 371/713, and Blackman to Grahame, 13 February 1909, FO 248/965.
266 Blackman to Grahame, 26 December 1908, FO 248/965, and Blackman to Grahame, 31 March 1909, FO 248/966.
267 Isfahan news, 10 March 1909, FO 248/966, and Blackman to Grahame, 20 March 1909, FO 248/966. Similarly, Zoroastrian firms were cautioned against giving financial help and weapons to the Qavami family in Shiraz, who were supporters of Mohammad 'Ali Shah (Bill to Tehran, 14 April 1909, FO 248/972). NB Amini has questioned Mehr's argument that there was widespread Zoroastrian involvement during the revolution (Amini, *Ta'amol Aqalliyyatha-ye Mazhabi va Enqelab-e Mashrutiyat-e Iran*, 50).
268 Afary, *The Iranian Constitutional Revolution*, 226–7.
269 Oberling, 'The Role of Religious Minorities in the Persian Revolution, 1906-1912', 26–8. For detailed analysis of Armenian participation in the revolution, see the work of Houri Berberian; for example, 'The Dashnaktsutiun and the Iranian Constitutional Revolution, 1905-1911', *Iranian Studies* 29, no. 2 (1996): 7–33, and *Armenians and the Iranian Constitutional Revolution of 1905–1911: 'The Love for Freedom Has no Fatherland'* (Boulder and Oxford: Westview Press, 2001).

Chapter 6

1 Majles 2:5, and Majles 2:8.
2 For detailed analysis of the period of the Second Majles, see Bayat, *Iran's Experiment with Parliamentary Governance*.
3 Katouzian, 'The Revolution for Law', 771–2. See also Bayat, *Iran's Experiment with Parliamentary Governance*, 110ff.
4 Afary, *The Iranian Constitutional Revolution*, 262–3.
5 NB only fifteen seats were allocated to Tehran (Browne, *The Persian Revolution of 1905–1909*, 397).
6 Chaqueri, 'The Armenian-Iranian Intelligentsia and Non-Armenian-Iranian Elites in Modern Times', 125.

7 Indeed, the Armenian representative later argued against communal representation for this reason (Bayat, *Iran's Experiment with Parliamentary Governance*, 388).
8 Shahrokh, *The Memoirs of Keikhosrow Shahrokh*, 39.
9 For example, see Majles 2:3, 2:13, 2:14, 2:40, 2:54, 2:67, 2:71, and 2:72. See also Shahrokh, *The Memoirs of Keikhosrow Shahrokh*, 89, and 99-103.
10 Shahrokh, *The Memoirs of Keikhosrow Shahrokh*, 58.
11 Amini, *Ta'amol Aqalliyyatha-ye Mazhabi va Enqelab-e Mashrutiyat-e Iran*, 72-3.
12 Shahrokh, *The Memoirs of Keikhosrow Shahrokh*, 29. Shahrokh played a key administrative role in the TZA; for example, he corresponded with Zoroastrians in India, supervised schools and raised funds. Meetings took place in a property belonging to Arbab Jamshid. Ardeshir Reporter also worked in the building, and there was a primary school on the ground floor.
13 Ibid., 26. At the request of Ardeshir Reporter, Shahrokh sent a copy of *A'ineh-ye A'in-e Mazdayasna* to Bhownaggree. In the accompanying letter, dated April 1907, Shahrokh described himself as a 'pure Parsi' from Kerman, and he outlined that one of his motives for writing the book had been to raise awareness of Zoroastrianism amongst those who criticized the religion (Mehr, 'Zoroastrians in Twentieth Century Iran', 290n13).
14 Shahmardan, *Farzanegan-e Zartoshti*, 434. In order to protect Shahrokh's dignity, Arbab Jamshid had also bought Shahrokh a house when he was elected to the Majles (ibid., 435).
15 *Parsi*, 19 May 1907, quoted in *RMM* 2, no. 8 (June 1907): 626.
16 Marashi, *Exile and the Nation*, 24. NB Shahrokh was interested in other religions and had even considered converting to Christianity (Shahrokh, *The Memoirs of Keikhosrow Shahrokh*, 9-10).
17 Marashi, *Exile and the Nation*, 24.
18 Ibid., 36ff. A later account described how the books were 'warmly welcomed by the Muslim educationalists' (*ILB* 1, no. 7 [September 1928]: 7).
19 Shahrokh quoted in Marashi, *Exile and the Nation*, 48.
20 Grigor, 'Freemasonry and the Architecture of the Persian Revival, 1843-1933', 173.
21 Bayat, *Iran's Experiment with Parliamentary Governance*, 31-2.
22 Ibid., 33.
23 Grigor, 'Freemasonry and the Architecture of the Persian Revival, 1843-1933', 159-60.
24 Hamid Algar, 'Introduction to the History of Freemasonry in Iran', *Middle Eastern Studies* 6, no. 3 (1970): 288-92.
25 Grigor, 'Parsi Patronage of the *Urheimat*', 57-8.
26 Bayat, *Iran's Experiment with Parliamentary Governance*, 32, and 386.
27 *Ma'rifat*, 16 Ramazan 1327 (1 October 1909), quoted in 'Ali Akbar Tashakori Bafqi, *Mashrutiyat dar Yazd: az Vorud-e Andishah-ye Navin ta Kudita-ye Sayyed Zia' al-Din Tabataba'i* (Tehran: Markaz-e Yazdshenasi, 1337/1998-9), 162-4. For details about the newspaper, see Edward Granville Browne, *The Press and Poetry of Modern Persia* (Cambridge: Cambridge University Press, 1914), 142.
28 For another positive contemporary reference to Zoroastrianism, see *Khabar*, quoted in *RMM* 12, no. 11 (November 1910): 495-9.
29 Grahame to Tehran, 25 September 1909, FO 248/967. Similarly, Shahmardan references an undated incident when Arbab Jamshid reportedly paid a sum to stop the execution of Ardeshir, the manager of the Jamshidian firm in Isfahan, who was accused of murdering a man (Shahmardan, *Farzanegan-e Zartoshti*, 434-5).

30 Barclay to Grey, 8 September 1909, 8 October 1909, and 4 November 1909, FO 416/42. See also Barclay to Grey, 16 July 1909, FO 416/41.
31 Blackman, 12 September 1909, FO 248/967.
32 Malcolm, *Five Years in a Persian Town*, 46.
33 Blackman to Grahame, 28 November 1909, FO 248/967.
34 Afary, *The Iranian Constitutional Revolution*, 316,
35 Blackman to Grahame, 12 December 1909, FO 248/967.
36 Majles 2:51. See also Majles 2:50, and 2:69. In 1907, Zoroastrians had successfully applied for the right to be represented in the provincial *anjoman* of Kerman, and, in 1909, having been thanked for their role in the restoration of constitutional rule, non-Muslims were assured representation on provincial councils (*RMM* 9 no. 11 [November 1909]: 479). See also Barclay to Grey, 4 November 1911, FO 416/42.
37 Shahrokh described receiving 'endless' requests from Zoroastrians (Shahrokh, *The Memoirs of Keikhosrow Shahrokh*, 60).
38 For example, Majles 2:51, 2:215, and 2:210.
39 Majles 2:215, and Bayat, *Iran's Experiment with Parliamentary Governance*, 296, and 133ff.
40 Afary, *The Iranian Constitutional Revolution*, 289. NB *Sharq* was edited by Sayyed Zia' al-Din Tabataba'i (Browne, *The Press and Poetry of Modern Persia*, 110), who later played a crucial role in the coup of Reza Khan.
41 Zia-Ebrahimi, *The Emergence of Iranian Nationalism*, 173.
42 *Iran-e Now*, 16 February 1910, quoted in Abrahamian, *Iran Between Two Revolutions*, 105. In October 1910, Mohammad Amin Rasulzadeh, editor of *Iran-e Now*, wrote a pamphlet that criticized the Moderates, specifically highlighting that they did not fully recognize non-Muslims as Iranian citizens (Afary, *The Iranian Constitutional Revolution*, 275, and 279). See also Bayat, *Iran's Experiment with Parliamentary Governance*, 143ff.
43 Bayat, *Iran's Experiment with Parliamentary Governance*, 217–19.
44 Ibid., 217.
45 *RMM* 11 no. 6 (June 1910): 340. See also Mateo Mohammad Farzaneh, *The Iranian Constitutional Revolution and the Clerical Leadership of Khurasani* (Syracuse: Syracuse University Press, 2015), 127, where Khorasani's order is linked to the concerns raised in the article in *Ma'rifat*.
46 Browne, *The Persian Revolution of 1905–1909*, 421.
47 Afary, 'The Place of *Shi'i* Clerics in the First Iranian Constitution', 333.
48 Kerman to Tehran, 7 April 1910, FO 248/998.
49 Kerman to Tehran, 14 April 1910, and 21 April 1910, FO 248/998. NB prior to this, Zoroastrians in Yazd and Kerman had written to the Majles regarding the discrimination they faced at the hands of local officials, and, in April 1910, government ministers were criticized by the Majles for not successfully implementing Article 8 (Bayat, *Iran's Experiment with Parliamentary Governance*, 182–3).
50 Mehmet Hacısalihoğlu, 'Inclusion and Exclusion: Conscription in the Ottoman Empire', *Journal of Modern European History* 5, no. 2 (2007): 277.
51 Majles 2:210. See also *RMM* 14 no. 4 (April 1911): 154–5, and Bayat, *Iran's Experiment with Parliamentary Governance*, 271–2. Yanes and Shahrokh also held differing views regarding the proposal that candidates for positions in the Registrar Bureau at the Ministry of Justice needed to have knowledge of Islamic law. Yanes was emphatic that all Iranians should be treated equally, and that knowledge of religious law was unnecessary, whereas Shahrokh took a more conciliatory approach, and

suggested that non-Muslims could learn Islamic law in order to be eligible for the role (Bayat, *Iran's Experiment with Parliamentary Governance*, 304–5).
52 Haig to Tehran, 7 December 1911, FO 248/1030.
53 Haig to Tehran, 11 December 1911, FO 248/1030.
54 For example, Ardeshir Reporter asked for British protection for a proposed Zoroastrian school in Tehran (British minister in Tehran to the Secretary to the Government of India Foreign Department, GI Proceedings September 1911, 300).
55 Barclay to Grey, 19 April 1911, FO 416/48. See Barclay to Grey, 18 May 1911, FO 416/48, for reference to anti-Zoroastrian views expressed in Isfahan in May 1911, and *Times*, 8 May 1911, 5.
56 Barclay to Grey, 13 July 1911, and 4 August 1911, FO 416/49, and Haig to Tehran, 2 July 1911, FO 248/1030.
57 Haig to Barclay, 27 July 1911, FO 248/1030. Likewise, when the Jewish quarter in Shiraz was attacked by a mob in October 1910, the British linked the events to local power politics (Bayat, *Iran's Experiment with Parliamentary Governance*, 277–8).
58 Haig to Barclay, 27 July 1911, FO 248/1030.
59 Shahrokh, *The Memoirs of Keikhosrow Shahrokh*, 40.
60 Haig to Tehran, 2 July 1911, FO 248/1030, and Barclay to Grey, 7 November 1911, FO 416/50.
61 Haig to Tehran, 2 July 1911, FO 248/1030, and Barclay to Grey, 7 November 1911, FO 416/50.
62 Shahrokh, *The Memoirs of Keikhosrow Shahrokh*, 41–2.
63 Modarres, *Modernizing Yazd*, 86.
64 Bayat, *Iran's Experiment with Parliamentary Governance*, 235ff.
65 Ibid., 254ff.
66 For information about the Gendarmerie, see Stephanie Cronin, 'Gendarmerie', https://www.iranicaonline.org/articles/gendarmerie (accessed on 18 March 2023).
67 W. Morgan Shuster, *The Strangling of Persia: Story of the European Diplomacy and Oriental Intrigue That Resulted in the Denationalization of Twelve Million Mohammedans, a Personal Narrative* (New York: The Century Co., 1912), 11, and 16. Arbab Jamshid's gardens were also enjoyed by Europeans living in Tehran, and the shah sometimes used the 'excellent tennis-court' (Dorothy de Warzée, *Peeps into Persia* [London: Hurst and Blackett Ltd, 1913], 99).
68 Bayat, *Iran's Experiment with Parliamentary Governance*, 326.
69 Ibid., 338, and 340.
70 Ibid., 333ff, and Martin, 'Constitutional Revolution ii. Events'.
71 Bayat, *Iran's Experiment with Parliamentary Governance*, 383.
72 NB whilst the restoration of constitutional rule was greeted with enthusiasm, this is not to say that the situation in Iran during the Lesser Despotism had not been reported in the Parsi press. For example, see: *HP*, 20 September 1908, 21; *HP*, 4 October 1908, 16; *HP*, 1 November 1908, 23; and, *HP*, 29 November 1908, 10. For examples of press coverage in India regarding the re-establishment of constitutional rule in Iran, see: *Jam-e Jamshed*, 25 August 1909, quoted in *Parsi Prakash* 4–5, 1909, 232; *ToI*, 4 June 1909, 9; *ToI*, 25 August 1909, 7; *HP*, 25 July 1909, 13 (Plate 5); and, *Modern Review* 6, no. 2 (August 1909): 180.
73 See *ToI*, 17 August 1911, 7, for biographical information.
74 See *ToI*, 13 April 1909, 7, where reference is made to Cooper visiting the Persian legation at Nowruz.

75 Ibid. NB the book was also printed in Bombay by Messrs. Th. and J. Cooper, who are likely to have been related to N. M. Cooper; three hundred copies were bought by the Bombay Parsi Panchayat.
76 Nasarvanji Maneckji Cooper, *The Imitation of Zoroaster: Quotations from Zoroastrian Literature* (London: Cooper Publishing Co., 1910), 1.
77 Nasarvanji Maneckji Cooper, *The Zoroastrian Code of Gentlehood* (London: Cooper Publishing Co., 1909), 8, and 32.
78 For example, a copy was presented to the First Dastur Meherjirana Library, Navsari, by the Parsi Panchayat.
79 Cooper, *The Zoroastrian Code of Gentlehood*, 2.
80 The venue was popular with Freemasons and it had also been used for a banquet in honour of athletes participating in the 1908 Olympic Games (*Times*, 2 July 1886, 7, and *Times*, 5 October 1908, 15).
81 *ToI*, 18 July 1910, 6. Moulton was a Wesleyan minister and academic; he argued that the *Gathas* provided evidence of monotheism in Zoroastrianism, an opinion welcomed by reformist Parsis (Hinnells, *Zoroastrian and Parsi Studies*, 246, and Ringer, *Pious Citizens*, 101–7).
82 Nasarvanji Maneckji Cooper (ed.), 'Addresses on Zoroastrianism delivered by Prof. James Hope Moulton, M.A., Prof. L. H. Mills, M.A., and Sir George Birdwood, K.C.I.E. at a reception held in the Holborn Restaurant, London, by Mr Nasarvanji Maneckji Cooper on June 30th, 1910' (London: Cooper Publishing Company, 1911), 35.
83 Ibid., 38–9.
84 Ibid., 7.
85 *RMM* 11, no. 6 (June 1910): 335.
86 Ibid. See also Majles 2:88.
87 *RMM* 11, no. 6 (June 1910): 335.
88 *MG*, 12 September 1910, 10.
89 Ibid. In the same year, Cooper published *For God and Iran*, an abridged version of Thomas Moore's *Lalla Rookh*, 'a thrilling story of Zoroastrian devotion and heroism with which all Parsees should be familiar' (Nasarvanji Maneckji Cooper, *For God and Iran* [London: Cooper Publishing Co., 1910], 5).
90 *MG*, 12 September 1910, 10.
91 Ibid.
92 Ibid.
93 P. Kershasp, *Studies in Ancient Persian History* (London: Kegan Paul, Trench, Trübner and Co., 1905).
94 *MG*, 12 September 1910, 10.
95 Bonakdarian, *Britain and the Iranian Constitutional Revolution of 1906–1911*, 129. See also page 456n93.
96 Bonakdarian, 'India ix, Relations: Qajar Period, Early 20th Century'.
97 *MG*, 12 September 1910, 10.
98 Ibid.
99 Ibid.
100 Bayat, *Iran's Experiment with Parliamentary Governance*, 197–8.
101 Ibid., 198.
102 For example, see 'Native Press Report', 6 March 1909, IOR/L/R/5/164.
103 *ToI*, 9 August 1910, 8.
104 Ibid. See also *ToI*, 28 May 1909, 10, for comments about the presumed physical decline of the Parsis made by someone outside the community.

105 *HP*, 11 September 1910, 20 (see Plate 6).
106 Ibid., 10.
107 Ibid.
108 This may be linked to the fact that there had been unrest in Iran in the preceding months; Behbahani was assassinated in July 1910, Taqizadeh was then expelled from the Majles, and there followed a series of violent incidents (for details, see Afary, *The Iranian Constitutional Revolution*, 292ff).
109 *HP*, 11 September 1910, 10, and *ToI*, 9 September 1910, 8.
110 *ToI*, 9 September 1910, 8, and *ToI*, 10 September 1910, 7. NB the previous year, J. J. Modi expressed the hope that some Parsis might 'return to their ancient fatherland' (*EW* 8, no. 2 [July 1909]: 670–1).
111 *HP*, 11 September 1910, 10. See also *ToI*, 9 September 1910, 8.
112 *HP*, 11 September 1910, 30.
113 Ibid., 20.
114 Ibid., 23.
115 *ToI*, 9 September 1910, 8. That year, the *Hindi Punch* reported that there were no Parsis on the Bombay Corporation, for the first time in its history (David Charles Mellor, 'The Parsis and the Press: An In-depth Study of the "Hindi Punch", 1906-1931' [MPhil Thesis, Victoria University of Manchester, Manchester, 1985], 57).
116 Mellor, 'The Parsis and the Press', 47–8. See also, Writer, *Contemporary Zoroastrians*, 91–2.
117 Sharafi, *Law and Identity in Colonial South Asia*, 275–6.
118 John R. Hinnells, 'Behramshah Naoroji Shroff', https://www.iranicaonline.org/articles/behramshah-naoroji-shroff-1858-1927 (accessed on 18 March 2023). See also Sharafi, *Law and Identity in Colonial South Asia*, 306–7; Rose, *Zoroastrianism*, 211–12; and, Luhrmann, 'Evil in the Sands of Time', 870ff.
119 Hinnells, 'Behramshah Naoroji Shroff'.
120 *RG*, 18 September 1910, 1.
121 Ibid.
122 Ibid.
123 *ToI*, 14 September 1910, 6.
124 *ToI*, 15 September 1910, 6.
125 *RG*, 18 September 1910, 2. The article suggested that instead of the colony plan, Parsis ought to focus on trade for the time being. It was also argued that a gradual increase in the number of Parsis in Iran would be more positively welcomed by Iranians than a sudden rise.
126 *RG*, 16 October 1910, 9–10.
127 Ibid.
128 *RG*, 18 September 1910, 1.
129 Ibid., 2.
130 *ToI*, 28 October 1910, 6.
131 Ibid. Iranian current affairs were covered in the Parsi press, and Parsi interest in contemporary Iran is reflected in the choice made by Pestonji Nasserwanji Dastur Meherjirana to present Curzon's 1892 volumes on Persia to the First Dastur Meherjirana Library, Navsari, to mark the occasion of his son's marriage in April 1908.
132 *ToI*, 28 October 1910, 6.
133 Ibid. Indeed, correspondence from the Foreign Office to the India Office referred to problems with trade due to insecurity (for example, 5 January 1910, FO 371/946).

134 *ToI*, 28 October 1910, 6.
135 Ibid.
136 *ToI*, 29 November 1910, 7, and *ToI*, 1 December 1910, 7. See Palsetia, *The Parsis of India*, 233-4, for further information about Karkaria, principally in relation to the question of the admission of converts to the community.
137 *ToI*, 1 December 1910, 7.
138 Ibid.
139 Ibid.
140 Ibid.
141 *RMM* 12, no. 10 (October 1910): 352.
142 Ibid.
143 *Parsi Prakash* 4-5, 1911, 10.
144 See Sharafi, *Law and Identity in Colonial South Asia*, 115, 139, and 280, for references to the legal work of P. B. Watcha (or Vachha).
145 P. B. Watcha, *Firdousi and the Parsis, reprinted from the 'Parsi'* (Bombay: P. B. Watcha, 1911), Preface.
146 See also *RG*, 19 January 1908, 2, which refers to a new translation of the *Shahnameh* by Alexander Rogers, dedicated to Bhownaggree's father. Rogers stated his hope that the text would 'foster laudable national sentiments in the descendants of those whose chivalrous deeds are perpetuated in it'.
147 Watcha, *Firdousi and the Parsis*, Preface.
148 *ToI*, 21 October 1910, 6.
149 Watcha, *Firdousi and the Parsis*, 1, and 65.
150 Ibid., 2, and 61.
151 Ibid., 2.
152 Ibid., 56. See also pages 55 and 57.
153 Ibid., 65.
154 Ibid., 2.
155 Ibid., 3.
156 *ToI*, 4 April 1911, 8.
157 Ringer, *Pious Citizens*, 107-9.
158 *ToI*, 3 April 1911, 5. For further references to Jackson's visit to Bombay, see: *ToI*, 31 March 1911, 6; *ToI*, 4 April 1911, 8; *ToI*, 6 May 1911, 10; *HP*, 2 April 1911, 20; *RG*, 2 April, 1911, 1-2, and 8; and, *Parsi Prakash* 4-5, 1911, 34.
159 *ToI*, 3 April 1911, 5.
160 *ToI*, 17 April 1911, 5.
161 Ibid.
162 *ToI*, 15 February 1911, 7.
163 Lyman Stebbins, 'British Imperialism, Regionalism, and Nationalism in Iran, 1890-1919', 160.
164 *ToI*, 15 February 1911, 7.
165 Ibid.
166 Ibid.
167 *ToI*, 17 July 1911, 6.
168 The involvement of Browne in campaigns against British foreign policy during this period has been discussed in depth by Mansour Bonakdarian. For example, see Mansour Bonakdarian, 'The Persia Committee and the Constitutional Revolution in Iran', and 'Edward G. Browne and the Iranian Constitutional Struggle: From Academic Orientalism to Political Activism', *Iranian Studies* 26, no. 1-2 (1993): 7-31.

169 *Times*, 24 June 1911, 3.
170 *ToI*, 15 July 1911, 11. In *RMM* 9, no. 11 (November 1909): 510, *Sharq* is described as ardently patriotic. See also Bonakdarian, *Britain and the Iranian Constitutional Revolution of 1906-1911*, 251, and 456n101.
171 *ToI*, 15 July 1911, 11.
172 Ibid.
173 *ToI*, 17 July 1911, 6.
174 *ToI*, 15 July 1911, 11.
175 *ToI*, 17 July 1911, 6.
176 Ibid.
177 Ibid.
178 Bayat, *Iran's Experiment with Parliamentary Governance*, 389.
179 *ToI*, 17 July 1911, 6.
180 *ToI*, 6 November 1911, 7. See also *ToI*, 16 August 1911, 7, where reference is made to challenges experienced by merchants from Yazd, including Zoroastrians.
181 The death of Cooper was reported in India; for example, *ToI*, 19 August 1911, 9, and *Daily Telegraph and Deccan Herald* (*DTDH*), 19 August 1911, 5.
182 *ToI*, 6 September 1911, 8, and *ToI*, 7 September 1911, 9. See also *ToI*, 17 August 1911, 7, and *DTDH*, 14 August 1911, 5. For references to 'insinuations' that were made in Cooper's newspaper, the *London Indian Chronicle*, about Bhownaggree and the Parsee Association, see Shapurji Saklatvala to Bhownaggree, 8 August 1911, ZTFE Archives.
183 *ToI*, 7 September 1911, 9.
184 For example, see *ToI*, 27 November 1911, 8, for an address delivered by the Parsis to mark the visit of the recently crowned King George V and Queen Mary.
185 Bonakdarian, 'India ix, Relations: Qajar Period, Early 20th Century'. For examples of cartoons depicting Russian aggression in Iran, see *HP*, 20 August 1911, 17; *HP*, 31 December 1911, 20 (Plate 7); and, *HP*, 28 January 1912, 17.
186 Bonakdarian, 'India ix, Relations: Qajar Period, Early 20th Century'.
187 *ToI*, 6 December 1911, 7 and *East & West* 11, no. 1 (January–June 1912): 102–3.
188 Mody, 'Madame Bhikhaiji Rustam Cama', 67.
189 Native Press Report, 21 October, and 18 November 1911, IOR L/R/5/166. The report for 18 November also refers to criticisms made of the British policy towards Persia in another Parsi publication, *Sanj Vartaman*. In addition, the *Parsi* had already voiced its disapproval of the presence of British troops in southern Iran in 1910 (Native Press Report, 5 November 1910, IOR L/R/5/165).
190 *Parsi*, 17 December 1911, quoted in *Parsi Prakash* 4–5, 1911, 62. See also Bonakdarian, 'India ix, Relations: Qajar Period, Early 20th Century'.
191 *ToI*, 14 December 1911, 7.
192 Martin, 'Constitutional Revolution ii. Events'.
193 Bayat, *Iran's Experiment with Parliamentary Governance*, 377–80.
194 Mansoureh Ettehadieh, 'Constitutional Revolution iv. The Aftermath', https://www.iranicaonline.org/articles/constitutional-revolution-iv (accessed on 18 March 2023).
195 For example, Abrahamian refers to the slightly longer period of 1909–21 as a 'Period of Disintegration' (Abrahamian, *Iran Between Two Revolution*, 102).
196 Oliver Bast, 'Disintegrating the "Discourse of Disintegration": Some Reflections on the Historiography of the Late Qajar Period and Iranian Cultural Memory', in Atabaki, *Iran in the Twentieth Century*, 60–1.

197 Stephanie Cronin, 'The Constitutional Revolution, Popular Politics, and State-Building in Iran', in *Iran's Constitutional Revolution: Popular Politics, Cultural Transformations and Transnational Connections*, ed. H. E. Chehabi and V. Martin (London: I.B. Tauris, 2010), 81–3. See also Bayat, *Iran's Experiment with Parliamentary Governance*, 401, regarding the continued urge for reform after 1911, and Enayat, *Law, State, and Society in Modern Iran*, 3–4, who outlines continuities in the legal sphere.
198 Marashi, *Nationalizing Iran*, 53–4, and 76–7.
199 For example, see Parliamentary Papers, Persia 5, 1912, 41; Haig to Tehran, 17 June 1912, FO 248/1052; and, Townley to Grey, 6 May 1912, FO 416/52.
200 Zoroastrian Anjoman of Yazd to Bhownaggree, 18 June 1912, IOR/L/PS/11/22, P2611/1912. The influence Bhownaggree was perceived to hold is reflected in a letter he received from Kaykhosrow Shahrokh in 1909. Shahrokh stated that Zoroastrians in Iran prayed for his success, as 'each step your Excellency advances in High ranks, the effects are our happy days and successions here' (quoted in Malcolm Deboo, 'Seth Maneckji Limji Hataria: The Martin Luther King of Zoroastrianism and the Struggle for Zoroastrian Civil Rights in Iran', http://www.zoroastrian.org.uk/vohuman/Article/Seth%20Maneckji%20Limji%20Hataria.htm [accessed on 18 March 2023]).
201 Bhownaggree to the Under Secretary of State, Foreign Office, and draft of the reply to Bhownaggree, 21 June 1912, IOR/L/PS/11/22, P2611/1912.
202 Townley to Grey, 29 October 1912, FO 416/54.
203 Townley to Grey, 11 June 1913, FO 416/56.
204 Smart to Townley, 20 June 1912, FO 416/53. For another reference to the Jamshidian firm dealing arms, see Political Diary of the Persian Gulf Residency, Lingah, February 1912, IOR/L/PS/10/827. Despite these criticisms, the British had appointed the Jamshidian firm as agents for the Anglo-Persian Oil Company (Political Diary of the Persian Gulf Residency, Lingah, January 1912, IOR/L/PS/10/827).
205 Mehrfar, 'Jamshid Bahman Jamshidian', 10–11. The devaluation of land was another contributing factor, as the Jamshidian company was heavily involved in issuing mortgages (*ToI*, 20 March 1913, 7). See also Amini, *Asnadi az Zartoshtiyan-e Mo'aser-e Iran*, 95–7; Townley to Grey, Persia: Annual Report, 1912, page 12, 18 March 1913, FO 416/111; Bamdad, *Sharh-e Hal-e Rejal-e Iran*, 1:280–1; 'Ali Akbar Tashakori Bafqi, 'Zamineha-ye Ejtema'a-ye va Eqtesadi-ye Zartoshtiyan-e Yazd dar Duran-e Qajar', *Siyasi-Eqtesadi* 277–8 (1389/2010): 112–14; and, Shahmardan, *Farzanegan-e Zartoshti*, 436–8, and 469.
206 Political Diary of the Persian Gulf Residency, Kerman and Bam, February 1913, IOR/L/PS/10/827. The Russians also asked the governor-general of Isfahan to close the Jamshidian office in Isfahan (Political Diary of the Persian Gulf Residency, Isfahan, March 1913, IOR/L/PS/10/827).
207 Political Diary of the Persian Gulf Residency, Kerman and Bam, February 1913, IOR/L/PS/10/827. The collapse of the Zoroastrian firms impacted the local economy, resulting in a rise in the price of imported goods (Political Diary of the Persian Gulf Residency, Kerman and Bam, May 1913, IOR/L/PS/10/827).
208 Shahrokh, *The Memoirs of Keikhosrow Shahrokh*, 58–9. Jamshid gave up Atabak Park as collateral for his debts with the Russian bank (Fischer, 'Zoroastrian Iran Between Myth and Praxis', 106n1).
209 Political Diary of the Persian Gulf Residency, Kerman and Bam, February 1913, IOR/L/PS/10/827.

210 Amighi, *The Zoroastrians of Iran*, 161–7.
211 Amini, *Asnadi az Zartoshtiyan-e Mo'aser-e Iran*, 161. For an overview of Shahrokh's responsibilities from 1909 to 1914, see Shahrokh, *The Memoirs of Keikhosrow Shahrokh*, 89–95.
212 Majles 4:21.
213 Shahrokh, *The Memoirs of Keikhosrow Shahrokh*, 69. See also Amini, *Asnadi az Zartoshtiyan-e Mo'aser-e Iran*, 178.
214 Ettehadieh, 'Constitutional Revolution iv. The Aftermath'.
215 *Journal of the Iranian Association (JIA)* 1, no. 9 (December 1912): 163.
216 Palsetia, *The Parsis of India*, 256–7, and Tanya M. Luhrmann, *The Good Parsi: The Fate of a Colonial Elite in a Postcolonial Society* (Cambridge, MA: Harvard University Press, 1996), 102–3.
217 *JIA* 1, no. 9 (December 1912): 166.
218 Ibid., 167.
219 Ibid.
220 Ibid.
221 *JIA*, 2 no. 5 (August 1913): 130. See also *ToI*, 8 August 1913, 7.
222 *JIA*, 2 no. 5 (August 1913): 131.
223 Ibid., 132.
224 Ibid., 130–1.
225 Ibid., 131.
226 *ToI*, 17 February 1915, 5. Another example of a Parsi donation towards all Iranians was that of 1,000 rupees given by Sir Shapurji Broacha of Bombay to the Persian Red Crescent Society, as 'a token of sympathy with the present misfortunes of Persia the original home of the Parsis and their civilisation' (*ToI*, 5 January 1912, 9). The words of Shapurji echo the justifications given in 1902 for the broad remit of the N. M. Wadia trust (see Chapter One), whose trustees were approached by Iranian Zoroastrians who wanted to found a school (*JIA* 2, no. 5 [August 1913]: 131).
227 *ToI*, 11 October 1913, 7. NB the person who laid the foundation stone was Reza Qoli Khan Hedayat, dean of Dar al-Fonun and Minister of Education (Grigor, 'Parsi Patronage of the *Urheimat*', 58). In an article by 'X', reference was made to Zoroastrian representation in the Majles, despite their small population, and to overall improvements for non-Muslims (*RMM* 27 [June 1914]: 268–9). NB 'X' was the signature used by Taqizadeh (Marashi, *Nationalizing Iran*, 50).
228 *ToI*, 11 October 1913, 7.
229 Ibid. The *Shahnameh* retained its popularity amongst Parsis and in the second decade of the twentieth century, two brothers, Faramarz and Mahiar Kutar, translated it into Gujarati (Kreyenbroek, 'The Role of the *Shăhnăme* in the Culture of the Parsi Community', 3). In December 1914, an illustrated Persian edition of the *Shahnameh* was presented to the Bombay Native General Library by the trustees of the Parsi Panchayat funds and Sir Jamsetjee Jejeebhoy translation fund. In addition to the poem there were biographical notes about influential contemporary Parsis and Iranian Zoroastrians, and other individuals who had helped fund the publication, seemingly creating a link between these figures and the heroes of the *Shahnameh*.
230 The idea that a strong government in Iran would benefit Britain was expounded by Curzon, who also referenced the ancient Persian past (George Nathaniel Curzon, *Persian Autonomy* [London: John Hogg, 1911]). For further details regarding the society, see Bonakdarian, *Britain and the Iranian Constitutional Revolution of 1906–1911* and, 'Great Britain iv. British influence in Persia, 1900–21'.

231 *ToI*, 3 December 1913, 6, and *ToI*, 26 November 1913, 6. Likewise, during the 1913 Nowruz celebrations, Rev. E. Clifton and Mrs Clifton encouraged Parsis to help Iranian Zoroastrians at this dawn of a 'new era' so that Persia might 'produce another Cyrus' (*IMR*, May 1913, 131, and *ToI*, 19 April, 1913, 8). Later that year, Sir Dinshaw Davar dismissed ideas of repatriation to Persia as 'chimerical', revealing that the issue remained a topic of debate within the Parsi community (*ToI*, 29 December 1913, 4). Davar may have been influenced by the 'very doleful stories' told by a group of Parsis about their treatment during their visit to Iran in 1913 (Report by the Commissioner of Police, Bombay, 7 July 1922, IOR/L/PS/11/214, P1728/1922).
232 *ToI*, 3 December 1913, 6.
233 *Times*, 16 November 1911, 7.
234 *ToI*, 13 April 1914, 8.
235 Bonakdarian, 'Great Britain iv. British influence in Persia, 1900-21'.
236 For further details, see George Lenczowski, 'Foreign Powers' Intervention in Iran during World War I', in *Qajar Iran: Political, Social and Cultural Change*, ed. Edmund Bosworth and Carole Hillenbrand (Edinburgh: Edinburgh University Press, 1983).
237 Ettehadieh, 'Constitutional Revolution: iv. The Aftermath'. NB the 1911 ultimatum issued by Russia was detrimental to Britain's reputation in Iran (Abbas Amanat, 'Through the Persian Eye: Anglophilia and Anglophobia in Modern Iranian History', in Amanat and Vejdani, *Iran Facing Others*, 144).
238 See Ettehadieh, 'The Iranian Provisional Government'.
239 Oshidari, *Tarikh-e Pahlavi va Zartoshtiyan*, 387.
240 Lyman Stebbins, 'British Imperialism, Regionalism, and Nationalism in Iran, 1890-1919', 162.
241 Bonakdarian, 'Great Britain iv. British influence in Persia, 1900-21'.
242 Lyman Stebbins, 'British Imperialism, Regionalism, and Nationalism in Iran, 1890-1919', 162ff, and Floreeda Safiri, 'South Persia Rifles', https://www.iranicaonline.org/articles/south-persia-rifles-militia (accessed on 18 March 2023).
243 Mina, 'Oil Agreements in Iran', and F. Kazemi, 'Anglo-Persian Oil Company', http://www.iranicaonline.org/articles/anglo-persian-oil-company (accessed on 18 May 2023).
244 Bonakdarian, 'Great Britain iv. British influence in Persia, 1900-21'.
245 For a detailed account, see Mohammad Gholi Majd, *The Great Famine and Genocide in Iran, 1917–1919*, 2nd edn (Lanham: University Press of America, 2013).
246 Shahrokh, *The Memoirs of Keikhosrow Shahrokh*, 62–9; Amini, *Asnadi az Zartoshtiyan-e Moʿaser-e Iran*, 167–77; Majd, *The Great Famine and Genocide in Iran*, xxxviii, and 54–5. NB Shahrokh had raised concerns in the Second Majles regarding the availability of grain (Majles 2:139, and Majles 2:187, quoted in Shahrokh, *The Memoirs of Keikhosrow Shahrokh*, 97–8).
247 Choksy, 'Despite Shāhs and Mollās', 145.
248 *MT* 20, no. 234 (1916): 127.
249 Report on the evacuation of Kerman station submitted by Superintendent J. W. Tanner, enclosed in the Director, Persian Gulf Section, Indo-European Telegraph Department, to the Secretary of the Government of India in the Foreign and Political Department, 14 April 1916, IOR/L/PS/10/591. For an overview of the position of the *kargozar*, see Morteza Nouraei, 'Kārgozār', https://www.iranicaonline.org/articles/kargozar-19th-century-term (accessed on 18 March 2023).
250 Report on the evacuation of Kerman station submitted by Superintendent J. W. Tanner, enclosed in the Director, Persian Gulf Section, Indo-European Telegraph

Department, to the Secretary of the Government of India in the Foreign and Political Department, 14 April 1916, IOR/L/PS/10/591.
251 Consul at Kerman to the Secretary to the Government of India in the Foreign and Political Department, Simla, 5 September 1915, IOR/L/PS/10/490.
252 Choksy, 'Despite Shāhs and Mollās', 145. See also May 1916, IOR/L/PS/10/475, page 3, and S. M. Edwardes, Commissioner of Police, Bombay, to the Secretary to the Government of India, Political Department, 20 December 1915, IOR/L/PS/10/493. In December 1915, a Zoroastrian in Yazd was killed by troops affiliated with the Germans. The murderers were subsequently arrested by members of the Gendarmerie (Confidential Summary News of His Majesty's Political Residency in the Persian Gulf for the month of January 1916, IOR/L/PS/10/827), even though the Gendarmerie was at this time becoming increasingly nationalistic and pro-German (Cronin, 'Gendarmerie').
253 Administration Report of His Majesty's Consulate, Kerman, for the Year 1931, IOR/R/15/1/715. See also Choksy, 'Despite Shāhs and Mollās', 146. For information about these companies, see Khosro Mehrfar, 'Sohrab Rostam Kaikhosrow Viraf Kianian', http://www.zoroastrian.org.uk/vohuman/Article/Sohrab%20Rostam%20Kaikhosow%20Viraf%20Kianian.htm (accessed on 25 May 2023). NB despite this incident, Sykes continued to have positive relations with Zoroastrians and encouraged Parsis to settle in Iran in the 1920s (*ILB* 1, no. 1 [March 1928]: 4).
254 Faraidun Bahram, Who's Who in Persia (Volume IV) Persian Baluchistan, Kerman, Bandar Abbas, Fars, Yezd and Laristan, IOR/L/MIL/17/15/11/7. See also Monthly Report from Shiraz, April 1918, IOR/L/PS/10/827, which refers to the arrest of three Zoroastrians who had been in correspondence with Wassmuss, and who were 'heavily in debt' to the British-owned Imperial Bank of Persia.
255 Extract from statement made by a British Agent, P5142/16, IOR/L/PS/10/475. For a reference to the pro-German sentiments of Sorabji, a representative of the Jamshidian firm, see S. M. Edwardes, Commissioner of Police, Bombay, to the Secretary to the Government of India, Political Department, 20 December 1915, enclosed in J. E. C. Jukes to the Foreign Secretary of the Government of India, 22 December 1915, IOR/L/PS/10/493.
256 Lieutenant Withers, Bandar Abbas to the Chief of the General Staff, Simla, 21 May 1916, IOR/L/PS/10/592. Hormusji's son, Kershasp, was also arrested (F. B. Prideaux, Sistan and Kain Consulate Diary, 12 August 1916, IOR/L/PS/10/210).
257 Bonakdarian, 'India ix, Relations: Qajar Period, Early 20th Century'.
258 Ibid.
259 Marashi, *Nationalizing Iran*, 52.
260 Ibid., 78. See also Iraj Afshar, 'Kāva Newspaper', https://www.iranicaonline.org/articles/kava (accessed on 18 March 2023).
261 Mohammed Alsulami, 'Iranian Journals in Berlin during the Interwar Period', in *Transnational Islam in Interwar Europe: Muslim Activists and Thinkers*, ed. Götz Nordbruch and Umar Ryad (New York: Palgrave Macmillan US, 2014), 162–5.
262 Ibid., 165–7.
263 Nassereddin Parvin, 'Rastḵiz', https://iranicaonline.org/articles/rastakhiz (accessed on 18 March 2023), and Marashi, *Exile and the Nation*, 153ff.
264 Quoted in Jehangir Barjorji Sanjana, *Ancient Persians and the Parsis: A Comprehensive History of the Parsis and their Religion from Primeval Times to the Present Age* (Bombay: Hosang T. Anklesaria at the Fort Printing Press, 1935), 607.

See Bayat, *Iran's Experiment with Parliamentary Governance*, 104–5, and 229, for references to views articulated by Danesh in earlier years.

265 *ToI*, 12 April 1917, 6 (NB this article was by G. K. Nariman, who likened the contemporary situation in Iran to the tolerance enjoyed by non-Muslims in the early years of Islam); Grigor, 'Parsi Patronage of the *Urheimat*', 58; Shahrokh, *The Memoirs of Keikhosrow Shahrokh*, 21; and, *ILB* 1, no. 7 (September 1928): 7. For details of the life of Hakimi, see Abbas Milani and *Encyclopædia Iranica*, 'Ḥakimi, Ebrāhim', https://www.iranicaonline.org/articles/hakimi-ebrahim (accessed on 18 March 2023).

266 Grigor, 'Parsi Patronage of the *Urheimat*', 58–9. See also Grigor, 'Freemasonry and the Architecture of the Persian Revival, 1843–1933', 168.

267 Grigor, 'Parsi Patronage of the *Urheimat*', 59.

268 Bayat, *Iran's Experiment with Parliamentary Governance*, 308–9. The electoral laws of 1906 and 1909 specified that Majles deputies must know Persian (Browne, *The Persian Revolution of 1905–1909*, 356, and 387).

269 For information about Azad Maraghah'i, see Vejdani, 'Indo-Iranian Linguistic, Literary, and Religious Entanglements', 445–6. Vejdani mentions that Azad Maraghah'i was a professor at Aligarh, and is thus likely to be the man referred to as 'Qasem Irani' earlier in this chapter.

270 *Nameh-ye Parsi: Nakhostin Ruznameh-ye Parsi dar Iran* 21, 27 Jumada Al-Thani 1335 (20 April 1917): 323–8. See also *Nameh-ye Parsi* 13, 20 Safar 1335 (16 December 1916): 195, and 199ff.

271 Shahrokh, *The Memoirs of Keikhosrow Shahrokh*, 28.

272 *Majles* 2:215, quoted in Shahrokh, *The Memoirs of Keikhosrow Shahrokh*, 105.

273 Amini, *Ta'amol Aqalliyyatha-ye Mazhabi va Enqelab-e Mashrutiyat-e Iran*, 72–3, and Shahrokh, *The Memoirs of Keikhosrow Shahrokh*, 28. *Neda-ye Vatan* had a regular column which often referred to Zoroastrians and to the Persian language, likely to have been written by Shahrokh; for example, see *Neda-ye Vatan* 5, 6 Zu al-Hijja 1324 (21 January 1907), 3–4.

274 Shahrokh, *The Memoirs of Keikhosrow Shahrokh*, 40–1; see also page 22. An instance of Muslims intervening in support of Zoroastrians was reported in the *RMM*, which noted that when a Zoroastrian man in Yazd was beaten to death in 1915 for being in a relationship with a Muslim woman, 'impartial Muslims' contacted the Minister of the Interior to express their disapproval (*RMM* 30 [1915]: 185–6). See also *MT* 19, no. 221 (1915): 134–5.

275 Shahrokh, *The Memoirs of Keikhosrow Shahrokh*, 18. Shahrokh was not alone in believing that Reporter was acting beyond his remit (see Amini, *Asnadi az Zartoshtiyan-e Mo'aser-e Iran*, 289–92). NB there are unclear accounts of the murder of Master Khodabakhsh, who was a rival of Shahrokh. Khodabakhsh was killed in Yazd *c*. 1918 and Shahrokh was rumoured to have ordered his assassination. Born in Yazd *c*. 1860, Khodabakhsh left Iran during the famine of the 1870s and went to Bombay. After completing his education in Bombay, he returned to teach in Yazd. He was also a member of the Zoroastrian Anjoman of Yazd and a scholar. Khodabakhsh was socially liberal but more religiously conservative than Shahrokh, he was also said to be sympathetic to the Bahá'ís (Fischer, 'Zoroastrian Iran Between Myth and Praxis', 108n1; Mehr, 'Zoroastrians in Twentieth Century Iran', 281n3; Stiles, 'Zoroastrian Conversions to the Bahá'í Faith in Yazd, Iran', 76–8; and, Shahmardan, *Farzanegan-e Zartoshti*, 611–16).

276 Shahrokh, *The Memoirs of Keikhosrow Shahrokh*, 18.

277 *ToI*, 23 November 1914, 9.

278 See *ToI*, 8 November 1918, 8. Here, Dr K. K. Dadachanji emphasized Parsi loyalty and proposed that a Parsi regiment be established. Meanwhile, in Britain, Ardeshir Kapadia served on the Ilford Urban District Council, and oversaw the recruitment department at the Town Hall. I am very grateful to Gerard Greene, manager of the Redbridge Museum & Heritage Centre, for sharing this information about Kapadia with me, in addition to Kapadia's 1927 obituary from the *Ilford Recorder*.
279 Sanjana, *Ancient Persians and the Parsis*, 625. See also pages 578, and 624–6, where Sanjana states that Karanjia went to Iran in 1913 where he became a naturalized Iranian and enlisted in the army. Foreign Office records suggest that Karanjia was linked to British forces stationed in Iran before the outbreak of the First World War (J. N. Merrill, 'Memoranda re Expedition to Kazerun', enclosed in Sir W. Townley to Sir Edward Grey, 28 May 1914, FO 416/60). It is possible that Karanjia then joined the British-led South Persia Rifles which, like the Cossack Brigade, operated as a 'Persian force' during the war, nominally under the command of the Persian War Ministry (Safiri, 'South Persia Rifles').
280 Indeed, Karanjia was later compared to ancient 'Parsi commanders' such as Artabanus (*ILQ* 3, no. 1 [October 1932]: 3).
281 *ToI*, 30 April, 1915, 12; *ToI*, 18 January 1916, 5; and, *ToI*, 16 February 1916, 8.
282 For instance, episodes from the *Shahnameh* were recited during celebrations for Aban Jashan in 1915. The event was presided over by J. J. Vimadalal, a Parsi lawyer who promoted eugenics (*ToI*, 17 April 1915, 7, and Sharafi, *Law and Identity in Colonial South Asia*, 251–2).
283 Hormasji T. Dadachanji, *First Steps in Persian* (Bombay, 1917).
284 Mellor, 'The Parsis and the Press', 63–4, and 69.
285 *ToI*, 13 December 1915, 8. J. J. Modi spearheaded the movement to erect a monument at Sanjan and raised over 20,000 rupees (*ToI*, 29 April 1916, 9); over 5,000 Parsis attended (*ToI*, 11 December 1916, 10). See *ToI*, 4 May 1910, 6, for an earlier reference to the plan.
286 Choksy, 'Despite Shāhs and Mollās', 153, and Amini, *Asnadi az Zartoshtiyan-e Mo'aser-e Iran*, 295–7.

Chapter 7

1 Kia, 'Persian Nationalism and the Campaign for Language Purification', 17–18.
2 Amanat, 'Through the Persian Eye', 144–5, and Kia, 'Persian Nationalism and the Campaign for Language Purification', 17–18.
3 Bonakdarian, 'Great Britain: British Influence in Persia, 1900-1921'.
4 For the text of the treaty see Hurewitz, *Diplomacy in the Near and Middle East*, 2:64–6. See also N. S. Fatemi, 'Anglo-Persian Agreement of 1919', http://www.iranicaonline.org/articles/anglo-persian-agreement-1919 (accessed on 18 March 2023).
5 Fatemi, 'Anglo-Persian Agreement of 1919'.
6 Philip Henning Grobien, 'The Origins and Intentions of the Anglo-Persian Agreement 1919: A Reassessment', *Iran: journal of the British Institute of Persian Studies* ahead-of-print, no. ahead-of-print (2022): 14.
7 Bast, 'Disintegrating the "Discourse of Disintegration"', 60–4.
8 Ali M. Ansari, *Modern Iran Since 1797: Reform and Revolution* (London; New York: Routledge, Taylor & Francis Group, 2019), 114–16.

9 Grobien, 'The Origins and Intentions of the Anglo-Persian Agreement 1919', 8–9, and 11–13.
10 Ibid., 11.
11 *New York Times*, 30 August 1919, 3. Shahrokh was supported by Shuster whilst in the US (Mehr, *Sahm-e Zartoshtiyan dar Enqelab-e Mashrutiyat-e Iran*, 26), and he was accompanied by Rostam Shahjahan (Shahrokh, *The Memoirs of Keikhosrow Shahrokh*, 43). See also Oshidari, *Tarikh-e Pahlavi va Zartoshtiyan*, 387, and Khosro Mehrfar, 'Keikhosrow Shahrokh', http://www.zoroastrian.org.uk/vohuman/Article/Keikhosrow%20Shahrokh.htm (accessed on 25 May 2023). NB in contrast to what was written in the American press, Shahrokh reportedly denied speaking against the agreement (His Britannic Majesty's Chargé d'Affaires and Special Commissioner, Tehran to His Excellency, the Viceroy, Simla, 15 September 1919, IOR/L/PS/10/614).
12 Sir R. W. Bullard to Viscount Halifax, 7 February 1940, FO 416/98.
13 Bonakdarian, 'India Relations: Qajar Period, Early 20th Century'.
14 Ibid.
15 Santanu Das, *India, Empire, and First World War Culture: Writings, Images, and Songs* (Cambridge: Cambridge University Press, 2018), 11.
16 Bonakdarian, 'India Relations: Qajar Period, Early 20th Century'. See also Kim A. Wagner, *Amritsar 1919: An Empire of Fear and the Making of a Massacre* (New Haven: Yale University Press, 2019), Chapter Two.
17 Wagner, *Amritsar 1919*, 54–6.
18 Bonakdarian, 'India Relations: Qajar Period, Early 20th Century'.
19 Heehs, *India's Freedom Struggle 1857–1947*, 90ff.
20 Palsetia, *The Parsis of India*, 307–9.
21 Kulke, *The Parsees in India*, 193–4, and 212, and Dinyar Patel, 'Beyond Hindu–Muslim Unity: Gandhi, the Parsis and the Prince of Wales Riots of 1921', *The Indian Economic and Social History Review* 55, no. 2 (2018): 226–8.
22 Kulke, *The Parsees in India*, 193–4
23 Ibid., 193–4, and 211–14. See for example, *ToI*, 26 January 1921, 14.
24 Patel, 'Beyond Hindu–Muslim Unity', 227.
25 *ToI*, 2 September 1919, 9.
26 *ToI*, 17 May 1919, 7.
27 Ibid.
28 *ToI*, 16 August 1919, 9. NB in 1919, the Iranian Association helped form the Iran Committee, which promoted 'cordial relations' between Zoroastrians in India and Iranians.
29 Hilary A. Langstaff, 'The Impact of Western Education and Political Changes upon the Religious Teachings of Indian Parsis in the Twentieth Century' (PhD Thesis, University of Manchester, Manchester, 1983), 153–4. See also *ToI*, 14 January 1919, 9, where an unnamed Parsi argued that Parsis ought to have territorial rights over Taq-e Kasra in Iraq, which was a 'symbol of ancient Persian sovereignty'.
30 S. H. Jhabvala, *A Brief History of Persia: Containing a Short Account of the Peshdadians, the Kayanians and the Achaemenians* (Bombay: N. Cursetjee at Union Press, 1920), 1.
31 *ToI*, 2 January 1920, 11. Kaveh was also a source of inspiration to Iranian nationalists in Berlin, who produced a journal called *Kaveh* in 1916–22.
32 *ToI*, 21 February 1920, 12.
33 *Times*, 3 November 1919, 17.
34 *ToI*, 29 November 1919, 11.

35 Ibid.
36 M. J. Sheikh-ol-Islami, 'Aḥmad Shah Qājār', http://www.iranicaonline.org/articles/ahmad-shah-qajar-1909-1925-the-seventh-and-last-ruler-of-the-qajar-dynasty (accessed on 18 March 2023).
37 *ToI*, 29 November 1919, 11.
38 Ibid.
39 Norman to Curzon, 24 November 1920, FO 416/68. See also Murali Ranganathan, 'Back to the Motherland? Parsi Gujarati Travelogues of Iran in the Qajar-Pahlavi Interregnum, 1921–1925', *Iranian Studies* 56, no. 1 (2023): 50–1.
40 Malcolm, *Five Years in a Persian Town*, 45–8.
41 Sivan Balslev, 'Dressed for Success: Hegemonic Masculinity, Elite Men and Westernisation in Iran, *c.* 1900-40', in *Gender, Imperialism and Global Exchanges*, ed. Stephan F. Miescher, Michele Mitchell, and Naoko Shibusawa (United Kingdom: John Wiley & Sons, Incorporated, 2015), 167. See also Baggaley to Barnham, 22 March 1907, FO 371/307, a report from Yazd which described how, for Zoroastrians, 'hats of all kinds are forbidden'.
42 Shahrokh, *The Memoirs of Keikhosrow Shahrokh*, 43. Prior to the Constitutional Revolution, Shahrokh had challenged clothing regulations whilst working for the Amelioration Society school in Kerman (Marashi, *Exile and the Nation*, 32, and Shahrokh, *The Memoirs of Keikhosrow Shahrokh*, 35–6).
43 Shahrokh, *The Memoirs of Keikhosrow Shahrokh*, 43.
44 Ibid., 43–4.
45 Norman to Curzon, 17 January 1921, FO 416/68.
46 Tashakkuri Bafqi, *Mashrutiyat dar Yazd*, 164–5. During this period, Shahrokh liaised with government ministers on behalf of Zoroastrians who left Yazd following the hostility over the uniforms, and who had encountered difficulties when they tried to emigrate to Bombay (Amini, *Asnadi az Zartoshtiyan-e Moʻaser-e Iran*, 313–20).
47 Kia, 'Persian Nationalism and the Campaign for Language Purification', 17–18. Edward Browne also referenced two novels published in 1919 which reflected 'recent tendencies to glorify Zoroastrian Persia' (*ILQ* 5 no. 4 [July 1935]: 229).
48 Alsulami, 'Iranian Journals in Berlin during the Interwar Period', 165–7.
49 Marashi, *Nationalizing Iran*, 76–7.
50 Ibid. See also Kia, 'Persian Nationalism and the Campaign for Language Purification', 19.
51 Pestanji Phirozshah Balsara, *Ancient Iran: Its Contribution to Human Progress* (Bombay: Iran League, 1936), vii.
52 Ansari, *Modern Iran Since 1797*, 121ff. NB it is unclear who held the most responsibility in planning the coup (Michael P. Zirinsky, 'Imperial Power and Dictatorship: Britain and the Rise of Reza Shah, 1921–1926', *International Journal of Middle East Studies* 24, no. 4 [1992]: 645).
53 Ansari, *Modern Iran Since 1797*, 125.
54 Ibid., 124–5.
55 Bonakdarian, 'India Relations: Qajar Period, Early 20th Century'. For further details, see Stephanie Cronin, 'Great Britain v. British influence during the Reżā Shah period, 1921-41', https://www.iranicaonline.org/articles/great-britain-v (accessed on 18 March 2023), and Zirinsky, 'Imperial Power and Dictatorship'.
56 Bonakdarian, 'India Relations: Qajar Period, Early 20th Century'.
57 Ibid. NB Bonakdarian also points out that there is no evidence that Reporter was acting as a British agent when he introduced Ironside to Reza Khan.

58 Ibid.
59 Ansari, *Modern Iran Since 1797*, 127–8.
60 Ibid., 132.
61 Ibid., 129–30. See also pages 121–2.
62 Ibid., 133–5.
63 Ibid., 135–6, and 140–1.
64 Ibid., 133.
65 For documents concerning Shahrokh's success in elections, see Amini, *Asnadi az Zartoshtiyan-e Moʻaser-e Iran*, 188–94.
66 Marashi, *Exile and the Nation*, 35.
67 *Majles* 4:29.
68 Kamyar Abdi, 'Nationalism, Politics, and the Development of Archaeology in Iran', *American Journal of Archaeology* 105, no. 1 (2001): 63. NB during the period of the Second Majles, Saniʻ al-Dowleh had suggested both celebrations for Nowruz and calendar reform (Bayat, *Iran's Experiment with Parliamentary Governance*, 286).
69 Stausberg, 'From Power to Powerlessness', 183.
70 Abdi, 'Nationalism, Politics, and the Development of Archaeology in Iran', 63.
71 Talinn Grigor, 'Recultivating "Good Taste": The Early Pahlavi Modernists and Their Society for National Heritage', *Iranian Studies* 37, no. 1 (2004): 21. See also, Abdi, 'Nationalism, Politics, and the Development of Archaeology in Iran', 56–7.
72 Shahrokh, *The Memoirs of Keikhosrow Shahrokh*, 44–5. In 1921, Zoroastrians in Kerman had also appealed to Shahrokh to ensure that the bandit Mashallah would be punished for his crimes (A. P. Trevor, 18 July 1921, IOR/L/PS/10/977). Shahrokh had personal reasons to hope for greater central government control; his son Shahrokh had been killed by bandits in 1921, whilst travelling between Isfahan and Shiraz (Shahrokh, *The Memoirs of Keikhosrow Shahrokh*, 4–6). Despite government support for the punishment of the bandits, they escaped (Amini, *Asnadi az Zartoshtiyan-e Moʻaser-e Iran*, 181–8).
73 Lyman Stebbins, *British Imperialism in Qajar Iran*, 224. NB there had been a rapid decrease in British influence in Tehran following the coup of 1921 (Cronin, 'Great Britain v. British influence during the Reżā Shah period, 1921-41').
74 Lieutenant-Colonel M. Saunders, 1 July 1923, FO 416/73.
75 8 March 1944, FO 371/40219. Zoroastrians had apparently demonstrated in favour of Reza Khan in 1922 (Amighi, *The Zoroastrians of Iran*, 168).
76 Kasheff, 'Anjoman-e Zartoštīān'.
77 Stephanie Cronin, 'Conscription and Popular Resistance in Iran, 1925-1941', *International Review of Social History* 43, no. 3 (1998): 454. See also Amini, *Asnadi az Zartoshtiyan-e Moʻaser-e Iran*, 145–6.
78 Ansari, *Modern Iran Since 1797*, 132.
79 Cronin, 'Conscription and Popular Resistance in Iran, 1925-1941', 454.
80 Ibid. NB the opinion expressed by Modarres echoes the terms of the *jezya*, a tax that had been imposed on non-Muslims in the past, which exempted them from military service. For further information about the views of Modarres, see Afary, 'The Place of Shiʻi Clerics in the First Iranian Constitution', 341.
81 Shahrokh, *The Memoirs of Keikhosrow Shahrokh*, 117–18.
82 Cronin, 'Conscription and Popular Resistance in Iran, 1925-1941', 455.
83 Ansari, *Modern Iran Since 1797*, 133, and 140–1.
84 *ToI*, 15 July 1921, 9.
85 Ibid.

86 *ToI*, 1 August 1921, 6.
87 Ibid.
88 Ibid.
89 For further details and an in-depth analysis of the visit of the Prince of Wales and the riots it provoked, see Patel, 'Beyond Hindu–Muslim Unity'.
90 Ibid., 223–4, and 231.
91 Ibid., 234.
92 Ibid., 237, and 222.
93 Ibid., 237–8.
94 Ibid., 238–9.
95 *ToI*, 23 August 1922, 11. See also Ranin Kazemi, 'Kāšef-al-Salṭana', https://www.iranicaonline.org/articles/kasef_al_saltana (accessed on 18 March 2023).
96 Temple referred to a book published in Tehran, in likelihood written by Kashef al-Saltaneh, which advocated a railway from Tabriz to Duzdab (Zahedan). According to Temple, this was the 'outcome of Parsi inspiration' (Report by Major B. Temple, 6 June 1922, IOR/L/PS/11/214, P1728/1922). Reza Khan was also keen to secure the involvement of the Tatas in the development of the Iranian railway system (Dinyar Patel, 'Caught Between Two Nationalisms: The Iran League of Bombay and the Political Anxieties of an Indian Minority', *Modern Asian Studies* 55, no. 3 [2021]: 784).
97 *Bombay Chronicle*, 22 November 1922, IOR/L/PS/11/214, P1728/1922.
98 Ibid.
99 Ibid. For further information about Irani, see Afshin Marashi, 'Irani, Dinshah Jijibhoy', http://www.iranicaonline.org/articles/irani-dinshah (accessed on 18 March 2023), and Marashi, *Exile and the Nation*, Chapter Two.
100 *Advocate of India*, 10 August 1922, IOR/L/PS/11/214, P1728/1922.
101 Ibid.
102 Ibid.
103 *Advocate of India*, 12 August 1922, IOR/L/PS/11/214, P1728/1922
104 Ibid. Similarly, an article from *Nameh-ye Bonavan*, dated 12 June 1921, suggested that 'competent Zoroastrians from India and Europe' could be invited to work in 'government and other offices' (Negin Nabavi, *Modern Iran: A History in Documents* [Princeton, NJ: Markus Wiener, 2016], 118–20).
105 *ToI*, 8 November 1923, 6.
106 *Farohar*, quoted in *ToI*, 8 November 1923, 6.
107 A letter signed by 'M. J. M.' exclaimed that the appeal was ridiculous and that after 1,300 years in India, Persia was no longer the fatherland of the Parsis (*ToI*, 10 November 1923, 10).
108 *ToI*, 25 May 1923, 9.
109 Report by the Commissioner of Police, Bombay, 7 July 1922, and *Advocate of India*, 15 August 1922, IOR/L/PS/11/214, P1728/1922.
110 S. G. Knox, 9 September 1923, IOR/L/PS/10/977.
111 A. P. Trevor, 14 July 1922, IOR/L/PS/10/977.
112 Ibid.
113 *Advocate of India*, 15 August 1922, IOR/L/PS/11/214, P1728/1922.
114 Ibid.
115 Report by Major B. Temple, 14 June 1922, IOR/L/PS/11/214, P1728/1922.
116 Ibid.
117 Ibid. Temple noted that Dady kept carried with him a copy of the *Bombay Chronicle*, dated 29 April 1922. This contained an article which outlined that although Iranians

opposed foreign interference, Parsis, who had always kept a 'strain of Persian patriotism', would be welcomed.
118 Report from Kerman, 17 April 1922, IOR/L/PS/11/214, P1728/1922.
119 Report by Major B. Temple, 14 June 1922, IOR/L/PS/11/214, P1728/1922.
120 Ibid.
121 Major B. Temple to the Secretary of State for Foreign Affairs, 19 June 1922, IOR/L/PS/11/214, P1728/1922, and G. F. W. Anson, 28 April 1922, IOR/L/PS/10/977. See A. P. Trevor, 21 May 1922, IOR/L/PS/10/977, for similar comments made to the British consul in Kerman. In March 1922, another Parsi doctor, whose name was not recorded, gave an address to Democrat leaders and members of the ulama at Shiraz. He stated that Parsis were keen to 'return' and would 'bring capital and set up factories'. The 'Rais-ul-Ulema' (head of the ulama) reassured him that Parsis would be safe if they did not interfere in religious matters (G. F. W. Anson, 28 April 1922, IOR/L/PS/10/977).
122 Report by the Commissioner of Police, Bombay, 18 August 1922, IOR/L/PS/11/214, P1728/1922.
123 Report by the Commissioner of Police, Bombay, 8 September 1922, IOR/L/PS/11/214, P1728/1922.
124 Report by the Commissioner of Police, Bombay, 18 August 1922, IOR/L/PS/11/214, P1728/1922.
125 Report by the Commissioner of Police, Bombay, 7 July 1922, IOR/L/PS/11/214, P1728/1922. The report stated that Parsis were not dissatisfied in Bombay, and noted that a group who had gone to Iran in 1913 had returned with 'very doleful stories'.
126 Kaikhusroo M. JamaspAsa, 'Iran League', https://www.iranicaonline.org/articles/iran-league (accessed on 18 March 2023). See Patel, 'Caught Between Two Nationalisms', for a detailed study of the Iran League.
127 G. K. Nariman, *Writings of G. K. Nariman*, compiled by R. B. Paymaster (Bombay: R. B. Paymaster, 1935), viii. For further details about Nariman, see Dinyar Patel, 'Gustaspshah Kaikhusroo Nariman: Improving Ties Between Zoroastrianism and Islam', *Fezana* 4 (2009): 43–5.
128 *ToI*, 1 March 1927, 14.
129 For instance, Dinshah Irani was president of the Iranian Zoroastrian Anjoman (Marashi, 'Irani, Dinshah Jijibhoy').
130 *ToI*, 25 November 1922, 11. Those present included Dady, as well as K. A. Fitter, G. K. Nariman, and other members of the Iran League and Iranian Zoroastrian Anjoman.
131 Shahrokh, *The Memoirs of Keikhosrow Shahrokh*, 185–7.
132 D. Irani to Treadwell, included in the report by C. E. Treadwell, 9 July 1923, IOR/L/PS/11/214, P1728/1922. In 1922, the Sir Ratan Tata trust donated 20,000 rupees for the equipped hall, and 5,000 rupees for other expenses, including the doctor's salary (*ToI*, 4 September 1922, 15).
133 Report by T. C. Tasker, included in C. E. Treadwell, 9 July 1923, IOR/L/PS/11/214, P1728/1922. NB Tasker made the complaint that funds were not being contributed by some wealthy Zoroastrians whose daughters were attending the CMS school.
134 Marashi, *Exile and the Nation*, 65.
135 Patel, 'Caught Between Two Nationalisms', 765. For biographical information about Marker, and the significance of his friendship with Dinshah Irani in respect to his decision to support Zoroastrians in Iran, see Marashi, *Exile and the Nation*, 75ff. See also Aban Rustomji, 'Peshotanji Dossabhai Marker', http://www.zoroastrian.org.uk/vohuman/Article/Marker,Peshotanji%20Dossabhai.htm (accessed on 25 May 2023).

136 See Afshin Marashi and Dinyar Patel, 'As Seen from Bombay: An Iranian Zoroastrian Photo Album from the 1930s', *Iranian Studies* 56, no. 1 (2023): 104–5. For contemporary references to P. D. Marker's philanthropic work, see *ToI*, 9 September 1924, 5; *ToI*, 24 June 1925, 8; and, *ILQ* 5, no. 4 (July 1935): 235.
137 Baggaley to Aganoor, 16 December 1908, FO 248/937.
138 C. E. Treadwell, 9 July 1923, IOR/L/PS/11/214, P1728/1922. The accumulation of wealth by some Iranian Zoroastrians is reflected in a notice regarding the large estate of Kaikobad Rustom Irani (*ToI*, 24 June 1924, 3). For references to charitable donations towards Iran in the will of a wealthy Iranian Zoroastrian resident in India, see *ToI*, 16 July 1924, 10.
139 D. Irani to C. E. Treadwell, enclosed in C. E. Treadwell, 9 July 1923, IOR/L/PS/11/214, P1728/1922. .
140 Report by T. C. Tasker, 30 March 1923, included in C. E. Treadwell, 9 July 1923, IOR/L/PS/11/214, P1728/1922. See also *Bombay Chronicle*, 22 November 1922, and *ToI*, 11 July 1924, 10. For later references to the non-denominational character of Zoroastrian philanthropy in Iran, see *ILB* 1, no. 1 (March 1928): 18, and *ILB* 1, no. 3 (May 1928): 21, which includes a letter of gratitude from Muslims in Yazd for the Sir Ratan Tata Medical and Surgical Hall.
141 Marashi, *Exile and the Nation*, 77.
142 *ToI*, 28 September 1929, 3.
143 *Advocate of India*, 15 August 1922, IOR/L/PS/11/214, P1728/1922.
144 Report by T. C. Tasker, 30 March 1923, included in C. E. Treadwell, 9 July 1923, IOR/L/PS/11/214, P1728/1922. This was not the only instance where Parsis criticized their co-religionists. For an account of tension in the Zoroastrian community of Kerman, see R. B. Prideaux, 23 June 1924, IOR/L/PS/10/977. Here, Dady is said to have asked Bombay Parsis to stop sending donations to Kerman because of the disagreements in the community. The local Anjoman had been dissolved, and disputes had ensued between two groups, the 'Young Men's Zoroastrian Association', and the 'Anjuman-i-Ithadieh-Milli-Zardushti' (Anjoman of the union of the nation of Zoroastrians). Ardeshir Reporter also highlighted the challenges of divisions amongst Zoroastrians in Iran (*ToI*, 17 May 1919, 7).
145 Nariman, *Persia and the Parsis Part I*, unnumbered page.
146 For detailed analysis of the collaboration between Purdavud and Zoroastrians in India, see Marashi, *Exile and the Nation*, Chapter Four.
147 Shahrokh, *The Memoirs of Keikhosrow Shahrokh*, 27.
148 Marashi, *Exile and the Nation*, 135–8.
149 Ibid., 166–70, and 212–13.
150 Marashi, *Nationalizing Iran*, 83.
151 Ibid., 84–5.
152 Marashi, *Exile and the Nation*, 172–3, and *ILB* 1, no. 3 (May 1928): 15.
153 Marashi, *Exile and the Nation*, 81–2.
154 Ibid., 4.
155 JamaspAsa, 'Iran League'. NB according to family history, the extensive collection of Persian books owned by Kaikhusro Maneckji B. Minocher Homji (1879–1929), proprietor of the *Bombay Samachar* newspaper, was sent to a library in Iran after his death (email communication with Avan Engineer, step-granddaughter of Homji, 10 June 2016).
156 Patel, 'Caught Between Two Nationalisms', 776, and Nariman, *Writings of G. K. Nariman*, iv.

157 G. K. Nariman (ed.), *The Ahad Nameh* (Bombay: Iran League, 1925), iii.
158 Ibid., vii–viii.
159 Patel, 'Caught Between Two Nationalisms', 776–7. For examples of the views expressed by Nariman, see *ToI*, 16 July 1919, 10, and *ToI*, 7 February 1920, 14. Criticisms were made of his arguments by J. J. Modi; for example, see *ToI*, 12 February 1920, 13. See also Kulke, *The Parsees in India*, 25.
160 *ToI*, 30 May 1925, 8.
161 *ToI*, 26 September 1925, 12. For other references to the use of the *Shahnameh*, see *ToI*, 31 December 1923, 5, and *ToI*, 12 September 1925, 16. See also Kreyenbroek, 'The Role of the *Shāhnāme* in the Culture of the Parsi Community', 3.
162 *ToI*, 21 March 1924, 7. See also Afshin Marashi, 'Patron and Patriot: Dinshah J. Irani and the Revival of Indo-Iranian Culture', *Iranian Studies* 46, no. 2 (2013): 193–5.
163 *ToI*, 12 November 1924, 5.
164 Ranganathan, 'Back to the Motherland?', 39–40, and 53–4.
165 Sir Percy Loraine to Sir Austen Chamberlain, 25 June 1926, FO 416/79. NB the British did warn Parsis about potential problems and asked the American financial mission, led by Arthur Millspaugh, to offer them support.
166 A. P. Trevor, 15 December 1923, IOR/L/PS/10/977.
167 A. P. Trevor, 10 April 1924, IOR/L/PS/10/977. See also Ranganathan, 'Back to the Motherland?', 41–3; H. B. M.'s Consulate, Kerman, Administration report for 1924, IOR/R/15/1/713; and, A. P. Trevor, 15 December 1923, IOR/L/PS/10/977. Santanu Das has examined the writings of Karkaria in relation to his experiences in the British army during the First World War, and has noted that Karkaria had a strong sense of his Parsi Gujarati identity. However, Das has also described the dawning of a 'dim sense of his Iranian ancestry', a factor that apparently led Karkaria to join the army (Das, *India, Empire, and First World War Culture*, 288).
168 H. D. G. Law, 14 March 1924, IOR/L/PS/10/977.
169 C. G. Crosthwaite, 5 June 1925, IOR/L/PS/10/977.
170 Ranganathan, 'Back to the Motherland?', 38–9, and 47. NB one of the travelogues was by a woman, Bai Kunvarbai Manekji Dhalla (1877–1942).
171 See Ranganathan, 'Back to the Motherland?', 51–2, regarding meetings between Reza Khan and Karkaria and Modi.
172 *ToI*, 11 July 1924, 10, and R. B. Prideaux, 23 June 1924, IOR/L/PS/10/977, who described how four members of the Iran League and Iranian Zoroastrian Anjoman arrived in Kerman in May 1924, including G. K. Nariman and P. S. Gazdar 'of the Cotton Industry'. See also Patel, 'Caught Between Two Nationalisms', 765–6.
173 *ToI*, 11 July 1924, 10.
174 Ibid.
175 F. B. Prideaux, November 1925, IOR/L/PS/10/977, and Ranganathan, 'Back to the Motherland?', 52–3.
176 *ToI*, 11 July 1924, 10.
177 H. G. Chick to Sir Percy Loraine, 9 June 1926, FO 416/79. NB by 1925, Dady, who had been promoting links with Iran, had been 'discredited' by the Iran League and had resigned from the organization (Bombay Police Commissioner, 5 October 1925, IOR/L/PS/262, P3990/1925).
178 *ToI*, 9 September 1925, 10.
179 H. G. Chick to Sir Percy Loraine, 9 June 1926, FO 416/79.
180 Ibid.
181 Ibid.

182 Ibid.
183 *ToI*, 3 December 1924, 15.
184 *ToI*, 10 December 1925, 13. For further information about the *hijrat*, see Dietrich Reetz, *Hijrat: The Flight of the Faithful. A British File on the Exodus of Muslim Peasants from North India to Afghanistan in 1920* (Berlin: Verlag Das Arabische Buch, 1995).
185 *ToI*, 10 December 1925, 13.
186 *ToI*, 21 December 1925, 14.
187 Ibid.
188 *ToI*, 10 December 1925, 7.
189 *ToI*, 21 December 1925, 14.
190 Sharafi, *Law and Identity in Colonial South Asia*, 309.
191 Ibid., 308. See *ILB* 2, no. 14 (April 1929): vi, for a reference to a Tehran newspaper, dated February 1925, which invited Parsis to return to their 'fatherland'.
192 *ToI*, 5 January 1926, 11.
193 Ibid.
194 *ToI*, 26 April 1926, 10.
195 *ToI*, 12 July 1926, 9. At a celebration organized by Parsis in Britain, the Persian chargé d'affaires stated that skilled Parsis, such as engineers, would have a 'hearty welcome' in Iran, emphasizing that it was not only the wealth of Parsis that was of interest to the Iranian government (*ToI*, 4 August 1926, 16). See also Hinnells, *Zoroastrians in Britain*, 113–14, regarding discussions that took place amongst Parsis about sending an illuminated address to congratulate Reza Shah. The reply from Reza Shah, dated December 1926, can be seen in the ZTFE file relating to Persia.
196 *ToI*, 26 April 1926, 10. See also *ToI*, 6 May 1926, 10, which refers to the revival of Parsi dreams of return, and to the 'intensive newspaper propaganda' aiming to nurture a love for Iran amongst Parsis. The idea of establishing an agency to relay news about Parsis to Iran, and vice versa, was also proposed. In view of all this talk of their 'motherland', the Persia Society encouraged Parsis to show their support for Iran by joining their society (*ToI*, 8 April 1926, 10).
197 This included calls for Parsis to learn Persian, and for Iranian history to be added to the curriculum in Parsi schools (*ToI*, 14 July 1926, 8).
198 *ToI*, 13 February 1926, 10. Tourism also drew Parsis to Iran; soon after the coronation, a group of twenty Parsis went to Iran to visit archaeological sites (*ToI*, 24 April 1926, 6).
199 JamaspAsa, 'Iran League'. Following some problems regarding his visa, Colonel M. S. Irani, the son of Iranian Zoroastrian immigrants to India, was able to attend the coronation (*ToI*, 13 April 1926,13; *ToI*, 21 April 1926, 15; *ToI*, 30 April 1926, 11; *ToI*, 11 May 1926, 15; *ToI*, 9 August 1926, 14; and, *ILQ* 4, no. 2–3 (January–April 1934): 94].
200 *ToI*, 9 January 1926, 11. NB the Aqa Khan had helped Parsis gain an audience with Mozaffar al-Din Shah in 1900 (*ToI*, 10 September 1900, 5). See Chapter Five of Green, *Bombay Islam*, for discussion about the Ismaili community in Bombay.
201 *ToI*, 25 January 1926, 11.
202 *ToI*, 1 February 1926, 10.
203 *ToI*, 21 June 1926, 13, and *ToI*, 22 August 1929, 5.
204 *ToI*, 21 June 1926, 13.
205 Ibid.

206 For an analytical overview of the rule of Reza Shah, see Ansari, *Modern Iran Since 1797*, Chapter Eight.
207 Marashi, *Exile and the Nation*, 23–4; Shahrokh, *The Memoirs of Keikhosrow Shahrokh*, 82; and, Amighi, *The Zoroastrians of Iran*, 173. NB Shahrokh had prior experience of managing large-scale projects, having been appointed managing director of the telephone company in 1916 (Shahrokh, *The Memoirs of Keikhosrow Shahrokh*, 60–2, and Amini, *Asnadi az Zartoshtiyan-e Moʻaser-e Iran*, 178–80).
208 Ansari, *Modern Iran Since 1797*, 151, and Ali M. Ansari, *The Politics of Nationalism in Modern Iran* (Cambridge: Cambridge University Press, 2012), 85–6. See also Sekandar Amanolahi, 'Reza Shah and the Lurs: The Impact of the Modern State on Luristan', *Iran & the Caucasus* 6, no. 1 (2002): 202.
209 Ansari, *Modern Iran Since 1797*, 168.
210 Ibid., 146.
211 Balslev, 'Dressed for Success', 174. See also ʻAlī-Akbar Saʻīdī Sīrjānī, 'Clothing xi. In the Pahlavi and post-Pahlavi periods', http://www.iranicaonline.org/articles/clothing-xi (accessed on 18 March 2023), and Houchang E. Chehabi, 'Staging the Emperor's New Clothes: Dress Codes and Nation-Building under Reza Shah', *Iranian Studies* 26, no. 3–4 (1993): 209–29.
212 Amighi, 'Zoroastrians in Iran iv. Between the Constitutional and the Islamic Revolutions'. However, there were instances where laws aiming to stop discrimination were contravened; in the year that Reza became shah, Zoroastrians in Yazd resorted to going on strike to secure their right to wear 'normal clothes' (Writer, *Contemporary Zoroastrians*, 49, and Fischer, 'Zoroastrian Iran Between Myth and Praxis', 100–1).
213 For detailed discussion, see Marashi, *Nationalizing Iran*, Chapter Three. NB the restrictions on schools also affected the schools of Zoroastrians and other non-Muslims (Sanasarian, *Religious Minorities in Iran*, 49).
214 Kia, 'Persian Nationalism and the Campaign for Language Purification', 19–27, and Monica Ringer, 'Iranian Nationalism and Zoroastrian Identity: Between Cyrus and Zoroaster', in Amanat and Vejdani, *Iran Facing Others*, 268. Discussions concerning language reform were reported by the Iran League, including the suggestion that the alphabet be changed to the Latin script. For example, see: *ILB* 1, no. 9 (November 1928): iv-v; *ILB* 1, no. 10 (December 1928-January 1929): 11; *ILQ* 3, no. 3 (April 1933): 191ff; *ILQ* 3, no. 4 (June 1933): 219; and, *ILQ* 5, no. 3 (April 1935): 137ff.
215 *ILB* 1, no. 2 (April 1928): 3.
216 Mehr, 'Zoroastrians in Twentieth Century Iran', 291–3, and 299, and Shahrokh, *The Memoirs of Keikhosrow Shahrokh*, 30. See also, Naser Yeganeh, 'Civil Code', https://www.iranicaonline.org/articles/civil-code (accessed on 23 March 2023).
217 Choksy, 'Despite Shāhs and Mollās', 160–1.
218 Administrative Report of His Majesty's Consulate, Kerman for 1929, page 36, IOR/R/15/1/714.
219 Cronin, 'Conscription and Popular Resistance in Iran, 1925-1941', 467. NB the number of Jews conscripted in Shiraz was also out of proportion to the size of their population (ibid.).
220 *ILB* 1, no. 1 (March 1928): 2–3.
221 References were made to changing conditions in Iran. For instance, after a Parsi couple visited Iran, it was reported that, 'The most impressive part of the Parsi travellers' experiences in his mother-country related to the patriotic and spontaneously liberal attitude of the Mussalmans' (*ILB* 1, no. 5 [July 1928]: 10–11).

See also *ILB* 1, no. 5 (July 1928): 14, which described how Reza Shah had elevated the Parsis 'to equality with Moslems', and *ILB* 1, no. 7 (September 1928): 28, which outlined that, 'National unity is increasing', and 'Order and security exist throughout the country'.
222 *ToI*, 7 August 1926, 12. 'N. M. D.' suggested that Parsis could act as 'peace-makers' to end the 'estrangement' between Hindus and Muslims, thereby following the example of Naoroji, who had helped heal divisions after the 1905-11 partition of Bengal (*ToI*, 9 September 1926, 10).
223 Heehs, *India's Freedom Struggle 1857-1947*, 103-5.
224 *ToI*, 28 December 1928, 9.
225 *ILB* 1, no. 8 (October 1928): 36, and Kulke, *The Parsees in India*, 194-8.
226 Ibid.
227 A key document in this respect was the Nehru Report, a draft constitution drawn up by a committee of Indian nationalists (Metcalf and Metcalf, *A Concise History of Modern India*, 190-1).
228 Ibid., 190.
229 Kulke, *The Parsees in India*, 196. Prior to the conferences, the Parsi Panchayat had written to the viceroy, requesting that Parsis be given 'adequate representation', as they had been resident in India so long as to 'entitle them to be regarded as one of the peoples of India' (*ToI*, 16 April 1930, 14).
230 *ToI*, 26 February 1930, 16.
231 Writer, *Contemporary Zoroastrians*, 94.
232 *ToI*, 31 May 1930, 16 (the author did express gratitude to the Hindus, referencing Jadi Rana from the *Qesse-ye Sanjan*, but argued that Parsis had repaid their debt). See *ToI*, 27 September 1930, 16, for a letter from a Parsi who expressed their loyalty to the British, and *ToI*, 8 November 1930, 14, where 'a Parsi' referenced a statement made by Ramanand Chaterji, that the only true inhabitants of India are Bengalis, and argued that without British help, the Zoroastrian community in Iran would have died out.
233 For example, see *ToI*, 3 October 1930, 6, for the views of K. K. Lalkaka, who argued that Parsis should support constitutional changes in India, yet should remain pro-British. Lalkaka also proposed they consider emigration to Australia and New Zealand. A suggestion was made in the *ILQ* that Parsis, who it was emphasized were loyal to both India and Iran, could join other minorities in India to form a league that would be a 'third power', balancing the influence of the Hindu and Muslim communities (*ILQ* 2, no. 1 [October 1931]: 3ff, and Kulke, *The Parsees in India*, 192-3).
234 In reference to a financial report concerning Iran, the *ILB* expressed greater optimism in the economic future of Iran than of India (*ILB* 1, no. 1 [March 1928]): 18).
235 *ToI*, 9 September 1927, 10.
236 Marashi, *Exile and the Nation*, 65-6; Shahrokh, *The Memoirs of Keikhosrow Shahrokh*, 23-4; and, *ToI*, 7 September 1929, 22.
237 *ToI*, 31 July 1929, 15. NB Bengali was rebuked by Lt.-Col. M. S. Irani (*ToI*, 7 September 1929, 22).
238 *ToI*, 22 August 1929, 5.
239 The *ILB* explicitly stated that the Iran League, IZA and Amelioration Society, 'will be always keen on helping forward, so far as in them lies, the interests of Persians without distinction of religion' (*ILB* 1, no. 3 [May 1928]: 21).
240 *ToI*, 31 July 1929, 15.

241 *ILB* 2, no. 20–21 (October-November 1929): 5. The *ILB* also reported that a girls' school was established in Khoramshah by Ardeshir Kaikhusrow Irani, who lived in India, in memory of his wife (*ILB* 1, no. 10 [December 1928–January 1929]: 21). Positive references to charitable donations towards educational projects were made in later years (for example: *ILQ* 3, no. 2 [January 1933]: 109; *ILQ* 3, no. 3 [April 1933]: 137; and, *ILQ* 5, no. 1 [October 1934]: 7).
242 *ILB* 2, no. 22–23 (December 1929–January 1930): i.
243 *ToI*, 7 August 1929, 12. B. S. Irani highlighted the poverty experienced by Iranian Zoroastrians in Bombay, and argued that Parsi funds would be better spent in Bombay, or alternatively in Yazd or Kerman, rather than Tehran (*ToI*, 27 August 1930, 11).
244 *ToI*, 7 August 1929, 12.
245 *ToI*, 17 August 1929, 19.
246 *ToI*, 28 September 1929, 3.
247 *ToI*, 21 July 1930, 15. Jehangir Mody also argued that the Parsis were focusing too much on establishing relations with Reza Shah, rather than recognizing their debt to the British (*ToI*, 14 October 1930, 6; *ToI*, 5 November 1930, 12, and *ToI*, 30 January 1933, 14).
248 *ILB* 2, no. 16–17 (June–July 1929): iv, and *ILB* 2, no. 18–19 (August–September 1929): 13. NB Parsis had also sent relief when an earthquake struck northeast Iran in 1923 (*ToI*, 17 July 1923, 3).
249 *ToI*, 25 December 1930, 16. NB later in the 1930s, S. A. Kaul, who was based in California, promoted conversion to Zoroastrianism and hoped for a revival of the religion in Iran (*ILQ* 3, no. 3 [April 1933], 157–8).
250 For details see, Writer, *Contemporary Zoroastrians*, 116–48, and Sharafi, *Law and Identity in Colonial South Asia*, 285ff.
251 *ToI*, 25 December 1930, 16. Cursetji likened Parsi plans to the ill-fated *hijrat* of 1920, which saw thousands of Muslims emigrate from India to Afghanistan.
252 *ToI*, 14 February 1931, 17. However, references were made to the idea of a Parsi colony (for example, *ILQ* 1, no. 1–2 [April–July 1930]: 37). Sykes also encouraged Parsis to settle in Iran, echoing his earlier proposals (*ILB* 1, no. 1 [March 1928]: 4), and it was proposed that Parsis might consider moving to the port of Bandar Shahpur (now Bandar Imam Khomeini) (*ILQ* 4, no. 2–3 [January–April 1934]: 117).
253 *ToI*, 4 February 1931, 12.
254 *ToI*, 21 February 1931, 16. For discussion of Reporter's promotion of 'Persia's re-Iranization', see Marashi, *Exile and the Nation*, 69ff.
255 Shahrokh, *The Memoirs of Keikhosrow Shahrokh*, 23–4. and Marashi, *Exile and the Nation*, 65ff. See also Mehr, 'Zoroastrians in Twentieth Century Iran', 296n22. Reporter had encouraged Parsis to support education in Iran in previous years (*ILB* 1, no. 1 [March 1928]: 18). The foundation stone for the school was laid by the Foreign Minister, H. H. Foroughi, and the *ILQ* described how 'His Highness took the opportunity of expressing pleasure at the diversion of a current of Parsi charity towards Persia, and extolled late Bai Ratanbai's interest in female education in that country' (*ILQ* 5, no. 1 [October 1934]: 7). For further information about this school, and others founded by the Iran League, see Patel, 'Caught Between Two Nationalisms', 772–4.
256 *ILQ* 5, no. 3 (April 1935): 163.
257 *ToI*, 14 February 1931, 17. An anonymous correspondent suggested that someone within the community was discouraging Parsi interest in Iran, and that letters

signed by Cursetji and other Parsis may have been drafted by this individual (*ToI*, 21 February 1931, 16).
258 NB one *lakh* is equivalent to one hundred thousand.
259 *ToI*, 3 December 1930, 5.
260 For an overview of the journal's aims, see *ILB* 1, no. 1 (March 1928): 1. By 1928, the Iran League had 600 ordinary members and 58 life members (*ILB* 1, no. 3 [May 1928]: 19).
261 Patel, 'Caught Between two Nationalisms', 771, and 774–5.
262 For example, see *ILQ* 2, no. 1 (October 1931): 48.
263 *ILB* 1, no. 4 (June 1928): i.
264 For example, reference was made to greater 'national unity' and the existence of 'order and security . . . throughout the country' (*ILB* 1, no. 7 [September 1928]: 28).
265 'Aref Qazvini also spoke of his 'firm kinship' with Zoroastrians (*ILQ* 1, no. 1–2 [April–July 1930]: 44).
266 For example, *ILB* 1, no. 10 (December 1928-January 1929): 15, and *ILB* 2, no. 22–23 (December 1929–January 1930): iii. NB apparently, some of the Muslims working in Irani cafes in Bombay and Calcutta, 'did not object to be counted Zoroastrians' (*ILB* 1, no. 9 [November 1928]: 29).
267 *ILB* 1, no. 8 (October 1928): 30. For example, the author Sadeq Hedayat (1903–51) studied Pahlavi with the Parsi scholar, B. T. Anklesaria (1873–1944) (Vejdani, 'Indo-Iranian Linguistic, Literary, and Religious Entanglements', 441).
268 Vejdani, 'Indo-Iranian Linguistic, Literary, and Religious Entanglements', 440.
269 *ToI*, 21 February 1931, 16. See Laura Fish, 'The Bombay Interlude: Parsi Transnational Aspirations in the First Persian Sound Film', *Transnational Cinemas* 9, no. 2 (2018): 199, regarding his choice of name.
270 Fish, 'The Bombay Interlude', 199, and 204, and Marashi, *Exile and the Nation*, 174.
271 For detailed discussion see Fish, 'The Bombay Interlude', and Golbar Rekabtalaei, 'Cinematic Modernity: Cosmopolitan Imaginaries in Twentieth Century Iran' (PhD Thesis, University of Toronto, Toronto, 2015), 79–83.
272 NB in an earlier version, the film ended with the couple's arrival in Bombay (Fish, 'The Bombay Interlude', 201).
273 Ibid., 198, 202–4, and 207–9. Interestingly, a few years earlier, an article in the *ILB* had suggested that Parsis consider becoming involved in film-making in Iran, noting that it might be profitable due to the 'present mood of the Parsis and Persia' (*ILB* 1, no. 10 [December 1928–January 1929]: 15).
274 Rekabtalaei, 'Cinematic Modernity', 80.
275 Ibid., 81–3. In 1934, the Iranian government commissioned the Imperial Film Company of Bombay, which had produced *Dokhtar-e Lor*, to produce a film about Ferdowsi (ibid., 90ff). See also *ToI*, 16 July 1934, 3.
276 J. M. Unvala, 'Observations on the Religious Conviction in Modern Persia', *Estratto da: Studie Materiali di Storia Delle Religioni* 9 (1933): 94.
277 Ibid., 91. Accusations made by Lalkaka, that Sepanta was conducting 'a crusade against priesthood' (*ToI*, 21 February 1931, 16), may reflect this increased interest in Zoroastrian ethics amongst non-Zoroastrian Iranians.
278 In 1925, Unvala had travelled to Iran with Manek Fardunji Mulla, who wanted to teach Iranian Zoroastrians about religious matters as he was concerned that they were not as devout as Parsis (F. B. Prideaux, November 1925, IOR/L/PS/10/977, and Bombay Police Commissioner, 5 October 1925, IOR/L/PS/262, P3990/1925). By 1928, Mulla had visited Iran twice and had published a 'Guide to Persia' in Gujarati

(*ILB* 1, no. 5 [July 1928]: 27). Ranganathan describes Mulla as a 'Zoroastrian missionary', who also directed his attention towards Zoroastrians who had converted to the Bahá'í faith (Ranganathan, 'Back to the Motherland?', 44, and 56).
279 Ringer, *Pious Citizens*, 188–9, and Shahrokh, *The Memoirs of Keikhosrow Shahrokh*, 11ff.
280 For details, see Stewart, 'The Politics of Zoroastrian Philanthropy and the Case of Qasr-e Firuzeh', 69–70.
281 Shahrokh, *The Memoirs of Keikhosrow Shahrokh*, 18.
282 Ringer, *Pious Citizens*, 189–92.
283 Ibid., 163.
284 *ILQ* 6, no. 2-3 (January–April 1936): 164, and Ringer, 'Iranian Nationalism and Zoroastrian Identity', 271–2. Similarly, an earlier article had stated that women held influential positions in pre-Islamic Iran (*ILB* 1–2, no. 12–13 [February–March 1929]: 1). The same reasoning was applied to other aspects of modernity; for instance, the editor of the *Iran League Quarterly*, Sohrab J. Bulsara, outlined that 'Constitutional Monarchy was always the method of state administration in ancient Iran' and argued that the example of the Parsis proved that modern Iranians also had the potential to succeed (*ILQ* 3, no. 2 [January 1933]: 119–29).
285 *ILQ* 3, no. 1 (October 1932): 2.
286 *ILQ* 5, no. 1 (October 1934): 36–9. See also Patel, 'Caught Between Two Nationalisms', 787.
287 Marashi, *Exile and the Nation*, 101.
288 Ibid., 107.
289 For detailed analysis of Tagore's tour, see ibid., Chapter Three.
290 Ibid., 101.
291 Ibid., 104–5. See also Vejdani, 'Indo-Iranian Linguistic, Literary, and Religious Entanglements', for an analysis of the complexity of Indo-Iranian connections.
292 Marashi, *Exile and the Nation*, 109–10. NB whilst the tour did incorporate cultural figures from the Islamic age, including the poet Hafez, in these instances an emphasis was placed on their role in preserving an authentic Iranian spirit dating from the pre-Islamic period (ibid., 118).
293 Ibid., 97. For further references to positive relations between Iranian diplomats and Zoroastrians in India, see *ILQ* 4, no. 1 (October 1933): photograph after page 30; *ILQ* 4, no. 2-3 (January–April 1934): 199; and, *ILQ* 4, no. 4 (July 1934): 85.
294 Marashi, *Exile and the Nation*, 113–14, 127, and 131. The school was funded by a Parsi, Bahram Bhikaji, in memory of his son who died during the First World War. For further details, see Mehr, 'Zoroastrians in Twentieth Century Iran', 296n21; *ILQ* 3, no. 2 (January 1933): 109; and, *ILQ* 3, no. 3 (April 1933): 137.
295 Marashi, *Exile and the Nation*, 102–4.
296 Mr Hoare to Sir John Simon, 24 May 1932, FO 416/90. See *ILQ* 2, no. 4 (July 1932): 191, for Irani's account of the trip.
297 Mr Hoare to Sir John Simon, 24 May 1932, FO 416/90. See also Marashi, '"Rich Fields in Persia"', 68–74.
298 Ibid.
299 Ibid.
300 For example, *Shafagh-Sorkh*, 5 June 1932, cited in *ToI*, 2 September 1932, 3.
301 For example, see the criticisms raised by Merwanji Cursetji (*ToI*, 20 July 1932, 11), and the response from Dinshah Irani (*ToI*, 29 July 1932, 5).
302 *ToI*, 2 September 1932, 3.

303 Mr Hoare to Sir John Simon, 24 May 1932, FO 416/90.
304 ToI, 8 July 1932, 5.
305 Mr Hoare to Sir John Simon, 24 May 1932, FO 416/90. NB for references to Dinshaw Navroji Pavri being deputed to Iran by the Iranian government to investigate the possibilities of establishing cotton mills, see *Byramjee Jeejeebhoy Parsee Charitable Institution Golden Jubilee 1891–1941* (1941), 127. See *ILQ* 3, no. 2 (January 1933): 89–94, for an article by Pavri, 'Renaissance of Persia'.
306 Willem Floor, 'Textile Industry in Iran', https://www.iranicaonline.org/articles/textile-industry-in-iran (accessed on 18 March 2023).
307 *ILQ* 3, no. 4 (June 1933): 197–8.
308 *ILQ* 4, no. 2–3 (January–April 1934): 45 (Persian numbers).
309 For example, Dr N. H. Bamboat, who had previously explored opportunities in Iran, went back in 1933 with the view of settling there (*ILQ* 4, no. 4 [July 1934]: 252ff). See also *ILQ* 3, no. 1 (October 1932): 1.
310 *ILQ* 3, no. 3 (April 1933): 183. See also *ILQ* 6, no.1 (October 1935): 3–5, and *ILQ* 3, no. 4 (June 1933): 183.
311 Phiroz D. Saklatvala, *The Rich Fields in Persia* (Bombay: Iran League, 1933); *ILQ* 5, no. 2 (January 1935): 136; and, Marashi, '"Rich Fields in Persia"', 65–8.
312 For example, see *ILQ* 4, no. 1 (October 1933): 29–30; *ILQ* 3, no. 4 (June 1933): 233–4; *ILQ* 6, no. 1 (October 1935): 57, which includes an Iranian Government Notification; and, *ILQ* 6, no. 2–3 (January–April 1936): 160. See also Marashi, *Exile and the Nation*, 72–5, and Marashi, '"Rich Fields in Persia"', 74–9.
313 Marashi, *Exile and the Nation*, 126.
314 Major Daly to Sir R. Clive, 8 December 1930, FO 416/88. See also *ILQ* 4, no. 2–3 (January–April 1934): 132, for a reference to Reza Shah's desire for Parsis to 'return'.
315 Masani, quoted in Marashi, *Exile and the Nation*, 125. See also the speech by Reza Shah, dated May 1932, printed on the inside cover of Ali Ashgar Hekmat, *Parsis of Iran, Their Past and Present* (Bombay: Iran League, 1956). For extracts from letters between Zoroastrians who were on the tour and 'Abdolhossein Teymurtash, Iranian Minister of Court, see *ILQ* 3, no. 1 (October 1932): 4–6.
316 Vejdani, 'Indo-Iranian Linguistic, Literary, and Religious Entanglements', 449–50. See also, Marashi, *Exile and the Nation*, 128–31. Nariman continued to criticize Pahlavi rhetoric until his death in 1933; for example, see his article in *The People*, Lahore, 1 January 1933, 'Does Iran Care for Zoroastrian Ideals?' (Papers of Alphonse Mingana, DA66/1/3/1/18, Cadbury Research Library, Special Collections).
317 Vejdani, 'Indo-Iranian Linguistic, Literary, and Religious Entanglements', 450.
318 C. K. Daly, Diary of Consul for Sistan and Kain for August 1931, IOR/L/PS/12/3403. For detailed analysis of the activities of Saif Azad in relation to Iranian nationalism and anti-imperialism, see Marashi, *Exile and the Nation*, Chapter Five.
319 *ILQ* 2, no. 2–3 (January–April 1932): 77.
320 Minister in Tehran, 10 February 1933, IOR/L/PS/12/3442.
321 *ILQ* 4, no. 2–3 (January–April 1934): 144.
322 Minister in Tehran, 10 February 1933, IOR/L/PS/12/3442, and 'Saif Azad alias Sheikh Abdul Rahman Seif', 14 September 1939, IOR/L/PS/12/3513.
323 Mr Hoare to Sir John Simon, Tehran, 24 May 1932, FO 416/90.
324 Marashi, *Exile and the Nation*, 214–15, 217, and 222.
325 Quoted by the Minister in Tehran, 10 February 1933, IOR/L/PS/12/3442.
326 *ILQ* 3, no. 3 (April 1933): 137–8.
327 Vejdani, 'Indo-Iranian Linguistic, Literary, and Religious Entanglements', 448–9.

328 *ILQ* 2, no. 2–3 (January–April 1932): 160.
329 Minister in Tehran, 10 February 1933, IOR/L/PS/12/3442.
330 Article from *Iran-e Bastan*, 28 January 1933, in a report from the Minister in Tehran, 10 February 1933, IOR/L/PS/12/3442.
331 Marashi, *Exile and the Nation*, 226–31, and Zia-Ebrahimi, *The Emergence of Iranian Nationalism*, 158–60. The opinions expressed in the journal and the frequent pictures of Nazi Germany printed in its pages led the British to suspect that it was financially supported by the German legation (Minister in Tehran to FO, 3 October, 1935, IOR/L/PS/12/3442). Saif Azad later returned to India and was arrested in 1939 on suspicion of being a German agent (Marashi, *Exile and the Nation*, 189–91, and 229–30). See also, 'Saif Azad alias Sheikh Abdul Rahman Seif', 14 September 1939, IOR/L/PS/12/3513.
332 For accounts of the Ferdowsi celebrations published in India, see issues of the *ILQ* from 1934 and 1935. See also *ToI*, 6 October 1934, 21; *ToI*, 8 October 1934, 8; *ToI*, 12 October 1934, 15; and, *ToI*, 13 October 1934, 16.
333 *ILQ* 4, no. 2–3 (January–April 1934): 185–7, and Marashi, *Nationalizing Iran*, 131. See also *ILQ* 5, no. 1 (October 1934): 20ff, as well as the earlier *ILB* 2, no. 22–23 (December 1929–January 1930): 17.
334 Shahrokh, *The Memoirs of Keikhosrow Shahrokh*, 72–81, and 147, and Marashi, *Exile and the Nation*, 24. See also A. Shahpur Shahbazi, 'Ferdowsi, Abu'l-Qāsem iii. Mausoleum', https://iranicaonline.org/articles/ferdowsi-iii (accessed on 18 March 2023), and 'Ferdowsi, Abu'l-Qāsem iv. Millenary Celebration', https://www.iranicaonline.org/articles/ferdowsi-iv (accessed on 18 March 2023). See Chapter Three of Talinn Grigor, *Identity Politics in Irano-Indian Modern Architecture* (Mumbai: K. R. Cama Oriental Institute, 2013), for detailed discussion about the mausoleum. For analysis of the celebrations, including the intended impact on an international audience, see Marashi, *Nationalizing Iran*, 124–32.
335 Shahbazi, 'Ferdowsi, Abu'l-Qāsem iv. Millenary Celebration'.
336 See Marashi and Patel, 'As Seen from Bombay', for photographs from this visit.
337 *ToI*, 8 July 1932, 11. In contrast, the following year the *ILQ* highlighted that due to the impact of floods and a decrease in trade, Zoroastrians in Kerman requested Parsi assistance for the upkeep of their schools (*ILQ* 3, no. 4 [June 1933]: 235–7). See also *ILQ* 4, no. 2–3 (January–April 1934): 172–4.
338 NB Purdavud was tutor of ancient Persian culture at Tagore's institution for one year (Vejdani, 'Indo-Iranian Linguistic, Literary, and Religious Entanglements', 441). Interestingly, the Iranian foreign minister, Mohammad 'Ali Foroughi, claimed that this funded position was to thank India for 'protecting Persia's children, the Parsis' (*ToI*, 8 July 1932, 5).
339 *ToI*, 8 July 1932, 11.
340 Kulke, *The Parsees in India*, 202, and references in, for example, *ToI*, 25 December 1930, 16; *ToI*, 28 June 1939, 17. See also David M. Fahey and Padma Manian, 'Poverty and Purification: The Politics of Gandhi's Campaign for Prohibition', *The Historian* 67, no. 3 (2005): 489–506.
341 Boyce, *Zoroastrians*, 216. See also Patel, 'Caught Between two Nationalisms', 793–4.
342 For example, see *ToI*, 5 September 1936, 11; *ToI*, 4 September 1937, 10; and, *ToI*, 6 September 1938, 8. See also Kulke, *The Parsees in India*, 58.
343 Kulke, *The Parsees in India*, 196–9.
344 Patel, 'Caught Between two Nationalisms', 783ff. Whereas in 1935, an article in the *ILQ* remained optimistic about future Parsi political success (*ILQ* 5, no. 4 [July 1935]: 216), by 1940, the mood had changed (*ILQ* 10, no.2 [January 1940]: 49–50).

345 For further details, see Marashi, '"Rich Fields in Persia"', particularly 61–3, and 72–4. See also *ILQ* 4, no. 4 (July 1934): 208.
346 Consulate-General, Meshed, to Commercial Secretariat, Tehran, 4 May 1937, IOR/L/PS/12/3415. See also C. H. Lincoln, 30 June 1933, IOR/L/PS/12/3444; *ILQ* 4, no. 1 (October 1933): 4; and, *ILQ* 4, no. 2–3 (January–April 1934): 82–3, and 144–5.
347 *ToI*, 28 March 1938, 12. For biographical details, see Kaikhusroo M. JamaspAsa, 'Coyajee, Jehangir Cooverji', http://www.iranicaonline.org/articles/coyajee-sir-jehangir-cooverji- (accessed on 18 March 2023).
348 *ToI*, 28 March 1938, 12.
349 Ranganathan, 'Back to the Motherland?', 56.
350 *ILQ* 6, no. 2–3 (January–April 1936): 157–8.
351 Marashi, '"Rich Fields in Persia"', 72.
352 *ToI*, 12 February 1936, 4.
353 *ToI*, 18 January 1936, 21.
354 *ToI*, 11 January 1937, 16. Likewise, in a lecture about Iran's influence on India, Ervad Framroze A. Bode outlined that the Parsis' mission in India was 'that of a mediator and peacemaker' (*ToI*, 3 October 1938, 12).
355 *ToI*, 15 September 1938, 13.
356 Marashi, *Exile and the Nation*, 25–6, and 49–53, and Patel, 'Caught Between two Nationalisms', 797–8.
357 Palsetia, *The Parsis of India*, 310.

Conclusion

1 *ToI*, 31 August 1946, 8.
2 *ToI*, 25 October 1947, 6.
3 *ToI*, 26 October 1947, 6.
4 *ToI*, 25 October 1947, 6. NB the conceptual position of Parsis as an 'exemplary' minority and the ongoing implications of this have been analysed by Jesse Buck (Jesse Buck, '"The World's Best Minority": Parsis and Hindutva's Ethnic Nationalism in India', *Ethnic and Racial Studies* 40, no. 15 (2017): 2806–22).
5 *ToI*, 26 October 1947, 6.
6 Balsara, *Ancient Iran*, v, and *ILB* 1, no. 2 (May 1928): 16.
7 *ILQ* 3 (October 1932): 18. See also Sanjana, *Ancient Persians and the Parsis*, v and 605.
8 For example, Unvala, 'Observations on the Religious Conviction in Modern Persia', 89.
9 *ILB* 1, no. 5 (July 1928): 14.
10 M. B. Pithawalla, *The Parsee Heritage* (Karachi: The Young Zoroastrian Circle, 1932), 19. See also e.g. *ILB* 1–2, no. 12–13 (February–March 1929): 14.
11 *ILB* 1, no. 7 (September 1928): 18.
12 *ToI*, 26 October 1947, 6.

Bibliography

Archives and unpublished documents

Amelioration Society Records: Typescript of 'A Report on the work of the Charitable Institution set up to Ameliorate the Condition of poor Zoroastrians in Iran', held at the K. R. Cama Oriental Institute Library ('Amelioration Society Typescript')
CMS: Church Missionary Society Archives (Cadbury Research Library, University of Birmingham).
FO: British Foreign Office Records (National Archives, Kew).
GI: Government of India Records (National Archives of India, New Delhi).
IOR: India Office Records (British Library, London).
Majles: Iranian Majles records
Parliamentary Papers, Persia
ZTFE: Archives of the Zoroastrian Trust Funds of Europe (Zoroastrian Centre, Harrow).

Newspapers and periodicals

Bombay Chronicle
Bombay Gazette
Bombay Guardian
Bombay Times and Journal of Commerce (*BTJC*)
Bombay Times and Standard (*BTS*)
Church Missionary Gleaner (*CMG*)
Church Missionary Intelligencer and Record (*CMIR*)
Daily Telegraph and Deccan Herald (*DTDH*)
East & West (*EW*)
Hindi Punch (*HP*)
Imperial and Asiatic Quarterly Review and Oriental and Colonial Record (*IAQROCR*)
Indian Magazine and Review (*IMR*)
Indian Sociologist (*IS*)
Iran League Bulletin (*ILB*)
Iran League Quarterly (*ILQ*)
Journal of the Iranian Association (*JIA*)
Journal of the Society of Arts (*JSA*)
Manchester Guardian (*MG*)
Men and Women of India (*MWI*)
Mercy and Truth (*MT*)
Modern Review
Nameh-ye Parsi

Neda-ye Vatan
Oriental Christian Spectator (OCS)
Parsi
Parsi Prakash
Pickings from Hindi Punch
Preaching and Healing (PH)
Rast Goftar (RG)
Revue du Monde Musulman (RMM)
Sobh-e Sadeq
Sur-e Esrafil
Times
Times of India (ToI)

Books and articles

Abdi, Kamyar. 'Nationalism, Politics, and the Development of Archaeology in Iran'. *American Journal of Archaeology* 105, no. 1 (2001): 51–76.
Abidi, A. H. H. 'Irano-Afghan Dispute over the Helmand Waters'. *International Studies* 16, no. 3 (1977): 357–78.
Abrahamian, Ervand. *Iran Between Two Revolutions*. Princeton, NJ: Princeton University Press, 1982.
Afary, Janet. *The Iranian Constitutional Revolution 1906-1911: Grassroots Democracy, Social Democracy, and the Origins of Feminism*. New York: Columbia University Press, 1996.
Afary, Janet. 'Civil Liberties and the Making of Iran's First Constitution'. *Comparative Studies of South Asia, Africa and the Middle East* 25, no. 2 (2005): 341–59.
Afary, Janet. 'The Place of Shi'i Clerics in the First Iranian Constitution'. *Critical Research on Religion* 1, no. 3 (2013): 327–46.
Afary, Janet. 'Performance of Justice in Qajar Society'. *International Journal of Humanities* 26, no. 1 (2019): 73–94.
Afshar, Iraj. 'Kāva Newspaper'. *Encyclopædia Iranica* 16.2 (2013): 132–5. Available online at https://www.iranicaonline.org/articles/kava (accessed on 18 March 2023).
Afshar, Iraj and *Encyclopædia Iranica*. 'Taqizadeh, Sayyed Ḥasan i. To the end of the Constitutional Revolution'. *Encyclopædia Iranica*, 2016. Available online at http://www.iranicaonline.org/articles/taqizadeh-sayyed-hasan (accessed on 3 February 2016).
Algar, Hamid. 'Introduction to the History of Freemasonry in Iran'. *Middle Eastern Studies* 6, no. 3 (1970): 276–96.
Algar, Hamid. *Mirza Malkum Khan: A Biographical Study in Iranian Modernism*. Berkeley and London: University of California Press, 1973.
Algar, Hamid. 'Āḵūndzāda'. *Encyclopædia Iranica* 1.7 (1984): 735–40 (updated in 2011). Available online at http://www.iranicaonline.org/articles/akundzada-playwright (accessed on 18 March 2023).
Algar, Hamid. 'Amīr Kabīr, Mīrzā Taqī Khan'. *Encyclopædia Iranica* 1.9 (1989): 959–63 (updated in 2011). Available online at http://www.iranicaonline.org/articles/amir-e-kabir-mirza-taqi-khan (accessed on 18 March 2023).
Algar, Hamid. 'Behbahānī, Moḥammad'. *Encyclopædia Iranica* 4.1 (1989): 96–7. Available online at http://www.iranicaonline.org/articles/behbahani-ayatollah-mohammad (accessed on 18 March 2023).

Algar, Hamid. 'Freemasonry ii. In the Qajar Period'. *Encyclopædia Iranica* 10.2 (2000): 208–12 (updated in 2012). Available online at https://www.iranicaonline.org/articles/freemasonry-ii-in-the-qajar-period (accessed on 18 March 2023).

Algar, Hamid. 'Ḥasan Širāzi'. *Encyclopædia Iranica* 12.1 (2003): 37–40 (updated in 2012). Available online at http://www.iranicaonline.org/articles/hasan-sirazi-mirza-mohammad (accessed on 30 December 2012).

Alsulami, Mohammed. 'Iranian Journals in Berlin during the Interwar Period'. In *Transnational Islam in Interwar Europe: Muslim Activists and Thinkers*, edited by Götz Nordbruch and Umar Ryad, 157–80. New York: Palgrave Macmillan US, 2014.

Amanat, Abbas (ed.). *Cities and Trade: Consul Abbott on the Economy and Society of Iran, 1847-1866*. London: Ithaca Press, 1983.

Amanat, Abbas. 'Constitutional Revolution i. Intellectual Background'. *Encyclopædia Iranica* 6.2 (1992): 163–76 (updated in 2011). Available online at https://www.iranicaonline.org/articles/constitutional-revolution-i (accessed on 18 March 2023).

Amanat, Abbas. 'Great Britain iii. British Influence in Persia in the 19th Century'. *Encyclopædia Iranica* 11.2 (2002): 208–18 (updated in 2012). Available online at https://iranicaonline.org/articles/great-britain-iii (accessed on 18 March 2023).

Amanat, Abbas. 'Through the Persian Eye: Anglophilia and Anglophobia in Modern Iranian History'. In *Iran Facing Others: Identity Boundaries in a Historical Perspective*, edited by Abbas Amanat and Farzin Vejdani, 127–51. New York: Palgrave Macmillan, 2012.

Amanat, Abbas and Farzin Vejdani. 'Jalāl-al-Din Mirzā'. *Encyclopædia Iranica* 14.4 (2008): 405–10 (updated in 2012). Available online at https://www.iranicaonline.org/articles/jalal-al-din-mirza (accessed on 18 March 2023).

Amanat, Abbas and Farzin Vejdani (eds). *Iran Facing Others: Identity Boundaries in a Historical Perspective*. New York: Palgrave Macmillan, 2012.

Amanolahi, Sekandar. 'Reza Shah and the Lurs: The Impact of the Modern State on Luristan'. *Iran & the Caucasus* 6, no. 1 (2002): 193–218.

Amighi, Janet Kestenberg. *The Zoroastrians of Iran: Conversion, Assimilation, or Persistence*. New York: AMS Press, 1990.

Amighi, Janet Kestenberg. 'Zoroastrians of 19th Century Yazd and Kerman'. *Encyclopædia Iranica*, 2014. Available online at http://www.iranicaonline.org/articles/kerman-13-zoroastrians (accessed on 18 March 2023).

Amighi, Janet Kestenberg. 'Zoroastrians in Iran iv. Between the Constitutional and the Islamic Revolutions'. *Encyclopædia Iranica*, 2016. Available online at http://www.iranicaonline.org/articles/zoroastrians-in-iran-parent (accessed on 18 March 2023).

Amini, Touraj. *Asnadi az Zartoshtiyan-e Moʻaser-e Iran*. Tehran: Entesharat-e Sazman-e Asnad-e Melli-ye Iran, 1380/2001.

Amini, Touraj. *Taʼamol Aqalliyyatha-ye Mazhabi va Enqelab-e Mashrutiyat-e Iran*. Los Angeles: Ketab Corp, 1387/2008.

Amirahmadi, Hooshang. *The Political Economy of Iran under the Qajars: Society, Politics, Economics and Foreign Relations, 1796 to 1926*. London: I.B. Tauris, 2012.

Andreeva, Elena. *Russia and the Great Game: Travelogues and Orientalism*. London and New York: Routledge, 2007.

Ansari, Ali M. *The Politics of Nationalism in Modern Iran*. Cambridge: Cambridge University Press, 2012.

Ansari, Ali M. *Modern Iran Since 1797: Reform and Revolution*. London and New York: Routledge, Taylor & Francis Group, 2019.

'Āqeli, Bāqer. "'Alā᾿-al-Salṭana'. *Encyclopædia Iranica*, 2002 (updated in 2011). Available online at http://www.iranicaonline.org/articles/ala-al-saltana-mohammad-ali-1 (accessed on 18 March 2023).

Arjomand, Said Amir. 'The Ulama's Traditionalist Opposition to Parliamentarianism: 1907-1909'. *Middle Eastern Studies* 17, no. 2 (1981): 174–90.

Arjomand, Said Amir. *Turban for the Crown: The Islamic Revolution in Iran*. New York: Oxford University Press, 1988.

Arjomand, Said Amir. 'Constitutional Revolution iii. The Constitution'. *Encyclopædia Iranica* 6.2 (1992): 187–92 (updated in 2011). Available online at https://iranicaonline.org/articles/constitutional-revolution-iii (accessed on 18 March 2023).

Ashraf, Ahmad. 'Faculties of the University of Tehran iii. Faculty of Law and Political Science'. *Encyclopædia Iranica* 9.2 (1999): 143–6 (updated in 2012). Available online at https://iranicaonline.org/articles/faculties-iii (accessed on 18 March 2023).

Ashraf, Ahmad and Ali Banuazizi. 'Class System v. Classes in the Qajar Period'. *Encyclopædia Iranica* 5.6 and 5.7 (1992): 667–72 and 673–7 (updated in 2011). Available online at https://iranicaonline.org/articles/class-system-v (accessed on 18 March 2023).

Atabaki, Touraj (ed.). *Iran in the Twentieth Century: Historiography and Political Culture*. London: I.B. Tauris, 2009.

Atkin, Muriel. 'Cossack Brigade'. *Encyclopædia Iranica* 6.3 (1993): 329–33 (updated in 2011). Available online at https://www.iranicaonline.org/articles/cossack-brigade (accessed on 18 March 2023).

Axelrod, Paul. 'Myth and Identity in the Indian Zoroastrian Community'. *Journal of Mithraic Studies* 3, no. 1–2 (1980): 150–65.

Back de Surany, Adolphe. *Essai sur la Constitution Persane*. Paris: A. Pedone, 1914.

Bakhash, Shaul. 'The Evolution of Qajar Bureaucracy: 1779-1879'. *Middle Eastern Studies* 7, no. 2 (1971): 139–68.

Balsara, Pestanji Phirozshah. *Ancient Iran: Its Contribution to Human Progress*. Bombay: Iran League, 1936.

Balslev, Sivan. 'Dressed for Success: Hegemonic Masculinity, Elite Men and Westernisation in Iran, c.1900-40'. In *Gender, Imperialism and Global Exchanges*, edited by Stephan F. Miescher, Michele Mitchell, and Naoko Shibusawa, 161–80. United Kingdom: John Wiley & Sons, Incorporated, 2015.

Bamdad, Mahdi. *Sharh-e Hal-e Rejal-e Iran*. Vol. 1. Tehran: Zuvvar, 1347/1968.

Bashir, Hassan. 'Qanun and the Modernisation of Political thought in Iran'. *Global Media Journal* 8, no. 14 (2009): 1–39.

Basseer, P. 'Banking in Iran i. History of Banking in Iran'. *Encyclopædia Iranica* 3.7 (1988): 698–709. Available online at https://www.iranicaonline.org/articles/banking-in-iran (accessed on 18 March 2023).

Bast, Oliver. 'Disintegrating the "Discourse of Disintegration": Some Reflections on the Historiography of the Late Qajar Period and Iranian Cultural Memory'. In *Iran in the Twentieth Century: Historiography and Political Culture*, edited by Touraj Atabaki, 55–68. London: I.B. Tauris, 2009.

Bayat (or Bayat-Philipp), Mangol. 'Mīrzā Āqā Khān Kirmānī: A Nineteenth Century Persian Nationalist'. *Middle Eastern Studies* 10, no. 1 (1974): 36–59.

Bayat (or Bayat-Philipp), Mangol. 'Women and Revolution in Iran, 1905-1911'. In *Women in the Muslim World*, edited by Lois Beck and Nikki Keddie, 295–308. Cambridge, MA: Harvard University Press, 1978.

Bayat (or Bayat-Philipp), Mangol. *Mysticism and Dissent: Socioreligious Thought in Qajar Iran*. Syracuse: Syracuse University Press, 1982.

Bayat (or Bayat-Philipp), Mangol. 'Āqā Khan Kermānī'. *Encyclopædia Iranica* 2.2 (1986): 175–7 (updated in 2011). Available online at http://www.iranicaonline.org/articles/aqa-khan-kermani (accessed on 18 March 2023).

Bayat (or Bayat-Philipp), Mangol. *Iran's First Revolution: Shi'ism and the Constitutional Revolution of 1905-1909*. New York and Oxford: Oxford University Press, 1991.

Bayat (or Bayat-Philipp), Mangol. *Iran's Experiment with Parliamentary Governance: The Second Majles, 1909-1911*. Syracuse, NY: Syracuse University Press, 2020.

Beck, Lois and Nikki Keddie (eds). *Women in the Muslim World*. Cambridge, MA: Harvard University Press, 1978.

Berberian, Houri. 'The Dashnaktsutiun and the Iranian Constitutional Revolution, 1905-1911'. *Iranian Studies* 29, no. 2 (1996): 7–33.

Berberian, Houri. *Armenians and the Iranian Constitutional Revolution of 1905-1911: 'The Love for Freedom has no Fatherland.'* Boulder and Oxford: Westview Press, 2001.

Bhagat, R. B. 'Census and the Construction of Communalism in India'. *Economic and Political Weekly* 36, no. 46/47 (24–30 November 2001): 4352–6.

Bhojak, Dinkar J. 'Kaikhushro Navroji Kabraji'. In *The Oxford Companion to Indian Theatre*, edited by Ananda Lal, 177–8. New Delhi: Oxford University Press, 2004.

Bonakdarian, Mansour. 'The Persia Committee and the Constitutional Revolution in Iran'. *British Journal of Middle Eastern Studies* 18, no. 2 (1991): 186–207.

Bonakdarian, Mansour. 'Edward G. Browne and the Iranian Constitutional Struggle: From Academic Orientalism to Political Activism'. *Iranian Studies* 26, no. 1–2 (1993): 7–31.

Bonakdarian, Mansour. 'Iranian Constitutional Exiles and British Foreign-Policy Dissenters, 1908–9'. *International Journal of Middle East Studies* 27, no. 2 (1995): 175–91.

Bonakdarian, Mansour. 'Great Britain iv. British Influence in Persia, 1900-21'. *Encyclopædia Iranica* 11.3 (2002): 225–31 (updated in 2012). Available online at https://www.iranicaonline.org/articles/great-britain-iv (accessed on 18 March 2023).

Bonakdarian, Mansour. 'India ix, Relations: Qajar Period, Early 20th Century'. *Encyclopædia Iranica* 13.1 (2004): 34–44 (updated in 2012). Available online at https://www.iranicaonline.org/articles/india-ix-relations-qajar-period-early-20th-century (accessed on 18 March 2023).

Bonakdarian, Mansour. *Britain and the Iranian Constitutional Revolution of 1906-1911: Foreign Policy, Imperialism, and Dissent*. New York: Syracuse University Press in association with Iran Heritage Foundation, 2006.

Borjian, Habib. 'Kashan vi. The Esbandi Festival'. *Encyclopædia Iranica* 16.1 (2012): 29–32. Available online at http://www.iranicaonline.org/articles/kashan-vi-the-esbandi-festival (accessed on 18 March 2023).

Bosworth, Edmund and Carole Hillenbrand (eds). *Qajar Iran: Political, Social and Cultural Change*. Edinburgh: Edinburgh University Press, 1983.

Boyce, Mary. *Zoroastrians: Their Religious Beliefs and Customs*. Abingdon: Routledge, 2001.

Boyce, Mary and Firoze M. Kotwal. 'Chāngā Āsā'. *Encyclopædia Iranica* 5.4 (1991): 362 (updated in 2011). Available online at https://www.iranicaonline.org/articles/changa-asa-an-eminent-parsi-layman-who-lived-in-the-15th-16th-centuries-a (accessed on 18 March 2023).

Boyce, Mary and D. N. MacKenzie. 'Darmesteter, James'. *Encyclopædia Iranica* 7.1 (1994): 56–9 (updated in 2011). Available online at https://iranicaonline.org/articles/darmesteter (accessed on 18 March 2023).

Brookshaw, Dominic Parviz and Seena B. Fazel (eds). *The Baha'is of Iran: Socio-Historical Studies*. London and New York: Routledge, 2008.
Browne, Edward Granville. *A Year Amongst the Persians*. London: Adam and Charles Black, 1893.
Browne, Edward Granville. *A Brief Narrative of Recent Events in Persia*. London: Luzac and Co., 1909.
Browne, Edward Granville. 'The Persian Constitutionalists: An Address'. In *Proceedings of the Central Asian Society*. London, 1909.
Browne, Edward Granville. *The Persian Revolution of 1905-1909*. Cambridge: Cambridge University Press, 1910.
Browne, Edward Granville. *The Press and Poetry of Modern Persia*. Cambridge: Cambridge University Press, 1914.
Buck, Jesse. '"The World's Best Minority": Parsis and Hindutva's Ethnic Nationalism in India'. *Ethnic and Racial Studies* 40, no. 15 (2017): 2806–22.
Busse, H. 'Abbās Mīrzā Qajar'. *Encyclopædia Iranica* 1.1 (1982): 79–84 (updated in 2011). Available online at http://www.iranicaonline.org/articles/abbas-mirza-qajar (accessed on 18 March 2023).
Byramjee Jeejeebhoy Parsee Charitable Institution Golden Jubilee 1891-1941, 1941.
Calmard, Jean. 'Anglo-Persian War (1856-57)'. *Encyclopædia Iranica* 2.1 (1985): 65–8 (updated in 2011). Available online at http://www.iranicaonline.org/articles/anglo-persian-war-1856-57 (accessed on 18 March 2023).
Calmard, Jean. 'Ayn-al-dawla, 'Abd-al-majīd'. *Encyclopædia Iranica* 3.2 (1987): 137–40 (updated in 2011). Available online at https://www.iranicaonline.org/articles/ayn-al-dawla-soltan-abd-al-majid-mirza (accessed on 18 March 2023).
Calmard, Jean. 'Gobineau, Joseph Arthur de'. *Encyclopædia Iranica* 11.1 (2001): 20–4 (updated in 2012). Available online at https://www.iranicaonline.org/articles/gobineau (accessed on 18 March 2023).
Cama, K. R. *A Discourse on Zoroastrians and Freemasonry*. Bombay: Times of India Steam Press, 1876.
Cereti, Carlo G. and Farrokh Vajifdar (eds), and Mehrborzin Soroushian (co-ordinator). *Ātaš-e Dorun: The Fire Within, Jamshid Soroush Soroushian Memorial Volume II*. United States: 1st Books, 2003.
Chaqueri, Cosroe. 'The Armenian-Iranian Intelligentsia and Non-Armenian-Iranian Elites in Modern Times: Reciprocal Outlooks'. In *The Armenians of Iran: The Paradoxical Role of a Minority in a Dominant Culture: Articles and Documents*, edited by Cosroe Chaqueri, 119–40. Cambridge, MA: Harvard University Press, 1998.
Chaqueri, Cosroe (ed.). *The Armenians of Iran: The Paradoxical Role of a Minority in a Dominant Culture: Articles and Documents*. Cambridge, MA: Harvard University Press, 1998.
Chehabi, Houchang E. 'Staging the Emperor's New Clothes: Dress Codes and Nation-Building under Reza Shah'. *Iranian Studies* 26, no. 3-4 (1993): 209–29.
Chehabi, Houchang E. and Vanessa Martin (eds). *Iran's Constitutional Revolution: Popular Politics, Cultural Transformations and Transnational Connections*. London: I.B. Tauris in association with the Iran Heritage Foundation, 2010.
Choksy, Jamsheed. 'Zoroastrians in Muslim Iran: Selected Problems of Coexistence and Interaction during the Early Medieval Period'. *Iranian Studies* 20, no. 1 (1987): 17–30.
Choksy, Jamsheed. 'Despite Shāhs and Mollās: Minority Sociopolitics in Premodern and Modern Iran'. *Journal of Asian History* 40, no. 2 (2006): 129–84.

Choksy, Jamsheed. 'Persian Literature of the Parsis in India'. In *Persian Literature from Outside Iran: The Indian Subcontinent, Anatolia, Central Asia, and in Judeo-Persian*, edited by J. R. Perry, 140–72. London: I.B. Tauris, 2018.
Cole, Juan R. I. 'Bahaism i. The Faith'. *Encyclopædia Iranica* 3.4 (1988): 438–46 (updated in 2011). Available online at http://www.iranicaonline.org/articles/bahaism-i (accessed on 18 March 2023).
Cole, Juan R. I. 'Conversion v. To Babism and the Bahai Faith'. *Encyclopædia Iranica* 6.3 (1993): 236–8 (updated in 2011). Available online at https://www.iranicaonline.org/articles/conversion-v (accessed on 18 March 2023).
Cole, Juan R. I. 'Marking Boundaries, Marking Time: The Iranian Past and the Construction of the Self by Qajar Thinkers'. *Iranian Studies* 29, no. 1 (1996): 35–56.
Cole, Juan R. I. 'Iranian Culture and South Asia, 1500-1900'. In *Iran and the Surrounding World: Interactions in Culture and Cultural Politics*, edited by Nikki R. Keddie and Rudi Matthee, 15–35. Seattle: University of Washington Press. 2002.
Cooper, Nasarvanji Maneckji. *The Zoroastrian Code of Gentlehood*. London: The Cooper Publishing Company, 1909.
Cooper, Nasarvanji Maneckji. *The Imitation of Zoroaster: Quotations from Zoroastrian Literature*. London: Cooper Publishing Company, 1910.
Cooper, Nasarvanji Maneckji. *For God and Iran*. London: Cooper Publishing Co., 1910.
Cooper, Nasarvanji Maneckji (ed.). *Addresses on Zoroastrianism delivered by Prof. James Hope Moulton, M.A., Prof. L. H. Mills, M.A., and Sir George Birdwood, K.C.I.E. at a reception held in the Holborn Restaurant, London, by Mr. Nasarvanji Maneckji Cooper on June 30th, 1910*. London: Cooper Publishing Company, 1911.
Copland, Ian. 'The Limits of Hegemony: Elite Responses to Nineteenth-Century Imperial and Missionary Acculturation Strategies in India'. *Comparative Studies in Society and History* 49, no. 3 (July 2007): 637–65.
Corbin, H. 'Āẕar Kayvān'. *Encyclopædia Iranica* 3.2 (1987): 183–7 (updated in 2011). Available online at https://iranicaonline.org/articles/azar-kayvan-priest (accessed on 18 March 2023).
Crawshay-Williams, Eliot. *Across Persia*. London: Edward Arnold, 1907.
Cronin, Stephanie. 'Conscription and Popular Resistance in Iran, 1925-1941'. *International Review of Social History* 43, no. 3 (1998): 451–71.
Cronin, Stephanie. 'Gendarmerie'. *Encyclopædia Iranica* 10.4 (2000): 398–405 (updated in 2012). Available online at https://www.iranicaonline.org/articles/gendarmerie (accessed on 18 March 2023).
Cronin, Stephanie. 'Great Britain v. British influence during the Reżā Shah period, 1921-41'. *Encyclopædia Iranica* 11.3 (2002): 231–4 (updated in 2012). Available online at https://www.iranicaonline.org/articles/great-britain-v (accessed on 18 March 2023).
Cronin, Stephanie. 'The Constitutional Revolution, Popular Politics, and State-Building in Iran'. In *Iran's Constitutional Revolution: Popular Politics, Cultural Transformations and Transnational Connections*, edited by H. E. Chehabi and V. Martin, 81–97. London: I.B. Tauris in association with the Iran Heritage Foundation, 2010.
Curzon, George Nathaniel. *Persia and the Persian Question*. 2 vols. London: Longmans, Green and Co., 1892.
Curzon, George Nathaniel. *Persian Autonomy*, London: John Hogg, 1911.
Dadachanji, Hormasji T. *First Steps in Persian*. Bombay, 1917.
Daniels, Peter T. 'Rawlinson, Henry ii. Contributions to Assyriology and Iranian Studies'. *Encyclopædia Iranica*, 2009 (updated in 2015). Available online at https://iranicaonline.org/articles/rawlinson-ii (accessed on 18 March 2023).

Daryaee, Touraj. 'Zoroastrianism under Islamic Rule'. In *The Wiley Blackwell Companion to Zoroastrianism*, edited by Michael Stausberg and Yuhan Sohrab-Dinshaw Vevaina, 103–18. Chichester: Wiley Blackwell, 2015.
Das, Santanu. *India, Empire, and First World War Culture: Writings, Images, and Songs*. Cambridge: Cambridge University Press, 2018.
Deboo, Malcolm M. 'The Amelioration of the Condition of Zoroastrians in Qajar Iran'. Unpublished paper.
Deboo, Malcolm M. 'Seth Maneckji Limji Hataria: the Martin Luther King of Zoroastrianism and the Struggle for Zoroastrian Civil Rights in Iran'. Available online at http://www.zoroastrian.org.uk/vohuman/Article/Seth%20Maneckji%20Limji %20Hataria.htm (accessed on 18 March 2023).
Destrée, Annette. 'Belgian-Iranian Relations'. *Encyclopædia Iranica* 4.2 (1989): 124–6. Available online at https://www.iranicaonline.org/articles/belgian-iranian-relations (accessed on 18 March 2023).
Dowlatabadi, Yahya. *Tarikh-e Moʿaser-e, ya Hayat-e Yahya*. Vol. 2. Tehran, 1331 (1952/3).
Duchesne-Guillemin, Jacques. 'Anquetil-Duperron'. *Encyclopædia Iranica* 2.1 (1985): 100–1 (updated in 2011). Available online at https://iranicaonline.org/articles/anquetil -duperron-abraham (accessed on 18 March 2023).
Durand, Ella R. *An Autumn Tour in Western Persia*. Westminster, London: A. Constable and Co., 1902.
Eastwick, Edward B. *Journal of a Diplomate's Three Years' Residence in Persia*. 2 vols. London: Smith, Elder and Co., 1864.
Edwardes, S. M. *Memoir of Sir Dinshaw Manockjee Petit, First Baronet (1823-1901)*. Oxford: Oxford University Press, 1923.
Egorova, Yulia. *Jews and Muslims in South Asia: Reflections on Difference, Religion, and Race*. New York: Oxford University Press, 2018.
Enayat, Hadi. *Law, State, and Society in Modern Iran: Constitutionalism, Autocracy, and Legal Reform, 1906-1941*. New York: Palgrave Macmillan, 2013.
Encyclopædia Iranica, based on an article submitted by Ali Modarres. 'Taft'. *Encyclopædia Iranica*, 2011. Available online at https://www.iranicaonline.org/articles/taft (accessed on 18 March 2023).
Ettehadieh, Mansoureh. 'Concessions ii. In the Qajar Period'. *Encyclopædia Iranica* 6.2 (1992): 119–22 (updated in 2011). Available online at https://www.iranicaonline.org/ articles/concessions#pt2 (accessed on 18 March 2023).
Ettehadieh, Mansoureh. 'Constitutional Revolution iv. The Aftermath'. *Encyclopædia Iranica* 6.2 (1992): 193–9 (updated in 2011). Available online at https://www .iranicaonline.org/articles/constitutional-revolution-iv (accessed on 18 March 2023).
Fahey, David M. and Padma Manian. 'Poverty and Purification: The Politics of Gandhi's Campaign for Prohibition'. *The Historian* 67, no. 3 (2005): 489–506.
Farmayan, H. F. 'Amīn-al-Dawla, Mīrzā ʿAlī Khan'. *Encyclopædia Iranica* 1.9 (1989): 943–5 (updated in 2011). Available online at http://www.iranicaonline.org/articles/amin-al -dawla-mirza-ali-khan (accessed on 18 March 2023).
Farridnejad, Shervin. 'The Royal Farmān and the Abolition of Zoroastrian Poll Tax in Qajar Iran'. *Himalayan and Central Asian Studies* 25, no. 1–3 (2021): 105–31.
Farzaneh, Mateo Mohammad. *The Iranian Constitutional Revolution and the Clerical Leadership of Khurasani*. Syracuse, NY: Syracuse University Press, 2015.
Fatemi, N. S. 'Anglo-Persian Agreement of 1919'. *Encyclopædia Iranica* 2.1 (1985): 59–61 (updated in 2011). Available online at http://www.iranicaonline.org/articles/anglo -persian-agreement-1919 (accessed on 18 March 2023).

Fathi, Asghar. 'Seyyed Jamal Vaez and the "Ajmal" Newspaper in Iran'. *Middle Eastern Studies* 33, no. 2 (1997): 216–25.
Fischer, Michael M. J. 'Zoroastrian Iran Between Myth and Praxis'. PhD Thesis, University of Chicago, 1973.
Fish, Laura. 'The Bombay Interlude: Parsi Transnational Aspirations in the First Persian Sound Film'. *Transnational Cinemas* 9, no. 2 (2018): 197–211.
Floor, Willem. 'Textile Industry in Iran'. *Encyclopædia Iranica*, 2005. Available online at https://www.iranicaonline.org/articles/textile-industry-in-iran (accessed on 18 March 2023).
Foltz, Richard. 'Zoroastrians in Iran: What Future in the Homeland?'. *The Middle East Journal* 65, no. 1 (2011): 73–84.
Foroutan, Kiyan. 'Yazd and Its Zoroastrians: A Review Paper of Ali Akbar Tashakori's *A Social History of the Zoroastrians of Yazd* (2019)'. *Iranian Studies* 56, no. 4 (2023): 811–36.
Francis-Dehqani, Gulnar E. 'Great Britain xv. British Schools in Persia'. *Encyclopædia Iranica* 11.3 (2002): 290–2 (updated in 2012). Available online at https://www.iranicaonline.org/articles/great-britain-xv (accessed on 18 March 2023).
Gaffary, F. 'Amīn-al-dawla, Farrok͟h Khan Ḡaffārī'. *Encyclopædia Iranica*, 2012. Available online at http://www.iranicaonline.org/articles/amin-al-dawla-farrok-khan-gaffari (accessed on 18 March 2023).
Geary, Grattan. *Through Asiatic Turkey: Narrative of a Journey from Bombay to the Bosphorus*. 2 vols. London: Sampson Low, 1878.
Gharipour, Mohammad (ed.). *The Bazaar in the Islamic City: Design, Culture, and History*. Cairo, London: American University in Cairo Press, 2012.
Gheissari, Ali. 'Despots of the World Unite! Satire in the Iranian Constitutional Press: The *Majalleh-ye Estebdad*, 1907-1908'. *Comparative Studies of South Asia, Africa and the Middle East* 25, no. 2 (2005): 360–76.
Ghereghlou, Kioumars. 'On the Margins of Minority Life: Zoroastrians and the State in Safavid Iran'. *Bulletin of the School of Oriental and African Studies* 80, no. 1 (2017): 45–71.
Giara, Marzban, Ramiyar P. Karanjia, and Michael Stausberg. 'Manekji on the Religious/ritual Practices of the Iranian Zoroastrians: An English Translation of a Passage from his Travel Report in Gujarati (1865)'. In *Zoroastrian Rituals in Context*, edited by Michael Stausberg, 481–515. Leiden and Boston: Brill, 2004.
Gilbar, Gad G. 'The Opening up of Qajar Iran: Some Economic and Social Aspects'. *Bulletin of the School of Oriental and African Studies* 49, no. 1 (1986): 76–89.
Gilbar, Gad G. 'Qajar Dynasty viii. "Big Merchants" in the Late Qajar Period'. *Encyclopædia Iranica*, 2015 (updated in 2019). Available online at http://www.iranicaonline.org/articles/qajar-big-merchants (accessed on 18 March 2023).
Gleave, Robert (ed.). *Religion and Society in Qajar Iran*. Abingdon: Routledge Curzon, 2005.
Godrej, Pheroza J. and Firoza Punthakey Mistree (eds). *A Zoroastrian Tapestry: Art, Religion and Culture*. Ahmedabad: Mapin Publishing, 2002.
Goldstein-Sabbah, S. R. and H. L. Murre-van den Berg (eds). *Modernity, Minority, and the Public Sphere: Jews and Christians in the Middle East*. Leiden: Brill, 2016.
Gordon, Thomas Edward. *Persia Revisited, 1895, With Remarks on M.I.M. Mozuffer-Ed-Din Shah, and the Present Situation, 1896*. London and New York: Edward Arnold, 1896.
Greaves, Rose L. 'Sīstān in British Indian Frontier Policy'. *Bulletin of the School of Oriental and African Studies* 49, no. 1 (1986): 90–102.

Green, Nile. *Bombay Islam: The Religious Economy of the West Indian Ocean, 1840-1915*. New York: Cambridge University Press, 2011.

Grigor, Talinn. 'Recultivating "Good Taste": The Early Pahlavi Modernists and Their Society for National Heritage'. *Iranian Studies* 37, no. 1 (2004), 17–45.

Grigor, Talinn. 'Parsi Patronage of the *Urheimat*'. *Getty Research Journal*, no. 2 (2010): 53–68.

Grigor, Talinn. *Identity Politics in Irano-Indian Modern Architecture*. Mumbai: K. R. Cama Oriental Institute, 2013.

Grigor, Talinn. 'Freemasonry and the Architecture of the Persian Revival, 1843–1933'. In *Freemasonry and the Visual Arts from the Eighteenth Century Forward: Historical and Global Perspectives*, edited by Reva Wolf and Alisa Luxenberg, 159–79. London: Bloomsbury, 2019.

Grobien, Philip Henning. 'The Origins and Intentions of the Anglo-Persian Agreement 1919: A Reassessment'. *Iran: journal of the British Institute of Persian Studies* ahead-of-print, no. ahead-of-print (2022): 1–16.

Gurney, John and Negin Nabavi. 'Dār al-Fonūn'. *Encyclopædia Iranica* 6.6 (1993): 662–8 (updated in 2011). Available online at https://www.iranicaonline.org/articles/dar-al-fonun-lit (accessed on 18 March 2023).

Gustafson, James M. 'Opium, Carpets and Constitutionalists: A Social History of the Elite Households of Kirman, 1859-1914'. PhD Thesis, University of Washington, Washington, 2010.

Gustafson, James M. 'Qajar Ambitions in the Great Game: Notes on the Embassy of 'Abbas Qoli Khan to the Amir of Bokhara, 1844'. *Iranian Studies* 46, no. 4 (2013): 535–52.

Hacısalihoğlu, Mehmet. 'Inclusion and Exclusion: Conscription in the Ottoman Empire'. *Journal of Modern European History* 5, no. 2 (2007): 264–86.

Hairi, Abdul-Hadi. 'European and Asian Influences on the Persian Revolution of 1906'. *Asian Affairs* 6, no. 2 (1975): 155–64.

Hairi, Abdul-Hadi. 'Shaykh Fażl Allāh Nūrī's Refutation of the Idea of Constitutionalism'. *Middle Eastern Studies* 13, no. 3 (1977): 327–39.

Hairi, Abdul-Hadi. *Shīʿism and Constitutionalism in Iran: A Study of the Role Played by the Persian Residents of Iraq in Iranian Politics*. Leiden: E. J. Brill, 1977.

Haji Akbari, Mozhgan. 'Naqsh-e Zartoshtiyan dar Eqtesad-e Dowreh-ye Qajari-ye ba Ta'kid bar Tojaratkhaneha-ye Zartoshti'. *Tarikh-e Now* 11 (Tabestan 1394/2015): 3–28.

Hakimian, Hassan. 'Economy viii. In the Qajar Period'. *Encyclopædia Iranica* 8.2 (1997): 138–43 (updated in 2011). Available online at https://www.iranicaonline.org/articles/economy-viii-in-the-qajar-period (accessed on 18 March 2023).

Hansen, Kathryn. 'Languages on Stage: Linguistic Pluralism and Community Formation in the Nineteenth-Century Parsi Theatre'. *Modern Asian Studies* 37, no. 2 (2003): 381–405.

Hanson, J. W. (ed.). *The World's Congress of Religions*. Chicago: Monarch Book Co., 1894.

Hasheminiasari, Hossein. 'The Newspaper and the Pulpit: Media, Religious Anxieties, and the Revolutionary Crowd Prior to Iran's Constitutional Revolution of 1905-1911'. MA Thesis, University of Colorado, Boulder, 2018.

Hataria, Manekji Limji. 'A Millennium of Misery: Travels in Iran: 2'. *Parsiana* 13, no. 3 (1990): 34–5. Abridged and edited by *Parsiana* from the English translation by Jamshed M. Bilmoria of M. L. Hataria, *Rishale Ej Har Shiyaate Iran* (1865).

Hataria, Manekji Limji. 'Rites of Passage: Travels in Iran: 3'. *Parsiana* 13, no. 4 (1990): 39–42. Abridged and edited by *Parsiana* from the English translation by Jamshed M. Bilmoria of M. L. Hataria, *Rishale Ej Har Shiyaate Iran* (1865).

Hataria, Manekji Limji. 'Support from the *Sethias*: Travels in Iran: 5'. *Parsiana* 13, no. 6 (1990): 29–32. Abridged and edited by *Parsiana* from the English translation by Jamshed M. Bilmoria of M. L. Hataria, *Rishale Ej Har Shiyaate Iran* (1865).

Hataria, Manekji Limji. 'The Land that Time Forgot: Travels in Iran: 1'. *Parsiana* 13, no. 2 (1990): 60–4. Abridged and edited by *Parsiana* from the English translation by Jamshed M. Bilmoria of M. L. Hataria, *Rishale Ej Har Shiyaate Iran* (1865).

Hataria, Manekji Limji. 'When the Parsis Intervened: Travels in Iran: 4'. *Parsiana* 13, no. 5 (1990): 25–6. Abridged and edited by *Parsiana* from the English translation by Jamshed M. Bilmoria of M. L. Hataria, *Rishale Ej Har Shiyaate Iran* (1865).

Hataria, Manekji Limji. 'Education for Amelioration: Travels in Iran: 6'. *Parsiana* 13, no. 7 (1991): 14–18. Abridged and edited by *Parsiana* from the English translation by Jamshed M. Bilmoria of M. L. Hataria, *Rishale Ej Har Shiyaate Iran* (1865).

Heehs, Peter. *India's Freedom Struggle 1857-1947: A Short History*. Delhi: Oxford University Press, 1991.

Hekmat, Ali Ashgar. *Parsis of Iran, Their Past and Present*. Bombay: Iran League, 1956.

Hinnells, John R. 'Social Change and Religious Transformation among Bombay Parsis in the Early 20th Century'. In *Traditions in Contact and Change*, edited by Peter Slater and Donald Wiebe, 105–25. Waterloo, Ontario, Canada: Wilfrid Laurier University Press, 1983.

Hinnells, John R. 'Behramshah Naoroji Shroff'. *Encyclopædia Iranica* 4.1 (1989): 109–10. Available online at https://www.iranicaonline.org/articles/behramshah-naoroji-shroff-1858-1927 (accessed on 18 March 2023).

Hinnells, John R. 'Bombay Parsi Panchayat'. *Encyclopædia Iranica* 4.4 (1989): 349–50. Available online at https://www.iranicaonline.org/articles/bombay-parsi-panchayat-the-largest-zoroastrian-institution-in-modern-history (accessed on 18 March 2023).

Hinnells, John R. 'Bombay, Persian Communities of. i. The Zoroastrian Community'. *Encyclopædia Iranica* 4.4 (1989): 339ff. Available online at https://www.iranicaonline.org/articles/bombay-persian-communities-of#pt1 (accessed on 18 March 2023).

Hinnells, John R. *Zoroastrians in Britain: The Ratanbai Katrak Lectures, University of Oxford, 1985*. Clarendon Press: Oxford, 1996.

Hinnells, John R. *Zoroastrian and Parsi Studies: Selected Works of John R. Hinnells*. Aldershot: Ashgate, 2000.

Hinnells, John R. 'Bombay Parsis and the Diaspora in the 18th and 19th Centuries' in Zoroastrian Tapestry'. In *A Zoroastrian Tapestry: Art, Religion and Culture*, edited by Pheroza J. Godrej and Firoza Punthakey Mistree, 458–77. Ahmedabad: Mapin Publishing, 2002.

Hinnells, John R. 'Parsi Communities i. Early History'. *Encyclopædia Iranica*, 2008. Available online at https://iranicaonline.org/articles/parsi-communities-i-early-history (accessed on 18 March 2023).

Hinnells, John R., Mary Boyce, and Shahrokh Shahrokh. 'Charitable Foundations ii. Among Zoroastrians in Islamic times'. *Encyclopædia Iranica* 5.4 (1991): 380–5 (updated in 2011). Available online at https://www.iranicaonline.org/articles/charitable-foundations-mpers#pt2 (accessed on 18 March 2023).

Hinnells, John R. and Alan Williams (eds). *Parsis in India and the Diaspora*. London: Routledge, 2007.

Hintze, Almut and Alan Williams (eds). *Holy Wealth: Accounting for this World and the Next in Religious Belief and Practice (Festschrift for John R. Hinnells)*. Wiesbaden: Harrassowitz Verlag, 2017.

Hopkins, B. D. *The Making of Modern Afghanistan*. New York: Palgrave Macmillan, 2008.

Hurewitz, J. C. *Diplomacy in the Near and Middle East: A Documentary Record*. 2 vols. Princeton: Van Nostrand, 1956.
Issawi, Charles. *The Economic History of Iran, 1800-1914*. Chicago: University of Chicago Press, 1971.
Jackson, A. V. Williams. *Persia Past and Present: A Book of Travel and Research*. New York and London: MacMillan, 1906.
JamaspAsa, Kaikhusroo M. 'Coyajee, Jehangir Cooverji'. *Encyclopædia Iranica* 6.4 (1993): 390 (updated in 2011). Available online at http://www.iranicaonline.org/articles/coyajee-sir-jehangir-cooverji- (accessed on 18 March 2023).
JamaspAsa, Kaikhusroo M. 'Iran League'. *Encyclopædia Iranica* 13.5 (2006): 486–7 (updated in 2012). Available online at https://www.iranicaonline.org/articles/iran-league (accessed on 18 March 2023).
Jhabvala, S. H. *A Brief History of Persia: Containing a Short Account of the Peshdadians, the Kayanians and the Achaemenians*. Bombay: N. Cursetjee at Union Press, 1920.
Kamaly, Hossein. 'Ḥāji Vāšangton'. *Encyclopædia Iranica* 11.5 (2002): 553–4 (updated in 2012). Available online at https://www.iranicaonline.org/articles/haji-vasangton (accessed on 18 March 2023).
Karaka, Dosabhai Framji. *The Parsees: Their History, Manners, Customs, and Religion*. London: Smith, Elder and Co.; Bombay: Smith, Taylor and Co., 1858.
Karaka, Dosabhai Framji. *History of the Parsis: Including Their Manners, Customs, Religion and Present Position*. 2 vols. London: MacMillan, 1884.
Kasheff, M. 'Anjoman-e Zartoštīān'. *Encyclopædia Iranica* 2.1 (1985): 90–5 (updated in 2011). Available online at http://www.iranicaonline.org/articles/anjoman-e-zartostian (accessed on 18 March 2023).
Kasravi, Ahmad. *Tarikh-e Mashruteh-ye Iran*. Vol. 1. Translated by Evan Siegel. Costa Mesa, CA: Mazda Publishers, 2006.
Katouzian, Homa. 'The Revolution for Law: A Chronographic Analysis of the Constitutional Revolution of Iran'. *Middle Eastern Studies* 47, no. 5 (2011): 757–77.
Kazemi, F. 'Anglo-Persian Oil Company'. *Encyclopædia Iranica* 2.1 (1985), 61–5 (updated in 2011). Available online at http://www.iranicaonline.org/articles/anglo-persian-oil-company (accessed on 18 May 2023).
Kazemi, Ranin. 'Kāšef-al-Salṭana'. *Encyclopædia Iranica* 15.6 (2011): 653–6 (updated in 2012). Available online at https://www.iranicaonline.org/articles/kasef_al_saltana (accessed on 18 March 2023).
Kazemzadeh, Firuz. *Russia and Britain in Persia, 1864-1914: A Study in Imperialism*. New Haven: Yale University Press, 1968.
Kazemzadeh, Firuz. 'Anglo-Russian Convention of 1907'. *Encyclopædia Iranica* 2.1 (1985): 68–70 (updated in 2011). Available online at http://www.iranicaonline.org/articles/anglo-russian-convention-of-1907-an-agreement-relating-to-persia-afghanistan-and-tibet (accessed on 18 March 2023).
Keddie, Nikki R. *Religion and Rebellion in Iran: The Iranian Tobacco Protest of 1891-1982*. London: Cass, 1966.
Keddie, Nikki R. 'Afġānī, Jamāl-al-Dīn'. *Encyclopædia Iranica* 1.5 (1983): 481–6 (updated in 2011). Available online at http://www.iranicaonline.org/articles/afgani-jamal-al-din (accessed on 18 March 2023).
Keddie, Nikki R. and Rudi Matthee (eds). *Iran and the Surrounding World: Interactions in Culture and Cultural Politics*. Seattle: University of Washington Press. 2002.
Kershasp, P. *Studies in Ancient Persian History*. London: Kegan Paul, Trench, Trübner and Co., 1905.

Khandalwala, Jamshedji Dorabji. *An Introduction to the Shah-Nameh of Firdousi from the French of Jules Mohl*. Veerkshetra Mudralay, 1898.

Kia, Mehrdad. 'Constitutionalism, Economic Modernization and Islam in the Writings of Mirza Yusef Khan Mostashar od-Dowle'. *Middle Eastern Studies* 30, no. 4 (1994): 751–77.

Kia, Mehrdad. 'Persian Nationalism and the Campaign for Language Purification'. *Middle Eastern Studies* 34, no. 2 (1998): 9–36.

Kidambi, Prashant, Manjiri Kamat, and Rachel Dwyer (eds). *Bombay Before Mumbai: Essays in Honour of Jim Masselos*. New York: Oxford University Press, 2019.

Kondo, Nobuaki. 'Migration and Multiethnic Coexistence in Qajar Tehran'. In *Human Mobility and Multiethnic Coexistence in Middle Eastern Urban Societies 1: Tehran, Aleppo, Istanbul, and Beirut*, edited by Hidemitsu Kuroki, 5–26. Tokyo: Research Institute for Languages and Cultures of Asia and Africa, 2014.

Kondo, Nobuaki. 'Non-Muslims at the Shari'a Court in Qajar Tehran'. In *Human Mobility and Multiethnic Coexistence in Middle Eastern Urban Societies 2: Tehran, Cairo, Istanbul, Aleppo, and Beirut*, edited by Hidemitsu Kuroki, 7–21. Tokyo: Research Institute for Languages and Cultures of Asia and Africa, 2018.

Kotwal, Firoze M., Jamsheed K. Choksy, Christopher J. Brunner, and Mahnaz Moazami. 'Hataria, Manekji Limji'. *Encyclopædia Iranica*, 2016. Available online at http://www.iranicaonline.org/articles/hataria-manekji-limji (accessed on 18 March 2023).

Kreyenbroek, Philip G. 'The Role of the Shāhnāme in the Culture of the Parsi Community'. Unpublished paper. Available online at http://misc.ilexfoundation.org/pdf/ferdowsi_2/kreyenbroek300.pdf (accessed on 19 June 2016).

Kulke, Eckehard. *The Parsees in India: A Minority as Agent of Social Change*. Munich: Welforum-Verlag, 1974.

Kuroki, Hidemitsu (ed.). *Human Mobility and Multiethnic Coexistence in Middle Eastern Urban Societies 1: Tehran, Aleppo, Istanbul, and Beirut*. Tokyo: Research Institute for Languages and Cultures of Asia and Africa, 2014.

Kuroki, Hidemitsu (ed.) *Human Mobility and Multiethnic Coexistence in Middle Eastern Urban Societies 2: Tehran, Cairo, Istanbul, Aleppo, and Beirut*. Tokyo: Research Institute for Languages and Cultures of Asia and Africa, 2018.

Lal, Ananda (ed.). *The Oxford Companion to Indian Theatre*. New Delhi: Oxford University Press, 2004.

Lambton, Ann K. S. *Landlord and Peasant in Persia: A Study of Land Tenure and Land Revenue Administration*. Oxford: Oxford University Press, 1953.

Lambton, Ann K. S. *Qajar Persia: Eleven Studies*. London: I.B. Tauris, 1987.

Landau, Jacob M. 'Arminius Vambéry: Traveller, Scholar, Politician'. *Middle Eastern Studies* 50, no. 6 (2014): 857–69.

Landor, Arnold Henry Savage. *Across Coveted Lands or a Journey from Flushing (Holland) to Calcutta, overland*. 2 vols. London: MacMillan, 1902.

Langstaff, Hilary A. 'The Impact of Western Education and Political Changes upon the Religious Teachings of Indian Parsis in the Twentieth Century'. PhD Thesis, University of Manchester, Manchester, 1983.

Laqueur, Walter. *The History of Zionism*. London: I.B. Tauris, 2003.

Laursen, Ole Birk. '"I Have Only One Country, It Is the World": Madame Cama, Anticolonialism, and Indian-Russian Revolutionary Networks in Paris, 1907–17'. *History Workshop Journal* 90 (2021): 96–114.

Lenczowski, George. 'Foreign Powers' Intervention in Iran during World War I'. In *Qajar Iran: Political, Social and Cultural Change*, edited by Edmund Bosworth and Carole Hillenbrand, 76–92. Edinburgh: Edinburgh University Press, 1983.

Loloi, Parvin. 'Eastwick, Edward Backhouse'. *Encyclopædia Iranica*, 2009. Available online at https://www.iranicaonline.org/articles/eastwick-edward-backhouse- (accessed on 18 March 2023).

Longva, Anh Nga. 'Introduction: Domination, Self-Empowerment, Accommodation'. In *Religious Minorities in the Middle East: Domination, Self-Empowerment, Accommodation*, edited by Anh Nga Longva and Anne Sofie Roald, 1–24. Leiden and Boston: Brill, 2012.

Longva, Anh Nga and Anne Sofie Roald (eds). *Religious Minorities in the Middle East: Domination, Self-Empowerment, Accommodation*. Leiden and Boston: Brill, 2012.

Luhrmann, Tanya M. *The Good Parsi: The Fate of a Colonial Elite in a Postcolonial Society*. Cambridge, MA: Harvard University Press, 1996.

Luhrmann, Tanya M. 'Evil in the Sands of Time: Theology and Identity Politics among the Zoroastrian Parsis'. *The Journal of Asiatic Studies* 61, no. 3 (2002): 861–89.

Lyman Stebbins, H. 'British Imperialism, Regionalism, and Nationalism in Iran, 1890-1919'. In *Iran Facing Others: Identity Boundaries in a Historical Perspective*, edited by Abbas Amanat and Farzin Vejdani, 153–69. New York: Palgrave Macmillan, 2012.

Lyman Stebbins, H. *British Imperialism in Qajar Iran: Consuls, Agents and Influence in the Middle East*. London and New York: I.B. Tauris, 2016.

MacEoin, D. M. 'Azali Babism'. *Encyclopaedia Iranica* 3.2 (1987): 179–81 (updated in 2011). Available online at http://www.iranicaonline.org/articles/azali-babism (accessed on 18 March 2023).

MacEoin, D. M. 'Babism'. *Encyclopædia Iranica* 3.3 (1988): 309–17 (updated in 2011). Available online at http://www.iranicaonline.org/articles/babism-index (accessed on 18 March 2023).

MacEoin, D. M. 'Bahaism vii. Bahai Persecutions'. *Encyclopædia Iranica* 3.5 (1988): 461–4 (updated in 2011). Available online at https://www.iranicaonline.org/articles/bahaism-vii (accessed on 18 March 2023).

Macuch, Maria. 'Charitable Foundations i. In the Sasanian Period'. *Encyclopædia Iranica* 5.4 (1991): 380–5 (updated in 2011). Available online at https://www.iranicaonline.org/articles/charitable-foundations-mpers#pt1 (accessed on 18 March 2023).

Majd, Mohammad Gholi. *The Great Famine and Genocide in Iran, 1917-1919*. 2nd edn. Lanham: University Press of America, 2013.

Majd, Mohammad Gholi. *A Victorian Holocaust: Iran in the Great Famine of 1869–1873*. Lanham, Boulder, New York, Toronto, Plymouth: Hamilton Books, 2017.

Malcolm, Napier. *Five Years in a Persian Town*. London: John Murray, 1908.

Malekzadeh, Mehdi. *Tarikh-e Enqelab-e Mashrutiyat-e Iran*. Vols 2 and 3. Tehran: Ketabkhaneh Soqrat, 1949.

Mama, Arnavaz S. 'Manekji Limji Hataria: Redeeming a Community'. *Parsiana* 12, no. 11 (1990): 26–30.

Marashi, Afshin. *Nationalizing Iran: Culture, Power, and the State, 1870-1940*. Seattle and London: University of Washington Press, 2008.

Marashi, Afshin. 'Patron and Patriot: Dinshah J. Irani and the Revival of Indo-Iranian Culture'. *Iranian Studies* 46, no. 2 (2013): 185–206.

Marashi, Afshin. 'Irani, Dinshah Jijibhoy'. *Encyclopædia Iranica*, 2015. Available online at http://www.iranicaonline.org/articles/irani-dinshah (accessed on 18 March 2023).

Marashi, Afshin. *Exile and the Nation: The Parsi Community of India and the Making of Modern Iran*. Austin, TX: University of Texas Press, 2020.

Marashi, Afshin. '"Rich Fields in Persia": Parsi Capital and the Origins of Economic Development in Pahlavi Iran, 1925–1941'. *Iranian Studies* 56, no. 1 (2023): 61–83.

Marashi, Afshin and Dinyar Patel. 'As Seen from Bombay: An Iranian Zoroastrian Photo Album from the 1930s'. *Iranian Studies* 56, no. 1 (2023): 101–13.

Marriott, John. *The Other Empire: Metropolis, India and Progress in the Colonial Imagination*. Manchester and New York: Manchester University Press, 2003.

Martin, Vanessa. *Islam and Modernism: The Iranian Revolution of 1906*. London: I.B. Tauris, 1989.

Martin, Vanessa. 'Constitutional Revolution ii. Events'. *Encyclopædia Iranica* 6.2 (1992): 176–87 (last updated in 2011). Available online at https://iranicaonline.org/articles/constitutional-revolution-ii (accessed on 18 March 2023).

Martin, Vanessa. *The Qajar Pact: Bargaining, Protest and the State in Nineteenth-Century Persia*. London: I.B. Tauris, 2005.

Martin, Vanessa. 'Aqa Najafi, Haj Aqa Nurullah, and the Emergence of Islamism in Isfahan 1889-1908'. *Iranian Studies* 41, no. 2 (2008): 155–72.

Martin, Vanessa. 'Nuri, Fażl-Allāh'. *Encyclopædia Iranica*, 2014. Available online at http://www.iranicaonline.org/articles/nuri-fazl-allah (accessed on 18 March 2023).

Martin, Vanessa. 'British Policy towards Iran 1809-1914: The Question of Cost'. *British Journal of Middle Eastern Studies* 48, no. 5 (2021): 1000–15.

Masani, R. P. *Dadabhai Naoroji: 'The Grand Old Man of India'*. London: George Allen & Unwin, 1939.

Massie, Eric and Janet Afary. 'Iran's 1907 Constitution and its Sources: A Critical Comparison'. *British Journal of Middle Eastern Studies* 46, no. 3 (2019): 464–80.

Massot, Anaïs. 'Ottoman Damascus during the Tanzimat: The New Visibility of Religious Distinctions'. In *Modernity, Minority, and the Public Sphere: Jews and Christians in the Middle East*, edited by S. R. Goldstein-Sabbah and H. L. Murre-van den Berg, 155–84. Leiden: Brill, 2016.

Matthee, Rudolph P. 'Facing a Rude and Barbarous Neighbor: Iranian Perceptions of Russia and the Russians from the Safavids to the Qajars'. In *Iran Facing Others: Identity Boundaries in a Historical Perspective*, edited by Abbas Amanat and Farzin Vejdani, 101–25. New York: Palgrave Macmillan, 2012.

Méchin, Ferdinand. *Lettres d'un voyageur en Perse: Djoulfa, Yesd, les Guèbres*. Bourges: A. Jollet, 1867.

Mehr, Farhang. *Sahm-e Zartoshtiyan dar Enqelab-e Mashrutiyat-e Iran*. Tehran: Hukht, 1348/1969.

Mehr, Farhang. 'Zoroastrians in Twentieth Century Iran'. In *A Zoroastrian Tapestry: Art, Religion and Culture*, edited by Pheroza J. Godrej and Firoza Punthakey Mistree, 278–99. Ahmedabad: Mapin Publishing, 2002.

Mehrfar, Khosro. 'Keikhosrow Shahrokh'. Available online at http://www.zoroastrian.org.uk/vohuman/Article/Keikhosrow%20Shahrokh.htm (accessed on 25 May 2023).

Mehrfar, Khosro. 'Sohrab Rostam Kaikhosow Viraf Kianian'. Available online at http://www.zoroastrian.org.uk/vohuman/Article/Sohrab%20Rostam%20Kaikhosow%20Viraf%20Kianian.htm (accessed on 25 May 2023).

Mehrfar, Khosro. 'Jamshid Bahman Jamshidian'. *Chehrehnama* 167 (2013): 7–11.

Mehri, Rastin. 'A Zoroastrian Historical Imaginary in India'. In *Time, History and the Religious Imaginary in South Asia*, edited by Anne Murphy, 70–83. Routledge: Abingdon, 2011.

Mellor, David Charles. 'The Parsis and the Press: An In-depth Study of the "Hindi Punch", 1906-1931'. MPhil Thesis, Victoria University of Manchester, Manchester, 1985.

Menant, Delphine (trans. Anthony D. Mango). *The Parsis*. Vol. 3. Bombay: Danai, 1996.

Metcalf, Barbara D. and Thomas R. Metcalf. *A Concise History of Modern India*. Cambridge: Cambridge University Press, 2006.

Micallef, Roberta and Sunil Sharma (eds). *On the Wonders of Land and Sea: Persianate Travel Writing*. Cambridge, MA: Harvard University Press, 2013.

Miescher, Stephan F., Michele Mitchell, and Naoko Shibusawa (eds). *Gender, Imperialism and Global Exchanges*. United Kingdom: John Wiley & Sons, Incorporated, 2015.

Milani, Abbas, and *Encyclopædia Iranica*. 'Ḥakimi, Ebrāhim'. *Encyclopædia Iranica* 11.6 (2003): 575–80 (updated in 2012). Available online at https://www.iranicaonline.org/articles/hakimi-ebrahim (accessed on 18 March 2023).

Mina, Parviz. 'Oil Agreements in Iran'. *Encyclopædia Iranica*, 2004. Available online at https://iranicaonline.org/articles/oil-agreements-in-iran (accessed on 18 March 2023).

Modarres, Ali. *Modernizing Yazd: Selective Historical Memory and the Fate of Vernacular Architecture*. Costa Mesa, California: Mazda Publishers, 2006.

Modarres, Ali. 'Form and Function: On Politics and the Morphology of the Bazaar in Yazd'. In *The Bazaar in the Islamic City: Design, Culture, and History*, edited by Mohammad Gharipour, 251–74. Cairo: London: American University in Cairo Press, 2012.

Modi, Jivanji Jamshedji. 'Belief and Ceremonies of the Followers of Zoroaster'. In *The World's Congress of Religions*, edited by J. W. Hanson, 452–65. Chicago: Monarch Book Co., 1894.

Modi, Jivanji Jamshedji. 'The Afghanistan of the Amir and the Ancient Mazdayaçnâns'. *East & West* 6, no. 1 (January-June 1907): 113–22.

Mody, Nawaz B. 'Madame Bhikhaiji Rustam Cama'. In *The Parsis in Western India: 1818-1920*, edited by Nawaz B. Mody, 46–106. Bombay: Allied Publishers Limited, 1998.

Mody, Nawaz B. (ed.). *The Parsis in Western India: 1818-1920*. Bombay: Allied Publishers Limited, 1998.

Mohajer, Nasser and Kaveh Yazdani. 'From Yazd to Bombay–Ardeshir Mehrabān 'Irani' and the Rise of Persia's Nineteenth-Century Zoroastrian Merchants'. *Journal of the Royal Asiatic Society* 34, no. 1 (2024): 1–25.

Mohammadzadeh, Hamid and Hamid Arasli (eds). *Mirza Fath 'ali Akhundov: Alefba-ye Jadid va Maktubat*. Baku: Izdatel'stvo Akademii Nauk Azerbaidzhanskoi SSR, 1963.

Mojtabāʾī, Fatḥ-Allāh. 'Dasātīr'. *Encyclopædia Iranica* 7.1 (1994): 84 (updated in 2011). Available online at https://iranicaonline.org/articles/dasatir (accessed on 18 March 2023).

Momen, M. 'Abu'l-Fażl Golpāyegānī'. *Encyclopædia Iranica* 1.3, 1983: 289–90 (updated in 2011). Available online at http://www.iranicaonline.org/articles/abul-fazl-or-abul-fazael-golpayegani-mirza-mohammad-prominent-bahai-scholar-and-apologist (accessed on 18 March 2023).

Momen, M. and B. T. Lawson. 'Lawḥ'. *Encyclopædia Iranica*, 2005. Available online at https://iranicaonline.org/articles/lawh (accessed on 18 March 2023).

Monier-Williams, Monier. 'The Pārsīs'. *The Nineteenth Century* 49 (March 1881): 500–16.

Moreen, Vera B. 'Jezya'. *Encyclopædia Iranica* 14.6 (2008): 643–5 (updated in 2012). Available online at http://www.iranicaonline.org/articles/jezya (accessed on 18 March 2023).

Mukherjee, Sumita and Rehana Ahmed (eds). *South Asian Resistances in Britain, 1858-1947*. London: Bloomsbury, 2012.

Murphy, Anne, (ed.). *Time, History and the Religious Imaginary in South Asia*. Abingdon: Routledge, 2011.

Murzban, M. M. *The Parsis in India: Being an Enlarged and Copiously Annotated, Up to Date English Edition of Mlle. Delphine Menant's 'Les Parsis'*. 2 vols. Bombay: Published by M. M. Murzban, 1917.

Nabavi, Negin. *Modern Iran: A History in Documents*. Princeton, NJ: Markus Wiener, 2016.

Nariman, G. K. (ed.). *Persia and the Parsis: Part I*. Bombay: Iran League, 1925.

Nariman, G. K. *The Ahad Nameh*. Bombay: Iran League, 1925.

Nariman, G. K. *Writings of G. K. Nariman, compiled by R. B. Paymaster*. Bombay: R. B. Paymaster, 1935.

Nashat, Guity. *The Origins of Modern Reform in Iran*. Urbana and London: University of Illinois Press, 1981.

Natesan, G. A. (ed.). *Congress Presidential Addresses: From the Foundation to the Silver Jubilee*. Madras: G. A. Natesan, 1935.

Nicholson, Rashna Darius. 'Corporeality, Aryanism, Race: The Theatre and Social Reform of the Parsis of Western India'. *South Asia Journal of South Asian Studies* 38, no. 4 (2015): 613–38.

Nicholson, Rashna Darius. 'The Picture, the Parable, the Performance and the Sword: Secularism's Demographic Imperatives'. *Ethnic and Racial Studies* 41, no. 12 (2018): 2197–214.

Nicholson, Rashna Darius. '"A Christy Minstrel, a Harlequin, or an Ancient Persian"?: Opera, Hindustani Classical Music, and the Origins of the Popular South Asian "Musical"'. *Theatre Survey* 61, no. 3 (2020): 331–50.

Nordbruch, Götz and Umar Ryad (eds). *Transnational Islam in Interwar Europe: Muslim Activists and Thinkers*. New York: Palgrave Macmillan US, 2014.

Nouraei, Morteza. 'Kārgozār'. *Encyclopædia Iranica* 15.5 (2010): 558–60 (updated in 2012). Available online at https://www.iranicaonline.org/articles/kargozar-19th-century-term (accessed on 18 March 2023).

Nouraie, Fereshte M. 'The Constitutional Ideas of a Shi'ite Mujtahid: Muhammad Husayn Na'ini'. *Iranian Studies* 8, no. 4 (1975): 234–47.

Oberling, Pierre. 'The Role of Religious Minorities in the Persian Revolution, 1906-1912'. *Journal of Asian History* 12, no. 1 (1978): 1–25.

Okazaki, Shoko. 'The Great Persian Famine of 1870-71'. *Bulletin of the School of Oriental and African Studies* 49, no.1 (1986): 183–92.

Oshidari, Jahangir. *Tarikh-e Pahlavi va Zartoshtiyan*. Tehran: Hukht, 2535/1976.

Palsetia, Jesse S. *The Parsis of India: Preservation of Identity in Bombay City*. Leiden: Brill, 2001.

Palsetia, Jesse S. 'Parsi and Hindu Traditional and Nontraditional Responses to Christian Conversion in Bombay, 1839–45'. *Journal of the American Academy of Religion* 74, no. 3 (2006): 615–45.

Palsetia, Jesse S. 'Parsi Communities ii. In Calcutta'. *Encyclopædia Iranica*, 2006. Available online at https://iranicaonline.org/articles/parsi-communities-ii-in-calcutta (accessed on 18 March 2023).

Palsetia, Jesse S. 'Parsi Charity: A Historical Perspective on Religion, Community, and Donor-Patron Relations among the Parsis of India'. In *Holy Wealth: Accounting for this World and the Next in Religious Belief and Practice. Festschrift for John R. Hinnells*, edited by Almut Hintze and Alan Williams, 175–92. Wiesbaden: Harrassowitz Verlag, 2017.

Parvin, Nassereddin. 'Ḥabl al-matin'. *Encyclopædia Iranica* 11.4 (2002): 431–4 (updated in 2012). Available online at https://www.iranicaonline.org/articles/habl-al-matin (accessed on 18 March 2023).

Parvin, Nassereddin. 'Rastkiz'. *Encyclopædia Iranica*, 2011. Available online at https://iranicaonline.org/articles/rastakhiz (accessed on 18 March 2023).

Patel, Dinyar. 'Gustaspshah Kaikhusroo Nariman: Improving Ties Between Zoroastrianism and Islam'. *Fezana* 4 (2009): 43–5.

Patel, Dinyar. 'Our Own Religion in Ancient Persia: Dadabhai Naoroji and Orientalist Scholarship on Zoroastrianism'. *Global Intellectual History* 2, no. 3 (2017): 311–28.

Patel, Dinyar. 'The Banaji and Mehta Families: Forging the Parsi Community in Calcutta'. In *Holy Wealth: Accounting for this World and the Next in Religious Belief and Practice. Festschrift for John R. Hinnells*, edited by Almut Hintze and Alan Williams, 211–30. Wiesbaden: Harrassowitz Verlag, 2017.

Patel, Dinyar. 'Beyond Hindu–Muslim Unity: Gandhi, the Parsis and the Prince of Wales Riots of 1921'. *The Indian Economic and Social History Review* 55, no. 2 (2018): 221–47.

Patel, Dinyar. *Naoroji: Pioneer of Indian Nationalism*. Cambridge, MA: Harvard University Press, 2020.

Patel, Dinyar. 'Caught Between Two Nationalisms: The Iran League of Bombay and the Political Anxieties of an Indian Minority'. *Modern Asian Studies* 55, no. 3 (2021): 764–800.

Patel, Dinyar. 'Power and Philanthropy: The Imperial Dimensions of Parsi Amelioration of the Iranian Zoroastrians'. *Iranian Studies* 56, no. 2 (2023): 205–29.

Patel, Simin. 'Cultural Intermediaries in a Colonial City: The Parsis of Bombay, c. 1860-1921'. DPhil Thesis, University of Oxford, Oxford, 2015.

Patel, Simin. 'The Great Persian Famine of 1871, Parsi Refugees and the Making of Irani Identity in Bombay'. In *Bombay Before Mumbai: Essays in Honour of Jim Masselos*, edited by Prashant Kidambi, Manjiri Kamat, and Rachel Dwyer, 57–76. New York: Oxford University Press, 2019.

Pavri, Jamshid. 'Arbab Rustam Bahman Guiv'. Available online at http://www.zoroastrian.org.uk/vohuman/Article/Rustam%20Guiv.htm (accessed on 18 March 2023).

Perry, John R. 'Zand Dynasty'. *Encyclopædia Iranica*, 2000 (updated in 2010). Available online at http://www.iranicaonline.org/articles/zand-dynasty (accessed on 18 March 2023).

Perry, John R. 'Karim Khan Zand'. *Encyclopædia Iranica* 15.6 (2011): 561–4 (updated in 2012). Available online at https://www.iranicaonline.org/articles/karim-khan-zand/ (accessed on 18 March 2023).

Perry, John R. (ed.). *Persian Literature from Outside Iran: The Indian Subcontinent, Anatolia, Central Asia, and in Judeo-Persian*. London: I.B. Tauris, 2018.

Pithawalla, M. B. *The Parsee Heritage*. Karachi: The Young Zoroastrian Circle, 1932.

de Planhol, Xavier. 'Famines'. *Encyclopædia Iranica* 9.2 (1999): 203–6 (updated in 2012). Available online at https://iranicaonline.org/articles/famines (accessed on 18 March 2023).

Ramanna, Mridula. 'Social Background of the Educated in Bombay City: 1824-58'. *Economic and Political Weekly* 24, no. 4 (1989): 203–11.

Ranganathan, Murali. 'Back to the Motherland? Parsi Gujarati Travelogues of Iran in the Qajar-Pahlavi Interregnum, 1921–1925'. *Iranian Studies* 56, no. 1 (2023): 37–59.

Reetz, Dietrich. *Hijrat: The Flight of the Faithful. A British File on the Exodus of Muslim Peasants from North India to Afghanistan in 1920*. Berlin: Verlag Das Arabische Buch, 1995.

Rekabtalaei, Golbarg. 'Cinematic Modernity: Cosmopolitan Imaginaries in Twentieth Century Iran'. PhD Thesis, University of Toronto, Toronto, 2015.

Ringer, Monica M. 'Reform Transplanted: Parsi Agents of Change amongst Zoroastrians in Nineteenth-Century Iran'. *Iranian Studies* 42, no. 4 (2009): 549–60.

Ringer, Monica M. *Pious Citizens: Reforming Zoroastrianism in India and Iran*. Syracuse, NY: Syracuse University Press, 2011.

Ringer, Monica M. 'Iranian Nationalism and Zoroastrian Identity: Between Cyrus and Zoroaster'. In *Iran Facing Others: Identity Boundaries in a Historical Perspective*, edited by Abbas Amanat and Farzin Vejdani, 267–78. New York: Palgrave Macmillan, 2012.

Rose, Jenny. *Zoroastrianism: An Introduction*. London and New York: I.B. Tauris, 2011.

Russell, James R. 'Cama, Kharshedji Rustamh'. *Encyclopædia Iranica* 4.7 (1990): 722. Available online at https://iranicaonline.org/articles/cama-kharshedji-rustamh-b (accessed on 18 March 2023).

Rustomji, Aban. 'Peshotanji Dossabhai Marker'. Available online at: http://www.zoroastrian.org.uk/vohuman/Article/Marker,Peshotanji%20Dossabhai.htm (accessed on 25 May 2023).

Safiri, Floreeda. 'South Persia Rifles'. *Encyclopædia Iranica*, 2008. Available online at: https://www.iranicaonline.org/articles/south-persia-rifles-militia (accessed on 18 March 2023).

Saʿīdī Sīrjānī, ʿAlī-Akbar. 'Clothing xi. In the Pahlavi and Post-Pahlavi Periods'. *Encyclopædia Iranica* 5.8 (1992): 808–11 (updated in 2012). Available online at http://www.iranicaonline.org/articles/clothing-xi (accessed on 18 March 2023).

Saʿīdī Sīrjānī, ʿAlī-Akbar. 'Constitutional Revolution vi. The Press'. *Encyclopædia Iranica* 6.2 (1992): 202–12 (updated in 2011). Available online at https://www.iranicaonline.org/articles/constitutional-revolution-vi (accessed on 18 March 2023).

Saklatvala, Phiroz D. *The Rich Fields in Persia*. Bombay: Iran League, 1933.

Sanasarian, Eliz. *Religious Minorities in Iran*. Cambridge: Cambridge University Press, 2000.

Sanjana, Darab Dastur Peshotan. *The Position of Zoroastrian Women in Remote Antiquity, as Illustrated in the Avesta, the Sacred Books of the Parsees*. Bombay: Education Society's Steam Press, 1892.

Sanjana, Jehangir Barjorji. *Ancient Persians and the Parsis: A Comprehensive History of the Parsis and their Religion from Primeval Times to the Present Age*. Bombay: Hosang T. Anklesaria at the Fort Printing Press, 1935.

Schmitt, Rüdiger. 'Westergaard, Niels Ludvig'. *Encyclopædia Iranica*, 2015. Available online at http://www.iranicaonline.org/articles/westergaard-niels-ludvig (accessed on 18 March 2023).

Seal, Anil. *The Emergence of Indian Nationalism: Competition and Collaboration in the Later Nineteenth Century*. Cambridge: Cambridge University Press, 1971.

Seoharvi, M. A. R. 'Proposed Reforms in Persia'. *East & West* 6, no. 1 (January-June 1907): 56–9.

Seyed-Gohrab, Ali-Asghar, and Sen McGlinn (eds). *The True Dream: Indictment of the Shiite clerics of Isfahan, an English Translation with Facing Persian Text*. London and New York: Routledge, 2017.

Seyf, Ahmad. 'Population and Agricultural Development in Iran, 1800-1906'. *Middle Eastern Studies* 45, no. 3 (2009): 447–60.

Shahmardan, Rashid. *Farzanegan-e Zartoshti*. Tehran: Sazman-e Javanan-e Zartoshti-ye Bamba'i, 1330/1961–2.
Shahnavaz, Shabaz. 'Afyūn'. *Encyclopædia Iranica* 1.6 (1984): 594–8 (updated in 2011). Available online at http://www.iranicaonline.org/articles/afyun-opium (accessed on 18 March 2023).
Shahnavaz, Shabaz. 'Karun River iii. The Opening of the Karun'. *Encyclopædia Iranica* 15.6 (2011): 633–40 (updated in 2012). Available online at https://www.iranicaonline.org/articles/karun_3 (accessed on 18 March 2023).
Shahpur Shahbazi, A. 'Ferdowsi, Abu'l-Qāsem iii. Mausoleum'. *Encyclopædia Iranica* 9.5 (1999): 524–7 (updated in 2012). Available online at https://iranicaonline.org/articles/ferdowsi-iii (accessed on 18 March 2023).
Shahpur Shahbazi, A. 'Ferdowsi, Abu'l-Qāsem iv. Millenary Celebration'. *Encyclopædia Iranica* 9.5 (1999): 527–30 (updated in 2012). Available online at https://www.iranicaonline.org/articles/ferdowsi-iv (accessed on 18 March 2023).
Shahrokh, Keikhosrow. *The Memoirs of Keikhosrow Shahrokh*. Edited and translated by Shahrokh Shahrokh and Rashna Writer. Lewiston, NY; Lampeter: Edwin Mellen Press, 1994.
Sharafi, Mitra. *Law and Identity in Colonial South Asia: Parsi Legal Culture, 1772-1947*. New York: Cambridge University Press, 2014.
Sheffield, Daniel J. 'Iran, the Mark of Paradise or the Land of Ruin?: Historical Approaches to Reading Two Parsi Zoroastrian Travelogues'. In *On the Wonders of Land and Sea: Persianate Travel Writing*, edited by Roberta Micallef and Sunil Sharma, 14–43. Cambridge, MA: Harvard University Press, 2013.
Sheikh-ol-Islami, M. J. 'Aḥmad Shah Qājār'. *Encyclopædia Iranica* 1.6 (1984): 657–60 (updated in 2011). Available online at http://www.iranicaonline.org/articles/ahmad-shah-qajar-1909-1925-the-seventh-and-last-ruler-of-the-qajar-dynasty (accessed on 18 March 2023).
Shuster, W. Morgan. *The Strangling of Persia: Story of the European Diplomacy and Oriental Intrigue That Resulted in the Denationalization of Twelve Million Mohammedans, a Personal Narrative*. New York: The Century Co., 1912.
Siegel, Evan. 'Shariatism versus Constitutionalism in the Iranian Constitutional Revolution'. *Asiatische Studien* 59, no. 3 (2005): 887.
Slater, Peter and Donald Wiebe (eds). *Traditions in Contact and Change*. Waterloo, Ontario, Canada: Wilfrid Laurier University Press, 1983.
Smith, P. 'Bahaism iv. The Bahai Communities'. *Encyclopædia Iranica* 3.5 (1988): 449–54 (updated in 2011). Available online at https://iranicaonline.org/articles/bahaism-iv (accessed on 23 March 2023).
Soudavar Farmanfarmaian, Fatema. 'Revisiting and Revising the Tobacco Rebellion'. *Iranian Studies* 47, no. 4 (2014): 595–625.
Stausberg, Michael. 'Manekji Limji Hatāriā and the Rediscovery of Ancient Iran'. In *Ātaš-e Dorun, The Fire Within: Jamshid Soroush Soroushian Memorial Volume II*, edited by Carlo G. Cereti and Farrokh Vajifdar and co-ordinated by Mehrborzin Soroushian, 439–46. United States: 1st Books, 2003.
Stausberg, Michael, (ed.). *Zoroastrian Rituals in Context*. Leiden and Boston: Brill, 2004.
Stausberg, Michael. 'From Power to Powerlessness: Zoroastrianism in Iranian History'. In *Religious Minorities in the Middle East: Domination, Self-Empowerment, Accommodation*, edited by Anh Nga Longva and Anne Sofie Roald, 171–93. Leiden and Boston: Brill, 2012.

Stausberg, Michael and Ramiyar P. Karanjia. 'Modi, Jivanji Jamshedji'. *Encyclopædia Iranica*, 2013. Available online at http://www.iranicaonline.org/articles/modi-jivanji-jamshedji (accessed on 18 March 2023).

Stausberg, Michael and Yuhan Sohrab-Dinshaw Vevaina (eds). *The Wiley Blackwell Companion to Zoroastrianism*. Chichester: Wiley Blackwell, 2015.

Stewart, Sarah. 'The Politics of Zoroastrian Philanthropy and the Case of Qasr-e Firuzeh'. *Iranian Studies* 45, no. 1 (2012): 59–80.

Stiles (Maneck), Susan Judith. 'Zoroastrian Conversions to the Bahá'í Faith in Yazd, Iran'. MA Thesis, University of Arizona, 1983.

Sykes, Ella C. *Persia and its People*. London: Methuen, 1910.

Sykes, Percy Molesworth. *Ten Thousand Miles in Persia or Eight Years in Iran*. London: John Murray, 1902.

Tashakori Bafqi, 'Ali Akbar. 'Zamineha-ye Ejtema'a-ye va Eqtesadi-ye Zartoshtiyan-e Yazd dar Duran-e Qajar'. *Siyasi-Eqtesadi* 277–278 (1389/2010): 104–15.

Tashakori Bafqi, 'Ali Akbar. *Mashrutiyat dar Yazd: az Vorud-e Andishah-ye Navin ta Kudita-ye Sayyed Zia' al-Din Tabataba'i*. Tehran: Markaz-e Yazdshenasi, 1337/1998–9.

Tavakoli-Targhi, Mohamad. *Refashioning Iran: Orientalism, Occidentalism and Historiography*. New York: Palgrave, 2001.

Tavakoli-Targhi, Mohamad. 'Historiography and Crafting Iranian National Identity'. In *Iran in the Twentieth Century: Historiography and Political Culture*, edited by Touraj Atabaki, 5–21. London: I.B. Tauris, 2009.

Tejani, Shabnum. *Indian Secularism: A Social and Intellectual History 1890-1950*. Bloomington and Indianapolis: Indiana University Press, 2008.

Tickell, Alex. 'Scholarship Terrorists: The India House Hostel and the "Student Problem" in Edwardian London'. In *South Asian Resistances in Britain, 1858-1947*, edited by Sumita Mukherjee and Rehana Ahmed, 29–43. London: Bloomsbury, 2012.

Torkman, Mohammad (ed.). *Rasa'el, e 'lamiyeh-ha, maktubat va ruznameh-ye Shaikh Shahid Fazl Allah Nuri*. 2 vols. Tehran: Rasa, 1983.

Tsadik, Daniel. 'The Legal Status of Religious Minorities: Imāmī Shī'īs Law and Iran's Constitutional Revolution'. *Islamic Law and Society* 10, no. 3 (2003): 376–408.

Tsadik, Daniel. *Between Foreigners and Shi'is: Nineteenth-Century Iran and its Jewish Minority*. Stanford, CA: Stanford University Press, 2007.

Tucker, Ernest. 'Nāder Shah'. *Encyclopædia Iranica*, 2006. Available online at https://www.iranicaonline.org/articles/nader-shah (accessed on 18 March 2023).

Unvala, J. M. 'Observations on the Religious Conviction in Modern Persia'. *Estratto da: Studie Materiali di Storia Delle Religioni* 9 (1933): 89–94.

Vafadari, Shahrokh R. 'A Note on Kerman and Dustur Jamasb'. In *Ātaš-e Dorun, The Fire Within: Jamshid Soroush Soroushian Memorial Volume II*, edited by Carlo G. Cereti and Farrokh Vajifdar and co-ordinated by Mehrborzin Soroushian, 447–53. United States: 1st Books, 2003.

Vahman, Fereydun. 'The Conversion of Zoroastrians to the Baha'i Faith'. In *The Baha'is of Iran: Socio-Historical Studies*, edited by Dominic Parviz Brookshaw and Seena B. Fazel, 30–48. London and New York: Routledge, 2008.

Veer, Peter van der. *Imperial Encounters: Religion and Modernity in India and Britain*. Princeton and Oxford: Princeton University Press, 2001.

Vejdani, Farzin. 'Indo-Iranian Linguistic, Literary, and Religious Entanglements: Between Nationalism and Cosmopolitanism, ca. 1900-1940'. *Comparative Studies of South Asia, Africa and the Middle East* 36, no. 3 (2016): 435–54.

Wacha, Dinsha Edulji. *Shells from the Sands of Bombay: Being my Recollections and Reminiscences, 1860-1875*. Bombay: K. T. Anklesaria, 1920.

Wadia, Rusheed. 'Bombay Parsi Merchants in the Eighteenth and Nineteenth Centuries'. In *Parsis in India and the Diaspora*, edited by John R. Hinnells and Alan Williams, 119–35. London: Routledge, 2007.

Wagner, Kim A. *Amritsar 1919: An Empire of Fear and the Making of a Massacre*. New Haven, CT: Yale University Press, 2019.

Warburg, Margit. 'Baha'is of Iran: Power, Prejudices and Persecutions'. In *Religious Minorities in the Middle East: Domination, Self-Empowerment, Accommodation*, edited by Anh Nga Longva and Anne Sofie Roald, 195–218. Leiden and Boston: Brill, 2012.

Warzée, Dorothy de. *Peeps into Persia*. London: Hurst and Blackett Ltd, 1913.

Watcha, P. B. *Firdousi and the Parsis, reprinted from the 'Parsi'*. Bombay: P. B. Watcha, 1911.

Waterfield, Henry. *Memorandum on the Census of British India of 1871-72*. London: Eyre and Spottiswoode for H.M. Stationery Office, 1875.

White, Benjamin Thomas. *The Emergence of Minorities in the Middle East: The Politics of Community in French Mandate Syria*. Edinburgh: Edinburgh University Press, 2011.

White, David L. 'From Crisis to Community Definition: The Dynamics of Eighteenth-Century Parsi Philanthropy'. *Modern Asian Studies* 25, no. 2 (1991): 303–20.

Wickens, G. Michael, Juan Cole, and Kamran Ekbal. 'Browne, Edward Granville'. *Encyclopædia Iranica* 4.5 (1989): 483–8. Available online at http://www.iraniaonline.org/articles/browne-edward-granville (accessed on 18 March 2023).

Williams, Alan. *The Zoroastrian Myth of Migration from Iran and Settlement in the Indian Diaspora: Text, Translation and Analysis of the 16th Century Qesse-ye Sanjān 'The Story of Sanjan'*. Leiden and Boston: Brill, 2009.

Willmer, David. 'Parsis and Public Space in 19th Century Bombay: A Different Formulation of "The Political" in a Non-European Context'. *Critical Horizons* 3, no. 2 (2002): 277–98.

Wolf, Reva and Alisa Luxenberg (eds). *Freemasonry and the Visual Arts from the Eighteenth Century Forward: Historical and Global Perspectives*. London: Bloomsbury, 2019.

Wright, Denis. 'Prince ʿAbd ul-Husayn Mirza Farman-Farma. Notes from British Sources'. *Iran* 38 (2000): 107–14.

Wright, Denis. *Britain and Iran, 1790-1980: Collected Essays of Sir Denis Wright*, edited by Sarah Searight. London: Iran Society, 2003.

Writer, Rashna. *Contemporary Zoroastrians: An Unstructured Nation*. Lanham, MD: University Press of America, 1994.

Writer, Rashna. 'Charity as a Means of Zoroastrian Self-Preservation'. *Iranian Studies* 49, no. 1 (2016): 117–36.

Wynn, Antony. *Persia in the Great Game: Sir Percy Sykes - Explorer, Consul, Soldier, Spy*. London: John Murray, 2004.

Yan, Kejia. 'Parsis in the Opium Trade in China'. *Shanghai Academy of Social Sciences*. Unpublished paper. Available online at https://asianscholarship.org/publications/ (accessed on 3 November 2023).

Yazdani, Sohrab. 'Heterodox Intellectuals of the Iranian Constitutional Revolution'. In *Religion and Society in Qajar Iran*, edited by Robert Gleave, 174–91. Abingdon: Routledge Curzon, 2005.

Yeganeh, Naser. 'Civil Code'. *Encyclopædia Iranica* 5.6 (1991): 648–50 (updated in 2011). Available online at https://www.iranicaonline.org/articles/civil-code (accessed on 23 March 2023).

Zia-Ebrahimi, Reza. 'An Emissary of the Golden Age: Manekji Limji Hataria and the Charisma of the Archaic in Pre-Nationalist Iran'. *Studies in Ethnicity and Nationalism* 10, no. 3 (2010): 377–90.

Zia-Ebrahimi, Reza. 'Self-Orientalization and Dislocation: The Uses and Abuses of the "Aryan" Discourse in Iran'. *Iranian Studies* 44, no. 4 (2010): 445–72.

Zia-Ebrahimi, Reza. '"Arab Invasion" and Decline, or the Import of European Racial Thought by Iranian Nationalists'. *Ethnic and Racial Studies* 37, no. 6 (2014): 1043–61.

Zia-Ebrahimi, Reza. *The Emergence of Iranian Nationalism: Race and the Politics of Dislocation*. New York: Columbia University Press, 2016.

Zirinsky, Michael P. 'Imperial Power and Dictatorship: Britain and the Rise of Reza Shah, 1921–1926'. *International Journal of Middle East Studies* 24, no. 4 (1992): 639–63.

Film

Naghashi, Hassan (writer, director, and producer). *Shahjahan*. 1392/2013.

Index

Abbas Mirza Qajar (1789-1833), crown prince 22, 33
Adenwalla, Hormusji Cowasji Dinshaw (1857-1939) 129, 156-7, 160, 167
Afghanistan 53, 88–90, 109, 140, 160. *See also* Kerman
Ahmad Qajar Shah (1898-1930, r. 1909–25) 123, 141, 143, 149, 151, 157
Akhundzadeh, Mirza Fath 'Ali (1812–78) 34–6, 40, 140
'Ala' al-Saltaneh, Mohammad-'Ali (d. 1918) 100–1, 116, 145
Amelioration Society. *See also* Hataria; *jezya*; Khansaheb; Reporter
  and the British 22, 65, 67–8, 71
  during the Constitutional Revolution 100–1, 108, 111–12, 114
  and education 18, 27–8, 67, 71, 73, 157
  establishment of 17
  and famine relief 19, 20
  financial support for 19, 31, 47, 73
  and religious reform 29
Amir Kabir, Mirza Taqi Khan Farahani (1807-52) 18, 55, 75
ancient Iran. *See* pre-Islamic Iran
Anglo-Persian Agreement (1919) 147–9, 151
Anglo-Russian Convention (1907) 109–12, 114, 127, 131, 143, 175–6
animal sacrifice 6, 29, 191 n.182. *See also* reform (religious and social)
Anjoman-e Asar-e Melli 152, 170
Anjoman-e Azerbaijan 112–14
Anjoman-e Elmi-e Farsi 38, 47
Anjoman-e Mavaddat 161, 163
*anjoman*s
  in Iran 81, 112–14, 117–18, 125
  Zoroastrian 18, 25–6, 30. *See also* Kerman; Tehran; Yazd
anti-Arab attitudes 33–6, 40, 42, 107, 124, 158. *See also* pre-Islamic Iran; Islam, attitudes towards

anti-Semitism 35, 42
Aqa Khan III, Sir Sultan Mahomed Shah (1872-1957, in office 1885-1957) 26, 93, 161
Arbab Fereydun Khosrow. *See* Fereydun
Arbab Jamshid Jamshidian (c. 1850-1932). *See also* Atabak Park
  and Bahá'ís 59
  and the British legation *bast* 79
  commercial activities of 57–8, 141 (*see also* Jamshidian firm)
  and the Majles 75, 80–3, 85, 87, 90, 105, 113, 117, 127, 129, 175
  and the National Bank 96
  and philanthropy 58–9, 124, 129
  reputation of 57–8, 127, 129
Arbab Khosrow Shahjahan. *See* Shahjahan, Arbab Khosrow
Armenian community 9, 100
  and the Constitutional Revolution 96, 101, 105–7, 118, 121
  Majles representative for 123, 126, 162
  and Russia 22, 59, 62
Article 8 103–7, 112, 116, 117, 123, 125, 173, 175, 227 n.141, 234 n.49. *See also* Supplementary Fundamental Laws
Aryan theory 35–6, 42, 167–9, 211 n.238, 229 n.192
Atabak-e A'zam, Mirza 'Ali Asghar Khan Amin al-Soltan (1858-1907) 25, 58, 111
Atabak Park 127, 228 n.171, 240 n.209
Azali Babis. *See* Babism and Babis

Babism and Babis 29–30, 77–8, 103, 117, 205 n.68, 206 n.82
Bahá'í faith and Bahá'ís 29–30, 59, 78, 86, 105, 135, 157, 244 n.276. *See also* conversion
Bakhtiyari tribe 121, 124

banking in Iran 54, 57–8, 60, 62, 107, 130, 140–1, 243 n.255. *See also* National Bank
Bast, Oliver 140, 147
Behbahani, Sayyed 'Abdollah (1840-1910) 79, 81, 82, 116, 117, 125, 127, 223 n.55, 224 n.74
Berlin 150, 158, 171. *See also* Germany
Bhownaggree, Mancherjee (1851-1933) 26–7, 47, 58, 65, 72, 82, 92, 101, 102, 107–9, 138, 140, 142, 149, 157, 233 n.13
Birdwood, George (1832-1917) 37, 65, 72, 83–6, 129, 130
Bombay
  growth of Parsi community in 4–5, 7, 15–16
  rise of 4
Bombay Parsi Panchayat (BPP) 5, 16, 18, 154, 156, 165
Bonakdarian, Mansour 11, 109, 118, 130, 138, 147, 148, 151
Brighty, Mary Ellen 'Nellie' (1874-1964) 28, 100, 102–3. *See also* Church Missionary Society
Britain
  Iranians in 23, 25, 76, 107–8, 118
  Zoroastrians in 1, 22–3, 25, 72–3, 82–3, 107–8, 128. *See also* Cooper
British involvement in Iranian affairs 76, 77, 79, 96, 100, 108, 112, 116, 137, 141, 143, 145–6, 156. *See also* Anglo-Persian Agreement; Anglo-Russian Convention; Great Game
Browne, Edward Granville (1862-1926) 25, 27, 42, 57, 96, 97, 99, 109, 118, 130–1, 137–8

calendar controversy, Parsi 4, 8, 18, 36
calendar reform, Iran 152
Cama, Bhikaji Rustom, 'Madame Cama' (1861-1936) 95, 138, 158
Cama, Kharshedji Rustomji, 'K. R.' (1831-1909) 6, 37, 73, 90
census, India 7, 10
charity. *See* philanthropy

China, Zoroastrian community in 2, 5, 51, 73, 102, 130, 164
Choksy, Jamsheed 8, 143–4
Christians. *See* Armenian community; Church Missionary Society; missionaries
Church Missionary Society (CMS) 28, 43, 100, 115. *See also* Brighty; Malcolm
cinema. *See* film
climate, perceived significance of 43, 50, 51, 71–2, 131
clothing regulations.
  in the Pahlavi period 162, 167
  for Zoroastrians in Iran 9, 57, 61, 100, 120, 126, 150. *See also* discrimination
colony, proposed Parsi 47–8, 50–3, 64–6, 72, 84–5, 109, 133–5, 137, 149, 164, 168, 212 n.245
Commercial Mission to Iran (1904) 64–8, 133
communalism, India 93, 95, 133, 148, 154, 161, 163, 165, 171
concessions, Iran 53–4, 63, 76–7, 109, 131, 201 n.205. *See also* Great Game; Tobacco Revolt
conscription, Iran 126, 153, 162, 173
Constantinople 23, 75, 76, 144–5. *See also* Ottoman Empire
Constitutional Revolution, Iran. *See also* names of particular individuals
  background to 75–80
  and India 92, 109
  and merchants 76–7, 79, 80, 96
  Parsi perception of 82–3, 85, 97, 107, 128, 134–5, 138–9, 149
  and recognised religious minorities 80–1, 123 (*see also* Article 8)
  and the ulama 76–7, 79, 81, 102 (*see also names of particular individuals*)
  and women 80, 96, 114, 117
  Zoroastrian involvement in 77, 79, 85, 96–7, 99, 113, 117
consulates, British
  in Iran 62 (*see also* Kerman)
  as a place of refuge 102, 114–15, 117, 119–20, 124, 126, 141

conversion
- to Babism and the Bahá'í faith   30, 59, 78, 257–8 n.278
- to Christianity   5, 16, 28, 233 n.16
- to Islam   2, 7, 8, 17, 18, 22, 24, 42, 43, 120, 121, 162
- to Zoroastrianism   2–3, 6, 41, 141, 164–5, 238 n.136

Cooper, Aimai (d. 1938)   1
Cooper, Nasarvanji Maneckji (d. 1911)   1, 84, 85, 128–30, 137–8, 175
Cossack Brigade   33, 103, 117, 141, 151
crime and violence   18, 77, 99, 103, 111–12, 114, 119–20, 126–7, 140. *See also names of particular individuals*
Curzon, George Nathaniel (1859-1925, Viceroy of India 1899-1905)   57, 61, 72, 73, 93, 147

Dady, Maneck (or Minocher)   155–7
*dakhmeh*s
- in India   4–5, 16, 44
- in Iran   18, 20, 29, 56, 58, 59, 166, 226 n.177

Dar al-Fonun   33, 34, 75–6, 80, 138
Dari   9, 28
Darmesteter, James (1849-94)   37, 39
Dasatiri texts   9, 34, 35
*dastur*s. *See* priests, Zoroastrian
Democrats (political party in Iran)   125, 127, 143, 250 n.121
Dhalla, Dastur Maneckji Nusserwanji (1875-1956)   171
*dhimmi*s   3. *See also specific religious communities in Iran*
diplomatic posts
- Iranians in India   44–8, 58, 71, 90, 100, 167
- Zoroastrians appointed to   46, 60–1, 168

discrimination against Zoroastrians and other non-Muslims, Iran   7–9, 23, 102, 120, 125, 152, 162. *See also* clothing regulations
Dixon & Company   115–16
Dowlatabadi, Yahya (1862-1940)   113, 137–8

economy, Iran   19, 54, 77, 79, 127
education. *See also* Amelioration Society
- female   7, 26, 28, 73, 114, 158, 163
- Zoroastrian priests   5–6, 29
- Zoroastrians in India   5, 16, 38
- Zoroastrians in Iran   18, 27–8, 47, 67–72, 156–7

electoral laws, Iran   80, 123, 244 n.268
Elphinstone College   5, 6, 61
emigration of Zoroastrians from Iran to India   10, 17, 19–22, 55, 77, 103, 109, 115, 120, 124, 143, 174, 204 n.45, 247 n.46. *See also* travel
equality, religious   59, 78, 81, 108, 118–19, 125, 153–6, 162. *See also* Article 8
'Eshqi, Mirzadeh (1893-1924)   159, 165

famine
- in India   5, 16
- in Iran   19–21, 23, 31, 55, 143, 157, 174, 206 n.87

Ferdowsi (Abol-Qasem Ferdowsi Tusi)   39–40, 52, 135–6, 149, 158–9
- millenary of   169–70

Fereydun (Arbab Fereydun Khosrow, d. 1908)   112–18, 175
film   165–7
fire temples
- in Bombay   16, 38
- in India   3, 15
- in Iran   8, 15
- in Kerman   7–8, 18, 193 n.1
- in Tehran   56, 142, 145
- in Yazd   17, 18, 28

First World War   142–6, 148
forced conversion to Islam. *See* conversion
France   22, 35, 124, 131, 147. *See also* Paris
Freemasonry   22, 34, 44, 46, 76–8, 124, 145. *See also* secret societies

Gandhi, Mohandas, 'Mahatma' (1869-1948)   83, 148, 154, 163, 170
*Gatha*s   2, 6, 129, 158, 165
Gendarmerie   127, 243 n.253
Germany   55, 109, 143–4. *See also* Berlin

Ginwalla, Nusserwanji Sheriarji 49, 208 n.143
girls' schools. *See* education
Gobineau, Joseph Arthur de (1816-82) 34-5, 55
Godrej, Manchershah Barjorji 94-5
Gordon, Thomas Edward (1832-1914) 56, 61, 62
Government of India 24, 55, 60, 62, 67-73, 79, 109, 148
Grahame, (Thomas) George (1861-1922) 100, 114-15
Great Game. *See also* Anglo-Russian Convention; British involvement in Iranian affairs; concessions
  and education 67-71
  and trade 53-5, 59-60, 62-7, 115
Grey, Edward (1862-1933) 109, 118, 137, 138, 142
Grigor, Talinn 11, 34, 38, 44, 124, 145, 152
Gujarati language 3, 38, 39, 136

Habibollah Khan (1872-1919), Amir of Afghanistan (1901-19) 88-90, 108
Habl al-Matin (newspaper) 81-2, 96, 106-7, 135, 161
Hataria, Manekji Limji (1813-90) 18, 22, 30, 33-6, 55, 56
Haug, Martin (1827-76) 6, 37
hijrat 160, 256 n.251
Hindi Punch (periodical) 73, 86-91, 109, 110, 128, 131, 132, 139, 160, 217 n.109, 219 n.183, 237 n.115
Hinduism 38, 43, 49, 148
Hormusji Cowasji Dinshaw. *See* Adenwalla, Hormusji Cowasji Dinshaw

Ilm-e Khshnoom 133
India Office 61, 101
India. *See also* Indian National Congress
  independence movement 50, 92, 94, 95, 144, 148, 154, 162-3
  political reform 93, 133, 163, 170
Indian National Congress (INC) 48-9, 93, 95, 148, 163, 170, 173
Indian Sociologist (periodical) 94-5

Iran League
  and education 164
  establishment of 156-7
  and Ferdowsi 158-9, 169-70
  and opportunities in Iran 159, 160, 167, 168
  publications 158, 162, 165
  and Reza Khan/Shah 159, 161, 162, 169
  and Saif Azad 169
  and the position of women 167
Iran-e Now (newspaper) 125, 130
Irani, Ardeshir (1886-1969) 165-6
Irani community 10, 20-1, 43, 68, 90, 100, 111, 146. *See also* emigration; Parsi community
Irani, Dinshah Jijibhoy (1881-1938) 146, 153-8, 165, 167
Iranian Association 141, 149
Iranian Muslim community in India 44, 160, 161, 165
Iranian Zoroastrian Anjoman (IZA) 146, 153, 156-7, 169, 173, 252 n.172, 255 n.239
Iraq 29, 81, 104, 125, 246 n.29
Isfahan 8, 81, 100, 121, 233 n.29, 235 n.55, 240 n.206
Islam, attitudes towards 35, 37, 42, 43, 62
Islamic law 56, 76, 77, 104-5, 116, 125, 162, 234-5 n.51
Istanbul. *See* Constantinople

Jackson, Abraham Valentine Williams (1862-1937) 29, 37, 42-3, 55-7, 136
Jahanian firm 57, 58, 66, 176, 203 n.65. *See also names of particular individuals*
  bankruptcy of 140-1, 143
  and the Constitutional Revolution 77, 99, 113, 115-17, 220 n.227
Jalal al-Din Mirza (1827-72) 34, 35, 40
Jalal al-Dowleh 58, 126, 205 n.68
Jam-e Jamshed (newspaper) 19, 48, 88, 92, 133, 156
Jamshidian, Arbab Jamshid. *See* Arbab Jamshid Jamshidian

Jamshidian firm   57–8, 66, 176, 205 n.65, 243 n.256. *See also* Arbab Jamshid Jamshidian
  bankruptcy of   140–1, 143
  and the Constitutional Revolution   77, 96, 121, 124
Jejeebhoy, Jamsetjee   1st Baronet (1783-1859)   5, 16, 17, 192 n.204
Jejeebhoy, Jamsetjee   3rd Baronet (1851-1898)   41
Jejeebhoy, Jamsetjee   4th Baronet (1852-1908)   27, 64, 73, 196 n.70
Jejeebhoy, Jamsetjee   5th Baronet (1878-1931)   137, 148, 160
Jewish community
  comparisons made with the Zoroastrian community   7, 23, 38, 42, 61, 72, 81, 86, 106–7, 137–8, 155, 169
  in Iran   2–3, 9, 58, 80–1, 96, 101, 105, 121, 123, 162, 204 n.38
jezya   3, 18, 19, 21–5, 27, 31, 45, 83, 126
justice, Zoroastrian demands for   56, 101–3, 111, 113, 115, 119. *See also* Article 8; *jezya*

Kabraji, Kaikhosro (*c.* 1842-1904)   40, 46, 47, 49
Karaka, Dosabhai Framji (1829-1902)   8, 29, 37, 42, 46
Karim Khan Zand (1705-79, r. 1751-79)   8–9, 21
Karkaria, Rustom P. (1869-1919)   135, 137
Kaveh (newspaper)   144, 150
Kayanians   44, 46, 124
Kerman
  Afghan attacks on   8
  British consuls in   62–3, 65, 67–70, 117, 126, 141, 143
  trade   7, 62–3, 67, 100
  Zoroastrian Anjoman of   18, 25–6, 66–70, 106, 114, 141, 225 n.91, 251 n.144
  Zoroastrian community of   8, 9, 17–18, 58, 63, 65, 71, 100, 125, 126, 138, 143–4, 162, 234 n.36
Kermani, Mirza Aqa Khan (1854-96)   35–6, 40, 106

Khansaheb, Kaykhosrow   25–6, 185 n.53
Khorasani, Mohammad Kazem (1839-1911)   104, 125
Kulke, Eckehard   6, 38, 51, 92, 148

landowners, Zoroastrian
  in India   7, 61
  in Iran   21, 57, 61, 111, 226 n.118
Lesser Despotism   117–21, 123, 130
libraries
  in India   42, 236 n.78, 237 n.131
  in Iran   31, 158
loans to Iran   26, 58, 77, 96, 109, 118, 131, 138, 147, 221 n.233, 227 n.153
loyalty of Zoroastrians
  to Britain   7, 45, 46, 49, 67–70, 92, 93, 144, 146, 148–9
  to India   92–5
  to Iran   46, 88–90, 92, 94, 99, 108–9, 131, 136, 149, 153
  reputation for   3, 27, 52, 91–2, 108

'Madame Cama'. *See* Cama, Bhikaji Rustom
Majles. *See also* Arbab Jamshid Jamshidian; Constitutional Revolution; Shahrokh, Kaykhosrow
  elections   80–1, 123, 141, 151, 162
  First   80
  in the Pahlavi period   151, 152
  Second   123, 127
  Third   141, 143
Malcolm, Napier (1870-1921)   30, 43, 55, 58, 63
Malek al-Motakallemin (1861-1908)   78, 116, 117
Malekzadeh, Mehdi   78, 79, 113
Marashi, Afshin   10, 11, 34, 40, 124, 140, 144, 150, 152, 157, 158, 167, 168, 171
Ma'rifat (newspaper)   124
Marker, Peshotanji D. (1871-1965)   157, 158, 170
Marling, Charles (1862-1933)   104, 113–16
marriage   3, 6, 16, 19, 42, 94, 120, 134
Masani, Rustom P. (1876-1966)   65, 133, 135, 137, 156, 167–8, 170, 197 n.89

Masons. *See* Freemasonry
Mehrban and Co.   19-21, 24, 57
Mehrban, Ardeshir   19, 60-2, 90, 191 n.176, 205 n.66
Mehrban, Gudarz (or Godrez)   19, 59, 77, 207 n.118
Mehrban, Rasheed (d. 1874)   23-4, 60, 102
Mehta, Pherozeshah (1845-1915)   48, 49, 94, 148
Menant, Delphine   59, 82
merchants. *See* Constitutional Revolution; trade; Zoroastrian community in Iran; *names of particular individuals and firms*
Miller, Alexander   67, 69-71
minorities, concept of   9-10
Mirza Fath 'Ali Akhundzadeh. *See* Akhundzadeh
Mirza Hosayn Khan. *See* Sepahsalar
Mirza Jahangir Khan (d. 1908)   78, 117, 130. *See also Sur-e Esrafil*
Mirza Malkam Khan (1833-1908)   33, 75-8
Mirza Mehdi Khan   107, 130-1, 134
missionaries, Christian in India   5, 16, 36. *See also* Wilson
For Christians in Iran, Church Missionary Society
modernity
  and Iran   23, 36, 86, 104, 145, 153, 166-7
  and Parsis   6, 36-8, 40, 166, 167
modernization in Iran   33, 46, 75, 83, 137, 145, 147, 150, 151, 161, 162
Modi, Jivanji Jamshedji, J. J. (1854-1933)   37, 38, 88-9, 90, 133, 135, 136-7, 138, 142, 146, 159, 161, 245 n.286, 252 nn.159, 171
Mohammad 'Ali Shah Qajar (1872-1925, r. 1907-9)
  accession of   90, 108
  as crown prince   79
  and the Lesser Despotism   117, 121
  and Russia   111, 121, 127
  and the Supplementary Fundamental Laws   104, 105
  and Zoroastrians   101, 108, 111-17
Mohammad Hasan Mirza Qajar, crown prince (1899-1943)   153

Moharram, month of   100, 120
Moshir al-Dowleh, Hasan Pirniya (1871-1935)   111-12, 114, 115, 229 n.192
mowbeds. See priests, Zoroastrian
Mozaffar al-Din Shah Qajar (1853-1907, r. 1896-1907)
  and the constitution   1, 80, 82-3, 93
  and Zoroastrians   26-7, 58, 68, 82-3, 88, 90-1
Mulla Firuz   8-9, 195 n.44, 196 n.78
Mulla Kaus   8-9
Mumbai. *See* Bombay
murders of Zoroastrians. *See* crime and violence; *names of particular individuals*
Muslim community, in India   49, 93, 133, 148, 168-9. *See also* Iranian Muslim community in India
Muslim League   93, 148

Naoroji, Dadabhai (1825-1917)   6, 22-3, 25, 26, 48, 82, 92-5, 200 n.173, 230 n.213
Nariman, Gushtaspshah Kaikhushro, G. K. (1873-1933)   142, 149, 156, 158, 159, 161, 169
Naser al-Din Shah Qajar (1831-96, r. 1848-96)   22-6, 45, 54, 56, 57, 76, 131, 132
National Bank (Iran)   95-7, 99, 101, 107, 114, 175. *See also* banking in Iran
nationalism
  Indian   38, 50, 93 148 (*see also* India; Indian National Congress)
  Iranian   33-6, 124, 125, 140, 144, 145, 147, 150-3, 158, 162, 166-70
Naus, Jospeh   77, 79
Neda-ye Vatan (newspaper)   1, 82-4, 106, 123, 145, 221 n.236
New Year
  Parsi (or Pateti)   39, 83, 131, 132, 160, 163
  Persian (or Jamshedji Nowruz)   107-8, 142, 159, 171, 200 n.177, 235 n.74, 242 n.232, 248 n.68
newspapers. *See also names of individual publications*
  English-language   101
  in India   6, 18, 20, 83, 92

in Iran   76, 82
with translated articles   1, 82–4
Non-Muslims in Iran. *See entries for specific communities*
Nowruz. *See* New Year
Nuri, Shaikh Fazlallah (1843-1909)   79, 104, 105, 112, 117, 123

opium   5, 19, 54–5, 159
Order of the Lion and the Sun   26, 47, 69
Oriental Review (journal)   67, 94, 226 n.128
Orientalism. *See* Western views and theories
Ottoman Empire   23, 59, 79, 126, 143, 144, 148. *See also* Constantinople; Iraq; Tanzimat reforms

Paris   22, 57, 76, 94, 95, 131, 138, 149, 158. *See also* France
Paris Peace Conference (1919)   147
Parsi community.
  early history in India   3 (*see also* Bombay)
  in 'exile'   38, 66, 86, 101, 106, 136, 146, 168, 174
  and ideas concerning race   40–1, 47, 51, 64, 72, 84, 86, 94, 129, 131, 133, 134, 136, 146, 155, 169
  opportunities in Iran   71–2, 82, 85–6, 97, 130–1, 133–7, 149, 153–5, 160, 165, 167–8, 170–1
  and politics   7, 82, 92–3, 95, 148, 160
  population size   7, 10, 163, 170
  position in India   133–5, 137, 148, 154, 158, 162–5, 168, 170, 171
  relations with the British   5–7, 16, 24–5, 41, 49, 59, 68, 138 (*see also* loyalty)
  'return' to Iran   49, 60, 63–4, 78, 82, 85–6, 94–5, 106, 124, 131–3, 136–7, 155–6, 160–1, 168 (*see also* colony)
  and the Zoroastrian community in Iran   21, 31–2, 50, 65, 68, 90–2, 129. *See also* Amelioration Society; Irani community; Iran League
Parsi (periodical)   37–8, 44, 51–2, 65, 69, 82, 83, 85, 124, 135, 138, 180 n.73

partition of Bengal (1905–11)   50, 92, 93, 148
Parveez, Naoroz   83–7, 109
Parviz Shahjahan. *See* Shahjahan, Parviz
Patel, Dinyar   5, 11, 148, 154, 158, 199 n.156, 202 n.2
Patel, Khan Bahadur Burjorjee Dorabjee   50, 51, 136, 137
patriotism. *See also* loyalty; nationalism
  Parsis towards India   48–9, 94–5, 162, 163, 171
  Parsis towards Iran   21, 27, 39, 45–6, 49, 66, 84, 97, 101–2, 130, 142, 149, 154, 161
Persia Committee   118, 142
Persia Society   142, 253 n.196
Persian Famine Relief Fund   19–20
Persian language
  and nationalism in Iran   35, 40, 52, 107, 145, 162
  and Parsis   38–9, 47, 52, 131, 136, 138, 141–2, 146, 156, 166
Petit, Dinshaw Maneckji   1st Baronet (1823-1901)   17, 31, 47, 49, 69
Petit, Dinshaw Maneckji   2nd Baronet (1873-1933)   65, 68, 70–3, 101, 108, 111, 133, 154
philanthropy. *See also* Amelioration Society; Persian Famine Relief Fund
  to Iran   17–18, 28, 31–2, 71–3, 101–2, 130, 145, 157, 160, 163–4
  non-sectarian   15–16, 130, 142, 157, 163–5, 168
  Parsi reputation for   15, 72, 134, 142
  textual   123, 158
  by women   17, 145, 164–5, 186 n.65
  in Zoroastrianism   15
  Zoroastrians in India   5, 15–17
  Zoroastrians in Iran   7–8, 58–9, 129, 157
pre-Islamic Iran
  and Freemasons   34, 44, 124
  as a golden age   33–4, 44, 65–6, 78, 86, 144–5, 149, 150, 153, 155, 158–9, 166, 169
  and Iranian Zoroastrians   24, 34, 81–2, 105–7, 113, 115, 167
  Parsi interest in   31, 33, 36–9, 84, 88–9, 133, 135, 142, 146, 159, 165

position of women in   7, 31, 37, 45, 136, 158, 167, 192 n.199
priests, Zoroastrian   3–6, 26, 28–30, 120, 190 n.163, 257 n.277
Prince of Wales, Edward (1894-1972, r. 1936)   154
Purdavud, Ebrahim (1885-1968)   144, 158, 165
purity, views regarding
  in Shi'ism   8, 9, 63
  in Zoroastrianism   3, 6, 41, 77, 181 n.87

Qajars   9, 123, 151, 174. *See also names of particular individuals*
Qesse-ye Sanjan   3, 15, 39, 188 n.105, 255 n.232
Quetta   50, 64, 66, 103, 109

Rast Goftar (newspaper)   6, 21, 49, 50, 83, 88, 90, 92, 93, 109, 112, 133, 134
Rawlinson, Henry (1810–95)   22, 23, 25, 34–5
reform (religious and social). *See also* animal sacrifice
  Parsis   6–7, 36–7, 40–1
  Zoroastrians in Iran   29, 30, 166
Renan, Ernest (1823–92)   35, 40
Reporter, Ardeshir Edulji (1865–1933)   26
  and the British   65–7, 79, 109, 235 n.54
  during the Constitutional Revolution   78–80, 82, 97, 101, 106, 111, 113, 119, 225 n.91
  and conversion   164
  and female education   26, 28, 164–5
  and Kaykhosrow Shahrokh   70, 145, 165, 233 n.13
  and Parsis   149, 164–5
  and Reza Khan (Shah)   151
  and Saif Azad   169
  and Zoroastrian Anjomans   66, 81
*Revayat*s   4, 9
Reza Shah Pahlavi (1878-1944, r. 1925–41)
  and nationalism   151–2, 166
  and reform   153, 161–2
  rise to power of   151–2
  and the ulama   152, 153, 162

and Zoroastrians   152, 155, 159–62, 168, 169, 171
Ringer, Monica   6, 7, 11, 37, 38, 136, 166
Rose, Jenny   2, 5–6, 213 n.24
Ross, Edward Charles (1836-1913)   25, 60, 63
Russia. *See also* Anglo-Russian Convention; Great Game; Zoroastrian community in Iran
  and Christians in Iran   22, 59, 62
  and Iranian affairs   77, 96, 110, 112, 117, 118, 121, 127, 138–41, 143
  revolution (1905)   79
  war with Japan (1904–5)   79

Safavid period   7–8, 18
Saif Azad, 'Abdulrahman (1884-1971)   169
Sasanian period   2, 9, 15, 36, 43, 52, 131, 150, 152, 155. *See also* pre-Islamic Iran
Sayyed Jamal al-Din Asadabadi, al-Afghani (1838/9–97)   76
Sayyed Jamal al-Din Va'ez Esfahani (1861-1908)   78, 96, 116, 117, 124
Sayyed Zia' al-Din Tabataba'i (1889-1969)   137, 151
schools. *See* education
secret societies (Iran)   78, 80. *See also* Freemasonry
secularism
  in India   93
  in Iran   78, 104, 125, 150, 162
Sepahsalar, Mirza Hosayn Khan (1827/8-81)   23, 75
Sepanta, Abdolhossein (1907–69)   165–7
separate electorates
  India   93–4, 133, 148, 163, 170, 173
  Iran   81, 123, 125, 173
Shahjahan, Arbab Khosrow   57, 81, 116–17
Shahjahan, Arbab Parviz (d. 1907)   57, 97, 99–103, 105–7
Shahjahan, Rostam   57, 114, 119, 246 n.11
Shahnameh   39–41, 44, 49, 85–7, 89, 113, 133, 136, 142, 144, 146, 149, 153, 158–9, 166, 169. *See also* Ferdowsi
Shahrokh, Kaykhosrow (1864-1939)
  and the British   69, 71, 147–8, 156

death of 171
early life of 69
and nationalism 124, 148, 152, 169–70
and the Persian language 145, 162
and politics 123, 125–7, 129–30, 141, 143, 152, 161
and religion 123–4, 145, 152, 166
and rights for Zoroastrians 69, 105, 125, 150, 153, 162
as a Russian agent 69–71
and the Tehran Zoroastrian Anjoman 81, 123, 145, 157
Sharafi, Mitra 6, 24–5, 41, 133
shari'a. *See* Islamic law
Sharq (newspaper) 125, 137
Sheffield, Daniel 4, 18, 21, 36, 38
Shi'i Islam in Iran 7, 8, 104. *See also* purity; ulama
Shiraz, Zoroastrian community of 100, 103, 114–15, 119, 160
Shroff, Behramshah Naoroji (1858-1927) 133
Shuster, William Morgan (1877-1960) 127
Sistan 50, 53, 64, 66, 86, 168, 208 n.147
Society for National Heritage (Iran). *See* Anjoman-e Asar-e Melli
Society for the Amelioration of the Conditions of the Zoroastrians of Persia. *See* Amelioration Society
Sorur Vakil 112, 114, 116
Spring-Rice, Cecil (1859-1918) 96, 100–2, 105, 109, 111
Stausberg, Michael 9, 11, 152
Sunni Muslims, Iran 7, 9, 105
Supplementary Fundamental Laws, Iran 103–5, 112, 124. *See also* Article 8
Sur-e Esrafil (newspaper) 105–6, 113, 117, 130
Sykes, Ella (1863-1939) 42
Sykes, Percy Molesworth (1867-1945) 42–4, 62–5, 67–73, 79, 84, 85, 142–4

Tabataba'i, Sayyed Mohammad (1842-1920) 79, 81, 101–5, 117, 124, 223 n.54

Tabriz 63, 117, 118, 121
Taft, bandits from 119–21, 127
Tagore, Rabindranath (1861-1941) 167–8, 170
Tanzimat reforms 23, 75
Taqizadeh, (Sayyed) Hasan (1878-1970) 104, 106, 111–13, 118–19, 124, 130–1, 144, 150, 241 n.228
Tata, Ratan (1871-1918) 73, 157
Tata, Ratanbanu Bamji (d. 1930) 164–5
Tehran
  Zoroastrian Anjoman of 81, 113, 123, 145, 152, 157, 158, 166, 224 n.73
  Zoroastrian community of 1, 20, 55–7
telegraph system (Iran) 54, 100, 120, 205 n.67, 221–2 n.15
theatre 40, 159, 165, 228 n.171. *See also* Kabraji
Theosophical movement 37, 141
Tilak, Bal Gangadhar (1856-1920) 93
Times (newspaper) 26, 118, 222 n.24
Times of India (newspaper)
  Parsi correspondence to 25, 49, 131, 134, 149, 163–5, 170
  regarding Iranian Zoroastrians 20, 21, 23, 43, 85, 90, 102
  regarding Parsis 20, 24, 28, 31, 45, 48, 49, 64, 67, 68, 133, 134, 149, 155, 159–61, 168
Tobacco Revolt 76–7
trade. *See also* Great Game; Parveez; Zoroastrian community in Iran
  between India and Iran 44, 54, 56, 61, 62, 83, 109 (*see also* Commercial Mission to Iran)
  between Parsis and Iran 49, 63–5, 68, 71–2, 83. *See also* Parsi community
Transcaucasia 79, 81, 117–18
translations
  of newspaper articles 1, 82–4
  of religious texts 5, 41, 188 n.100
travel. *See also* emigration
  Zoroastrians from India to Iran 4, 8–9, 83–5, 130, 142, 154, 159, 167–8, 170

Zoroastrians from Iran to India 3-4, 10, 56, 61
tribes in Iran 9, 54, 123, 143, 161-2, 205 n.65. *See also* Bakhtiyari tribe
Turkey 151. *See also* Constantinople; Ottoman Empire
Twelver Shi'ism. *See* Shi'ism

ulama 76-8, 104. *See also* Constitutional Revolution; Islamic law; Zoroastrian community in Iran
United States of America 57, 147, 148

Vámbéry, Ármin (1832-1913) 38-9, 51-2
Vaughan, Henry Bathurst 24, 59-60
Vimadalal, J. J. 37-8, 41, 154, 160, 198 n.135, 245 n.283
violence. *See* crime and violence

Wacha, Dinshaw Edulji (1844-1936) 48, 148
Wadia Trust 31, 164
Wassmuss, Wilhelm (1880-1931) 143, 144
Watcha, P. B. 135-6
Westergaard, Niels Ludvig (1815-78) 17-18, 29
Western views and theories 6, 34-7, 39, 40, 42-4, 51-2, 76, 124, 136
Wilson, John (1804-75) 5, 6, 16, 17

Yazd
and trade 54, 59, 62
Zoroastrian Anjoman of 18, 25-6, 30, 61, 99, 101, 111, 120, 140, 145, 157-8
Zoroastrian community of 8, 9, 28, 47, 55-60, 99, 102-3, 119-20, 125-7, 150, 152, 157-8
Yazdegird III (624-51, r. 632-51) 30, 131, 132
Young Turks 118, 126

Zaheer, Syed Ali (1896-1983) 173, 176
Zarathustra 2, 30, 42, 129, 144, 159, 199 n.138, 219 n.181
Zarbanu Dinshah Molla 158
Zel al-Soltan (1850-1919) 47, 58
Zia-Ebrahimi, Reza 11, 33-6, 40, 42, 125
Zionism 50-2, 154
Zoroastrian community in Iran
attitudes towards 23-5, 34-5, 42-3, 56, 60, 68, 85, 96, 115, 141-2, 168
class divisions 28, 101, 120
landownership 21, 57, 61, 226 n.118
naturalized British subjects 24, 56, 59, 61, 67, 116-17, 125, 140, 226 n.118
political and economic influence 100, 101, 105-6, 113, 115, 124, 126-7, 130 (*see also names of particular individuals*)
population size 7, 9, 17-19, 101, 164-5
relations with Iranian ruling classes 57-8, 68, 69, 90, 99, 115, 126-7
relations with Muslims 60, 61, 82, 102-3, 106-7, 113, 141, 143, 150, 157-8, 164
relations with the British 55, 56-7, 59-61, 63, 66, 68-71, 84, 100-2, 106, 111-12, 114-15, 119-20, 140-1, 143-4 (*see also* consulates; Great Game)
relations with the Russians 62, 66-7, 69-71, 84
relations with the ulama 22, 25-6, 56, 58, 63, 77-8, 81, 99, 102, 103, 125 (*see also* Nuri)
trade 7, 19-20, 55-7, 59-60, 66-7, 77, 115. *See also particular individuals and companies*
Zoroastrian Funds of Europe (ZFE) 82-3, 107-8
Zoroastrianism 2, 5-6, 124. *See also* reform